LUNAR RETURNS AND EARTH RETURNS

a Daniela

Ciro Discepolo

LUNAR RETURNS AND EARTH RETURNS

Two supporting methodologies for Active Astrology

Ricerca '90 Publisher

Translation and editing: Luciano Drusetta and Ram Ramakrishnan
Graphic design: Pino Valente
Cover picture: Courtesy NASA/JPL-Caltech.

Let me express my special acknowledgments to my favourite proof-reader, my friend Lorenzo Vancheri: with affection, yet without any trace of indulgence for any sort of typo, he helps improving the quality of my works with highly precious suggestions and remarks.

Further acknowledgments to:

Dr. Stefano Briganti
Maestro Pino Valente

Copyright © 2009 Edizioni Ricerca '90
Viale Gramsci, 16
80122 Napoli - ITALY
info@cirodiscepolo.it
www.solarreturns.com
www.cirodiscepolo.it

There are some aspects, in Active Astrology and in Astrogeography, that very much resemble pure mathematics.

Ciro Discepolo

The only certain basis for accurate and reproducible astrological forecasting, in my opinion, is the parallel and wise usage of transits, Solar Returns, Lunar Returns, and Earth Returns according to the rules of *Active Astrology* – the whole to be read with comparative readings of more than one group of people belonging to the same 'family': being it genetic, political, sporting, business and so on…

Ciro Discepolo

The birth data of the people mentioned in this book proceed mainly from Lois M. Rodden's database and from Ciro Discepolo's archives. Other birth data are taken from web-based databases.

Astral maps and calculations are produced by the exceptionally precise astrological software **Astral** and **Aladino** (also referred to as *Module for the Automatized Research of the Aimed Solar Returns* '*RSMA*').

Preface to the English Edition

In almost forty years of passionate studies, many of my books have been read and studied by dozens of thousands of readers all over the world.

One of my luckier volumes (*Transits and Solar Returns* is its title in English) has been published once in English, in German, and in Spanish; and twice in Italian and French. It may be claimed that, especially thanks to that wonderful virtual shop called Amazon, this book is now being read all over the world including Mongolia, the Philippines, Australia, Canada, etc.

Other volumes of mine on Solar Returns or on Lunar Returns are presently studied in Slovenia, in Hungary, in Russia…

Soon further versions of my books will be available in other minor languages.

What you are browsing is my most recent book, since it was first sold in Italian bookshops in September, 2008. This is its second English edition, containing slight but significant amendments.

Since they are usually particularly attentive to this kind of technical astrology, I trust that my English-speaking readers will appreciate this new 'Northwest Passage' of astrological research, which may lead you to heuristic paths of great interest – as it is the case of Earth Returns, a subject that I consider to be extremely interesting.

Other subjects of mine are presently widely applied here in Italy: I trust that one day they might become useful also to my American or anyway English-speaking colleagues. I am referring to different astrological threads, such as the protocol for a rectification of the time of birth of an individual; the method for the dating of events within a year; my rules of medical astrology; my concept of the exorcism of symbols; and many other subjects.

Nice reading to you all.

Ciro Discepolo
Naples, the 2nd of January 2009

Preface

Predictive astrology is the most fascinating branch of our discipline. Within predictive astrology, the study of the Solar Returns and of the Lunar Returns represents the milestone of all the theoretical and practical scaffolding for the benefit of those moved by the ambition of casting fairly exact forecasts.

This book analyzes some of the most critical subjects for this kind of study: those chapters that – in my opinion – rightfully legitimizes the consideration of the segment called 'Solar and Lunar Returns' as the ultimate course in the study of astrology.

We'll come back to this point. First, let me develop a few theoretical digressions apparently farther off from this point which, I believe, may be of a great interest within the work that you have just started reading now.

And so I begin with discussing two wonderful masterpieces of literature – *One Thousand and One Nights* and the *Odyssey* – and then will draw a parallel with the movie *The Devil's Advocate* (USA 1997, with Keanu Reeves and Charlize Theron, directed by Taylor Hackford) to eventually come back to what was mentioned in the first lines of this preface.

For the sake of those who have never read the *One Thousand and One Nights*[1], let me explain in brief what it is about. It is undoubtedly one of the most precious masterpieces of the literature of all the times: a collection of tales that is in no way inferior to William Shakespeare's, Dante Alighieri's or Giovanni Boccaccio's *opera omnia*.

In a way, the tale of Shahrazad is the core of the *One Thousand and One Nights*. The following passage is made up of fragments taken from *The Book of The Thousand Nights and a Night*, translated by Richard F. Burton.

In the Name of Allah, the Compassionating, the Compassionate!

PRAISE BE TO ALLAH * THE BENEFICENT KING * THE CREATOR OF THE UNIVERSE * [...] AND GRACE, AND PRAYER-BLESSING BE UPON OUR LORD MOHAMMED * LORD OF APOSTOLIC MEN * AND UPON HIS FAMILY AND COMPANION TRAIN * PRAYER AND BLESSINGS ENDURING AND GRACE WHICH UNTO THE DAY OF DOOM SHALL REMAIN * AMEN!

Verily the works and words of those gone before us have become instances and examples to men of our modern day, that folk may view what admonishing chances befel other folk and may therefrom take warning; and that they may peruse the annals of antique peoples and all that hath betided them, and be thereby ruled and restrained [...]. Now of such instances are the tales called *'A Thousand Nights and a Night'*, together with their far famed legends and wonders.

Therein it is related (but Allah is All knowing of His hidden things and All ruling and All honoured and All giving and All gracious and All merciful) that, in tide of yore and in time long gone before, there was a King of the Kings of the Banu Sásán in the Islands of India and China, a Lord of armies and guards and servants and dependents. He left only two sons, one in the prime of manhood and the other yet a youth, while both were Knights and Braves, albeit the elder was a doughtier horseman than the younger. So he succeeded to the empire; when he ruled the land and lorded it over his lieges with justice so exemplary that he was beloved by all the peoples of his capital and of his kingdom. His name was King Shahryár, and he made his younger brother, Shah Zamán hight, King of Samarcand in Barbarian land.

These two ceased not to abide in their several realms and the law was ever carried out in their dominions; and each ruled his own kingdom, with equity and fair dealing to his subjects, in extreme solace and enjoyment; and this condition continually endured for a score of years.

But at the end of the twentieth twelvemonth the elder King yearned for a sight of his younger brother and felt that he must look upon him once more. So he took counsel with his Wazír about visiting him, [...] «Harkening and obedience!» quoth the Minister, who fell to making ready without stay and packed up his loads and prepared all his requisites without delay. When he entered the city he proceeded straightway to the palace, where he presented himself in the royal presence; and, after kissing ground and praying for the King's health and happiness and for victory over all his enemies, he informed him that his brother was yearning to see him, and prayed for the pleasure of a visit. [...] when the King had fully comprehended its import, he said, «I hear and I obey the commands of the beloved brother!» He [...] stablished his chief Wazir viceroy of the land during his absence. Then he caused his tents and camels and mules to be brought forth and encamped, with their bales and loads, attendants and guards, within sight of the city, in readiness to set out next morning for his brother's capital.

But when the night was half spent he bethought him that he had forgotten in his palace somewhat which he should have brought with him, so he returned privily and entered his apartments, where he found the Queen, his wife, asleep on his own carpet bed, embracing with both arms a black cook of loathsome aspect and foul with kitchen grease and grime. When he saw this the world waxed black before his sight and he said, «If such case happen while I am yet within sight of the city what will be the doings of this damned whore during my long absence at my brother's court?» So he drew his scymitar and, cutting the two in four pieces with a single blow, left them on the carpet and returned presently to his camp without letting anyone know of what had happened. Then he gave orders for immediate departure and set out at once and began his travel; […] Now when Shah Zaman drew near the capital of his brother he despatched vaunt couriers and messengers of glad tidings to announce his arrival, and Shahryar came forth to meet him with his Wazirs and Emirs and Lords and Grandees of his realm; and saluted him and joyed with exceeding joy and caused the city to be decorated in his honour. When, however, the brothers met, the elder could not but see the change of complexion in the younger and questioned him of his case whereto he replied, «'Tis caused by the travails of wayfare and my case needs care, for I have suffered from the change of water and air! […]» So he let him wend his own ways and asked no questions of him till one day when he again said, «O my brother, I see thou art grown weaker of body and yellower of colour.» «O my brother,» replied Shah Zaman «I have an internal wound.» still he would not tell him what he had witnessed in his wife. One day his elder brother said to him, «I am going forth to hunt and course and to take my pleasure and pastime; maybe this would lighten thy heart.»

Shah Zaman, however, refused, […]

So King Shah Zaman passed his night in the palace and, next morning, when his brother had fared forth, he removed from his room and sat him down at one of the lattice windows overlooking the pleasure grounds; […] Thereupon Shah Zaman drew back from the window, but he kept the bevy in sight espying them from a place whence he could not be espied. They walked under the very lattice and advanced a little way into the garden till they came to a jetting fountain amiddlemost a great basin of water; then they stripped off their clothes and behold, ten of them were women, concubines of the King, and the other ten were white slaves. Then they all paired off, each with each: but the Queen, who was left alone, presently cried out in a loud voice, «Here to me, O my lord Saeed!» and then sprang with a drop leap from one of the trees a big slobbering blackamoor with rolling eyes which showed the whites, a truly hideous sight. He walked boldly up to her and threw his arms round her neck while she embraced him as warmly; then he bussed her and winding his legs round hers, as a button loop clasps a button, he threw her and enjoyed her. On like wise did the other slaves with the girls till all had satisfied their passions, and they ceased not from kissing and clipping, coupling and carousing till day began to wane; [...]

Now, when Shah Zaman saw this conduct of his sister in law he said in himself, «By Allah, my calamity is lighter than this!» So he put away his melancholy and despondency, regret and repine, and allayed his sorrow by constantly repeating those words, adding, «'Tis my conviction that no man in this world is safe from their malice!» [...] Next day he broke his fast heartily and began to recover health and strength, and presently regained excellent condition.

His brother came back from the chase ten days after, when he rode out to meet him and they saluted each other; and when King Shahryar looked at King Shah Zaman he saw how the hue of health had returned to him, how his face had waxed ruddy and how he ate with an appetite after his late scanty diet. He wondered much and said, «[...] I was desirous to carry thee with me to the chase but I saw thee changed in hue, pale and wan to view, and in sore trouble of mind too. But now Alham-dolillah—glory be to God!— I see thy natural colour hath returned to thy face and that thou art again in the best of case. [...] So speak out and hide naught!» When Shah Zaman heard this he bowed groundwards awhile his head, then raised it and said, «I will tell thee what caused my complaint and my loss of colour; but excuse my acquainting thee with the cause of its return to me and the reason of my complete recovery: indeed I pray thee not to press me for a reply.»» Said Shahryar, who was much surprised by these words, «Let me hear first what produced thy pallor and thy poor condition.» «Know, then, O my brother,» rejoined Shah Zaman, «that when thou sentest thy Wazir with the invitation to place myself between thy hands, I made ready and marched out of my city; but presently I minded me having left behind me in the palace a string of jewels intended as a gift to thee. I returned for it alone and found my wife on my carpet bed and in the arms of a hideous black cook. So I slew the twain and came to thee, yet my thoughts brooded over this business and I lost my bloom and became weak.

But excuse me if I still refuse to tell thee what was the reason of my complexion returning.» Shahryar shook his head, marvelling with extreme marvel, [...] «That were but a better reason,» quoth Shahryar, «for telling me the whole history, and I conjure thee by Allah not to keep back aught from me.» Thereupon Shah Zaman told him all he had seen, from commencement to con elusion, [...] When King Shahryar heard this he waxed wroth with exceeding wrath, and rage was like to strangle him; but presently he recovered himself and said, «O my brother, I would not give thee the lie in this matter, but I cannot credit it till I see it with mine own eyes.» «And thou wouldst look upon thy calamity,» quoth Shah Zaman, «rise at once and make ready again for hunting and coursing, and then hide thyself with me, so shalt thou witness it and shine eyes shall verify it.»

«True,» quoth the King; whereupon he let make proclamation of his in tent to travel, and the troops and tents fared forth without the city, camping within sight, and Shahryar sallied out with them and took seat amidmost his host, bidding the slaves admit no man to him. When night came on […] the brothers disguised themselves and returned by night with all secrecy to the palace, where they passed the dark hours: and at dawn they seated themselves at the lattice overlooking the pleasure grounds, when presently the Queen and her handmaids came out as before, and passing under the windows made for the fountain. Here they stripped, ten of them being men to ten women, and the King's wife cried out, «Where art thou, O Saeed?» […]

When King Shahryar saw this infamy of his wife and concubines he became as one distraught and he cried out, «Only in utter solitude can man be safe from the doings of this vile world! […] Let us up as we are and depart forthright hence, for we have no concern with Kingship, and let us overwander Allah's earth, worshipping the Almighty till we find some one to whom the like calamity hath happened; and if we find none then will death be more welcome to us than life.» So the two brothers issued from a second private postern of the palace; and they never stinted wayfaring by day and by night, until they reached a tree a middle of a meadow hard by a spring of sweet water on the shore of the salt sea. Both drank of it and sat down to take their rest; and when an hour of the day had gone by: lo! they heard a mighty roar and uproar in the middle of the main as though the heavens were falling upon the earth; and the sea brake with waves before them, and from it towered a black pillar, which grew and grew till it rose skywards and began making for that meadow.

Seeing it, they waxed fearful exceedingly and climbed to the top of the tree, which was a lofty; whence they gazed to see what might be the matter. And behold, it was a Jinni, huge of height and burly of breast and bulk, broad of brow and black of blee, bearing on his head a coffer of crystal. He strode to land, wading through the deep, and coming to the tree whereupon were the two Kings, seated himself beneath it. He then set down the coffer on its bottom and out it drew a casket, […] which he unlocked […] and out of it a young lady to come was seen, white-skinned and of winsomest mien, of stature fine and thin, and bright as though a moon of the fourteenth night she had been, or the sun raining lively sheen. The Jinni seated her under the tree by his side and looking at her said, «O choicest love of this heart of mine! O dame of noblest line, whom I snatched away on thy bride night […]: O my sweetheart! I would fief sleep a little while.» He then laid his head upon the lady's thighs; and, stretching out his legs which extended down to the sea, slept and snored and sparked like the roll of thunder. Presently she raised her head towards the tree top and saw the two Kings perched near the summit; then she softly lifted off her lap the Jinni's pate which she was tired of supporting and placed it upon the ground; then standing upright under the tree signed to the Kings, «Come ye down, ye two, and fear naught from this Ifrit.» They were in a terrible fright when they found that she had seen them and answered her in the same manner, «Allah upon thee and by thy modesty, O lady, excuse us from coming down!» But she rejoined by saying, «Allah upon you both, that ye come down forthright, and if ye come not, I will rouse upon you my husband, this Ifrit, and he shall do you to die by the illest of deaths.» So, being afraid, they came down to her and she rose be fore them and said, «Stroke me a strong stroke, without stay or delay, otherwise will I arouse and set upon you this Ifrit who shall slay you straightway.» [...] Whereupon out of fear King Shahryar said to King Shah Zaman, «O my brother, do thou what she biddeth thee do;» but he replied, «I will not do it till thou do it before I do.» And they began disputing about futtering her. Then quoth she to the twain, «How is it I see you disputing and demurring; if ye do not come forward like men and do the deed of kind ye two, I will arouse upon you the Ifrit.» At this, by reason of their sore dread of the Jinni, both did by her what she bade them do; and, when they had dismounted from her, she said, «Well done!» She then took from her pocket a purse and drew out a knotted string, whereon were strung five hundred and seventy seal rings, and asked, «Know ye what be these?» They answered her saying, «We know not!» Then quoth she; «These be the signets of five hundred and seventy men who have all futtered me upon the horns of this foul, this foolish, this filthy Ifrit; so give me also your two seal rings, ye pair of brothers.» When they had drawn their two rings from their hands and given them to her, she said to them, «Of a truth this If rit bore me off on my bride night, and put me into a casket and set the casket in a coffer and to the coffer he affixed seven strong padlocks of steel and deposited me on the deep bottom of the sea that raves, dashing and clashing with waves; [...] But [...] this wretched Jinni wotteth not that Des tiny may not be averted nor hindered by aught, and that whatso woman willeth the same she fulfilleth however man nilleth.» [...] Hearing these words they marvelled with exceeding marvel, and she went from them to the Ifrit and, taking up his head on her thigh as before, said to them softly, «Now wend your ways and bear yourselves beyond the bounds of his malice.» [...] Thereupon they rode back to the tents of King Shahryar, which they reached on the morning of the third day; [...]

There he sat him upon his throne [...] he carried her [wife] to the place of execution and did her die. [...] He also sware himself by a binding oath that whatever wife he married he would abate her maidenhead at night and slay her next morning to make sure of his honour; [...] On this wise he continued for the space of three years; marrying a maiden every night and killing her the next morning, till folk raised an outcry against him and cursed him, praying Allah utterly to destroy him and his rule; and women made an uproar and mothers wept and parents fled with their daughters till there remained not in the city a young person fit for carnal copulation. Presently the King ordered his Chief Wazir [...] to bring him a virgin as was his wont; and the Minister went forth and searched and found none; so he returned home in sorrow and anxiety fearing for his life from the King.

Now he had two daughters, Shahrazad and Dunyazad hight, of whom the elder had perused the books, annals and legends of preceding Kings, and the stories, examples and instances of by gone men and things; [...] and she was pleasant and polite, wise and witty, well read and well bred. Now on that day she said to her father, «Why do I see thee thus changed and laden with cark and care? Concerning this matter quoth one of the poets.— Tell whoso hath sorrow * Grief never shall last [...]» When the Wazir heard from his daughter these words he related to her, from first to last, all that had happened between him and the King. Thereupon said she, «By Allah, O my father [...] I wish thou wouldst give me in marriage to this King Shahryar; either I shall live or I shall be a ransom for the virgin daughters of Moslems and the cause of their deliverance from his hands and thine.» «Allah upon thee!» cried he in wrath exceeding that lacked no feeding, «O scanty of wit, expose not thy life to such peril!» [...] and she answered, «O my father it must be, come of it what will!» [...] Hereupon the Wazir being weary of lamenting and contending, persuading and dissuading her, all to no purpose, went up to King Shahryar and [...] told him all about his dispute with his daughter from first to last and how he designed to bring her to him that night. [...] But Shahrazed rejoiced with exceeding joy and get ready all she required and said to her younger sister, Dunyazad, «Note well what directions I entrust to thee! When I have gone in to the King I will send for thee and when thou comest to me and seest that he hath had his carnal will of me, do thou say to me:—O my sister, an thou be not sleepy, relate to me some new story, delectable and delightsome, the better to speed our waking hours;— and I will tell thee a tale which shall be our deliverance, if so Allah please, and which shall turn the King from his blood thirsty custom.»

[...] So when it was night their father the Wazir carried Shahrazad to the King who was gladdened at the sight and asked,

«Hast thou brought me my need?» and he answered, «I have.»

But when the King took her to his bed and fell to toying with her and wished to go in to her she wept; [...] «O King of the age, I have a younger sister and fief would I take leave of her this night before I see the dawn.

« So he sent at once for Dunyazad and she came and kissed the ground between his hands, when he permitted her to take her seat near the foot of the couch. Then the King arose and did away with his bride's maidenhead and [...] when it was midnight Shahrazad awoke and signalled to her sister Dunyazad who sat up and said, «Allah upon thee, O my sister, recite to us some new story, delightsome and delectable, wherewith to while away the waking hours of our latter night.» «With joy and goodly gree,» answered Shahrazad, «if this pious and auspicious King permit me.» «Tell on,» quoth the King who chanced to be sleepless and restless and therefore was pleased with the prospect of hearing her story. So Shahrazad rejoiced; and thus, on the first night of the Thousand Nights and a Night, she began... [2]

The undercurrent that the reader can perceive throughout the book – and also while watching its fantastic film version by Pier Paolo Pasolini[3] – is the sense of Fate, the theme of this work being the notion of an already written and immutable destiny which man fulfils from his very birth. Every single action had been already announced; the presence of good and evil genies – resembling the angels and the devils of the Catholic religion – represents a sort of bureaucratic administration regulating a traffic of destinies crossing each other like the clogging of many cogwheels.

The same can be told of Homer's masterpiece[4], in which virile and battling men such as the incomparable Ulysses bow to the will of the gods and to what had already been written at the moment of their own birth. The king of Ithaca struggles against Polyphemus and against the enchantress Circe and against the Sirens, and against the thousands of traps set for him by Poseidon. But he knows his doom already: coming back to Ithaca after an odyssey of twenty years just to briefly enjoy the coveted embrace with Penelope and their son Telemachus, and eventually leaving again for the final sea journey in which he faces death – a death forecast even by his protectress, Athena.

Do not fear – I don't have the presumption of racking my brain over the world's most ancient riddle: the chance that a human being stands to escape from a destiny that, as it is also projected by the two mentioned works of literature, seems to be based on a timeless willing that not only has already decided everything for us, but has also timed them[5].

Now let's add some consideration about the film *The Devil's Advocate*, starring a superb Al Pacino. The protagonist of this film is a young, unknown small-town-attorney who sets the whole country's tongues wagging because of his good track record of having never lost a case. He's made an offer to work in New York City joining the largest law firm in the Big Apple, by one of its founders, John Milton. This latter character, starred by Al Pacino, is actually an allusion to the Devil. The young attorney may in fact be considered as the son of Satan: John Milton is planning to have him coupled with another of his daughters – an attorney herself – to eventually rule the world.

Among other things, I find it interesting to see the obsessive demonization of the role of attorneys in the fiction filmed in the States.

Eventually the young attorney realizes what's going on. In an attempt to escape from this hellish plot he attempts suicide shooting himself – but the Devil had foreseen that too, so...

As you can easily understand, this is actually like an *uroboro* eating its own tail; i.e. it is a self-reproducing process without any escape; a general intrigue which represents the synthesis of a written, unmodifiable destiny.

Of course I do not personally agree with it, neither am I trying to convince you. Those who firmly believe that they are already crucified since their birth, are free to genuflect and live in a hopeless Middle Age. Those who think otherwise will try to do like those gazelles in the savannah – maybe they are conscious of the fact that their destiny is to become food for predators, yet they attempt to escape anyway – and many of them do survive.

Also the strongest lions in Africa and the terrible tigers probably are automatically aware of being obliged to winning and predating forever, without any chance of living a different destiny. Nonetheless many of them become prey themselves: killed by other predators or by a mistaken movement, or victims of the predator *par excellence* – man.

So then, perhaps there's a small degree of freedom within the frame of destinies that are apparently fully prefabricated and unalterable. I happen to remember the considerations that my friend and astrological researcher Enzo Barillà[6] wrote once when he was asked to express his opinion about the chance of changing our destiny by means of the Aimed Solar Returns. In that occasion he proposed – cleverly, I dare say – a parallel with the answers given by the Swiss Jungian psychologist Marie-Louise von Franz when she was once asked about the chance of eluding destiny. More or less she answered, «If we the depth-psychologists didn't believe so, why should we apply depth psychology to our patients?»

Now, with these simple words the problem is solved – at least it is solved for a good portion of Humankind – barring the narrow domain of philosophical conjectures without solution and joining the even less vast realm of a universe in which our will represents a real value – not a chimera, as in the imaginary world of *Matrix* or in Gabriele Salvatores' *Nirvana*.

Within the several books that I have written, you can find many examples of biological or astrological twins in which – on the day of their Solar Return – one of them chose to leave for an Aimed SR while the other one chose to spend that day at home. As a result, the following twelve months for each of them was completely different. All the rest is philosophy.

As I mentioned earlier, in my opinion the subject 'Solar and Lunar

Returns' represents, in a way, the University of Astrology. I know that many colleagues do not agree, and I don't mean to argue in any way. The Reader – free from any sort of conditioning – will read/taste a little of everything and eventually – and being under no pressure – will choose his own author and his own school.

Notes
1) Many decades ago, I had the pleasure of reading many editions of this book – which is, without any doubt, one of my favourites. The last that I read it was in the winter of 2007, in the excellent edition of publisher Einaudi, supervised by Mirella Cassarono, including an essay by Abdelfattah Kilito.
2) In fact, the bearing frame of *One Thousand and One Nights* is based on the expediency of the beautiful and cultured woman giving her 'literary drogue' to the king, night after night, in order to save thousands of other maids from certain death.
3) *Arabian Nights*, an Italian-French film directed by Pier Paolo Pasolini in 1974, starring Ninetto Davoli and Franco Citti.
4) The RAI edition of this DVD is really splendid! You will be amazed by watching it in *Full Definition* (1900 x 1080 pixels) – wonderful pictures and a wonderful definition.
5) Nonetheless I cannot but remark that even in such a religious (the term being used in the context of the notion of 'destiny') work like the *One Thousand and One Nights* the charming Shahrazad seems to have found the way to fool destiny: with the narration of tales for her king, telling a different story every night in order to delay her own execution.
6) See A *Few Facts on Aimed Birthdays*, Blue Diamond Publisher: it can be downloaded free from website www.cirodiscepolo.it.

Naples, the 5th of October 2007

PART I

LUNAR RETURNS

1.
The unconscious roots of my passion for the Aimed Solar Returns

Perhaps I have found out the unconscious – and that goes back quite a long time – roots of my irrepressible passion for ASRs. Be assured that my main motivation is their unquestionable value: ASRs do work perfectly (despite the disagreement of a few) thus representing a reality which is very close to pure mathematics: almost at the same level as Relocations.

We all know the value of symbols, and it hasn't been impossible for me to keep trace of the starting point of my profound interest towards this subject. I might remark, with certain bemusement, that nothing of this had ever emerged during three long-lasting sessions of depth analysis which I undertook approximately from the age of 20 until the age of 40. Only in recent times – within the frame of a magical period of my life – has it popped out in my mind; the clear, the crystal-clear, the impressively limpid memory of the very moment in which the trigger of the 'aimed birthday' clicked inside me.

I do not expect that everybody believes it – only those who have studied or read much of psychology.

I was three or four years old – no less and no more – it was my mother's birthday.

Keep in mind that the day of our birthday or the day of the birthday of a dear one, is always an extraordinary day of good or evil.

It is needless to explain what my mother represented for me. I am a Cancerian with my Ascendant also being Cancer (even though, having the Sun in my First House I am also an Aries to all intents and purposes): hence she was my everything, for me she was the world spinning around me, the air I used to breathe, love, tenderness, protection…

It is not by chance that I was her favourite son, the third of four.

I used to spend many hours of the day with her. As any good Cancerian, I absorbed all that she said without loosing a single word.

That day she upset me with her words, «Today is my birthday.» «What does it mean?», I asked. «It means – she answered – that your mum today gets a little older. Every year, on the day of her birthday, mummy gets a little older…» I got into a panic. I remember it as if it were yesterday. Disproportional emotional reactions broke out inside me, and I felt a sort of menace, a danger in those words – the fear that somebody or something could take her away from me.

I instinctively thought of an expedient, and that cruelly immature age made me exclaim, «No, mum – every year on the day of your birthday I will tie you to a chair with ropes so that you are not going to grow (in my childish mind getting old was a synonym for growing, also in the length of bones). This is what I'll do and you won't get older!»

It was very soothing for me to remember that episode, for it explains in a very simple and exhaustive way the fundamental direction of my life.

Let us repeat once again that the symbol is not a mark written on the paper with a pen – no, it is actually a dinosaur living inside us. This dinosaur might even devour us if we didn't grab it by the horns.

Later on I my life, other symbols would strike by force before my path, forecasting the precise route of my destiny.

By the age of 8 I used to be a pupil in the primary school of the Barnabite in Posillipo. Every morning a claret schoolbus would stop just before our door to take me to the top of the most picturesque hill of Naples. During the trip, in turn, little boys and girls used to sit by my side to express their personal, familiar, delicate problems. I did not understand that situation, yet I was already able to realize that something was going on – although I could not recognize that it was a symbol pressing strongly from inside myself, urging me to understand which direction my life would take.

Approximately four years later, as a student of junior secondary school I used to trace strange drawings with a little mitre square and a stencil with circles of different dimensions. I would cross circles and triangles and colour them in a particular way. Several times my teachers sent for my parents and asked them what those strange drawings represent. Several years later, at the age of 22, I started drawing freehand astral maps of people, and I used a little square and a stencil of circles: then I connected the two things.

2.
Why and how do Solar Returns and Lunar Returns work

There is a question that I've asked often to myself. Several times I have also been asked the same question by my readers or by people attending my seminars and lectures. The question is, in what physical or universal principle is it possible to set the functioning of Solar and Lunar Returns, thus accepting – already seen to be working in their theoretical formulation – that they actually operate in practice?

Let us forget for the time being what I have repeated several times – i.e. that an astrologer should not really care for the theoretical justification of the functioning of the Aimed Solar Returns and of the Aimed Lunar Returns, after having successfully experimented thousands of times that ASRs and ALRs do really work in practice. Yet over the years I do have developed a theory of my own, a theory that seems to have been validated by different schools of thought, some of them strictly scientific and some others, non-scientific.

For example we know that Carl Gustav Jung discussed for long the question of astrology being considered under the principle of cause and effect or under the principle of synchronicity. He also worked together with Wolfgang Ernst Pauli, a Nobel laureate in physics, and all his doubts on this subject started to pervade his works, beginning with his study on synchronicity[1] through all the following publications in which he faced such subjects. Almost until the day of his death – as described by Emma Baumann Jung[2] herself – he continued being uncertain about 'that strange thing called astrology', but he never doubted its validity: he was simply uncertain about how to classify it – as a 'causal' or as a 'synchronistic' phenomenon. Unfortunarely the great Swiss psychologist and thinker left us with this doubt.

Personally, for some years now I have been developing the conviction that our discipline should be explained in a causal way.

Before exposing my whole thought on this point, particularly referring to the Solar and Lunar Returns, I would urge you to read something important (at least in my opinion). It's a series of articles that appeared between 2005 and 2007 in my quarterly *Ricerca '90*. It is my belief that the following articles have an exceptional importance, especially if you consider that they contain certain coherent aspects that characterize them all in a sort of cross-party or bipartisan alignment.

I believe that the 3rd, 4th, and 5th of June 2005 are bound to be historical days for astrology. Those days, in the *XII Yearly Congress of Astrology* promoted and organized by *Ricerca '90* in Vico Equense (not far from Naples), some scientists 'out of the halls of power' held exceptionally interesting lectures.

I wish to express my gratefulness once again to those extraordinary researchers for their highly valued contributions – a special acknowledgement to my master and friend, engineer Vincenzo Di Napoli who has left this life. Now those scientists sat down at the same table without knowing each other. They exposed some aspects of a possible vision of the world and its laws: a sort of *Weltanschauung* that you may consider following a criterion which I'll explain later on. This idea picks up a little bit from each of the following lectures and may become the ground for a general theory on a possible functioning of astrology – a new theory never conjectured before, which in my opinion may be of particular interest and a quite convincing one.

Please read their lectures and also what they wrote on *Ricerca '90*: I will comment upon them later on.

It's science that should validate itself – by Renato Palmieri[3]

As it always happens in the conferences of 'heretical' disciplines, when you face the problem of their relationship with 'official' science they show a disposition of reclaiming their own validation on the basis of principles taken from the disciplines currently in force – whereas we should overturn the question and ask the academic science to show 'its own' credentials on the basis of heretical principles. The paradox is only apparent: in fact, it is precisely the anomalies presented by the so-called 'scientific heresies' that are the 'heel of Achilles' of the normal paradigm, which is unable to explain them and therefore – simply denies them. An emblematic example is given by 'cold fusion': in 1989 it marked the beginning of a series of experiments on a global scale, each of them confirming its validity, followed by a progressive wave of resistance at a theoretical level – or rather at an 'economical' level, and at the level of the power of the Establishment.

Two considerations can be put on the table in the frame of our congress. Astrology researches its effectual motivations in two orders of influences: those of a gravitational kind, and those of an electromagnetic kind. Let us consider then what current science really 'knows' of the essence of gravitation and of electromagnetism. Well, it can be easily shown that it actually knows absolutely 'nothing'.

1) In this congress the Zodiac is your daily bread. Zodiac implies ecliptic. The plane of the ecliptic is that of the whole solar system, with an axis centred on the Sun and a vast equatorial plane on which the planets rotate: the giant planets with their whole parade of satellites, Saturn with its rings, and so on. This structure, in its whole, has a discoidal shape similar to that of the immense galactic discs, and a general rotation which is prospectivally anticlockwise or clockwise as regards the two poles – North and South – of the central axis. Such an immediately evident feature has a very clear name: it is called *dipolarity* and it is present without ambiguity in any celestial body having enough size. However, gravitation is incredibly ignored from this scheme. It is ignored in every book of theoretical physics, of cosmology and of history of science, starting from the theorems of Kepler and of Newton throughout the experiment of Cavendish for the measurement of the gravitational constant and up to Einstein. Even more: it is even denied when they talk about the 'spherical symmetry' and the 'unipolar field' of gravitation (cfr. Phillips, *La Geofisica*, Biblioteca EST Mondatori, page 168). This implies that all the discussions and the calculations that have been made or that they are making about gravitation are approximate: the proof being that the so-called G-'constant' or gravitational 'constant' is reckoned with only three significant figures (6.67), while other cosmological constants have eight or nine figures.

2) Here are two pieces of magnetic chess: a queen and a king. They have the same polarity, being opposite to the polarity of the magnetic board. Let us pull the two bottoms of the pieces closer. Immediately it becomes evident that the so-called 'repulsion' between them does not manifest along an axis – as it is shown in any book of physics – but with a sort or rotational 'sliding' that no theory is able to explain to us. Now, such a phenomenon is exactly identical to the behaviour of a comet with a very stretched-out ellipse: when it reaches the perihelion, it also 'slides' rotating around the Sun and then it goes back to outer space with an overall movement which nobody would ever define 'repulsive' as regards the Sun.

As a consequence, the general scene of the pieces of knowledge 'proven' by current science with respect to the so-called 'heretical' notions is similar to Pieter Bruegel the Elder's painting *The Blind leading the Blind*. The roped-party leader, who's already fallen into the ditch, is the academic science – despite Popper's 'falsifiability', which Professor Emilio Del Giudice has rightly criticized in his previous lecture. The following blind men, unless they resolve to leave the roped party as soon as possible, will follow as the heretical disciplines do looking for the support of science.

And to sum up with a general proposal, may I invite you to found the CCCONS as a counterpart to the notorious CSICOP (TN: today's CSI, *Committee for Skeptical Inquiry*): where the latter is the *Committee for the Scientific Investigation of Claims of the Paranormal*, the former would be the *Committee for the Control of Claims of the Normal Science* – it should pass judgment on many of the most sensational articles of the academic magazines like the *Scientific American*.

Vico Equense, the 4th of June 2005

On Fibonacci, pyramids and environs – by Vincenzo Di Napoli[4]

This lecture can be seen to be the continuation of what – some time ago – I happened to claim on the implication of the fatal Fibonacci number on architecture. The dimensioning of the building elements according to the classical golden dimensions, both on plan and on elevation, implies an important consequence in the field of hertz microwaves: a building element, with its planoaltimetric conformation, builds up a volume; as regards to microwaves, this volume behaves just like a resonance box – it resonates on frequencies corresponding to the frequencies of the various colours of the Helmholtz spectrum. The induction of such frequencies is of a cosmogeographical kind; their value not only depends on dimensions, but also on shape as well as on the orientation of the building element in space. At his point let us add that such frequencies, when dimensioned in accordance with the golden elements, fall in the band corresponding to orange yellow. How could ancient architects reach such results? It is a mystery.

In order to understand the importance of what we are talking about, we must notice that, according to the medical theories of chromotherapy, all the colours ranging from orange yellow to red are bioaccelerator, while all the colours towards violet are bioretardant[1]. Hence, we have a standstill in correspondence of orange yellow. Thus, we have opened a new chapter of environmental health: a chapter that considers even the nature of building materials as a corollary – this is particularly true with the sands used as a component of the different kinds of concrete, and those used for colouring the internal walls. So, during the design of new objects or the renewal of existing ones, there's the need of a technique that allows to determine and to measure the following elements:

1) Sensibility to cosmogeophysical radiations of the premises for their planoaltimetric conformation.

2) Nature of the materials with which we intend to build.

3) Colours of the walls delimiting a room.

If the volume of the room can be inscribed into a sphere, the accumulation of energy can be studied also on a diagram, representing its planimetry. This I have personally carried out by using the Callegari machine as a hertz-microwave detector – see the previous issues of our quarterly. In a following issue we'll describe its technique of employment.

At this point let me make a digression, due to its historical character within my studies and because of its astrological implications.

Originally I focused my attention on these subjects when I resolved to investigate certain, still unknown aspects of the Egyptian pyramids.

I built a model on the same proportions (i.e. the same ratio between its perimeter and the double of its altitude) of the Great Pyramid of Giza, and I found out that its volume was resonating on a frequency around orange yellow, and that it changed in plus or minus depending on its orientation and on the day. This implied important considerations:

1) Its builders knew very well that the entity of the inductional cosmogeographical energy was a function of its planoaltimetric dimensions…

2) …and that it was variable with the orientation as regards to determined constellations – which testifies the perfect knowledge of astrology[2], if not something else.

Searching for the meaning of this all, I assumed that the explanation might hide in the aim those mastodontic objects had been built for, which was undoubtedly the conservation of the Pharaohs' mummies. Now, the conservation of a corpse implied a struggle against the enemies of the flesh provoking its putrefaction, namely water and micro organisms (fungi). Against water they performed a biopsy that allowed withdrawing all the inner organs from the corpse; and substituting them with cotton wool drenched in perfumes. The corpse itself was wrapped up in cotton bandages drenched in sea salt. Against micro organisms, there was the energy accumulated inside the pyramid: as we have seen, it fell in a colour range close to the orange yellow; hence it was also able to keep them sedated, therefore inactive.

This justifies, for example, the mishaps of the French archaeologists who first violated the pyramids and withdrew some mummies, now exposed at the Louvre in Paris. In fact, as they entered inside the pyramids they became victims of the micro organisms; once outside, the micro organisms resumed their virulence provoking even the death of certain members of the expedition – the death later on explained as 'the Pharaoh's curse'.

An astrological consequence is that it would be helpful and interesting to analyze the levels of geocosmic energy depending on the day and the hours, taking photographs of the celestial vault using the Callegari control unit. It would be another piece of corroboration, if needed, of the physical-scientific fundamentals of astrology.

I propose to develop a research on this, hoping to be able to report some positive result on the following issues of this quarterly.

In mathematics, the **Fibonacci numbers** are a sequence of numbers [...] The first number of the sequence is 0, the second number is *1* (NT: F0 =*0* and F1 =*1*), and each subsequent number is equal to the sum of the previous two numbers of the sequence itself, yielding the sequence 0, 1, 1, 2, 3, 5, 8, etc. [...] The sequence extended to negative index *n* satisfies $F_n = F_{n»1} + F_{n»2}$ for *all* integers *n*, and $F_{»n} = («1)^{n+1} F_n$ [...]

The sequence is named after *Leonardo of Pisa*, known as Fibonacci, who introduced this sequence in his 1202 book *Liber Abaci*. Fibonacci's intention was to describe a law describing the growth of a population of rabbits. It is assumed that each rabbit takes a month before it becomes fertile, and that each couple of fertile rabbits produce a couple of bunnies each month. So if we start with a single couple, after the first month we have two rabbit couples, of which only one is fertile. The following month we have 2+1=3 couples, because only the fertile couple delivered: and of the three couples, only two are fertile. Thus the following month we have 3+2=5 couples. Thus the number of rabbit couples each month describes the sequence of Fibonacci numbers.

The first 41 Fibonacci numbers are:

0, 1, <u>1</u>, <u>2</u>, <u>3</u>, <u>5</u>, <u>8</u>, <u>13</u>, <u>21</u>, <u>34</u>, <u>55</u> (=F10), <u>89</u>, <u>144</u>, 233, 377, 610, 987, 1597, 2584, 4181, 6765 (=F20), 10946, 17711, 28657, 46368, 75025, 121393, 196418, 317811, 514229, 32040 (=F30), 1346269, 2178309, 3524578, 5702887, 9227465, 14930352, 24157817, 39088169, 63245986, 102334155 (=F40)

Fibonacci sequence is called sequence A000045 in OEIS. Fibonacci numbers possess an amazing wide range of properties; they can be found in the mathematical models of several phenomena, and they are used in many computational procedures. Moreover, they possess several interesting

generalizations. A scientific magazine, *The Fibonacci Quarterly*, is specifically devoted to these subjects.
(Partly quoted from English Wikipedia and partly retranslated from Italian Wikipedia)

Notes of the Author
1) Those who ever dealt with chromotherapy know very well that if you suffer, say, from a molar toothache, wearing a red scarf would be like adding fuel to the flames. On the other hand, any garment whose colour tended to violet (i.e. the opposite direction in the spectrum of electromagnetic-waves frequencies) would certainly relieve your pain.
2) In my opinion, this is another topical passage of engineer Di Napoli's lecture: it has a great importance also considering what he and his esteemed colleagues have been telling us on these pages in the last few months. I believe that they have been disclosing cores of an extraordinary truth in the field of Knowledge: such Knowledge that is not polluted by the blind fundamentalist hatred of certain pseudo scientists who are moved by prejudice or – even worse – perhaps they're in somebody's pay… Here the author refers generically to 'constellations' while we astrologers know that it has to be referred to the transit of celestial bodies along the ecliptic. These few lines are pregnant with extraordinary importance, for they allow us to understand wonderful aspects of how the universe, the Earth, and the stars work – not to mention their mutual interactions. Anybody, let me underline *anybody*, can prove with his/her own eyes that if you build up a small pyramid with the figures suggested by engineer Di Napoli, he/she would observe, for example, the 'prodigy' of the split apple. Let us cut an apple in two halves and put one half into a pyramid made of transparent Plexiglas, made according to the ratios of the Great Pyramid of Giza. Now let us place the other half of the apple under another pyramid – built up with *wrong* measures. After a few days you'll see that the first half preserved perfectly, while the other one putrefied completely. I am perfectly convinced, at this point, that fundamentally important things have been written down in the recent issues of *Ricerca '90* – extremely important for the understanding of astrology as well, of how astrology works. Suggested by Pino Valente, by the engineer Giuseppe Callegari and others, the grounds have been established for a possible test of the frequencies of the different celestial bodies in the Callegari scale and using the Callegari Control Unit, and any possible future employment of such frequencies. The notion that one day you may deploy an aimed birthday in a laboratory is much closer to reality than to a science-fiction novel. Once again let me express my gratefulness to engineer Di Napoli for such pearls of knowledge!

Callegari radionics and astrology – by Giuseppe Callegari[5]

I fully agree with those, like professor Palmieri and others who held their lectures before me, who claim that ASTROLOGY has its own life and it has no need for the official consent from whomsoever. Emilio Segré, Nobel laureate in physics, the discoverer of the antiproton, in a congress titled «The Physics of the XX century» declared in public, «[…] without the bravery of men capable of thinking and reasoning in an unconventional and untraditional way, detaching from the so-called 'fundamental laws' we would not have today the radio, the television, the telephone, the airplane, the space missions… So any time that the practical experience suggested not to consider some of the 'consolidated' certainties of the Official Science, or even to consider them as questionable...» This Science even today wants to ignore, or at least it pretends it ignores, the existence of the Other Science, parallel to itself: that science that amazes and excites you; that makes you rejoice at the beauty of the Creations; that makes you dream and fancy; that elevate the spirits; that should be taught to everybody from the very first years of school. The father of radionics, Giambattista Callegari warns, «[...] The incontrovertibly established results of experience are authoritative upon the theoretical propositions... Theories in general can be considered with certain detachment, leaving to time the task of affirming them, of perfecting them or burying them according with the results of further experiences... **Theories may change, but the facts and the results of experience remain still, and cannot be ignored...**» But as you can easily guess, there's a precise will, tenaciously working against the common man, to keep tight the strings of profit, cost what it may. What's systematically going on in the world is before everybody's eye. The most absurd wars, the most dissolute abandonment (despite the frenetic consumerism of many) of suffering populations that run the risk of disappearing. The foolish clearing of trees and the huge deforestation, having the consequence of eliminating the great present that God has given to us. The green of plants and trees not only is a pulsing tank of oxygen and chlorophyll: it is also a natural defence against the constant, unceasing bombing of neutrons from outer space. So I ask, where have all the Mighty, the Chiefs of the Nations, those 'in the know' gone? They are actually absent, minding only of their own – political and financial – business, careful not to loose their own power, cost what it may... You'll forgive me for this digression, but I believe that it's not a bad thing to keep our eyes on these subjects, especially when you are facing other subjects, so pleasant and fascinating ones like what Astrology offers today to us, in this gorgeous day in Vico Equense. So let us stick to our subject: «**Possible hypotheses on how Astrology works**» Six thousands of years ago Fo-hi, a Chinese enlightened mind claimed, «**Man is the synthesis between the Celestial Strenghts and the Earthly Strengths.**» In particular, «[...] *the celestial bodies [...] are points of reference for the motion of the earth in the Universe. Such motion corresponds to periodical variations in the energy of the space, affecting the phenomena that weigh both upon organic and inorganic substance – therefore affecting, in particular, Man. That is to say, there are variations in the fields of strengths that affect man.*» (Translated from G. Callegari's work: «La mia opinione, fondata sulla K-analisi, intorno al contenuto del volume: Mario Pincherle, *Fonti archeologiche della magia*, Edizioni Filelpo, 1977»). Giambattista Callegari's radionics confirmed, after six thousands years, the transcendental truth expressed by Fo-hi. The discovery of the K-effect or Radionical effect, and the «Radionical principle» (1938-1945), together with the results of a relentless, unceasing experimentation confirm that, as the consequence of the 'Cosmogeographical Conjuncture' – i.e. the simultaneousness of natural phenomena weighing on the Earth and the Universe to which the Earth belongs – particular processes of natural ionization take place in space, and such phenomena make it possible the activation of the phenomenon called '**resonance**'. *In other words, in the non-impedant (i.e. more transparent) space it becomes possible for the exchange of energy between the radio oscillating-broadcasting structures (in our case **the planets, the stars, the constellations**) and man.* Anyway, such a phenomenon concerns all living beings: besides man, the animals and the plants, as well as the inorganic substances. *Hence the manifestation – in that sky and in that time – of phenomena and events that interfere and interact with the 'earthly day' of the human being, both at a material level and at a psychical-emotional level.* From the results of Callegari's experimentation, man is nothing more than a particular 'naturally oscillating circuit': a sort of Callegari circuit, with an antenna to pick up the waves arriving from the space surrounding him. In this natural circuit the **coil** is made up of nervous strands departing from the spinal cord, while the **capacitor** or **condenser** is made up of the grounds scattered all over the body. The average value of the radionical frequency of the human being, based on the original Callegari scale, is fk = 5.751. This value it is not expressed in hertz, but its value in hertz can be calculated. This value is the sum of the two following frequencies fk = 3.753 (biophysical wave) and fk = 9.001 (photopsychonic wave). There would be so much to tell about the radiations arriving from the celestial bodies: to each wavelength and frequency corresponds a different colour and musical note – by the way, the amusing configuration and the equilibrium of our solar system are governed by a musical order. For example, our Earth 'colours in blue' and it 'sounds in sol'. Giambattista Callegari determined the radionical values of the energy of the Sun, of the stars, of Galaxies and Comets (fk = 8.001); of the interstellar, interplanetary and endoatomic space (fk = 9.000); of the planets, the satellites, the asteroids, meteors and sunspots (fk = 0.001). The Sun and the Moon influence man, having him participate of the masculine nature of the former and the feminine nature of the latter. Just consider that a red blood cell performs a complete tour inside our body while the heart beats 28 times and you breathe 7 times. This ratio between the number of heartbeats and the number of breaths you take is constant, and it is equal to the ratio between the solar cycle and the lunar cycle. This means that the rhythms of man follow the same laws of the rhythms of our Galaxy – i.e., there's a perfect analogy between macrocosm and microcosm. As if that wasn't enough, all this is complicated (and enhanced, for our amusement) by the almost 'persistent' presence of certain figures, in Nature, in the Universe and in the artistic or non-artistic artefacts created by man. For example, the divine golden figure or Fibonacci number Æ = **1,618...** – we find it in the disposition of the leaves of plants; in the logarithmic spirals of sunflowers; in shells; in vortexes; in the spiral-shaped galaxies; in Leonardo da Vinci's, Piero della Francesca's and Albrecht Dürer's masterpieces... Incidentally, or strangely, the radionical value of water measured by Callegari is fk = 1.600... Another repeating figure is ð = 3.14... – it can be found in the structure of the Great Pyramid of Giza. Callegari found that in correspondence of the radionical number fk = 3.333 – which is also close to the double of 1.618... – the images becomes stronger, i.e. they appear in natural relief. In fact if you have a light beam pass through a Callegari radionical circuit, thus creating a radionical channel, you have variations in the Fraunhofer lines. Unfortunately there isn't time to go into these facts now. The CRC (Callegari Radiobiological Central unit) that you can see down here on this table is the prototype of the new model called CRC 75/05 Super Original New. It is produced exclusively in the Laboratory of Callegari Radionics and Radiobiology that I direct and supervise. Today I introduce it officially for the first time. Now with this model it is possible to 'pick up' a substance in general – and in particular, the human being. In other words, it is possible (also with a photo) to establish a radionical resonance with the object or the subject, and to study its/his/her energetic status of that moment: surplus, deficit, equilibrium. Once you determine the imbalance and you discover the causes of such phase-shifts, it is then possible to restore phase, i.e. to re-balance trying to re-establish the isoenergeticism of the individual being examined. From this table of the XII Vico Congress on Astrology I announce to you the birth of **Radionical Astrology**. As regards to that I am working on a new instrument of Callegari radionics: the first central unit for Radionical Astrology called 'PC/05 ASTRAL RADIONIC CALLEGARI', an equipment unique in its genre, especially developed for astrological applications. Through a holographic technique, this unit allows the radionical verification of the typical determinations of the astrological technique. It allows ascertaining the current status of resonance or lack of resonance between the subject and the result of the astrological calculations represented by the graphics. In case of negative result – namely, the lack of resonance – it will be necessary to determine the probable data of origin, for example the complete birth data of the subject: day, month, year, time, place, environmental conditions, relevant local and/or general events, etc. Subsequently you'll be able to perform the required corrections in order to re-modulate the astrological determination. In case of negative result – namely, the presence of resonance – you will be able to determine the complementary radionical frequency (*fkc* or *fkr*) and intervene positively with the application of the K-method (Callegari's radionical method) on the energetic status of the subject in a natural way, using subtle, non-destructive and non-invasive energies without any collateral effect and which is absolutely not damaging. In other words, it will be possible to verify whether the 'astrological remedy' recommended by the operational protocol is really necessary and applicable, or if it is not compatible with the subject considered. This verification will be performed by reckoning, with the already mentioned PC/05 Callegari unit, the value of radionical frequency *fk* on the recommended astrological remedy; and checking up with the very same equipment whether such a frequency is complementary or not complementary for the subject. For example, if the astrological remedy implies an environmental-geographical relocation (a change of both spatial-terrestrial and energetic-magnetic co-ordinates) you determine the radionical frequency of the place recommended [NT, for an Aimed Solar Return] with reference with a time interval close to the foreseen one, and you verify whether such a frequency is complementary, that's to say, whether it is the right one for the overall re-equilibration of the subject. If this is not the case, you have to re-examine the proposed case and find out another astrological remedy. For example, it might be solved with the direct and unique application of the complementary radionical frequency (the already mentioned *fkc*) with the aforementioned CRC 75/05. It is time now for me to conclude my lecture, for I don't wish to take time from other lecturers at this table. However, let me express my deep approval and my special gratefulness to Ciro Discepolo. With his usual elegance and passion, he has been able to describe to you all some experiences of radionics that he personally had with my father Giambattista Callegari – and he has done it with conviction and with a wealth of affectional details. I am deeply grateful to him for that.

Astrology, prejudice and a 'gem' on Guglielmo Marconi – by Emilio Del Giudice[6]

Let me begin with William Shakespeare, a quote from Hamlet: «There are more things in heaven and earth, Horatio – Than are dreamt of in your philosophy.» It has almost nothing to do with philosophy, but listen to me for five minutes and I'll be able to tell you a tendentious story of the birth of radio at the end of the 19th century.

Around 1870 Scottish theoretical physicist James Clerk Maxwell proved that, based on the functions of electromagnetism, it is possible that the field energy propagates in space through the electromagnetic waves, the latter not being the same as the electric field and the magnetic field; as it were, they are in fact its 'travelling component'.

In other words, the comprehensive field has this travelling component as well as the component called *near field*, which propagates much less, being the field closer to the source.

How did this idea get into his head? As long as everything is static, nothing propagates. But let us argue that the field source is modified by somebody close to the source.

Since this field acts at a distance, and it acts over electric charges, the natural question is, how much time after the modification of the source does the charge receiving the action 'realize' that something has been modified? Does it realize it immediately or after a while?

Let us put this in a simpler way. Guess you have a pool full of water. A ball is floating on the surface. You wish to move the ball but you are at a distance from it. So what you do is take an oar and smash the water with it to create waves on the surface. Waves reach the ball and it moves. If you hit the water properly, you'll have the ball move.

In this example you modify an infinite medium and it takes a while to get a result at a distance. Which is the vehicle in this case? It's the propagating wave.

Now, the electromagnetic wave acts more or less the same way – to make a long story short, you have a field generated down here, with a charge, and it acts over there. So you take this charge and instead of keeping it still, you move it. As a consequence, also the acting strength fluctuates. The question is: does fluctuation appear at the same time or a little later?

Well, the answer given by Maxwell theory is that it takes a little time. The speed of propagation of this wave, according to the parameters of his theory, is equal to the speed of light. This arouses the suspicion of light being a particular form of the electromagnetic field.

About thirty years later, this appeared to be a mere theoretical construction. Then Heinrich Rudolf Hertz experimentally verified Maxwell's theories. In his studies, Hertz was assisted by Augusto Righi, an Italian after whom squares, street, and schools are named here in Italy – so that we can project Hertz to be a 'validated' person. So – by using electromagnetic waves it is possible to send messages at a distance. How come it took a number of years before the electromagnetic waves found their practical applications?

Because one of the consequences of the theory confirmed by Hertz's experiment was that the electromagnetic waves propagate along a straight line with lateral fluctuations – the so-called refractive effects – as large as the wavelength.

So if you consider the antennas available at the time, if you used electromagnetic waves whose wavelength is as long as a few hundred metres to one kilometre, the refractive effects made it possible that the waves overcame a hill – but not certainly the curvature of the Earth. Hence the notion of transmitting an electromagnetic wave from Europe to America or vice-versa was a foolish nonsense.

Luckily Guglielmo Marconi wanted to try this foolishness out. He had a very rich family background. As a rich boy, he was also arrogant. So he resolved to carry out this attempt. He was certainly clever but also ignorant. In fact, he did not study because he was rich. So he confused the 'electromagnetic' field with the 'electric' field. He thought «In the books it is said that when an electric field is close to a conductor, it arranges itself parallel to the surface of the conductor. Hence, the Earth is a conductor and the electric field must arrange itself parallel to the soil. If so, the curvature of Earth is not a problem.» So did he rightly surmise – or better said, unrightly: because as an ignorant boy, he wasn't aware that the electric field arranging itself parallel is the near field – not the electromagnetic field which has nothing to do with that. Anyway he knocked at Augusto Righi's door who was teaching in Milan by the time. And if Hertz is the father of the electromagnetic waves, certainly Righi was its uncle. So Marconi addressed Righi more or less this manner: «Professor, I've found a way to transmit a radio signal from Europe to America.» As a successful scientist, Righi was arrogant too and replied, «Oh really? And how would this thing work?» Marconi confided to him what I've just detailed.

Then Righi replied icily, «Get out of here right now, I haven't got time to waste on these things, come back after having had some education!» kicking him out.

Luckily, Marconi had no need to ask for funds from the State – which would have been refused for sure – so he asked his mother instead, who would have certainly gouged Righi's eyes out had she known of Righi's negative reaction. So his mother sponsored the enterprise and Guglielmo left for England, where he placed an antenna in Cornwall. Then, considering that his mother's money was much but not endless, he rented a plot of land – and not buy it – in Terranova, Canada; and placed another antenna there. Meanwhile the press began spreading the news of an Italian young man working on a wireless telegraph.

Journalists started polling various scientists on this subject. On the front page of *Le Monde* (the most important French daily at that time) an interview with the most important theoretical physician of France, Henry Poincaré, was published. He was a great scientist. Those whom I am mentioning were not simple people, were not ignorant; they were not Piero Angela [NT, Italian science journalist and a member of CICAP, the Italian council of sceptical organizations]; each of them had discovered something.

So back to Henry Poincaré declaring to *Le Monde*, with all his French condescension, «Has anybody explained to this Italian guy that the Earth is a sphere? Perhaps he thinks that the Earth is flat, like the ancients did? Haven't they told him?» (A note of the Author: This resembles, somehow, the story of the bumblebee – according to scientific calculation it should be unable to fly, yet nobody told it so that it flies anyway. See Ciro Discepolo's *I fondamenti dell'astrologia medica*, Armenia)

Marconi didn't care, the day arrived and he sent the signal, and the signal arrived! How embarrassing!

Then, if we were to take 'Popper the bighead' seriously we could wonder, «Did Marconi falsify the theory on electromagnetism? On one hand the theory says that the electromagnetic waves propagate approximately along a straight line; on the other hand the Earth is round. If you put these two things together, an electromagnetic wave starting from Europe cannot arrive in America.»

If it does arrive, according to Karl Popper one of the two statements has been falsified.

Which of the two assertions is correct? «Is it not true that the electromagnetic waves propagate on a straight line?» or «Is it not true that the Earth is round?»

It is absolutely true that the electromagnetic waves propagate in a straight line; and it is also true that the Earth is round (it is also proven by photographs now) – so what is the explanation?

The explanation is always the same: there's something unknown at the time of the events, something deceiving people – in our case, it's the ionosphere. At the time of the events neither Righi nor Marconi knew that there is an ionosphere – a layer of the atmosphere surrounding our planet at several scores of kilometres from its surface. The ionosphere is made up of gases that are ionized by radiation from outer space: the result is a layer of ionized molecules.

That layer behaves like a mirror with regard to those electromagnetic waves whose wavelength, let us put it this way, corresponds to the density of that plasma.

Therefore, with frequencies lower than the so-called plasma frequency of a gas, the ionosphere behaves like a mirror. That is to say that that layer of gas is opaque to radiations. So, luckily – fortune favours the brave – the frequencies that Marconi employed fell into the right range. Hence the wave of Marconi started from Terranova; proceeding on a straight line, it went up and up; it met the mirror; it was reflected down to Earth; and it eventually reached Europe.

So you can see that Righi's theory was absolutely right; Poincaré's statements were indisputable; yet Marconi was right despite them all.

Why?

Because of the intervention of a different circumstance, unknown to his contemporaries, that conspired to make things work as they did.

In fact there's a saying: If an old professor says that something is not possible he's almost certainly wrong, but if he says that it is possible he's almost certainly right.

That is, if you say that something isn't possible it is the greatest piece of nonsense that one can say, because there is always a way to overcome the obstacle.

I do not mean to say that the hypothesis that I'm offering to you is the right one; perhaps it isn't so, but in any case this makes you realize that it is not impossible to think of mechanisms that explain… Now that I think about it again, what is certainly impossible is to say, «it is not possible…».

Just to say that ignorance does not always help: the first time things went well for Marconi, but the second time they went wrong, definitely wrong. It was the case of the radar, whose idea first occurred to Marconi. In fact, during a conference held at the headquarters staff of the Italian

Navy in 1922, he proposed to place an antenna on a ship to 'shoot' an electromagnetic wave which would glance off another ship, if it came across one, thus coming back and revealing the alien ship's presence. It is the same principle on which a modern the radar works.

But as we have seen, Marconi could not differentiate between an electrical field and an electromagnetic field. He lacked the knowledge about wavelengths.

He had a liking for long waves, so he projected a radar tool (or had it projected) based on a radio wave whose length was some hundreds of metres. It is therefore not true that the Italian Navy did not possess a radar instrument during the War – in fact the Navy had radar, and we called it 'gufo' (owl). But the Italian 'owl' was useless because the electromagnetic wave that it employed had a wavelength of some hundred of metres, while the ships were much shorter than that! As a consequence, the refractive effect, i.e. the lateral deviation, invested the whole ship and the result was that you could see nothing. The resolution of a radar instrument, that's to say, the length of the smallest object visible, is given by the wavelength employed.

Thus, the ships being shorter than the employed wavelength, the Italian Navy's 'owl' was a fiasco.

Two such equipment were mounted, one on the battleship *Littorio* and one on the destroyer *Lince*, but a few months later they got dismounted because they detected nothing.

The Englishmen used electromagnetic waves with a 10-centimetre length for their radar and they could see not only ships but also airplanes.

Although the very idea of radar first occurred to Marconi, thanks to the fact that he hadn't a clear notion of the undulatory theories, the equipment created by him proved to be ineffectual.

Coming back to Astrology and to many other related phenomena – I would say that usually a series of factors that would make the phenomenon plausible are not considered and worse: they are neglected. In fact during the last years we have seen the flowering of many impossible things: cold fusion is one of them, i.e. the posibility of conducting nuclear reactions at room temperature, and without huge machines. We also learn – and it is true – that the armies of a certain countries employ strange weapons, called depleted uranium weapons even though depleted uranium has nothing to do with them – it is only a sort of smokescreen operation. These weapons produce a flow of neutrons, a flood of nuclear reactions – let us put it this way – in an unconventional way. This is what the armies of the major countries do, such as the United States, leading me to suspect (among other things) that the hostility manifested by the Establishment against new discoveries is actually the wish – inspired by the armed forces – of avoiding a particular concentration of the public attention on them, so that somebody may exercise a monopoly on them.

You are right: I haven't talked about Astrology. But I did talk to you about conditioning and prejudice, about the reasons why scientists or the scientific community are not always worth being listened to. Sometimes, in fact, they rather deserve to be ignored or disbelieved.

The miraculously healing water – by Nicola Del Giudice[7]

Let me digress a little bit from the subjects dwelt upon so far. As a homeopath doctor, I happen to face paradoxical aspects, such as the miraculous healing water, the absence of molecules as a *condicio sine qua non* of a therapeutic phenomenon that science cannot simply explain – therefore I mainly refer to the actions and the events happening within my field of expertise.

Certainly, science has been meeting many strange phenomena: once they belonged to magicians and charlatans, now they are the fundament of science.

One of the interesting phenomena is cold fusion [...]. I know Ciro since we were kids, so several times we have discussed about things that are going on; certainly one of the most important features of any researcher should be – being curious. Curiosity means not to deny *a priori* any phenomenon, and not to look for a scientific explanation at any rate. I've seen many scientific theories falling before an empirical event, but I've never seen an empirical event falling because of a theory.

Let's accept empirical events then without the need of denying them later on, or as you can see some times, without the need of a self-objection, as it were, just because we do not want to devaluate the physical theory.

This is precisely what happened to me some time ago. One of my female patients with a disease, she was discovered to have a serious disease: multiple sclerosis. As it happens quite frequently, her condition developed a month after a pregnancy. It affected the lower parts of her body, and she was desperate. She was a good acquaintance of mine; she told me that the diagnosis had been made in a famous medical centre in Milan. Of course, she was very fond of homeopathic medicine, and she also had an undeserved faith in me; she asked what we could do, considering that traditional science could do nothing.

Then we treated her with specific magnetic fields for six months. At the end of this treatment she went back to that medical centre in Milan: after a session of nuclear magnetic resonance she was told that her scars had totally disappeared, and she had recovered movement and sensitivity.

Perhaps this case is peculiar compared to other ones, because it just happened a little time ago. But the thing was striking. In fact I remember that at the first session of electromagnetic field therapy I tried testing her sensitivity by piercing a needle on her foot, and she had no reaction at all.

After some treatment I repeated the test and the lady immediately reacted to the stimulus, showing that she had recovered sensitivity.

When my patient went back to that diagnostical centre in Milan, the person who had previously diagnosed her disease (he was a good friend of hers, too) could not deny the facts. Yet, in an attempt to stick to the traditional theory and medicine, he claimed he had made a wrong diagnosis initially: she had never really suffered from multiple sclerosis.

In other words, he preferred to make a fool of himself rather than admitting that a homeopathic treatment could have really given any benefit to the lady.

I might enumerate several cases like this. There are also cases of mutual irradiation with our neighbours, people we meet, and such exchange may also have a therapeutic function. It may be the case of a guru or Jesus Christ healing the cripple or it may be somebody healing a headache with the imposition of his or her hand, or whatever. We irradiate in any case, and we can have a practical demonstration of this too.

As an example, let us take a Kirlian camera and take a picture of a patient and of his/her therapist. You'll see that the photographs of their aura are different if you take them before and after treatment. Paradoxically the therapist's aura after treatment tends to assume the patient's characters – as if the negative influence of the patient affected the therapist, as if there was a resonance.

And this is another amazing fact that would need to be analyzed.

For sure, official science denies itself the possibility of facing such themes, although – let us put it bluntly – when the problems touch their personal spheres they don't hesitate to ask even for the homeopaths' help secretly crowding their clinics – like a famous pharmacologist from

Naples who used to pontificate against homeopathy in his classes.

One day a student went to a homeopath doctor; where he noticed – guess who? – his professor of pharmacology and asked him, «Professor! How come you are here now, if you keep on denigrating homeopathy?» The professor looked into the student's eye and answered, «My son, bread is bread but skin is skin!»

Another case happened during a confrontation between the adherents of allopathic medicine and homeopathic medicine, the former represented among others, by professor Garattini. First the allopaths spoke. I don't wish to repeat everything that was said against us the homeopaths – that we are swindlers, magicians, charlatans and you name it. […] In particular, Garattini spoke ironically on the lack of understanding about how molecules recognize each other within a living organism. Although it has been ascertained that molecules move to find an appropriate equal to react with, the manner in which they accomplish this is still unknown.

How can molecules recognize each other among millions of molecules within an organism? How do they know which one of them is their 'soulmate', their second self with which they can mutually entangle giving an oncological effect? They don't explain it.

Of course we too would not have an answer to this question. So I said, «You see Professor, if you give me an explanation on how molecules move, I swear I'll stroll in the very centre of Naples with a poster saying, 'Homeopathy is nonsense, and I am a fool'.»

He answered, «Are you bull****ting me or what?» and I said, «No, I am not».

Said I, «On the contrary, let us suppose, that you take a plane and fly to the United States to take part in a congress. There you browse a newspaper and you see a short article saying that 'a certain professor…' has died in a car accident: at that point your hand goes to your breast and you fall down to the ground due to a heart attack. Then Professor Garattini, can you explain to me which one was the molecule that hit your eyes from the paper? The molecule that through your eyes arrived to the midollary zone of the suprarenal gland, that activated the production of adrenaline there, the adrenaline entered into circulation, it caused the vasorestriction and you had a heart attack? Could you explain this to me, doctor Garattini?» […]

Of course I had no answer from Professor Garattini. But I can attempt one and give it to you now. Here is an evident example of it. There are two people suffering from the same pathology, they go to two different homeopath doctors. Both doctors know homeopathic medicine perfectly, both prescribe the treatment correctly – the same treatment for both patients – but one patient recovers while the other does not.

Could you explain to me why one patient recovers while the other doesn't? It is because homeopathy recognises an effect – the therapist-medicine effect. Even the therapist is a medicine, and a powerful one! So the very same drug does not have an affect if provided by one doctor, but it does if provided by another. The reason is that a resonant irradiation exchange has been activated, and this exchange is the first source of healing. The same happened, for example, with a patient of mine suffering from asthma: he arrived in the surgery breathing in a horrible way; he took a seat in the waiting room and started chatting with the others. When the time arrived to see him, he simply told me that the crisis was over.

That is, the very fact of discovering inside the clinic the possibility of opening himself to others and exchanging information – therefore important feelings, sensations and emotions – had made it possible for him to relax his body without any need of taking cortisone or other drugs.

So what we are learning – in conclusion – and we are trying to enhance by means of homeopathy are those apparently strange aspects that this science proposes. We find similar underlying notions in astrology, in acupuncture and other such disciplines. Interestingly these concepts not only provide an acceptable basis for the subjects but they are also able to explain the great discoveries of the official science. In other words, perhaps it hasn't been possible to demonstrate, for example, how molecules meet – but it's a matter of fact that the molecules do meet.

If we are able to advance this thought process further it would be a big step forward for science and diseases would no longer need the types of drugs we are using nowadays.

Thank you all (AN, audience applauses).

A scientist's thought on Astrology – by Renato Palmieri

Sirius rising, a leaf moves on my balcony. Of course it does not move only because of the influence of Sirius, but for the infinite magneto-gravitational components coeval to the rising of Sirius. They change every moment in a non identifiable way, therefore the leaf palpitates at every puff of wind and it rustles together with all the other leaves.

Although it is true that it is impossible to sever all the innumerable influences of the astronomical firmament, yet many of them possess a cyclic nature as regards to the position of the Earth in the solar system and the 'other stars' – as Dante Alighieri used to call them – and their cyclicity may determine sensitive, periodical variations of those influences in quantity and mode, thus contributing to imprinting those who were born under the light of the birthday with different characters.

This is what a man like me can recognize in Astrology: one who is not a scientist, but one who knows – from history – that this is a branch of learning whose students were thinkers and scientists. Moreover, I do not exclude *a priori* a symbolic and supersensitive value of the astral references on the human experience. *Homo sum: humani nihil a me alienum puto*, as Terence said..

Anyway, it is a matter of fact that – as it has been proven very well somewhere else – that as far as knowledge is concerned, academic 'science' is as qualified as the roughest of the astrologers. This is particularly true for those subjects, such as gravitation and electromagnetism, whose essential nature science completely ignores, yet using these subjects for its arrogant refutation of the loathed astrological 'heresy'.

A few notes of remark – by Ciro Discepolo

Instances of two interventions from unbiased and open mided scientists whose research into normal phenomena is branded to be paranormal only because they are not accepted by the Establishment.

We thank professors Vincenzo Di Napoli and Renato Palmieri very much for the elucidation of knowledge and wisdom they bestow upon us each time they accept to collaborate with our quarterly magazine.

It is my opinion that in the past year we have hosted extraordinarily interesting articles by them, as well as other articles having similar content. I am referring to several articles and brief essays of scientist who made us reflect on certain contentious subjects which I would like to mention in a concise list:

- Engineer and professor Di Napoli, together with engineer Callegari and other students of Giambattista Callegari's method have taught us – among other facts – that when two bodies in the space are in resonance (i.e. their energies are in resonance), impedance (in the 'transmission between the two energies') is equal to zero. This means that distance hasn't value any longer. The consequences of this fact are enormous, for it explains, among other things, how is it that Pluto may have the same astrological value as the Moon or Mars.

- Professor Palmieri has made us notice that modern physics does not take into consideration the question of polarity of the gravitational field of the Earth and of other planets. Moreover, in his *Unigravitational Physics*, professor Palmieri unifies the nature of the electromagnetic and gravitational waves, with the insertion of fundamental distinctions where most other physicists are in a confusion claiming, for example, that Pluto cannot have an influence on human beings because its gravitational strength is virtually zero.

- Scientists and researchers Emilio Del Giudice and Nicola Del Giudice has made it clear – with several very clear details – the notion of the memory of water, and the fact that a newborn baby, before developing a magnetic filed of its own, takes the magnetic field that is 'gravitating around it' at the moment of its birth. That's to say, the water molecules are oriented by the magnetic field and they preserve 'forevermore' such orientation – and this may help us very much explain how astrology works.

Yet in these pages our friends have written this and much more. Do not forget it, for in my opinion, *Ricerca '90* made it possible to seal up an important chapter of history in the huge book of philosophy of science.

cd (Forgive me for my excessive vulgarization; perhaps it was necessary for a non-insider audience.)

As you can easily understand, we are really facing a topical milestone in the heuristic path in general and in particular in the study of astrology. The three notions that I have just recollected for your attention may be the fundaments for a universal theory that we might call the **Callegari-Palmieri-Del Giudice's theory**. This theory may be sufficient to explain a possible way of the functioning of astrology from a purely physical point of view, without mentioning either Jung's synchronicity or the so-called paranormal phenomena that amuse the minds (?) of the member of CICAP (TN, the Italian CSICOP).

The points that have been discussed so far are constitute just the tip of the proverbial iceberg. I believe that compared to the day prior to this *XII Congress of Astrological Studies* in Vico Equense, a new and extremely important *Weltanschauung* has been established before the world and particularly for open-minded people.

It will be necessary to come back again and again several times in the future, to study and to have a debate in this field. For the time being, considering the subject of this book, we can consider this question closed in order to say something even more specific about Solar and Lunar Returns.

Approximately fifty years ago the scientific study of biorhythms started to spread among medical doctors.[8]

In fact, even after the end of WWII, medical doctors went on giving medicines to patients without giving any particular importance to the moment of the day in which it was administered[9] that resulted in wasteful consumptions like concentrates of vitamins and dietary minerals at night just before going to sleep; or melatonin in the morning.

When doctors got aware of the importance of biorhythms, they could avoid most of such mistakes.

Today we are aware that there are different biorhythms, among which the following three are the most important:[10]

1) A circadian rhythm lasting, as its Latin etymology says, approximately one day. Obviously this corresponds with the time that the Earth takes to rotate once around its own axis. We have innumerable evidence of such biorhythm associated with the life of human beings, animals, and plants. For example, it can be easily proven that there is a precise reproducibility of the peaks in the curve of certain biological functions of the human being as observed during the day: such as the frequency of the daily peaks of urination, of arterial pressure, of the index of blood flocculation, and so on. For example, we know that our body produces melatonin constantly, but there's a peak of 'overproduction' about half an hour after sunset. This is why – among other things – melatonin induces an antidepressant action, which is extremely important when the sun lights up our day no more; and melatonin also induces sleep. Hence you can understand why it was a mistake on the part of certain doctors to give artificial melatonin early in the morning. Let me mention at this point poor professor Luigi Di Bella, the physiologist who developed the so-called Di Bella therapy, an unorthodox cancer treatment which caused collective discussions during 1997 and 1998 in Italy. He was literally 'slaughtered' by the Medical establishment because his therapy went against the interests of pharmaceutical companies. In fact Professor Di Bella, together with other alternative scientist, believed that it was extremely useful to give patients – as well as healthy people – 'industrial' quantities of melatonin and vitamin C. (It's for similar sentences that I have to go to the stake. See the shameful episode of the Italian Wikipedia at this

website: http://www.cirodiscepolo.it/wikipedia.htm. Don't be surprised then, if one day some supporter of CICAP or of the *Italian Wikipedia* would manage to have cocaine found on my writing-table in order to get rid of such an uncomfortable and unpleasant person like me.)

2) A monthly rhythm of about 29 days clearly connected with the complete passage of the Moon around the Earth. We have incontrovertible evidence of this too, despite the opposite opinion of 'scientists': even children can see them, such as tides, or the menstrual cycle.

3) A yearly rhythm linked with the complete orbit of the Earth around the Sun. Examples of this are the animals hibernating always during the same period of the year; others migrating or being moved by sexual desire always in a precise period of the year. Trees bear fruits always in the same time of the year, and so on.

Now consider the sine wave below and pay attention to point **A**. This sine wave can represent the development of any biorhythm. Let us consider two of them in particular: the wave could draw the development of the lunar biorhythm and of the solar biorhythm. Let us start with the solar one. In the very moment of our birth, with our first breath, our first yearly biorhythm starts: it begins at the point **A** and it ends at the point **A**.

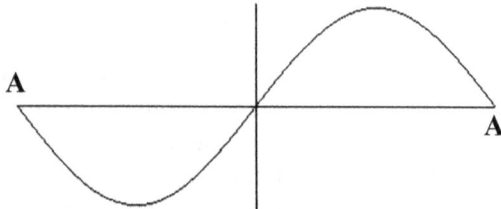

So we should not be surprised if somebody (i.e. me the Author) claims that in the moment of the yearly solar return, exactly at the point **A**, the imprinting that we receive from the sky is not the same as that of the rest of the days of the year. In fact it is very special, not because of analogies, but because the moment A is a sort of 'reset' or zeroing of a whole yearly cycle to start with another yearly cycle. In my opinion this widely justifies the importance of each of us being under that particular sky of the world in that moment and not in any other moment – according to criteria whose real literature (I mean the literature originated by practice, not by theory) suggests that thus our year might be qualitatively enhanced – but also spoiled if we are not careful.

It seems quite obvious to me that the same may be said about the sine wave of the monthly cycle, where point **A** corresponds to the return of the Moon to the precise point it was in at the moment of birth with regard to the native in focus.

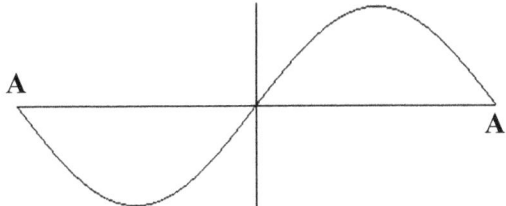

I believe that such an explanation is plausible. Nevertheless it is left to the students, pupils, colleagues and denigrators to use or not to use such wonderful tools of quality enhancement to one's life: namely, the Aimed Solar Returns and the Aimed Lunar Returns.

Note
1) Carl Gustav Jung, *La Sincronicità [Synchronicity]*, Editore Boringhieri S.p.A., Torino, 1980, 124 pages.
2) Gret Baumann-Jung, *Alcune riflessioni sull'oroscopo di Carl Gustav Jung [Some considerations on Carl Gustav Jung's horoscope]*, Ricerca '90 #5 of January 1991, translated into Italian by Enzo Barillà
3) Renato Palmieri is an excellent physicist from Naples. I had suggested to the Italian Institution of Philosophical Studies [Istituto Italiano per gli Studi Filosofici] – a wonderful institution of Knowledge conceived, founded, and directed by Gerardo Marotta – to publish Professor Palmieri's precious volume: otherwise it would have never seen the light of day. There was no special need in urging them to it, because when I talked to the secretary general of the institution Professor Antonio Gargano and my friend Professor Aldo Tonini, they immediately accepted my request, and this way they added another gem to their already huge list of Cultural works. Thus, at last his book *La fisica unigravitazionale e l'equazione cosmologica [Unigravitational Physics and the Cosmologic Equation]* is a reality now, and certainly one of the things I am most proud of.
4) Engineer Vincenzo Di Napoli died in Novembre 2007. He was a great researcher; his life crossed mine several times. He used to be my teacher of electronics in the school «Augusto Righi» of Naples. He was a simple man, who used to reach the core of any subject; everybody used to understand his lessons immediately. Later on, we met again when he was the president of the Association of Ham Radios of Naples. I was trying to get a CB licence then, but I did not succeed because by those times they required a quite difficult exam on radiotelegraphy, and my lack of 'an ear for music' for such things, was a hindrance in distinguishing 'dots' and 'dashes' of the Morse code. We met yet again when he was the president of the Centre of Studies «Callegari» concerning Callegari Radiobiology. I have written of this latter event in a brief note in my book on the interpretation of the natal map *L'interpretazione del tema natale*, Armenia editore, Milano, 2007, 350 pages, in pages # 87-90. And to conclude, I would like to add – it doesn't seem a mere coincidence – that Professor Di Napoli had always lived not farther off than fifty metres from my place. I remember him with gratefulness and affection.
5) Engineer Giuseppe Callegari is the son of Giovanbattista Callegari. I have written briefly

about the latter in my book *L'interpretazione del tema natale*, in pages # 87-90. I am very glad to see that Engineer Callegari is trying to further develop his father's great discoveries.

6) Emilio Del Giudice is professor of Physics at the *Istituto Superiore di Fisica* in Milan, Italy. Together with his brother, homeopathic medical doctor Nicola Del Giudice, he has written books of great scientific interest. They also tried (in my opinion, with great efficiency) to develop the question of the memory of water – a subject of extraordinary interest that may help in understanding the mechanisms of the influence of the sky over the life of terrestrial creatures.

7) Apply to him the same considerations about his activity together with his brother. Nicola Del Giudice is a well known and appreciated homeopathic doctor, endocrinologist and researcher in a broad sense. He wrote together with his brother the book *Omeopatia e bioenergetica. Le medicine alternative: dalla stregoneria alla scienza [Homeopathy and bioenergetics. The alternative medicines: from sorcery to science]*, Cortina editore, Verona, 1999, 302 pages; and also the volume *Omeopatia. Un ponte tra biologia e psicologia. Vent'anni di ricerca della Fondazione omeopatica italiana [Homeopathy: a bridge between biology and psychology. Twenty years of research of the Italian Homeopathic Foundation]*, edizioni Nuova IPSA, Palermo, 1998, 334 pages.

8) Lyall Watson, *SuperNatura [SuperNature]*, Rizzoli editore, Milano, 1974.
9) Ibidem.
10) Ibidem

Left to right: Nicola Del Giudice, Renato Palmieri, Emilio Del Giudice, Ciro Discepolo, Andrea Rossetti, Massimo Troise, Giuseppe Callegari

Right: Callegari Radiobiological Central unit and Vincenzo Di Napoli

3.
Lunar Returns

Lunar Returns have a fairly high value in predictive astrology, provided that you are able to read them correctly. In particular, they help date the events in a highly precise way.

I am often surprised because some readers ask me why I haven't written much about them so far.

Well, I do believe that no other author on Earth has written even a portion of what I have published on this subject.

For those who do not really remember, let me summarize my most important contributions in this field:

- Some articles in the magazine *Gli Arcani*, ed. Armenia, Milan, at the beginning of the '70s.

- *Guida all'astrologia*, 1979, Armenia, Milan

- *Guida ai transiti*, 1984, Armenia, Milan

- Several articles in the magazines *Astra* and *Sirio*, Milan, between 1977 and the early '80s.

- *Trattato pratico di Rivoluzioni solari*, 1993, Blue Diamond Publisher, Milan

- *Transiti e Rivoluzioni Solari*, 1997, Armenia, Milan. As it is explained in several passages of this volume, those sections may be used also for the interpretation of the Lunar Returns.

- Several articles on the quarterly *Ricerca '90*, ed. Ricerca '90, Naples, from 1990 onwards.

- *Nuovo Dizionario di Astrologia*, 1996, Armenia, Milan

- *Nuovo Trattato delle Rivoluzioni Solari,* 2003, Armenia, Milan

- *Nuovo Trattato di Astrologia,* 2004, Armenia, Milan. This is a volume of almost 800 pages: of them, approximately 500 pages are devoted to the dating of events. Within that section of the volume, there are several examples of Lunar Returns and how to read them.

- *L'interpretazione del tema natale*, 2007, Armenia, Milan

…and many more.

Everybody knows my opinion on the usage of LRs, yet it may be good to repeat it in short. I believe that LRs should mainly help us dating the events within the frame of the 12 months covered by a Solar Return. While SRs may be aimed, I find it much less useful aiming LRs if you have already aimed your SR. In fact, no matter how much daunting or alluring may be the Lunar Returns within the year, they could never overcome the limits imposed by their ruling Solar Return.

In other words, if you protect yourself with a good Aimed Solar Return, within the frame of the following twelve months even two or more apparently frightful Lunar Returns wouldn't be able to produce devastating effects, if there is no trace of them in the Solar Return. The same can be said on the other side as well: if a SR announces a detrimental year you wouldn't be able to overcome the predicted events of the SR even if you aimed every single Lunar Return of the following twelve months.

If anything, we could talk of 'modulation' – a slightly positive and/or negative effect which might be algebraically added to the effect of the relevant Solar Return.

So, in what circumstances is it convenient to relocate, or better said, to aim a LR?

Certainly it is not expedient to do so to counter the misjudgement of not having aimed your Solar Return: for you could face such a negative experience in the next twelve months, that the conviction would grow strong in your mind to relocate for every single aimed birthday in the following years from then on.

Nonetheless we could plan a sort of partial repentance. This would be the case, say, of a subject who had the chance to select among a range of possible locations for an ASR, and opted for the cheapest one and/or the closest one. Such a subject might wish to mend this decision by aiming the Lunar Returns of the most difficult months. Be clear that even so, this is not a completely logical thing to do, but one can try.

There is a third possibility: a good example of which is one of my only two aimed LRs in my life (up to summer 2007).

Please consider the following charts: one is my birth chart and the other one is my ASR of 2006 in Petropavlovsk, Kamtchatka. I must say that it was a really important and positive ASR for me.

On the 11th of February 2007 in Naples I would have faced the LR that you can see in these pages.

In that case, with a really negligible displacement, I could have enhanced that LR with two really positive results:

- keeping Saturn out of the 10th House, and

- considering that my birth time – 5:40 am – is almost certain, I could have placed Venus on the very cusp between the 5th and the 6th House.

I could have made all this by simply taking a flight to Genoa; I would have remained far from home for a few hours only, with not even the need of going out of the airport. In fact, there was a flight Naples to Genoa scheduled for the late afternoon on that day. Once there, I could have waited a couple of hours at the airport and then flown back home, spending less than 200 Euros.

If I remember well, the flight was scheduled to take off at 9:30 pm while I would have had my Lunar Return at 21:59 pm. Now a consideration must be made for the fact that I have been flying more than a civilian pilot, and know that it's quite a rare event having a flight taking off less than half an hour after the scheduled time.

In order to avoid any intervention of the devil, who's always waiting in ambush in these instances, I resolved to fly Naples to Turin, and to take the return flight Turin to Naples at 9:30 pm. This way, thought I, my flight would almost certainly take off later; and if it took off on time, roughly reckoning I would have been flying over Genoa at the moment of my Lunar Return.

But you know, the devil is always on duty 24/7 – and my flight took off from Turin at 9:30 pm sharp!

I was disappointed to see that the flight commander, who perhaps had a gallant meeting in Naples, resolved to speed up the aircraft southward at an incredible pace. Thus I noticed with great dissatisfaction that in twelve minutes of flight we had already overpassed the gulf of Genoa.

Quite upset, I asked the flight assistant to request the commander to let me know the geographical coordinates of the place that we would overfly at 9:59 pm.

Needless to say, the hostess stared at me with a strange light in her eyes; yet she complied and asked the commander. The commander denied giving me such a precious piece of information, probably fearing that I was a terrorist aiming to have the aircraft struck by a surface-to-air missile exactly at 9:59 pm.

I understood that I would never receive any assistance in this. So I opened my notebook and zoomed on a map of the area over which we were flying. I thought that the lights of the isle of Elba and of the town of Piombino would help me locate the exact place of my Lunar Return at 9:59 pm. I was right: at that time we would fly – roughly – somewhere between Piombino and Elba. Hence I realized, as you can see for yourselves, that the operation had been a partial success. Saturn had remained on the cusp between the 10th and the 11th House, while Venus had hit the centre, namely the cusp between the 5th and the 6th House.

It was a calculated risk: had I wanted my ALR in Genoa explicitly, I could have spent a night there and take the return flight the next day. But I took the exercise rather as an experiment than a serious attempt at aimed relocation. Saturn in the 10th House did not produce serious damage, while I derived some benefit from the position of Venus.

I think that this is a correct usage of an Aimed Lunar Return, with all the considerations already expressed in this chapter.

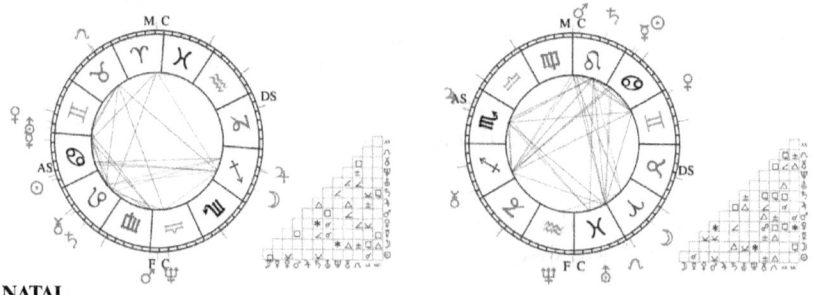

NATAL

ASR, Petropavlosvk

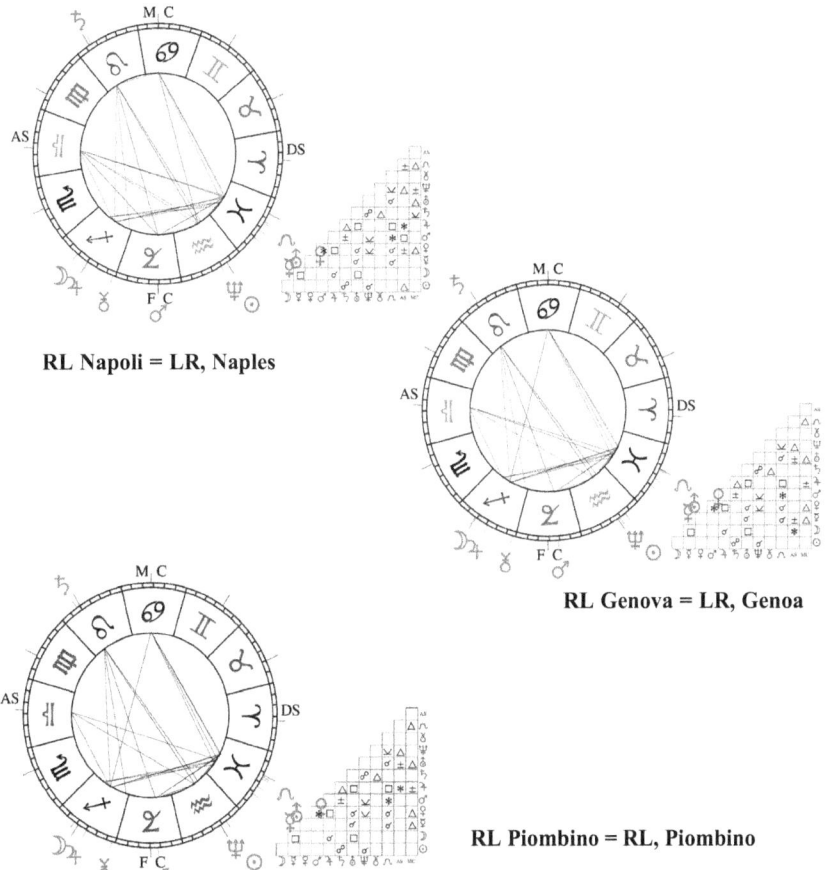

RL Napoli = LR, Naples

RL Genova = LR, Genoa

RL Piombino = RL, Piombino

Now let us consider a more extensive example concerning the subject we are discussing. We'll make use of random data, but they could be real as well. Say that the subject to whom these data refer left in March 2007 for an aimed birthday and that the ASR is bringing good results. The subject wishes to further enhance the benefits of his relocation of March, and in August 2007 he asks me to help him aim his future Lunar Returns. In my opinion, this course of action may be excessively expensive and time-consuming and I would suggest it only for those special events in which the subject has got plenty of time and money, or if he/she is in the absolute need of conceiving really special goals during a certain year. I am writing down a report on this hypothetical subject with short remarks of the subject's base sky and his LRs, month after month. In each of the following pages you'll see, on the left: his birth chart, and on the right: his sky of BLR (Base

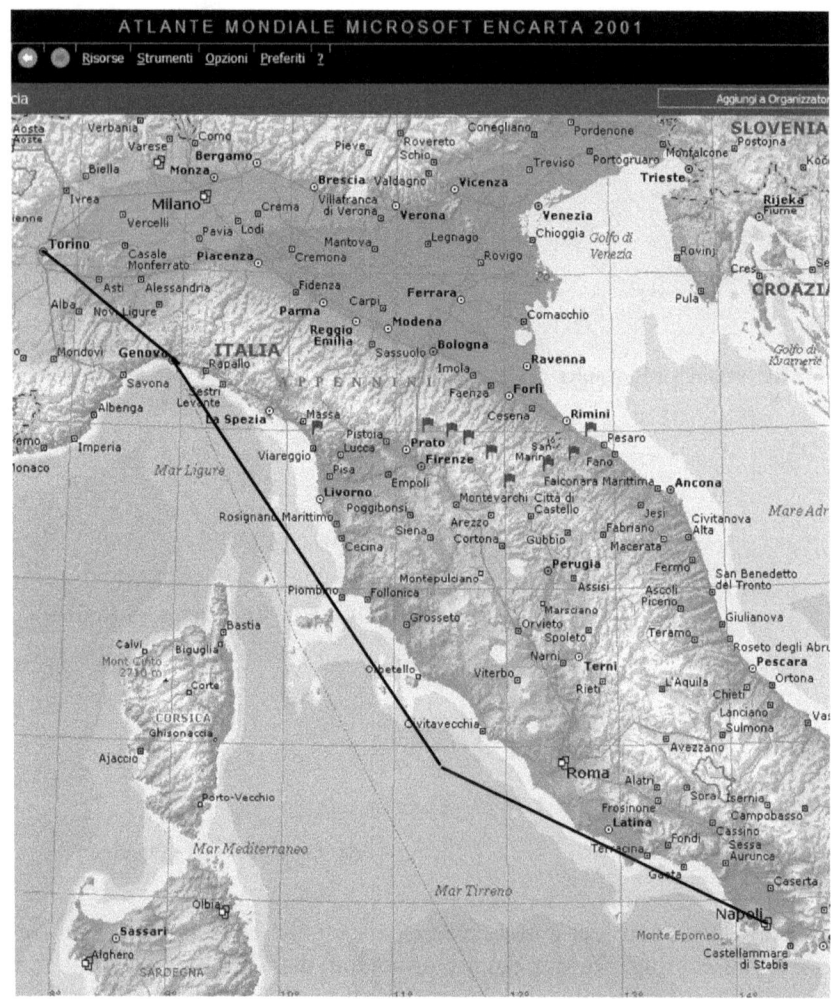

Lunar Return). Below them you'll see his natal chart once again, and on its right: the sky of the ALR that I suggested to him. In the first case I asked him to relocate to Oslo, thus avoiding two positions detrimental for his health and for any sort of trouble in general. Moreover, I have also placed a gorgeous Venus on the cusp between the 1st and the 2nd House. All this could be attained spending that LR in Oslo, Europe.

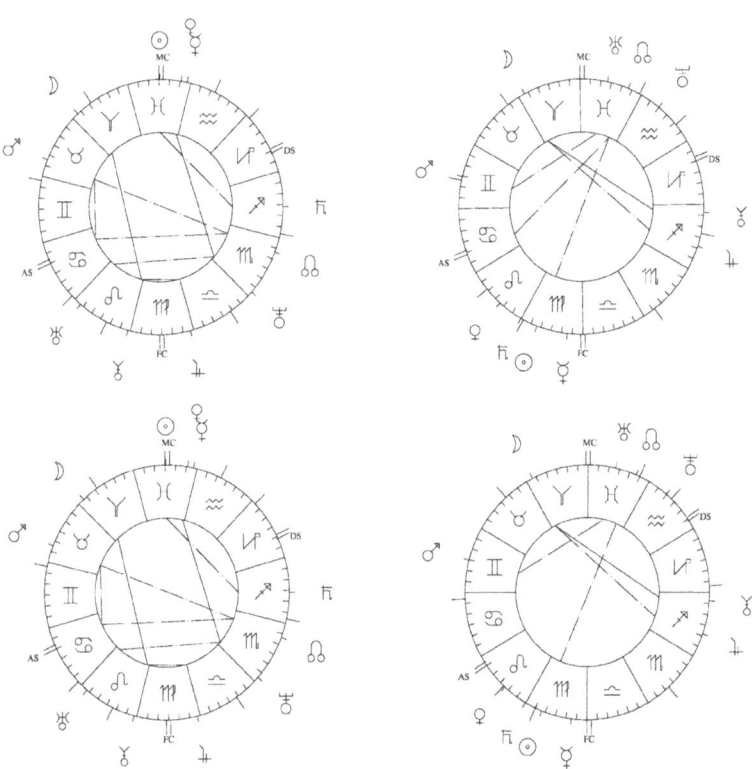

Below you can see the subject's ALR for October 2007: in Karachi not only do we avoid a Mars sticking to the Ascendant of the LR – we can also get two wonderful cusps, namely Venus on the delimiter 1st / 2nd House, and Jupiter on the 4th / 5th House! For the scope of this exercise it is not important to consider the ASR of that year: we have already explained that compared to the LRs, the SR is absolutely overriding as far as the events of the year are concerned. Possible supporting ALRs would only perform the task of not hindering the ASR and of enhancing the effects of the ASR. Any other consideration or speculation follows well behind, as it is something absolutely ancillary in the scope of this volume. Please note that in this case I also suggested to the subject to aim the LR with a modest level of travel. The effort to reach Karachi (which is the largest city of Pakistan, but not its capital) is minimal – compared with a travel to North Canada or to Alaska or to Micronesia or Polynesia.

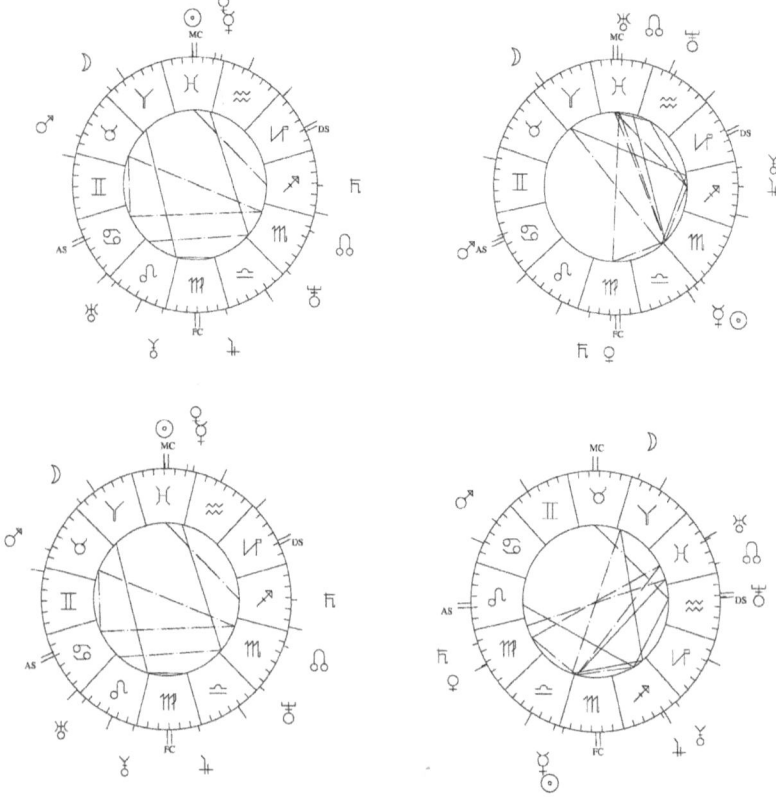

ALR of November. The Base LR would have the Sun in the 12th House, the Ascendant in the natal 6th House, and a stellium spanned over the 12th and the 1st House. The SR aimed in Mauritius (similar to the previous one, in Karachi) completely shuffles the celestials. All the detrimental or even dangerous positions of the BSR are gone with the wind. The Sun moves to the 10th House, we have a splendid cuspidal position of Jupiter between the 10th and the 11th House and – the cherry on the cake: Venus in the 8th House, certainly announcing incoming money.

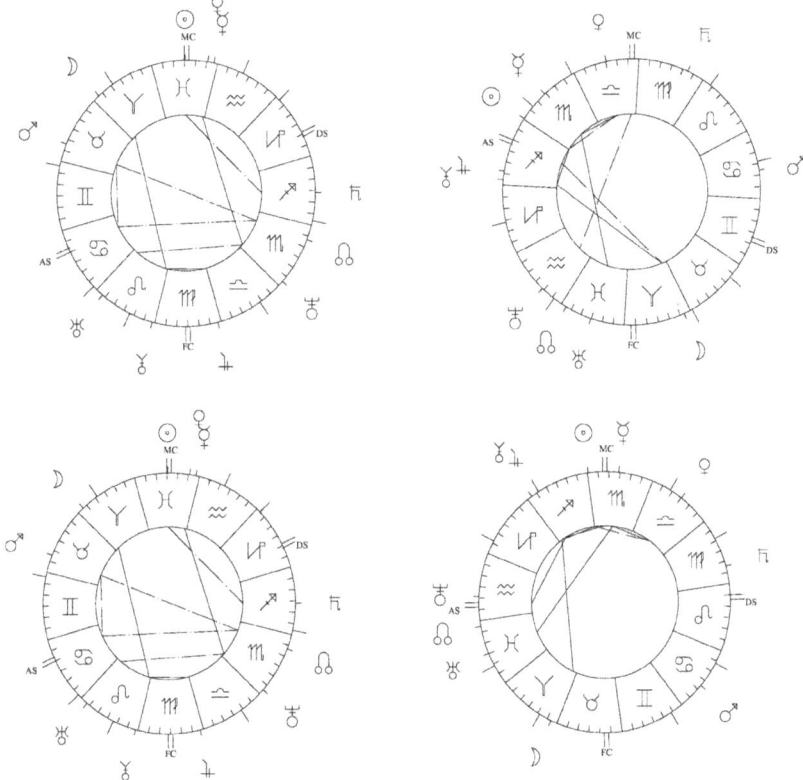

ALR of December. Mars is once again very close to the Ascendant, and there is a strong stellium with the Sun in the 6th House. Yet, since his ASR is good, nothing would happen to the subject even if he didn't relocate. I had a Mars in the 6th House of a LR myself recently. But I had protected my year with a good ASR, so the only problem I experienced during that month was three-four days of colic on account of bad food.

Nonetheless, for the same reasons already expressed – and I hope, almost definitely clear – I suggested the subject an ALR in Caracas in order to place that magnificent 'lining up' exactly over the Medium Coeli, besides Venus in the 8th House. Also in this case, travel was not particularly expensive or demanding.

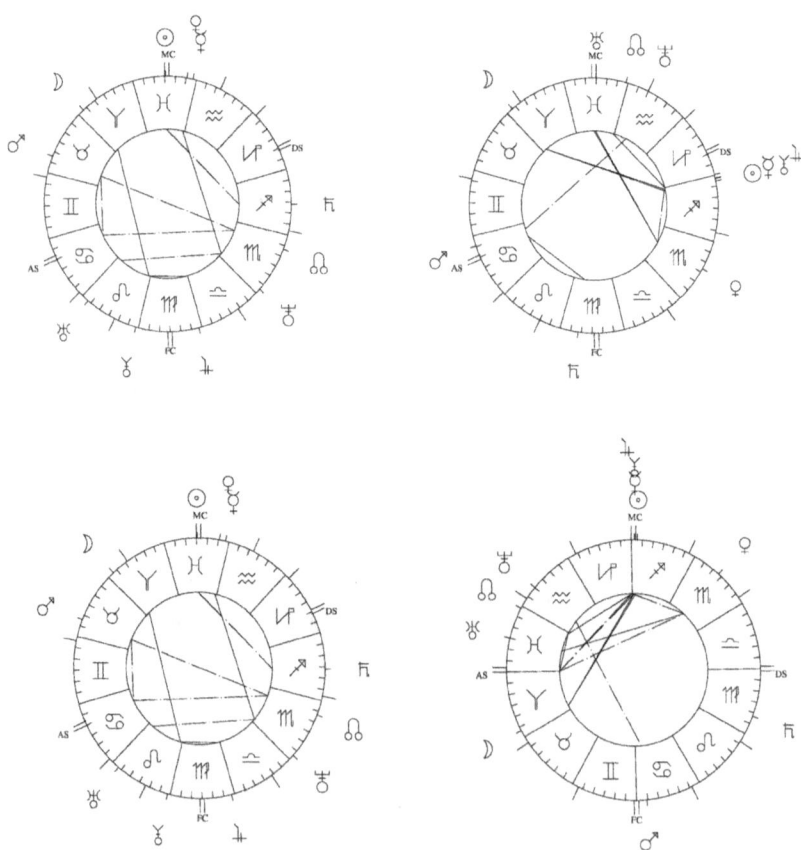

LUNAR RETURNS

BLR of January 2008: no reason at all to have it changed.

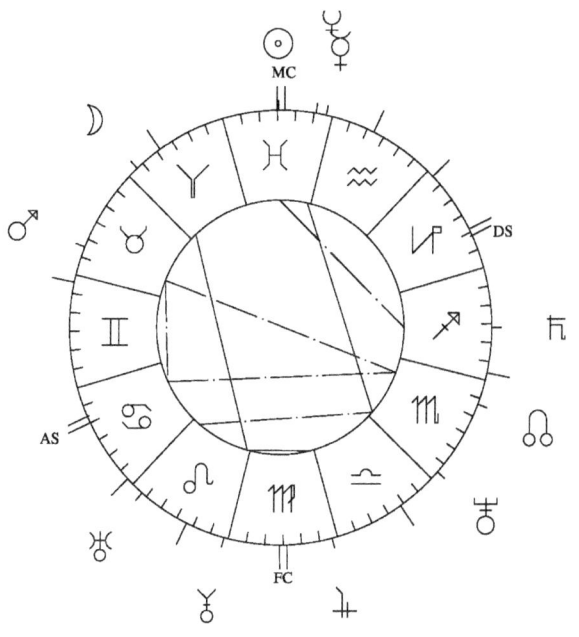

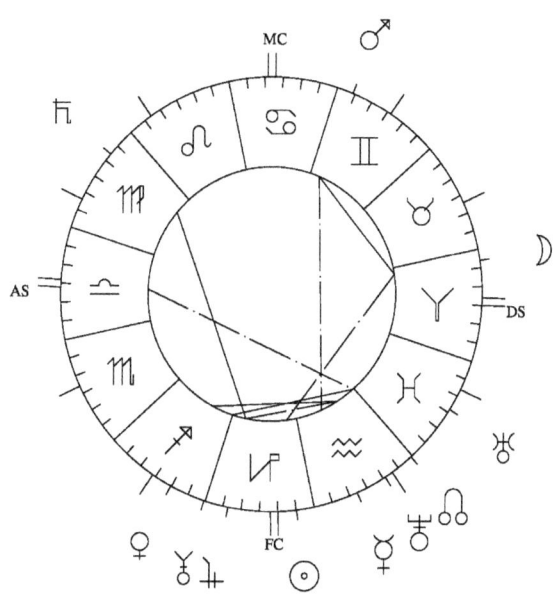

ALR of February 2008: a massive stellium over the 1st and the 12th House, as well as Mars in the 6th House. By relocating to Reykjavík, Europe, the whole stellium moves to the 2nd House and we keep Mars out of the 6th House.

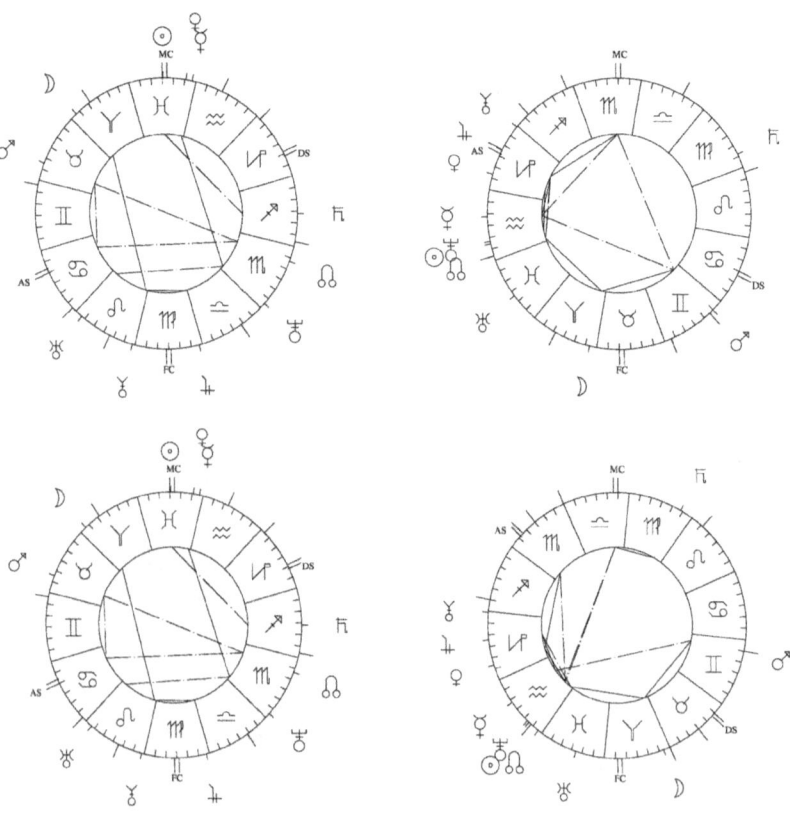

4.
Twenty trustworthy rules

The rules you are about to read, similar to the 'sibling' rules that you can find in the volume *Transits and Solar Returns*, haven't been written as a Bible or a Koran or any other scripture – they simply descend from my own experience on the field.

The reduction of their explanation to a sequence of single sentences allows you to avoid useless sophistry, hot air and haughty descriptions that explain nothing. By means of them you can also nail the author to his responsibilities: for you can study your own natal chart and that of your closest relatives and their Returns of the last, say, five years – and verify whether the following rules do work or not.

If these rules are trustworthy, you'll get several instances of corroboration and you might also suggest your friends and colleagues to follow them. If not so, I myself suggest that you burn off this book.

1) In terms of operational and expressive power, the effects of Lunar Returns are much lesser than the Solar Return under which they take place.

2) A Lunar Return can never overturn or subvert the general reading of the Solar Return under which the LR takes place.

3) The Lunar Return can only act as a modulation – see the following chapter – of the current Solar Return; or as the enhancement of a specific aspect of the SR, referring to the month of validity of the LR.

4) The Lunar Return helps us very much in dating the events within the frame of the current Solar Return (see the almost 500 pages of practical examples in my volume *Nuovo Trattato di Astrologia*, ed. Armenia)).

5) An Aimed Lunar Return can not replace the Aimed Solar Return. So

if subject *A* does not relocate his SR and repents later on, he can not flatter himself with the illusion of replacing the missed aimed birthday with 12 or 13 Aimed Lunar Returns.

6) By exploiting the effect of synergy as explained in the innumerable examples of my volume *Nuovo Trattato di Astrologia* published by Armenia editore, it is possible and useful, too, to perform a single Aimed Lunar Return for a specific month in harmony with good transits and a previously performed ASR. This way it is possible to achieve – during that month and not in other months – what we most expect from this combination of active relocations.

7) Those who can afford it and have enough time to do so, can certainly achieve wonderful results by performing a good ASR and aiming all the LRs of the following twelve months.

8) Rule #7 is certainly true, nevertheless it must be underlined that – for the reason already mentioned – in the majority of the cases it is quite useless, superfluous, and redundant to aim all the LRs.

9) Even the most apparently awful LR can not imply serious damage if it takes place in the twelve months following a good SR.

10) Even an apparently wonderful LR would imply very little results if it takes place in the twelve months following a feeble SR.

11) As a consequence of rule #9 we might even perform an Aimed Lunar Return in order to place, say, a wonderful conjunction of Venus and Jupiter in the 5th House of the LR even if by doing so, say, the Ascendant of the LR would lie in the 12th natal House. In fact, if the reading of the current SR allows to forecast so, such a LR might announce the arrival of a new and happy love affair, while at most its Asc. in the 12th House might imply a bad cold – certainly not a stay in hospital.

12) With the exception of the rules listed in these pages, reading a Lunar Return is basically the same as reading a Solar Return: thus – with the exception of the rules listed in these pages – the relevant sections of my volume *Transits and Solar Returns* can be also applied to LRs.

13) A Lunar Return, just like the Solar Return, is always 'aimed' – even if you make up your mind to spend that moment at home, i.e. in the place where you usually live.

14) For an ASR it is enough to stay in the place of the Solar Return for a single minute; and for an ALR it is also enough to stay in the place of the Lunar Return for a single minute. If you aren't sure of your time of birth,

you can reach the place one hour before the Return and you can leave one hour after the Return. There's no use in remaining there 24 hours or even longer (see my volume *A Few Facts on Aimed Birthdays*, Blue Diamond Publisher: it can be downloaded free from my website).

15) In the volume mentioned in rule #14 you can also find several cases of criticism that may be directed both to ASRs and to ALRs, and my answers to them.

16) If an ALR contains exactly opposite elements compared with the SR under which it takes place, the aimed result would be virtually zero. For example, assume that the SR contains a strict conjunction of Mars and Saturn in the 4th House (I'd never leave it there!) and you try and perform an ALR to place Jupiter and Venus in the 4th House of the chart of Lunar Return because, you possibly wish to buy or to sell an estate that month – the result would be close to absolute vacuum.

17) This rule is an attempt to explain better a notion that is not always easy to understand. I refer to placing, for example, Mars in the 4th House of an ALR. Many people refuse to do so, because they fear it might harm their parents. This is not possible! If it were, we should admit that it is possible to get rid of a hostile subject by simply sticking pins into dolls. At most, with Mars in the 4th House of the Return, we enhance our level of concern towards our parents' problems – not their real, practical problems. The same can be said, on the opposite side, for Venus in the 4th House of a Return. Having clarified this, let me add that if my parents lived, and if I could do so without it being detrimental to other elements of the Return, I would place Venus in the 4th House…

18) As with ASRs, ALRs too can help you to correct (i.e. rectify) your time of birth. Assume that we have a map of LR with Mars on the cusp between the 3rd and the 4th House. Don't you think that one month after, analyzing the events that happened, any astrologer would be able to understand whether that Mars was actually in the 3rd House or in the 4th House?

19) Nevertheless, remember that one swallow does not make a summer: a single event is not enough to rectify the time of birth. Rectification should be done following the protocol that I have defined in the first hundred pages of my volume *Nuovo Trattato di Astrologia,* Armenia. So, placing a celestial on a cusp of an ALR may help you very much in this sense, but in my opinion its possible implication as regards to the time of birth should be added to – not replacing – the mentioned protocol of rectification.

20) In this volume you'll find examples of two Aimed Lunar Returns of mine in which I was in mid-flight at the very moment of the Return. I hadn't planned so, it was by mere chance: but they have helped me rectify my time of birth.

Ciro Discepolo

A Few Facts on Aimed Birthdays

Blue Diamond Publisher

Free Download of this book from:
http://www.cirodiscepolo.it/english_corner/English_corner.htm

5.
The concept of modulation

An example that we may well define 'biological' will help me explain to the Reader how – from my point of view and above all, according to my experience – an Aimed Lunar Return stands a chance of interacting with the current Solar Return.

Everybody knows that the human body produces melatonin: it is a substance that favours sleep and helps fight against depression. The production of melatonin in human beings has a peak – in a cycle of 24 hours – approximately half an hour after sunset. This is quite logical, if you think that one hand, the lack of sunlight should prepare the body to sleep, and on the other hand it can also induce a slight depression in human beings.

99%, this reflects the situation regarding the production of melatonin in the human body – a situation that can be verified with laboratory analyses.

Now – for the sake of simplicity and clarity – let us suppose that our melatonin production draws a perfectly sinusoidal wave as in the illustration below:

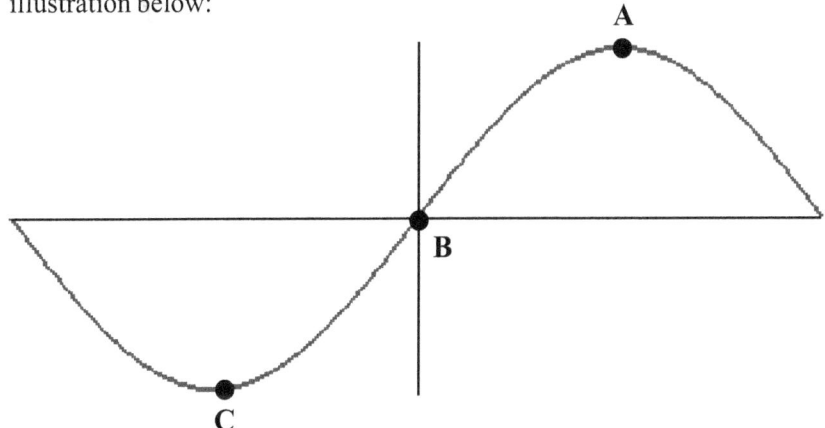

The peak marked with a capital letter A corresponds to the maximum endogen production of melatonin approximately half an hour after sunset. As I said, for the sake of simplicity you can take this wave to be perfectly sinusoidal. In this case the trough marked as C approximately corresponds to dawn which would have been roughly 12 hours earlier (if you were on the Equator and close to the equinox of autumn). It's the time when you wake up and your body does not need to produce melatonin: it 'knows' that it doesn't have to do so, for if it did it would spoil its own circadian cycle that induces, at that time of the day, a sharp awakening and a state of euphoria induced by sunlight. The medium point marked B corresponds to ca. 6 hours before the peak A.

The next day and all the following days, a similar situation would repeat itself.

Now let us assume that the subject whose melatonin production wave we are considering, resolves to take a small pill of artificial melatonin at the time of the day marked A. The content of melatonin of the pill would be a very small portion of our natural production.

Yet it would be enough to modify the perfect sinusoidal wave like this:

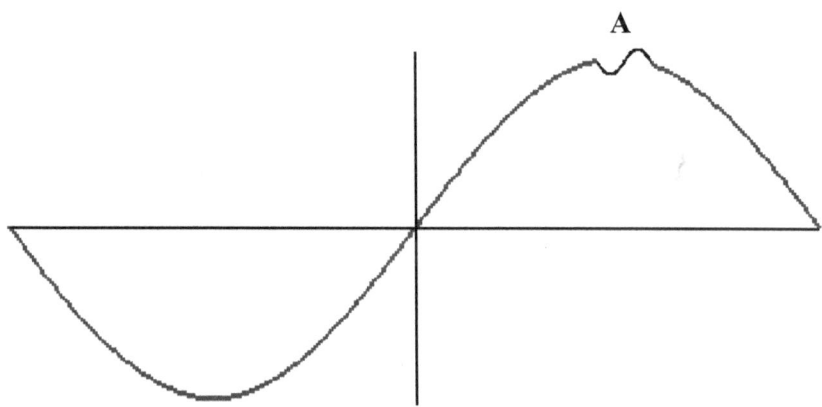

As you can see, the point marked A has slightly moved upwards. Perhaps the following diagram would make things even clearer:

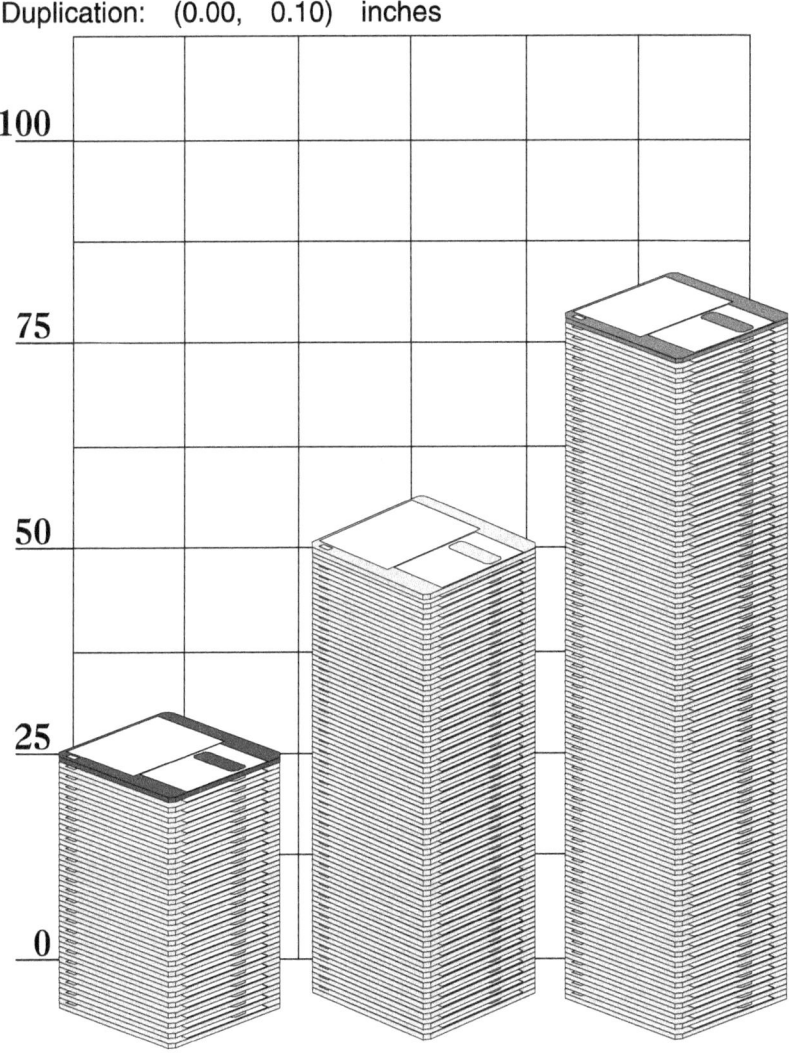

Duplication: (0.00, 0.10) inches

This chart is called a 'bar chart'. Now do not consider the numeric values of the three bars of the diagrams, but concentrate on their relative height, that represents quite well what I am trying to explain. The highest bar on the right may represent the point A after taking a pill of melatonin. The lower central bar may represent the point A before or without the assumption of the pill. In this diagram the central bar corresponds to a value of 55, but please make an effort and imagine that it is actually around 73.

Now it should be clear that I have tried to prove that the action of the drug has slightly altered the level of melatonin in our blood.

If the pill had had active ingredients other than melatonin, say for example stimulating ones such as caffeine and slightly depressive ones such as those that you can find in a variety of vegetal plants, the result would have been a slight reduction of the level of melatonin in our blood.

Such a general action, which I have simply outlined here, is called *modulation*. It indicates the process by means of which a little input is able to lower or to raise a certain threshold.

We can say that the Aimed Lunar Return work in the same way as regards to the Solar Return governing them during the year.

Let me be even clearer and say that if Helen's current SR is wonderful – especially for health – and one of her LRs of the same year is apparently very detrimental for her health, at most such a bad LR could only 'slightly modulate' Helen's current SR. The bad LR might simply give Helen a bad cold, but considering the overall year, Helen would have very good health.

In my opinion, this concept is extremely important. This is the notion that led to the enunciation of the main rules of the previous chapter, which – according to my practical experience and my research on past events – you should always keep in mind when you intend to change a Lunar Return for an Aimed Lunar Return.

6.
Do ALRs work?

It is such a meaningless question that it would neither be worth an answer nor consideration. It is a matter of fact that all astrology – from the Western to the Vedic: considering all its variety – is fundamentally based on the principle of 'here and now', which is also the banner of Gestalt psychological analysis as well as the main subject dwelt upon by that wonderful movie starring Robin Williams and directed by Peter Weir: *Dead Poets Society*.

As I have written several times, in my opinion there are some aspects, in the study of Solar and Lunar Returns, that resemble pure mathematics – which makes it parallel to Astrogeography, the latter discipline being accepted even by those who question the effectiveness of the aimed birthdays (a term that I apply either to Solar or Lunar Returns). Yet both afore mentioned branches of astrology take their origin in the very same theoretical assumptions, and they do work in an absolutely identical way.

This time I'll skip the innumerable practical examples that I have given to my readers in at least a dozen of my books on these matters. I believe that such examples are so crystal-clear that nobody has ever tried to criticize them. So this time I'll propose one example only: an empirical one; one that any of you could fully manage independently; one whose starting point and whose point of conclusion is *you*; one on which you'll be able to give your unambiguous opinion.

It is such a clear and simple example – at least in my opinion it is so – that it can wipe away in one blow whatever residual doubt in both protagonists and antagonists. The latter will go on denying what I am writing, if that they have particular reasons to do so – but at least they might be convinced that they declare false things.

Now here is the experiment. Let us assume that Tanya, a female friend of yours, lives in Chicago, Illinois.

The following data are not real, yet they help us understand how the experiment I propose to you works; you can also use any other set of data, even real ones.

Now let us assume that Tanya was born in Chicago on the 24th of August 1968 at 11:15 am.

Consider Tanya's LR of January 2008, in Chicago: we can see Mars placed in the very middle of the 7th House.

Let us further assume that Tanya aims her LR and spends it in Denver, Colorado. Everybody knows that in the States it is possible to cover such a distance in very short time, spending less than $100 for a return trip. In the map of the ALR in Denver, Mars has clearly left the 7th House – it is in fact in the 8th House of LR.

This example is particularly directed at practising astrologers and students of astrology: if they decide to perform this experiment, a month later they would certainly be able to say whether during those 30 days Mars acted as a 'Mars in the 7th House' or as a 'Mars in the 8th House'. TThe effect of Mars being so utterly different in these Houses, even if an astrologer applies the most convoluted of rules – he would not mistake the behaviour of a Mars in the 7th House of Return with that of a Mars in the 8th House of Return.

Now, I believe that such a simple experiment will prove to you and convince you that this thing works... unless you intend to give evidence of it to a group of *fundamentalist scientifists* who would deny even the transit of the sun at the MC for the sake of running down astrology and astrologers.

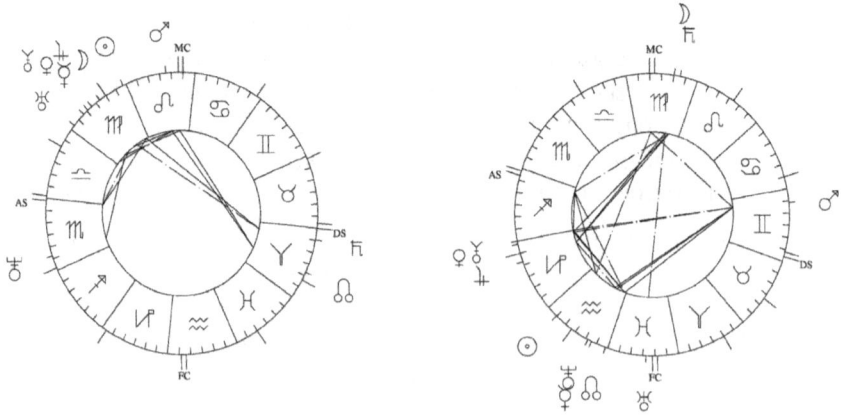

Natal **BLR, Chicago**

DO ALRS WORK?

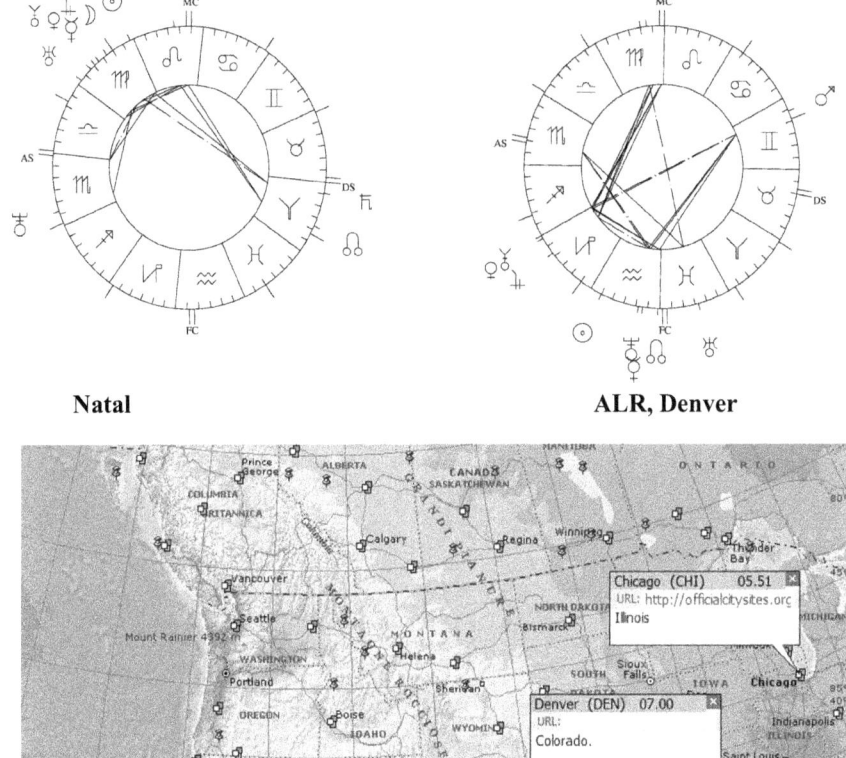

Natal   **ALR, Denver**

Translator's note:
Scientifist: I have tried to translate a non-existing Italian word which has actually been created by Ciro Discepolo to define a narrow-minded scientist.
In the Author's mind, a 'scientifist' is basically a scientist who scrictly follow a sort of '*scientism*' or '*scientifism*' consisting in a sort of religion, denying anything that he doesn't know or accept, despite any evidence, unless it's officially considered as 'scientific' by the scientific community – hence the word *scientifist*.

7.
New fields of research for Lunar Returns

As I have written in another section of this volume, many students of astrology at different levels are showing a growing interest in LRs. As for me, I first started to study them in the early '70s. I am aware that at that time LRs could not have become popular among readers – the reason being that it took more than thirty years for me to convince most of my colleagues about the extraordinary importance and power of Solar Returns and of Aimed Solar Returns.

In this context, I would like to show you a new kind of research that I have performed with Lunar Returns thanks to a little but exceptional – at least I find it exceptional – modification to my already wonderful software *Aladino* (*also refereed to as Module for the Automatized Research of the Aimed Solar Returns 'RSMA'*: http://www.programmiastral.com/guide/rsma.htm).

For the sake of simplicity I'll show you an example using my own data of birth.

Let us consider my Base LR of February 2008, in Naples:

Now let us assume that I wish to attain extraordinary results, for that month, concerning the 5th and the 7th House. What would I do if it were a SR? Well, obviously I'd try to place Venus and Jupiter in the 5th House and the stellium with the Sun in the 7th House. Taken for granted that I know that my time of birth is absolutely correct to the minute, I'd also try to have the conjunction of Venus and Jupiter – one degree, that very day! – exactly on the cusp between the 5th and 6th House: this way I'd protect both Houses, the 5th and 6th, as well as all the direct and indirect meanings covered by these two sectors of the sky. Now you can proceed with a series of attempts until you attain this result. Using the 'old' software Astral in fact, and after a number of trials, I could achieve it in Bordeaux, France. But if you really

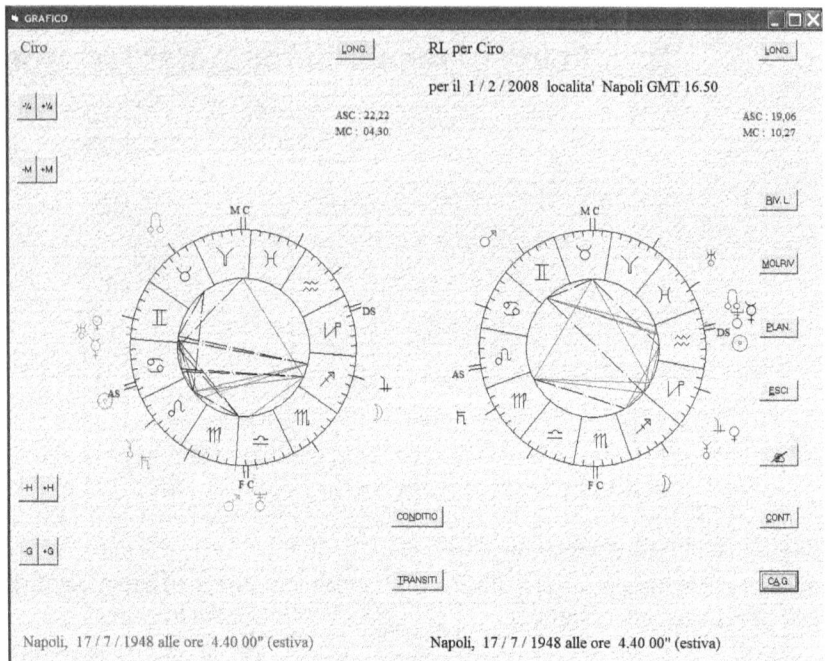

wanted to *choose*, and to choose freely, you should be able to compare a good amount of charts with the desired features: this way you'd be able to select a place where that LR could offer you an extra advantage.

This is exactly where *Aladino* can help you with its incredible power of calculations. Of course the example that we are considering can also be solved reckoning by hand (or by heart[1]), the advantage of *Aladino* being the fact that in its newer release, this application helps you spare hours, if not days of work. By the way the newer version of *Aladino* is freely available for its registered users. Of course, new users paying the registration fee will be given this newer version.

Back to our experiment now.

As you can see from the following illustration, I wrote my own data of birth in the section *Molriv* of *Aladino*, and then I selected the LR of February 2008. *Aladino* told me that the LR would take place on the 1st of February 2008 at 4:52 pm

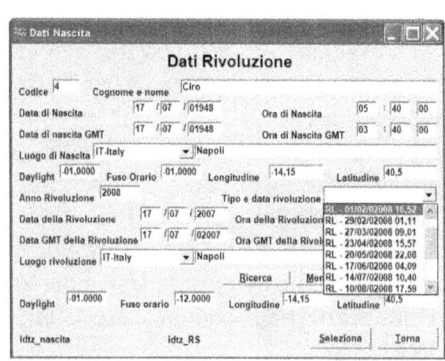

Greenwich Time. The old *Astral* would have said 4:50 pm, but keep in mind that *Aladino* is much more precise – anyway, such a difference of two minutes would not have any practical effect.

BLR longitudes listed by Aladino

RS per prova , GMT: 01/02/02008 ore 16:52
RS per Napoli (NA) (IT)

Sole :in Aquario 12°12'10,8739
Sole :in Aquario 12°12'10,8739
Luna :in Sagittario 09°18'49,8420
Luna :in Sagittario 09°18'49,8420
Mercurio :in Aquario 22°29'36,1176   Retrogrado
Mercurio :in Aquario 22°29'36,1176
Venere :in Capricorno 10°17'18,7113
Venere :in Capricorno 10°17'18,7113
Marte :in Gemelli 24°05'50,3053
Marte :in Gemelli 24°05'50,3053
Giove :in Capricorno 10°03'46,2521
Giove :in Capricorno 10°03'46,2521
Saturno :in Vergine 06°54'11,1663   Retrogrado
Saturno :in Vergine 06°54'11,1663
Urano :in Pesci 16°39'57,8631
Urano :in Pesci 16°39'57,8631
Nettuno :in Aquario 21°21'39,1485
Nettuno :in Aquario 21°21'39,1485
Plutone :in Capricorno 00°12'00,9084
Plutone :in Capricorno 00°12'00,9084
Nodo Medio :in Aquario 28°39'50,7313   Retrogrado
Nodo Medio :in Aquario 28°39'50,7313
Nodo Vero :in Aquario 27°50'49,7316   Retrogrado
Nodo Vero :in Aquario 27°50'49,7316
Lilith(Apogeo Medio) :in Scorpione 22°19'40,4759
Lilith(Apogeo Medio) :in Scorpione 22°19'40,4759
Apogeo Osculante :in Scorpione 19°15'19,0544   Retrogrado
Apogeo Osculante :in Scorpione 19°15'19,0544
Terra :in Ariete 00°00'00,0000
Terra :in Ariete 00°00'00,0000
Chirone :in Aquario 15°32'08,6671
Chirone :in Aquario 15°32'08,6671
Pholus :in Sagittario 09°43'55,6753
Pholus :in Sagittario 09°43'55,6753
Ceres :in Toro 13°21'03,3248
Ceres :in Toro 13°21'03,3248
Pallas :in Pesci 19°09'59,5204
Pallas :in Pesci 19°09'59,5204
Juno :in Sagittario 17°10'29,8993
Juno :in Sagittario 17°10'29,8993
Vesta :in Aquario 21°46'40,2456
Vesta :in Aquario 21°46'40,2456
Casa 1 :in Leone 19°28'47,2689
Casa 2 :in Vergine 11°19'49,6739
Casa 3 :in Bilancia 08°15'28,7284
Casa 4 :in Scorpione 10°57'17,8303
Casa 5 :in Sagittario 16°45'59,8765
Casa 6 :in Capricorno 20°24'32,9715
Casa 7 :in Aquario 19°28'47,2689
Casa 8 :in Pesci 11°19'49,6739
Casa 9 :in Ariete 08°15'28,7284
Casa 10 :in Toro 10°57'17,8303
Casa 11 :in Gemelli 16°45'59,8765
Casa 12 :in Cancro 20°24'32,9715

Now let us input in Aladino the data of a baby born on the 1st of February 2008, in Naples, at 5:52 pm (Italian time corresponding to 4:52 pm Greenwich Time).

Something is still missing, but my brilliant programmer Stefano Briganti has added it to *Aladino* under my strict supervision: namely, the possibility of reckoning such an ASR (OK, this is an ALR – but *Aladino* doesn't know and it doesn't even need to know) in which a cusp, say the cusp of the 1st House, or of the 2nd House, or of any other House) is placed exactly where we want it to be.

I say that the amendment has been done 'under my strict control' because *Aladino* is a piece of software of incredible complexity: the risk is that by modifying a section of the programme any other section might begin malfunctioning.

In this case we bypassed the risk with a delicate sort of 'grafting'. Believe me, Dr. Briganti and I almost worked like surgeons, with a sterile mask on our mouth and the eyes glued to a microscope...

I am writing this at the beginning of September 2007: I won't give my OK to this new release of *Aladino* before one year, and certainly not before I have verified that all the other features of this piece of software haven't been damaged in any way.

Nonetheless there was still another problem left.

Wanting to position Jupiter and Venus on the cusp between the 5th and the 6th House and the stellium with the Sun in the 7th House, we should have accepted also an Ascendant of LR in the 12th natal House (of course the 'natal' of this LR is not my own natal chart, but this doesn't change what we are trying to achieve). Could we? Of course we can. In fact I have explained it several times: if the SR is good, even a bad LR taking place under that SR can not cause serious damage – not even if there is a Sun in the 12th House of LR. In the worst case the unfavourable elements of a bad LR within a good SR can simply announce some cold, with no detriment for its advantages given by the positive elements in the 5th and in the 7th House. Moreover – you should not undervalue it, although this refers to LRs only, not to SRs – we have placed a wonderful protection in the 6th House, the House of health.

Now all this shows the kind of open-mindedness that you need if you wish to create a condition of synergy between an ASR and an ALR. Nevertheless since its birth Aladino was programmed to block any possible 'solution to the equation' if it broke any of the 'taboo-rules' within the 'thirty rules' given in the volume *Transits and Solar Returns*.

So we performed a second amendment – together with the previous one – in order to be able to unblock the 'lock' of the 'thirty rules'. Now Aladino – only when we give it the desired longitude for a cusp – may also propose a Return with detrimental elements such as the Sun in the 12th House or Mars in the 6th House, or a stellium of celestials in the 8th House and so on.

To make a long story short, this is what the genius of the *One Thousand and One Nights* has been able to offer to us after a scan of a few seconds: a list of several dozens of places. We show you the relevant charts for few of these locations. Please consider them, study them and then try to understand which one I would have chosen if I had resolved to relocate this LR. Elaborate: why would I have chosen that place and not any other?

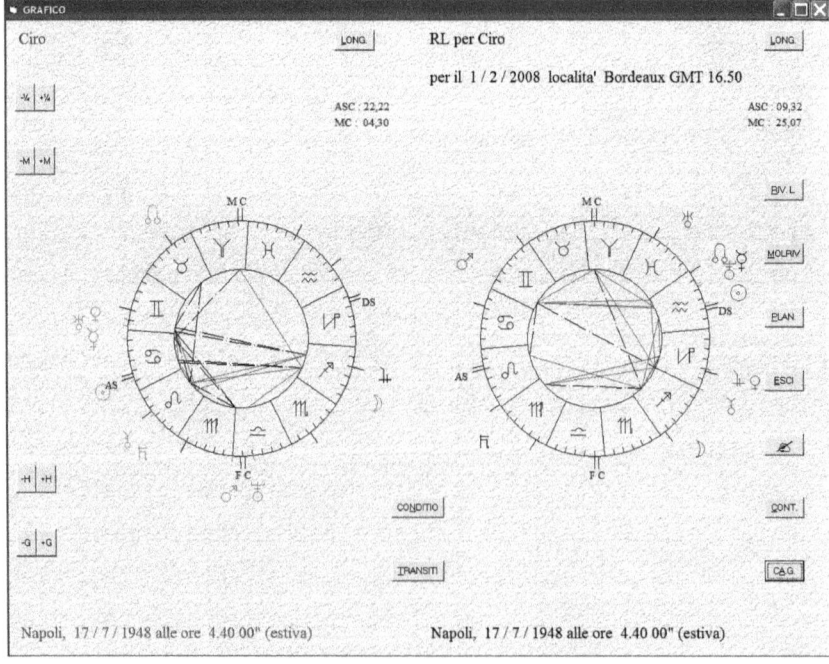

NEW FIELDS OF RESEARCH FOR LUNAR RETURNS

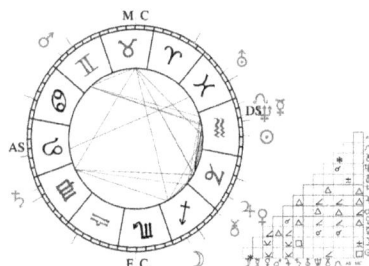

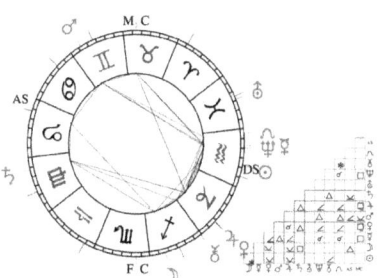

ALR in Queenstown, South Africa

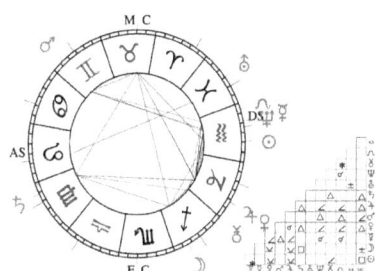

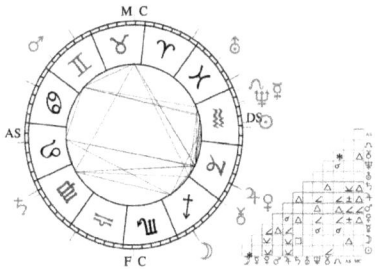

ALR in Djanet, Algeria

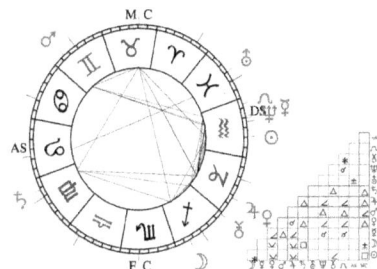

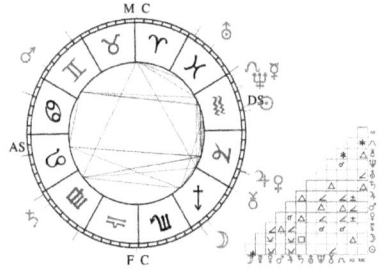

ALR in Palma de Majorca, Spain

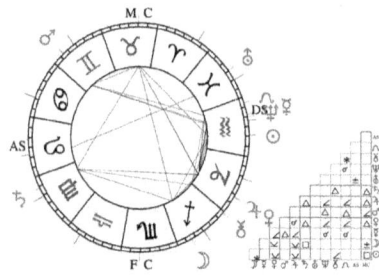
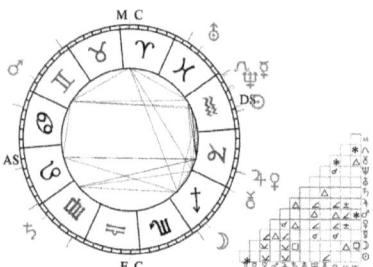

ALR in Bordeaux, France

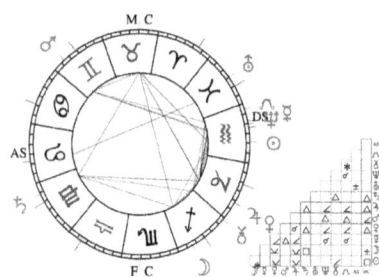
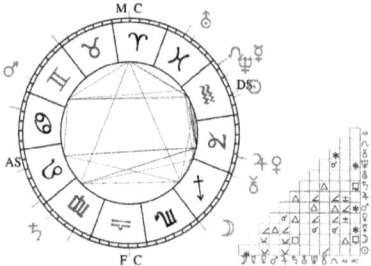

ALR in Plymouth, UK

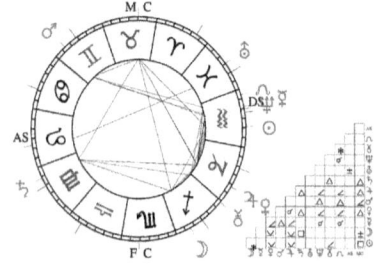
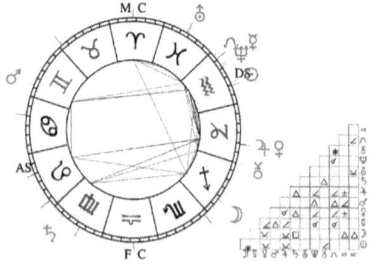

ALR in Carrickfinn, Ireland

NEW FIELDS OF RESEARCH FOR LUNAR RETURNS

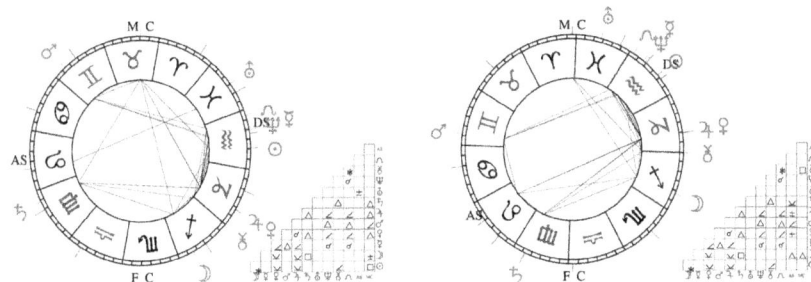

ALR in Reykjavik, Iceland

My choice would have been certainly Queenstown: there, relying on a very good 7th House and a very good 5th house, with Uranus also in the 7th House I would have increased the chances for the turn of events concerning the 7th House.

Notes
1) During a congress of Astrology in Lavagna, Genoa, in October 2006, half-jokingly I proposed to the audience that I select one subject among them to reckon his/her ASR by heart, and to modify it according to the rules of my school, still by heart. That day only a few good colleagues of mine did understand that I was not joking: it was in fact a piece of bravura that you could hardly witness in the future... The episode has been described with plenty of details in my volume on the interpretation of the natal map *L'interpretazione del tema natale*, Armenia editore.

8.
A thrilling Lunar Return

With this Lunar Return of mine I wished to achieve a precise aim: to support with an appropriate astral configuration a series of publishing projects in which I would be involved during the second half of the month of October.

First of all, it is important to remark that in the overwhelming majority of my own aimed birthdays, I use the 3rd House and the 9th House of the SR as a recipient for the malefic planets, and this probably explains it well why my books have been published abroad so late. Nevertheless, in 2007 I aimed my SR otherwise and I spent it in Río Gallegos, Patagonia, Argentina: where I placed Venus exactly on the cusp between the 2nd and the 3rd House of SR – this way I would achieve important goals in the field of publishing during the following twelve months, especially with regard to publishing my books abroad.

In this case my goal was achievable because I would aim a LR that was already supported by a promising SR in the field of publishing, and a LR of this kind would work in synergy with the existing SR.

So it was easy for me to select a good location and I spent my LR in Istanbul, Turkey, where I placed Jupiter in conjunction with the Medium Coeli – immediately after the MC, in the so-called Gauquelin zone where the planet is supposed to be stronger – and at the same time I avoided the Sun falling in the 8th House and I also avoided possible harm to my daughters by putting Mars in the 4th House instead of the 5th House.

It is common knowledge that with low-cost airlines it is possible to relocate a Solar or Lunar Return with a one-day return ticket, with a relatively low fare.

II opted for this course of action as well but didn't know that I would have a thrilling Lunar Return...

This is what happened.

My LR was to take place at 4:44 pm, local time of Istanbul; my flight back home would take off at 5:30 pm, local time.

I was in the airport already at 10 o'clock in the morning. With good anticipation, a flight to Milan Malpensa scheduled for 2 pm was announced to be rescheduled to 4:30 pm. But I had booked a seat on a flight to Rome Fiumicino, and there was no news about my flight. Usually, having no news of a flight is a bad sign: especially when Alitalia, our flag carrier, was facing a period of workers' union unrest because of its serious financial and corporate situation (still existing on the date I am writing these lines, on the 16th of October 2007). So I thought to myself, if it's 10 am and they already announce a two-hour delay for the flight Istanbul to Milan, when I'm supposed to take off in the afternoon there will surely be further delays and my flight to Rome Fiumicino might even be cancelled. So I resolved to take a seat on the flight to Milan, where I could catch an evening flight home to Naples. Of course I considered the chance that – with the devil's help – the 16:30 flight could actually take off on time, but the probability theory was against this remote chance, so I eventually determined that it would be a good decision to fly to Milan.

Of course things shaped otherwise. More than an hour before the scheduled departure, the aircraft was already connected to the terminal and 60 minutes before departure, two ground hostesses were already standing at the gate, ready to check the passports and the tickets.

Twenty minutes before departure we were embarking. The strangest thing of all is that, beyond any reasonable forecast everybody got on board immediately, nobody was missing.

Another incredible fact happened: the control tower gave an immediate OK for take off! It was as if Alitalia was making a demonstration of its own efficiency for a TV coverage...

Moreover, Istanbul has a huge airport, and in huge airports the aircrafts usually queue one after another on the runway. Well, not even this happened! There was no queue so that we took off at 16:30.

Now, I had the chart of my monthly Return clearly in my mind, and I feared missing the main goal that I intended to achieve by aiming it in Istanbul: namely, Jupiter in the 9th House in conjunction with the Medium Coeli. For if the aircraft had moved westward in the following minutes,

Jupiter would have been placed very clearly in the 10th House of the LR, which would have simply spoiled my Aimed Lunar Return.

At this point, while all my mental antennas were trying to capture any indication of the direction that our flight was taking, I understood that something was happening in my favour. We were taking off and, as it is logical in these cases, we were taking off keeping the sun *behind* the aircraft – in other words, we were flying eastward. I could not be mistaken on such an elementary thing; I only wondered whether the captain would make a large or a narrow turn in order to take the final direction – westward. Minutes ticked away and it was like being in a thrilling movie film: the airplane went on rising up in the sky, still going eastward. Eventually we started a slow turn in an westward direction. At this point, I was in the need to know over which part of the globe I would be at 4:44 pm. In this search I have been shamelessly lucky, I dare say. I switched on my notebook, opened *MS Encarta World Atlas* and I zoomed the window around Istanbul. The sky was slightly clouded but I could see the ground from my seat.

At 4:44 pm just under me, a little bit on the right side of the window by which I was seated, I could see the portion of the Black Sea – a bay of an unmistakable shape (you can see it in the following maps). More or less we were flying somewhere between Igneada and Avcýlar, approx. 41°54' N and 27°56' East. Without loosing a minute, I immediately opened my astrology software and after typing the information in its module Molriv I got the chart reproduced down here. Ironically, this Lunar Return might even be better than the one planned for relocation in Istanbul. In fact I had Jupiter glued to the Medium Coeli but still in the 9th House, while Venus was touching the borderline of the conjunction, two and a half degree below the Descendant. The Sun as well as the Ascendant of the LR hadn't fallen into the 8th House. I had one doubt left: perhaps it was closer than 2.5 degree from the cusp between the 4th and the 5th House, what I had wished to avoid not to cause any harm to my daughter, nor to have troubles related with them. Nonetheless we have to remember that this LR and all the LRs of the period June 2007 to July 2008 stood under the frame of an ASR that contained no dangerous element of this kind: so, even if something would take place related to my daughters, it could not be anything serious.

In fact as soon as I reached home I got to know that my daughter Luna had had a tumble on the street at around 3 pm in Naples – but she only got slight scratches on her knee and on her lower lip. Those who haven't fully understood how LRs and SRs work would cry out, «This is the proof that the Mars of your LR was in the 5th House!» But it is not so – in fact we are talking of an event that took place in Naples at 3 'o clock pm, that is to say, *before* the Lunar Return of Istanbul. In fact at that time, the previous LR of mine was effective, the one I had spent in San Severo di Foggia – the one with Uranus in the 5th House and Mars in the 7th House!

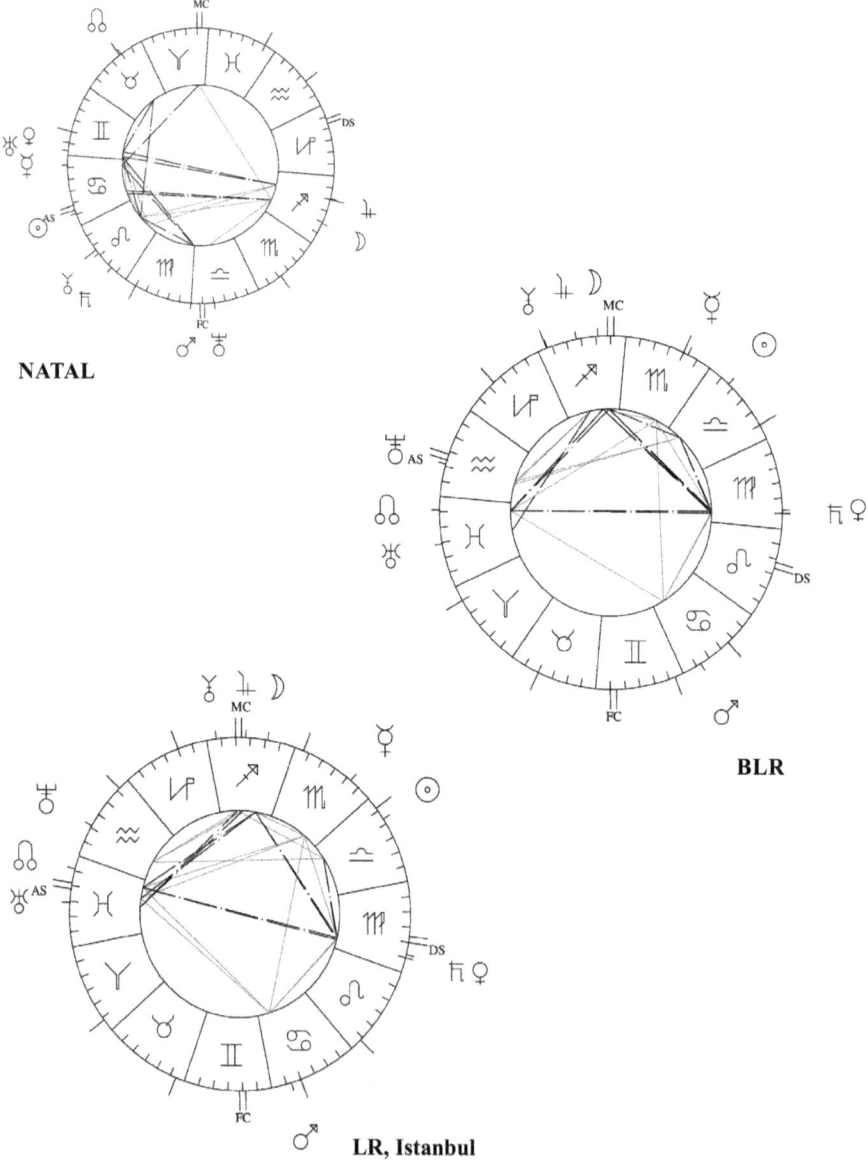

NATAL

BLR

LR, Istanbul

A THRILLING LUNAR RETURN

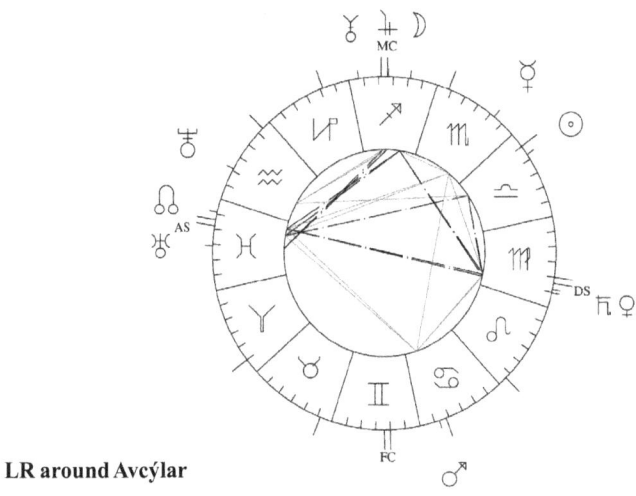

LR around Avcýlar

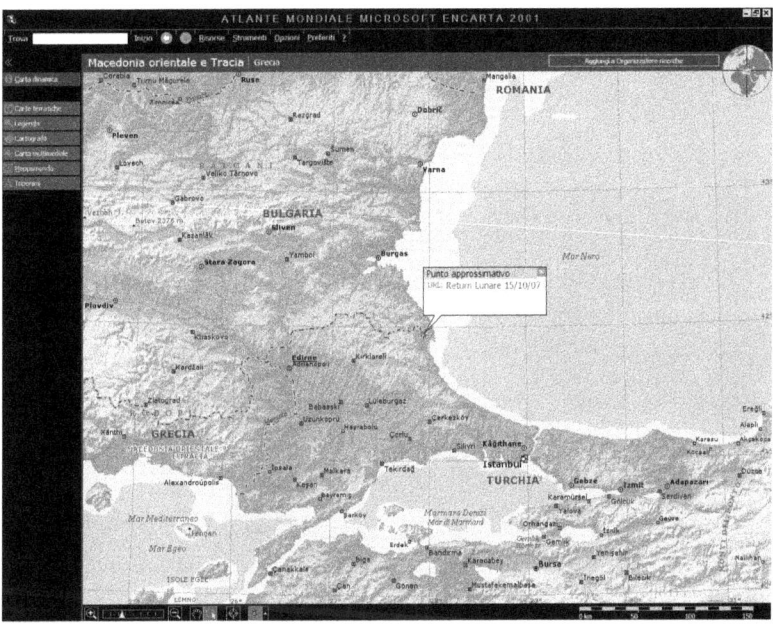

88   LUNAR RETURNS AND EARTH RETURNS

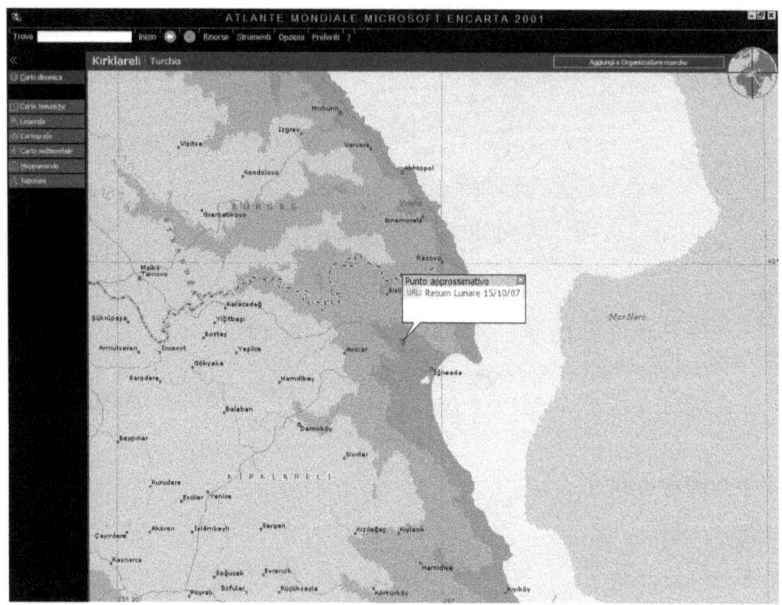

9.
An Aimed Lunar Return for an intervention of rhinoplasty

While I am writing these lines, the subject to whom the following charts refer is having the Aimed Solar Return that you can see in the following pages: he had himself chosen the place to relocate it. Now the subject is deeply concerned because he would like to undergo rhinoplasty: not only for aesthetic reasons, but also for functional ones.

He asks me the following questions:

1) During such a SR can I undergo this kind of a surgical intervention?

2) Can I hope that such an intervention will have a favourable result?

3) Only one of the two candidate surgeons has given me his full data of birth: which one should I choose to perform the intervention?

4) Both surgeons wants to operate somewhere between the 10th and the 20th of December. Would it be helpful for me to aim a LR in order to achieve better results from this rhinoplasty? Keep in mind that I need it very much, but on the other hand it makes me deeply anguished.

These are my answers, the answers that I gave to myself and that I subsequently sent to the subject.

1) Obviously, I wouldn't have chosen *that* ASR knowing that I would have to undergo surgery; knowing that it would be an important operation for me, an intervention that would consist in liberation from the particularly annoying problems that prevent me from breathing and sleeping well. Considering that, such a SR is not the best one – because it has Saturn in the 10th House, which does not favour any sort of emancipation or liberation. Nevertheless we have certain elements in this SR that make me say «yes» to surgery. First of all, generally speaking, the SR itself is not a bad one. Then we have Venus on the Medium Coeli, and Jupiter in the 2nd

House: both favour specifically what we have enumerated so far.

2) Yes – especially if we sum the effects of the Aimed Lunar Return that I'm about to suggest you.

3) Not knowing the time of birth of one of them, I can only consider the other surgeon, the former being 'nothing' for me from an astrological point of view. Now I can consider the selected surgeon's natal chart, his LR and his SR and I can see that he's probably going to face huge legal troubles and/or troubles connected with his sentimental or marital life in the following months. Yet I would exclude that it could be a trial connected with the intervention that the querying subject wishes to undergo: in fact he is a famous surgeon, well known in this field; almost certainly he must be insured against the risks of errors in such a kind of intervention. Now, if he would make a mistake – a bad mistake – while operating Brad Pitt's nose, two or three insurance companies wouldn't be enough to cover the damage, and the surgeon would certainly undergo a sensational trial, resounding in all the media. My querying subject, however, is a rather modest man from the financial-professional point of view. It is not logical to think that if he resolved to bring a suit against the surgeon, such a 'war' would be announced so clearly in the surgeon's chart of Solar and Lunar Returns. Moreover, in my subject's SR there is no element announcing wars or battles of any sort, especially not legal suits – so I must think that the risks of mistaken surgery are quite reduced. Still in connection with the selected surgeon, the sinastry with my subject gives 8 points over 44 according to the algorithm that I have elaborated – the same that I use for the calculation of a sinastry that I offer free-of-charge to the visitors of my web pages. This result is soothing for me: in fact, if their index of sinastry would have been much higher, it might have represented a piece of common destiny between the two of them – and this would have been the case if they would face a long-lasting trial connected with compensation for damage. On the contrary, a low index of sinastry is typical of any person who enters in your life and goes out from it almost immediately, without leaving any significant track of his/her passage.

4) Certainly yes, because in this case we can sum a good Aimed Lunar Return to protect 'appearance' (especially following the subject's query) and, as the saying goes, the game is worth the candle. Below these lines you can see the Base Lunar Return (a quite bad one) and the Aimed Lunar Return, relocated in the Cocos Islands, where we can place a wonderful Venus in the 2nd House with a tolerance of 12 minutes, just in case the subject had actually be born before the given time (although he assures that he is absolutely confident of his own time of birth). With these 12 minutes we would not loose the effect of Venus in the 2nd House even considering an extension of two and

AN AIMED LUNAR RETURN FOR AN INTERVENTION OF RHINOPLASTY

a half degrees beyond the cusp. Lastly you must consider that the Moon will be in Capricorn on the date chosen by the surgeon for the intervention. This is not the ideal position in these cases; I would have avoided Scorpio above all (there are different schools of thought about it, but I think that Scorpio is the Sign which is more strictly related to the nose), as well as Aries (the face) and Capricorn (the bones). On the other hand, the greatest percentage of surgical interventions has to do with bones, so it's OK.

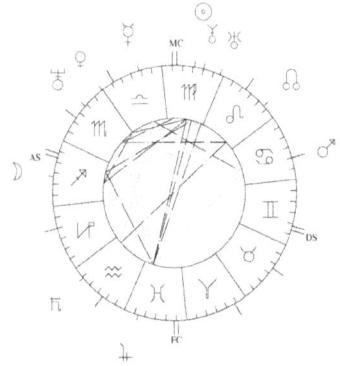

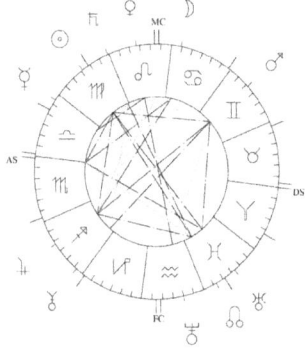

SR

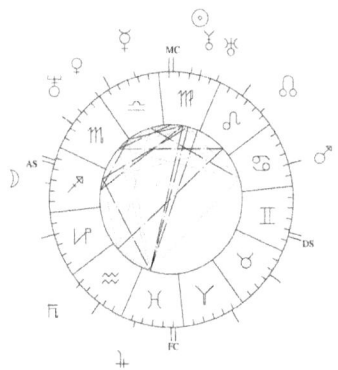

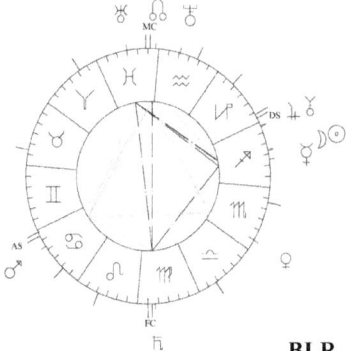

BLR

LUNAR RETURNS AND EARTH RETURNS

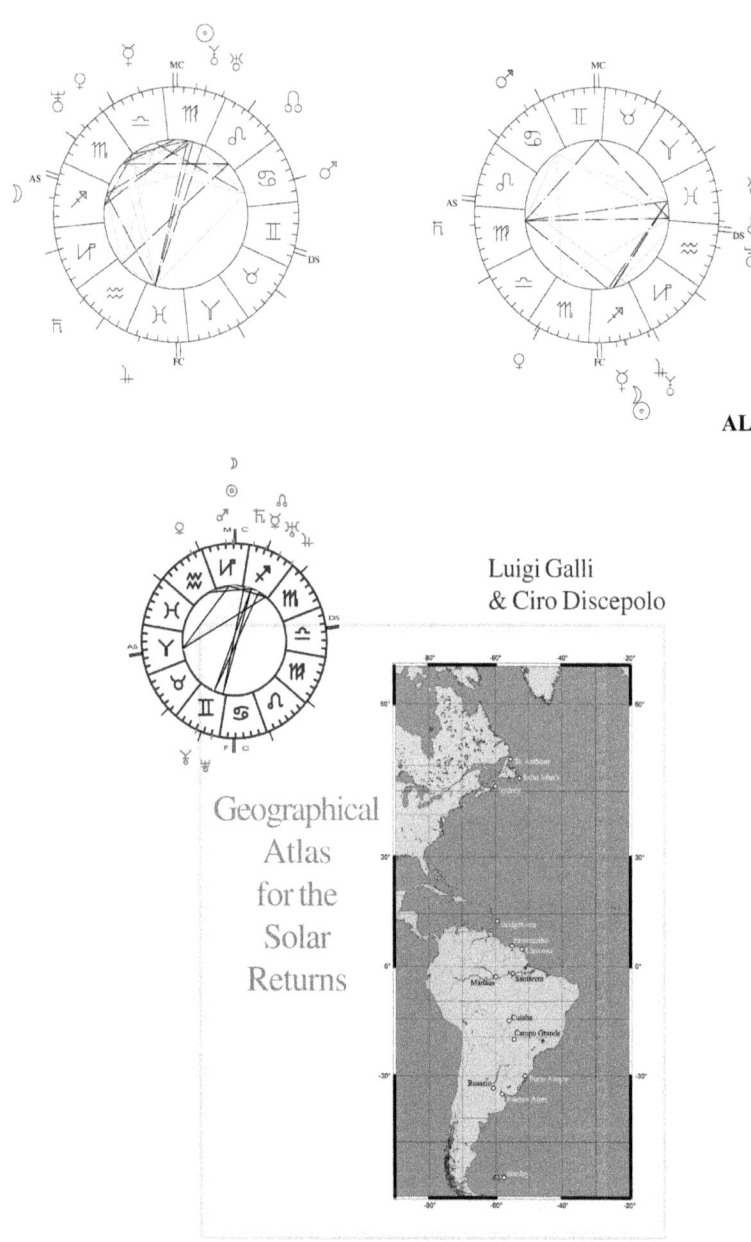

ALR

Luigi Galli
& Ciro Discepolo

Geographical Atlas for the Solar Returns

Ricerca '90 Publisher
Free Download of this book from:
http://www.cirodiscepolo.it/english_corner/English_corner.htm

10.
Lunar Return in San Severo di Foggia

The chart shows my LR of the 18th of September 2007, at 7:03 am Greenwich Mean Time, corresponding to 9:03[1] am Italian time.

The drawing itself doesn't change much if you cast it for Naples or for San Severo di Foggia, but the latter place is where I actually went to, that morning. I'd say it's almost impossible to see the difference in the distance of Sun and Saturn from the cusps. In Naples I ran the risk of having a LR with the Sun in the 12th House or with Saturn in the 10th House, considering the rule of the 2.5 degrees from the cusp – see Ciro Discepolo's *Nuovo Trattato di Astrologia*, Armenia editore. In such a case I detected a valuable place that was about 250 kms from home, where I could avoid both the Sun in the 12th House and Saturn in the 10th House – and not going there I would have felt like throwing a piece of good luck out of the window. After all, it was a matter of driving a few hours and staying there only five minutes. Moreover, a few days later two books of mine would be published: *L'interpretazione del tema natale*, Armenia editore, and *Transits and Solar Returns*, Ricerca '90 Publishing.

In other words, I was convinced then and I am still convinced now, that it was an alluring marketing action, because I could achieve the utmost result with the least effort.

So I selected the location with the help of *Aladino*, and I cross-checked the calculation by hand:

Longitudes of San Severo di Foggia:

Sun: 25°00'01" Virgo

Cusp of the 12th House: 28°13'57" Virgo

Difference: 3° 13' 56" 00, that is to say much larger then the range of 2.5 degrees.

Saturn: 1°56'43" Virgo

Cusp between the 10 and the 11th House: 29°22'58" Leo

Difference: 2° 33' 45" 00, not very much larger than 2.5 degrees – but larger.

Please note that in my case I am assured that there is no doubt about my real time of birth, having verified it several times in the last decades – nonetheless, if it had been a Solar Return I would have kept a much larger margin in order to avoid any risk of the Sun falling in the 12th House.

In this case, as I have already explained, the game was worth the candle. But if you work at such a level of accuracy, saying «San Severo» is not enough – you have to find out the very exact longitude of the location and you have to reach that very point inside the little town of San Severo corresponding to that longitude.

As you can see from the screenshots of Aladino reproduced in the following page, this piece of software is based on a huge database of localities that I have bought from American geographical institutions, which have obtained the coordinates directly from a satellite that has measured them. Now all this procedure assures me that the longitude of that place called 'San Severo' is 15°23' East and 41°41' North.

The next step was to open *Google Earth*, a wonderful tool for my work, and finding out that the point of my interest corresponds exactly to a shop called *Catalano* placed in Corso Amedeo d'Aosta #45. According to Google Earth the geographical coordinates of that point corresponded to the longitude of 15°22'59"86 E and to the latitude of 41°40'54"79 N: more or less, with the precision of a few metres, exactly the point that I was looking for, and where I eventually stayed during my LR.

At this point, I had only to drive my car and set up my GPS receiver to the address desired – all the rest was almost automatic...

Notes
1) If you cast my LR of September with the old version of *Astral*, the GMT time would result to be 7:00 am. If you do the same with *Aladino*, the result is 7:03. The slight difference is due to the different geographical coordinates of my place of birth in the different databases of geographical coordinates that have been published in Italy and abroad – but it's a difference of few hundred metres after all. In order to overcome even this non-existing problem, I remained before Mr. Catalano's shop from 8:45 to 9:03.

LUNAR RETURN IN SAN SEVERO DI FOGGIA

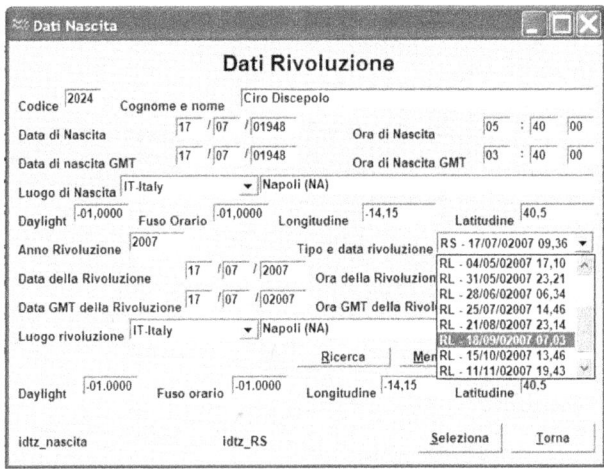

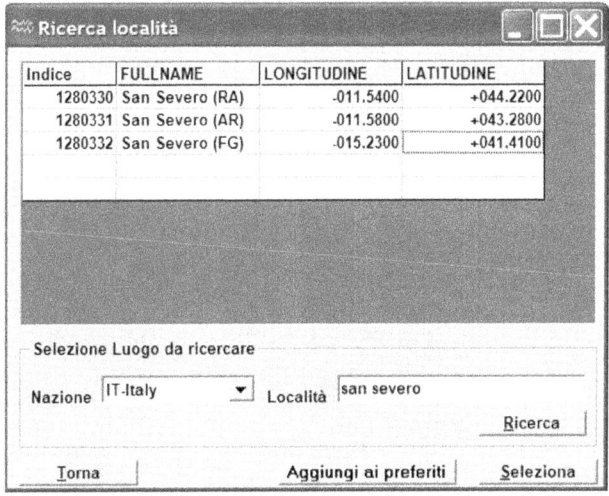

These are the two screenshots of *Aladino* that led me to casting my sky of LR for relocation in San Severo di Foggia.

RS per RL per settembre 2007, GMT: 18/09/02007 ore 07:03
RS per San Severo (FG) (IT)

Sole : in Vergine 25°00'01,4657
Luna : in Sagittario 09°18'51,9247
Mercurio : in Bilancia 18°40'59,5083
Venere : in Leone 18°17'03,7163
Marte : in Gemelli 24°48'11,4737
Giove : in Sagittario 12°32'36,0637
Saturno : in Vergine 01°56'43,5332
Urano : in Pesci 16°22'18,6200 Retrogrado
Nettuno : in Aquario 19°44'22,4983 Retrogrado
Plutone : in Sagittario 26°19'54,8911
Nodo Medio : in Pesci 05°53'11,6032 Retrogrado
Nodo Vero : in Pesci 06°54'31,0811 Retrogrado
Lilith(Apogeo Medio) : in Scorpione 07°03'29,7593
Apogeo Osculante : in Scorpione 11°25'45,9676 Retrogrado
Chirone : in Aquario 11°00'11,5014 Retrogrado
Pholus : in Sagittario 03°30'28,7015
Ceres : in Toro 23°55'01,6216
Pallas : in Pesci 06°18'09,3834 Retrogrado
Juno : in Scorpione 02°47'51,5418
Vesta : in Sagittario 17°13'10,4707
Casa 1 : in Bilancia 21°55'47,8647
Casa 2 : in Scorpione 19°28'24,9939
Casa 3 : in Sagittario 21°16'17,7155
Casa 4 : in Capricorno 25°58'02,5701
Casa 5 : in Aquario 29°22'58,0410
Casa 6 : in Pesci 28°13'57,2768
Casa 7 : in Ariete 21°55'47,8647
Casa 8 : in Toro 19°28'24,9939
Casa 9 : in Gemelli 21°16'17,7155
Casa 10 : in Cancro 25°58'02,5701
Casa 11 : in Leone 29°22'58,0410
Casa 12 : in Vergine 28°13'57,2768

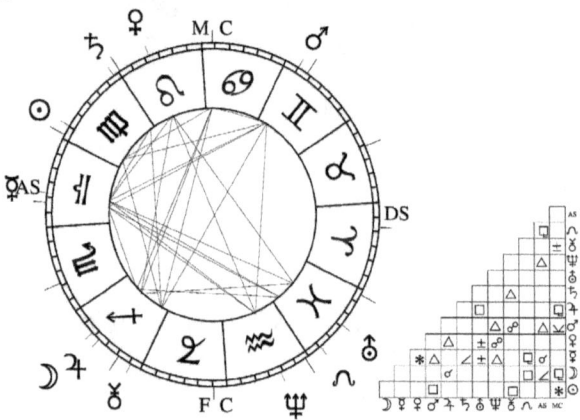

LUNAR RETURN IN SAN SEVERO DI FOGGIA

This picture was taken before Mr. Catalano's shop in the very moment of the Lunar Return

11.
How to choose an ALR for eye surgery

This practical lesson is about a subject who had recently spent his SR at home in Italy, but after a few days repented it because he had the Sun of SR in the 1st House of SR and Uranus in the 6th House of SR – not the very best for safety as far as one's health is concerned. And the very day of his birthday, he was told that he needed eye surgery not only to improve his health, but also to improve his sight.

So the subject contacted me asking in which period he should undergo such surgery. He also asked me for the most suitable month to found a commercial society with a female friend of his, before a notary.

The answer to this latter question is: never! In fact he had a quite dangerous Saturn in the natal 7th House, which we may compare to a sleeping dog. There was no reason to wake this dog up creating a new commercial enterprise while the subject's main activity is already a good, stable, and sure one.

So let us focus on the main scope of this practical lesson and let's begin with recollecting all the 20 rules already listed in another section of this book. First of all, the rule that says that you had better avoid any surgery during the 20 days immediately following one's birthday.

Now you'll see all his following LRs one by one. For each of them I'll write down some remark, without repeating what we have already discussed so far.

After this exercise we'll take stock of his general situation, also considering his transits as well as the subject's field of activity.

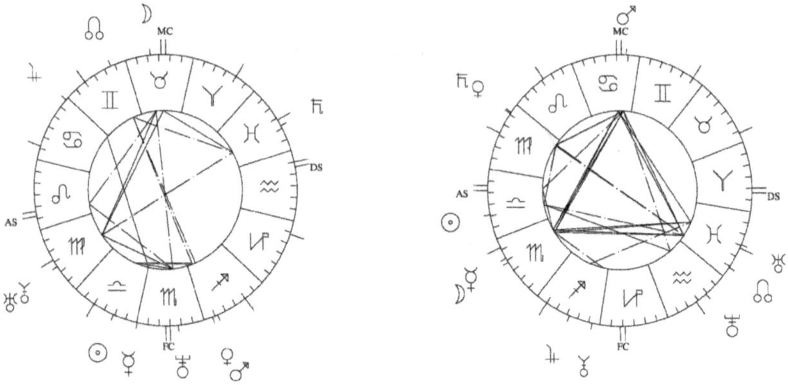

NATAL and BLR

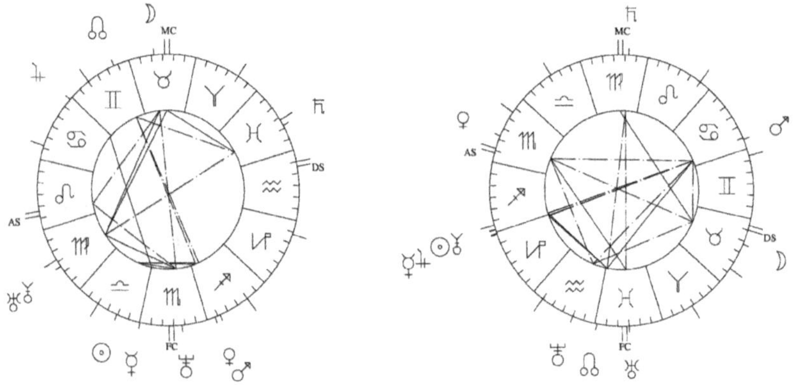

The Base Lunar Return is quite detrimental, much in conflict with the subject's aims. With a low cost flight to Madrid, it's another kettle of fish… Remember that with Ryanair, for example, it is possible to reach several capitals of Europe with 25 Euro / ticket, and fly back to Italy for 1 •!

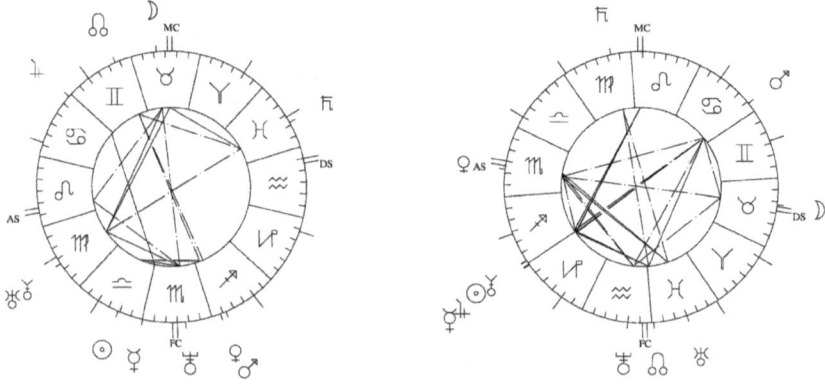

Almost the same can be said for his following LR: with a flight of a few hours, and a very cheap one at that, it is possible to improve his situation very much by spending the LR in Lisbon.

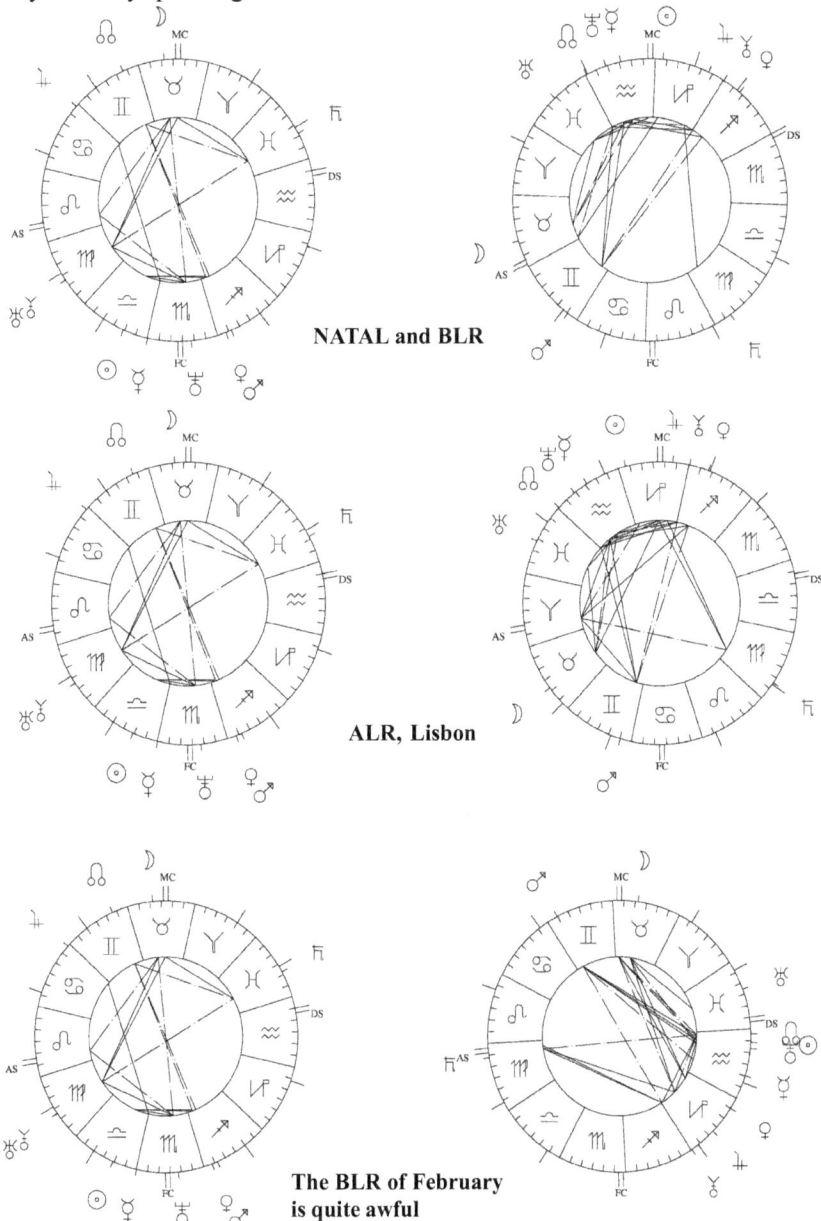

NATAL and BLR

ALR, Lisbon

The BLR of February is quite awful

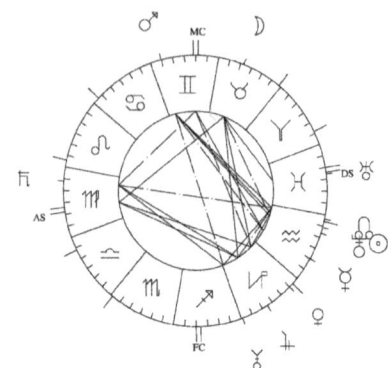

But in Rovaniemi, Finland, things change a lot.

The following three BLRs don't need to be changed

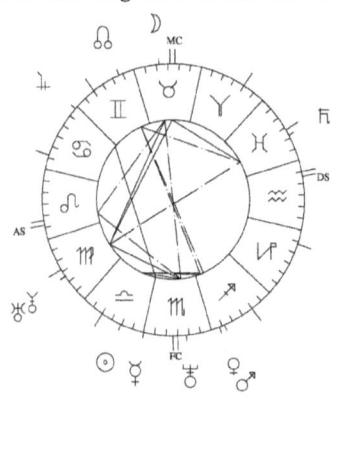
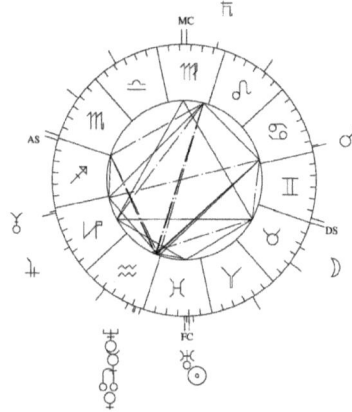

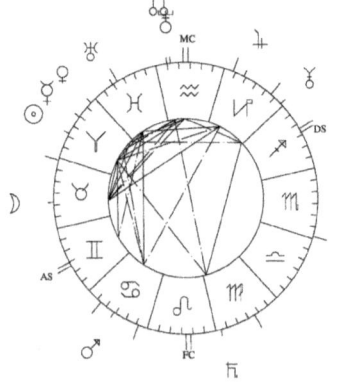

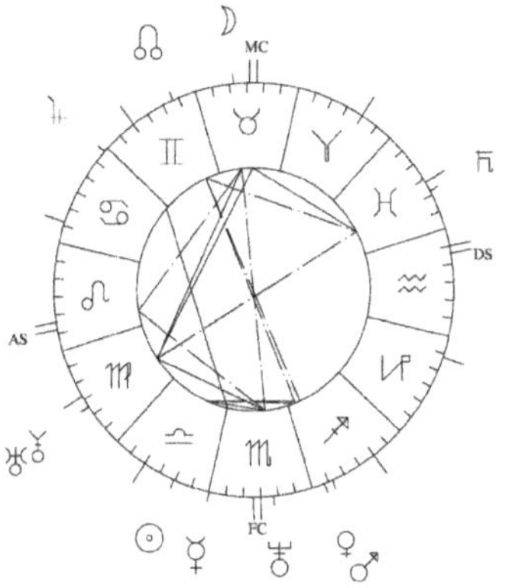

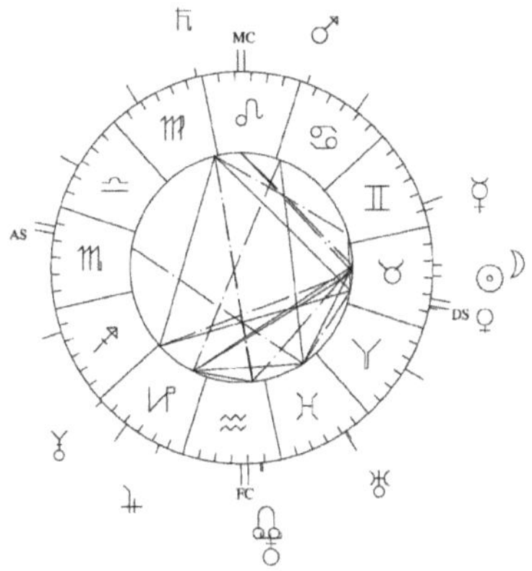

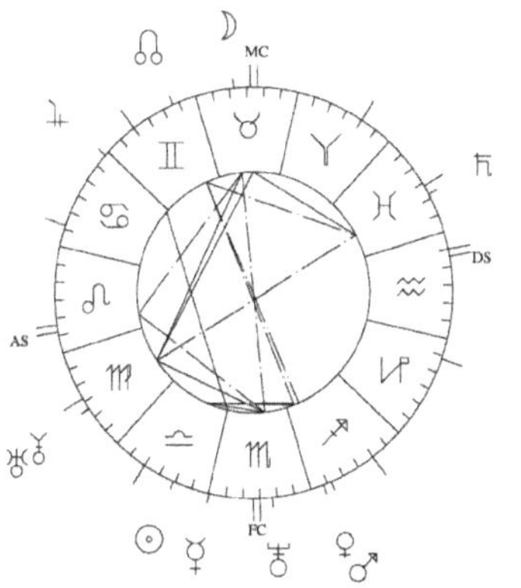

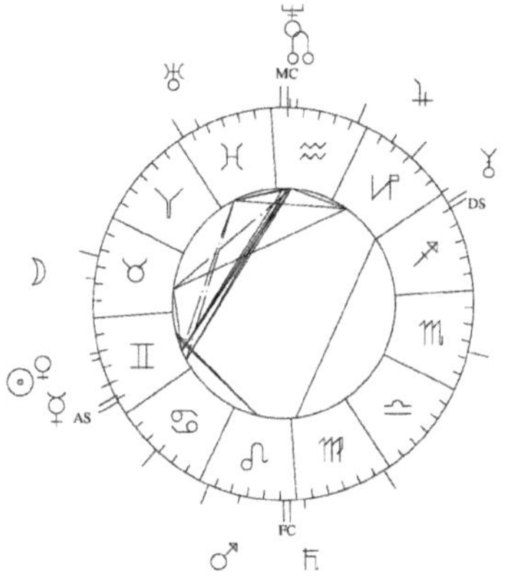

HOW TO CHOOSE AN ALR FOR EYE SURGERY

But the LR of June can be improved...

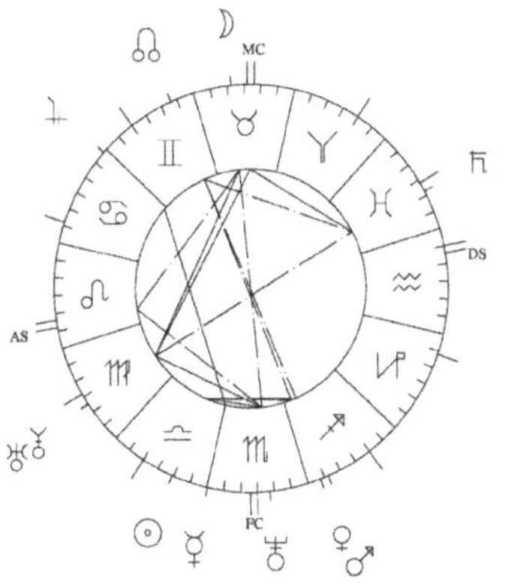

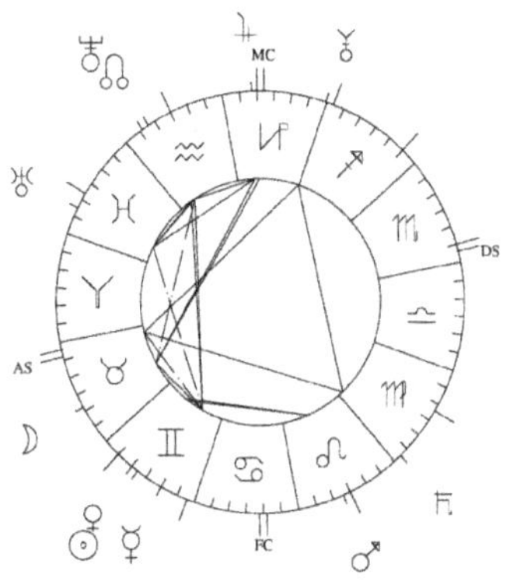

..**by relocating it in Ponta Delgada, in the isles Azores (Portugal).**

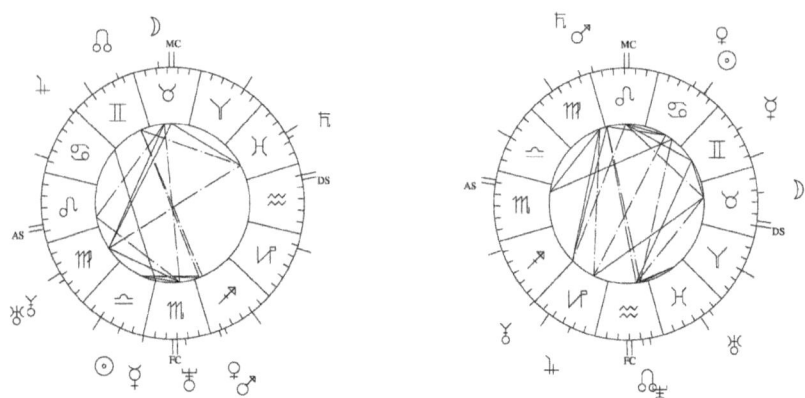

The above LR should be avoided because of its conjunction of Mars and Saturn in the 10th House. By relocating or aiming it to Madeira, Portugal, things become much better (see chart below).

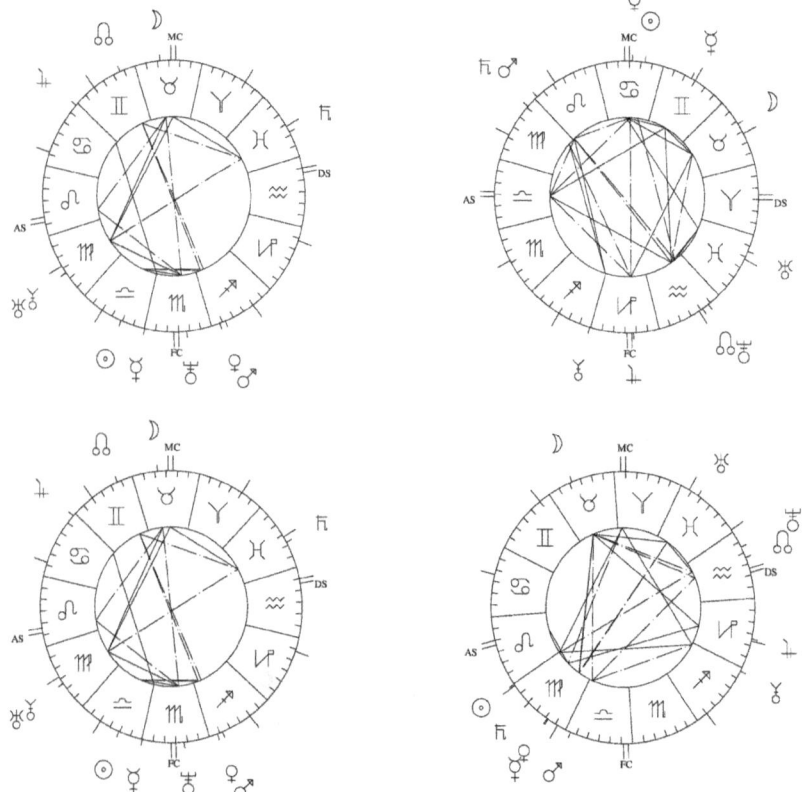

Ascendant in the 12th House and Sun in the 1st House: no good.

HOW TO CHOOSE AN ALR FOR EYE SURGERY

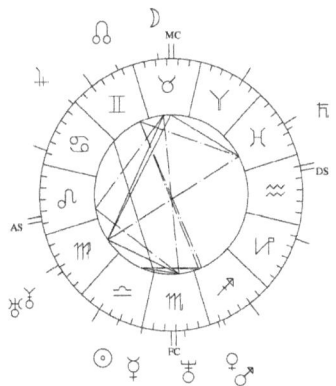

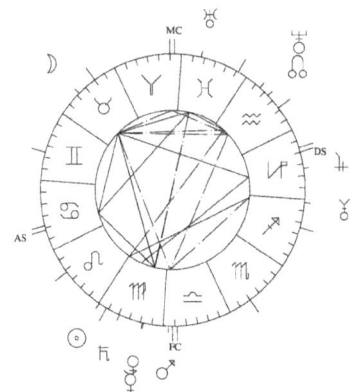

In Lisbon it is much better.

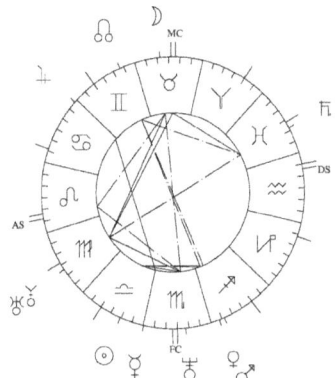

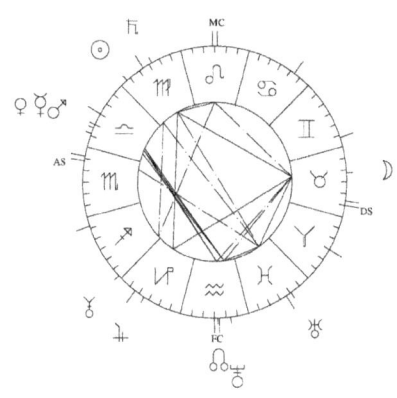

The stellium in the 12th House should be avoided.

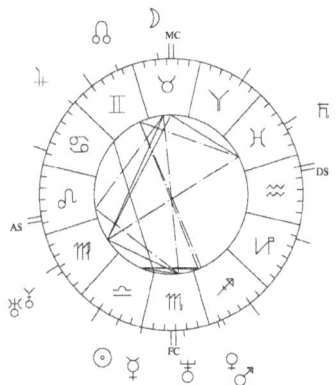

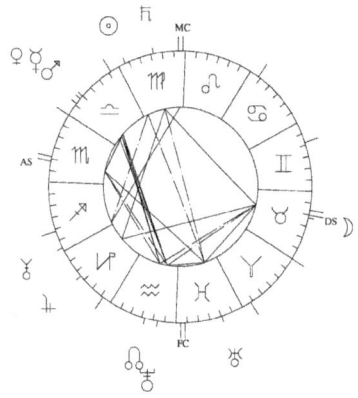

Relocating in Istanbul improves much.

106   LUNAR RETURNS AND EARTH RETURNS

Considering the rules expressed in this volume and those listed in my previous works; also keeping in mind that we should avoid surgery in the 20 days after the subject's birthday – but on the other hand it wasn't advisable to wait too long, otherwise it would be the stars who 'would cause any surgery, by chance' – I stated that the best LR within whose frame the subject should undergo surgery was the LR of the 21st of December 2007 in Madrid. I believe so also for the following reasons:

- We position Venus on the Ascendant of LR, thus protecting health very much

- The stellium of prevailingly harmonic celestials in the 2nd House is very good, because – as we stated before – surgery had also an aesthetical implication.

- In the days following the LR of Madrid, transiting Sun and Mercury would be trine to the subject's Medium Coeli, while Jupiter would still be trine to his Ascendant.

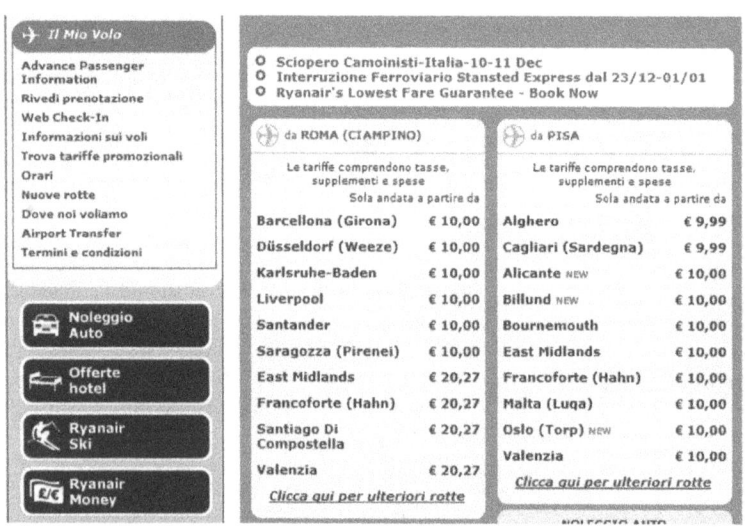

This is a detail from the website www.ryanair.com: try and test it!

12.
A few practical exercises on the dating of events

Starting from the 70s to date, I have written plenty of material explaining how to use LRs for the dating of events: among them half a dozen books and several articles. In particular, about 500 of 800 pages of my volume *Nuovo Trattato di Astrologia*, Armenia, are devoted to practical exercises on the dating of important events: there you can find dozens of charts of LR that help achieving this goal.

Considering that, I'll include only a few examples here.

Let us start with the election of the current Pontiff: Pope Benedict XVI, born Joseph Alois Ratzinger, was elected on the 19th of April 2005, exactly three days after his birthday.

The most interesting this about this fact is that, according to all the expert Vatican correspondents, he became the Pope exactly on the day of his birthday.

In fact, still as a cardinal, on the 16th of April 2005 Joseph Ratzinger was asked to make a speech before the World: where he said exactly what his opinion was and what he would do if he was elected. By doing so he was convinced that he was actually deleting his own name from the list of the possible candidates to the papacy.

To make a long story short, he clearly stated – opposing the general trend – that he would not follow the stream of great ecumenicalism of his predecessor Pope John Paul II. Although he intended to respect the essence and the role of other religions, he said, he would virtually seal the borders among the different credo. He would not mix up Christians, Jews, Muslims and so on.

It seems that most of the voting cardinals in the papal conclave heartily agreed with him – almost certainly they would elect him thanks to the essence of his speech.

Now let us consider his SR, cast for Rome on the 16th April 2005. We can see there is a conjunction of the Sun with Venus, in the 3rd House. This shows his main asset for that year, namely – according to the experts of Vatican – his speech (the 3rd House). Now let us consider his LR covering the same period of the events we are describing: we can see that the LR also 'speaks' the same way. There we have the Moon and Jupiter in strict conjunction in the 3rd House, and the conjunction of Sun, Venus, and Mercury in the 9th House. So you see both Houses connected with communication are strongly occupied by magnificent celestials.

Unluckily I don't know the birth data of his family members, so I cannot use another software called *AstralDetector* to produce a graph on the most important events of his family – but in any case this graph would have simply confirmed what we have already described.

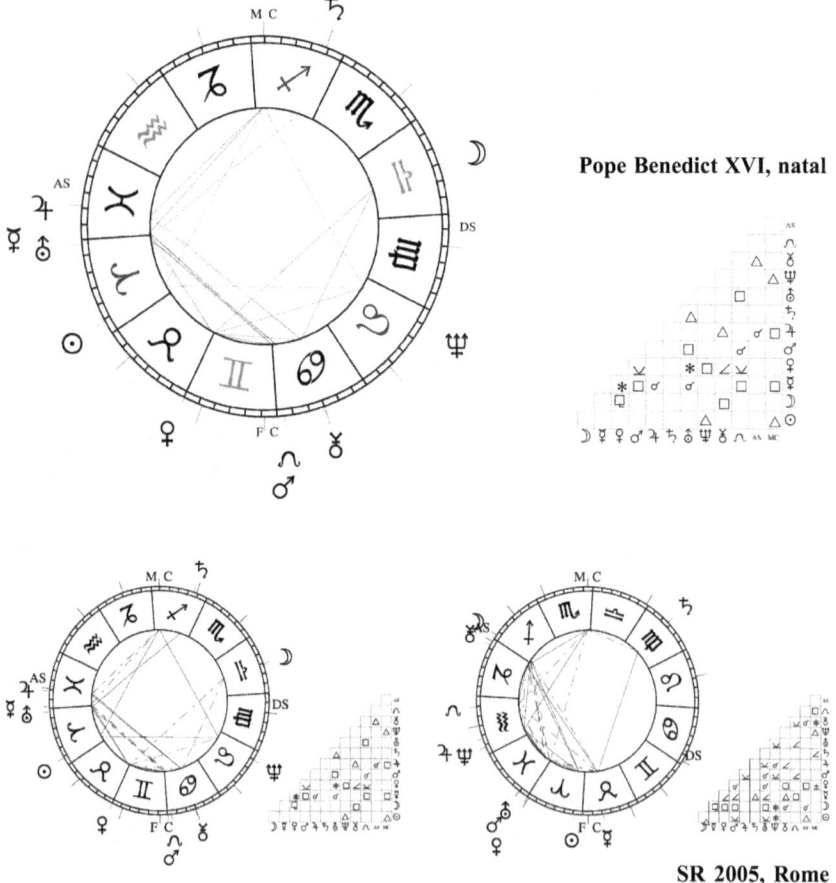

Pope Benedict XVI, natal

SR 2005, Rome

A FEW PRACTICAL EXERCISES ON THE DATING OF EVENTS

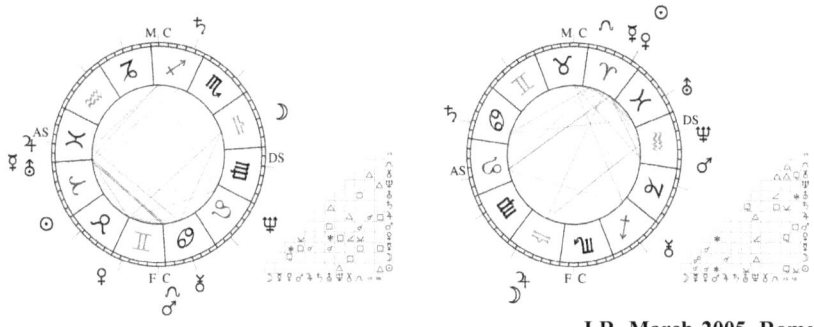

LR, March 2005, Rome

Silvio Berlusconi announces the birth of a new political party

On the 18th of November 2007, without giving any prior notice Silvio Berlusconi announced the birth of a new political party: the People of Freedom. This took by surprise even his most intimate collaborators.

I am not certain about his SR – I know for sure that even his closest collaborators asked him where he had spent his birthday, but he replied with a laugh.

Nonetheless, you can cast his SR for Milan or Rome and there wouldn't be any significant difference. This SR seems to be the most representative of the events: Saturn is on the Medium Coeli is typical of a 'dismissal', the end of an activity, a 'discharge', as the one described in *The Missing Star*, an Italian film directed by Gianni Amelio in 2006. Nonetheless Jupiter in the 1st House and the Sun in the 10th House make you think that – from Berlusconi's point of view – it was a winning move.

His LR of October is clearly significant of the described event – without distinction if you cast it for Rome or Milan. In fact we see indication of a very strong radicalism (Uranus at the Medium Coeli and Mars close to the Ascendant), which induced a huge change of profession for him (Uranus at the Medium Coeli). While Jupiter and Pluto in the 6th House confirm what the SR says: a winning move at a professional level.

Last, let us consider the graph produced by *AstralDetector* based on a group of four birth dates: Silvio Berlusconi, Gianfranco Fini, Pierferdinando Casini, and Umberto Bossi – the leaders of the three allies of Berlusconi by that time. As you can see, the wonderful instrument of analysis of the dating of events called *AstralDetector* misses the real date by only two days: it draws a net negative peak in the graph on the 20th of November 2007. Keep in mind that the 'negative' or the 'positive' peaks cast by this software indicate important events for the subject – they can be favourable or unfavourable for the subject in both cases.

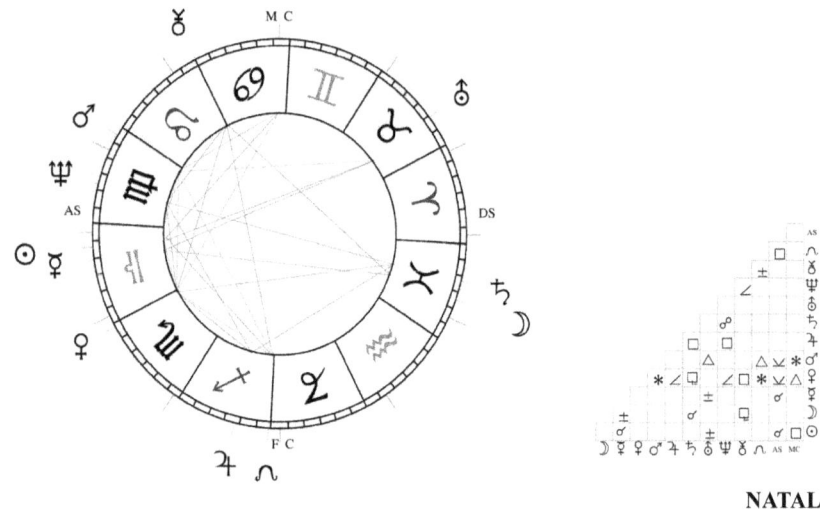

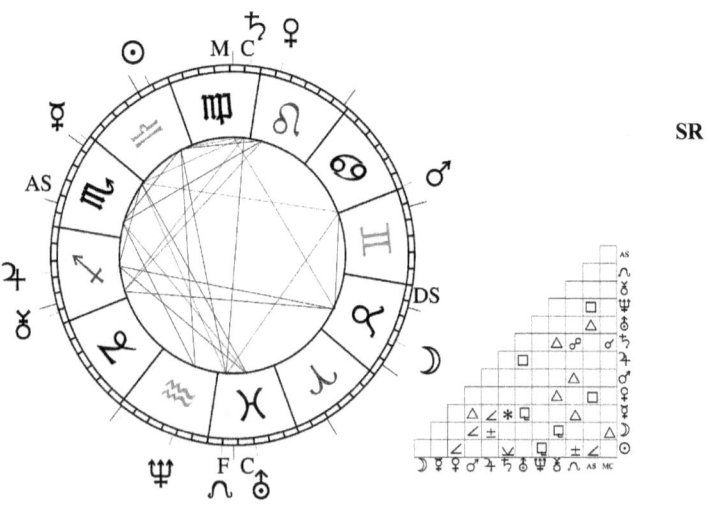

A FEW PRACTICAL EXERCISES ON THE DATING OF EVENTS 111

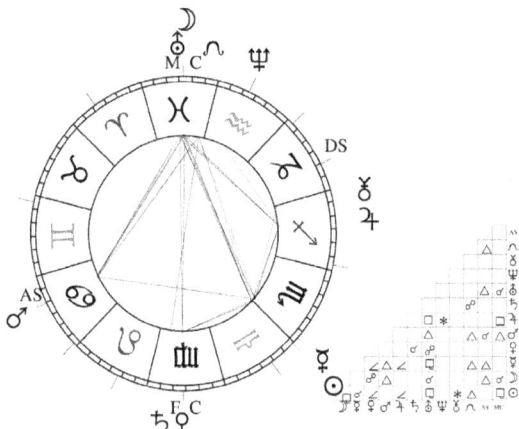

LR, October 2007

The graph elaborated by the software programme AstralDetector

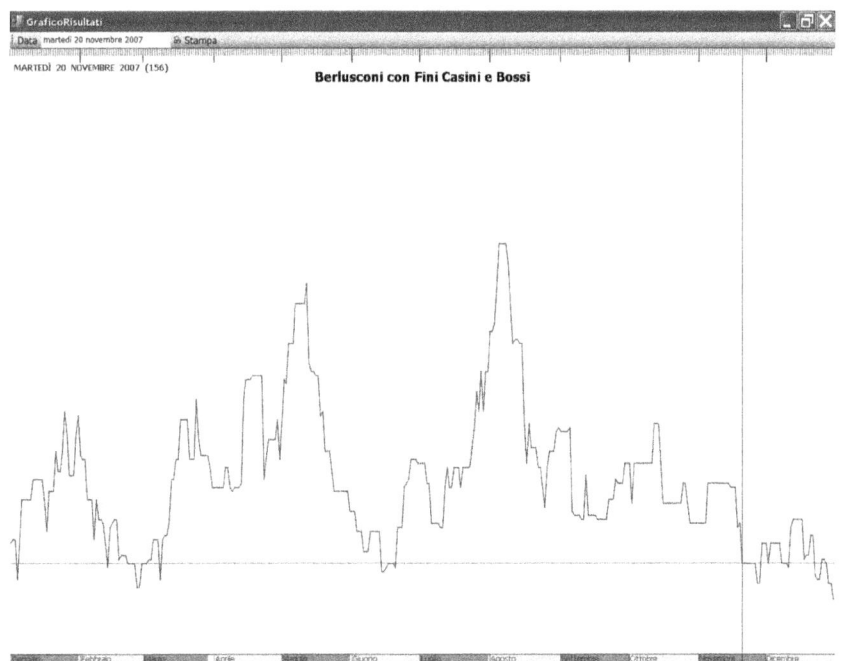

The arrest of Stefano Ricucci

On the 18th of April 2006 all the Italian media reported in their first pages the arrest of entrepreneur Stefano Ricucci, accused of rigging the market and revealing classified information. He was involved in a process but this is not very interesting from the astrological point of view. What is really interesting in this case is the astral positions underlining his arrest in a very striking way.

Stefano Ricucci's SR of 2005 in Rome – where we suppose he spent his birthday – shows the Sun in the 1st House and the Ascendant of SR in the 6th Natal House. These are positions that, according to certain fellow astrologers, correspond to the growth of the chest in male subjects and of the breast in female subject. The followers of *Active Astrology*, on the contrary, believe that before certain positions of the SR it is better not to grow too much but avoid jail as well as other possible unpleasant situations instead – and they act in order to avoid such positions in the Return chart. Let us consider his LR of April 2006 – a few days before his arrest – and we realize that it is really striking in its precision. In fact the Ascendant of LR lies in his 6th Natal House, while Saturn is placed exactly on the Medium Coeli (announcing a very bad social fall) and the Sun is in the 7th House (possible troubles with law).

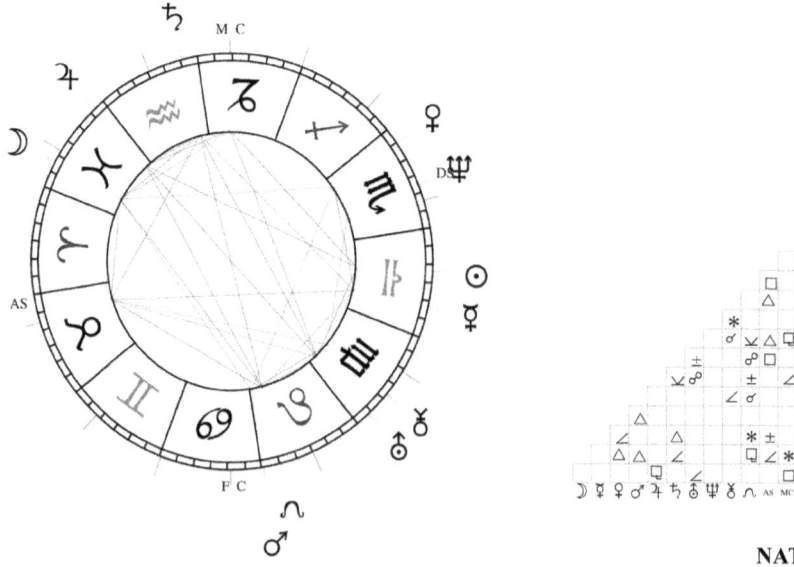

NATAL

A FEW PRACTICAL EXERCISES ON THE DATING OF EVENTS   113

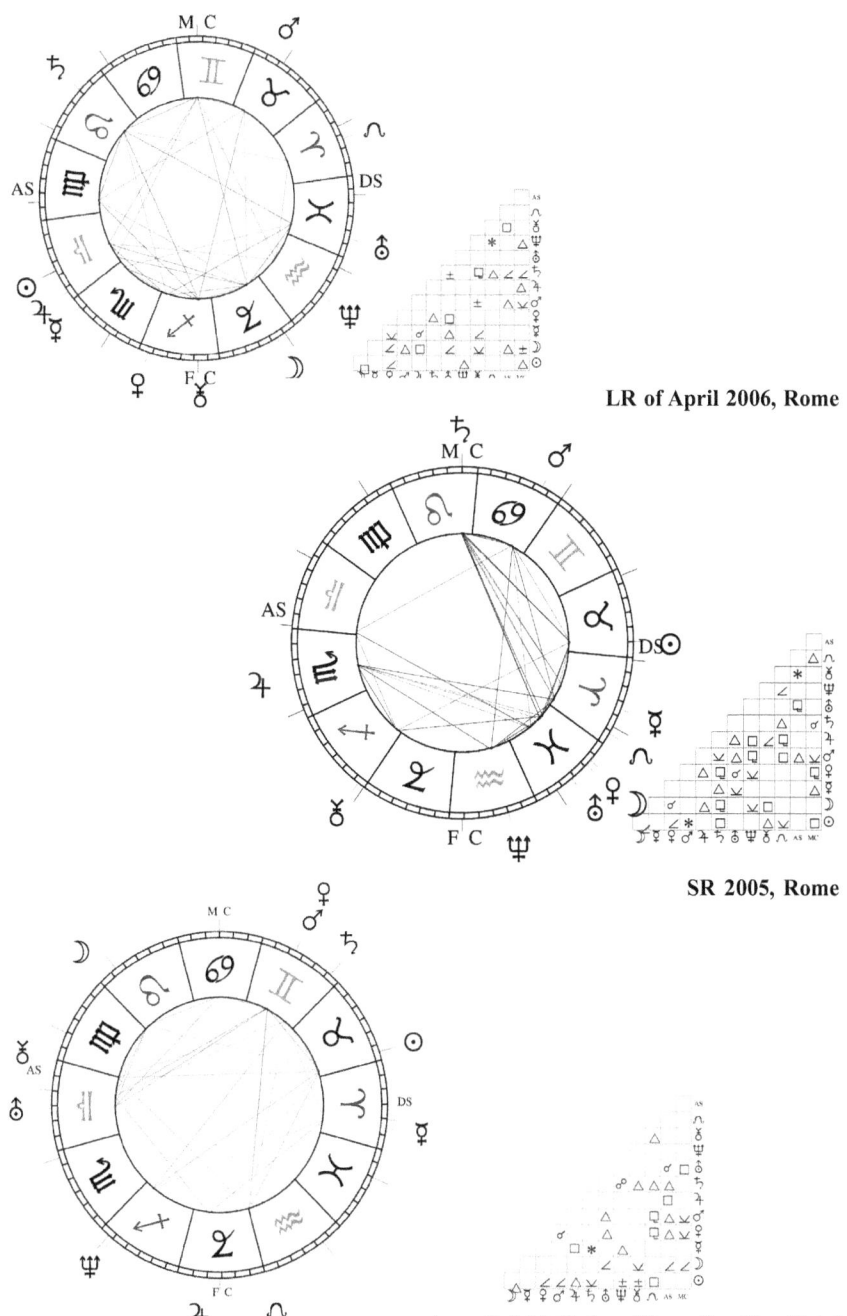

LR of April 2006, Rome

SR 2005, Rome

Anna Falchi, Stefano Ricucci's wife – Natal

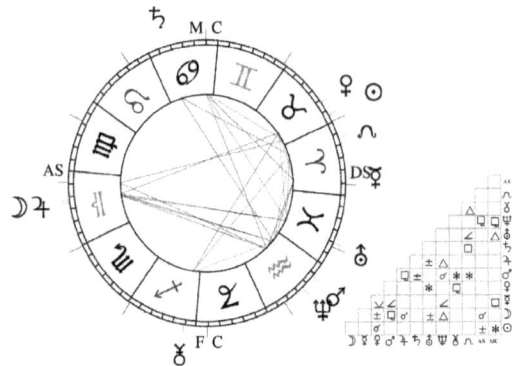

Anna Falchi's SR of 2005, Rome

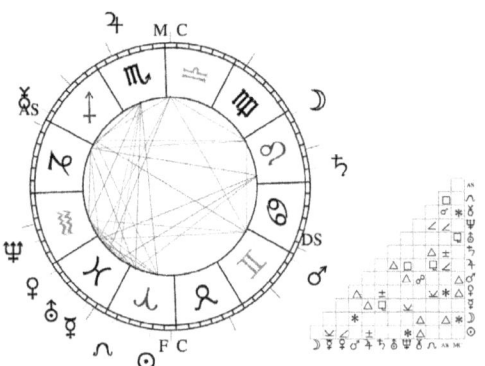

Anna Falchi's LR of April 2006

If we consider his wife's celestials, the event becomes even clearer. First of all, his husband is arrested four days before her birthday – see the rule #1 of the thirty rules listed in my volume *Transits and Solar Returns*.

Her Solar Return of 2005 has the Ascendant falling in her 12th Natal House; the conjunction Sun-Venus in the 8th House (rule #26 warns that similar positions have something to do with jail, especially if there are other 'dissonant' elements); and eventually the cherry on the cake: Saturn in the 10th House heralding a very bad, brutal fall in society.

Her Lunar Return of April 2005 is considerable as well, with its Mars in the 6th House and Saturn in the 7th House: a copybook LR, announcing legal troubles for her husband. In this case Jupiter in the 10th House and the Sun in the 3rd House acted as a megaphone – the media covering the event.

In the following lines you'll find four of the thirty rules published in my volume *Transits and Solar Returns*: they can explain in full what happened to the pair Ricucci-Falchi in April 2006. Needless to say that I wrote those thirty rules several years before the arrest of Stefano Ricucci, and that you'll be able to use them to explain any future event without any need for fixed stars, Chiron, Arabian Parts, secondary or tertiary progressions, lunar nodes, and other rules invented on the spot.

1) The twenty days before one's birthday and the twenty days after one's birthday are extremely important days, both positively and negatively. Often the most important events of one's year take place exactly on those days.

4) Remember that if the Ascendant, a stellium, or the Sun of the Solar Return lies in the 1st, the 6th, or the 12th House, with almost no difference of strength between them, you should expect to have a very burdensome, dangerous, critical and gloomy year in one or more aspects of your life – not just specifically concerning your health, work or love alone. Almost in 100% of the cases, it would be a bad year, a detrimental one – a year that you'll never forget even though you would want to. I realize that this way I underline, I stress, I emphasize it – but it's exactly what I want to do. It is my opinion that no author has ever declared this fact with such a stress, but I find it correct to write down certain rules with exclamation marks – and this is one rule that needs to be written down so, more than all the others. Some author expressed himself in a fairly negative way in connection with the 12th House, but no one before me has ever demonized this House as much as I do. And nobody else has also treated as a criminal the 6th and the 1st House as well. Simply try and follow this rule, and then let me know. When these three Houses play a role in the Solar Return, you can face trouble and unpleasant situations of any kind: in your affections, your health, with justice, money, possible mourning, and so on.

5) The very same rule applies to Mars in the 12th, 6th, or 1st House of the Solar Return. This position alone can spoil a year even if other elements of the Solar Return may be positive, and even if during the year there are other gorgeous transits.

26) Remember: often the 8th House refers to jail.

At the end of this chapter let me repeat something important for me.

As I have written several times, in other books and articles of mine, it is my opinion that all the branches of Astrology deserve respect and closer examination from any student of this discipline.

But if we talk about Predictive Astrology I believe that my colleagues making forecasts on the basis of different schools of thought other than mine, they should show their loyalty and transparency towards readers by stating, at the very beginning of their works, what are the rules to be followed in order to be able to follow them in their heuristic path. Otherwise, if there aren't starting rules, everybody can claim anything and its opposite at the same time, whatever private or public event they analyze under that method.

Galileo Galilei watching the celestials through his telescope did so not only to study their shape and motions, but also to elaborate his astrological forecasts.

13.
SRs and LRs in the attack on Pearl Harbor

This exercise allows throwing further light on certain details of the reading of SRs and LRs.

Let us consider the attack on Pearl Harbor, where the Japanese navy and air force conducted a surprise military strike against the United States' naval base in Hawaii on the morning of the 7th of December 1941, destroying several ships and causing personnel losses in thousands. Thanks to those manoeuvres, the Japanese won supremacy over the entire Pacific Ocean during the World War II – at least, for a short period.

Let us watch that event in the eyes of the four main leading actors of the time: namely the President of the United States of America; Winston Churchill; Benito Mussolini, and Adolf Hitler.

Let us begin with the President of the USA.

Franklin Delano Roosevelt was born in Hyde Park, New York, on the 30th of January 1882 at 8:45 pm. Nowadays the President of the United States spends a large amount of time flying on board the presidential airplane, mainly for security reasons. There he holds crucial meetings all the time, always connected with the most strategic locations of the world. But you can be reasonably confident that Roosevelt used to spend almost all his time in the White House or not far from there. We can presume that he spent his birthday previous to the 7th of December 1941, there.

His SR is quite clear. Mars in the 12th House conjunct with the Ascendant clearly announces a year of war and heavy concerns in relationship with foreign people and foreign countries (Neptune in the 9th House).

There had been rumours in the States of a possible future Japanese attack, and if anybody had studied Roosevelt's LRs it would have been possible to forecast the time of the attack with good accuracy. The most important element

118 LUNAR RETURNS AND EARTH RETURNS

of the LR cast for the 5th of December (two days before the attack) is the Ascendant falling in the 9th House radix (foreign people). There is also a very detrimental stellium spanning the 12th and the 1st Houses as well as the Sun in the 6th House. That's really too much! Also consider that Mars is in the 11th House of the LR. Its meaning is similar to that of Mars in the 7th House, only a little bit less detrimental: war, attacks, marked tensions.

The only favourable point of this LR is Jupiter close to the Ascendant from the stronger side, i.e. in the 12th House. We all know that the consequences of that attack were very serious. On the other hand, we may say that the United States was quite lucky because there was no American aircraft carrier in the harbour that day. Was it by chance – many historians suggest so – or is it the evidence that the USA let Japan attack them in order to push U.S. public opinion from isolationism to the acceptance of participation in the war being unavoidable. We'll probably never know. Anyway, President Roosevelt's LR announces a little moment of good luck within a period marked by a very potent celestial situation.

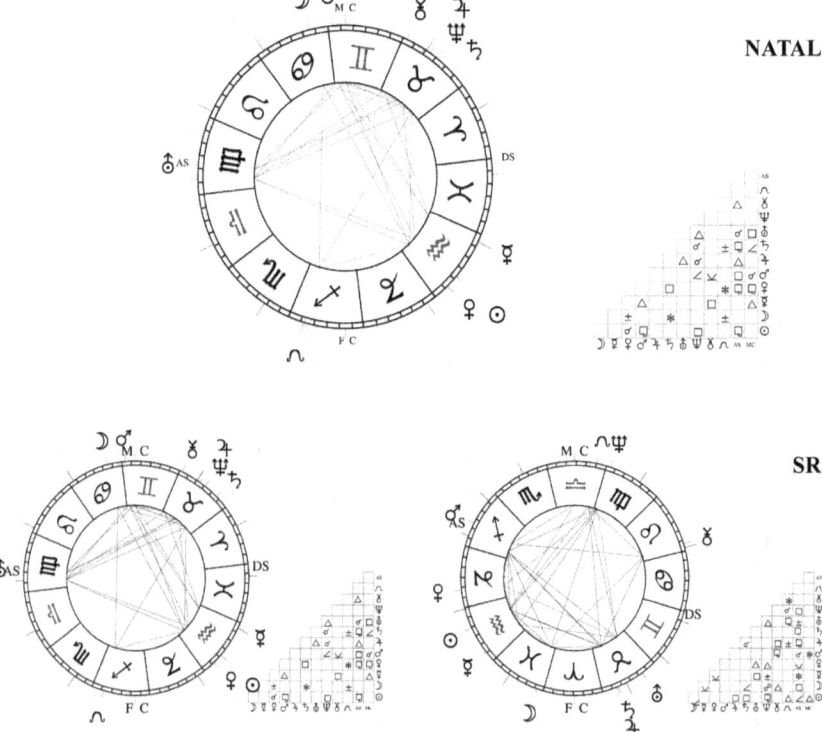

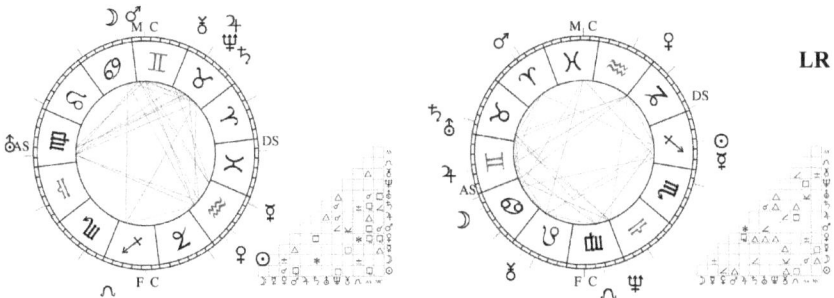

Let us consider now the same event through the celestials of the English Prime Minister. **Winston Churchill**'s SR took place a few days before the attack on Pearl Harbor: he was surely in London that day. In fact he was born in Woodstock on the 30th of November 1874 at 1:30 am. It is a matter of fact that things of an extraordinary importance take place during the days close to one's birthday. For example, Adolf Hitler died 10 days after his own birthday and got married somewhen between his birthday and his suicide. This fact is now accepted and reported by all my fellow astrologers. Unluckily they forget to mention who actually found out this fact – but luckily my books are preserved in the public libraries, and there is a date in each of them.

Now back to Sir Churchill's terrible SR. The Sun was in conjunction with the Ascendant of the SR, and it's not so important whether it lies in the 12th House or in the 1st House. There's also a stellium spanned over the 12th and the 1st House. Mars is in the 7th House and Saturn is in the 9th House, and they speak for themselves. Nevertheless there's something strange in it. Churchill knew that after such an attack, America's huge war machine would finally intervene giving an essential hand to the English, who had so far been the only nation struggling for the defence of Western civilization. So why was Churchill's SR so detrimental? The news arrived in London via radio, and probably made superoptimist Winston Churchill's blood run cold, because he probably feared that the USA had suffered such a terrible damage that had left Japan virtually unbeatable.

On the other hand, celestials are impartial: the presence of Venus in the 10th House of his SR announced a sort of emancipation for him and for the United Kingdom.

His LR of the 12th November 1941 is also significant: a strict conjunction of Saturn and Uranus in the 10th House of LR is very detrimental for the Prime Minister's position before the entire world, but on the other had Jupiter in the 10th House recalls the same reading of that Venus in the 10th House of SR.

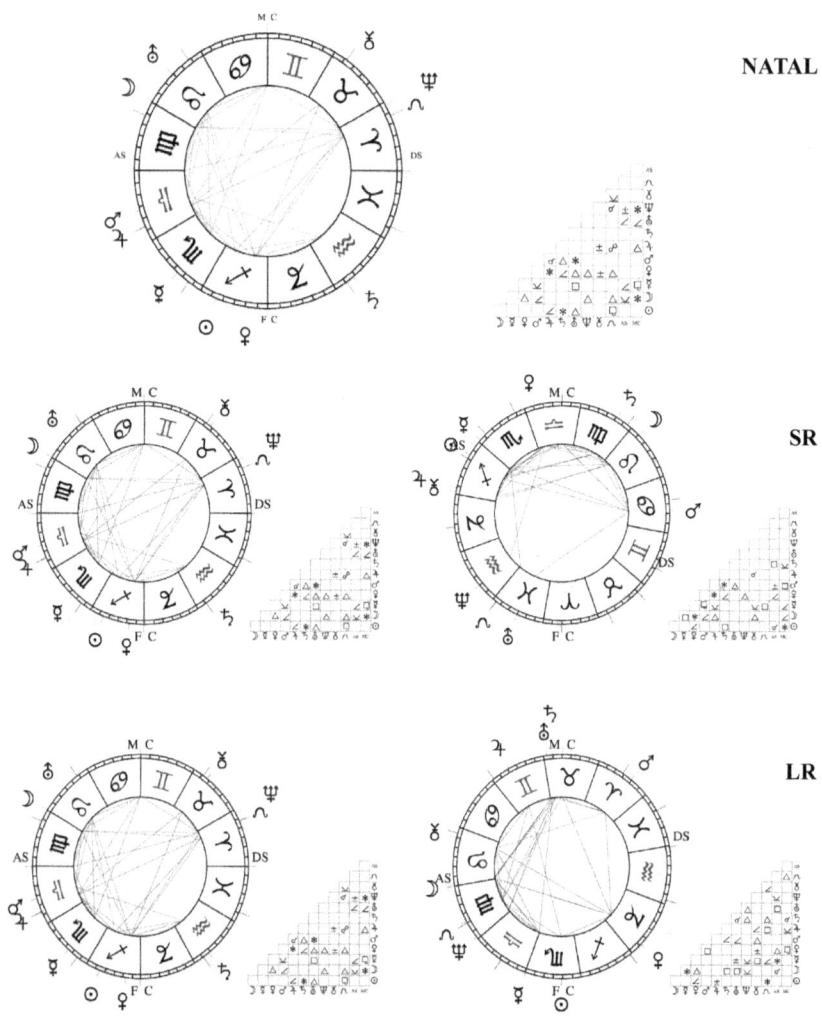

Let us study now **Adolf Hitler**'s stars. He was born in Braunau on the 20th April 1889 at 6:30 pm. Even in this case, there is almost no doubt on where he spent his birthday. We know that he had had his headquarters built on the Eagles' Nest, on a mountain peak from where he could see his birth village, Braunau. In astrological terms, there is a minimal difference between his spending his SR there or in Berlin.

Now Hitler's SR is remarkable. The Ascendant and Mars in the 9th House, but above all: a striking and quite positive stellium in the 11th House! It is evident for an astrologer that the *Fürher* – who in his madness believed that there were non-existing army corps ready to save him a few days before his final defeat – greeted the attack on Pearl Harbor as the sign of destiny of a very certain victory of the Triple, diabolic Alliance. The presence of Jupiter in the 1st House conjunct with the Ascendant in his LR shows the same kind of optimism. Venus might have been over the cusp of the 9th House.

Please note that other elements of this LR are really detrimental, but do not forget the rules already given in this volume for a correct reading of a Lunar Return: very dangerous positions of LR falling within the frame of a good SR – and Hitler had had a good SR fore sure – which can not and must not worry anybody.

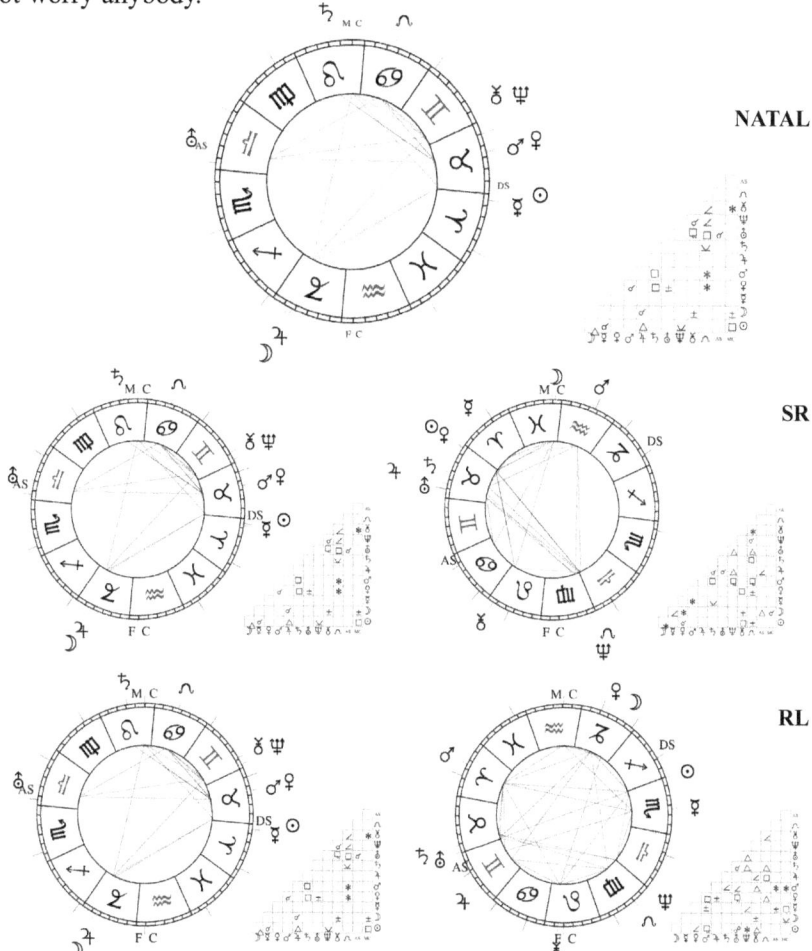

Now it's **Benito Mussolini**'s turn. Here we find ambivalence due to the fact that from certain points of view the Italian *Duce* was less mad than Hitler; in fact the former used to reason with more clarity of mind, compared with the latter. Also in Mussolini's SR we can find elements of joy for alleged victories abroad: the Sun, Pluto, and Venus are in the 9th House, and Venus is conjunct with the Medium Coeli. Yet the SR itself is still detrimental, due to its Ascendant falling in Mussolini's natal 1st House and because of a stellium in the 7th House of SR (announcing that a new, powerful enemy would soon arrive to fight).

We can cast similar considerations from his LR too.

And to conclude, consider the graph produced by *AstralDetector* for the year 1941 based on the birth data of the aforementioned subjects. It clearly shows a serious crisis on the 7th December, the day of the attack on Pearl Harbor; it is a net, negative peak. I mention it to arouse your curiosity, because the dating of the events through the graphs of *AstralDetector* is not within the scopes of this volume. To get to know more on this subject visit this webpage (in Italian): http://www.cirodiscepolo.it/AstralDetector.htm

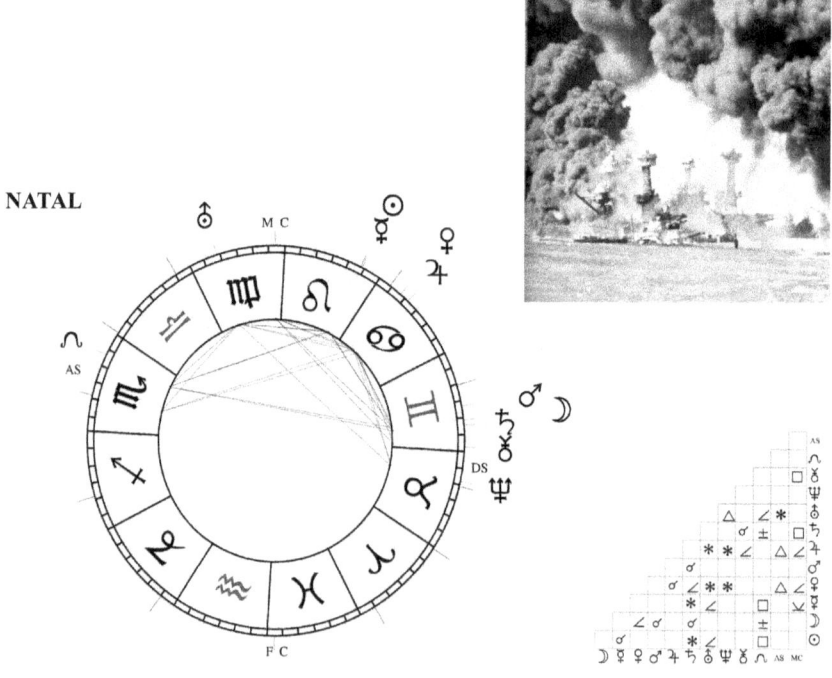

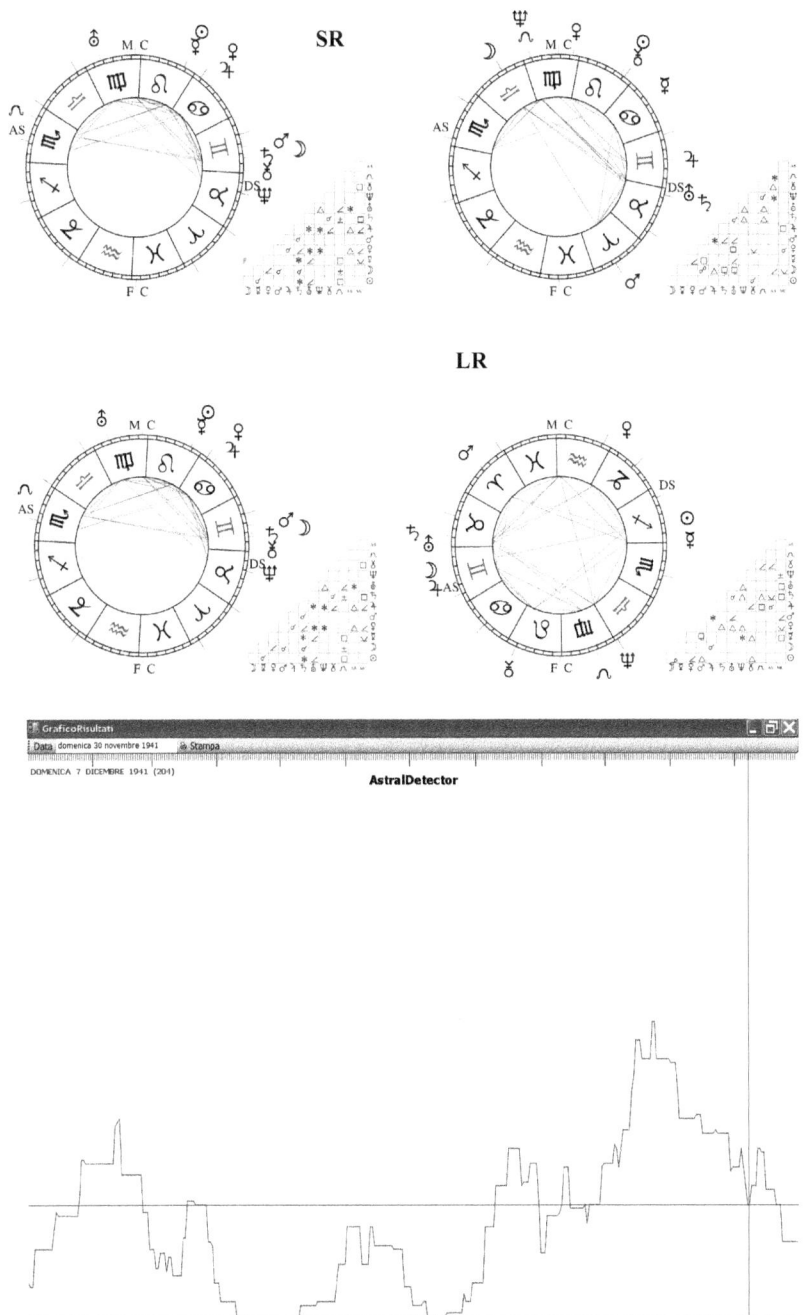

14.
Lunar Return on airliners

Several times, with practical examples both in my books and in my magazine *Ricerca '90*, I have shown how to aim a Solar Return and/or a Lunar Return 'on the fly' – or better said: 'on the flight' – in order to reach places that one could not reach on the dry land.

Remember that in such events (which are the subject of one whole chapter of my book *I fondamenti dell'astrologia medica*, Armenia editore) you usually have two options: taking a taxi plane or hiring a private aircraft with a pilot from a flying club.

I would avoid the first because it would be quite expensive – although of course the notion of 'expensive' is a relative one, depending also from the subject's needs and financial situations. In fact, a rich man seeking desperately to save his own life would certainly choose this solution instead of the other, perhaps less expensive but unsure ways.

Usually it's easier to contact a flying club, where you'd certainly meet a keen flyer whose main dream is to be allowed to fly for free for hours: he'd be only glad if you refund the cost of fuel and give him an extra income of some Euros.

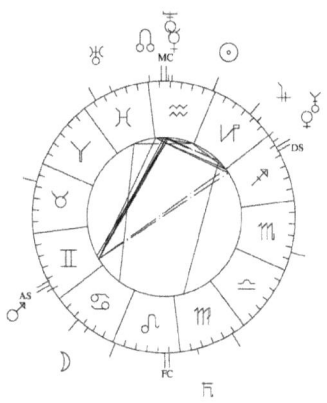

Now let me introduce a brand new method; something that – to my knowledge – nobody has ever tried before. Nonetheless it is something that, being pure mathematics, can be said to be self-proven.

Say that a David Smith wants to spend his Lunar Return in Milan, Italy, on the 21st of January 2008 at 1:02 pm GMT. As you can see from the relevant chart, it is a very bad Return. Say that David's current SR is detrimental too, so that he wants to aim (i.e. relocate according to the rules given in my books) this bad LR in order to avoid further risks for himself. The ideal place for such relocation would be an isle in the very middle of the Ocean between Senegal (on the West coast of Central Africa) and Brazil (to be more precise, the North-East point of Brazil). This is one of the emptiest portions of this planet. If Our Lord had been passionately fond of Aimed Solar Returns, he would have certainly filled up this void with at least one island in the middle.

Alas, there's no island in there. Yet, our brain often can be better than an island – so I made up my mind and invented the method that I'm going to expose. In my opinion, it's something that has very solid theoretical basis and can be applied without spending 50,000 Euros for a taxi plane, but only 1,000 Euros on an airliner.

It consists of tracing the route of an airliner, say flying Lisbon to Recife, provided that you know ALL the points touched by the route during the flight, and at what time you'll be flying over any of them.

It is not a 'mission impossible'! I'm going to show you how, and after the following single example, you'll be able to do the same for any area of the world and apply it to any Aimed SR and/or Aimed LR.

The most difficult point is getting the precise route of the flight. Forget about asking the airlines: they aren't going to tell you anything for security reasons because of the hazard posed by terrorism.

My friend Pino Valente was smart enough to find out, on the Internet, the webpage of the fans of flight simulation. As everybody knows, people like these can become really manic in their wish to create a perfect simulation of flights; therefore they get to know whatever may be needed to be known as far as routes are concerned. Also on 'normal' webpages devoted to travels, like for example www.opodo.it, you can get to know the kind of aircraft, the departure & arrival time, the time needed to reach there, and everything else that you need for the purposes that I'm explaining to you.

Now this is the URL of the webpage for flight simulators:

http://rfinder.asalink.net/

It is necessary to subscribe and login; you'll have access to this area:

http://rfinder.asalink.net/free/autoroute_rt.php

From www.opodo.it I got to know that there's a flight TAP TP151 Lisbon to Recife leaving Lisbon on the 21st January 2008 at 10:50; the flight takes 7 hours and 45 minutes. Hence you can get, from the Route Finder webpage, the following table containing really *all* the information that you need. We'll consider only the second part of the table, listing all the virtual points of the sky that are used by air traffic controllers to guide the aircrafts along very narrow skyways: Nakos, Barok, Bentu, Nevel, Mitla...

In the following map we have traced all these virtual nodes of the sky and we have connected them to form a line.

RouteFinder

*Route generator for PC flight simulation use - **NOT FOR REAL WORLD NAVIGATION***
(C)2005-2007 ASA srl - Italy

Computed route from **LISBOA** (LPPT, LP) to **GUARARAPES GILBERTO FREYRE INTSB** (

```
Cruise altitude between FL330 and FL330
LPPT  (0.0nm)    -SID->   NAKOS  (47.8nm)   -UZ4->   BAROK  (174.3nm)  -UN873->
BENTU (274.5nm)  -UN873-> NEVEL  (395.5nm)  -UN873-> MITLA  (519.8nm)  -UN873->
SAMAR (549.7nm)  -UN873-> GDV    (727.2nm)  -UN729-> REMGI  (787.1nm)  -UN729->
DEREV (809.3nm)  -UN857-> BIPET  (930.0nm)  -UN857-> ETIBA  (1184.4nm) -UN857->
GUNET (1304.7nm) -UN857-> ORABI  (1555.9nm) -UN857-> BOTNO  (1722.6nm) -UN857->
DELAX (2074.0nm) -UN857-> MAROA  (2203.1nm) -UN857-> ERETU  (2427.2nm) -UN857->
NOISE (2544.7nm) -UN857-> CLOVE  (2564.9nm) -UN857-> NEURA  (2702.3nm) -UN857->
FNO   (2900.5nm) -UB623-> ESGUM  (3091.8nm) -B623->  ISADO  (3148.0nm) -DCT->
SBRF  (3196.2nm)
```

Details:

```
ID      FREQ    TRK   DIST   Coords                              Name/Remarks
LPPT             0      0    N38°46'52.72"  W009°08'09.31"  LISBOA
NAKOS          198     48    N38°00'00.00"  W009°20'04.18"  NAKOS
BAROK          202    126    N35°58'00.00"  W010°01'24.00"  BAROK
BENTU          224    100    N34°37'42.00"  W011°14'37.00"  BENTU
NEVEL          223    121    N32°59'51.00"  W012°40'18.00"  NEVEL
MITLA          223    124    N31°18'30.00"  W014°04'56.00"  MITLA
SAMAR          223     30    N30°53'59.00"  W014°24'56.00"  SAMAR
GDV     112.9  206    178    N28°04'37.49"  W015°25'44.35"  GRAN CANARIA
REMGI          180     60    N27°05'24.72"  W015°16'10.57"
DEREV          180     22    N26°43'23.42"  W015°12'39.79"
BIPET          220    121    N25°00'00.00"  W016°21'31.67"  BIPET
ETIBA          220    254    N21°20'17.75"  W018°40'43.63"  ETIBA
GUNET          220    120    N19°35'42.00"  W019°44'06.00"  GUNET
ORABI          221    251    N15°56'18.00"  W021°52'12.00"  ORABI
BOTNO          222    167    N13°30'00.00"  W023°14'30.00"  BOTNO
DELAX          223    351    N08°20'12.00"  W026°03'06.00"  DELAX
MAROA          225    129    N06°26'08.00"  W027°03'44.00"  MAROA
ERETU          225    224    N03°07'42.00"  W028°48'00.00"  ERETU
NOISE          227    118    N01°23'40.20"  W029°42'33.00"  NOISE
CLOVE          227     20    N01°05'42.60"  W029°51'39.00"  CLOVE
NEURA          227    137    S00°56'10.80"  W030°54'51.00"  NEURA
FNO     113.7  228    198    S03°52'12.72"  W032°25'45.55"  FERNANDO
ESGUM          231    191    S06°37'33.00"  W034°02'14.40"  ESGUM
ISADO          232     56    S07°26'03.60"  W034°30'45.60"  ISADO
SBRF           233     48    S08°07'36.46"  W034°55'22.94"  GUARARAPES GILBERTO
```

On Giovanna Bianco & Pino Valente's website www.bianco-valente.com you can see their work of 2005 titled *Relational Domain* – it's a beautiful work of art resembling the world of synapses, the connections between the sky and human mind, the air traffic controllers' celestial nodes, the communication between our brain and the reality of universe...

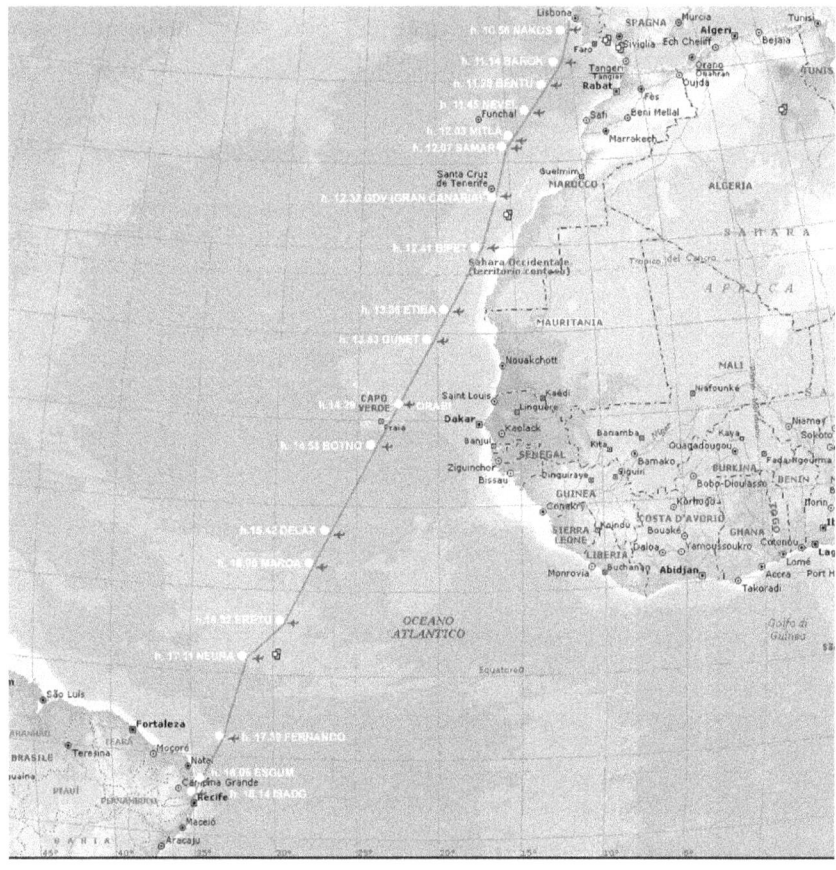

Back to our scope. After drawing this line on the map you proceed as follows. You open the astrological software that you use to calculate Solar returns and/or Lunar Returns. There you add new 'locations' in its database, say: Nakos Radar, longitude 9°20'W and latitude 38°00'N, Barok Radar longitude 10°01'W and latitude 35°58'N and so on.

As you already know, the time zone is not required while casting SRs and LRs, so when you're asked to input the Time Zone, you can simply digit '1'.

Now consider the following four maps of ALR that I have cast to explain this method.

Compare them with the already given map of BLR of Milan, Italy – a very bad one. Having added the additional locations to our software program, it is now able to cast a LR for Maroa. Taken for granted that the map of SR and the map of LR must have the domification of the place where the subject is there in that moment – neither the place of his birth nor the place of his usual residence – nobody can deny that the result is striking. It isn't important to know what time will it be there in their local time, because our software calculates the GMT of the LR and relocates the map of that moment on to Maroa. Those who still doubt about this method, may cast the Aimed LR for Cape Verde (for example, Sale) and they can see that the resulting map is almost identical to the map cast for Orabi Radar (in fact, the geographic coordinates of the two locations are very close).

With the tables given here you can calculate anything. We know that the aircraft, an Airbus A330-220, flying at an average cruise speed of 412 Mph (nautical miles per hour) takes 7 hours and 45 minutes to fly the whole route Lisbon to Recife, corresponding to 3,196 nautical miles. Knowing the distance between the single points of the line that we have traced on our map, we can also know at what time we'll be flying over each of those points.

The method's only drawback is that the aircraft may take off later than the scheduled time, but you can always recalculate the route by heart. In fact, consider our map with the dotted line. Say that you had reckoned to be over Maroa for your Aimed LR. Now being late, instead of flying over Maroa, you'll be flying over Delax in the very moment in which the LR takes place. An as you can see from the chart cast for Delax, it's good anyway.

If you wish to get a safe calculation, you can apply larger margins of tolerance and reckon that if the aircraft takes off with a delay of, say, less than 30 minutes, the pilots are able to make up time by flying a little more than the usual cruise speed.

I believe that you have now a new tool, and a very feasible one, to achieve the goals that you wish: moreover, spending no more than one hundred Euros instead of, say, fifty thousand Euros.

130 LUNAR RETURNS AND EARTH RETURNS

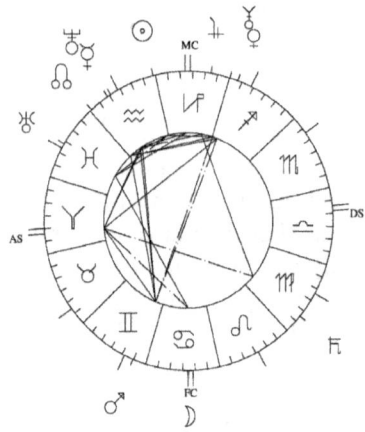

ALR, Maroa

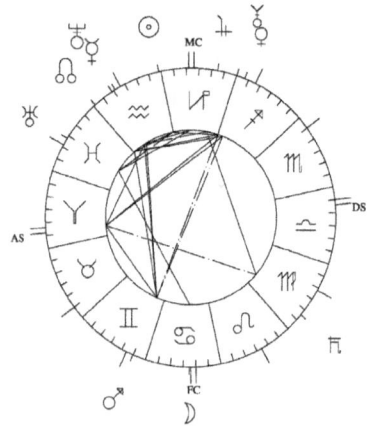

ALR, Delax

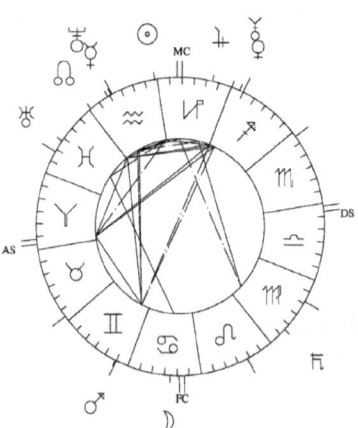

ALR, Cape Verde

ALR, Orabi

15.
Lunar Return in Flores

My LR of the 1st of February was quite difficult to aim. Or better said: while at a first sight its relocation appeared extremely simple to be planned and calculated, when I proceeded with the exercise I realized that it would be a kind of benchmark, or a sort of *summa*, of all my studies in astrology so far.

First of all, I'd like to make some preliminary remarks of personal character.

Some of you may perhaps be aware that I separated from my wife in spring 2006. We went on living together in separate rooms for a couple of years, deferring judicial separation because our daughter Luna, despite having already grown up to be a little woman (at the end of august 1984) strongly opposed our decision by means of a series of self-injuring actions that prevented me from proceeding effectively.

It is my opinion that a parting is never a positive event, but in certain cases it is the lesser of two evils when two partners become convinced that the daily micro conflicts overpass the positivity of living as a couple.

Considering that I got engaged at the age of twenty and I separated judicially with official signatures at the age of sixty, at the end of my marital path I can say that very few subjects born – like me – with the conjunction of Venus and Uranus in their 12th Natal House would have been able to carry on one relationship for more than forty years.

Most of my male and female friends offered me their condolences on this event, but my answer to them was that I have considered this situation not as a mourning but as an opportunity that life has offered to me.

I don't know to whom I should be more grateful for the life that I've received as a present and that I have lived in a winning way in almost all its fields. I have no regrets; I believe that I've been lucky beyond reason.

Yet one cannot forget that separation from a lawyer is not the same as separation from a steelworker – I know hundreds of people whom have been tortured and flayed alive in separation suits that have lasted up to six or seven years.

In my case, from the day in which I charged a lawyer to start this procedure for me, I have finished with it in about one month. Many people were surprised, saying that I hadn't even to go and sleep under a bridge!

Well, if I wasn't able to improve my own life and to achieve particularly positive results using my AA (Active Astrology), how could I pretend to try and improve the others' life with the same tools?

I am not claiming that I achieved my goal for free – I am saying that obviously I have paid a fee for it, especially as far as stress, time, money, and battles are concerned: but it has been a much lower toll than what life would have collected from me.

So back to my Aimed LR of the beginning of February 2006. By that time I had a couple of meetings with the lawyer, whom I hadn't charged yet to act for me. There were two LRs left to relocate and I felt that I must not make a mistake.

This is why I first considered the possibility of aiming my LR in Bordeaux, France. There I would have placed a marvellous, very strict conjunction of Venus and Jupiter on the cusp between the 5th and the 6th House of LR. One should not expect more from life… especially if in that moment what you care for most is your own health, your daughters' health, the chance of meeting the right partner, a little help in your activity and in your working relationships, and so on. Yet I had another completely different goal, namely: closing as soon as possible a situation that prevented me from putting all my energies into something more constructive.

Now, from this point of view the ALR of Bordeaux was the worst one could imagine, for how could I have reached separation by mutual consent with a stellium in the 7th House and Mars in the 11th House? Even considering that the Ascendant of the LR falling in my natal 1st House – for the reasons that I've explained in several points of this volume – didn't worry me at all, I couldn't have stood the least chance of achieving such goal.

So I started scanning the whole surface of the globe in search of a suitable location where I could have aimed my LR, but I wasn't able to find one. I felt that a radical change in my approach was required, in order to reach a brand new dimension even if, at a first sight, it might appear to be absurd. And in fact, in part, it was absurd: it was the island of Flores, in the Azores

(Portugal). I would have obtained the greatest celestial protection there concerning a possible legal agreement that nobody – lawyers included – believed possible.

On the other hand, the sky over Flores might have represented the sum of the worst meanings of the 6th House; and I also had the Ascendant falling in the 12th House, and Mars in the 12th House of LR. Perhaps Flores could have been the worst Aimed LR ever: I wouldn't have suggested it even to my worst enemy. Some of you would claim that, with the protection of a previous good SR, for the reasons explained in other sections of this volume I shouldn't have feared from anything terrible. Well, terrible perhaps not, mortal perhaps not – but something detrimental, perhaps a little bit less dangerous than mortal, yes! Do not forget the fact that in my SR, which I had aimed to Río Gallego, there was Uranus in the 9th House, and above all the Ascendant and Mars in the 12th House. This might have caused even a stroke to me, keeping in mind that I am sixty years old now and that I have always been very active all my life.

So I was uncertain about this decision. This is quite unusual of me, for I usually take even important decisions in less than a minute.

Eventually I resolved to leave and to reach there. I took five flights to reach there and five more on my way back (still spending a paltry amount: 700 Euros altogether). I remained there many days because it's necessary to be there several days in advance: in fact, due to strong winds, sometimes the flights are also suspended for two-three days. I stayed at a bed & breakfast hotel (I think it's the only one open on the island): it was so chilly that I had to sleep without taking my clothes off. Food – you had better forget about it: I ate only the bread and jam that they served for breakfast. I don't mean to offend the Portuguese, but that was the only edible thing in the middle of the Atlantic Ocean.

As soon as my LR took place, troubles arrived as forecast. I resolved to try and leave by an earlier flight than the one I had booked. Twice they registered me into a waiting list and only at the very last minute they would tell me whether I could fly or not. So I had to run for hundreds of metres in Flores and for kilometres in Lisbon in a sea of sweat with my only one, extremely heavy (due to my heavy clothes) hand luggage and I could not drink a drop of water for a long while. In Lisbon I literally got very close to having a heart attack. Once back home I started preparations for the legal 'battle' that perhaps would not be a real battle – for I virtually accepted all the conditions that the opposite lawyer imposed upon me – but when the time arrived to reach a written agreement, promises were broken and new claims arrived. To make a long story short, few days before my new Return, after a sequel of events in which I was forced to take part in actions of great tensions, I charged my lawyer to proceed and during my transit in Heathrow (London) I phoned him. He told me that my brother had intervened – and I wish to express here my gratefulness to him for his brotherly and affectionate mediation – and this would eventually lead to an agreement (Venus and Jupiter on the Descendant of the RL, i.e. within a distance of 2.5 degrees from the Descendant).

I am not certain about my willingness to repeat such an experience. I also had the flu, which I haven't had in the last twenty years, as well as strong pain in my arms all along during that lunar month. You can be sure that I would reflect very much before repeating such an experience. And if I met those who claim that an Ascendant of Return in the natal 12th House and Mars of Return in the 12th House of Return make you grow – well I think that I'd imitate Hannibal Lecter and eat them up, on the spot and without cooking them.

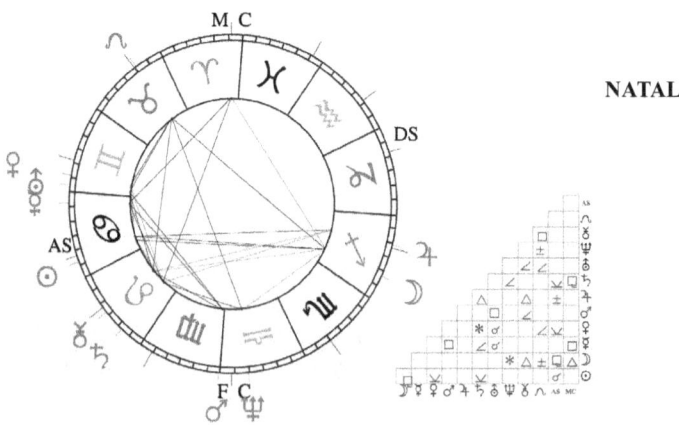

NATAL

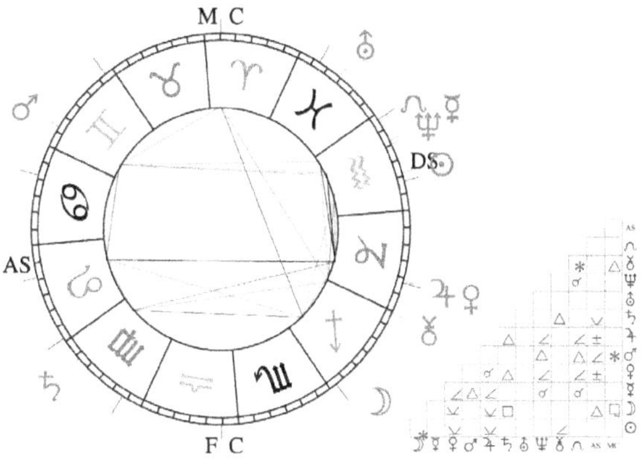

LUNAR RETURN IN FLORES

ALR, Bordeaux

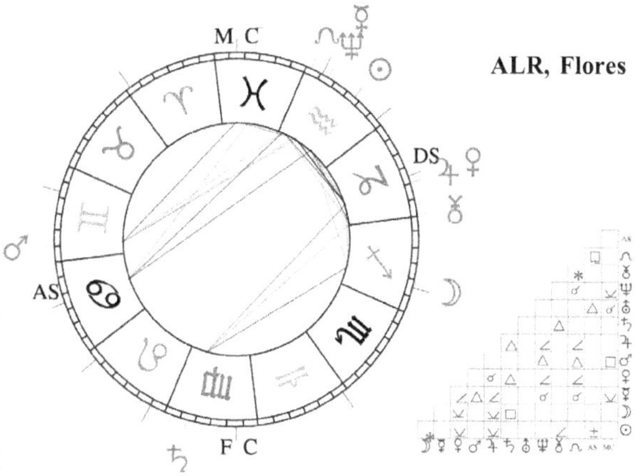

ALR, Flores

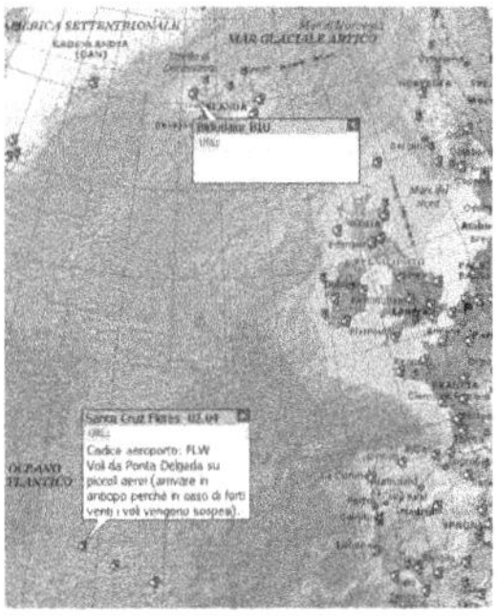

Icelanders claim to possess a small western portion of European land, somewhere close to Bildudalur. Portuguese claim the same in connection with the island of Flores, in the Azores. I've been personally to both places and if I say that the Portuguese are right, it's because the geographic map proves so, as you can see here.

16.
Lunar Return in Peterhead

This Aimed Lunar Return followed the one of Flores, and it was intended to seal up the result of the ALR of Flores. My friend Pino Valente was there as I thought about it – he actually knew and knows everything about me and my astrological plans: one day he could become my official biographer. So this is how I was reasoning: Placing several celestials in the 2nd and in the 8th House of LR, meant that there will be a significant flow of outgoing money. Considering that my financial possibilities are not really huge, a 'significant flow' can only mean that I'll reach an agreement for separation by mutual consent – what else if not that?

Once again it seemed to be a quite an easy thing to be put into practice, but in reality it turned out to be extremely difficult to find out the proper place I believe that I couldn't have succeeded without help from *Aladino*.

The place I chose for this ALR was Peterhead, Scotland. It's an approximately 45-minute drive from Dyce where Aberdeen airport is. Beside the already mentioned goal, in this ALR I would also have Venus on the cusp of the 2nd-3rd House, which would relieve me from certain expenses and would help me spread my books abroad, where in fact I am attaining very important results. On the other hand I would prevent Mars from even getting close (within the range of 2.5 degrees) from the cusp of the 7th-8th House of the LR – for I was aiming an agreement, not a battle.

Keep in mind that I can swear on the precision of my time of birth, as well as on a wonderful piece of software that is able to calculate the cusps of the Houses with a precision of ten thousandths of seconds, although I am satisfied to reach a precision to the minutes of degrees. Thus, assisted by that wonderful tool called *Google Earth*) I selected a specific road in Peterhead in which I could attain that astounding result, which also let me prove once again the correctness of my time of birth. While all the protagonists of this story forecast

6 or 7 years of harsh legal battles, on Wednesday the 17th of March at 12:57 I signed all the papers related with my legal separation.

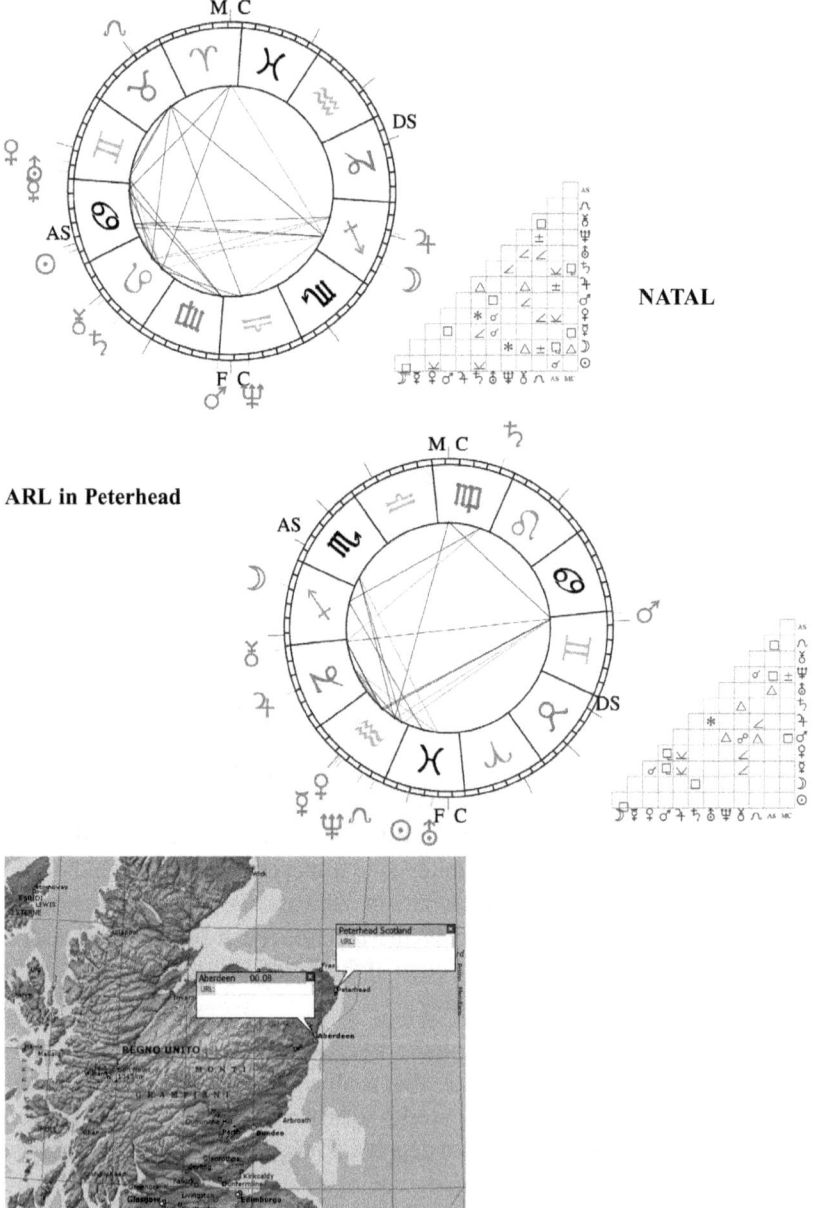

NATAL

ARL in Peterhead

LUNAR RETURN IN PETERHEAD

Tema natale per 2 29 Nato a Seaview Hotel Peterhead (00) (GB) il 29/02/02008 ore: 01.10

Sole :in Pesci 09°49'30,3722
Luna :in Sagittario 09°18'32,7389
Mercurio :in Aquario 12°57'28,1330
Venere :in Aquario 14°02'40,5650
Marte :in Gemelli 28°40'45,2434
Giove :in Capricorno 15°25'47,6642
Saturno :in Vergine 04°47'14,0445 Retrogrado
Urano :in Pesci 18°08'24,0756
Nettuno :in Aquario 22°23'28,5678
Plutone :in Capricorno 00°51'03,9673
Nodo Medio :in Aquario 27°12'57,6428 Retrogrado
Nodo Vero :in Aquario 27°38'20,6285
Lilith(Apogeo Medio) :in Scorpione 25°23'32,2720
Apogeo Osculante :in Scorpione 26°28'54,2498 Retrogrado
Chirone :in Aquario 17°35'10,2343
Pholus :in Sagittario 10°16'23,4081
Ceres :in Toro 20°13'56,0746
Pallas :in Pesci 28°32'17,7328
Juno :in Sagittario 23°55'01,1651
Vesta :in Pesci 05°35'08,3763
Casa 1 :in Scorpione 24°05'02,2154
Casa 2 :in Sagittario 25°52'57,0279
Casa 3 :in Aquario 11°46'56,6985
Casa 4 :in Pesci 23°25'08,2824
Casa 5 :in Ariete 21°10'49,0746
Casa 6 :in Toro 10°01'27,7247
Casa 7 :in Toro 24°05'02,2154
Casa 8 :in Gemelli 25°52'57,0279
Casa 9 :in Leone 11°46'56,6985
Casa 10 :in Vergine 23°25'08,2824
Casa 11 :in Bilancia 21°10'49,0746
Casa 12 :in Scorpione 10°01'27,7247

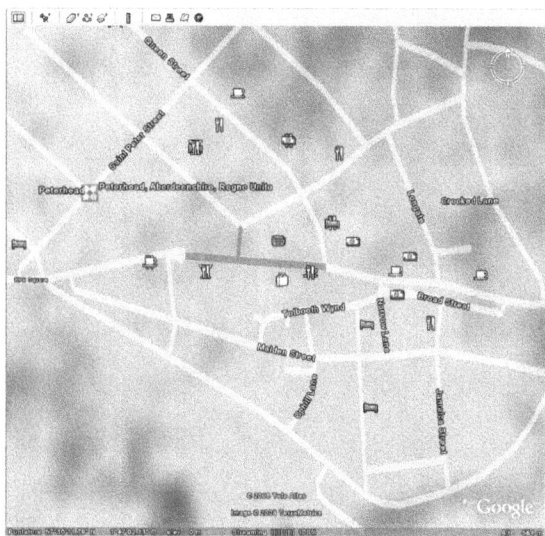

This is the area of my hotel in Peterhead, which I was able to select thanks to the extremely high level of precision of Google Earth.

PART II
EARTH RETURNS

17.
What Earth Returns are and how they work

Important preliminary remarks

The chapter you are about to read is rather difficult: it addresses only highly experienced astrologers.

It explains an experimental study of mine – as experimental as nothing else, I dare say.

For the first time in my life as a researcher of astrology I have followed a completely different method of research and work. Years ago I used to perform tests for several years, and then publish the results.

Let me show you an example taken from my book *Nuovo Trattato di Astrologia*, ed. Armenia. It is one of my most voluminous books and possibly one of my best ones. Before writing it I was searching for the correct measure to assign to the borders of a cusp. Later on I mentioned – as I am recollecting it here and now – the fact that for many, long years I had considered an orb of 3.5 degrees before and after the cusp of any House. For the following years I tried and considered only 3 degrees. Then I started considering 2.5 degrees, then 2 degrees; then I increased it once again; eventually, after many years of attempts, I resolved that the measure closest to reality is 2.5 degrees before and 2.5 degrees after the cusp.

I must underline that by then I had 'all my life before me' or at least I thought so. In other words I hadn't concerns other than studying, researching, 'testing' my hypotheses on myself and on other subjects and only then, after several tests, I resolved to publish the results of my studies.

Today I feel that I cannot proceed any longer this way. It is not because I feel death approaching – but it is a matter of fact that I have no longer 'all my life before me' and I run the risk of sowing something that nobody could ever mow, unless I advertise it at once.

This is why I resolved to change strategy, although it is evident that this exposes me to the risk of drawing a blank and find myself in a deadlock after years of long-lasting research.

Such a dilemma has afflicted me during the recent months so that I resolved to follow this new path.

This is why I am going to write about a new research which, I believe, could lead to concrete results that everybody would be able to use in practice – as it has turned out to be with almost all my studies: and I thank the Heavens for having granted me this 'wildcard' in this branch and not in any other.

I am referring to **Earth Returns**.

What ERs (Earth Returns) are and how they can be explained

I don't remember them having being conjectured or studied by any other author. On the other hand, this is not so important: in fact my approach is surely original and their possible applications are also original; and I'm not afraid of being belied. Of course, provided that I live long enough, in the coming years I'll go on with this research and I'll be glad to compare them with yours. If not, I'll have left a trace for you to investigate on it.

In order to understand what ERs are it is important that you have read and understood the chapter describing what SRs and LRs are and how they work.

If you don't study that chapter attentively, I believe it useless for you to read this one: you'd understand very little of what I am about to tell you.

First of all, we must start with certain premises which – in my opinion – are fundamental for going along this path.

- As the background of the entire dissertation on ERs we must start with a conceptual base where causality is predominant as regards to synchronicity. In other words you must accept that astrology has an explanation at a physical level, and not – in this specific case – an explanation based on Carl Gustav Jung's principle of synchronicity.

- In my opinion it is essential that you create a strict and ideal link between biorhythms and the Returns: SRs, LRs, and ERs.

- And among the innumerable biorhythms governing us, in my opinion you must consider mainly three. The first one is connected with the yearly rhythm: animals hibernate always during the same period of the year; they also migrate or mate always in a precise period of the year; trees bear fruits always in the same month of the year, and so on – we could list scores of known natural phenomena that have been studied and proven. The second rhythm is connected with the monthly cycle which can be verified through the phenomena of tides, menstruation, metabolic activity of micro organisms, etc. Lastly we have the circadian rhythm lasting approximately one day, where we can prove that such physiological functions as urination, arterial pressure or the endogenous production of melatonin follow highly predictable peaks in determined hours of the day.

- The yearly rhythm can be gorgeously visualised through the Solar Return. It is easy to draw it by taking the Sun, in its geocentric view, as the reference point in the very instant of its yearly return onto its birth position: i.e. on the same degree, minutes, and seconds, of one's birth.

- The monthly rhythm can also easily be visualised through the Lunar Return, i.e. the return of our satellite, the Moon – always considered in a geocentric view of the sky – on the precise point that it occupied at one's birth[1].

Now the problem – in my opinion it is not an easy point to be solved – is the circadian rhythm, which should be visualised – and this is the point – by the Earth Return. In fact we can detect the position of the Earth (which occupies the precisely opposite longitude to the one of the Sun) at one's birth. This is an important starting point. And for the sake of simplicity, the rhythm can be compared to that of a sine wave. In this case we'll place a number n of sine waves side by side that help us detect which is the point A within the day whose Earth Return we wish to cast. Now, how can we quantify this timing? And above all how can we transpose it into a chart of an astrological interest? This is a really complex dilemma and I admit that I have banged my head against this 'brick wall' for long. I chose two ways.

I started with a first working hypothesis, the one that I'm going to describe right now. I don't think that this is the correct one: I believe that the following one is the right one, or the potentially right one. As I told you, it is an experimental work in which I am writing before having studied it for several years, unlike my habit until now. As I mentioned, the base is the rotation of the Earth, i.e. the spinning motion around its own axis. A complete rotation is carried out in approximately one day, but it does not correspond to exactly 24 hours. In fact sidereal rotation (that's to say, taking an external reference point outside Earth, say a star) lasts 23 hours, 56 minutes, 4 seconds and 905 ten thousandths of a second: 23h56'04".0905.

I'll expose you to this first working hypothesis with an example whose starting parameters are extremely exact. It is the assassination of Mahatma Gandhi. His time of birth is well known as well as his time of death. For example you can find it in the wonderful on-line encyclopaedia www.britannica.com – I suggest it to you all because with a fee of a few Euros per years you can enter a kind of Pandora's Box of any individual of any culture. It is a treasure of knowledge compiled by competent people, not by occasional editors whose common feature is ignorance and arrogance rather than any other virtue. In fact the Britannica has always been the absolute reference point for knowledge in the world. Mohandas Karamchand Gandhi was born in Porbandar, India, on the 2nd of October 1869 at 7:08 am, corresponding to 2:30 Zulu (Universal Time of Greenwich).

My first idea was to create a table (you'll find it in the following pages; it has been prepared by Stefano Briganti and Pino Valente) showing, day after day, the multiples of 23h56'04".0905 starting from a date of birth. This corresponds to placing many sine waves one after another as the one reproduced in the previous page, in order to detect the exact time of point *A* in a given day of the life of a subject. Once we get to know that, we draw the chart of the ER of the subject. Let us proceed step by step though. The webpage http://www.astronomy.villanova.edu/links/jd.htm gives us the chance of entering a certain date and calculating its relevant *Julian Day* or Julian Date: a sort of absolute reference point not depending on the centuries. The Julian Date of the Mahatma's date of birth corresponds to 2403972.5 – we could proceed with our calculation in such a way, but we have found out a more comfortable one. There's another website (http://xoomer.alice.it/esongi/duration.htm) in which we can get to know how many days has passed since two dates: the first one being a date of birth, and the second one being the day for which we wish to cast the ER. Thus we get to know that between the 2/10/1869 and the 30/1/1948 (day of the assassination of the spiritual father of India) passed 28,608 days. Just look for this number in the table prepared by Pino Valente and Stefano Briganti and you'll find the value corresponding to the multiple of 23h56'04".0905: namely 28,529.88774 days of 23h56'04".0905 each.

All this led us to know that the margin of 0.88774 days is the Greenwich Time (remember? the two URLs that I have mentioned before calculate always with reference to 00:00 GMT) in which, when we start from 00:00

GMT of the 30th of January 1948, the nth sine-wave-like cycle repeats starting from point A. If you wish to get to know to how many hours & minutes 0.88774 days correspond, you should set the following proportion 0.88774 : 1 = x : 86,400 – where 86,400 is the number of seconds that make up a day. The solution of this proportion gives x = 76,700.736 which is the quantity of seconds corresponding to 21.3058 hours, that's to say, 21 hours and 18 minutes. Nevertheless we must not forget that we started from time 00:00 of the 2nd of October 1869, while we should have actually started from 02:30 GMT, matching 7:08 Indian time, i.e. the local time of birth of Gandhi in Porbandar. To finish with, we can cast a chart of Earth Return for 23h48' (21h18'+2h30') of the 30/1/1948, in Greenwich. Entering these data in any software of astrology you can get the chart relevant to Delhi, the one that you can also see in these pages.

Yet this chart is not correct. Let us see why. If a baby was born on 30/1/1948 at 23:48 GMT, its astral map corresponds to that of another baby who was born in Delhi 5h30' later (for this is the time span between the two locations). Now, we know that the leader of non-violence was murdered at 17:41 of Delhi, on the 30th of January. This means that we have cast the ER of the day following his death. Thus we have to go into reverse and recalculate, this time considering 28,607 days instead of 28,608. To make a long story short I don't detail all the steps and I jump to the result. In order to cast this map of Earth Return you should consider Delhi time of the 29th (not the 30th) of January 1948: 23 hours and 52 minutes. As you can see for yourselves, the latter chart contains many elements of concern, perfectly relevant with Gandhi's murder. It goes without saying that if you consider this latter astral map, if the pacifist leader would have been anywhere else on that moment, he could have changed his ER completely – and almost certainly he would not have been killed then. There can be several objections yet.

1) Can Earth Returns be 'aimed' (i.e. relocated) just like Solar and Lunar Returns? The answer is no. In 99.99% of the events, it isn't necessary. But if we consider that we are studying the stars of a great political and intellectual leader during a quite dangerous period for him (as you can see in page #267 and following ones of the above mentioned book), then I believe that not only should he have taken into due consideration this possibility: even more, he should have performed such a relocation (or *aiming*) in order to avoid to the huge multitude of his followers such a horrible loss that cannot be filled. 2) It is also evident that if Gandhi would have aimed his ER travelling to a location several time zones away from there, he wouldn't

have been killed also for logistical reasons. In fact the fanatic Hindu who killed him wouldn't probably have followed his victim to Oslo, Dallas, or the Fijis where Gandhi could have relocated his Earth Return. 3) On the other hand it appears clear that the map of ER for the same location changes very little day by day, over a period of several months. This is the reason why I started considering a different working hypothesis, under a new light.

For I said to myself, what is the condition that gives you the exact and quick measure of the spinning of the Earth around its own axis during a (sidereal) day? The answer is the classical egg of Columbus: it's the precise point where the Ascendant lies, possibly expressed in degrees, minutes, and seconds. I am certain that reading these lines, a high percentage of colleagues would claim that it is obvious, that they had already known and used it. But of course this research, even if it's in an early experimental phase, is intended for me and for those three or four people who haven't already understood it all. Unluckily, those who claim that they have already known this whole matter will not be able to prove it because they would be unable to show any written evidence of it. In this case, as it often happens when astrologers talk about SRs and ASRs, we face that particular situation which jurisprudence defines as *false pretences*. Let us stick to more serious facts and try to develop our line of reasoning by setting the fundamental points for the casting and the usage of Earth Returns, a new technique which I could compare to a sort of new Northwest Passage of astrological research applied to absolutely practical goals, not theoretical ones.

Now the Ascendant of the Great Soul is 00°43'16.8269 Virgo but we can consider it 0°43' Virgo – as far as the birth relocated to Greenwich is concerned. For what is important for us is the timing of ER, thus we have to transpose it to Universal Time. When we look for the hour & minutes in which the sine wave of the birth starting from the point A completes a precise multiple of itself on the day that we wish to consider, we'll have to repeat the calculation for Greenwich (adding to or subtracting from 12 as many minutes as the minutes required to get an astral map whose Ascendant lies on 0°43' Virgo). This way we'll get a given time to which (or from which) we add (or subtract) the difference of longitude of the different places that we'll be considering. If we did otherwise (for example if we calculated at what time of the day we can get an Ascendant on 0°43' Virgo in New Delhi on 30/1/1948) we would get an invariable chart even if we relocate to Dallas or Perth: for even in the latter places we should always get an astral map whose Ascendant lies on 0°43' Virgo. This way Mars would always remain in the 11th House of ER, Uranus always in the 8th

House of ER, and Saturn always in the 10th House of ER.

Hence, according to this second working hypothesis, an ER is calculated starting from the time in which the daily Ascendant has the same value that it had when the subject was born, referred to Greenwich. Once you detect that moment and transpose it to Greenwich, you can then relocate the astral map to the place where the subject actually is at that moment.

Now let us look at some examples using the module *Molriv* of my software package *Astral*. Even if Astral doesn't reach the precision (and the 'miracles') that you can attain with *Aladino* (also refereed to as Module for the Automated Research of the Aimed Solar Returns 'RSMA' – see www.cirodiscepolo.it/astral.htm), Astral is more suitable for different, more immediate elaborations. By pressing on the icons of + and – (hours, minutes, or quarters) you can easily find out that on the 29th of January 1948 the return of the Ascendant takes places at 6:42 pm Greenwich time (we have already explained why we must consider the day before Gandhi's murder). The shown Ascendant lies on 0°47' – it's a quite minimal difference, but if you really wish you can also calculate it to a precision of ten thousandths of a second. Now we take these data for granted and we add 5 hours and 30 minutes (corresponding to the difference between GMT and the time zone of India) and we cast the natal chart of a baby born in Delhi on the 30/1/1948 at 00:12. What we get is an 'astral map' (actually the map of ER) with the Ascendant on the 1st House radix, Mars in the 11th House, Uranus in the 8th House, Saturn in the 10th House, and the Sun in the 4th House of ER. Consider that the Sun in the 4th often can be found in the astral charts of many Solar Returns and/or Lunar Returns corresponding to deadly events. Just to make another example – what if we want to cast the map for Perth? In this case we should have cast the sky of a baby born in Perth on the 30/1/1948 at 02:42 (corresponding to 18:42 + a time span of 8 hours). There the Ascendant of ER would have been in the 3rd natal House, Mars and Saturn in the 9thh House of ER, Uranus in the 6th House of ER, Pluto in the 8th House of ER, the Sun in the 2nd House of ER, and Jupiter in the 12th House of ER conjunct to the Ascendant. I would have bet anything that the latter sky of ER could not correspond to any deadly event for the subject.

Notes
1) In this regard I would like to underline that I personally use the very same mathematical procedure suggested by Henri J. Gouchon. He said, cast an astral map for the moment in which the Moon passes exactly over its own natal position. One could also use other methods (for example, when the Moon passes over the subject's natal Sun every month) but I have always

150   LUNAR RETURNS AND EARTH RETURNS

considered the former way more suitable, for it also corresponds to the causal theory that I mention in the chapter relevant to a possible 'physical' functioning of Solar and Lunar Returns. I have searched for Alexandre Volguine's opinion in his only one book on SRs, but I have found nothing in this regard.

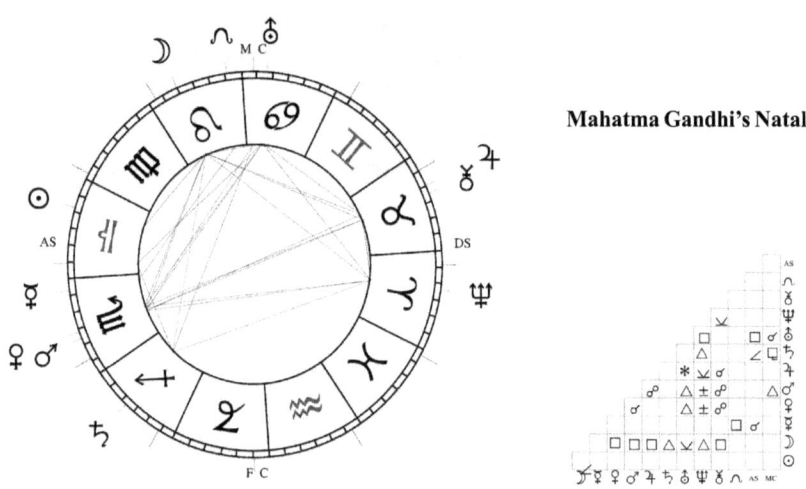

Mahatma Gandhi's Natal

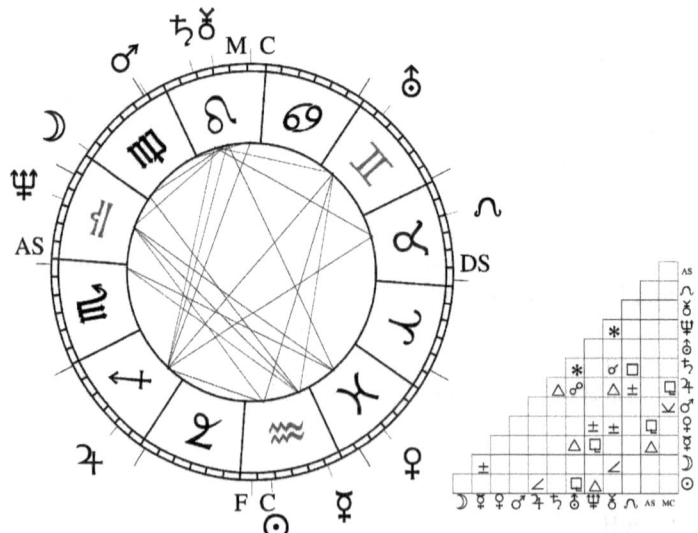

ER of the assassination of Gandhi, Delhi

WHAT EARTH RETURNS ARE AND HOW THEY WORK

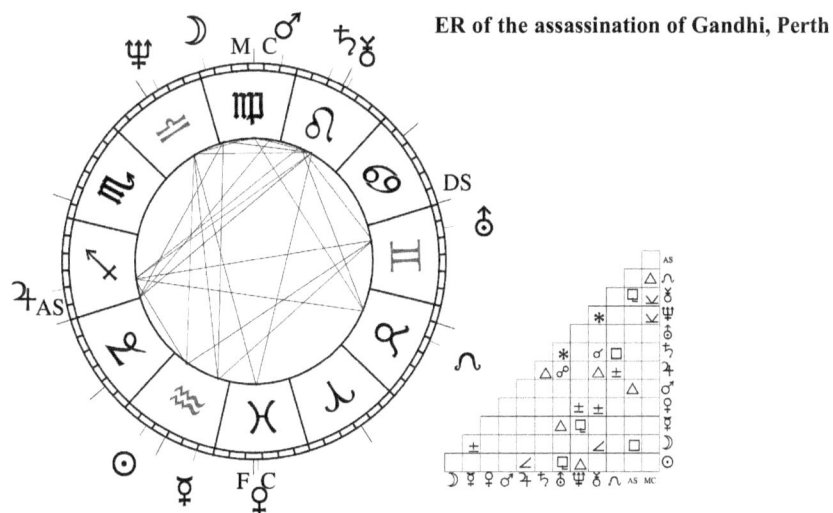

ER of the assassination of Gandhi, Perth

Let us consider another example, a quite significant one: the arrest of **Benito Mussolini** which took place in Rome on the 25th of July 1943. The following chart shows his natal sky – he was born in Predappio (Forlì) on the 29th July of 1883 at 1:54 pm. You can also see the map of ER of the day of the arrest, cast in Rome. I'll also show you how that map would have looked like if he had spent that day, say in Santo Domingo – in this case I am confident that he would have not been arrested on that day. And to conclude, just to give you an idea of how the maps of ER change (they actually show a difference of approximately 4' of the clock as far as its Ascendant is considered) I'll show you Mussolini's map of ER ten days before his arrest.

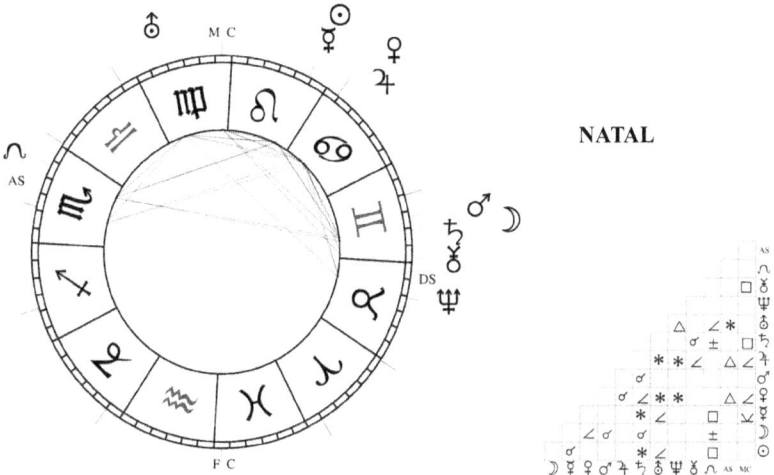

NATAL

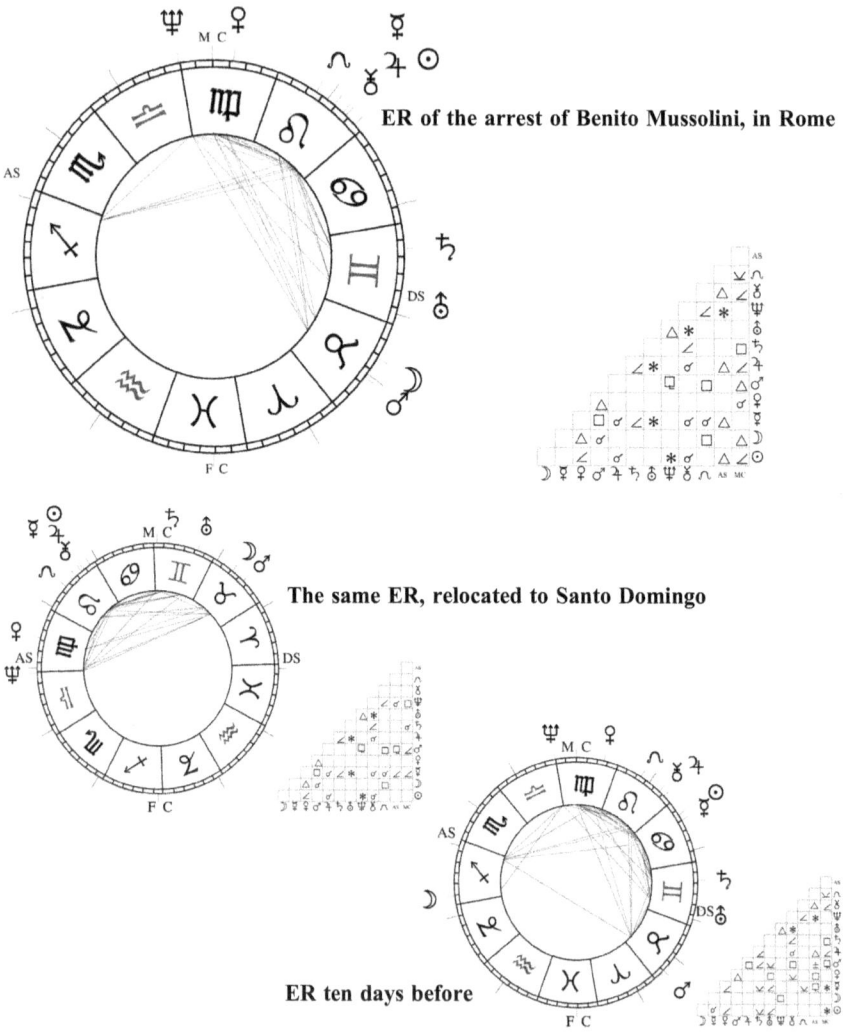

ER of the arrest of Benito Mussolini, in Rome

The same ER, relocated to Santo Domingo

ER ten days before

Example of a practical application of an ER with no need for geographical relocation

Now let us consider an example that helps throw light over another possible usage of ERs with no need for the subject to aim, or relocate, them. We are still considering a case of Predictive Astrology in which it is possible to evaluate the great value that an ER could have in choosing a favourable day for a given event. So let us create a male subject born in Naples on the 2nd of February 1976 at 11 am. Let us say that he had an ASR in Reykjavík in 2008.

WHAT EARTH RETURNS ARE AND HOW THEY WORK

The aim of this exercise is to select a very favourable day during the twelve months of his SR, in which he could reach an agreement with members of his family in connection with a lawsuit related with real estate.

Here are the charts:

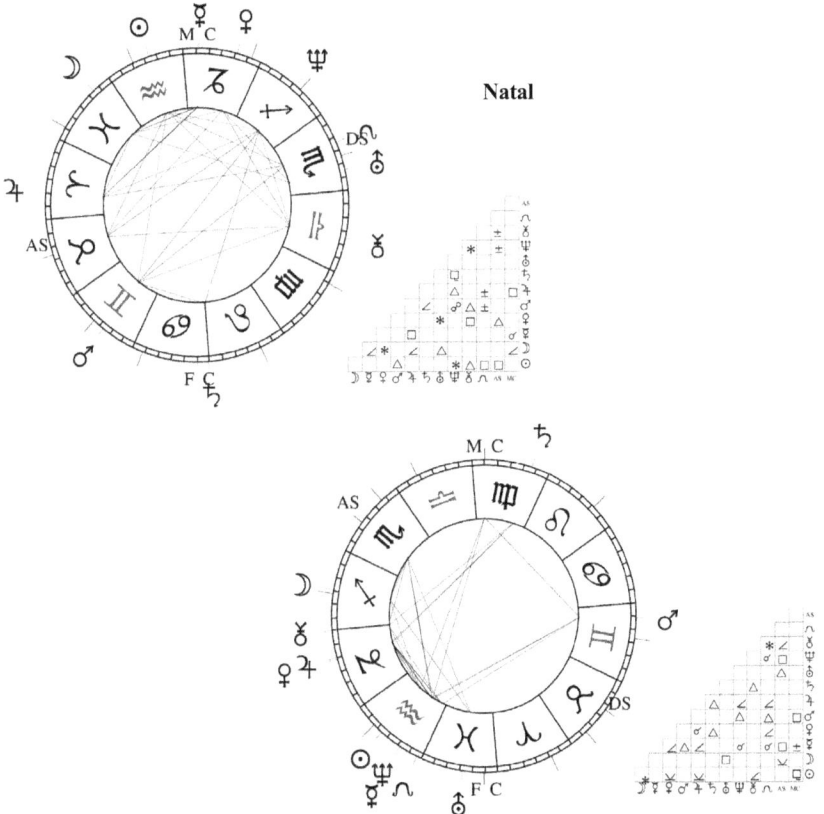

- his Natal chart

- his Aimed Solar Return in Reykjavik

- his Earth Return in Naples, cast for the 2nd of February 2008 at 10:02 Greenwich time. A remark: it is theoretically possible to be there in Reykjavik at approximately 2 o'clock in the morning, and then in Naples at 10:02 of the same day).

- his Earth Return in Naples, on the 2nd of April 2008 at 7:06 Greenwich time.

- his Earth Return in Naples, on the 2nd of August 2008 at 23:02 Greenwich time.

- his Earth Return in Naples, on the 2nd of December 2008 at 14:03 Greenwich time.

ER, Naples, on the 2nd of February 2008

ER, Naples, on the 2nd of April 2008

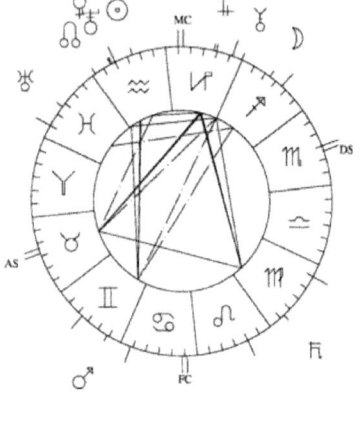

ER, Naples, on the 2nd of August 2008

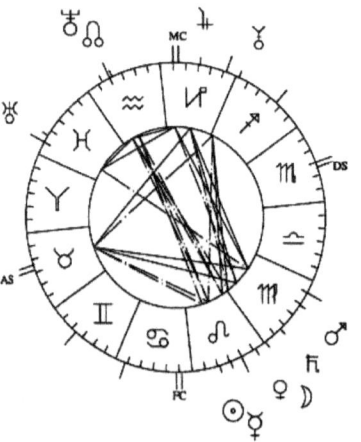

ER, Naples, on the 2nd of December 2008

As you can see, the Earth Return of the 2nd of December is perfect in Naples with no need for relocation, because it has a strict conjunction of Venus and Jupiter on the Medium Coeli.

At this point you consider the subject's Base Lunar Return in Naples for November 2008: such a LR contains this Earth Return, and we can see that it is not the very best to achieve our astrological goals.

So what we can do is to relocate the Lunar Return of November to Recife, where Jupiter is placed in the 7th House of LR. This way we attain a wonderful example of complete synergy among Solar Return, Lunar Return, and Earth Return.

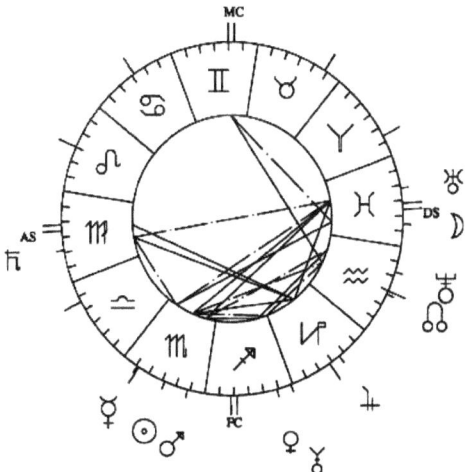

BLR, Naples, on the 11th of November 2008

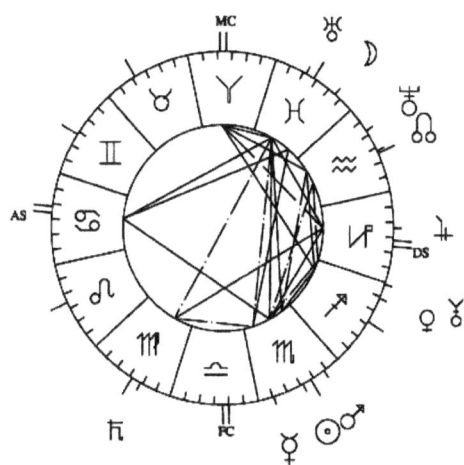

ALR, Recife, on the 11th of November 2008

18.
Table to find out the point A in Earth Returns

1	0,997269566	80	79,78156528	159	158,565861	238	237,3501567	317	316,1344524	396	394,9187481
2	1,994539132	81	80,77883484	160	159,5631306	239	238,3474263	318	317,131722	397	395,9160177
3	2,991808698	82	81,77610441	161	160,5604001	240	239,3446958	319	318,1289915	398	396,9132873
4	3,989078264	83	82,77337398	162	161,5576697	241	240,3419654	320	319,1262611	399	397,9105568
5	4,98634783	84	83,77064354	163	162,5549393	242	241,339235	321	320,1235307	400	398,9078264
6	5,983617396	85	84,76791311	164	163,5522088	243	242,3365045	322	321,1208002	401	399,905096
7	6,980886962	86	85,76518267	165	164,5494784	244	243,3337741	323	322,1180698	402	400,9023655
8	7,978156528	87	86,76245224	166	165,546748	245	244,3310437	324	323,1153394	403	401,8996351
9	8,975426094	88	87,75972181	167	166,5440175	246	245,3283132	325	324,1126089	404	402,8969047
10	9,97269566	89	88,75699137	168	167,5412871	247	246,3255828	326	325,1098785	405	403,8941742
11	10,96996523	90	89,75426094	169	168,5385566	248	247,3228524	327	326,1071481	406	404,8914438
12	11,96723479	91	90,7515305	170	169,5358262	249	248,3201219	328	327,1044176	407	405,8887134
13	12,96450436	92	91,74880007	171	170,5330958	250	249,3173915	329	328,1016872	408	406,8859829
14	13,96177392	93	92,74606964	172	171,5303653	251	250,3146611	330	329,0989568	409	407,8832525
15	14,95904349	94	93,7433392	173	172,5276349	252	251,3119306	331	330,0962263	410	408,880522
16	15,95631306	95	94,74060877	174	173,5249045	253	252,3092002	332	331,0934959	411	409,8777916
17	16,95358262	96	95,73787833	175	174,522174	254	253,3064698	333	332,0907655	412	410,8750612
18	17,95085219	97	96,7351479	176	175,5194436	255	254,3037393	334	333,088035	413	411,8723307
19	18,94812175	98	97,73241747	177	176,5167132	256	255,3010089	335	334,0853046	414	412,8696003
20	19,94539132	99	98,72968703	178	177,5139827	257	256,2982785	336	335,0825742	415	413,8668699
21	20,94266089	100	99,7269566	179	178,5112523	258	257,295548	337	336,0798437	416	414,8641394
22	21,93993045	101	100,7242262	180	179,5085219	259	258,2928176	338	337,0771133	417	415,861409
23	22,93720002	102	101,7214957	181	180,5057914	260	259,2900872	339	338,0743829	418	416,8586786
24	23,93446958	103	102,7187653	182	181,503061	261	260,2873567	340	339,0716524	419	417,8559481
25	24,93173915	104	103,7160349	183	182,5003306	262	261,2846263	341	340,068922	420	418,8532177
26	25,92900872	105	104,7133044	184	183,4976001	263	262,2818959	342	341,0661916	421	419,8504873
27	26,92627828	106	105,710574	185	184,4948697	264	263,2791654	343	342,0634611	422	420,8477568
28	27,92354785	107	106,7078436	186	185,4921393	265	264,276435	344	343,0607307	423	421,8450264
29	28,92081741	108	107,7051131	187	186,4894088	266	265,2737045	345	344,0580003	424	422,842296
30	29,91808698	109	108,7023827	188	187,4866784	267	266,2709741	346	345,0552698	425	423,8395655
31	30,91535655	110	109,6996523	189	188,483948	268	267,2682437	347	346,0525394	426	424,8368351
32	31,91262611	111	110,6969218	190	189,4812175	269	268,2655132	348	347,049809	427	425,8341047
33	32,90989568	112	111,6941914	191	190,4784871	270	269,2627828	349	348,0470785	428	426,8313742
34	33,90716524	113	112,691461	192	191,4757567	271	270,2600524	350	349,0443481	429	427,8286438
35	34,90443481	114	113,6887305	193	192,4730262	272	271,2573219	351	350,0416177	430	428,8259134
36	35,90170438	115	114,6860001	194	193,4702958	273	272,2545915	352	351,0388872	431	429,8231829
37	36,89897394	116	115,6832697	195	194,4675654	274	273,2518611	353	352,0361568	432	430,8204525
38	37,89624351	117	116,6805392	196	195,4648349	275	274,2491306	354	353,0334264	433	431,8177221
39	38,89351307	118	117,6778088	197	196,4621045	276	275,2464002	355	354,0306959	434	432,8149916
40	39,89078264	119	118,6750784	198	197,4593741	277	276,2436698	356	355,0279655	435	433,8122612
41	40,8880522	120	119,6723479	199	198,4566436	278	277,2409393	357	356,0252351	436	434,8095308
42	41,88532177	121	120,6696175	200	199,4539132	279	278,2382089	358	357,0225046	437	435,8068003
43	42,88259134	122	121,666887	201	200,4511828	280	279,2354785	359	358,0197742	438	436,8040699
44	43,8798609	123	122,6641566	202	201,4484523	281	280,232748	360	359,0170438	439	437,8013395
45	44,87713047	124	123,6614262	203	202,4457219	282	281,2300176	361	360,0143133	440	438,798609
46	45,87440003	125	124,6586957	204	203,4429915	283	282,2272872	362	361,0115829	441	439,7958786
47	46,8716696	126	125,6559653	205	204,440261	284	283,2245567	363	362,0088524	442	440,7931482
48	47,86893917	127	126,6532349	206	205,4375306	285	284,2218263	364	363,006122	443	441,7904177
49	48,86620873	128	127,6505044	207	206,4348002	286	285,2190959	365	364,0033916	444	442,7876873
50	49,8634783	129	128,647774	208	207,4320697	287	286,2163654	366	365,0006611	445	443,7849569
51	50,86074786	130	129,6450436	209	208,4293393	288	287,213635	367	365,9979307	446	444,7822264
52	51,85801743	131	130,6423131	210	209,4266089	289	288,2109046	368	366,9952003	447	445,779496
53	52,855287	132	131,6395827	211	210,4238784	290	289,2081741	369	367,9924698	448	446,7767656
54	53,85255656	133	132,6368523	212	211,421148	291	290,2054437	370	368,9897394	449	447,7740351
55	54,84982613	134	133,6341218	213	212,4184176	292	291,2027133	371	369,987009	450	448,7713047
56	55,84709569	135	134,6313914	214	213,4156871	293	292,1999828	372	370,9842785	451	449,7685743
57	56,84436526	136	135,628661	215	214,4129567	294	293,1972524	373	371,9815481	452	450,7658438
58	57,84163483	137	136,6259305	216	215,4102263	295	294,194522	374	372,9788177	453	451,7631134
59	58,83890439	138	137,6232001	217	216,4074958	296	295,1917915	375	373,9760872	454	452,760383
60	59,83617396	139	138,6204697	218	217,4047654	297	296,1890611	376	374,9733568	455	453,7576525
61	60,83344352	140	139,6177392	219	218,4020349	298	297,1863307	377	375,9706264	456	454,7549221
62	61,83071309	141	140,6150088	220	219,3993045	299	298,1836002	378	376,9678959	457	455,7521916
63	62,82798266	142	141,6122784	221	220,3965741	300	299,1808698	379	377,9651655	458	456,7494612
64	63,82525222	143	142,6095479	222	221,3938436	301	300,1781394	380	378,9624351	459	457,7467308
65	64,82252179	144	143,6068175	223	222,3911132	302	301,1754089	381	379,9597046	460	458,7440003
66	65,81979135	145	144,6040871	224	223,3883828	303	302,1726785	382	380,9569742	461	459,7412699
67	66,81706092	146	145,6013566	225	224,3856523	304	303,1699481	383	381,9542438	462	460,7385395
68	67,81433049	147	146,5986262	226	225,3829219	305	304,1672176	384	382,9515133	463	461,735809
69	68,81160005	148	147,5958958	227	226,3801915	306	305,1644872	385	383,9487829	464	462,7330786
70	69,80886962	149	148,5931653	228	227,377461	307	306,1617568	386	384,9460525	465	463,7303482
71	70,80613918	150	149,5904349	229	228,3747306	308	307,1590263	387	385,943322	466	464,7276177
72	71,80340875	151	150,5877045	230	229,3720002	309	308,1562959	388	386,9405916	467	465,7248873
73	72,80067832	152	151,584974	231	230,3692697	310	309,1535655	389	387,9378612	468	466,7221569
74	73,79794788	153	152,5822436	232	231,3665393	311	310,150835	390	388,9351307	469	467,7194264
75	74,79521745	154	153,5795132	233	232,3638089	312	311,1481046	391	389,9324003	470	468,716696
76	75,79248701	155	154,5767827	234	233,3610784	313	312,1453741	392	390,9296699	471	469,7139656
77	76,78975658	156	155,5740523	235	234,358348	314	313,1426437	393	391,9269394	472	470,7112351
78	77,78702615	157	156,5713219	236	235,3556176	315	314,1399133	394	392,924209	473	471,7085047
79	78,78429571	158	157,5685914	237	236,3528871	316	315,1371828	395	393,9214786	474	472,7057743

475	473,7030438	565	563,4573048	655	653,2115657	745	742,9658266	835	832,7200876	925	922,4743485
476	474,7003134	566	564,4545743	656	654,2088353	746	743,9630962	836	833,7173572	926	923,4716181
477	475,697583	567	565,4518439	657	655,2061048	747	744,9603658	837	834,7146267	927	924,4688877
478	476,6948525	568	566,4491135	658	656,2033744	748	745,9576353	838	835,7118963	928	925,4661572
479	477,6921221	569	567,446383	659	657,200644	749	746,9549049	839	836,7091659	929	926,4634268
480	478,6893917	570	568,4436526	660	658,1979135	750	747,9521745	840	837,7064354	930	927,4606964
481	479,6866612	571	569,4409222	661	659,1951831	751	748,949444	841	838,703705	931	928,4579659
482	480,6839308	572	570,4381917	662	660,1924527	752	749,9467136	842	839,7009745	932	929,4552355
483	481,6812004	573	571,4354613	663	661,1897222	753	750,9439832	843	840,6982441	933	930,4525051
484	482,6784699	574	572,4327309	664	662,1869918	754	751,9412527	844	841,6955137	934	931,4497746
485	483,6757395	575	573,4300004	665	663,1842614	755	752,9385223	845	842,6927832	935	932,4470442
486	484,6730091	576	574,427 27	666	664,1815309	756	753,9357919	846	843,6900528	936	933,4443138
487	485,6702786	577	575,4245396	667	665,1788005	757	754,9330614	847	844,6873224	937	934,4415833
488	486,6675482	578	576,4218091	668	666,1760701	758	755,930331	848	845,6845919	938	935,4388529
489	487,6648178	579	577,4190787	669	667,1733396	759	756,9276006	849	846,6818615	939	936,4361224
490	488,6620873	580	578,4163483	670	668,1706092	760	757,9248701	850	847,6791311	940	937,433392
491	489,6593569	581	579,4136178	671	669,1678788	761	758,9221397	851	848,6764006	941	938,4306616
492	490,6566265	582	580,4108874	672	670,1651483	762	759,9194093	852	849,6736702	942	939,4279311
493	491,653896	583	581,408157	673	671,1624179	763	760,9166788	853	850,6709398	943	940,4252007
494	492,6511656	584	582,4054265	674	672,1596875	764	761,9139484	854	851,6682093	944	941,4224703
495	493,6484352	585	583,4026961	675	673,156957	765	762,911218	855	852,6654789	945	942,4197398
496	494,6457047	586	584,3999657	676	674,1542266	766	763,9084875	856	853,6627485	946	943,4170094
497	495,6429743	587	585,3972352	677	675,1514962	767	764,9057571	857	854,660018	947	944,414279
498	496,6402439	588	586,3945048	678	676,1487657	768	765,9030267	858	855,6572876	948	945,4115485
499	497,6375134	589	587,3917744	679	677,1460353	769	766,9002962	859	856,6545572	949	946,4088181
500	498,634783	590	588,3890439	680	678,1433049	770	767,8975658	860	857,6518267	950	947,4060877
501	499,6320526	591	589,3863135	681	679,1405744	771	768,8948354	861	858,6490963	951	948,4033572
502	500,6293221	592	590,3835831	682	680,137844	772	769,8921049	862	859,6463659	952	949,4006268
503	501,6265917	593	591,3808526	683	681,1351136	773	770,8893745	863	860,6436354	953	950,3978964
504	502,6238613	594	592,3781222	684	682,1323831	774	771,8866441	864	861,640905	954	951,3951659
505	503,6211308	595	593,3753918	685	683,1296527	775	772,8839136	865	862,6381746	955	952,3924355
506	504,6184004	596	594,3726613	686	684,1269223	776	773,8811832	866	863,6354441	956	953,3897051
507	505,6156699	597	595,3699309	687	685,1241918	777	774,8784528	867	864,6327137	957	954,3869746
508	506,6129395	598	596,3672005	688	686,1214614	778	775,8757223	868	865,6299833	958	955,3842442
509	507,6102091	599	597,36447	689	687,118731	779	776,8729919	869	866,6272528	959	956,3815138
510	508,6074786	600	598,3617396	690	688,1160005	780	777,8702615	870	867,6245224	960	957,3787833
511	509,6047482	601	599,3590091	691	689,1132701	781	778,867531	871	868,621792	961	958,3760529
512	510,6020178	602	600,3562787	692	690,1105397	782	779,8648006	872	869,6190615	962	959,3733225
513	511,5992873	603	601,3535483	693	691,1078092	783	780,8620702	873	870,6163311	963	960,370592
514	512,5965569	604	602,3508178	694	692,1050788	784	781,8593397	874	871,6136007	964	961,3678616
515	513,5938265	605	603,3480874	695	693,1023484	785	782,8566093	875	872,6108702	965	962,3651312
516	514,591096	606	604,345357	696	694,0996179	786	783,8538789	876	873,6081398	966	963,3624007
517	515,5883656	607	605,3426265	697	695,0968875	787	784,8511484	877	874,6054094	967	964,3596703
518	516,5856352	608	606,3398961	698	696,094157	788	785,848418	878	875,6026789	968	965,3569399
519	517,5829047	609	607,3371657	699	697,0914266	789	786,8456876	879	876,5999485	969	966,3542094
520	518,5801743	610	608,3344352	700	698,0886962	790	787,8429571	880	877,597218	970	967,351479
521	519,5774439	611	609,3317048	701	699,0859657	791	788,8402267	881	878,5944876	971	968,3487486
522	520,5747134	612	610,3289744	702	700,0832353	792	789,8374963	882	879,5917572	972	969,3460181
523	521,571983	613	611,3262439	703	701,0805049	793	790,8347658	883	880,5890268	973	970,3432877
524	522,5692526	614	612,3235135	704	702,0777744	794	791,8320354	884	881,5862963	974	971,3405573
525	523,5665221	615	613,3207831	705	703,075044	795	792,8293049	885	882,5835659	975	972,3378268
526	524,5637917	616	614,3180526	706	704,0723136	796	793,8265745	886	883,5808355	976	973,3350964
527	525,5610613	617	615,3153222	707	705,0695831	797	794,8238441	887	884,578105	977	974,332366
528	526,5583308	618	616,3125918	708	706,0668527	798	795,8211136	888	885,5753746	978	975,3296355
529	527,5556004	619	617,3098613	709	707,0641223	799	796,8183832	889	886,5726441	979	976,3269051
530	528,55287	620	618,3071309	710	708,0613918	800	797,8156528	890	887,5699137	980	977,3241747
531	529,5501395	621	619,3044005	711	709,0586614	801	798,8129223	891	888,5671833	981	978,3214442
532	530,5474091	622	620,30167	712	710,055931	802	799,8101919	892	889,5644528	982	979,3187138
533	531,5446787	623	621,2989396	713	711,0532005	803	800,8074615	893	890,5617224	983	980,3159834
534	532,5419482	624	622,2962092	714	712,0504701	804	801,804731	894	891,558992	984	981,3132529
535	533,5392178	625	623,2934787	715	713,0477397	805	802,8020006	895	892,5562615	985	982,3105225
536	534,5364874	626	624,2907483	716	714,0450092	806	803,7992702	896	893,5535311	986	983,307792
537	535,5337569	627	625,2880179	717	715,0422788	807	804,7965397	897	894,5508007	987	984,3050616
538	536,5310265	628	626,2852874	718	716,0395484	808	805,7938093	898	895,5480702	988	985,3023312
539	537,5282961	629	627,282557	719	717,0368179	809	806,7910789	899	896,5453398	989	986,2996007
540	538,5255656	630	628,2798266	720	718,0340875	810	807,7883484	900	897,5426094	990	987,2968703
541	539,5228352	631	629,2770961	721	719,0313571	811	808,785618	901	898,5398789	991	988,2941399
542	540,5201048	632	630,2743657	722	720,0286266	812	809,7828876	902	899,5371485	992	989,2914094
543	541,5173743	633	631,2716353	723	721,0258962	813	810,7801571	903	900,5344181	993	990,288679
544	542,5146439	634	632,2689048	724	722,0231658	814	811,7774267	904	901,5316876	994	991,2859486
545	543,5119135	635	633,2661744	725	723,0204353	815	812,7746963	905	902,5289572	995	992,2832181
546	544,509183	636	634,263444	726	724,0177049	816	813,7719658	906	903,5262268	996	993,2804877
547	545,5064526	637	635,2607135	727	725,0149745	817	814,7692354	907	904,5234963	997	994,2777573
548	546,5037222	638	636,2579831	728	726,012244	818	815,766505	908	905,5207659	998	995,2750268
549	547,5009917	639	637,2552527	729	727,0095136	819	816,7637745	909	906,5180355	999	996,2722964
550	548,4982613	640	638,2525222	730	728,0067832	820	817,7610441	910	907,515305	1000	997,269566
551	549,4955309	641	639,2497918	731	729,0040527	821	818,7583137	911	908,5125746	1001	998,2668355
552	550,4928004	642	640,2470614	732	730,0013223	822	819,7555832	912	909,5098442	1002	999,2641051
553	551,49007	643	641,2443309	733	730,9985919	823	820,7528528	913	910,5071137	1003	1000,261375
554	552,4873395	644	642,2416005	734	731,9958614	824	821,7501224	914	911,5043833	1004	1001,258644
555	553,4846091	645	643,2388701	735	732,993131	825	822,7473919	915	912,5016529	1005	1002,255914
556	554,4818787	646	644,2361396	736	733,9904006	826	823,7446615	916	913,4989224	1006	1003,253183
557	555,4791482	647	645,2334092	737	734,9876701	827	824,7419311	917	914,496192	1007	1004,250453
558	556,4764178	648	646,2306788	738	735,9849397	828	825,7392006	918	915,4934616	1008	1005,247723
559	557,4736874	649	647,2279483	739	736,9822093	829	826,7364702	919	916,4907311	1009	1006,244992
560	558,4709569	650	648,2252179	740	737,9794788	830	827,7337398	920	917,4880007	1010	1007,242262
561	559,4682265	651	649,2224874	741	738,9767484	831	828,7310093	921	918,4852703	1011	1008,239531
562	560,4654961	652	650,219757	742	739,974018	832	829,7282789	922	919,4825398	1012	1009,236801
563	561,4627656	653	651,2170266	743	740,9712875	833	830,7255485	923	920,4798094	1013	1010,23407
564	562,4600352	654	652,2142961	744	741,9685571	834	831,722818	924	921,477079	1014	1011,23134

TABLE TO FIND OUT THE POINT A IN EARTH RETURNS 159

1015	1012,228609	1105	1101,98287	1195	1191,737131	1285	1281,491392	1375	1371,245653	1465	1460,999914
1016	1013,225879	1106	1102,98014	1196	1192,734401	1286	1282,488662	1376	1372,242923	1466	1461,997184
1017	1014,223149	1107	1103,97741	1197	1193,73167	1287	1283,485931	1377	1373,240192	1467	1462,994453
1018	1015,220418	1108	1104,974679	1198	1194,72894	1288	1284,483201	1378	1374,237462	1468	1463,991723
1019	1016,217688	1109	1105,971949	1199	1195,72621	1289	1285,480471	1379	1375,234731	1469	1464,988992
1020	1017,214957	1110	1106,969218	1200	1196,723479	1290	1286,47774	1380	1376,232001	1470	1465,986262
1021	1018,212227	1111	1107,966488	1201	1197,720749	1291	1287,47501	1381	1377,229271	1471	1466,983532
1022	1019,209496	1112	1108,963757	1202	1198,718018	1292	1288,472279	1382	1378,22654	1472	1467,980801
1023	1020,206766	1113	1109,961027	1203	1199,715288	1293	1289,469549	1383	1379,22381	1473	1468,978071
1024	1021,204036	1114	1110,958296	1204	1200,712557	1294	1290,466818	1384	1380,221079	1474	1469,97534
1025	1022,201305	1115	1111,955566	1205	1201,709827	1295	1291,464088	1385	1381,218349	1475	1470,97261
1026	1023,198575	1116	1112,952836	1206	1202,707097	1296	1292,461358	1386	1382,215618	1476	1471,969879
1027	1024,195844	1117	1113,950105	1207	1203,704366	1297	1293,458627	1387	1383,212888	1477	1472,967149
1028	1025,193114	1118	1114,947375	1208	1204,701636	1298	1294,455897	1388	1384,210158	1478	1473,964419
1029	1026,190383	1119	1115,944644	1209	1205,698905	1299	1295,453166	1389	1385,207427	1479	1474,961688
1030	1027,187653	1120	1116,941914	1210	1206,696175	1300	1296,450436	1390	1386,204697	1480	1475,958958
1031	1028,184923	1121	1117,939183	1211	1207,693444	1301	1297,447705	1391	1387,201966	1481	1476,956227
1032	1029,182192	1122	1118,936453	1212	1208,690714	1302	1298,444975	1392	1388,199236	1482	1477,953497
1033	1030,179462	1123	1119,933723	1213	1209,687984	1303	1299,442244	1393	1389,196505	1483	1478,950766
1034	1031,176731	1124	1120,930992	1214	1210,685253	1304	1300,439514	1394	1390,193775	1484	1479,948036
1035	1032,174001	1125	1121,928262	1215	1211,682523	1305	1301,436784	1395	1391,191045	1485	1480,945305
1036	1033,17127	1126	1122,925531	1216	1212,679792	1306	1302,434053	1396	1392,188314	1486	1481,942575
1037	1034,16854	1127	1123,922801	1217	1213,677062	1307	1303,431323	1397	1393,185584	1487	1482,939845
1038	1035,165809	1128	1124,92007	1218	1214,674331	1308	1304,428592	1398	1394,182853	1488	1483,937114
1039	1036,163079	1129	1125,91734	1219	1215,671601	1309	1305,425862	1399	1395,180123	1489	1484,934384
1040	1037,160349	1130	1126,91461	1220	1216,66887	1310	1306,423131	1400	1396,177392	1490	1485,931653
1041	1038,157618	1131	1127,911879	1221	1217,66614	1311	1307,420401	1401	1397,174662	1491	1486,928923
1042	1039,154888	1132	1128,909149	1222	1218,66341	1312	1308,417671	1402	1398,171931	1492	1487,926192
1043	1040,152157	1133	1129,906418	1223	1219,660679	1313	1309,41494	1403	1399,169201	1493	1488,923462
1044	1041,149427	1134	1130,903688	1224	1220,657949	1314	1310,41221	1404	1400,166471	1494	1489,920732
1045	1042,146696	1135	1131,900957	1225	1221,655218	1315	1311,409479	1405	1401,16374	1495	1490,918001
1046	1043,143966	1136	1132,898227	1226	1222,652488	1316	1312,406749	1406	1402,16101	1496	1491,915271
1047	1044,141236	1137	1133,895497	1227	1223,649757	1317	1313,404018	1407	1403,158279	1497	1492,91254
1048	1045,138505	1138	1134,892766	1228	1224,647027	1318	1314,401288	1408	1404,155549	1498	1493,90981
1049	1046,135775	1139	1135,890036	1229	1225,644297	1319	1315,398558	1409	1405,152818	1499	1494,907079
1050	1047,133044	1140	1136,887305	1230	1226,641566	1320	1316,395827	1410	1406,150088	1500	1495,904349
1051	1048,130314	1141	1137,884575	1231	1227,638836	1321	1317,393097	1411	1407,147358	1501	1496,901619
1052	1049,127583	1142	1138,881844	1232	1228,636105	1322	1318,390366	1412	1408,144627	1502	1497,898888
1053	1050,124853	1143	1139,879114	1233	1229,633375	1323	1319,387636	1413	1409,141897	1503	1498,896158
1054	1051,122123	1144	1140,876383	1234	1230,630644	1324	1320,384905	1414	1410,139166	1504	1499,893427
1055	1052,119392	1145	1141,873653	1235	1231,627914	1325	1321,382175	1415	1411,136436	1505	1500,890697
1056	1053,116662	1146	1142,870923	1236	1232,625184	1326	1322,379444	1416	1412,133705	1506	1501,887966
1057	1054,113931	1147	1143,868192	1237	1233,622453	1327	1323,376714	1417	1413,130975	1507	1502,885236
1058	1055,111201	1148	1144,865462	1238	1234,619723	1328	1324,373984	1418	1414,128245	1508	1503,882505
1059	1056,10847	1149	1145,862731	1239	1235,616992	1329	1325,371253	1419	1415,125514	1509	1504,879775
1060	1057,10574	1150	1146,860001	1240	1236,614262	1330	1326,368523	1420	1416,122784	1510	1505,877045
1061	1058,103009	1151	1147,85727	1241	1237,611531	1331	1327,365792	1421	1417,120053	1511	1506,874314
1062	1059,100279	1152	1148,85454	1242	1238,608801	1332	1328,363062	1422	1418,117323	1512	1507,871584
1063	1060,097549	1153	1149,85181	1243	1239,606071	1333	1329,360331	1423	1419,114592	1513	1508,868853
1064	1061,094818	1154	1150,849079	1244	1240,60334	1334	1330,357601	1424	1420,111862	1514	1509,866123
1065	1062,092088	1155	1151,846349	1245	1241,60061	1335	1331,354871	1425	1421,109132	1515	1510,863392
1066	1063,089357	1156	1152,843618	1246	1242,597879	1336	1332,35214	1426	1422,106401	1516	1511,860662
1067	1064,086627	1157	1153,840888	1247	1243,595149	1337	1333,34941	1427	1423,103671	1517	1512,857932
1068	1065,083896	1158	1154,838157	1248	1244,592418	1338	1334,346679	1428	1424,10094	1518	1513,855201
1069	1066,081166	1159	1155,835427	1249	1245,589688	1339	1335,343949	1429	1425,09821	1519	1514,852471
1070	1067,078436	1160	1156,832697	1250	1246,586957	1340	1336,341218	1430	1426,095479	1520	1515,84974
1071	1068,075705	1161	1157,829966	1251	1247,584227	1341	1337,338488	1431	1427,092749	1521	1516,84701
1072	1069,072975	1162	1158,827236	1252	1248,581497	1342	1338,335758	1432	1428,090018	1522	1517,844279
1073	1070,070244	1163	1159,824505	1253	1249,578766	1343	1339,333027	1433	1429,087288	1523	1518,841549
1074	1071,067514	1164	1160,821775	1254	1250,576036	1344	1340,330297	1434	1430,084558	1524	1519,838819
1075	1072,064783	1165	1161,819044	1255	1251,573305	1345	1341,327566	1435	1431,081827	1525	1520,836088
1076	1073,062053	1166	1162,816314	1256	1252,570575	1346	1342,324836	1436	1432,079097	1526	1521,833358
1077	1074,059323	1167	1163,813583	1257	1253,567844	1347	1343,322105	1437	1433,076366	1527	1522,830627
1078	1075,056592	1168	1164,810853	1258	1254,565114	1348	1344,319375	1438	1434,073636	1528	1523,827897
1079	1076,053862	1169	1165,808123	1259	1255,562384	1349	1345,316644	1439	1435,070905	1529	1524,825166
1080	1077,051131	1170	1166,805392	1260	1256,559653	1350	1346,313914	1440	1436,068175	1530	1525,822436
1081	1078,048401	1171	1167,802662	1261	1257,556923	1351	1347,311184	1441	1437,065445	1531	1526,819706
1082	1079,04567	1172	1168,799931	1262	1258,554192	1352	1348,308453	1442	1438,062714	1532	1527,816975
1083	1080,04294	1173	1169,797201	1263	1259,551462	1353	1349,305723	1443	1439,059984	1533	1528,814245
1084	1081,04021	1174	1170,79447	1264	1260,548731	1354	1350,302992	1444	1440,057253	1534	1529,811514
1085	1082,037479	1175	1171,79174	1265	1261,546001	1355	1351,300262	1445	1441,054523	1535	1530,808784
1086	1083,034749	1176	1172,78901	1266	1262,543271	1356	1352,297531	1446	1442,051792	1536	1531,806053
1087	1084,032018	1177	1173,786279	1267	1263,54054	1357	1353,294801	1447	1443,049062	1537	1532,803323
1088	1085,029288	1178	1174,783549	1268	1264,53781	1358	1354,292071	1448	1444,046332	1538	1533,800592
1089	1086,026557	1179	1175,780818	1269	1265,535079	1359	1355,28934	1449	1445,043601	1539	1534,797862
1090	1087,023827	1180	1176,778088	1270	1266,532349	1360	1356,28661	1450	1446,040871	1540	1535,795132
1091	1088,021096	1181	1177,775357	1271	1267,529618	1361	1357,283879	1451	1447,03814	1541	1536,792401
1092	1089,018366	1182	1178,772627	1272	1268,526888	1362	1358,281149	1452	1448,03541	1542	1537,789671
1093	1090,015636	1183	1179,769897	1273	1269,524157	1363	1359,278418	1453	1449,032679	1543	1538,78694
1094	1091,012905	1184	1180,767166	1274	1270,521427	1364	1360,275688	1454	1450,029949	1544	1539,78421
1095	1092,010175	1185	1181,764436	1275	1271,518697	1365	1361,272958	1455	1451,027218	1545	1540,781479
1096	1093,007444	1186	1182,761705	1276	1272,515966	1366	1362,270227	1456	1452,024488	1546	1541,778749
1097	1094,004714	1187	1183,758975	1277	1273,513236	1367	1363,267497	1457	1453,021758	1547	1542,776019
1098	1095,001983	1188	1184,756244	1278	1274,510505	1368	1364,264766	1458	1454,019027	1548	1543,773288
1099	1095,999253	1189	1185,753514	1279	1275,507775	1369	1365,262036	1459	1455,016297	1549	1544,770558
1100	1096,996523	1190	1186,750784	1280	1276,505044	1370	1366,259305	1460	1456,013566	1550	1545,767827
1101	1097,993792	1191	1187,748053	1281	1277,502314	1371	1367,256575	1461	1457,010836	1551	1546,765097
1102	1098,991062	1192	1188,745323	1282	1278,499584	1372	1368,253845	1462	1458,008105	1552	1547,762366
1103	1099,988331	1193	1189,742592	1283	1279,496853	1373	1369,251114	1463	1459,005375	1553	1548,759636
1104	1100,985601	1194	1190,739862	1284	1280,494123	1374	1370,248384	1464	1460,002645	1554	1549,756906

1555	1550,754175	1645	1640,508436	1735	1730,262697	1825	1820,016958	1915	1909,771219	2005	1999,52548
1556	1551,751445	1646	1641,505706	1736	1731,259967	1826	1821,014227	1916	1910,768488	2006	2000,522749
1557	1552,748714	1647	1642,502975	1737	1732,257236	1827	1822,011497	1917	1911,765758	2007	2001,520019
1558	1553,745984	1648	1643,500245	1738	1733,254506	1828	1823,008767	1918	1912,763028	2008	2002,517288
1559	1554,743253	1649	1644,497514	1739	1734,251775	1829	1824,006036	1919	1913,760297	2009	2003,514558
1560	1555,740523	1650	1645,494784	1740	1735,249045	1830	1825,003306	1920	1914,757567	2010	2004,511828
1561	1556,737792	1651	1646,492053	1741	1736,246314	1831	1826,000575	1921	1915,754836	2011	2005,509097
1562	1557,735062	1652	1647,489323	1742	1737,243584	1832	1826,997845	1922	1916,752106	2012	2006,506367
1563	1558,732332	1653	1648,486593	1743	1738,240853	1833	1827,995114	1923	1917,749375	2013	2007,503636
1564	1559,729601	1654	1649,483862	1744	1739,238123	1834	1828,992384	1924	1918,746645	2014	2008,500906
1565	1560,726871	1655	1650,481132	1745	1740,235393	1835	1829,989654	1925	1919,743914	2015	2009,498175
1566	1561,72414	1656	1651,478401	1746	1741,232662	1836	1830,986923	1926	1920,741184	2016	2010,495445
1567	1562,72141	1657	1652,475671	1747	1742,229932	1837	1831,984193	1927	1921,738454	2017	2011,492715
1568	1563,718679	1658	1653,47294	1748	1743,227201	1838	1832,981462	1928	1922,735723	2018	2012,489984
1569	1564,715949	1659	1654,47021	1749	1744,224471	1839	1833,978732	1929	1923,732993	2019	2013,487254
1570	1565,713219	1660	1655,46748	1750	1745,22174	1840	1834,976001	1930	1924,730262	2020	2014,484523
1571	1566,710488	1661	1656,464749	1751	1746,21901	1841	1835,973271	1931	1925,727532	2021	2015,481793
1572	1567,707758	1662	1657,462019	1752	1747,21628	1842	1836,970541	1932	1926,724801	2022	2016,479062
1573	1568,705027	1663	1658,459288	1753	1748,213549	1843	1837,96781	1933	1927,722071	2023	2017,476332
1574	1569,702297	1664	1659,456558	1754	1749,210819	1844	1838,96508	1934	1928,719341	2024	2018,473602
1575	1570,699566	1665	1660,453827	1755	1750,208088	1845	1839,962349	1935	1929,71661	2025	2019,470871
1576	1571,696836	1666	1661,451097	1756	1751,205358	1846	1840,959619	1936	1930,71388	2026	2020,468141
1577	1572,694106	1667	1662,448366	1757	1752,202627	1847	1841,956888	1937	1931,711149	2027	2021,46541
1578	1573,691375	1668	1663,445636	1758	1753,199897	1848	1842,954158	1938	1932,708419	2028	2022,46268
1579	1574,688645	1669	1664,442906	1759	1754,197167	1849	1843,951427	1939	1933,705688	2029	2023,459949
1580	1575,685914	1670	1665,440175	1760	1755,194436	1850	1844,948697	1940	1934,702958	2030	2024,457219
1581	1576,683184	1671	1666,437445	1761	1756,191706	1851	1845,945967	1941	1935,700228	2031	2025,454488
1582	1577,680453	1672	1667,434714	1762	1757,188975	1852	1846,943236	1942	1936,697497	2032	2026,451758
1583	1578,677723	1673	1668,431984	1763	1758,186245	1853	1847,940506	1943	1937,694767	2033	2027,449028
1584	1579,674993	1674	1669,429253	1764	1759,183514	1854	1848,937775	1944	1938,692036	2034	2028,446297
1585	1580,672262	1675	1670,426523	1765	1760,180784	1855	1849,935045	1945	1939,689306	2035	2029,443567
1586	1581,669532	1676	1671,423793	1766	1761,178054	1856	1850,932314	1946	1940,686575	2036	2030,440836
1587	1582,666801	1677	1672,421062	1767	1762,175323	1857	1851,929584	1947	1941,683845	2037	2031,438106
1588	1583,664071	1678	1673,418332	1768	1763,172593	1858	1852,926854	1948	1942,681115	2038	2032,435375
1589	1584,66134	1679	1674,415601	1769	1764,169862	1859	1853,924123	1949	1943,678384	2039	2033,432645
1590	1585,65861	1680	1675,412871	1770	1765,167132	1860	1854,921393	1950	1944,675654	2040	2034,429915
1591	1586,655879	1681	1676,41014	1771	1766,164401	1861	1855,918662	1951	1945,672923	2041	2035,427184
1592	1587,653149	1682	1677,40741	1772	1767,161671	1862	1856,915932	1952	1946,670193	2042	2036,424454
1593	1588,650419	1683	1678,40468	1773	1768,15894	1863	1857,913201	1953	1947,667462	2043	2037,421723
1594	1589,647688	1684	1679,401949	1774	1769,15621	1864	1858,910471	1954	1948,664732	2044	2038,418993
1595	1590,644958	1685	1680,399219	1775	1770,15348	1865	1859,907741	1955	1949,662001	2045	2039,416262
1596	1591,642227	1686	1681,396488	1776	1771,150749	1866	1860,90501	1956	1950,659271	2046	2040,413532
1597	1592,639497	1687	1682,393758	1777	1772,148019	1867	1861,90228	1957	1951,656541	2047	2041,410802
1598	1593,636766	1688	1683,391027	1778	1773,145288	1868	1862,899549	1958	1952,65381	2048	2042,408071
1599	1594,634036	1689	1684,388297	1779	1774,142558	1869	1863,896819	1959	1953,65108	2049	2043,405341
1600	1595,631306	1690	1685,385566	1780	1775,139827	1870	1864,894088	1960	1954,648349	2050	2044,40261
1601	1596,628575	1691	1686,382836	1781	1776,137097	1871	1865,891358	1961	1955,645619	2051	2045,39988
1602	1597,625845	1692	1687,380106	1782	1777,134367	1872	1866,888628	1962	1956,642888	2052	2046,397149
1603	1598,623114	1693	1688,377375	1783	1778,131636	1873	1867,885897	1963	1957,640158	2053	2047,394419
1604	1599,620384	1694	1689,374645	1784	1779,128906	1874	1868,883167	1964	1958,637428	2054	2048,391689
1605	1600,617653	1695	1690,371914	1785	1780,126175	1875	1869,880436	1965	1959,634697	2055	2049,388958
1606	1601,614923	1696	1691,369184	1786	1781,123445	1876	1870,877706	1966	1960,631967	2056	2050,386228
1607	1602,612193	1697	1692,366453	1787	1782,120714	1877	1871,874975	1967	1961,629236	2057	2051,383497
1608	1603,609462	1698	1693,363723	1788	1783,117984	1878	1872,872245	1968	1962,626506	2058	2052,380767
1609	1604,606732	1699	1694,360993	1789	1784,115254	1879	1873,869514	1969	1963,623775	2059	2053,378036
1610	1605,604001	1700	1695,358262	1790	1785,112523	1880	1874,866784	1970	1964,621045	2060	2054,375306
1611	1606,601271	1701	1696,355532	1791	1786,109793	1881	1875,864054	1971	1965,618315	2061	2055,372575
1612	1607,59854	1702	1697,352801	1792	1787,107062	1882	1876,861323	1972	1966,615584	2062	2056,369845
1613	1608,59581	1703	1698,350071	1793	1788,104332	1883	1877,858593	1973	1967,612854	2063	2057,367115
1614	1609,593079	1704	1699,34734	1794	1789,101601	1884	1878,855862	1974	1968,610123	2064	2058,364384
1615	1610,590349	1705	1700,34461	1795	1790,098871	1885	1879,853132	1975	1969,607393	2065	2059,361654
1616	1611,587619	1706	1701,34188	1796	1791,09614	1886	1880,850401	1976	1970,604662	2066	2060,358923
1617	1612,584888	1707	1702,339149	1797	1792,09341	1887	1881,847671	1977	1971,601932	2067	2061,356193
1618	1613,582158	1708	1703,336419	1798	1793,09068	1888	1882,844941	1978	1972,599201	2068	2062,353462
1619	1614,579427	1709	1704,333688	1799	1794,087949	1889	1883,84221	1979	1973,596471	2069	2063,350732
1620	1615,576697	1710	1705,330958	1800	1795,085219	1890	1884,83948	1980	1974,593741	2070	2064,348002
1621	1616,573966	1711	1706,328227	1801	1796,082488	1891	1885,836749	1981	1975,59101	2071	2065,345271
1622	1617,571236	1712	1707,325497	1802	1797,079758	1892	1886,834019	1982	1976,58828	2072	2066,342541
1623	1618,568506	1713	1708,322767	1803	1798,077027	1893	1887,831288	1983	1977,585549	2073	2067,33981
1624	1619,565775	1714	1709,320036	1804	1799,074297	1894	1888,828558	1984	1978,582819	2074	2068,33708
1625	1620,563045	1715	1710,317306	1805	1800,071567	1895	1889,825828	1985	1979,580088	2075	2069,334349
1626	1621,560314	1716	1711,314575	1806	1801,068836	1896	1890,823097	1986	1980,577358	2076	2070,331619
1627	1622,557584	1717	1712,311845	1807	1802,066106	1897	1891,820367	1987	1981,574628	2077	2071,328889
1628	1623,554853	1718	1713,309114	1808	1803,063375	1898	1892,817636	1988	1982,571897	2078	2072,326158
1629	1624,552123	1719	1714,306384	1809	1804,060645	1899	1893,814906	1989	1983,569167	2079	2073,323428
1630	1625,549393	1720	1715,303653	1810	1805,057914	1900	1894,812175	1990	1984,566436	2080	2074,320697
1631	1626,546662	1721	1716,300923	1811	1806,055184	1901	1895,809445	1991	1985,563706	2081	2075,317967
1632	1627,543932	1722	1717,298193	1812	1807,052454	1902	1896,806714	1992	1986,560975	2082	2076,315236
1633	1628,541201	1723	1718,295462	1813	1808,049723	1903	1897,803984	1993	1987,558245	2083	2077,312506
1634	1629,538471	1724	1719,292732	1814	1809,046993	1904	1898,801254	1994	1988,555515	2084	2078,309775
1635	1630,53574	1725	1720,290001	1815	1810,044262	1905	1899,798523	1995	1989,552784	2085	2079,307045
1636	1631,53301	1726	1721,287271	1816	1811,041532	1906	1900,795793	1996	1990,550054	2086	2080,304315
1637	1632,530279	1727	1722,28454	1817	1812,038801	1907	1901,793062	1997	1991,547323	2087	2081,301584
1638	1633,527549	1728	1723,28181	1818	1813,036071	1908	1902,790332	1998	1992,544593	2088	2082,298854
1639	1634,524819	1729	1724,27908	1819	1814,033341	1909	1903,787601	1999	1993,541862	2089	2083,296123
1640	1635,522088	1730	1725,276349	1820	1815,03061	1910	1904,784871	2000	1994,539132	2090	2084,293393
1641	1636,519358	1731	1726,273619	1821	1816,02788	1911	1905,782141	2001	1995,536402	2091	2085,290662
1642	1637,516627	1732	1727,270888	1822	1817,025149	1912	1906,77941	2002	1996,533671	2092	2086,287932
1643	1638,513897	1733	1728,268158	1823	1818,022419	1913	1907,77668	2003	1997,530941	2093	2087,285202
1644	1639,511166	1734	1729,265427	1824	1819,019688	1914	1908,773949	2004	1998,52821	2094	2088,282471

TABLE TO FIND OUT THE POINT A IN EARTH RETURNS 161

2095	2089,279741	2185	2179,034002	2275	2268,788263	2365	2358,542524	2455	2448,296784	2545	2538,051045
2096	2090,27701	2186	2180,031271	2276	2269,785532	2366	2359,539793	2456	2449,294054	2546	2539,048315
2097	2091,27428	2187	2181,028541	2277	2270,782802	2367	2360,537063	2457	2450,291324	2547	2540,045585
2098	2092,271549	2188	2182,02581	2278	2271,780071	2368	2361,534332	2458	2451,288593	2548	2541,042854
2099	2093,268819	2189	2183,02308	2279	2272,777341	2369	2362,531602	2459	2452,285863	2549	2542,040124
2100	2094,266089	2190	2184,020349	2280	2273,77461	2370	2363,528871	2460	2453,283132	2550	2543,037393
2101	2095,263358	2191	2185,017619	2281	2274,77188	2371	2364,526141	2461	2454,280402	2551	2544,034663
2102	2096,260628	2192	2186,014889	2282	2275,76915	2372	2365,52341	2462	2455,277671	2552	2545,031932
2103	2097,257897	2193	2187,012158	2283	2276,766419	2373	2366,52068	2463	2456,274941	2553	2546,029202
2104	2098,255167	2194	2188,009428	2284	2277,763689	2374	2367,51795	2464	2457,272211	2554	2547,026471
2105	2099,252436	2195	2189,006697	2285	2278,760958	2375	2368,515219	2465	2458,26948	2555	2548,023741
2106	2100,249706	2196	2190,003967	2286	2279,758228	2376	2369,512489	2466	2459,26675	2556	2549,021011
2107	2101,246976	2197	2191,001236	2287	2280,755497	2377	2370,509758	2467	2460,264019	2557	2550,01828
2108	2102,244245	2198	2191,998506	2288	2281,752767	2378	2371,507028	2468	2461,261289	2558	2551,01555
2109	2103,241515	2199	2192,995776	2289	2282,750037	2379	2372,504297	2469	2462,258558	2559	2552,012819
2110	2104,238784	2200	2193,993045	2290	2283,747306	2380	2373,501567	2470	2463,255828	2560	2553,010089
2111	2105,236054	2201	2194,990315	2291	2284,744576	2381	2374,498837	2471	2464,253098	2561	2554,007358
2112	2106,233323	2202	2195,987584	2292	2285,741845	2382	2375,496106	2472	2465,250367	2562	2555,004628
2113	2107,230593	2203	2196,984854	2293	2286,739115	2383	2376,493376	2473	2466,247637	2563	2556,001898
2114	2108,227862	2204	2197,982123	2294	2287,736384	2384	2377,490645	2474	2467,244906	2564	2556,999167
2115	2109,225132	2205	2198,979393	2295	2288,733654	2385	2378,487915	2475	2468,242176	2565	2557,996437
2116	2110,222402	2206	2199,976663	2296	2289,730923	2386	2379,485184	2476	2469,239445	2566	2558,993706
2117	2111,219671	2207	2200,973932	2297	2290,728193	2387	2380,482454	2477	2470,236715	2567	2559,990976
2118	2112,216941	2208	2201,971202	2298	2291,725463	2388	2381,479724	2478	2471,233984	2568	2560,988245
2119	2113,21421	2209	2202,968471	2299	2292,722732	2389	2382,476993	2479	2472,231254	2569	2561,985515
2120	2114,21148	2210	2203,965741	2300	2293,720002	2390	2383,474263	2480	2473,228524	2570	2562,982785
2121	2115,208749	2211	2204,96301	2301	2294,717271	2391	2384,471532	2481	2474,225793	2571	2563,980054
2122	2116,206019	2212	2205,96028	2302	2295,714541	2392	2385,468802	2482	2475,223063	2572	2564,977324
2123	2117,203289	2213	2206,957549	2303	2296,71181	2393	2386,466071	2483	2476,220332	2573	2565,974593
2124	2118,200558	2214	2207,954819	2304	2297,70908	2394	2387,463341	2484	2477,217602	2574	2566,971863
2125	2119,197828	2215	2208,952089	2305	2298,70635	2395	2388,460611	2485	2478,214871	2575	2567,969132
2126	2120,195097	2216	2209,949358	2306	2299,703619	2396	2389,45788	2486	2479,212141	2576	2568,966402
2127	2121,192367	2217	2210,946628	2307	2300,700889	2397	2390,45515	2487	2480,209411	2577	2569,963672
2128	2122,189636	2218	2211,943897	2308	2301,698158	2398	2391,452419	2488	2481,20668	2578	2570,960941
2129	2123,186906	2219	2212,941167	2309	2302,695428	2399	2392,449689	2489	2482,20395	2579	2571,958211
2130	2124,184176	2220	2213,938436	2310	2303,692697	2400	2393,446958	2490	2483,201219	2580	2572,95548
2131	2125,181445	2221	2214,935706	2311	2304,689967	2401	2394,444228	2491	2484,198489	2581	2573,95275
2132	2126,178715	2222	2215,932976	2312	2305,687237	2402	2395,441497	2492	2485,195758	2582	2574,950019
2133	2127,175984	2223	2216,930245	2313	2306,684506	2403	2396,438767	2493	2486,193028	2583	2575,947289
2134	2128,173254	2224	2217,927515	2314	2307,681776	2404	2397,436037	2494	2487,190298	2584	2576,944558
2135	2129,170523	2225	2218,924784	2315	2308,679045	2405	2398,433306	2495	2488,187567	2585	2577,941828
2136	2130,167793	2226	2219,922054	2316	2309,676315	2406	2399,430576	2496	2489,184837	2586	2578,939098
2137	2131,165062	2227	2220,919323	2317	2310,673584	2407	2400,427845	2497	2490,182106	2587	2579,936367
2138	2132,162332	2228	2221,916593	2318	2311,670854	2408	2401,425115	2498	2491,179376	2588	2580,933637
2139	2133,159602	2229	2222,913863	2319	2312,668123	2409	2402,422384	2499	2492,176645	2589	2581,930906
2140	2134,156871	2230	2223,911132	2320	2313,665393	2410	2403,419654	2500	2493,173915	2590	2582,928176
2141	2135,154141	2231	2224,908402	2321	2314,662663	2411	2404,416924	2501	2494,171184	2591	2583,925445
2142	2136,15141	2232	2225,905671	2322	2315,659932	2412	2405,414193	2502	2495,168454	2592	2584,922715
2143	2137,14868	2233	2226,902941	2323	2316,657202	2413	2406,411463	2503	2496,165724	2593	2585,919985
2144	2138,145949	2234	2227,90021	2324	2317,654471	2414	2407,408732	2504	2497,162993	2594	2586,917254
2145	2139,143219	2235	2228,89748	2325	2318,651741	2415	2408,406002	2505	2498,160263	2595	2587,914524
2146	2140,140489	2236	2229,89475	2326	2319,64901	2416	2409,403271	2506	2499,157532	2596	2588,911793
2147	2141,137758	2237	2230,892019	2327	2320,64628	2417	2410,400541	2507	2500,154802	2597	2589,909063
2148	2142,135028	2238	2231,889289	2328	2321,64355	2418	2411,397811	2508	2501,152071	2598	2590,906332
2149	2143,132297	2239	2232,886558	2329	2322,640819	2419	2412,39508	2509	2502,149341	2599	2591,903602
2150	2144,129567	2240	2233,883828	2330	2323,638089	2420	2413,39235	2510	2503,146611	2600	2592,900872
2151	2145,126836	2241	2234,881097	2331	2324,635358	2421	2414,389619	2511	2504,14388	2601	2593,898141
2152	2146,124106	2242	2235,878367	2332	2325,632628	2422	2415,386889	2512	2505,14115	2602	2594,895411
2153	2147,121376	2243	2236,875636	2333	2326,629897	2423	2416,384158	2513	2506,138419	2603	2595,89268
2154	2148,118645	2244	2237,872906	2334	2327,627167	2424	2417,381428	2514	2507,135689	2604	2596,88995
2155	2149,115915	2245	2238,870176	2335	2328,624437	2425	2418,378697	2515	2508,132958	2605	2597,887219
2156	2150,113184	2246	2239,867445	2336	2329,621706	2426	2419,375967	2516	2509,130228	2606	2598,884489
2157	2151,110454	2247	2240,864715	2337	2330,618976	2427	2420,373237	2517	2510,127498	2607	2599,881758
2158	2152,107723	2248	2241,861984	2338	2331,616245	2428	2421,370506	2518	2511,124767	2608	2600,879028
2159	2153,104993	2249	2242,859254	2339	2332,613515	2429	2422,367776	2519	2512,122037	2609	2601,876298
2160	2154,102263	2250	2243,856523	2340	2333,610784	2430	2423,365045	2520	2513,119306	2610	2602,873567
2161	2155,099532	2251	2244,853793	2341	2334,608054	2431	2424,362315	2521	2514,116576	2611	2603,870837
2162	2156,096802	2252	2245,851063	2342	2335,605324	2432	2425,359584	2522	2515,113845	2612	2604,868106
2163	2157,094071	2253	2246,848332	2343	2336,602593	2433	2426,356854	2523	2516,111115	2613	2605,865376
2164	2158,091341	2254	2247,845602	2344	2337,599863	2434	2427,354124	2524	2517,108385	2614	2606,862645
2165	2159,08861	2255	2248,842871	2345	2338,597132	2435	2428,351393	2525	2518,105654	2615	2607,859915
2166	2160,08588	2256	2249,840141	2346	2339,594402	2436	2429,348663	2526	2519,102924	2616	2608,857185
2167	2161,083149	2257	2250,83741	2347	2340,591671	2437	2430,345932	2527	2520,100193	2617	2609,854454
2168	2162,080419	2258	2251,83468	2348	2341,588941	2438	2431,343202	2528	2521,097463	2618	2610,851724
2169	2163,077689	2259	2252,83195	2349	2342,58621	2439	2432,340471	2529	2522,094732	2619	2611,848993
2170	2164,074958	2260	2253,829219	2350	2343,58348	2440	2433,337741	2530	2523,092002	2620	2612,846263
2171	2165,072228	2261	2254,826489	2351	2344,58075	2441	2434,335011	2531	2524,089271	2621	2613,843532
2172	2166,069497	2262	2255,823758	2352	2345,578019	2442	2435,33228	2532	2525,086541	2622	2614,840802
2173	2167,066767	2263	2256,821028	2353	2346,575289	2443	2436,32955	2533	2526,083811	2623	2615,838072
2174	2168,064036	2264	2257,818297	2354	2347,572558	2444	2437,326819	2534	2527,08108	2624	2616,835341
2175	2169,061306	2265	2258,815567	2355	2348,569828	2445	2438,324089	2535	2528,07835	2625	2617,832611
2176	2170,058576	2266	2259,812836	2356	2349,567097	2446	2439,321358	2536	2529,075619	2626	2618,82988
2177	2171,055845	2267	2260,810106	2357	2350,564367	2447	2440,318628	2537	2530,072889	2627	2619,82715
2178	2172,053115	2268	2261,807376	2358	2351,561637	2448	2441,315898	2538	2531,070158	2628	2620,824419
2179	2173,050384	2269	2262,804645	2359	2352,558906	2449	2442,313167	2539	2532,067428	2629	2621,821689
2180	2174,047654	2270	2263,801915	2360	2353,556176	2450	2443,310437	2540	2533,064698	2630	2622,818959
2181	2175,044923	2271	2264,799184	2361	2354,553445	2451	2444,307706	2541	2534,061967	2631	2623,816228
2182	2176,042193	2272	2265,796454	2362	2355,550715	2452	2445,304976	2542	2535,059237	2632	2624,813498
2183	2177,039463	2273	2266,793723	2363	2356,547984	2453	2446,302245	2543	2536,056506	2633	2625,810767
2184	2178,036732	2274	2267,790993	2364	2357,545254	2454	2447,299515	2544	2537,053776	2634	2626,808037

LUNAR RETURNS AND EARTH RETURNS

2635	2627,805306	2725	2717,559567	2815	2807,313828	2905	2897,068089	2995	2986,82235	3085	3076,576611
2636	2628,802576	2726	2718,556837	2816	2808,311098	2906	2898,065359	2996	2987,81962	3086	3077,573881
2637	2629,799845	2727	2719,554106	2817	2809,308367	2907	2899,062628	2997	2988,816889	3087	3078,57115
2638	2630,797115	2728	2720,551376	2818	2810,305637	2908	2900,059898	2998	2989,814159	3088	3079,56842
2639	2631,794385	2729	2721,548646	2819	2811,302906	2909	2901,057167	2999	2990,811428	3089	3080,565689
2640	2632,791654	2730	2722,545915	2820	2812,300176	2910	2902,054437	3000	2991,808698	3090	3081,562959
2641	2633,788924	2731	2723,543185	2821	2813,297446	2911	2903,051707	3001	2992,805967	3091	3082,560228
2642	2634,786193	2732	2724,540454	2822	2814,294715	2912	2904,048976	3002	2993,803237	3092	3083,557498
2643	2635,783463	2733	2725,537724	2823	2815,291985	2913	2905,046246	3003	2994,800507	3093	3084,554768
2644	2636,780732	2734	2726,534993	2824	2816,289254	2914	2906,043515	3004	2995,797776	3094	3085,552037
2645	2637,778002	2735	2727,532263	2825	2817,286524	2915	2907,040785	3005	2996,795046	3095	3086,549307
2646	2638,775272	2736	2728,529533	2826	2818,283793	2916	2908,038054	3006	2997,792315	3096	3087,546576
2647	2639,772541	2737	2729,526802	2827	2819,281063	2917	2909,035324	3007	2998,789585	3097	3088,543846
2648	2640,769811	2738	2730,524072	2828	2820,278333	2918	2910,032594	3008	2999,786854	3098	3089,541115
2649	2641,76708	2739	2731,521341	2829	2821,275602	2919	2911,029863	3009	3000,784124	3099	3090,538385
2650	2642,76435	2740	2732,518611	2830	2822,272872	2920	2912,027133	3010	3001,781394	3100	3091,535655
2651	2643,761619	2741	2733,51588	2831	2823,270141	2921	2913,024402	3011	3002,778663	3101	3092,532924
2652	2644,758889	2742	2734,51315	2832	2824,267411	2922	2914,021672	3012	3003,775933	3102	3093,530194
2653	2645,756159	2743	2735,510419	2833	2825,26468	2923	2915,018941	3013	3004,773202	3103	3094,527463
2654	2646,753428	2744	2736,507689	2834	2826,26195	2924	2916,016211	3014	3005,770472	3104	3095,524733
2655	2647,750698	2745	2737,504959	2835	2827,25922	2925	2917,01348	3015	3006,767741	3105	3096,522002
2656	2648,747967	2746	2738,502228	2836	2828,256489	2926	2918,01075	3016	3007,765011	3106	3097,519272
2657	2649,745237	2747	2739,499498	2837	2829,253759	2927	2919,00802	3017	3008,762281	3107	3098,516541
2658	2650,742506	2748	2740,496767	2838	2830,251028	2928	2920,005289	3018	3009,75955	3108	3099,513811
2659	2651,739776	2749	2741,494037	2839	2831,248298	2929	2921,002559	3019	3010,75682	3109	3100,511081
2660	2652,737045	2750	2742,491308	2840	2832,245567	2930	2921,999828	3020	3011,754089	3110	3101,50835
2661	2653,734315	2751	2743,488576	2841	2833,242837	2931	2922,997098	3021	3012,751359	3111	3102,50562
2662	2654,731585	2752	2744,485846	2842	2834,240106	2932	2923,994367	3022	3013,748628	3112	3103,502889
2663	2655,728854	2753	2745,483115	2843	2835,237376	2933	2924,991637	3023	3014,745898	3113	3104,500159
2664	2656,726124	2754	2746,480385	2844	2836,234646	2934	2925,988907	3024	3015,743168	3114	3105,497428
2665	2657,723393	2755	2747,477654	2845	2837,231915	2935	2926,986176	3025	3016,740437	3115	3106,494698
2666	2658,720663	2756	2748,474924	2846	2838,229185	2936	2927,983446	3026	3017,737707	3116	3107,491968
2667	2659,717932	2757	2749,472193	2847	2839,226454	2937	2928,980715	3027	3018,734976	3117	3108,489237
2668	2660,715202	2758	2750,469463	2848	2840,223724	2938	2929,977985	3028	3019,732246	3118	3109,486507
2669	2661,712472	2759	2751,466733	2849	2841,220993	2939	2930,975254	3029	3020,729515	3119	3110,483776
2670	2662,709741	2760	2752,464002	2850	2842,218263	2940	2931,972524	3030	3021,726785	3120	3111,481046
2671	2663,707011	2761	2753,461272	2851	2843,215533	2941	2932,969794	3031	3022,724054	3121	3112,478315
2672	2664,70428	2762	2754,458541	2852	2844,212802	2942	2933,967063	3032	3023,721324	3122	3113,475585
2673	2665,70155	2763	2755,455811	2853	2845,210072	2943	2934,964333	3033	3024,718594	3123	3114,472855
2674	2666,698819	2764	2756,45308	2854	2846,207341	2944	2935,961602	3034	3025,715863	3124	3115,470124
2675	2667,696089	2765	2757,45035	2855	2847,204611	2945	2936,958872	3035	3026,713133	3125	3116,467394
2676	2668,693359	2766	2758,447619	2856	2848,20188	2946	2937,956141	3036	3027,710402	3126	3117,464663
2677	2669,690628	2767	2759,444889	2857	2849,19915	2947	2938,953411	3037	3028,707672	3127	3118,461933
2678	2670,687898	2768	2760,442159	2858	2850,19642	2948	2939,95068	3038	3029,704941	3128	3119,459202
2679	2671,685167	2769	2761,439428	2859	2851,193689	2949	2940,94795	3039	3030,702211	3129	3120,456472
2680	2672,682437	2770	2762,436698	2860	2852,190959	2950	2941,94522	3040	3031,699481	3130	3121,453741
2681	2673,679706	2771	2763,433967	2861	2853,188228	2951	2942,942489	3041	3032,69675	3131	3122,451011
2682	2674,676976	2772	2764,431237	2862	2854,185498	2952	2943,939759	3042	3033,69402	3132	3123,448281
2683	2675,674246	2773	2765,428506	2863	2855,182767	2953	2944,937028	3043	3034,691289	3133	3124,44555
2684	2676,671515	2774	2766,425776	2864	2856,180037	2954	2945,934298	3044	3035,688559	3134	3125,44282
2685	2677,668785	2775	2767,423046	2865	2857,177307	2955	2946,931567	3045	3036,685828	3135	3126,440089
2686	2678,666054	2776	2768,420315	2866	2858,174576	2956	2947,928837	3046	3037,683098	3136	3127,437359
2687	2679,663324	2777	2769,417585	2867	2859,171846	2957	2948,926107	3047	3038,680368	3137	3128,434628
2688	2680,660593	2778	2770,414854	2868	2860,169115	2958	2949,923376	3048	3039,677637	3138	3129,431898
2689	2681,657863	2779	2771,412124	2869	2861,166385	2959	2950,920646	3049	3040,674907	3139	3130,429168
2690	2682,655132	2780	2772,409393	2870	2862,163654	2960	2951,917915	3050	3041,672176	3140	3131,426437
2691	2683,652402	2781	2773,406663	2871	2863,160924	2961	2952,915185	3051	3042,669446	3141	3132,423707
2692	2684,649672	2782	2774,403933	2872	2864,158193	2962	2953,912454	3052	3043,666715	3142	3133,420976
2693	2685,646941	2783	2775,401202	2873	2865,155463	2963	2954,909724	3053	3044,663985	3143	3134,418246
2694	2686,644211	2784	2776,398472	2874	2866,152733	2964	2955,906994	3054	3045,661254	3144	3135,415515
2695	2687,64148	2785	2777,395741	2875	2867,150002	2965	2956,904263	3055	3046,658524	3145	3136,412785
2696	2688,63875	2786	2778,393011	2876	2868,147272	2966	2957,901533	3056	3047,655794	3146	3137,410055
2697	2689,636019	2787	2779,39028	2877	2869,144541	2967	2958,898802	3057	3048,653063	3147	3138,407324
2698	2690,633289	2788	2780,38755	2878	2870,141811	2968	2959,896072	3058	3049,650333	3148	3139,404594
2699	2691,630559	2789	2781,384819	2879	2871,13908	2969	2960,893341	3059	3050,647602	3149	3140,401863
2700	2692,627828	2790	2782,382089	2880	2872,13635	2970	2961,890611	3060	3051,644872	3150	3141,399133
2701	2693,625098	2791	2783,379359	2881	2873,13362	2971	2962,887881	3061	3052,642141	3151	3142,396402
2702	2694,622367	2792	2784,376628	2882	2874,130889	2972	2963,88515	3062	3053,639411	3152	3143,393672
2703	2695,619637	2793	2785,373898	2883	2875,128159	2973	2964,88242	3063	3054,636681	3153	3144,390942
2704	2696,616906	2794	2786,371167	2884	2876,125428	2974	2965,879689	3064	3055,63395	3154	3145,388211
2705	2697,614176	2795	2787,368437	2885	2877,122698	2975	2966,876959	3065	3056,63122	3155	3146,385481
2706	2698,611446	2796	2788,365706	2886	2878,119967	2976	2967,874228	3066	3057,628489	3156	3147,38275
2707	2699,608715	2797	2789,362976	2887	2879,117237	2977	2968,871498	3067	3058,625759	3157	3148,38002
2708	2700,605985	2798	2790,360246	2888	2880,114507	2978	2969,868767	3068	3059,623028	3158	3149,377289
2709	2701,603254	2799	2791,357515	2889	2881,111776	2979	2970,866037	3069	3060,620298	3159	3150,374559
2710	2702,600524	2800	2792,354785	2890	2882,109046	2980	2971,863307	3070	3061,617568	3160	3151,371828
2711	2703,597793	2801	2793,352054	2891	2883,106315	2981	2972,860576	3071	3062,614837	3161	3152,369098
2712	2704,595063	2802	2794,349324	2892	2884,103585	2982	2973,857846	3072	3063,612107	3162	3153,366368
2713	2705,592332	2803	2795,346593	2893	2885,100854	2983	2974,855115	3073	3064,609376	3163	3154,363637
2714	2706,589602	2804	2796,343863	2894	2886,098124	2984	2975,852385	3074	3065,606646	3164	3155,360907
2715	2707,586872	2805	2797,341133	2895	2887,095393	2985	2976,849654	3075	3066,603915	3165	3156,358176
2716	2708,584141	2806	2798,338402	2896	2888,092663	2986	2977,846924	3076	3067,601185	3166	3157,355446
2717	2709,581411	2807	2799,335672	2897	2889,089933	2987	2978,844194	3077	3068,598454	3167	3158,352715
2718	2710,57868	2808	2800,332941	2898	2890,087202	2988	2979,841463	3078	3069,595724	3168	3159,349985
2719	2711,57595	2809	2801,330211	2899	2891,084472	2989	2980,838733	3079	3070,592994	3169	3160,347255
2720	2712,573219	2810	2802,32748	2900	2892,081741	2990	2981,836002	3080	3071,590263	3170	3161,344524
2721	2713,570489	2811	2803,32475	2901	2893,079011	2991	2982,833272	3081	3072,587533	3171	3162,341794
2722	2714,567759	2812	2804,32202	2902	2894,07628	2992	2983,830541	3082	3073,584802	3172	3163,339063
2723	2715,565028	2813	2805,319289	2903	2895,07355	2993	2984,827811	3083	3074,582072	3173	3164,336333
2724	2716,562298	2814	2806,316559	2904	2896,07082	2994	2985,825081	3084	3075,579341	3174	3165,333602

TABLE TO FIND OUT THE POINT A IN EARTH RETURNS

3175	3166,330872	3265	3256,085133	3355	3345,839394	3445	3435,593655	3535	3525,347916	3625	3615,102177
3176	3167,328142	3266	3257,082402	3356	3346,836663	3446	3436,590924	3536	3526,345185	3626	3616,099446
3177	3168,325411	3267	3258,079672	3357	3347,833933	3447	3437,588194	3537	3527,342455	3627	3617,096716
3178	3169,322681	3268	3259,076942	3358	3348,831203	3448	3438,585463	3538	3528,339724	3628	3618,093985
3179	3170,31995	3269	3260,074211	3359	3349,828472	3449	3439,582733	3539	3529,336994	3629	3619,091255
3180	3171,31722	3270	3261,071481	3360	3350,825742	3450	3440,580003	3540	3530,334264	3630	3620,088524
3181	3172,314489	3271	3262,06875	3361	3351,823011	3451	3441,577272	3541	3531,331533	3631	3621,085794
3182	3173,311759	3272	3263,06602	3362	3352,820281	3452	3442,574542	3542	3532,328803	3632	3622,083064
3183	3174,309028	3273	3264,063289	3363	3353,81755	3453	3443,571811	3543	3533,326072	3633	3623,080333
3184	3175,306298	3274	3265,060559	3364	3354,81482	3454	3444,569081	3544	3534,323342	3634	3624,077603
3185	3176,303568	3275	3266,057829	3365	3355,812089	3455	3445,56635	3545	3535,320611	3635	3625,074872
3186	3177,300837	3276	3267,055098	3366	3356,809359	3456	3446,56362	3546	3536,317881	3636	3626,072142
3187	3178,298107	3277	3268,052368	3367	3357,806629	3457	3447,56089	3547	3537,315151	3637	3627,069411
3188	3179,295376	3278	3269,049637	3368	3358,803898	3458	3448,558159	3548	3538,31242	3638	3628,066681
3189	3180,292646	3279	3270,046907	3369	3359,801168	3459	3449,555429	3549	3539,30969	3639	3629,063951
3190	3181,289915	3280	3271,044176	3370	3360,798437	3460	3450,552698	3550	3540,306959	3640	3630,06122
3191	3182,287185	3281	3272,041446	3371	3361,795707	3461	3451,549968	3551	3541,304229	3641	3631,05849
3192	3183,284455	3282	3273,038716	3372	3362,792976	3462	3452,547237	3552	3542,301498	3642	3632,055759
3193	3184,281724	3283	3274,035985	3373	3363,790246	3463	3453,544507	3553	3543,298768	3643	3633,053029
3194	3185,278994	3284	3275,033255	3374	3364,787516	3464	3454,541777	3554	3544,296037	3644	3634,050298
3195	3186,276263	3285	3276,030524	3375	3365,784785	3465	3455,539046	3555	3545,293307	3645	3635,047568
3196	3187,273533	3286	3277,027794	3376	3366,782055	3466	3456,536316	3556	3546,290577	3646	3636,044838
3197	3188,270802	3287	3278,025063	3377	3367,779324	3467	3457,533585	3557	3547,287846	3647	3637,042107
3198	3189,268072	3288	3279,022333	3378	3368,776594	3468	3458,530855	3558	3548,285116	3648	3638,039377
3199	3190,265342	3289	3280,019602	3379	3369,773863	3469	3459,528124	3559	3549,282385	3649	3639,036646
3200	3191,262611	3290	3281,016872	3380	3370,771133	3470	3460,525394	3560	3550,279655	3650	3640,033916
3201	3192,259881	3291	3282,014142	3381	3371,768403	3471	3461,522663	3561	3551,276924	3651	3641,031185
3202	3193,25715	3292	3283,011411	3382	3372,765672	3472	3462,519933	3562	3552,274194	3652	3642,028455
3203	3194,25442	3293	3284,008681	3383	3373,762942	3473	3463,517203	3563	3553,271464	3653	3643,025724
3204	3195,251689	3294	3285,00595	3384	3374,760211	3474	3464,514472	3564	3554,268733	3654	3644,022994
3205	3196,248959	3295	3286,00322	3385	3375,757481	3475	3465,511742	3565	3555,266003	3655	3645,020264
3206	3197,246229	3296	3287,000489	3386	3376,75475	3476	3466,509011	3566	3556,263272	3656	3646,017533
3207	3198,243498	3297	3287,997759	3387	3377,75202	3477	3467,506281	3567	3557,260542	3657	3647,014803
3208	3199,240768	3298	3288,995029	3388	3378,74929	3478	3468,50355	3568	3558,257811	3658	3648,012072
3209	3200,238037	3299	3289,992298	3389	3379,746559	3479	3469,50082	3569	3559,255081	3659	3649,009342
3210	3201,235307	3300	3290,989568	3390	3380,743829	3480	3470,49809	3570	3560,252351	3660	3650,006611
3211	3202,232576	3301	3291,986837	3391	3381,741098	3481	3471,495359	3571	3561,24962	3661	3651,003881
3212	3203,229846	3302	3292,984107	3392	3382,738368	3482	3472,492629	3572	3562,24689	3662	3652,001151
3213	3204,227115	3303	3293,981376	3393	3383,735637	3483	3473,489898	3573	3563,244159	3663	3652,99842
3214	3205,224385	3304	3294,978646	3394	3384,732907	3484	3474,487168	3574	3564,241429	3664	3653,99569
3215	3206,221655	3305	3295,975916	3395	3385,730176	3485	3475,484437	3575	3565,238698	3665	3654,992959
3216	3207,218924	3306	3296,973185	3396	3386,727446	3486	3476,481707	3576	3566,235968	3666	3655,990229
3217	3208,216194	3307	3297,970455	3397	3387,724716	3487	3477,478977	3577	3567,233237	3667	3656,987498
3218	3209,213463	3308	3298,967724	3398	3388,721985	3488	3478,476246	3578	3568,230507	3668	3657,984768
3219	3210,210733	3309	3299,964994	3399	3389,719255	3489	3479,473516	3579	3569,227777	3669	3658,982038
3220	3211,208002	3310	3300,962263	3400	3390,716524	3490	3480,470785	3580	3570,225046	3670	3659,979307
3221	3212,205272	3311	3301,959533	3401	3391,713794	3491	3481,468055	3581	3571,222316	3671	3660,976577
3222	3213,202542	3312	3302,956803	3402	3392,711063	3492	3482,465324	3582	3572,219585	3672	3661,973846
3223	3214,199811	3313	3303,954072	3403	3393,708333	3493	3483,462594	3583	3573,216855	3673	3662,971116
3224	3215,197081	3314	3304,951342	3404	3394,705603	3494	3484,459864	3584	3574,214124	3674	3663,968385
3225	3216,19435	3315	3305,948611	3405	3395,702872	3495	3485,457133	3585	3575,211394	3675	3664,965655
3226	3217,19162	3316	3306,945881	3406	3396,700142	3496	3486,454403	3586	3576,208664	3676	3665,962925
3227	3218,188889	3317	3307,94315	3407	3397,697411	3497	3487,451672	3587	3577,205933	3677	3666,960194
3228	3219,186159	3318	3308,94042	3408	3398,694681	3498	3488,448942	3588	3578,203203	3678	3667,957464
3229	3220,183429	3319	3309,937689	3409	3399,69195	3499	3489,446211	3589	3579,200472	3679	3668,954733
3230	3221,180698	3320	3310,934959	3410	3400,68922	3500	3490,443481	3590	3580,197742	3680	3669,952003
3231	3222,177968	3321	3311,932229	3411	3401,68649	3501	3491,44075	3591	3581,195011	3681	3670,949272
3232	3223,175237	3322	3312,929498	3412	3402,683759	3502	3492,43802	3592	3582,192281	3682	3671,946542
3233	3224,172507	3323	3313,926768	3413	3403,681029	3503	3493,43529	3593	3583,189551	3683	3672,943811
3234	3225,169776	3324	3314,924037	3414	3404,678298	3504	3494,432559	3594	3584,18682	3684	3673,941081
3235	3226,167046	3325	3315,921307	3415	3405,675568	3505	3495,429829	3595	3585,18409	3685	3674,938351
3236	3227,164315	3326	3316,918576	3416	3406,672837	3506	3496,427098	3596	3586,181359	3686	3675,93562
3237	3228,161585	3327	3317,915846	3417	3407,670107	3507	3497,424368	3597	3587,178629	3687	3676,93289
3238	3229,158855	3328	3318,913116	3418	3408,667376	3508	3498,421637	3598	3588,175898	3688	3677,930159
3239	3230,156124	3329	3319,910385	3419	3409,664646	3509	3499,418907	3599	3589,173168	3689	3678,927429
3240	3231,153394	3330	3320,907655	3420	3410,661916	3510	3500,416177	3600	3590,170438	3690	3679,924698
3241	3232,150663	3331	3321,904924	3421	3411,659185	3511	3501,413446	3601	3591,167707	3691	3680,921968
3242	3233,147933	3332	3322,902194	3422	3412,656455	3512	3502,410716	3602	3592,164977	3692	3681,919238
3243	3234,145202	3333	3323,899463	3423	3413,653724	3513	3503,407985	3603	3593,162246	3693	3682,916507
3244	3235,142472	3334	3324,896733	3424	3414,650994	3514	3504,405255	3604	3594,159516	3694	3683,913777
3245	3236,139742	3335	3325,894003	3425	3415,648263	3515	3505,402524	3605	3595,156785	3695	3684,911046
3246	3237,137011	3336	3326,891272	3426	3416,645533	3516	3506,399794	3606	3596,154055	3696	3685,908316
3247	3238,134281	3337	3327,888542	3427	3417,642803	3517	3507,397064	3607	3597,151324	3697	3686,905585
3248	3239,13155	3338	3328,885811	3428	3418,640072	3518	3508,394333	3608	3598,148594	3698	3687,902855
3249	3240,12882	3339	3329,883081	3429	3419,637342	3519	3509,391603	3609	3599,145864	3699	3688,900125
3250	3241,126089	3340	3330,88035	3430	3420,634611	3520	3510,388872	3610	3600,143133	3700	3689,897394
3251	3242,123359	3341	3331,87762	3431	3421,631881	3521	3511,386142	3611	3601,140403	3701	3690,894664
3252	3243,120629	3342	3332,874889	3432	3422,62915	3522	3512,383411	3612	3602,137672	3702	3691,891933
3253	3244,117898	3343	3333,872159	3433	3423,62642	3523	3513,380681	3613	3603,134942	3703	3692,889203
3254	3245,115168	3344	3334,869429	3434	3424,62369	3524	3514,37795	3614	3604,132211	3704	3693,886472
3255	3246,112437	3345	3335,866698	3435	3425,620959	3525	3515,37522	3615	3605,129481	3705	3694,883742
3256	3247,109707	3346	3336,863968	3436	3426,618229	3526	3516,37249	3616	3606,126751	3706	3695,881011
3257	3248,106976	3347	3337,861237	3437	3427,615498	3527	3517,369759	3617	3607,12402	3707	3696,878281
3258	3249,104246	3348	3338,858507	3438	3428,612768	3528	3518,367029	3618	3608,12129	3708	3697,875551
3259	3250,101516	3349	3339,855776	3439	3429,610037	3529	3519,364298	3619	3609,118559	3709	3698,87282
3260	3251,098785	3350	3340,853046	3440	3430,607307	3530	3520,361568	3620	3610,115829	3710	3699,87009
3261	3252,096055	3351	3341,850316	3441	3431,604577	3531	3521,358837	3621	3611,113098	3711	3700,867359
3262	3253,093324	3352	3342,847585	3442	3432,601846	3532	3522,356107	3622	3612,110368	3712	3701,864629
3263	3254,090594	3353	3343,844855	3443	3433,599116	3533	3523,353377	3623	3613,107638	3713	3702,861898
3264	3255,087863	3354	3344,842124	3444	3434,596385	3534	3524,350646	3624	3614,104907	3714	3703,859168

3715	3704,856438	3805	3794,610699	3895	3884,364959	3985	3974,11922	4075	4063,873481	4165	4153,627742
3716	3705,853707	3806	3795,607968	3896	3885,362229	3986	3975,11649	4076	4064,870751	4166	4154,625012
3717	3706,850977	3807	3796,605238	3897	3886,359499	3987	3976,11376	4077	4065,86802	4167	4155,622281
3718	3707,848246	3808	3797,602507	3898	3887,356768	3988	3977,111029	4078	4066,86529	4168	4156,619551
3719	3708,845516	3809	3798,599777	3899	3888,354038	3989	3978,108299	4079	4067,86256	4169	4157,616821
3720	3709,842785	3810	3799,597046	3900	3889,351307	3990	3979,105568	4080	4068,859829	4170	4158,61409
3721	3710,840055	3811	3800,594316	3901	3890,348577	3991	3980,102838	4081	4069,857099	4171	4159,61136
3722	3711,837325	3812	3801,591585	3902	3891,345846	3992	3981,100107	4082	4070,854368	4172	4160,608629
3723	3712,834594	3813	3802,588855	3903	3892,343116	3993	3982,097377	4083	4071,851638	4173	4161,605899
3724	3713,831864	3814	3803,586125	3904	3893,340386	3994	3983,094646	4084	4072,848907	4174	4162,603168
3725	3714,829133	3815	3804,583394	3905	3894,337655	3995	3984,091916	4085	4073,846177	4175	4163,600438
3726	3715,826403	3816	3805,580664	3906	3895,334925	3996	3985,089186	4086	4074,843447	4176	4164,597708
3727	3716,823672	3817	3806,577933	3907	3896,332194	3997	3986,086455	4087	4075,840716	4177	4165,594977
3728	3717,820942	3818	3807,575203	3908	3897,329464	3998	3987,083725	4088	4076,837986	4178	4166,592247
3729	3718,818212	3819	3808,572472	3909	3898,326733	3999	3988,080994	4089	4077,835255	4179	4167,589516
3730	3719,815481	3820	3809,569742	3910	3899,324003	4000	3989,078264	4090	4078,832525	4180	4168,586786
3731	3720,812751	3821	3810,567012	3911	3900,321273	4001	3990,075533	4091	4079,829794	4181	4169,584055
3732	3721,81002	3822	3811,564281	3912	3901,318542	4002	3991,072803	4092	4080,827064	4182	4170,581325
3733	3722,80729	3823	3812,561551	3913	3902,315812	4003	3992,070073	4093	4081,824334	4183	4171,578594
3734	3723,804559	3824	3813,55882	3914	3903,313081	4004	3993,067342	4094	4082,821603	4184	4172,575864
3735	3724,801829	3825	3814,55609	3915	3904,310351	4005	3994,064612	4095	4083,818873	4185	4173,573134
3736	3725,799098	3826	3815,553359	3916	3905,30762	4006	3995,061881	4096	4084,816142	4186	4174,570403
3737	3726,796368	3827	3816,550629	3917	3906,30489	4007	3996,059151	4097	4085,813412	4187	4175,567673
3738	3727,793638	3828	3817,547899	3918	3907,302159	4008	3997,05642	4098	4086,810681	4188	4176,564942
3739	3728,790907	3829	3818,545168	3919	3908,299429	4009	3998,05369	4099	4087,807951	4189	4177,562212
3740	3729,788177	3830	3819,542438	3920	3909,296699	4010	3999,05096	4100	4088,80522	4190	4178,559481
3741	3730,785446	3831	3820,539707	3921	3910,293968	4011	4000,048229	4101	4089,80249	4191	4179,556751
3742	3731,782716	3832	3821,536977	3922	3911,291238	4012	4001,045499	4102	4090,79976	4192	4180,554021
3743	3732,779985	3833	3822,534246	3923	3912,288507	4013	4002,042768	4103	4091,797029	4193	4181,55129
3744	3733,777255	3834	3823,531516	3924	3913,285777	4014	4003,040038	4104	4092,794299	4194	4182,54856
3745	3734,774525	3835	3824,528786	3925	3914,283046	4015	4004,037307	4105	4093,791568	4195	4183,545829
3746	3735,771794	3836	3825,526055	3926	3915,280316	4016	4005,034577	4106	4094,788838	4196	4184,543099
3747	3736,769064	3837	3826,523325	3927	3916,277586	4017	4006,031847	4107	4095,786107	4197	4185,540368
3748	3737,766333	3838	3827,520594	3928	3917,274855	4018	4007,029116	4108	4096,783377	4198	4186,537638
3749	3738,763603	3839	3828,517864	3929	3918,272125	4019	4008,026386	4109	4097,780647	4199	4187,534908
3750	3739,760872	3840	3829,515133	3930	3919,269394	4020	4009,023655	4110	4098,777916	4200	4188,532177
3751	3740,758142	3841	3830,512403	3931	3920,266664	4021	4010,020925	4111	4099,775186	4201	4189,529447
3752	3741,755412	3842	3831,509672	3932	3921,263933	4022	4011,018194	4112	4100,772455	4202	4190,526716
3753	3742,752681	3843	3832,506942	3933	3922,261203	4023	4012,015464	4113	4101,769725	4203	4191,523986
3754	3743,749951	3844	3833,504212	3934	3923,258473	4024	4013,012733	4114	4102,766994	4204	4192,521255
3755	3744,74722	3845	3834,501481	3935	3924,255742	4025	4014,010003	4115	4103,764264	4205	4193,518525
3756	3745,74449	3846	3835,498751	3936	3925,253012	4026	4015,007273	4116	4104,761534	4206	4194,515794
3757	3746,741759	3847	3836,49602	3937	3926,250281	4027	4016,004542	4117	4105,758803	4207	4195,513064
3758	3747,739029	3848	3837,49329	3938	3927,247551	4028	4017,001812	4118	4106,756073	4208	4196,510334
3759	3748,736298	3849	3838,490559	3939	3928,24482	4029	4017,999081	4119	4107,753342	4209	4197,507603
3760	3749,733568	3850	3839,487829	3940	3929,24209	4030	4018,996351	4120	4108,750612	4210	4198,504873
3761	3750,730838	3851	3840,485099	3941	3930,239359	4031	4019,99362	4121	4109,747881	4211	4199,502142
3762	3751,728107	3852	3841,482368	3942	3931,236629	4032	4020,99089	4122	4110,745151	4212	4200,499412
3763	3752,725377	3853	3842,479638	3943	3932,233899	4033	4021,98816	4123	4111,742421	4213	4201,496681
3764	3753,722646	3854	3843,476907	3944	3933,231168	4034	4022,985429	4124	4112,73969	4214	4202,493951
3765	3754,719916	3855	3844,474177	3945	3934,228438	4035	4023,982699	4125	4113,73696	4215	4203,491221
3766	3755,717185	3856	3845,471446	3946	3935,225707	4036	4024,979968	4126	4114,734229	4216	4204,48849
3767	3756,714455	3857	3846,468716	3947	3936,222977	4037	4025,977238	4127	4115,731499	4217	4205,48576
3768	3757,711725	3858	3847,465986	3948	3937,220246	4038	4026,974507	4128	4116,728768	4218	4206,483029
3769	3758,708994	3859	3848,463255	3949	3938,217516	4039	4027,971777	4129	4117,726038	4219	4207,480299
3770	3759,706264	3860	3849,460525	3950	3939,214786	4040	4028,969047	4130	4118,723307	4220	4208,477568
3771	3760,703533	3861	3850,457794	3951	3940,212055	4041	4029,966316	4131	4119,720577	4221	4209,474838
3772	3761,700803	3862	3851,455064	3952	3941,209325	4042	4030,963586	4132	4120,717847	4222	4210,472108
3773	3762,698072	3863	3852,452333	3953	3942,206594	4043	4031,960855	4133	4121,715116	4223	4211,469377
3774	3763,695342	3864	3853,449603	3954	3943,203864	4044	4032,958125	4134	4122,712386	4224	4212,466647
3775	3764,692612	3865	3854,446872	3955	3944,201133	4045	4033,955394	4135	4123,709655	4225	4213,463916
3776	3765,689881	3866	3855,444142	3956	3945,198403	4046	4034,952664	4136	4124,706925	4226	4214,461186
3777	3766,687151	3867	3856,441412	3957	3946,195673	4047	4035,949933	4137	4125,704194	4227	4215,458455
3778	3767,68442	3868	3857,438681	3958	3947,192942	4048	4036,947203	4138	4126,701464	4228	4216,455725
3779	3768,68169	3869	3858,435951	3959	3948,190212	4049	4037,944473	4139	4127,698734	4229	4217,452994
3780	3769,678959	3870	3859,43322	3960	3949,187481	4050	4038,941742	4140	4128,696003	4230	4218,450264
3781	3770,676229	3871	3860,43049	3961	3950,184751	4051	4039,939012	4141	4129,693273	4231	4219,447534
3782	3771,673499	3872	3861,427759	3962	3951,18202	4052	4040,936281	4142	4130,690542	4232	4220,444803
3783	3772,670768	3873	3862,425029	3963	3952,17929	4053	4041,933551	4143	4131,687812	4233	4221,442073
3784	3773,668038	3874	3863,422299	3964	3953,17656	4054	4042,93082	4144	4132,685081	4234	4222,439342
3785	3774,665307	3875	3864,419568	3965	3954,173829	4055	4043,92809	4145	4133,682351	4235	4223,436612
3786	3775,662577	3876	3865,416838	3966	3955,171099	4056	4044,92536	4146	4134,679621	4236	4224,433881
3787	3776,659846	3877	3866,414107	3967	3956,168368	4057	4045,922629	4147	4135,67689	4237	4225,431151
3788	3777,657116	3878	3867,411377	3968	3957,165638	4058	4046,919899	4148	4136,67416	4238	4226,428421
3789	3778,654385	3879	3868,408646	3969	3958,162907	4059	4047,917168	4149	4137,671429	4239	4227,42569
3790	3779,651655	3880	3869,405916	3970	3959,160177	4060	4048,914438	4150	4138,668699	4240	4228,42296
3791	3780,648925	3881	3870,403186	3971	3960,157446	4061	4049,911707	4151	4139,665968	4241	4229,420229
3792	3781,646194	3882	3871,400455	3972	3961,154716	4062	4050,908977	4152	4140,663238	4242	4230,417499
3793	3782,643464	3883	3872,397725	3973	3962,151986	4063	4051,906247	4153	4141,660507	4243	4231,414768
3794	3783,640733	3884	3873,394994	3974	3963,149255	4064	4052,903516	4154	4142,657777	4244	4232,412038
3795	3784,638003	3885	3874,392264	3975	3964,146525	4065	4053,900786	4155	4143,655047	4245	4233,409308
3796	3785,635272	3886	3875,389533	3976	3965,143794	4066	4054,898055	4156	4144,652316	4246	4234,406577
3797	3786,632542	3887	3876,386803	3977	3966,141064	4067	4055,895325	4157	4145,649586	4247	4235,403847
3798	3787,629812	3888	3877,384073	3978	3967,138333	4068	4056,892594	4158	4146,646855	4248	4236,401116
3799	3788,627081	3889	3878,381342	3979	3968,135603	4069	4057,889864	4159	4147,644125	4249	4237,398386
3800	3789,624351	3890	3879,378612	3980	3969,132873	4070	4058,887134	4160	4148,641394	4250	4238,395655
3801	3790,62162	3891	3880,375881	3981	3970,130142	4071	4059,884403	4161	4149,638664	4251	4239,392925
3802	3791,61889	3892	3881,373151	3982	3971,127412	4072	4060,881673	4162	4150,635934	4252	4240,390195
3803	3792,616159	3893	3882,37042	3983	3972,124681	4073	4061,878942	4163	4151,633203	4253	4241,387464
3804	3793,613429	3894	3883,36769	3984	3973,121951	4074	4062,876212	4164	4152,630473	4254	4242,384734

TABLE TO FIND OUT THE POINT A IN EARTH RETURNS

4255	4243,382003	4345	4333,136264	4435	4422,890525	4525	4512,644786	4615	4602,399047	4705	4692,153308
4256	4244,379273	4346	4334,133534	4436	4423,887795	4526	4513,642056	4616	4603,396317	4706	4693,150577
4257	4245,376542	4347	4335,130803	4437	4424,885064	4527	4514,639325	4617	4604,393586	4707	4694,147847
4258	4246,373812	4348	4336,128073	4438	4425,882334	4528	4515,636595	4618	4605,390856	4708	4695,145117
4259	4247,371081	4349	4337,125342	4439	4426,879603	4529	4516,633864	4619	4606,388125	4709	4696,142386
4260	4248,368351	4350	4338,122612	4440	4427,876873	4530	4517,631134	4620	4607,385395	4710	4697,139656
4261	4249,365621	4351	4339,119882	4441	4428,874142	4531	4518,628403	4621	4608,382664	4711	4698,136925
4262	4250,36289	4352	4340,117151	4442	4429,871412	4532	4519,625673	4622	4609,379934	4712	4699,134195
4263	4251,36016	4353	4341,114421	4443	4430,868682	4533	4520,622943	4623	4610,377203	4713	4700,131464
4264	4252,357429	4354	4342,11169	4444	4431,865951	4534	4521,620212	4624	4611,374473	4714	4701,128734
4265	4253,354699	4355	4343,10896	4445	4432,863221	4535	4522,617482	4625	4612,371743	4715	4702,126004
4266	4254,351968	4356	4344,106229	4446	4433,86049	4536	4523,614751	4626	4613,369012	4716	4703,123273
4267	4255,349238	4357	4345,103499	4447	4434,85776	4537	4524,612021	4627	4614,366282	4717	4704,120543
4268	4256,346508	4358	4346,100769	4448	4435,855029	4538	4525,60929	4628	4615,363551	4718	4705,117812
4269	4257,343777	4359	4347,098038	4449	4436,852299	4539	4526,60656	4629	4616,360821	4719	4706,115082
4270	4258,341047	4360	4348,095308	4450	4437,849569	4540	4527,60383	4630	4617,35809	4720	4707,112351
4271	4259,338316	4361	4349,092577	4451	4438,846838	4541	4528,601099	4631	4618,35536	4721	4708,109621
4272	4260,335586	4362	4350,089847	4452	4439,844108	4542	4529,598369	4632	4619,35263	4722	4709,106891
4273	4261,332855	4363	4351,087116	4453	4440,841377	4543	4530,595638	4633	4620,349899	4723	4710,10416
4274	4262,330125	4364	4352,084386	4454	4441,838647	4544	4531,592908	4634	4621,347169	4724	4711,10143
4275	4263,327395	4365	4353,081655	4455	4442,835916	4545	4532,590177	4635	4622,344438	4725	4712,098699
4276	4264,324664	4366	4354,078925	4456	4443,833186	4546	4533,587447	4636	4623,341708	4726	4713,095969
4277	4265,321934	4367	4355,076195	4457	4444,830456	4547	4534,584716	4637	4624,338977	4727	4714,093238
4278	4266,319203	4368	4356,073464	4458	4445,827725	4548	4535,581986	4638	4625,336247	4728	4715,090508
4279	4267,316473	4369	4357,070734	4459	4446,824995	4549	4536,579256	4639	4626,333517	4729	4716,087777
4280	4268,313742	4370	4358,068003	4460	4447,822264	4550	4537,576525	4640	4627,330786	4730	4717,085047
4281	4269,311012	4371	4359,065273	4461	4448,819534	4551	4538,573795	4641	4628,328056	4731	4718,082317
4282	4270,308281	4372	4360,062542	4462	4449,816803	4552	4539,571064	4642	4629,325325	4732	4719,079586
4283	4271,305551	4373	4361,059812	4463	4450,814073	4553	4540,568334	4643	4630,322595	4733	4720,076856
4284	4272,302821	4374	4362,057082	4464	4451,811343	4554	4541,565603	4644	4631,319864	4734	4721,074125
4285	4273,30009	4375	4363,054351	4465	4452,808612	4555	4542,562873	4645	4632,317134	4735	4722,071395
4286	4274,29736	4376	4364,051621	4466	4453,805882	4556	4543,560143	4646	4633,314404	4736	4723,068664
4287	4275,294629	4377	4365,04889	4467	4454,803151	4557	4544,557412	4647	4634,311673	4737	4724,065934
4288	4276,291899	4378	4366,04616	4468	4455,800421	4558	4545,554682	4648	4635,308943	4738	4725,063204
4289	4277,289168	4379	4367,043429	4469	4456,79769	4559	4546,551951	4649	4636,306212	4739	4726,060473
4290	4278,286438	4380	4368,040699	4470	4457,79496	4560	4547,549221	4650	4637,303482	4740	4727,057743
4291	4279,283708	4381	4369,037969	4471	4458,792229	4561	4548,54649	4651	4638,300751	4741	4728,055012
4292	4280,280977	4382	4370,035238	4472	4459,789499	4562	4549,54376	4652	4639,298021	4742	4729,052282
4293	4281,278247	4383	4371,032508	4473	4460,786769	4563	4550,54103	4653	4640,29529	4743	4730,049551
4294	4282,275516	4384	4372,029777	4474	4461,784038	4564	4551,538299	4654	4641,29256	4744	4731,046821
4295	4283,272786	4385	4373,027047	4475	4462,781308	4565	4552,535569	4655	4642,28983	4745	4732,044091
4296	4284,270055	4386	4374,024316	4476	4463,778577	4566	4553,532838	4656	4643,287099	4746	4733,04136
4297	4285,267325	4387	4375,021586	4477	4464,775847	4567	4554,530108	4657	4644,284369	4747	4734,03863
4298	4286,264595	4388	4376,018855	4478	4465,773116	4568	4555,527377	4658	4645,281638	4748	4735,035899
4299	4287,261864	4389	4377,016125	4479	4466,770386	4569	4556,524647	4659	4646,278908	4749	4736,033169
4300	4288,259134	4390	4378,013395	4480	4467,767656	4570	4557,521916	4660	4647,276177	4750	4737,030438
4301	4289,256403	4391	4379,010664	4481	4468,764925	4571	4558,519186	4661	4648,273447	4751	4738,027708
4302	4290,253673	4392	4380,007934	4482	4469,762195	4572	4559,516456	4662	4649,270717	4752	4739,024978
4303	4291,250942	4393	4381,005203	4483	4470,759464	4573	4560,513725	4663	4650,267986	4753	4740,022247
4304	4292,248212	4394	4382,002473	4484	4471,756734	4574	4561,510995	4664	4651,265256	4754	4741,019517
4305	4293,245482	4395	4382,999742	4485	4472,754003	4575	4562,508264	4665	4652,262525	4755	4742,016786
4306	4294,242751	4396	4383,997012	4486	4473,751273	4576	4563,505534	4666	4653,259795	4756	4743,014056
4307	4295,240021	4397	4384,994282	4487	4474,748543	4577	4564,502803	4667	4654,257064	4757	4744,011325
4308	4296,23729	4398	4385,991551	4488	4475,745812	4578	4565,500073	4668	4655,254334	4758	4745,008595
4309	4297,23456	4399	4386,988821	4489	4476,743082	4579	4566,497343	4669	4656,251604	4759	4746,005864
4310	4298,231829	4400	4387,98609	4490	4477,740351	4580	4567,494612	4670	4657,248873	4760	4747,003134
4311	4299,229099	4401	4388,98336	4491	4478,737621	4581	4568,491882	4671	4658,246143	4761	4748,000404
4312	4300,226368	4402	4389,980629	4492	4479,73489	4582	4569,489151	4672	4659,243412	4762	4748,997673
4313	4301,223638	4403	4390,977899	4493	4480,73216	4583	4570,486421	4673	4660,240682	4763	4749,994943
4314	4302,220908	4404	4391,975169	4494	4481,729429	4584	4571,48369	4674	4661,237951	4764	4750,992212
4315	4303,218177	4405	4392,972438	4495	4482,726699	4585	4572,48096	4675	4662,235221	4765	4751,989482
4316	4304,215447	4406	4393,969708	4496	4483,723969	4586	4573,47823	4676	4663,23249	4766	4752,986751
4317	4305,212716	4407	4394,966977	4497	4484,721238	4587	4574,475499	4677	4664,22976	4767	4753,984021
4318	4306,209986	4408	4395,964247	4498	4485,718508	4588	4575,472769	4678	4665,22703	4768	4754,981291
4319	4307,207255	4409	4396,961516	4499	4486,715777	4589	4576,470038	4679	4666,224299	4769	4755,97856
4320	4308,204525	4410	4397,958786	4500	4487,713047	4590	4577,467308	4680	4667,221569	4770	4756,97583
4321	4309,201795	4411	4398,956056	4501	4488,710316	4591	4578,464577	4681	4668,218838	4771	4757,973099
4322	4310,199064	4412	4399,953325	4502	4489,707586	4592	4579,461847	4682	4669,216108	4772	4758,970369
4323	4311,196334	4413	4400,950595	4503	4490,704856	4593	4580,459117	4683	4670,213377	4773	4759,967638
4324	4312,193603	4414	4401,947864	4504	4491,702125	4594	4581,456386	4684	4671,210647	4774	4760,964908
4325	4313,190873	4415	4402,945134	4505	4492,699395	4595	4582,453656	4685	4672,207917	4775	4761,962178
4326	4314,188142	4416	4403,942403	4506	4493,696664	4596	4583,450925	4686	4673,205186	4776	4762,959447
4327	4315,185412	4417	4404,939673	4507	4494,693934	4597	4584,448195	4687	4674,202456	4777	4763,956717
4328	4316,182682	4418	4405,936942	4508	4495,691203	4598	4585,445464	4688	4675,199725	4778	4764,953986
4329	4317,179951	4419	4406,934212	4509	4496,688473	4599	4586,442734	4689	4676,196995	4779	4765,951256
4330	4318,177221	4420	4407,931482	4510	4497,685743	4600	4587,440003	4690	4677,194264	4780	4766,948525
4331	4319,17449	4421	4408,928751	4511	4498,683012	4601	4588,437273	4691	4678,191534	4781	4767,945795
4332	4320,17176	4422	4409,926021	4512	4499,680282	4602	4589,434543	4692	4679,188804	4782	4768,943064
4333	4321,169029	4423	4410,92329	4513	4500,677551	4603	4590,431812	4693	4680,186073	4783	4769,940334
4334	4322,166299	4424	4411,92056	4514	4501,674821	4604	4591,429082	4694	4681,183343	4784	4770,937604
4335	4323,163568	4425	4412,917829	4515	4502,67209	4605	4592,426351	4695	4682,180612	4785	4771,934873
4336	4324,160838	4426	4413,915099	4516	4503,66936	4606	4593,423621	4696	4683,177882	4786	4772,932143
4337	4325,158108	4427	4414,912369	4517	4504,666629	4607	4594,42089	4697	4684,175151	4787	4773,929412
4338	4326,155377	4428	4415,909638	4518	4505,663899	4608	4595,41816	4698	4685,172421	4788	4774,926682
4339	4327,152647	4429	4416,906908	4519	4506,661169	4609	4596,41543	4699	4686,169691	4789	4775,923951
4340	4328,149916	4430	4417,904177	4520	4507,658438	4610	4597,412699	4700	4687,16696	4790	4776,921221
4341	4329,147186	4431	4418,901447	4521	4508,655708	4611	4598,409969	4701	4688,16423	4791	4777,918491
4342	4330,144455	4432	4419,898716	4522	4509,652977	4612	4599,407238	4702	4689,161499	4792	4778,91576
4343	4331,141725	4433	4420,895986	4523	4510,650247	4613	4600,404508	4703	4690,158769	4793	4779,91303
4344	4332,138995	4434	4421,893256	4524	4511,647516	4614	4601,401777	4704	4691,156038	4794	4780,910299

4795	4781,907569	4885	4871,66183	4975	4961,416091	5065	5051,170352	5155	5140,924613	5245	5230,678874
4796	4782,904838	4886	4872,659099	4976	4962,41336	5066	5052,167621	5156	5141,921882	5246	5231,676143
4797	4783,902108	4887	4873,656369	4977	4963,41063	5067	5053,164891	5157	5142,919152	5247	5232,673413
4798	4784,899378	4888	4874,653638	4978	4964,407899	5068	5054,16216	5158	5143,916421	5248	5233,670682
4799	4785,896647	4889	4875,650908	4979	4965,405169	5069	5055,15943	5159	5144,913691	5249	5234,667952
4800	4786,893917	4890	4876,648178	4980	4966,402439	5070	5056,156699	5160	5145,91096	5250	5235,665221
4801	4787,891186	4891	4877,645447	4981	4967,399708	5071	5057,153969	5161	5146,90823	5251	5236,662491
4802	4788,888456	4892	4878,642717	4982	4968,396978	5072	5058,151239	5162	5147,9055	5252	5237,65976
4803	4789,885725	4893	4879,639986	4983	4969,394247	5073	5059,148508	5163	5148,902769	5253	5238,65703
4804	4790,882995	4894	4880,637256	4984	4970,391517	5074	5060,145778	5164	5149,900039	5254	5239,6543
4805	4791,880264	4895	4881,634525	4985	4971,388786	5075	5061,143047	5165	5150,897308	5255	5240,651569
4806	4792,877534	4896	4882,631795	4986	4972,386056	5076	5062,140317	5166	5151,894578	5256	5241,648839
4807	4793,874804	4897	4883,629065	4987	4973,383326	5077	5063,137586	5167	5152,891847	5257	5242,646108
4808	4794,872073	4898	4884,626334	4988	4974,380595	5078	5064,134856	5168	5153,889117	5258	5243,643378
4809	4795,869343	4899	4885,623604	4989	4975,377865	5079	5065,132126	5169	5154,886387	5259	5244,640647
4810	4796,866612	4900	4886,620873	4990	4976,375134	5080	5066,129395	5170	5155,883656	5260	5245,637917
4811	4797,863882	4901	4887,618143	4991	4977,372404	5081	5067,126665	5171	5156,880926	5261	5246,635187
4812	4798,861151	4902	4888,615412	4992	4978,369673	5082	5068,123934	5172	5157,878195	5262	5247,632456
4813	4799,858421	4903	4889,612682	4993	4979,366943	5083	5069,121204	5173	5158,875465	5263	5248,629726
4814	4800,855691	4904	4890,609952	4994	4980,364212	5084	5070,118473	5174	5159,872734	5264	5249,626995
4815	4801,85296	4905	4891,607221	4995	4981,361482	5085	5071,115743	5175	5160,870004	5265	5250,624265
4816	4802,85023	4906	4892,604491	4996	4982,358752	5086	5072,113013	5176	5161,867273	5266	5251,621534
4817	4803,847499	4907	4893,60176	4997	4983,356021	5087	5073,110282	5177	5162,864543	5267	5252,618804
4818	4804,844769	4908	4894,59903	4998	4984,353291	5088	5074,107552	5178	5163,861813	5268	5253,616074
4819	4805,842038	4909	4895,596299	4999	4985,35056	5089	5075,104821	5179	5164,859082	5269	5254,613343
4820	4806,839308	4910	4896,593569	5000	4986,34783	5090	5076,102091	5180	5165,856352	5270	5255,610613
4821	4807,836578	4911	4897,590838	5001	4987,345099	5091	5077,09936	5181	5166,853621	5271	5256,607882
4822	4808,833847	4912	4898,588108	5002	4988,342369	5092	5078,09663	5182	5167,850891	5272	5257,605152
4823	4809,831117	4913	4899,585378	5003	4989,339639	5093	5079,093899	5183	5168,84816	5273	5258,602421
4824	4810,828386	4914	4900,582647	5004	4990,336908	5094	5080,091169	5184	5169,84543	5274	5259,599691
4825	4811,825656	4915	4901,579917	5005	4991,334178	5095	5081,088439	5185	5170,8427	5275	5260,596961
4826	4812,822925	4916	4902,577186	5006	4992,331447	5096	5082,085708	5186	5171,839969	5276	5261,59423
4827	4813,820195	4917	4903,574456	5007	4993,328717	5097	5083,082978	5187	5172,837239	5277	5262,5915
4828	4814,817465	4918	4904,571725	5008	4994,325986	5098	5084,080247	5188	5173,834508	5278	5263,588769
4829	4815,814734	4919	4905,568995	5009	4995,323256	5099	5085,077517	5189	5174,831778	5279	5264,586039
4830	4816,812004	4920	4906,566265	5010	4996,320526	5100	5086,074786	5190	5175,829047	5280	5265,583308
4831	4817,809273	4921	4907,563534	5011	4997,317795	5101	5087,072056	5191	5176,826317	5281	5266,580578
4832	4818,806543	4922	4908,560804	5012	4998,315065	5102	5088,069326	5192	5177,823587	5282	5267,577847
4833	4819,803812	4923	4909,558073	5013	4999,312334	5103	5089,066595	5193	5178,820856	5283	5268,575117
4834	4820,801082	4924	4910,555343	5014	5000,309604	5104	5090,063865	5194	5179,818126	5284	5269,572387
4835	4821,798351	4925	4911,552612	5015	5001,306873	5105	5091,061134	5195	5180,815395	5285	5270,569656
4836	4822,795621	4926	4912,549882	5016	5002,304143	5106	5092,058404	5196	5181,812665	5286	5271,566926
4837	4823,792891	4927	4913,547152	5017	5003,301412	5107	5093,055673	5197	5182,809934	5287	5272,564195
4838	4824,79016	4928	4914,544421	5018	5004,298682	5108	5094,052943	5198	5183,807204	5288	5273,561465
4839	4825,78743	4929	4915,541691	5019	5005,295952	5109	5095,050213	5199	5184,804473	5289	5274,558734
4840	4826,784699	4930	4916,53896	5020	5006,293221	5110	5096,047482	5200	5185,801743	5290	5275,556004
4841	4827,781969	4931	4917,53623	5021	5007,290491	5111	5097,044752	5201	5186,799013	5291	5276,553274
4842	4828,779238	4932	4918,533499	5022	5008,28776	5112	5098,042021	5202	5187,796282	5292	5277,550543
4843	4829,776508	4933	4919,530769	5023	5009,28503	5113	5099,039291	5203	5188,793552	5293	5278,547813
4844	4830,773778	4934	4920,528039	5024	5010,282299	5114	5100,03656	5204	5189,790821	5294	5279,545082
4845	4831,771047	4935	4921,525308	5025	5011,279569	5115	5101,03383	5205	5190,788091	5295	5280,542352
4846	4832,768317	4936	4922,522578	5026	5012,276839	5116	5102,0311	5206	5191,78536	5296	5281,539621
4847	4833,765586	4937	4923,519847	5027	5013,274108	5117	5103,028369	5207	5192,78263	5297	5282,536891
4848	4834,762856	4938	4924,517117	5028	5014,271378	5118	5104,025639	5208	5193,7799	5298	5283,534161
4849	4835,760125	4939	4925,514386	5029	5015,268647	5119	5105,022908	5209	5194,777169	5299	5284,53143
4850	4836,757395	4940	4926,511656	5030	5016,265917	5120	5106,020178	5210	5195,774439	5300	5285,5287
4851	4837,754665	4941	4927,508925	5031	5017,263186	5121	5107,017447	5211	5196,771708	5301	5286,525969
4852	4838,751934	4942	4928,506195	5032	5018,260456	5122	5108,014717	5212	5197,768978	5302	5287,523239
4853	4839,749204	4943	4929,503465	5033	5019,257726	5123	5109,011986	5213	5198,766247	5303	5288,520508
4854	4840,746473	4944	4930,500734	5034	5020,254995	5124	5110,009256	5214	5199,763517	5304	5289,517778
4855	4841,743743	4945	4931,498004	5035	5021,252265	5125	5111,006526	5215	5200,760787	5305	5290,515047
4856	4842,741012	4946	4932,495273	5036	5022,249534	5126	5112,003795	5216	5201,758056	5306	5291,512317
4857	4843,738282	4947	4933,492543	5037	5023,246804	5127	5113,001065	5217	5202,755326	5307	5292,509587
4858	4844,735551	4948	4934,489812	5038	5024,244073	5128	5113,998334	5218	5203,752595	5308	5293,506856
4859	4845,732821	4949	4935,487082	5039	5025,241343	5129	5114,995604	5219	5204,749865	5309	5294,504126
4860	4846,730091	4950	4936,484352	5040	5026,238613	5130	5115,992873	5220	5205,747134	5310	5295,501395
4861	4847,72736	4951	4937,481621	5041	5027,235882	5131	5116,990143	5221	5206,744404	5311	5296,498665
4862	4848,72463	4952	4938,478891	5042	5028,233152	5132	5117,987413	5222	5207,741674	5312	5297,495934
4863	4849,721899	4953	4939,47616	5043	5029,230421	5133	5118,984682	5223	5208,738943	5313	5298,493204
4864	4850,719169	4954	4940,47343	5044	5030,227691	5134	5119,981952	5224	5209,736213	5314	5299,490474
4865	4851,716438	4955	4941,470699	5045	5031,22496	5135	5120,979221	5225	5210,733482	5315	5300,487743
4866	4852,713708	4956	4942,467969	5046	5032,22223	5136	5121,976491	5226	5211,730752	5316	5301,485013
4867	4853,710978	4957	4943,465239	5047	5033,219499	5137	5122,97376	5227	5212,728021	5317	5302,482282
4868	4854,708247	4958	4944,462508	5048	5034,216769	5138	5123,97103	5228	5213,725291	5318	5303,479552
4869	4855,705517	4959	4945,459778	5049	5035,214039	5139	5124,9683	5229	5214,72256	5319	5304,476821
4870	4856,702786	4960	4946,457047	5050	5036,211308	5140	5125,965569	5230	5215,71983	5320	5305,474091
4871	4857,700056	4961	4947,454317	5051	5037,208578	5141	5126,962839	5231	5216,7171	5321	5306,471361
4872	4858,697325	4962	4948,451586	5052	5038,205847	5142	5127,960108	5232	5217,714369	5322	5307,46863
4873	4859,694595	4963	4949,448856	5053	5039,203117	5143	5128,957378	5233	5218,711639	5323	5308,4659
4874	4860,691865	4964	4950,446125	5054	5040,200386	5144	5129,954647	5234	5219,708908	5324	5309,463169
4875	4861,689134	4965	4951,443395	5055	5041,197656	5145	5130,951917	5235	5220,706178	5325	5310,460439
4876	4862,686404	4966	4952,440665	5056	5042,194926	5146	5131,949186	5236	5221,703447	5326	5311,457708
4877	4863,683673	4967	4953,437934	5057	5043,192195	5147	5132,946456	5237	5222,700717	5327	5312,454978
4878	4864,680943	4968	4954,435204	5058	5044,189465	5148	5133,943726	5238	5223,697987	5328	5313,452248
4879	4865,678212	4969	4955,432473	5059	5045,186734	5149	5134,940995	5239	5224,695256	5329	5314,449517
4880	4866,675482	4970	4956,429743	5060	5046,184004	5150	5135,938265	5240	5225,692526	5330	5315,446787
4881	4867,672752	4971	4957,427012	5061	5047,181273	5151	5136,935534	5241	5226,689795	5331	5316,444056
4882	4868,670021	4972	4958,424282	5062	5048,178543	5152	5137,932804	5242	5227,687065	5332	5317,441326
4883	4869,667291	4973	4959,421552	5063	5049,175813	5153	5138,930073	5243	5228,684334	5333	5318,438595
4884	4870,66456	4974	4960,418821	5064	5050,173082	5154	5139,927343	5244	5229,681604	5334	5319,435865

TABLE TO FIND OUT THE POINT A IN EARTH RETURNS

5335	5320,433134	5425	5410,187395	5515	5499,941656	5605	5589,695917	5695	5679,450178	5785	5769,204439
5336	5321,430404	5426	5411,184665	5516	5500,938926	5606	5590,693187	5696	5680,447448	5786	5770,201709
5337	5322,427674	5427	5412,181935	5517	5501,936195	5607	5591,690456	5697	5681,444717	5787	5771,198978
5338	5323,424943	5428	5413,179204	5518	5502,933465	5608	5592,687726	5698	5682,441987	5788	5772,196248
5339	5324,422213	5429	5414,176474	5519	5503,930735	5609	5593,684996	5699	5683,439256	5789	5773,193517
5340	5325,419482	5430	5415,173743	5520	5504,928004	5610	5594,682265	5700	5684,436526	5790	5774,190787
5341	5326,416752	5431	5416,171013	5521	5505,925274	5611	5595,679535	5701	5685,433796	5791	5775,188057
5342	5327,414021	5432	5417,168282	5522	5506,922543	5612	5596,676804	5702	5686,431065	5792	5776,185326
5343	5328,411291	5433	5418,165552	5523	5507,919813	5613	5597,674074	5703	5687,428335	5793	5777,182596
5344	5329,408561	5434	5419,162821	5524	5508,917082	5614	5598,671343	5704	5688,425604	5794	5778,179865
5345	5330,40583	5435	5420,160091	5525	5509,914352	5615	5599,668613	5705	5689,422874	5795	5779,177135
5346	5331,4031	5436	5421,157361	5526	5510,911622	5616	5600,665883	5706	5690,420143	5796	5780,174404
5347	5332,400369	5437	5422,15463	5527	5511,908891	5617	5601,663152	5707	5691,417413	5797	5781,171674
5348	5333,397639	5438	5423,1519	5528	5512,906161	5618	5602,660422	5708	5692,414683	5798	5782,168944
5349	5334,394908	5439	5424,149169	5529	5513,90343	5619	5603,657691	5709	5693,411952	5799	5783,166213
5350	5335,392178	5440	5425,146439	5530	5514,9007	5620	5604,654961	5710	5694,409222	5800	5784,163483
5351	5336,389448	5441	5426,143708	5531	5515,897969	5621	5605,65223	5711	5695,406491	5801	5785,160752
5352	5337,386717	5442	5427,140978	5532	5516,895239	5622	5606,6495	5712	5696,403761	5802	5786,158022
5353	5338,383987	5443	5428,138248	5533	5517,892509	5623	5607,646769	5713	5697,40103	5803	5787,155291
5354	5339,381256	5444	5429,135517	5534	5518,889778	5624	5608,644039	5714	5698,3983	5804	5788,152561
5355	5340,378526	5445	5430,132787	5535	5519,887048	5625	5609,641309	5715	5699,39557	5805	5789,14983
5356	5341,375795	5446	5431,130056	5536	5520,884317	5626	5610,638578	5716	5700,392839	5806	5790,1471
5357	5342,373065	5447	5432,127326	5537	5521,881587	5627	5611,635848	5717	5701,390109	5807	5791,14437
5358	5343,370334	5448	5433,124595	5538	5522,878856	5628	5612,633117	5718	5702,387378	5808	5792,141639
5359	5344,367604	5449	5434,121865	5539	5523,876126	5629	5613,630387	5719	5703,384648	5809	5793,138909
5360	5345,364874	5450	5435,119135	5540	5524,873395	5630	5614,627656	5720	5704,381917	5810	5794,136178
5361	5346,362143	5451	5436,116404	5541	5525,870665	5631	5615,624926	5721	5705,379187	5811	5795,133448
5362	5347,359413	5452	5437,113674	5542	5526,867935	5632	5616,622196	5722	5706,376456	5812	5796,130717
5363	5348,356682	5453	5438,110943	5543	5527,865204	5633	5617,619465	5723	5707,373726	5813	5797,127987
5364	5349,353952	5454	5439,108213	5544	5528,862474	5634	5618,616735	5724	5708,370996	5814	5798,125257
5365	5350,351221	5455	5440,105482	5545	5529,859743	5635	5619,614004	5725	5709,368265	5815	5799,122526
5366	5351,348491	5456	5441,102752	5546	5530,857013	5636	5620,611274	5726	5710,365535	5816	5800,119796
5367	5352,345761	5457	5442,100022	5547	5531,854282	5637	5621,608543	5727	5711,362804	5817	5801,117065
5368	5353,34303	5458	5443,097291	5548	5532,851552	5638	5622,605813	5728	5712,360074	5818	5802,114335
5369	5354,3403	5459	5444,094561	5549	5533,848822	5639	5623,603083	5729	5713,357343	5819	5803,111604
5370	5355,337569	5460	5445,09183	5550	5534,846091	5640	5624,600352	5730	5714,354613	5820	5804,108874
5371	5356,334839	5461	5446,0891	5551	5535,843361	5641	5625,597622	5731	5715,351883	5821	5805,106144
5372	5357,332108	5462	5447,086369	5552	5536,84063	5642	5626,594891	5732	5716,349152	5822	5806,103413
5373	5358,329378	5463	5448,083639	5553	5537,8379	5643	5627,592161	5733	5717,346422	5823	5807,100683
5374	5359,326648	5464	5449,080908	5554	5538,835169	5644	5628,58943	5734	5718,343691	5824	5808,097952
5375	5360,323917	5465	5450,078178	5555	5539,832439	5645	5629,5867	5735	5719,340961	5825	5809,095222
5376	5361,321187	5466	5451,075448	5556	5540,829709	5646	5630,583969	5736	5720,33823	5826	5810,092491
5377	5362,318456	5467	5452,072717	5557	5541,826978	5647	5631,581239	5737	5721,3355	5827	5811,089761
5378	5363,315726	5468	5453,069987	5558	5542,824248	5648	5632,578509	5738	5722,33277	5828	5812,08703
5379	5364,312995	5469	5454,067256	5559	5543,821517	5649	5633,575778	5739	5723,330039	5829	5813,0843
5380	5365,310265	5470	5455,064526	5560	5544,818787	5650	5634,573048	5740	5724,327309	5830	5814,08157
5381	5366,307534	5471	5456,061795	5561	5545,816056	5651	5635,570317	5741	5725,324578	5831	5815,078839
5382	5367,304804	5472	5457,059065	5562	5546,813326	5652	5636,567587	5742	5726,321848	5832	5816,076109
5383	5368,302074	5473	5458,056335	5563	5547,810596	5653	5637,564856	5743	5727,319117	5833	5817,073378
5384	5369,299343	5474	5459,053604	5564	5548,807865	5654	5638,562126	5744	5728,316387	5834	5818,070648
5385	5370,296613	5475	5460,050874	5565	5549,805135	5655	5639,559396	5745	5729,313657	5835	5819,067917
5386	5371,293882	5476	5461,048143	5566	5550,802404	5656	5640,556665	5746	5730,310926	5836	5820,065187
5387	5372,291152	5477	5462,045413	5567	5551,799674	5657	5641,553935	5747	5731,308196	5837	5821,062457
5388	5373,288421	5478	5463,042682	5568	5552,796943	5658	5642,551204	5748	5732,305465	5838	5822,059726
5389	5374,285691	5479	5464,039952	5569	5553,794213	5659	5643,548474	5749	5733,302735	5839	5823,056996
5390	5375,282961	5480	5465,037222	5570	5554,791482	5660	5644,545743	5750	5734,300004	5840	5824,054265
5391	5376,28023	5481	5466,034491	5571	5555,788752	5661	5645,543013	5751	5735,297274	5841	5825,051535
5392	5377,2775	5482	5467,031761	5572	5556,786022	5662	5646,540283	5752	5736,294543	5842	5826,048804
5393	5378,274769	5483	5468,02903	5573	5557,783291	5663	5647,537552	5753	5737,291813	5843	5827,046074
5394	5379,272039	5484	5469,0263	5574	5558,780561	5664	5648,534822	5754	5738,289083	5844	5828,043344
5395	5380,269308	5485	5470,023569	5575	5559,77783	5665	5649,532091	5755	5739,286352	5845	5829,040613
5396	5381,266578	5486	5471,020839	5576	5560,7751	5666	5650,529361	5756	5740,283622	5846	5830,037883
5397	5382,263848	5487	5472,018108	5577	5561,772369	5667	5651,52663	5757	5741,280891	5847	5831,035152
5398	5383,261117	5488	5473,015378	5578	5562,769639	5668	5652,5239	5758	5742,278161	5848	5832,032422
5399	5384,258387	5489	5474,012648	5579	5563,766909	5669	5653,521169	5759	5743,27543	5849	5833,029691
5400	5385,255656	5490	5475,009917	5580	5564,764178	5670	5654,518439	5760	5744,2727	5850	5834,026961
5401	5386,252926	5491	5476,007187	5581	5565,761448	5671	5655,515709	5761	5745,26997	5851	5835,024231
5402	5387,250195	5492	5477,004456	5582	5566,758717	5672	5656,512978	5762	5746,267239	5852	5836,0215
5403	5388,247465	5493	5478,001726	5583	5567,755987	5673	5657,510248	5763	5747,264509	5853	5837,01877
5404	5389,244735	5494	5478,998995	5584	5568,753256	5674	5658,507517	5764	5748,261778	5854	5838,016039
5405	5390,242004	5495	5479,996265	5585	5569,750526	5675	5659,504787	5765	5749,259048	5855	5839,013309
5406	5391,239274	5496	5480,993535	5586	5570,747796	5676	5660,502056	5766	5750,256317	5856	5840,010578
5407	5392,236543	5497	5481,990804	5587	5571,745065	5677	5661,499326	5767	5751,253587	5857	5841,007848
5408	5393,233813	5498	5482,988074	5588	5572,742335	5678	5662,496596	5768	5752,250857	5858	5842,005117
5409	5394,231082	5499	5483,985343	5589	5573,739604	5679	5663,493865	5769	5753,248126	5859	5843,002387
5410	5395,228352	5500	5484,982613	5590	5574,736874	5680	5664,491135	5770	5754,245396	5860	5843,999657
5411	5396,225621	5501	5485,979882	5591	5575,734143	5681	5665,488404	5771	5755,242665	5861	5844,996926
5412	5397,222891	5502	5486,977152	5592	5576,731413	5682	5666,485674	5772	5756,239935	5862	5845,994196
5413	5398,220161	5503	5487,974422	5593	5577,728682	5683	5667,482943	5773	5757,237204	5863	5846,991465
5414	5399,21743	5504	5488,971691	5594	5578,725952	5684	5668,480213	5774	5758,234474	5864	5847,988735
5415	5400,2147	5505	5489,968961	5595	5579,723222	5685	5669,477483	5775	5759,231743	5865	5848,986004
5416	5401,211969	5506	5490,96623	5596	5580,720491	5686	5670,474752	5776	5760,229013	5866	5849,983274
5417	5402,209239	5507	5491,9635	5597	5581,717761	5687	5671,472022	5777	5761,226283	5867	5850,980544
5418	5403,206508	5508	5492,960769	5598	5582,71503	5688	5672,469291	5778	5762,223552	5868	5851,977813
5419	5404,203778	5509	5493,958039	5599	5583,7123	5689	5673,466561	5779	5763,220822	5869	5852,975083
5420	5405,201048	5510	5494,955309	5600	5584,709569	5690	5674,46383	5780	5764,218091	5870	5853,972352
5421	5406,198317	5511	5495,952578	5601	5585,706839	5691	5675,4611	5781	5765,215361	5871	5854,969622
5422	5407,195587	5512	5496,949848	5602	5586,704109	5692	5676,45837	5782	5766,21263	5872	5855,966891
5423	5408,192856	5513	5497,947117	5603	5587,701378	5693	5677,455639	5783	5767,2099	5873	5856,964161
5424	5409,190126	5514	5498,944387	5604	5588,698648	5694	5678,452909	5784	5768,20717	5874	5857,961431

LUNAR RETURNS AND EARTH RETURNS

5875	5858,9587	5965	5948,712961	6055	6038,467222	6145	6128,221483	6235	6217,975744	6325	6307,730005
5876	5859,95597	5966	5949,710231	6056	6039,464492	6146	6129,218752	6236	6218,973013	6326	6308,727274
5877	5860,953239	5967	5950,7075	6057	6040,461761	6147	6130,216022	6237	6219,970283	6327	6309,724544
5878	5861,950509	5968	5951,70477	6058	6041,459031	6148	6131,213292	6238	6220,967553	6328	6310,721813
5879	5862,947778	5969	5952,702039	6059	6042,4563	6149	6132,210561	6239	6221,964822	6329	6311,719083
5880	5863,945048	5970	5953,699309	6060	6043,45357	6150	6133,207831	6240	6222,962092	6330	6312,716353
5881	5864,942317	5971	5954,696578	6061	6044,450839	6151	6134,2051	6241	6223,959361	6331	6313,713622
5882	5865,939587	5972	5955,693848	6062	6045,448109	6152	6135,20237	6242	6224,956631	6332	6314,710892
5883	5866,936857	5973	5956,691118	6063	6046,445378	6153	6136,199639	6243	6225,9539	6333	6315,708161
5884	5867,934126	5974	5957,688387	6064	6047,442648	6154	6137,196909	6244	6226,95117	6334	6316,705431
5885	5868,931396	5975	5958,685657	6065	6048,439918	6155	6138,194179	6245	6227,948439	6335	6317,7027
5886	5869,928665	5976	5959,682926	6066	6049,437187	6156	6139,191448	6246	6228,945709	6336	6318,69997
5887	5870,925935	5977	5960,680196	6067	6050,434457	6157	6140,188718	6247	6229,942979	6337	6319,69724
5888	5871,923204	5978	5961,677465	6068	6051,431726	6158	6141,185987	6248	6230,940248	6338	6320,694509
5889	5872,920474	5979	5962,674735	6069	6052,428996	6159	6142,183257	6249	6231,937518	6339	6321,691779
5890	5873,917744	5980	5963,672005	6070	6053,426265	6160	6143,180526	6250	6232,934787	6340	6322,689048
5891	5874,915013	5981	5964,669274	6071	6054,423535	6161	6144,177796	6251	6233,932057	6341	6323,686318
5892	5875,912283	5982	5965,666544	6072	6055,420805	6162	6145,175066	6252	6234,929326	6342	6324,683587
5893	5876,909552	5983	5966,663813	6073	6056,418074	6163	6146,172335	6253	6235,926596	6343	6325,680857
5894	5877,906822	5984	5967,661083	6074	6057,415344	6164	6147,169605	6254	6236,923866	6344	6326,678127
5895	5878,904091	5985	5968,658352	6075	6058,412613	6165	6148,166874	6255	6237,921135	6345	6327,675396
5896	5879,901361	5986	5969,655622	6076	6059,409883	6166	6149,164144	6256	6238,918405	6346	6328,672666
5897	5880,898631	5987	5970,652891	6077	6060,407152	6167	6150,161413	6257	6239,915674	6347	6329,669935
5898	5881,8959	5988	5971,650161	6078	6061,404422	6168	6151,158683	6258	6240,912944	6348	6330,667205
5899	5882,89317	5989	5972,647431	6079	6062,401692	6169	6152,155952	6259	6241,910213	6349	6331,664474
5900	5883,890439	5990	5973,6447	6080	6063,398961	6170	6153,153222	6260	6242,907483	6350	6332,661744
5901	5884,887709	5991	5974,64197	6081	6064,396231	6171	6154,150492	6261	6243,904753	6351	6333,659013
5902	5885,884978	5992	5975,639239	6082	6065,3935	6172	6155,147761	6262	6244,902022	6352	6334,656283
5903	5886,882248	5993	5976,636509	6083	6066,39077	6173	6156,145031	6263	6245,899292	6353	6335,653553
5904	5887,879518	5994	5977,633778	6084	6067,388039	6174	6157,1423	6264	6246,896561	6354	6336,650822
5905	5888,876787	5995	5978,631048	6085	6068,385309	6175	6158,13957	6265	6247,893831	6355	6337,648092
5906	5889,874057	5996	5979,628318	6086	6069,382579	6176	6159,136839	6266	6248,8911	6356	6338,645361
5907	5890,871326	5997	5980,625587	6087	6070,379848	6177	6160,134109	6267	6249,88837	6357	6339,642631
5908	5891,868596	5998	5981,622857	6088	6071,377118	6178	6161,131379	6268	6250,88564	6358	6340,6399
5909	5892,865865	5999	5982,620126	6089	6072,374387	6179	6162,128648	6269	6251,882909	6359	6341,63717
5910	5893,863135	6000	5983,617396	6090	6073,371657	6180	6163,125918	6270	6252,880179	6360	6342,63444
5911	5894,860404	6001	5984,614665	6091	6074,368926	6181	6164,123187	6271	6253,877448	6361	6343,631709
5912	5895,857674	6002	5985,611935	6092	6075,366196	6182	6165,120457	6272	6254,874718	6362	6344,628979
5913	5896,854944	6003	5986,609205	6093	6076,363465	6183	6166,117726	6273	6255,871987	6363	6345,626248
5914	5897,852213	6004	5987,606474	6094	6077,360735	6184	6167,114996	6274	6256,869257	6364	6346,623518
5915	5898,849483	6005	5988,603744	6095	6078,358005	6185	6168,112266	6275	6257,866526	6365	6347,620787
5916	5899,846752	6006	5989,601013	6096	6079,355274	6186	6169,109535	6276	6258,863796	6366	6348,618057
5917	5900,844022	6007	5990,598283	6097	6080,352544	6187	6170,106805	6277	6259,861066	6367	6349,615327
5918	5901,841291	6008	5991,595552	6098	6081,349813	6188	6171,104074	6278	6260,858335	6368	6350,612596
5919	5902,838561	6009	5992,592822	6099	6082,347083	6189	6172,101344	6279	6261,855605	6369	6351,609866
5920	5903,835831	6010	5993,590091	6100	6083,344352	6190	6173,098613	6280	6262,852874	6370	6352,607135
5921	5904,8331	6011	5994,587361	6101	6084,341622	6191	6174,095883	6281	6263,850144	6371	6353,604405
5922	5905,83037	6012	5995,584631	6102	6085,338892	6192	6175,093153	6282	6264,847413	6372	6354,601674
5923	5906,827639	6013	5996,5819	6103	6086,336161	6193	6176,090422	6283	6265,844683	6373	6355,598944
5924	5907,824909	6014	5997,57917	6104	6087,333431	6194	6177,087692	6284	6266,841953	6374	6356,596214
5925	5908,822178	6015	5998,576439	6105	6088,3307	6195	6178,084961	6285	6267,839222	6375	6357,593483
5926	5909,819448	6016	5999,573709	6106	6089,32797	6196	6179,082231	6286	6268,836492	6376	6358,590753
5927	5910,816718	6017	6000,570978	6107	6090,325239	6197	6180,0795	6287	6269,833761	6377	6359,588022
5928	5911,813987	6018	6001,568248	6108	6091,322509	6198	6181,07677	6288	6270,831031	6378	6360,585292
5929	5912,811257	6019	6002,565518	6109	6092,319779	6199	6182,074039	6289	6271,8283	6379	6361,582561
5930	5913,808526	6020	6003,562787	6110	6093,317048	6200	6183,071309	6290	6272,82557	6380	6362,579831
5931	5914,805796	6021	6004,560057	6111	6094,314318	6201	6184,068579	6291	6273,82284	6381	6363,5771
5932	5915,803065	6022	6005,557326	6112	6095,311587	6202	6185,065848	6292	6274,820109	6382	6364,57437
5933	5916,800335	6023	6006,554596	6113	6096,308857	6203	6186,063118	6293	6275,817379	6383	6365,57164
5934	5917,797604	6024	6007,551865	6114	6097,306126	6204	6187,060387	6294	6276,814648	6384	6366,568909
5935	5918,794874	6025	6008,549135	6115	6098,303396	6205	6188,057657	6295	6277,811918	6385	6367,566179
5936	5919,792144	6026	6009,546405	6116	6099,300665	6206	6189,054926	6296	6278,809187	6386	6368,563448
5937	5920,789413	6027	6010,543674	6117	6100,297935	6207	6190,052196	6297	6279,806457	6387	6369,560718
5938	5921,786683	6028	6011,540944	6118	6101,295205	6208	6191,049466	6298	6280,803726	6388	6370,557987
5939	5922,783952	6029	6012,538213	6119	6102,292474	6209	6192,046735	6299	6281,800996	6389	6371,555257
5940	5923,781222	6030	6013,535483	6120	6103,289744	6210	6193,044005	6300	6282,798266	6390	6372,552527
5941	5924,778491	6031	6014,532752	6121	6104,287013	6211	6194,041274	6301	6283,795535	6391	6373,549796
5942	5925,775761	6032	6015,530022	6122	6105,284283	6212	6195,038544	6302	6284,792805	6392	6374,547066
5943	5926,773031	6033	6016,527292	6123	6106,281552	6213	6196,035813	6303	6285,790074	6393	6375,544335
5944	5927,7703	6034	6017,524561	6124	6107,278822	6214	6197,033083	6304	6286,787344	6394	6376,541605
5945	5928,76757	6035	6018,521831	6125	6108,276092	6215	6198,030353	6305	6287,784613	6395	6377,538874
5946	5929,764839	6036	6019,5191	6126	6109,273361	6216	6199,027622	6306	6288,781883	6396	6378,536144
5947	5930,762109	6037	6020,51637	6127	6110,270631	6217	6200,024892	6307	6289,779153	6397	6379,53414
5948	5931,759378	6038	6021,513639	6128	6111,2679	6218	6201,022161	6308	6290,776422	6398	6380,530683
5949	5932,756648	6039	6022,510909	6129	6112,26517	6219	6202,019431	6309	6291,773692	6399	6381,527953
5950	5933,753918	6040	6023,508178	6130	6113,262439	6220	6203,0167	6310	6292,770961	6400	6382,525222
5951	5934,751187	6041	6024,505448	6131	6114,259709	6221	6204,01397	6311	6293,768231	6401	6383,522492
5952	5935,748457	6042	6025,502718	6132	6115,256979	6222	6205,011239	6312	6294,7655	6402	6384,519761
5953	5936,745726	6043	6026,499987	6133	6116,254248	6223	6206,008509	6313	6295,76277	6403	6385,517031
5954	5937,742996	6044	6027,497257	6134	6117,251518	6224	6207,005779	6314	6296,76004	6404	6386,5143
5955	5938,740265	6045	6028,494526	6135	6118,248787	6225	6208,003048	6315	6297,757309	6405	6387,51157
5956	5939,737535	6046	6029,491796	6136	6119,246057	6226	6209,000318	6316	6298,754579	6406	6388,50884
5957	5940,734804	6047	6030,489065	6137	6120,243326	6227	6209,997587	6317	6299,751848	6407	6389,506109
5958	5941,732074	6048	6031,486335	6138	6121,240596	6228	6210,994857	6318	6300,749118	6408	6390,503379
5959	5942,729344	6049	6032,483605	6139	6122,237866	6229	6211,992126	6319	6301,746387	6409	6391,500648
5960	5943,726613	6050	6033,480874	6140	6123,235135	6230	6212,989396	6320	6302,743657	6410	6392,497918
5961	5944,723883	6051	6034,478144	6141	6124,232405	6231	6213,986666	6321	6303,740927	6411	6393,495187
5962	5945,721152	6052	6035,475413	6142	6125,229674	6232	6214,983935	6322	6304,738196	6412	6394,492457
5963	5946,718422	6053	6036,472683	6143	6126,226944	6233	6215,981205	6323	6305,735466	6413	6395,489727
5964	5947,715691	6054	6037,469952	6144	6127,224213	6234	6216,978474	6324	6306,732735	6414	6396,486996

TABLE TO FIND OUT THE POINT A IN EARTH RETURNS 169

6415	6397,484266	6505	6487,238527	6595	6576,992788	6685	6666,747049	6775	6756,501309	6865	6846,25557
6416	6398,481535	6506	6488,235796	6596	6577,990057	6686	6667,744318	6776	6757,498579	6866	6847,25284
6417	6399,478805	6507	6489,233066	6597	6578,987327	6687	6668,741588	6777	6758,495849	6867	6848,25011
6418	6400,476074	6508	6490,230335	6598	6579,984596	6688	6669,738857	6778	6759,493118	6868	6849,247379
6419	6401,473344	6509	6491,227605	6599	6580,981866	6689	6670,736127	6779	6760,490388	6869	6850,244649
6420	6402,470614	6510	6492,224874	6600	6581,979135	6690	6671,733396	6780	6761,487657	6870	6851,241918
6421	6403,467883	6511	6493,222144	6601	6582,976405	6691	6672,730666	6781	6762,484927	6871	6852,239188
6422	6404,465153	6512	6494,219414	6602	6583,973675	6692	6673,727935	6782	6763,482196	6872	6853,236457
6423	6405,462422	6513	6495,216683	6603	6584,970944	6693	6674,725205	6783	6764,479466	6873	6854,233727
6424	6406,459692	6514	6496,213953	6604	6585,968214	6694	6675,722475	6784	6765,476736	6874	6855,230996
6425	6407,456961	6515	6497,211222	6605	6586,965483	6695	6676,719744	6785	6766,474005	6875	6856,228266
6426	6408,454231	6516	6498,208492	6606	6587,962753	6696	6677,717014	6786	6767,471275	6876	6857,225536
6427	6409,451501	6517	6499,205761	6607	6588,960022	6697	6678,714283	6787	6768,468544	6877	6858,222805
6428	6410,44877	6518	6500,203031	6608	6589,957292	6698	6679,711553	6788	6769,465814	6878	6859,220075
6429	6411,44604	6519	6501,200301	6609	6590,954562	6699	6680,708822	6789	6770,463083	6879	6860,217344
6430	6412,443309	6520	6502,19757	6610	6591,951831	6700	6681,706092	6790	6771,460353	6880	6861,214614
6431	6413,440579	6521	6503,19484	6611	6592,949101	6701	6682,703362	6791	6772,457623	6881	6862,211883
6432	6414,437848	6522	6504,192109	6612	6593,94637	6702	6683,700631	6792	6773,454892	6882	6863,209153
6433	6415,435118	6523	6505,189379	6613	6594,94364	6703	6684,697901	6793	6774,452162	6883	6864,206423
6434	6416,432387	6524	6506,186648	6614	6595,940909	6704	6685,69517	6794	6775,449431	6884	6865,203692
6435	6417,429657	6525	6507,183918	6615	6596,938179	6705	6686,69244	6795	6776,446701	6885	6866,200962
6436	6418,426927	6526	6508,181188	6616	6597,935448	6706	6687,689709	6796	6777,44397	6886	6867,198231
6437	6419,424196	6527	6509,178457	6617	6598,932718	6707	6688,686979	6797	6778,44124	6887	6868,195501
6438	6420,421466	6528	6510,175727	6618	6599,929988	6708	6689,684249	6798	6779,438509	6888	6869,19277
6439	6421,418735	6529	6511,172996	6619	6600,927257	6709	6690,681518	6799	6780,435779	6889	6870,19004
6440	6422,416005	6530	6512,170266	6620	6601,924527	6710	6691,678788	6800	6781,433049	6890	6871,18731
6441	6423,413274	6531	6513,167535	6621	6602,921796	6711	6692,676057	6801	6782,430318	6891	6872,184579
6442	6424,410544	6532	6514,164805	6622	6603,919066	6712	6693,673327	6802	6783,427588	6892	6873,181849
6443	6425,407814	6533	6515,162074	6623	6604,916335	6713	6694,670596	6803	6784,424857	6893	6874,179118
6444	6426,405083	6534	6516,159344	6624	6605,913605	6714	6695,667866	6804	6785,422127	6894	6875,176388
6445	6427,402353	6535	6517,156614	6625	6606,910875	6715	6696,665136	6805	6786,419396	6895	6876,173657
6446	6428,399622	6536	6518,153883	6626	6607,908144	6716	6697,662405	6806	6787,416666	6896	6877,170927
6447	6429,396892	6537	6519,151153	6627	6608,905414	6717	6698,659675	6807	6788,413936	6897	6878,168197
6448	6430,394161	6538	6520,148422	6628	6609,902683	6718	6699,656944	6808	6789,411205	6898	6879,165466
6449	6431,391431	6539	6521,145692	6629	6610,899953	6719	6700,654214	6809	6790,408475	6899	6880,162736
6450	6432,388701	6540	6522,142961	6630	6611,897222	6720	6701,651483	6810	6791,405744	6900	6881,160005
6451	6433,38597	6541	6523,140231	6631	6612,894492	6721	6702,648753	6811	6792,403014	6901	6882,157275
6452	6434,38324	6542	6524,137501	6632	6613,891762	6722	6703,646022	6812	6793,400283	6902	6883,154544
6453	6435,380509	6543	6525,13477	6633	6614,889031	6723	6704,643292	6813	6794,397553	6903	6884,151814
6454	6436,377779	6544	6526,13204	6634	6615,886301	6724	6705,640562	6814	6795,394823	6904	6885,149083
6455	6437,375048	6545	6527,129309	6635	6616,88357	6725	6706,637831	6815	6796,392092	6905	6886,146353
6456	6438,372318	6546	6528,126579	6636	6617,88084	6726	6707,635101	6816	6797,389362	6906	6887,143623
6457	6439,369587	6547	6529,123848	6637	6618,878109	6727	6708,63237	6817	6798,386631	6907	6888,140892
6458	6440,366857	6548	6530,121118	6638	6619,875379	6728	6709,62964	6818	6799,383901	6908	6889,138162
6459	6441,364127	6549	6531,118388	6639	6620,872648	6729	6710,626909	6819	6800,38117	6909	6890,135431
6460	6442,361396	6550	6532,115657	6640	6621,869918	6730	6711,624179	6820	6801,37844	6910	6891,132701
6461	6443,358666	6551	6533,112927	6641	6622,867188	6731	6712,621449	6821	6802,375709	6911	6892,12997
6462	6444,355935	6552	6534,110196	6642	6623,864457	6732	6713,618718	6822	6803,372979	6912	6893,12724
6463	6445,353205	6553	6535,107466	6643	6624,861727	6733	6714,615988	6823	6804,370249	6913	6894,12451
6464	6446,350474	6554	6536,104735	6644	6625,858996	6734	6715,613257	6824	6805,367518	6914	6895,121779
6465	6447,347744	6555	6537,102005	6645	6626,856266	6735	6716,610527	6825	6806,364788	6915	6896,119049
6466	6448,345014	6556	6538,099275	6646	6627,853535	6736	6717,607796	6826	6807,362057	6916	6897,116318
6467	6449,342283	6557	6539,096544	6647	6628,850805	6737	6718,605066	6827	6808,359327	6917	6898,113588
6468	6450,339553	6558	6540,093814	6648	6629,848075	6738	6719,602336	6828	6809,356596	6918	6899,110857
6469	6451,336822	6559	6541,091083	6649	6630,845344	6739	6720,599605	6829	6810,353866	6919	6900,108127
6470	6452,334092	6560	6542,088353	6650	6631,842614	6740	6721,596875	6830	6811,351136	6920	6901,105397
6471	6453,331361	6561	6543,085622	6651	6632,839883	6741	6722,594144	6831	6812,348405	6921	6902,102666
6472	6454,328631	6562	6544,082892	6652	6633,837153	6742	6723,591414	6832	6813,345675	6922	6903,099936
6473	6455,325901	6563	6545,080161	6653	6634,834422	6743	6724,588683	6833	6814,342944	6923	6904,097205
6474	6456,32317	6564	6546,077431	6654	6635,831692	6744	6725,585953	6834	6815,340214	6924	6905,094475
6475	6457,32044	6565	6547,074701	6655	6636,828962	6745	6726,583222	6835	6816,337483	6925	6906,091744
6476	6458,317709	6566	6548,07197	6656	6637,826231	6746	6727,580492	6836	6817,334753	6926	6907,089014
6477	6459,314979	6567	6549,06924	6657	6638,823501	6747	6728,577762	6837	6818,332023	6927	6908,086283
6478	6460,312248	6568	6550,066509	6658	6639,82077	6748	6729,575031	6838	6819,329292	6928	6909,083553
6479	6461,309518	6569	6551,063779	6659	6640,81804	6749	6730,572301	6839	6820,326562	6929	6910,080823
6480	6462,306788	6570	6552,061048	6660	6641,815309	6750	6731,56957	6840	6821,323831	6930	6911,078092
6481	6463,304057	6571	6553,058318	6661	6642,812579	6751	6732,56684	6841	6822,321101	6931	6912,075362
6482	6464,301327	6572	6554,055588	6662	6643,809849	6752	6733,564109	6842	6823,31837	6932	6913,072631
6483	6465,298596	6573	6555,052857	6663	6644,807118	6753	6734,561379	6843	6824,31564	6933	6914,069901
6484	6466,295866	6574	6556,050127	6664	6645,804388	6754	6735,558649	6844	6825,31291	6934	6915,06717
6485	6467,293135	6575	6557,047396	6665	6646,801657	6755	6736,555918	6845	6826,310179	6935	6916,06444
6486	6468,290405	6576	6558,044666	6666	6647,798927	6756	6737,553188	6846	6827,307449	6936	6917,06171
6487	6469,287674	6577	6559,041935	6667	6648,796196	6757	6738,550457	6847	6828,304718	6937	6918,058979
6488	6470,284944	6578	6560,039205	6668	6649,793466	6758	6739,547727	6848	6829,301988	6938	6919,056249
6489	6471,282214	6579	6561,036475	6669	6650,790735	6759	6740,544996	6849	6830,299257	6939	6920,053518
6490	6472,279483	6580	6562,033744	6670	6651,788005	6760	6741,542266	6850	6831,296527	6940	6921,050788
6491	6473,276753	6581	6563,031014	6671	6652,785275	6761	6742,539536	6851	6832,293796	6941	6922,048057
6492	6474,274022	6582	6564,028283	6672	6653,782544	6762	6743,536805	6852	6833,291066	6942	6923,045327
6493	6475,271292	6583	6565,025553	6673	6654,779814	6763	6744,534075	6853	6834,288336	6943	6924,042597
6494	6476,268561	6584	6566,022822	6674	6655,777083	6764	6745,531344	6854	6835,285605	6944	6925,039866
6495	6477,265831	6585	6567,020092	6675	6656,774353	6765	6746,528614	6855	6836,282875	6945	6926,037136
6496	6478,263101	6586	6568,017361	6676	6657,771622	6766	6747,525883	6856	6837,280144	6946	6927,034405
6497	6479,26037	6587	6569,014631	6677	6658,768892	6767	6748,523153	6857	6838,277414	6947	6928,031675
6498	6480,25764	6588	6570,011901	6678	6659,766162	6768	6749,520423	6858	6839,274683	6948	6929,028944
6499	6481,254909	6589	6571,00917	6679	6660,763431	6769	6750,517692	6859	6840,271953	6949	6930,026214
6500	6482,252179	6590	6572,00644	6680	6661,760701	6770	6751,514962	6860	6841,269223	6950	6931,023484
6501	6483,249448	6591	6573,003709	6681	6662,75797	6771	6752,512231	6861	6842,266492	6951	6932,020753
6502	6484,246718	6592	6574,000979	6682	6663,75524	6772	6753,509501	6862	6843,263762	6952	6933,018023
6503	6485,243988	6593	6574,998248	6683	6664,752509	6773	6754,50677	6863	6844,261031	6953	6934,015292
6504	6486,241257	6594	6575,995518	6684	6665,749779	6774	6755,50404	6864	6845,258301	6954	6935,012562

6955	6936,009831	7045	7025,764092	7135	7115,518353	7225	7205,272614	7315	7295,026875	7405	7384,781136
6956	6937,007101	7046	7026,761362	7136	7116,515623	7226	7206,269884	7316	7296,024145	7406	7385,778406
6957	6938,00437	7047	7027,758631	7137	7117,512892	7227	7207,267153	7317	7297,021414	7407	7386,775675
6958	6939,00164	7048	7028,755901	7138	7118,510162	7228	7208,264423	7318	7298,018684	7408	7387,772945
6959	6939,99891	7049	7029,753171	7139	7119,507431	7229	7209,261692	7319	7299,015953	7409	7388,770214
6960	6940,996179	7050	7030,75044	7140	7120,504701	7230	7210,258962	7320	7300,013223	7410	7389,767484
6961	6941,993449	7051	7031,74771	7141	7121,501971	7231	7211,256232	7321	7301,010492	7411	7390,764753
6962	6942,990718	7052	7032,744979	7142	7122,49924	7232	7212,253501	7322	7302,007762	7412	7391,762023
6963	6943,987988	7053	7033,742249	7143	7123,49651	7233	7213,250771	7323	7303,005032	7413	7392,759293
6964	6944,985257	7054	7034,739518	7144	7124,493779	7234	7214,24804	7324	7304,002301	7414	7393,756562
6965	6945,982527	7055	7035,736788	7145	7125,491049	7235	7215,24531	7325	7304,999571	7415	7394,753832
6966	6946,979797	7056	7036,734058	7146	7126,488318	7236	7216,242579	7326	7305,99684	7416	7395,751101
6967	6947,977066	7057	7037,731327	7147	7127,485588	7237	7217,239849	7327	7306,99411	7417	7396,748371
6968	6948,974336	7058	7038,728597	7148	7128,482858	7238	7218,237119	7328	7307,991379	7418	7397,74564
6969	6949,971605	7059	7039,725866	7149	7129,480127	7239	7219,234388	7329	7308,988649	7419	7398,74291
6970	6950,968875	7060	7040,723136	7150	7130,477397	7240	7220,231658	7330	7309,985919	7420	7399,74018
6971	6951,966144	7061	7041,720405	7151	7131,474666	7241	7221,228927	7331	7310,983188	7421	7400,737449
6972	6952,963414	7062	7042,717675	7152	7132,471936	7242	7222,226197	7332	7311,980458	7422	7401,734719
6973	6953,960684	7063	7043,714944	7153	7133,469205	7243	7223,223466	7333	7312,977727	7423	7402,731988
6974	6954,957953	7064	7044,712214	7154	7134,466475	7244	7224,220736	7334	7313,974997	7424	7403,729258
6975	6955,955223	7065	7045,709484	7155	7135,463745	7245	7225,218005	7335	7314,972266	7425	7404,726527
6976	6956,952492	7066	7046,706753	7156	7136,461014	7246	7226,215275	7336	7315,969536	7426	7405,723797
6977	6957,949762	7067	7047,704023	7157	7137,458284	7247	7227,212545	7337	7316,966806	7427	7406,721066
6978	6958,947031	7068	7048,701292	7158	7138,455553	7248	7228,209814	7338	7317,964075	7428	7407,718336
6979	6959,944301	7069	7049,698562	7159	7139,452823	7249	7229,207084	7339	7318,961345	7429	7408,715606
6980	6960,94157	7070	7050,695831	7160	7140,450092	7250	7230,204353	7340	7319,958614	7430	7409,712875
6981	6961,93884	7071	7051,693101	7161	7141,447362	7251	7231,201623	7341	7320,955884	7431	7410,710145
6982	6962,93611	7072	7052,690371	7162	7142,444631	7252	7232,198892	7342	7321,953153	7432	7411,707414
6983	6963,933379	7073	7053,68764	7163	7143,441901	7253	7233,196162	7343	7322,950423	7433	7412,704684
6984	6964,930649	7074	7054,68491	7164	7144,439171	7254	7234,193432	7344	7323,947693	7434	7413,701953
6985	6965,927918	7075	7055,682179	7165	7145,43644	7255	7235,190701	7345	7324,944962	7435	7414,699223
6986	6966,925188	7076	7056,679449	7166	7146,43371	7256	7236,187971	7346	7325,942232	7436	7415,696493
6987	6967,922457	7077	7057,676718	7167	7147,430979	7257	7237,18524	7347	7326,939501	7437	7416,693762
6988	6968,919727	7078	7058,673988	7168	7148,428249	7258	7238,18251	7348	7327,936771	7438	7417,691032
6989	6969,916997	7079	7059,671258	7169	7149,425518	7259	7239,179779	7349	7328,93404	7439	7418,688301
6990	6970,914266	7080	7060,668527	7170	7150,422788	7260	7240,177049	7350	7329,93131	7440	7419,685571
6991	6971,911536	7081	7061,665797	7171	7151,420058	7261	7241,174319	7351	7330,928579	7441	7420,68284
6992	6972,908805	7082	7062,663066	7172	7152,417327	7262	7242,171588	7352	7331,925849	7442	7421,68011
6993	6973,906075	7083	7063,660336	7173	7153,414597	7263	7243,168858	7353	7332,923119	7443	7422,67738
6994	6974,903344	7084	7064,657605	7174	7154,411866	7264	7244,166127	7354	7333,920388	7444	7423,674649
6995	6975,900614	7085	7065,654875	7175	7155,409136	7265	7245,163397	7355	7334,917658	7445	7424,671919
6996	6976,897884	7086	7066,652144	7176	7156,406405	7266	7246,160666	7356	7335,914927	7446	7425,669188
6997	6977,895153	7087	7067,649414	7177	7157,403675	7267	7247,157936	7357	7336,912197	7447	7426,666458
6998	6978,892423	7088	7068,646684	7178	7158,400945	7268	7248,155205	7358	7337,909466	7448	7427,663727
6999	6979,889692	7089	7069,643953	7179	7159,398214	7269	7249,152475	7359	7338,906736	7449	7428,660997
7000	6980,886962	7090	7070,641223	7180	7160,395484	7270	7250,149745	7360	7339,904006	7450	7429,658266
7001	6981,884231	7091	7071,638492	7181	7161,392753	7271	7251,147014	7361	7340,901275	7451	7430,655536
7002	6982,881501	7092	7072,635762	7182	7162,390023	7272	7252,144284	7362	7341,898545	7452	7431,652806
7003	6983,878771	7093	7073,633031	7183	7163,387292	7273	7253,141553	7363	7342,895814	7453	7432,650075
7004	6984,87604	7094	7074,630301	7184	7164,384562	7274	7254,138823	7364	7343,893084	7454	7433,647345
7005	6985,87331	7095	7075,627571	7185	7165,381832	7275	7255,136092	7365	7344,890353	7455	7434,644614
7006	6986,870579	7096	7076,62484	7186	7166,379101	7276	7256,133362	7366	7345,887623	7456	7435,641884
7007	6987,867849	7097	7077,62211	7187	7167,376371	7277	7257,130632	7367	7346,884893	7457	7436,639153
7008	6988,865118	7098	7078,619379	7188	7168,37364	7278	7258,127901	7368	7347,882162	7458	7437,636423
7009	6989,862388	7099	7079,616649	7189	7169,37091	7279	7259,125171	7369	7348,879432	7459	7438,633693
7010	6990,859657	7100	7080,613918	7190	7170,368179	7280	7260,12244	7370	7349,876701	7460	7439,630962
7011	6991,856927	7101	7081,611188	7191	7171,365449	7281	7261,11971	7371	7350,873971	7461	7440,628232
7012	6992,854197	7102	7082,608458	7192	7172,362718	7282	7262,116979	7372	7351,87124	7462	7441,625501
7013	6993,851466	7103	7083,605727	7193	7173,359988	7283	7263,114249	7373	7352,86851	7463	7442,622771
7014	6994,848736	7104	7084,602997	7194	7174,357258	7284	7264,111519	7374	7353,865779	7464	7443,62004
7015	6995,846005	7105	7085,600266	7195	7175,354527	7285	7265,108788	7375	7354,863049	7465	7444,61731
7016	6996,843275	7106	7086,597536	7196	7176,351797	7286	7266,106058	7376	7355,860319	7466	7445,61458
7017	6997,840544	7107	7087,594805	7197	7177,349066	7287	7267,103327	7377	7356,857588	7467	7446,611849
7018	6998,837814	7108	7088,592075	7198	7178,346336	7288	7268,100597	7378	7357,854858	7468	7447,609119
7019	6999,835084	7109	7089,589344	7199	7179,343605	7289	7269,097866	7379	7358,852127	7469	7448,606388
7020	7000,832353	7110	7090,586614	7200	7180,340875	7290	7270,095136	7380	7359,849397	7470	7449,603658
7021	7001,829623	7111	7091,583884	7201	7181,338145	7291	7271,092406	7381	7360,846666	7471	7450,600927
7022	7002,826892	7112	7092,581153	7202	7182,335414	7292	7272,089675	7382	7361,843936	7472	7451,598197
7023	7003,824162	7113	7093,578423	7203	7183,332684	7293	7273,086945	7383	7362,841206	7473	7452,595467
7024	7004,821431	7114	7094,575692	7204	7184,329953	7294	7274,084214	7384	7363,838475	7474	7453,592736
7025	7005,818701	7115	7095,572962	7205	7185,327223	7295	7275,081484	7385	7364,835745	7475	7454,590006
7026	7006,815971	7116	7096,570231	7206	7186,324492	7296	7276,078753	7386	7365,833014	7476	7455,587275
7027	7007,81324	7117	7097,567501	7207	7187,321762	7297	7277,076023	7387	7366,830284	7477	7456,584545
7028	7008,81051	7118	7098,564771	7208	7188,319032	7298	7278,073292	7388	7367,827553	7478	7457,581814
7029	7009,807779	7119	7099,56204	7209	7189,316301	7299	7279,070562	7389	7368,824823	7479	7458,579084
7030	7010,805049	7120	7100,55931	7210	7190,313571	7300	7280,067832	7390	7369,822093	7480	7459,576353
7031	7011,802318	7121	7101,556579	7211	7191,31084	7301	7281,065101	7391	7370,819362	7481	7460,573623
7032	7012,799588	7122	7102,553849	7212	7192,30811	7302	7282,062371	7392	7371,816632	7482	7461,570893
7033	7013,796857	7123	7103,551118	7213	7193,305379	7303	7283,05964	7393	7372,813901	7483	7462,568162
7034	7014,794127	7124	7104,548388	7214	7194,302649	7304	7284,05691	7394	7373,811171	7484	7463,565432
7035	7015,791397	7125	7105,545658	7215	7195,299918	7305	7285,054179	7395	7374,80844	7485	7464,562701
7036	7016,788666	7126	7106,542927	7216	7196,297188	7306	7286,051449	7396	7375,80571	7486	7465,559971
7037	7017,785936	7127	7107,540197	7217	7197,294458	7307	7287,048719	7397	7376,802979	7487	7466,55724
7038	7018,783205	7128	7108,537466	7218	7198,291727	7308	7288,045988	7398	7377,800249	7488	7467,55451
7039	7019,780475	7129	7109,534736	7219	7199,288997	7309	7289,043258	7399	7378,797519	7489	7468,55178
7040	7020,777744	7130	7110,532005	7220	7200,286266	7310	7290,040527	7400	7379,794788	7490	7469,549049
7041	7021,775014	7131	7111,529275	7221	7201,283536	7311	7291,037797	7401	7380,792058	7491	7470,546319
7042	7022,772284	7132	7112,526545	7222	7202,280805	7312	7292,035066	7402	7381,789327	7492	7471,543588
7043	7023,769553	7133	7113,523814	7223	7203,278075	7313	7293,032336	7403	7382,786597	7493	7472,540858
7044	7024,766823	7134	7114,521084	7224	7204,275345	7314	7294,029606	7404	7383,783866	7494	7473,538127

TABLE TO FIND OUT THE POINT A IN EARTH RETURNS 171

7495	7474,535397	7585	7564,289658	7675	7654,043919	7765	7743,79818	7855	7833,552441	7945	7923,306702
7496	7475,532667	7586	7565,286927	7676	7655,041188	7766	7744,795449	7856	7834,54971	7946	7924,303971
7497	7476,529936	7587	7566,284197	7677	7656,038458	7767	7745,792719	7857	7835,54698	7947	7925,301241
7498	7477,527206	7588	7567,281467	7678	7657,035728	7768	7746,789988	7858	7836,544249	7948	7926,29851
7499	7478,524475	7589	7568,278736	7679	7658,032997	7769	7747,787258	7859	7837,541519	7949	7927,29578
7500	7479,521745	7590	7569,276006	7680	7659,030267	7770	7748,784528	7860	7838,538789	7950	7928,293049
7501	7480,519014	7591	7570,273275	7681	7660,027536	7771	7749,781797	7861	7839,536058	7951	7929,290319
7502	7481,516284	7592	7571,270545	7682	7661,024806	7772	7750,779067	7862	7840,533328	7952	7930,287589
7503	7482,513553	7593	7572,267814	7683	7662,022075	7773	7751,776336	7863	7841,530597	7953	7931,284858
7504	7483,510823	7594	7573,265084	7684	7663,019345	7774	7752,773606	7864	7842,527867	7954	7932,282128
7505	7484,508093	7595	7574,262354	7685	7664,016614	7775	7753,770875	7865	7843,525136	7955	7933,279397
7506	7485,505362	7596	7575,259623	7686	7665,013884	7776	7754,768145	7866	7844,522406	7956	7934,276667
7507	7486,502632	7597	7576,256893	7687	7666,011154	7777	7755,765415	7867	7845,519676	7957	7935,273936
7508	7487,499901	7598	7577,254162	7688	7667,008423	7778	7756,762684	7868	7846,516945	7958	7936,271206
7509	7488,497171	7599	7578,251432	7689	7668,005693	7779	7757,759954	7869	7847,514215	7959	7937,268476
7510	7489,49444	7600	7579,248701	7690	7669,002962	7780	7758,757223	7870	7848,511484	7960	7938,265745
7511	7490,49171	7601	7580,245971	7691	7670,000232	7781	7759,754493	7871	7849,508754	7961	7939,263015
7512	7491,48898	7602	7581,243241	7692	7670,997501	7782	7760,751762	7872	7850,506023	7962	7940,260284
7513	7492,486249	7603	7582,24051	7693	7671,994771	7783	7761,749032	7873	7851,503293	7963	7941,257554
7514	7493,483519	7604	7583,23778	7694	7672,992041	7784	7762,746302	7874	7852,500562	7964	7942,254823
7515	7494,480788	7605	7584,235049	7695	7673,98931	7785	7763,743571	7875	7853,497832	7965	7943,252093
7516	7495,478058	7606	7585,232319	7696	7674,98658	7786	7764,740841	7876	7854,495102	7966	7944,249363
7517	7496,475327	7607	7586,229588	7697	7675,983849	7787	7765,73811	7877	7855,492371	7967	7945,246632
7518	7497,472597	7608	7587,226858	7698	7676,981119	7788	7766,73538	7878	7856,489641	7968	7946,243902
7519	7498,469867	7609	7588,224127	7699	7677,978388	7789	7767,732649	7879	7857,48691	7969	7947,241171
7520	7499,467136	7610	7589,221397	7700	7678,975658	7790	7768,729919	7880	7858,48418	7970	7948,238441
7521	7500,464406	7611	7590,218667	7701	7679,972928	7791	7769,727188	7881	7859,481449	7971	7949,23571
7522	7501,461675	7612	7591,215936	7702	7680,970197	7792	7770,724458	7882	7860,478719	7972	7950,23298
7523	7502,458945	7613	7592,213206	7703	7681,967467	7793	7771,721728	7883	7861,475989	7973	7951,230249
7524	7503,456214	7614	7593,210475	7704	7682,964736	7794	7772,718997	7884	7862,473258	7974	7952,227519
7525	7504,453484	7615	7594,207745	7705	7683,962006	7795	7773,716267	7885	7863,470528	7975	7953,224789
7526	7505,450754	7616	7595,205014	7706	7684,959275	7796	7774,713536	7886	7864,467797	7976	7954,222058
7527	7506,448023	7617	7596,202284	7707	7685,956545	7797	7775,710806	7887	7865,465067	7977	7955,219328
7528	7507,445293	7618	7597,199554	7708	7686,953815	7798	7776,708075	7888	7866,462336	7978	7956,216597
7529	7508,442562	7619	7598,196823	7709	7687,951084	7799	7777,705345	7889	7867,459606	7979	7957,213867
7530	7509,439832	7620	7599,194093	7710	7688,948354	7800	7778,702615	7890	7868,456876	7980	7958,211136
7531	7510,437101	7621	7600,191362	7711	7689,945623	7801	7779,699884	7891	7869,454145	7981	7959,208406
7532	7511,434371	7622	7601,188632	7712	7690,942893	7802	7780,697154	7892	7870,451415	7982	7960,205676
7533	7512,43164	7623	7602,185901	7713	7691,940162	7803	7781,694423	7893	7871,448684	7983	7961,202945
7534	7513,42891	7624	7603,183171	7714	7692,937432	7804	7782,691693	7894	7872,445954	7984	7962,200215
7535	7514,42618	7625	7604,180441	7715	7693,934701	7805	7783,688962	7895	7873,443223	7985	7963,197484
7536	7515,423449	7626	7605,17771	7716	7694,931971	7806	7784,686232	7896	7874,440493	7986	7964,194754
7537	7516,420719	7627	7606,17498	7717	7695,929241	7807	7785,683502	7897	7875,437762	7987	7965,192023
7538	7517,417988	7628	7607,172249	7718	7696,92651	7808	7786,680771	7898	7876,435032	7988	7966,189293
7539	7518,415258	7629	7608,169519	7719	7697,92378	7809	7787,678041	7899	7877,432302	7989	7967,186563
7540	7519,412527	7630	7609,166788	7720	7698,921049	7810	7788,67531	7900	7878,429571	7990	7968,183832
7541	7520,409797	7631	7610,164058	7721	7699,918319	7811	7789,67258	7901	7879,426841	7991	7969,181102
7542	7521,407067	7632	7611,161328	7722	7700,915588	7812	7790,669849	7902	7880,42411	7992	7970,178371
7543	7522,404336	7633	7612,158597	7723	7701,912858	7813	7791,667119	7903	7881,42138	7993	7971,175641
7544	7523,401606	7634	7613,155867	7724	7702,910128	7814	7792,664389	7904	7882,418649	7994	7972,17291
7545	7524,398875	7635	7614,153136	7725	7703,907397	7815	7793,661658	7905	7883,415919	7995	7973,17018
7546	7525,396145	7636	7615,150406	7726	7704,904667	7816	7794,658928	7906	7884,413189	7996	7974,16745
7547	7526,393414	7637	7616,147675	7727	7705,901936	7817	7795,656197	7907	7885,410458	7997	7975,164719
7548	7527,390684	7638	7617,144945	7728	7706,899206	7818	7796,653467	7908	7886,407728	7998	7976,161989
7549	7528,387954	7639	7618,142214	7729	7707,896475	7819	7797,650736	7909	7887,404997	7999	7977,159258
7550	7529,385223	7640	7619,139484	7730	7708,893745	7820	7798,648006	7910	7888,402267	8000	7978,156528
7551	7530,382493	7641	7620,136754	7731	7709,891015	7821	7799,645275	7911	7889,399536	8001	7979,153797
7552	7531,379762	7642	7621,134023	7732	7710,888284	7822	7800,642545	7912	7890,396806	8002	7980,151067
7553	7532,377032	7643	7622,131293	7733	7711,885554	7823	7801,639815	7913	7891,394076	8003	7981,148336
7554	7533,374301	7644	7623,128562	7734	7712,882823	7824	7802,637084	7914	7892,391345	8004	7982,145606
7555	7534,371571	7645	7624,125832	7735	7713,880093	7825	7803,634354	7915	7893,388615	8005	7983,142876
7556	7535,36884	7646	7625,123101	7736	7714,877362	7826	7804,631623	7916	7894,385884	8006	7984,140145
7557	7536,36611	7647	7626,120371	7737	7715,874632	7827	7805,628893	7917	7895,383154	8007	7985,137415
7558	7537,36338	7648	7627,117641	7738	7716,871901	7828	7806,626162	7918	7896,380423	8008	7986,134684
7559	7538,360649	7649	7628,11491	7739	7717,869171	7829	7807,623432	7919	7897,377693	8009	7987,131954
7560	7539,357919	7650	7629,11218	7740	7718,866441	7830	7808,620702	7920	7898,374963	8010	7988,129223
7561	7540,355188	7651	7630,109449	7741	7719,86371	7831	7809,617971	7921	7899,372232	8011	7989,126493
7562	7541,352458	7652	7631,106719	7742	7720,86098	7832	7810,615241	7922	7900,369502	8012	7990,123763
7563	7542,349727	7653	7632,103988	7743	7721,858249	7833	7811,61251	7923	7901,366771	8013	7991,121032
7564	7543,346997	7654	7633,101258	7744	7722,855519	7834	7812,60978	7924	7902,364041	8014	7992,118302
7565	7544,344267	7655	7634,098528	7745	7723,852788	7835	7813,607049	7925	7903,36131	8015	7993,115571
7566	7545,341536	7656	7635,095797	7746	7724,850058	7836	7814,604319	7926	7904,35858	8016	7994,112841
7567	7546,338806	7657	7636,093067	7747	7725,847328	7837	7815,601589	7927	7905,355849	8017	7995,11011
7568	7547,336075	7658	7637,090336	7748	7726,844597	7838	7816,598858	7928	7906,353119	8018	7996,10738
7569	7548,333345	7659	7638,087606	7749	7727,841867	7839	7817,596128	7929	7907,350389	8019	7997,10465
7570	7549,330614	7660	7639,084875	7750	7728,839136	7840	7818,593397	7930	7908,347658	8020	7998,101919
7571	7550,327884	7661	7640,082145	7751	7729,836406	7841	7819,590667	7931	7909,344928	8021	7999,099189
7572	7551,325154	7662	7641,079414	7752	7730,833675	7842	7820,587936	7932	7910,342197	8022	8000,096458
7573	7552,322423	7663	7642,076684	7753	7731,830945	7843	7821,585206	7933	7911,339467	8023	8001,093728
7574	7553,319693	7664	7643,073954	7754	7732,828215	7844	7822,582475	7934	7912,336736	8024	8002,090997
7575	7554,316962	7665	7644,071223	7755	7733,825484	7845	7823,579745	7935	7913,334006	8025	8003,088267
7576	7555,314232	7666	7645,068493	7756	7734,822754	7846	7824,577015	7936	7914,331276	8026	8004,085536
7577	7556,311501	7667	7646,065762	7757	7735,820023	7847	7825,574284	7937	7915,328545	8027	8005,082806
7578	7557,308771	7668	7647,063032	7758	7736,817293	7848	7826,571554	7938	7916,325815	8028	8006,080076
7579	7558,306041	7669	7648,060301	7759	7737,814562	7849	7827,568823	7939	7917,323084	8029	8007,077345
7580	7559,30331	7670	7649,057571	7760	7738,811832	7850	7828,566093	7940	7918,320354	8030	8008,074615
7581	7560,30058	7671	7650,054841	7761	7739,809102	7851	7829,563362	7941	7919,317623	8031	8009,071884
7582	7561,297849	7672	7651,05211	7762	7740,806371	7852	7830,560632	7942	7920,314893	8032	8010,069154
7583	7562,295119	7673	7652,04938	7763	7741,803641	7853	7831,557902	7943	7921,312163	8033	8011,066423
7584	7563,292388	7674	7653,046649	7764	7742,80091	7854	7832,555171	7944	7922,309432	8034	8012,063693

LUNAR RETURNS AND EARTH RETURNS

8035	8013,060963	8125	8102,815224	8215	8192,569484	8305	8282,323745	8395	8372,078006	8485	8461,832267
8036	8014,058232	8126	8103,812493	8216	8193,566754	8306	8283,321015	8396	8373,075276	8486	8462,829537
8037	8015,055502	8127	8104,809763	8217	8194,564024	8307	8284,318285	8397	8374,072545	8487	8463,826806
8038	8016,052771	8128	8105,807032	8218	8195,561293	8308	8285,315554	8398	8375,069815	8488	8464,824076
8039	8017,050041	8129	8106,804302	8219	8196,558563	8309	8286,312824	8399	8376,067085	8489	8465,821346
8040	8018,04731	8130	8107,801571	8220	8197,555832	8310	8287,310093	8400	8377,064354	8490	8466,818615
8041	8019,04458	8131	8108,798841	8221	8198,553102	8311	8288,307363	8401	8378,061624	8491	8467,815885
8042	8020,04185	8132	8109,79611	8222	8199,550371	8312	8289,304632	8402	8379,058893	8492	8468,813154
8043	8021,039119	8133	8110,79338	8223	8200,547641	8313	8290,301902	8403	8380,056163	8493	8469,810424
8044	8022,036389	8134	8111,79065	8224	8201,544911	8314	8291,299171	8404	8381,053432	8494	8470,807693
8045	8023,033658	8135	8112,787919	8225	8202,54218	8315	8292,296441	8405	8382,050702	8495	8471,804963
8046	8024,030928	8136	8113,785189	8226	8203,53945	8316	8293,293711	8406	8383,047972	8496	8472,802233
8047	8025,028197	8137	8114,782458	8227	8204,536719	8317	8294,29098	8407	8384,045241	8497	8473,799502
8048	8026,025467	8138	8115,779728	8228	8205,533989	8318	8295,28825	8408	8385,042511	8498	8474,796772
8049	8027,022737	8139	8116,776997	8229	8206,531258	8319	8296,285519	8409	8386,03978	8499	8475,794041
8050	8028,020006	8140	8117,774267	8230	8207,528528	8320	8297,282789	8410	8387,03705	8500	8476,791311
8051	8029,017276	8141	8118,771537	8231	8208,525798	8321	8298,280058	8411	8388,034319	8501	8477,78858
8052	8030,014545	8142	8119,768806	8232	8209,523067	8322	8299,277328	8412	8389,031589	8502	8478,78585
8053	8031,011815	8143	8120,766076	8233	8210,520337	8323	8300,274598	8413	8390,028859	8503	8479,783119
8054	8032,009084	8144	8121,763345	8234	8211,517606	8324	8301,271867	8414	8391,026128	8504	8480,780389
8055	8033,006354	8145	8122,760615	8235	8212,514876	8325	8302,269137	8415	8392,023398	8505	8481,777659
8056	8034,003623	8146	8123,757884	8236	8213,512145	8326	8303,266406	8416	8393,020667	8506	8482,774928
8057	8035,000893	8147	8124,755154	8237	8214,509415	8327	8304,263676	8417	8394,017937	8507	8483,772198
8058	8035,998163	8148	8125,752424	8238	8215,506684	8328	8305,260945	8418	8395,015206	8508	8484,769467
8059	8036,995432	8149	8126,749693	8239	8216,503954	8329	8306,258215	8419	8396,012476	8509	8485,766737
8060	8037,992702	8150	8127,746963	8240	8217,501224	8330	8307,255485	8420	8397,009745	8510	8486,764006
8061	8038,989971	8151	8128,744232	8241	8218,498493	8331	8308,252754	8421	8398,007015	8511	8487,761276
8062	8039,987241	8152	8129,741502	8242	8219,495763	8332	8309,250024	8422	8399,004285	8512	8488,758546
8063	8040,98451	8153	8130,738771	8243	8220,493032	8333	8310,247293	8423	8400,001554	8513	8489,755815
8064	8041,98178	8154	8131,736041	8244	8221,490302	8334	8311,244563	8424	8400,998824	8514	8490,753085
8065	8042,97905	8155	8132,733311	8245	8222,487571	8335	8312,241832	8425	8401,996093	8515	8491,750354
8066	8043,976319	8156	8133,73058	8246	8223,484841	8336	8313,239102	8426	8402,993363	8516	8492,747624
8067	8044,973589	8157	8134,72785	8247	8224,482111	8337	8314,236372	8427	8403,990632	8517	8493,744893
8068	8045,970858	8158	8135,725119	8248	8225,47938	8338	8315,233641	8428	8404,987902	8518	8494,742163
8069	8046,968128	8159	8136,722389	8249	8226,47665	8339	8316,230911	8429	8405,985172	8519	8495,739433
8070	8047,965397	8160	8137,719658	8250	8227,473919	8340	8317,22818	8430	8406,982441	8520	8496,736702
8071	8048,962667	8161	8138,716928	8251	8228,471189	8341	8318,22545	8431	8407,979711	8521	8497,733972
8072	8049,959937	8162	8139,714197	8252	8229,468458	8342	8319,222719	8432	8408,97698	8522	8498,731241
8073	8050,957206	8163	8140,711467	8253	8230,465728	8343	8320,219989	8433	8409,97425	8523	8499,728511
8074	8051,954476	8164	8141,708737	8254	8231,462998	8344	8321,217258	8434	8410,971519	8524	8500,72578
8075	8052,951745	8165	8142,706006	8255	8232,460267	8345	8322,214528	8435	8411,968789	8525	8501,72305
8076	8053,949015	8166	8143,703276	8256	8233,457537	8346	8323,211798	8436	8412,966059	8526	8502,720319
8077	8054,946284	8167	8144,700545	8257	8234,454806	8347	8324,209067	8437	8413,963328	8527	8503,717589
8078	8055,943554	8168	8145,697815	8258	8235,452076	8348	8325,206337	8438	8414,960598	8528	8504,714859
8079	8056,940823	8169	8146,695084	8259	8236,449345	8349	8326,203606	8439	8415,957867	8529	8505,712128
8080	8057,938093	8170	8147,692354	8260	8237,446615	8350	8327,200876	8440	8416,955137	8530	8506,709398
8081	8058,935363	8171	8148,689624	8261	8238,443884	8351	8328,198145	8441	8417,952406	8531	8507,706667
8082	8059,932632	8172	8149,686893	8262	8239,441154	8352	8329,195415	8442	8418,949676	8532	8508,703937
8083	8060,929902	8173	8150,684163	8263	8240,438424	8353	8330,192685	8443	8419,946946	8533	8509,701206
8084	8061,927171	8174	8151,681432	8264	8241,435693	8354	8331,189954	8444	8420,944215	8534	8510,698476
8085	8062,924441	8175	8152,678702	8265	8242,432963	8355	8332,187224	8445	8421,941485	8535	8511,695746
8086	8063,92171	8176	8153,675971	8266	8243,430232	8356	8333,184493	8446	8422,938754	8536	8512,693015
8087	8064,91898	8177	8154,673241	8267	8244,427502	8357	8334,181763	8447	8423,936024	8537	8513,690285
8088	8065,91625	8178	8155,670511	8268	8245,424771	8358	8335,179032	8448	8424,933293	8538	8514,687554
8089	8066,913519	8179	8156,66778	8269	8246,422041	8359	8336,176302	8449	8425,930563	8539	8515,684824
8090	8067,910789	8180	8157,66505	8270	8247,419311	8360	8337,173572	8450	8426,927832	8540	8516,682093
8091	8068,908058	8181	8158,662319	8271	8248,41658	8361	8338,170841	8451	8427,925102	8541	8517,679363
8092	8069,905328	8182	8159,659589	8272	8249,41385	8362	8339,168111	8452	8428,922372	8542	8518,676633
8093	8070,902597	8183	8160,656858	8273	8250,411119	8363	8340,16538	8453	8429,919641	8543	8519,673902
8094	8071,899867	8184	8161,654128	8274	8251,408389	8364	8341,16265	8454	8430,916911	8544	8520,671172
8095	8072,897137	8185	8162,651397	8275	8252,405658	8365	8342,159919	8455	8431,91418	8545	8521,668441
8096	8073,894406	8186	8163,648667	8276	8253,402928	8366	8343,157189	8456	8432,91145	8546	8522,665711
8097	8074,891676	8187	8164,645937	8277	8254,400198	8367	8344,154458	8457	8433,908719	8547	8523,66298
8098	8075,888945	8188	8165,643206	8278	8255,397467	8368	8345,151728	8458	8434,905989	8548	8524,66025
8099	8076,886215	8189	8166,640476	8279	8256,394737	8369	8346,148998	8459	8435,903259	8549	8525,657519
8100	8077,883484	8190	8167,637745	8280	8257,392006	8370	8347,146267	8460	8436,900528	8550	8526,654789
8101	8078,880754	8191	8168,635015	8281	8258,389276	8371	8348,143537	8461	8437,897798	8551	8527,652059
8102	8079,878024	8192	8169,632284	8282	8259,386545	8372	8349,140806	8462	8438,895067	8552	8528,649328
8103	8080,875293	8193	8170,629554	8283	8260,383815	8373	8350,138076	8463	8439,892337	8553	8529,646598
8104	8081,872563	8194	8171,626824	8284	8261,381085	8374	8351,135345	8464	8440,889606	8554	8530,643867
8105	8082,869832	8195	8172,624093	8285	8262,378354	8375	8352,132615	8465	8441,886876	8555	8531,641137
8106	8083,867102	8196	8173,621363	8286	8263,375624	8376	8353,129885	8466	8442,884146	8556	8532,638406
8107	8084,864371	8197	8174,618632	8287	8264,372893	8377	8354,127154	8467	8443,881415	8557	8533,635676
8108	8085,861641	8198	8175,615902	8288	8265,370163	8378	8355,124424	8468	8444,878685	8558	8534,632946
8109	8086,85891	8199	8176,613171	8289	8266,367432	8379	8356,121693	8469	8445,875954	8559	8535,630215
8110	8087,85618	8200	8177,610441	8290	8267,364702	8380	8357,118963	8470	8446,873224	8560	8536,627485
8111	8088,85345	8201	8178,607711	8291	8268,361971	8381	8358,116232	8471	8447,870493	8561	8537,624754
8112	8089,850719	8202	8179,60498	8292	8269,359241	8382	8359,113502	8472	8448,867763	8562	8538,622024
8113	8090,847989	8203	8180,60225	8293	8270,356511	8383	8360,110772	8473	8449,865032	8563	8539,619293
8114	8091,845258	8204	8181,599519	8294	8271,35378	8384	8361,108041	8474	8450,862302	8564	8540,616563
8115	8092,842528	8205	8182,596789	8295	8272,35105	8385	8362,105311	8475	8451,859572	8565	8541,613833
8116	8093,839797	8206	8183,594058	8296	8273,348319	8386	8363,10258	8476	8452,856841	8566	8542,611102
8117	8094,837067	8207	8184,591328	8297	8274,345589	8387	8364,09985	8477	8453,854111	8567	8543,608372
8118	8095,834337	8208	8185,588597	8298	8275,342858	8388	8365,097119	8478	8454,85138	8568	8544,605641
8119	8096,831606	8209	8186,585867	8299	8276,340128	8389	8366,094389	8479	8455,84865	8569	8545,602911
8120	8097,828876	8210	8187,583137	8300	8277,337398	8390	8367,091659	8480	8456,845919	8570	8546,60018
8121	8098,826145	8211	8188,580406	8301	8278,334667	8391	8368,088928	8481	8457,843189	8571	8547,59745
8122	8099,823415	8212	8189,577676	8302	8279,331937	8392	8369,086198	8482	8458,840459	8572	8548,59472
8123	8100,820684	8213	8190,574945	8303	8280,329206	8393	8370,083467	8483	8459,837728	8573	8549,591989
8124	8101,817954	8214	8191,572215	8304	8281,326476	8394	8371,080737	8484	8460,834998	8574	8550,589259

TABLE TO FIND OUT THE POINT A IN EARTH RETURNS 173

8575	8551,586528	8665	8641,340789	8755	8731,09505	8845	8820,849311	8935	8910,603572	9025	9000,357833
8576	8552,583798	8666	8642,338059	8756	8732,09232	8846	8821,846581	8936	8911,600842	9026	9001,355102
8577	8553,581067	8667	8643,335328	8757	8733,089589	8847	8822,84385	8937	8912,598111	9027	9002,352372
8578	8554,578337	8668	8644,332598	8758	8734,086859	8848	8823,84112	8938	8913,595381	9028	9003,349642
8579	8555,575606	8669	8645,329867	8759	8735,084128	8849	8824,838389	8939	8914,59265	9029	9004,346911
8580	8556,572876	8670	8646,327137	8760	8736,081398	8850	8825,835659	8940	8915,58992	9030	9005,344181
8581	8557,570146	8671	8647,324407	8761	8737,078667	8851	8826,832928	8941	8916,587189	9031	9006,34145
8582	8558,567415	8672	8648,321676	8762	8738,075937	8852	8827,830198	8942	8917,584459	9032	9007,33872
8583	8559,564685	8673	8649,318946	8763	8739,073207	8853	8828,827468	8943	8918,581728	9033	9008,335989
8584	8560,561954	8674	8650,316215	8764	8740,070476	8854	8829,824737	8944	8919,578998	9034	9009,333259
8585	8561,559224	8675	8651,313485	8765	8741,067746	8855	8830,822007	8945	8920,576268	9035	9010,330529
8586	8562,556493	8676	8652,310754	8766	8742,065015	8856	8831,819276	8946	8921,573537	9036	9011,327798
8587	8563,553763	8677	8653,308024	8767	8743,062285	8857	8832,816546	8947	8922,570807	9037	9012,325068
8588	8564,551033	8678	8654,305294	8768	8744,059554	8858	8833,813815	8948	8923,568076	9038	9013,322337
8589	8565,548302	8679	8655,302563	8769	8745,056824	8859	8834,811085	8949	8924,565346	9039	9014,319607
8590	8566,545572	8680	8656,299833	8770	8746,054094	8860	8835,808355	8950	8925,562615	9040	9015,316876
8591	8567,542841	8681	8657,297102	8771	8747,051363	8861	8836,805624	8951	8926,559885	9041	9016,314146
8592	8568,540111	8682	8658,294372	8772	8748,048633	8862	8837,802894	8952	8927,557155	9042	9017,311416
8593	8569,53738	8683	8659,291641	8773	8749,045902	8863	8838,800163	8953	8928,554424	9043	9018,308685
8594	8570,53465	8684	8660,288911	8774	8750,043172	8864	8839,797433	8954	8929,551694	9044	9019,305955
8595	8571,53192	8685	8661,28618	8775	8751,040441	8865	8840,794702	8955	8930,548963	9045	9020,303224
8596	8572,529189	8686	8662,28345	8776	8752,037711	8866	8841,791972	8956	8931,546233	9046	9021,300494
8597	8573,526459	8687	8663,28072	8777	8753,034981	8867	8842,789241	8957	8932,543502	9047	9022,297763
8598	8574,523728	8688	8664,277989	8778	8754,03225	8868	8843,786511	8958	8933,540772	9048	9023,295033
8599	8575,520998	8689	8665,275259	8779	8755,02952	8869	8844,783781	8959	8934,538042	9049	9024,292302
8600	8576,518267	8690	8666,272528	8780	8756,026789	8870	8845,78105	8960	8935,535311	9050	9025,289572
8601	8577,515537	8691	8667,269798	8781	8757,024059	8871	8846,77832	8961	8936,532581	9051	9026,286842
8602	8578,512806	8692	8668,267067	8782	8758,021328	8872	8847,775589	8962	8937,52985	9052	9027,284111
8603	8579,510076	8693	8669,264337	8783	8759,018598	8873	8848,772859	8963	8938,52712	9053	9028,281381
8604	8580,507346	8694	8670,261607	8784	8760,015868	8874	8849,770128	8964	8939,524389	9054	9029,27865
8605	8581,504615	8695	8671,258876	8785	8761,013137	8875	8850,767398	8965	8940,521659	9055	9030,27592
8606	8582,501885	8696	8672,256146	8786	8762,010407	8876	8851,764668	8966	8941,518929	9056	9031,273189
8607	8583,499154	8697	8673,253415	8787	8763,007676	8877	8852,761937	8967	8942,516198	9057	9032,270459
8608	8584,496424	8698	8674,250685	8788	8764,004946	8878	8853,759207	8968	8943,513468	9058	9033,267729
8609	8585,493693	8699	8675,247954	8789	8765,002215	8879	8854,756476	8969	8944,510737	9059	9034,264998
8610	8586,490963	8700	8676,245224	8790	8765,999485	8880	8855,753746	8970	8945,508007	9060	9035,262268
8611	8587,488233	8701	8677,242494	8791	8766,996754	8881	8856,751015	8971	8946,505276	9061	9036,259537
8612	8588,485502	8702	8678,239763	8792	8767,994024	8882	8857,748285	8972	8947,502546	9062	9037,256807
8613	8589,482772	8703	8679,237033	8793	8768,991294	8883	8858,745555	8973	8948,499815	9063	9038,254076
8614	8590,480041	8704	8680,234302	8794	8769,988563	8884	8859,742824	8974	8949,497085	9064	9039,251346
8615	8591,477311	8705	8681,231572	8795	8770,985833	8885	8860,740094	8975	8950,494355	9065	9040,248616
8616	8592,47458	8706	8682,228841	8796	8771,983102	8886	8861,737363	8976	8951,491624	9066	9041,245885
8617	8593,47185	8707	8683,226111	8797	8772,980372	8887	8862,734633	8977	8952,488894	9067	9042,243155
8618	8594,46912	8708	8684,22338	8798	8773,977641	8888	8863,731902	8978	8953,486163	9068	9043,240424
8619	8595,466389	8709	8685,22065	8799	8774,974911	8889	8864,729172	8979	8954,483433	9069	9044,237694
8620	8596,463659	8710	8686,21792	8800	8775,972181	8890	8865,726441	8980	8955,480702	9070	9045,234963
8621	8597,460928	8711	8687,215189	8801	8776,96945	8891	8866,723711	8981	8956,477972	9071	9046,232233
8622	8598,458198	8712	8688,212459	8802	8777,96672	8892	8867,720981	8982	8957,475242	9072	9047,229503
8623	8599,455467	8713	8689,209728	8803	8778,963989	8893	8868,71825	8983	8958,472511	9073	9048,226772
8624	8600,452737	8714	8690,206998	8804	8779,961259	8894	8869,71552	8984	8959,469781	9074	9049,224042
8625	8601,450007	8715	8691,204267	8805	8780,958528	8895	8870,712789	8985	8960,46705	9075	9050,221311
8626	8602,447276	8716	8692,201537	8806	8781,955798	8896	8871,710059	8986	8961,46432	9076	9051,218581
8627	8603,444546	8717	8693,198807	8807	8782,953068	8897	8872,707328	8987	8962,461589	9077	9052,21585
8628	8604,441815	8718	8694,196076	8808	8783,950337	8898	8873,704598	8988	8963,458859	9078	9053,21312
8629	8605,439085	8719	8695,193346	8809	8784,947607	8899	8874,701868	8989	8964,456129	9079	9054,210389
8630	8606,436354	8720	8696,190615	8810	8785,944876	8900	8875,699137	8990	8965,453398	9080	9055,207659
8631	8607,433624	8721	8697,187885	8811	8786,942146	8901	8876,696407	8991	8966,450668	9081	9056,204929
8632	8608,430893	8722	8698,185154	8812	8787,939415	8902	8877,693676	8992	8967,447937	9082	9057,202198
8633	8609,428163	8723	8699,182424	8813	8788,936685	8903	8878,690946	8993	8968,445207	9083	9058,199468
8634	8610,425433	8724	8700,179694	8814	8789,933954	8904	8879,688215	8994	8969,442476	9084	9059,196737
8635	8611,422702	8725	8701,176963	8815	8790,931224	8905	8880,685485	8995	8970,439746	9085	9060,194007
8636	8612,419972	8726	8702,174233	8816	8791,928494	8906	8881,682755	8996	8971,437015	9086	9061,191276
8637	8613,417241	8727	8703,171502	8817	8792,925763	8907	8882,680024	8997	8972,434285	9087	9062,188546
8638	8614,414511	8728	8704,168772	8818	8793,923033	8908	8883,677294	8998	8973,431555	9088	9063,185816
8639	8615,41178	8729	8705,166041	8819	8794,920302	8909	8884,674563	8999	8974,428824	9089	9064,183085
8640	8616,40905	8730	8706,163311	8820	8795,917572	8910	8885,671833	9000	8975,426094	9090	9065,180355
8641	8617,40632	8731	8707,160581	8821	8796,914841	8911	8886,669102	9001	8976,423363	9091	9066,177624
8642	8618,403589	8732	8708,15785	8822	8797,912111	8912	8887,666372	9002	8977,420633	9092	9067,174894
8643	8619,400859	8733	8709,15512	8823	8798,909381	8913	8888,663642	9003	8978,417902	9093	9068,172163
8644	8620,398128	8734	8710,152389	8824	8799,90665	8914	8889,660911	9004	8979,415172	9094	9069,169433
8645	8621,395398	8735	8711,149659	8825	8800,90392	8915	8890,658181	9005	8980,412442	9095	9070,166703
8646	8622,392667	8736	8712,146928	8826	8801,901189	8916	8891,65545	9006	8981,409711	9096	9071,163972
8647	8623,389937	8737	8713,144198	8827	8802,898459	8917	8892,65272	9007	8982,406981	9097	9072,161242
8648	8624,387207	8738	8714,141467	8828	8803,895728	8918	8893,649989	9008	8983,40425	9098	9073,158511
8649	8625,384476	8739	8715,138737	8829	8804,892998	8919	8894,647259	9009	8984,40152	9099	9074,155781
8650	8626,381746	8740	8716,136007	8830	8805,890268	8920	8895,644528	9010	8985,398789	9100	9075,15305
8651	8627,379015	8741	8717,133276	8831	8806,887537	8921	8896,641798	9011	8986,396059	9101	9076,15032
8652	8628,376285	8742	8718,130546	8832	8807,884807	8922	8897,639068	9012	8987,393329	9102	9077,147589
8653	8629,373554	8743	8719,127815	8833	8808,882076	8923	8898,636337	9013	8988,390598	9103	9078,144859
8654	8630,370824	8744	8720,125085	8834	8809,879346	8924	8899,633607	9014	8989,387868	9104	9079,142129
8655	8631,368093	8745	8721,122354	8835	8810,876615	8925	8900,630876	9015	8990,385137	9105	9080,139398
8656	8632,365363	8746	8722,119624	8836	8811,873885	8926	8901,628146	9016	8991,382407	9106	9081,136668
8657	8633,362633	8747	8723,116894	8837	8812,871154	8927	8902,625415	9017	8992,379676	9107	9082,133937
8658	8634,359902	8748	8724,114163	8838	8813,868424	8928	8903,622685	9018	8993,376946	9108	9083,131207
8659	8635,357172	8749	8725,111433	8839	8814,865694	8929	8904,619955	9019	8994,374216	9109	9084,128476
8660	8636,354441	8750	8726,108702	8840	8815,862963	8930	8905,617224	9020	8995,371485	9110	9085,125746
8661	8637,351711	8751	8727,105972	8841	8816,860233	8931	8906,614494	9021	8996,368755	9111	9086,123016
8662	8638,34898	8752	8728,103241	8842	8817,857502	8932	8907,611763	9022	8997,366024	9112	9087,120285
8663	8639,34625	8753	8729,100511	8843	8818,854772	8933	8908,609033	9023	8998,363294	9113	9088,117555
8664	8640,34352	8754	8730,097781	8844	8819,852041	8934	8909,606302	9024	8999,360563	9114	9089,114824

LUNAR RETURNS AND EARTH RETURNS

9115	9090,112094	9205	9179,866355	9295	9269,620616	9385	9359,374877	9475	9449,129138	9565	9538,883399
9116	9091,109363	9206	9180,863624	9296	9270,617885	9386	9360,372146	9476	9450,126407	9566	9539,880668
9117	9092,106633	9207	9181,860894	9297	9271,615155	9387	9361,369416	9477	9451,123677	9567	9540,877938
9118	9093,103903	9208	9182,858163	9298	9272,612424	9388	9362,366685	9478	9452,120946	9568	9541,875207
9119	9094,101172	9209	9183,855433	9299	9273,609694	9389	9363,363955	9479	9453,118216	9569	9542,872477
9120	9095,098442	9210	9184,852703	9300	9274,606964	9390	9364,361224	9480	9454,115485	9570	9543,869746
9121	9096,095711	9211	9185,849972	9301	9275,604233	9391	9365,358494	9481	9455,112755	9571	9544,867016
9122	9097,092981	9212	9186,847242	9302	9276,601503	9392	9366,355764	9482	9456,110025	9572	9545,864285
9123	9098,09025	9213	9187,844511	9303	9277,598772	9393	9367,353033	9483	9457,107294	9573	9546,861555
9124	9099,08752	9214	9188,841781	9304	9278,596042	9394	9368,350303	9484	9458,104564	9574	9547,858825
9125	9100,084789	9215	9189,83905	9305	9279,593311	9395	9369,347572	9485	9459,101833	9575	9548,856094
9126	9101,082059	9216	9190,83632	9306	9280,590581	9396	9370,344842	9486	9460,099103	9576	9549,853364
9127	9102,079329	9217	9191,83359	9307	9281,587851	9397	9371,342111	9487	9461,096372	9577	9550,850633
9128	9103,076598	9218	9192,830859	9308	9282,58512	9398	9372,339381	9488	9462,093642	9578	9551,847903
9129	9104,073868	9219	9193,828129	9309	9283,58239	9399	9373,336651	9489	9463,090912	9579	9552,845172
9130	9105,071137	9220	9194,825398	9310	9284,579659	9400	9374,33392	9490	9464,088181	9580	9553,842442
9131	9106,068407	9221	9195,822668	9311	9285,576929	9401	9375,33119	9491	9465,085451	9581	9554,839712
9132	9107,065676	9222	9196,819937	9312	9286,574198	9402	9376,328459	9492	9466,08272	9582	9555,836981
9133	9108,062946	9223	9197,817207	9313	9287,571468	9403	9377,325729	9493	9467,07999	9583	9556,834251
9134	9109,060216	9224	9198,814477	9314	9288,568737	9404	9378,322998	9494	9468,077259	9584	9557,83152
9135	9110,057485	9225	9199,811746	9315	9289,566007	9405	9379,320268	9495	9469,074529	9585	9558,82879
9136	9111,054755	9226	9200,809016	9316	9290,563277	9406	9380,317538	9496	9470,071798	9586	9559,826059
9137	9112,052024	9227	9201,806285	9317	9291,560546	9407	9381,314807	9497	9471,069068	9587	9560,823329
9138	9113,049294	9228	9202,803555	9318	9292,557816	9408	9382,312077	9498	9472,066338	9588	9561,820599
9139	9114,046563	9229	9203,800824	9319	9293,555085	9409	9383,309346	9499	9473,063607	9589	9562,817868
9140	9115,043833	9230	9204,798094	9320	9294,552355	9410	9384,306616	9500	9474,060877	9590	9563,815138
9141	9116,041103	9231	9205,795363	9321	9295,549624	9411	9385,303885	9501	9475,058146	9591	9564,812407
9142	9117,038372	9232	9206,792633	9322	9296,546894	9412	9386,301155	9502	9476,055416	9592	9565,809677
9143	9118,035642	9233	9207,789903	9323	9297,544164	9413	9387,298424	9503	9477,052685	9593	9566,806946
9144	9119,032911	9234	9208,787172	9324	9298,541433	9414	9388,295694	9504	9478,049955	9594	9567,804216
9145	9120,030181	9235	9209,784442	9325	9299,538703	9415	9389,292964	9505	9479,047225	9595	9568,801486
9146	9121,02745	9236	9210,781711	9326	9300,535972	9416	9390,290233	9506	9480,044494	9596	9569,798755
9147	9122,02472	9237	9211,778981	9327	9301,533242	9417	9391,287503	9507	9481,041764	9597	9570,796025
9148	9123,02199	9238	9212,77625	9328	9302,530511	9418	9392,284772	9508	9482,039033	9598	9571,793294
9149	9124,019259	9239	9213,77352	9329	9303,527781	9419	9393,282042	9509	9483,036303	9599	9572,790564
9150	9125,016529	9240	9214,77079	9330	9304,525051	9420	9394,279311	9510	9484,033572	9600	9573,787833
9151	9126,013798	9241	9215,768059	9331	9305,52232	9421	9395,276581	9511	9485,030842	9601	9574,785103
9152	9127,011068	9242	9216,765329	9332	9306,51959	9422	9396,273851	9512	9486,028112	9602	9575,782372
9153	9128,008337	9243	9217,762598	9333	9307,516859	9423	9397,27112	9513	9487,025381	9603	9576,779642
9154	9129,005607	9244	9218,759868	9334	9308,514129	9424	9398,26839	9514	9488,022651	9604	9577,776912
9155	9130,002876	9245	9219,757137	9335	9309,511398	9425	9399,265659	9515	9489,01992	9605	9578,774181
9156	9131,000146	9246	9220,754407	9336	9310,508668	9426	9400,262929	9516	9490,01719	9606	9579,771451
9157	9131,997416	9247	9221,751677	9337	9311,505937	9427	9401,260198	9517	9491,014459	9607	9580,76872
9158	9132,994685	9248	9222,748946	9338	9312,503207	9428	9402,257468	9518	9492,011729	9608	9581,76599
9159	9133,991955	9249	9223,746216	9339	9313,500477	9429	9403,254738	9519	9493,008998	9609	9582,763259
9160	9134,989224	9250	9224,743485	9340	9314,497746	9430	9404,252007	9520	9494,006268	9610	9583,760529
9161	9135,986494	9251	9225,740755	9341	9315,495016	9431	9405,249277	9521	9495,003538	9611	9584,757799
9162	9136,983763	9252	9226,738024	9342	9316,492285	9432	9406,246546	9522	9496,000807	9612	9585,755068
9163	9137,981033	9253	9227,735294	9343	9317,489555	9433	9407,243816	9523	9496,998077	9613	9586,752338
9164	9138,978303	9254	9228,732564	9344	9318,486824	9434	9408,241085	9524	9497,995346	9614	9587,749607
9165	9139,975572	9255	9229,729833	9345	9319,484094	9435	9409,238355	9525	9498,992616	9615	9588,746877
9166	9140,972842	9256	9230,727103	9346	9320,481364	9436	9410,235625	9526	9499,989885	9616	9589,744146
9167	9141,970111	9257	9231,724372	9347	9321,478633	9437	9411,232894	9527	9500,987155	9617	9590,741416
9168	9142,967381	9258	9232,721642	9348	9322,475903	9438	9412,230164	9528	9501,984425	9618	9591,738686
9169	9143,96465	9259	9233,718911	9349	9323,473172	9439	9413,227433	9529	9502,981694	9619	9592,735955
9170	9144,96192	9260	9234,716181	9350	9324,470442	9440	9414,224703	9530	9503,978964	9620	9593,733225
9171	9145,95919	9261	9235,71345	9351	9325,467711	9441	9415,221972	9531	9504,976233	9621	9594,730494
9172	9146,956459	9262	9236,71072	9352	9326,464981	9442	9416,219242	9532	9505,973503	9622	9595,727764
9173	9147,953729	9263	9237,70799	9353	9327,462251	9443	9417,216511	9533	9506,970772	9623	9596,725033
9174	9148,950998	9264	9238,705259	9354	9328,45952	9444	9418,213781	9534	9507,968042	9624	9597,722303
9175	9149,948268	9265	9239,702529	9355	9329,45679	9445	9419,211051	9535	9508,965312	9625	9598,719572
9176	9150,945537	9266	9240,699798	9356	9330,454059	9446	9420,20832	9536	9509,962581	9626	9599,716842
9177	9151,942807	9267	9241,697068	9357	9331,451329	9447	9421,20559	9537	9510,959851	9627	9600,714112
9178	9152,940076	9268	9242,694337	9358	9332,448598	9448	9422,202859	9538	9511,95712	9628	9601,711381
9179	9153,937346	9269	9243,691607	9359	9333,445868	9449	9423,200129	9539	9512,95439	9629	9602,708651
9180	9154,934616	9270	9244,688877	9360	9334,443138	9450	9424,197398	9540	9513,951659	9630	9603,70592
9181	9155,931885	9271	9245,686146	9361	9335,440407	9451	9425,194668	9541	9514,948929	9631	9604,70319
9182	9156,929155	9272	9246,683416	9362	9336,437677	9452	9426,191938	9542	9515,946199	9632	9605,700459
9183	9157,926424	9273	9247,680685	9363	9337,434946	9453	9427,189207	9543	9516,943468	9633	9606,697729
9184	9158,923694	9274	9248,677955	9364	9338,432216	9454	9428,186477	9544	9517,940738	9634	9607,694999
9185	9159,920963	9275	9249,675224	9365	9339,429485	9455	9429,183746	9545	9518,938007	9635	9608,692268
9186	9160,918233	9276	9250,672494	9366	9340,426755	9456	9430,181016	9546	9519,935277	9636	9609,689538
9187	9161,915503	9277	9251,669764	9367	9341,424024	9457	9431,178285	9547	9520,932546	9637	9610,686807
9188	9162,912772	9278	9252,667033	9368	9342,421294	9458	9432,175555	9548	9521,929816	9638	9611,684077
9189	9163,910042	9279	9253,664303	9369	9343,418564	9459	9433,172825	9549	9522,927085	9639	9612,681346
9190	9164,907311	9280	9254,661572	9370	9344,415833	9460	9434,170094	9550	9523,924355	9640	9613,678616
9191	9165,904581	9281	9255,658842	9371	9345,413103	9461	9435,167364	9551	9524,921625	9641	9614,675886
9192	9166,90185	9282	9256,656111	9372	9346,410372	9462	9436,164633	9552	9525,918894	9642	9615,673155
9193	9167,89912	9283	9257,653381	9373	9347,407642	9463	9437,161903	9553	9526,916164	9643	9616,670425
9194	9168,89639	9284	9258,65065	9374	9348,404911	9464	9438,159172	9554	9527,913433	9644	9617,667694
9195	9169,893659	9285	9259,64792	9375	9349,402181	9465	9439,156442	9555	9528,910703	9645	9618,664964
9196	9170,890929	9286	9260,64519	9376	9350,399451	9466	9440,153711	9556	9529,907972	9646	9619,662233
9197	9171,888198	9287	9261,642459	9377	9351,39672	9467	9441,150981	9557	9530,905242	9647	9620,659503
9198	9172,885468	9288	9262,639729	9378	9352,39399	9468	9442,148251	9558	9531,902512	9648	9621,656773
9199	9173,882737	9289	9263,636998	9379	9353,391259	9469	9443,14552	9559	9532,899781	9649	9622,654042
9200	9174,880007	9290	9264,634268	9380	9354,388529	9470	9444,14279	9560	9533,897051	9650	9623,651312
9201	9175,877277	9291	9265,631537	9381	9355,385798	9471	9445,140059	9561	9534,89432	9651	9624,648581
9202	9176,874546	9292	9266,628807	9382	9356,383068	9472	9446,137329	9562	9535,89159	9652	9625,645851
9203	9177,871816	9293	9267,626077	9383	9357,380338	9473	9447,134598	9563	9536,888859	9653	9626,64312
9204	9178,869085	9294	9268,623346	9384	9358,377607	9474	9448,131868	9564	9537,886129	9654	9627,64039

TABLE TO FIND OUT THE POINT A IN EARTH RETURNS

9655	9628,637659	9745	9718,39192	9835	9808,146181	9925	9897,900442	10015	9987,654703	10105	10077,40896
9656	9629,634929	9746	9719,38919	9836	9809,143451	9926	9898,897712	10016	9988,651973	10106	10078,40623
9657	9630,632199	9747	9720,38646	9837	9810,14072	9927	9899,894981	10017	9989,649242	10107	10079,4035
9658	9631,629468	9748	9721,383729	9838	9811,13799	9928	9900,892251	10018	9990,646512	10108	10080,40077
9659	9632,626738	9749	9722,380999	9839	9812,13526	9929	9901,889521	10019	9991,643781	10109	10081,39804
9660	9633,624007	9750	9723,378268	9840	9813,132529	9930	9902,88679	10020	9992,641051	10110	10082,39531
9661	9634,621277	9751	9724,375538	9841	9814,129799	9931	9903,88406	10021	9993,638321	10111	10083,39258
9662	9635,618546	9752	9725,372807	9842	9815,127068	9932	9904,881329	10022	9994,63559	10112	10084,38985
9663	9636,615816	9753	9726,370077	9843	9816,124338	9933	9905,878599	10023	9995,63286	10113	10085,38712
9664	9637,613086	9754	9727,367346	9844	9817,121607	9934	9906,875868	10024	9996,630129	10114	10086,38439
9665	9638,610355	9755	9728,364616	9845	9818,118877	9935	9907,873138	10025	9997,627399	10115	10087,38166
9666	9639,607625	9756	9729,361886	9846	9819,116147	9936	9908,870408	10026	9998,624668	10116	10088,37893
9667	9640,604894	9757	9730,359155	9847	9820,113416	9937	9909,867677	10027	9999,621938	10117	10089,3762
9668	9641,602164	9758	9731,356425	9848	9821,110686	9938	9910,864947	10028	10000,61921	10118	10090,37347
9669	9642,599433	9759	9732,353694	9849	9822,107955	9939	9911,862216	10029	10001,61648	10119	10091,37074
9670	9643,596703	9760	9733,350964	9850	9823,105225	9940	9912,859486	10030	10002,61375	10120	10092,36801
9671	9644,593973	9761	9734,348233	9851	9824,102494	9941	9913,856755	10031	10003,61102	10121	10093,36528
9672	9645,591242	9762	9735,345503	9852	9825,099764	9942	9914,854025	10032	10004,60829	10122	10094,36255
9673	9646,588512	9763	9736,342773	9853	9826,097034	9943	9915,851294	10033	10005,60556	10123	10095,35982
9674	9647,585781	9764	9737,340042	9854	9827,094303	9944	9916,848564	10034	10006,60282	10124	10096,35709
9675	9648,583051	9765	9738,337312	9855	9828,091573	9945	9917,845834	10035	10007,60009	10125	10097,35436
9676	9649,58032	9766	9739,334581	9856	9829,088842	9946	9918,843103	10036	10008,59736	10126	10098,35163
9677	9650,57759	9767	9740,331851	9857	9830,086112	9947	9919,840373	10037	10009,59463	10127	10099,34889
9678	9651,574859	9768	9741,32912	9858	9831,083381	9948	9920,837642	10038	10010,5919	10128	10100,34616
9679	9652,572129	9769	9742,32639	9859	9832,080651	9949	9921,834912	10039	10011,58917	10129	10101,34343
9680	9653,569399	9770	9743,32366	9860	9833,07792	9950	9922,832181	10040	10012,58644	10130	10102,3407
9681	9654,566668	9771	9744,320929	9861	9834,07519	9951	9923,829451	10041	10013,58371	10131	10103,33797
9682	9655,563938	9772	9745,318199	9862	9835,07246	9952	9924,826721	10042	10014,58098	10132	10104,33524
9683	9656,561207	9773	9746,315468	9863	9836,069729	9953	9925,82399	10043	10015,57825	10133	10105,33251
9684	9657,558477	9774	9747,312738	9864	9837,066999	9954	9926,82126	10044	10016,57552	10134	10106,32978
9685	9658,555746	9775	9748,310007	9865	9838,064268	9955	9927,818529	10045	10017,57279	10135	10107,32705
9686	9659,553016	9776	9749,307277	9866	9839,061538	9956	9928,815799	10046	10018,57006	10136	10108,32432
9687	9660,550286	9777	9750,304547	9867	9840,058807	9957	9929,813068	10047	10019,56733	10137	10109,32159
9688	9661,547555	9778	9751,301816	9868	9841,056077	9958	9930,810338	10048	10020,5646	10138	10110,31886
9689	9662,544825	9779	9752,299086	9869	9842,053347	9959	9931,807608	10049	10021,56187	10139	10111,31613
9690	9663,542094	9780	9753,296355	9870	9843,050616	9960	9932,804877	10050	10022,55914	10140	10112,3134
9691	9664,539364	9781	9754,293625	9871	9844,047886	9961	9933,802147	10051	10023,55641	10141	10113,31067
9692	9665,536633	9782	9755,290894	9872	9845,045155	9962	9934,799416	10052	10024,55368	10142	10114,30794
9693	9666,533903	9783	9756,288164	9873	9846,042425	9963	9935,796686	10053	10025,55095	10143	10115,30521
9694	9667,531173	9784	9757,285433	9874	9847,039694	9964	9936,793955	10054	10026,54822	10144	10116,30248
9695	9668,528442	9785	9758,282703	9875	9848,036964	9965	9937,791225	10055	10027,54549	10145	10117,29975
9696	9669,525712	9786	9759,279973	9876	9849,034234	9966	9938,788494	10056	10028,54276	10146	10118,29702
9697	9670,522981	9787	9760,277242	9877	9850,031503	9967	9939,785764	10057	10029,54002	10147	10119,29429
9698	9671,520251	9788	9761,274512	9878	9851,028773	9968	9940,783034	10058	10030,53729	10148	10120,29156
9699	9672,51752	9789	9762,271781	9879	9852,026042	9969	9941,780303	10059	10031,53456	10149	10121,28883
9700	9673,51479	9790	9763,269051	9880	9853,023312	9970	9942,777573	10060	10032,53183	10150	10122,28609
9701	9674,512059	9791	9764,26632	9881	9854,020581	9971	9943,774842	10061	10033,5291	10151	10123,28336
9702	9675,509329	9792	9765,26359	9882	9855,017851	9972	9944,772112	10062	10034,52637	10152	10124,28063
9703	9676,506599	9793	9766,26086	9883	9856,015121	9973	9945,769381	10063	10035,52364	10153	10125,2779
9704	9677,503868	9794	9767,258129	9884	9857,01239	9974	9946,766651	10064	10036,52091	10154	10126,27517
9705	9678,501138	9795	9768,255399	9885	9858,00966	9975	9947,763921	10065	10037,51818	10155	10127,27244
9706	9679,498407	9796	9769,252668	9886	9859,006929	9976	9948,76119	10066	10038,51545	10156	10128,26971
9707	9680,495677	9797	9770,249938	9887	9860,004199	9977	9949,75846	10067	10039,51272	10157	10129,26698
9708	9681,492946	9798	9771,247207	9888	9861,001468	9978	9950,755729	10068	10040,50999	10158	10130,26425
9709	9682,490216	9799	9772,244477	9889	9861,998738	9979	9951,752999	10069	10041,50726	10159	10131,26152
9710	9683,487486	9800	9773,241747	9890	9862,996007	9980	9952,750268	10070	10042,50453	10160	10132,25879
9711	9684,484755	9801	9774,239016	9891	9863,993277	9981	9953,747538	10071	10043,5018	10161	10133,25606
9712	9685,482025	9802	9775,236286	9892	9864,990547	9982	9954,744808	10072	10044,49907	10162	10134,25333
9713	9686,479294	9803	9776,233555	9893	9865,987816	9983	9955,742077	10073	10045,49634	10163	10135,2506
9714	9687,476564	9804	9777,230825	9894	9866,985086	9984	9956,739347	10074	10046,49361	10164	10136,24787
9715	9688,473833	9805	9778,228094	9895	9867,982355	9985	9957,736616	10075	10047,49088	10165	10137,24514
9716	9689,471103	9806	9779,225364	9896	9868,979625	9986	9958,733886	10076	10048,48815	10166	10138,24241
9717	9690,468373	9807	9780,222633	9897	9869,976894	9987	9959,731155	10077	10049,48542	10167	10139,23968
9718	9691,465642	9808	9781,219903	9898	9870,974164	9988	9960,728425	10078	10050,48269	10168	10140,23695
9719	9692,462912	9809	9782,217173	9899	9871,971434	9989	9961,725694	10079	10051,47996	10169	10141,23422
9720	9693,460181	9810	9783,214442	9900	9872,968703	9990	9962,722964	10080	10052,47723	10170	10142,23149
9721	9694,457451	9811	9784,211712	9901	9873,965973	9991	9963,720234	10081	10053,47449	10171	10143,22876
9722	9695,45472	9812	9785,208981	9902	9874,963242	9992	9964,717503	10082	10054,47176	10172	10144,22603
9723	9696,45199	9813	9786,206251	9903	9875,960512	9993	9965,714773	10083	10055,46903	10173	10145,22329
9724	9697,44926	9814	9787,20352	9904	9876,957781	9994	9966,712042	10084	10056,4663	10174	10146,22056
9725	9698,446529	9815	9788,20079	9905	9877,955051	9995	9967,709312	10085	10057,46357	10175	10147,21783
9726	9699,443799	9816	9789,19806	9906	9878,952321	9996	9968,706581	10086	10058,46084	10176	10148,2151
9727	9700,441068	9817	9790,195329	9907	9879,94959	9997	9969,703851	10087	10059,45811	10177	10149,21237
9728	9701,438338	9818	9791,192599	9908	9880,94686	9998	9970,701121	10088	10060,45538	10178	10150,20964
9729	9702,435607	9819	9792,189868	9909	9881,944129	9999	9971,69839	10089	10061,45265	10179	10151,20691
9730	9703,432877	9820	9793,187138	9910	9882,941399	10000	9972,69566	10090	10062,44992	10180	10152,20418
9731	9704,430146	9821	9794,184407	9911	9883,938668	10001	9973,692929	10091	10063,44719	10181	10153,20145
9732	9705,427416	9822	9795,181677	9912	9884,935938	10002	9974,690199	10092	10064,44446	10182	10154,19872
9733	9706,424686	9823	9796,178947	9913	9885,933207	10003	9975,687468	10093	10065,44173	10183	10155,19599
9734	9707,421955	9824	9797,176216	9914	9886,930477	10004	9976,684738	10094	10066,439	10184	10156,19326
9735	9708,419225	9825	9798,173486	9915	9887,927747	10005	9977,682008	10095	10067,43627	10185	10157,19053
9736	9709,416494	9826	9799,170755	9916	9888,925016	10006	9978,679277	10096	10068,43354	10186	10158,1878
9737	9710,413764	9827	9800,168025	9917	9889,922286	10007	9979,676547	10097	10069,43081	10187	10159,18507
9738	9711,411033	9828	9801,165294	9918	9890,919555	10008	9980,673816	10098	10070,42808	10188	10160,18234
9739	9712,408303	9829	9802,162564	9919	9891,916825	10009	9981,671086	10099	10071,42535	10189	10161,17961
9740	9713,405573	9830	9803,159834	9920	9892,914094	10010	9982,668355	10100	10072,42262	10190	10162,17688
9741	9714,402842	9831	9804,157103	9921	9893,911364	10011	9983,665625	10101	10073,41989	10191	10163,17415
9742	9715,400112	9832	9805,154373	9922	9894,908634	10012	9984,662895	10102	10074,41716	10192	10164,17142
9743	9716,397381	9833	9806,151642	9923	9895,905903	10013	9985,660164	10103	10075,41443	10193	10165,16869
9744	9717,394651	9834	9807,148912	9924	9896,903173	10014	9986,657434	10104	10076,41169	10194	10166,16596

LUNAR RETURNS AND EARTH RETURNS

10195	10167,16323	10285	10256,91749	10375	10346,67175	10465	10436,42601	10555	10526,18027	10645	10615,93453
10196	10168,16049	10286	10257,91476	10376	10347,66902	10466	10437,42328	10556	10527,17754	10646	10616,9318
10197	10169,15776	10287	10258,91203	10377	10348,66629	10467	10438,42055	10557	10528,17481	10647	10617,92907
10198	10170,15503	10288	10259,90929	10378	10349,66356	10468	10439,41782	10558	10529,17208	10648	10618,92634
10199	10171,1523	10289	10260,90656	10379	10350,66083	10469	10440,41509	10559	10530,16935	10649	10619,92361
10200	10172,14957	10290	10261,90383	10380	10351,65809	10470	10441,41236	10560	10531,16662	10650	10620,92088
10201	10173,14684	10291	10262,9011	10381	10352,65536	10471	10442,40963	10561	10532,16389	10651	10621,91815
10202	10174,14411	10292	10263,89837	10382	10353,65263	10472	10443,40689	10562	10533,16116	10652	10622,91542
10203	10175,14138	10293	10264,89564	10383	10354,6499	10473	10444,40416	10563	10534,15843	10653	10623,91269
10204	10176,13865	10294	10265,89291	10384	10355,64717	10474	10445,40143	10564	10535,15569	10654	10624,90996
10205	10177,13592	10295	10266,89018	10385	10356,64444	10475	10446,3987	10565	10536,15296	10655	10625,90723
10206	10178,13319	10296	10267,88745	10386	10357,64171	10476	10447,39597	10566	10537,15023	10656	10626,9045
10207	10179,13046	10297	10268,88472	10387	10358,63898	10477	10448,39324	10567	10538,1475	10657	10627,90176
10208	10180,12773	10298	10269,88199	10388	10359,63625	10478	10449,39051	10568	10539,14477	10658	10628,89903
10209	10181,125	10299	10270,87926	10389	10360,63352	10479	10450,38778	10569	10540,14204	10659	10629,8963
10210	10182,12227	10300	10271,87653	10390	10361,63079	10480	10451,38505	10570	10541,13931	10660	10630,89357
10211	10183,11954	10301	10272,8738	10391	10362,62806	10481	10452,38232	10571	10542,13658	10661	10631,89084
10212	10184,11681	10302	10273,87107	10392	10363,62533	10482	10453,37959	10572	10543,13385	10662	10632,88811
10213	10185,11408	10303	10274,86834	10393	10364,6226	10483	10454,37686	10573	10544,13112	10663	10633,88538
10214	10186,11135	10304	10275,86561	10394	10365,61987	10484	10455,37413	10574	10545,12839	10664	10634,88265
10215	10187,10862	10305	10276,86288	10395	10366,61714	10485	10456,3714	10575	10546,12566	10665	10635,87992
10216	10188,10589	10306	10277,86015	10396	10367,61441	10486	10457,36867	10576	10547,12293	10666	10636,87719
10217	10189,10316	10307	10278,85742	10397	10368,61168	10487	10458,36594	10577	10548,1202	10667	10637,87446
10218	10190,10043	10308	10279,85469	10398	10369,60895	10488	10459,36321	10578	10549,11747	10668	10638,87173
10219	10191,09769	10309	10280,85196	10399	10370,60622	10489	10460,36048	10579	10550,11474	10669	10639,869
10220	10192,09496	10310	10281,84923	10400	10371,60349	10490	10461,35775	10580	10551,11201	10670	10640,86627
10221	10193,09223	10311	10282,84649	10401	10372,60076	10491	10462,35502	10581	10552,10928	10671	10641,86354
10222	10194,0895	10312	10283,84376	10402	10373,59803	10492	10463,35229	10582	10553,10655	10672	10642,86081
10223	10195,08677	10313	10284,84103	10403	10374,59529	10493	10464,34956	10583	10554,10382	10673	10643,85808
10224	10196,08404	10314	10285,8383	10404	10375,59256	10494	10465,34683	10584	10555,10109	10674	10644,85535
10225	10197,08131	10315	10286,83557	10405	10376,58983	10495	10466,34409	10585	10556,09836	10675	10645,85262
10226	10198,07858	10316	10287,83284	10406	10377,5871	10496	10467,34136	10586	10557,09563	10676	10646,84989
10227	10199,07585	10317	10288,83011	10407	10378,58437	10497	10468,33863	10587	10558,09289	10677	10647,84716
10228	10200,07312	10318	10289,82738	10408	10379,58164	10498	10469,3359	10588	10559,09016	10678	10648,84443
10229	10201,07039	10319	10290,82465	10409	10380,57891	10499	10470,33317	10589	10560,08743	10679	10649,8417
10230	10202,06766	10320	10291,82192	10410	10381,57618	10500	10471,33044	10590	10561,0847	10680	10650,83896
10231	10203,06493	10321	10292,81919	10411	10382,57345	10501	10472,32771	10591	10562,08197	10681	10651,83623
10232	10204,0622	10322	10293,81646	10412	10383,57072	10502	10473,32498	10592	10563,07924	10682	10652,8335
10233	10205,05947	10323	10294,81373	10413	10384,56799	10503	10474,32225	10593	10564,07651	10683	10653,83077
10234	10206,05674	10324	10295,811	10414	10385,56526	10504	10475,31952	10594	10565,07378	10684	10654,82804
10235	10207,05401	10325	10296,80827	10415	10386,56253	10505	10476,31679	10595	10566,07105	10685	10655,82531
10236	10208,05128	10326	10297,80554	10416	10387,5598	10506	10477,31406	10596	10567,06832	10686	10656,82258
10237	10209,04855	10327	10298,80281	10417	10388,55707	10507	10478,31133	10597	10568,06559	10687	10657,81985
10238	10210,04582	10328	10299,80008	10418	10389,55434	10508	10479,3086	10598	10569,06286	10688	10658,81712
10239	10211,04309	10329	10300,79735	10419	10390,55161	10509	10480,30587	10599	10570,06013	10689	10659,81439
10240	10212,04036	10330	10301,79462	10420	10391,54888	10510	10481,30314	10600	10571,0574	10690	10660,81166
10241	10213,03763	10331	10302,79189	10421	10392,54615	10511	10482,30041	10601	10572,05467	10691	10661,80893
10242	10214,03489	10332	10303,78916	10422	10393,54342	10512	10483,29768	10602	10573,05194	10692	10662,8062
10243	10215,03216	10333	10304,78643	10423	10394,54069	10513	10484,29495	10603	10574,04921	10693	10663,80347
10244	10216,02943	10334	10305,78369	10424	10395,53796	10514	10485,29222	10604	10575,04648	10694	10664,80074
10245	10217,0267	10335	10306,78096	10425	10396,53523	10515	10486,28949	10605	10576,04375	10695	10665,79801
10246	10218,02397	10336	10307,77823	10426	10397,53249	10516	10487,28676	10606	10577,04102	10696	10666,79528
10247	10219,02124	10337	10308,7755	10427	10398,52976	10517	10488,28403	10607	10578,03829	10697	10667,79255
10248	10220,01851	10338	10309,77277	10428	10399,52703	10518	10489,28129	10608	10579,03556	10698	10668,78982
10249	10221,01578	10339	10310,77004	10429	10400,5243	10519	10490,27856	10609	10580,03283	10699	10669,78709
10250	10222,01305	10340	10311,76731	10430	10401,52157	10520	10491,27583	10610	10581,03009	10700	10670,78436
10251	10223,01032	10341	10312,76458	10431	10402,51884	10521	10492,2731	10611	10582,02736	10701	10671,78163
10252	10224,00759	10342	10313,76185	10432	10403,51611	10522	10493,27037	10612	10583,02463	10702	10672,7789
10253	10225,00486	10343	10314,75912	10433	10404,51338	10523	10494,26764	10613	10584,0219	10703	10673,77616
10254	10226,00213	10344	10315,75639	10434	10405,51065	10524	10495,26491	10614	10585,01917	10704	10674,77343
10255	10226,9994	10345	10316,75366	10435	10406,50792	10525	10496,26218	10615	10586,01644	10705	10675,7707
10256	10227,99667	10346	10317,75093	10436	10407,50519	10526	10497,25945	10616	10587,01371	10706	10676,76797
10257	10228,99394	10347	10318,7482	10437	10408,50246	10527	10498,25672	10617	10588,01098	10707	10677,76524
10258	10229,99121	10348	10319,74547	10438	10409,49973	10528	10499,25399	10618	10589,00825	10708	10678,76251
10259	10230,98848	10349	10320,74274	10439	10410,497	10529	10500,25126	10619	10590,00552	10709	10679,75978
10260	10231,98575	10350	10321,74001	10440	10411,49427	10530	10501,24853	10620	10591,00279	10710	10680,75705
10261	10232,98302	10351	10322,73728	10441	10412,49154	10531	10502,2458	10621	10592,00006	10711	10681,75432
10262	10233,98029	10352	10323,73455	10442	10413,48881	10532	10503,24307	10622	10592,99733	10712	10682,75159
10263	10234,97756	10353	10324,73182	10443	10414,48608	10533	10504,24034	10623	10593,9946	10713	10683,74886
10264	10235,97483	10354	10325,72909	10444	10415,48335	10534	10505,23761	10624	10594,99187	10714	10684,74613
10265	10236,97209	10355	10326,72636	10445	10416,48062	10535	10506,23488	10625	10595,98914	10715	10685,7434
10266	10237,96936	10356	10327,72363	10446	10417,47789	10536	10507,23215	10626	10596,98641	10716	10686,74067
10267	10238,96663	10357	10328,7209	10447	10418,47516	10537	10508,22942	10627	10597,98368	10717	10687,73794
10268	10239,9639	10358	10329,71816	10448	10419,47243	10538	10509,22669	10628	10598,98095	10718	10688,73521
10269	10240,96117	10359	10330,71543	10449	10420,4697	10539	10510,22396	10629	10599,97822	10719	10689,73248
10270	10241,95844	10360	10331,7127	10450	10421,46696	10540	10511,22123	10630	10600,97549	10720	10690,72975
10271	10242,95571	10361	10332,70997	10451	10422,46423	10541	10512,2185	10631	10601,97276	10721	10691,72702
10272	10243,95298	10362	10333,70724	10452	10423,4615	10542	10513,21576	10632	10602,97003	10722	10692,72429
10273	10244,95025	10363	10334,70451	10453	10424,45877	10543	10514,21303	10633	10603,96729	10723	10693,72156
10274	10245,94752	10364	10335,70178	10454	10425,45604	10544	10515,2103	10634	10604,96456	10724	10694,71883
10275	10246,94479	10365	10336,69905	10455	10426,45331	10545	10516,20757	10635	10605,96183	10725	10695,7161
10276	10247,94206	10366	10337,69632	10456	10427,45058	10546	10517,20484	10636	10606,9591	10726	10696,71336
10277	10248,93933	10367	10338,69359	10457	10428,44785	10547	10518,20211	10637	10607,95637	10727	10697,71063
10278	10249,9366	10368	10339,69086	10458	10429,44512	10548	10519,19938	10638	10608,95364	10728	10698,7079
10279	10250,93387	10369	10340,68813	10459	10430,44239	10549	10520,19665	10639	10609,95091	10729	10699,70517
10280	10251,93114	10370	10341,6854	10460	10431,43966	10550	10521,19392	10640	10610,94818	10730	10700,70244
10281	10252,92841	10371	10342,68267	10461	10432,43693	10551	10522,19119	10641	10611,94545	10731	10701,69971
10282	10253,92568	10372	10343,67994	10462	10433,4342	10552	10523,18846	10642	10612,94272	10732	10702,69698
10283	10254,92295	10373	10344,67721	10463	10434,43147	10553	10524,18573	10643	10613,93999	10733	10703,69425
10284	10255,92022	10374	10345,67448	10464	10435,42874	10554	10525,183	10644	10614,93726	10734	10704,69152

TABLE TO FIND OUT THE POINT A IN EARTH RETURNS 177

10735	10705,68879	10825	10795,44305	10915	10885,19731	11005	10974,95157	11095	11064,70583	11185	11154,4601
10736	10706,68606	10826	10796,44032	10916	10886,19458	11006	10975,94884	11096	11065,7031	11186	11155,45736
10737	10707,68333	10827	10797,43759	10917	10887,19185	11007	10976,94611	11097	11066,70037	11187	11156,45463
10738	10708,6806	10828	10798,43486	10918	10888,18912	11008	10977,94338	11098	11067,69764	11188	11157,4519
10739	10709,67787	10829	10799,43213	10919	10889,18639	11009	10978,94065	11099	11068,69491	11189	11158,44917
10740	10710,67514	10830	10800,4294	10920	10890,18366	11010	10979,93792	11100	11069,69218	11190	11159,44644
10741	10711,67241	10831	10801,42667	10921	10891,18093	11011	10980,93519	11101	11070,68945	11191	11160,44371
10742	10712,66968	10832	10802,42394	10922	10892,1782	11012	10981,93246	11102	11071,68672	11192	11161,44098
10743	10713,66695	10833	10803,42121	10923	10893,17547	11013	10982,92973	11103	11072,68399	11193	11162,43825
10744	10714,66422	10834	10804,41848	10924	10894,17274	11014	10983,927	11104	11073,68126	11194	11163,43552
10745	10715,66149	10835	10805,41575	10925	10895,17001	11015	10984,92427	11105	11074,67853	11195	11164,43279
10746	10716,65876	10836	10806,41302	10926	10896,16728	11016	10985,92154	11106	11075,6758	11196	11165,43006
10747	10717,65603	10837	10807,41029	10927	10897,16455	11017	10986,91881	11107	11076,67307	11197	11166,42733
10748	10718,6533	10838	10808,40756	10928	10898,16182	11018	10987,91608	11108	11077,67034	11198	11167,4246
10749	10719,65056	10839	10809,40483	10929	10899,15909	11019	10988,91335	11109	11078,66761	11199	11168,42187
10750	10720,64783	10840	10810,4021	10930	10900,15636	11020	10989,91062	11110	11079,66488	11200	11169,41914
10751	10721,6451	10841	10811,39936	10931	10901,15363	11021	10990,90789	11111	11080,66215	11201	11170,41641
10752	10722,64237	10842	10812,39663	10932	10902,1509	11022	10991,90516	11112	11081,65942	11202	11171,41368
10753	10723,63964	10843	10813,3939	10933	10903,14816	11023	10992,90243	11113	11082,65669	11203	11172,41095
10754	10724,63691	10844	10814,39117	10934	10904,14543	11024	10993,8997	11114	11083,65396	11204	11173,40822
10755	10725,63418	10845	10815,38844	10935	10905,1427	11025	10994,89696	11115	11084,65123	11205	11174,40549
10756	10726,63145	10846	10816,38571	10936	10906,13997	11026	10995,89423	11116	11085,6485	11206	11175,40276
10757	10727,62872	10847	10817,38298	10937	10907,13724	11027	10996,8915	11117	11086,64576	11207	11176,40003
10758	10728,62599	10848	10818,38025	10938	10908,13451	11028	10997,88877	11118	11087,64303	11208	11177,3973
10759	10729,62326	10849	10819,37752	10939	10909,13178	11029	10998,88604	11119	11088,6403	11209	11178,39456
10760	10730,62053	10850	10820,37479	10940	10910,12905	11030	10999,88331	11120	11089,63757	11210	11179,39183
10761	10731,6178	10851	10821,37206	10941	10911,12632	11031	11000,88058	11121	11090,63484	11211	11180,3891
10762	10732,61507	10852	10822,36933	10942	10912,12359	11032	11001,87785	11122	11091,63211	11212	11181,38637
10763	10733,61234	10853	10823,3666	10943	10913,12086	11033	11002,87512	11123	11092,62938	11213	11182,38364
10764	10734,60961	10854	10824,36387	10944	10914,11813	11034	11003,87239	11124	11093,62665	11214	11183,38091
10765	10735,60688	10855	10825,36114	10945	10915,1154	11035	11004,86966	11125	11094,62392	11215	11184,37818
10766	10736,60415	10856	10826,35841	10946	10916,11267	11036	11005,86693	11126	11095,62119	11216	11185,37545
10767	10737,60142	10857	10827,35568	10947	10917,10994	11037	11006,8642	11127	11096,61846	11217	11186,37272
10768	10738,59869	10858	10828,35295	10948	10918,10721	11038	11007,86147	11128	11097,61573	11218	11187,36999
10769	10739,59596	10859	10829,35022	10949	10919,10448	11039	11008,85874	11129	11098,613	11219	11188,36726
10770	10740,59323	10860	10830,34749	10950	10920,10175	11040	11009,85601	11130	11099,61027	11220	11189,36453
10771	10741,5905	10861	10831,34476	10951	10921,09902	11041	11010,85328	11131	11100,60754	11221	11190,3618
10772	10742,58776	10862	10832,34203	10952	10922,09629	11042	11011,85055	11132	11101,60481	11222	11191,35907
10773	10743,58503	10863	10833,3393	10953	10923,09356	11043	11012,84782	11133	11102,60208	11223	11192,35634
10774	10744,5823	10864	10834,33656	10954	10924,09083	11044	11013,84509	11134	11103,59935	11224	11193,35361
10775	10745,57957	10865	10835,33383	10955	10925,0881	11045	11014,84236	11135	11104,59662	11225	11194,35088
10776	10746,57684	10866	10836,3311	10956	10926,08536	11046	11015,83963	11136	11105,59389	11226	11195,34815
10777	10747,57411	10867	10837,32837	10957	10927,08263	11047	11016,8369	11137	11106,59116	11227	11196,34542
10778	10748,57138	10868	10838,32564	10958	10928,0799	11048	11017,83416	11138	11107,58843	11228	11197,34269
10779	10749,56865	10869	10839,32291	10959	10929,07717	11049	11018,83143	11139	11108,5857	11229	11198,33996
10780	10750,56592	10870	10840,32018	10960	10930,07444	11050	11019,8287	11140	11109,58296	11230	11199,33723
10781	10751,56319	10871	10841,31745	10961	10931,07171	11051	11020,82597	11141	11110,58023	11231	11200,3345
10782	10752,56046	10872	10842,31472	10962	10932,06898	11052	11021,82324	11142	11111,5775	11232	11201,33177
10783	10753,55773	10873	10843,31199	10963	10933,06625	11053	11022,82051	11143	11112,57477	11233	11202,32903
10784	10754,555	10874	10844,30926	10964	10934,06352	11054	11023,81778	11144	11113,57204	11234	11203,3263
10785	10755,55227	10875	10845,30653	10965	10935,06079	11055	11024,81505	11145	11114,56931	11235	11204,32357
10786	10756,54954	10876	10846,3038	10966	10936,05806	11056	11025,81232	11146	11115,56658	11236	11205,32084
10787	10757,54681	10877	10847,30107	10967	10937,05533	11057	11026,80959	11147	11116,56385	11237	11206,31811
10788	10758,54408	10878	10848,29834	10968	10938,0526	11058	11027,80686	11148	11117,56112	11238	11207,31538
10789	10759,54135	10879	10849,29561	10969	10939,04987	11059	11028,80413	11149	11118,55839	11239	11208,31265
10790	10760,53862	10880	10850,29288	10970	10940,04714	11060	11029,8014	11150	11119,55566	11240	11209,30992
10791	10761,53589	10881	10851,29015	10971	10941,04441	11061	11030,79867	11151	11120,55293	11241	11210,30719
10792	10762,53316	10882	10852,28742	10972	10942,04168	11062	11031,79594	11152	11121,5502	11242	11211,30446
10793	10763,53043	10883	10853,28469	10973	10943,03895	11063	11032,79321	11153	11122,54747	11243	11212,30173
10794	10764,5277	10884	10854,28196	10974	10944,03622	11064	11033,79048	11154	11123,54474	11244	11213,299
10795	10765,52496	10885	10855,27923	10975	10945,03349	11065	11034,78775	11155	11124,54201	11245	11214,29627
10796	10766,52223	10886	10856,2765	10976	10946,03076	11066	11035,78502	11156	11125,53928	11246	11215,29354
10797	10767,5195	10887	10857,27376	10977	10947,02803	11067	11036,78229	11157	11126,53655	11247	11216,29081
10798	10768,51677	10888	10858,27103	10978	10948,0253	11068	11037,77956	11158	11127,53382	11248	11217,28808
10799	10769,51404	10889	10859,2683	10979	10949,02256	11069	11038,77683	11159	11128,53109	11249	11218,28535
10800	10770,51131	10890	10860,26557	10980	10950,01983	11070	11039,7741	11160	11129,52836	11250	11219,28262
10801	10771,50858	10891	10861,26284	10981	10951,0171	11071	11040,77136	11161	11130,52563	11251	11220,27989
10802	10772,50585	10892	10862,26011	10982	10952,01437	11072	11041,76863	11162	11131,5229	11252	11221,27716
10803	10773,50312	10893	10863,25738	10983	10953,01164	11073	11042,7659	11163	11132,52016	11253	11222,27443
10804	10774,50039	10894	10864,25465	10984	10954,00891	11074	11043,76317	11164	11133,51743	11254	11223,2717
10805	10775,49766	10895	10865,25192	10985	10955,00618	11075	11044,76044	11165	11134,5147	11255	11224,26897
10806	10776,49493	10896	10866,24919	10986	10956,00345	11076	11045,75771	11166	11135,51197	11256	11225,26623
10807	10777,4922	10897	10867,24646	10987	10957,00072	11077	11046,75498	11167	11136,50924	11257	11226,2635
10808	10778,48947	10898	10868,24373	10988	10957,99799	11078	11047,75225	11168	11137,50651	11258	11227,26077
10809	10779,48674	10899	10869,241	10989	10958,99526	11079	11048,74952	11169	11138,50378	11259	11228,25804
10810	10780,48401	10900	10870,23827	10990	10959,99253	11080	11049,74679	11170	11139,50105	11260	11229,25531
10811	10781,48128	10901	10871,23554	10991	10960,9898	11081	11050,74406	11171	11140,49832	11261	11230,25258
10812	10782,47855	10902	10872,23281	10992	10961,98707	11082	11051,74133	11172	11141,49559	11262	11231,24985
10813	10783,47582	10903	10873,23008	10993	10962,98434	11083	11052,7386	11173	11142,49286	11263	11232,24712
10814	10784,47309	10904	10874,22735	10994	10963,98161	11084	11053,73587	11174	11143,49013	11264	11233,24439
10815	10785,47036	10905	10875,22462	10995	10964,97888	11085	11054,73314	11175	11144,4874	11265	11234,24166
10816	10786,46763	10906	10876,22189	10996	10965,97615	11086	11055,73041	11176	11145,48467	11266	11235,23893
10817	10787,4649	10907	10877,21916	10997	10966,97342	11087	11056,72768	11177	11146,48194	11267	11236,2362
10818	10788,46216	10908	10878,21643	10998	10967,97069	11088	11057,72495	11178	11147,47921	11268	11237,23347
10819	10789,45943	10909	10879,2137	10999	10968,96796	11089	11058,72222	11179	11148,47648	11269	11238,23074
10820	10790,4567	10910	10880,21096	11000	10969,96523	11090	11059,71949	11180	11149,47375	11270	11239,22801
10821	10791,45397	10911	10881,20823	11001	10970,9625	11091	11060,71676	11181	11150,47102	11271	11240,22528
10822	10792,45124	10912	10882,2055	11002	10971,95976	11092	11061,71403	11182	11151,46829	11272	11241,22255
10823	10793,44851	10913	10883,20277	11003	10972,95703	11093	11062,7113	11183	11152,46556	11273	11242,21982
10824	10794,44578	10914	10884,20004	11004	10973,9543	11094	11063,70856	11184	11153,46283	11274	11243,21709

11275 11244,21436	11365 11333,96862	11455 11423,72288	11545 11513,47714	11635 11603,2314	11725 11692,98566
11276 11245,21163	11366 11334,96589	11456 11424,72015	11546 11514,47441	11636 11604,22867	11726 11693,98293
11277 11246,2089	11367 11335,96316	11457 11425,71742	11547 11515,47168	11637 11605,22594	11727 11694,9802
11278 11247,20617	11368 11336,96043	11458 11426,71469	11548 11516,46895	11638 11606,22321	11728 11695,97747
11279 11248,20343	11369 11337,9577	11459 11427,71196	11549 11517,46622	11639 11607,22048	11729 11696,97474
11280 11249,2007	11370 11338,95497	11460 11428,70923	11550 11518,46349	11640 11608,21775	11730 11697,97201
11281 11250,19797	11371 11339,95223	11461 11429,7065	11551 11519,46076	11641 11609,21502	11731 11698,96928
11282 11251,19524	11372 11340,9495	11462 11430,70377	11552 11520,45803	11642 11610,21229	11732 11699,96655
11283 11252,19251	11373 11341,94677	11463 11431,70103	11553 11521,4553	11643 11611,20956	11733 11700,96382
11284 11253,18978	11374 11342,94404	11464 11432,6983	11554 11522,45257	11644 11612,20683	11734 11701,96109
11285 11254,18705	11375 11343,94131	11465 11433,69557	11555 11523,44983	11645 11613,2041	11735 11702,95836
11286 11255,18432	11376 11344,93858	11466 11434,69284	11556 11524,4471	11646 11614,20137	11736 11703,95563
11287 11256,18159	11377 11345,93585	11467 11435,69011	11557 11525,44437	11647 11615,19863	11737 11704,9529
11288 11257,17886	11378 11346,93312	11468 11436,68738	11558 11526,44164	11648 11616,1959	11738 11705,95017
11289 11258,17613	11379 11347,93039	11469 11437,68465	11559 11527,43891	11649 11617,19317	11739 11706,94743
11290 11259,1734	11380 11348,92766	11470 11438,68192	11560 11528,43618	11650 11618,19044	11740 11707,9447
11291 11260,17067	11381 11349,92493	11471 11439,67919	11561 11529,43345	11651 11619,18771	11741 11708,94197
11292 11261,16794	11382 11350,9222	11472 11440,67646	11562 11530,43072	11652 11620,18498	11742 11709,93924
11293 11262,16521	11383 11351,91947	11473 11441,67373	11563 11531,42799	11653 11621,18225	11743 11710,93651
11294 11263,16248	11384 11352,91674	11474 11442,671	11564 11532,42526	11654 11622,17952	11744 11711,93378
11295 11264,15975	11385 11353,91401	11475 11443,66827	11565 11533,42253	11655 11623,17679	11745 11712,93105
11296 11265,15702	11386 11354,91128	11476 11444,66554	11566 11534,4198	11656 11624,17406	11746 11713,92832
11297 11266,15429	11387 11355,90855	11477 11445,66281	11567 11535,41707	11657 11625,17133	11747 11714,92559
11298 11267,15156	11388 11356,90582	11478 11446,66008	11568 11536,41434	11658 11626,1686	11748 11715,92286
11299 11268,14883	11389 11357,90309	11479 11447,65735	11569 11537,41161	11659 11627,16587	11749 11716,92013
11300 11269,1461	11390 11358,90036	11480 11448,65462	11570 11538,40888	11660 11628,16314	11750 11717,9174
11301 11270,14337	11391 11359,89763	11481 11449,65189	11571 11539,40615	11661 11629,16041	11751 11718,91467
11302 11271,14063	11392 11360,8949	11482 11450,64916	11572 11540,40342	11662 11630,15768	11752 11719,91194
11303 11272,1379	11393 11361,89217	11483 11451,64643	11573 11541,40069	11663 11631,15495	11753 11720,90921
11304 11273,13517	11394 11362,88943	11484 11452,6437	11574 11542,39796	11664 11632,15222	11754 11721,90648
11305 11274,13244	11395 11363,8867	11485 11453,64097	11575 11543,39523	11665 11633,14949	11755 11722,90375
11306 11275,12971	11396 11364,88397	11486 11454,63823	11576 11544,3925	11666 11634,14676	11756 11723,90102
11307 11276,12698	11397 11365,88124	11487 11455,6355	11577 11545,38977	11667 11635,14403	11757 11724,89829
11308 11277,12425	11398 11366,87851	11488 11456,63277	11578 11546,38703	11668 11636,1413	11758 11725,89556
11309 11278,12152	11399 11367,87578	11489 11457,63004	11579 11547,3843	11669 11637,13857	11759 11726,89283
11310 11279,11879	11400 11368,87305	11490 11458,62731	11580 11548,38157	11670 11638,13583	11760 11727,8901
11311 11280,11606	11401 11369,87032	11491 11459,62458	11581 11549,37884	11671 11639,1331	11761 11728,88737
11312 11281,11333	11402 11370,86759	11492 11460,62185	11582 11550,37611	11672 11640,13037	11762 11729,88463
11313 11282,1106	11403 11371,86486	11493 11461,61912	11583 11551,37338	11673 11641,12764	11763 11730,8819
11314 11283,10787	11404 11372,86213	11494 11462,61639	11584 11552,37065	11674 11642,12491	11764 11731,87917
11315 11284,10514	11405 11373,8594	11495 11463,61366	11585 11553,36792	11675 11643,12218	11765 11732,87644
11316 11285,10241	11406 11374,85667	11496 11464,61093	11586 11554,36519	11676 11644,11945	11766 11733,87371
11317 11286,09968	11407 11375,85394	11497 11465,6082	11587 11555,36246	11677 11645,11672	11767 11734,87098
11318 11287,09695	11408 11376,85121	11498 11466,60547	11588 11556,35973	11678 11646,11399	11768 11735,86825
11319 11288,09422	11409 11377,84848	11499 11467,60274	11589 11557,357	11679 11647,11126	11769 11736,86552
11320 11289,09149	11410 11378,84575	11500 11468,60001	11590 11558,35427	11680 11648,10853	11770 11737,86279
11321 11290,08876	11411 11379,84302	11501 11469,59728	11591 11559,35154	11681 11649,1058	11771 11738,86006
11322 11291,08603	11412 11380,84029	11502 11470,59455	11592 11560,34881	11682 11650,10307	11772 11739,85733
11323 11292,0833	11413 11381,83756	11503 11471,59182	11593 11561,34608	11683 11651,10034	11773 11740,8546
11324 11293,08057	11414 11382,83483	11504 11472,58909	11594 11562,34335	11684 11652,09761	11774 11741,85187
11325 11294,07783	11415 11383,8321	11505 11473,58636	11595 11563,34062	11685 11653,09488	11775 11742,84914
11326 11295,0751	11416 11384,82937	11506 11474,58363	11596 11564,33789	11686 11654,09215	11776 11743,84641
11327 11296,07237	11417 11385,82663	11507 11475,5809	11597 11565,33516	11687 11655,08942	11777 11744,84368
11328 11297,06964	11418 11386,8239	11508 11476,57817	11598 11566,33243	11688 11656,08669	11778 11745,84095
11329 11298,06691	11419 11387,82117	11509 11477,57543	11599 11567,3297	11689 11657,08396	11779 11746,83822
11330 11299,06418	11420 11388,81844	11510 11478,5727	11600 11568,32697	11690 11658,08123	11780 11747,83549
11331 11300,06145	11421 11389,81571	11511 11479,56997	11601 11569,32423	11691 11659,0785	11781 11748,83276
11332 11301,05872	11422 11390,81298	11512 11480,56724	11602 11570,3215	11692 11660,07577	11782 11749,83003
11333 11302,05599	11423 11391,81025	11513 11481,56451	11603 11571,31877	11693 11661,07303	11783 11750,8273
11334 11303,05326	11424 11392,80752	11514 11482,56178	11604 11572,31604	11694 11662,0703	11784 11751,82457
11335 11304,05053	11425 11393,80479	11515 11483,55905	11605 11573,31331	11695 11663,06757	11785 11752,82183
11336 11305,0478	11426 11394,80206	11516 11484,55632	11606 11574,31058	11696 11664,06484	11786 11753,8191
11337 11306,04507	11427 11395,79933	11517 11485,55359	11607 11575,30785	11697 11665,06211	11787 11754,81637
11338 11307,04234	11428 11396,7966	11518 11486,55086	11608 11576,30512	11698 11666,05938	11788 11755,81364
11339 11308,03961	11429 11397,79387	11519 11487,54813	11609 11577,30239	11699 11667,05665	11789 11756,81091
11340 11309,03688	11430 11398,79114	11520 11488,5454	11610 11578,29966	11700 11668,05392	11790 11757,80818
11341 11310,03415	11431 11399,78841	11521 11489,54267	11611 11579,29693	11701 11669,05119	11791 11758,80545
11342 11311,03142	11432 11400,78568	11522 11490,53994	11612 11580,2942	11702 11670,04846	11792 11759,80272
11343 11312,02869	11433 11401,78295	11523 11491,53721	11613 11581,29147	11703 11671,04573	11793 11760,79999
11344 11313,02596	11434 11402,78022	11524 11492,53448	11614 11582,28874	11704 11672,043	11794 11761,79726
11345 11314,02323	11435 11403,77749	11525 11493,53175	11615 11583,28601	11705 11673,04027	11795 11762,79453
11346 11315,0205	11436 11404,77476	11526 11494,52902	11616 11584,28328	11706 11674,03754	11796 11763,7918
11347 11316,01777	11437 11405,77203	11527 11495,52629	11617 11585,28055	11707 11675,03481	11797 11764,78907
11348 11317,01503	11438 11406,7693	11528 11496,52356	11618 11586,27782	11708 11676,03208	11798 11765,78634
11349 11318,0123	11439 11407,76657	11529 11497,52083	11619 11587,27509	11709 11677,02935	11799 11766,78361
11350 11319,00957	11440 11408,76383	11530 11498,5181	11620 11588,27236	11710 11678,02662	11800 11767,78088
11351 11320,00684	11441 11409,7611	11531 11499,51537	11621 11589,26963	11711 11679,02389	11801 11768,77815
11352 11321,00411	11442 11410,75837	11532 11500,51263	11622 11590,2669	11712 11680,02116	11802 11769,77542
11353 11322,00138	11443 11411,75564	11533 11501,5099	11623 11591,26417	11713 11681,01843	11803 11770,77269
11354 11322,99865	11444 11412,75291	11534 11502,50717	11624 11592,26143	11714 11682,0157	11804 11771,76996
11355 11323,99592	11445 11413,75018	11535 11503,50444	11625 11593,2587	11715 11683,01297	11805 11772,76723
11356 11324,99319	11446 11414,74745	11536 11504,50171	11626 11594,25597	11716 11684,01023	11806 11773,7645
11357 11325,99046	11447 11415,74472	11537 11505,49898	11627 11595,25324	11717 11685,0075	11807 11774,76177
11358 11326,98773	11448 11416,74199	11538 11506,49625	11628 11596,25051	11718 11686,00477	11808 11775,75904
11359 11327,985	11449 11417,73926	11539 11507,49352	11629 11597,24778	11719 11687,00204	11809 11776,7563
11360 11328,98227	11450 11418,73653	11540 11508,49079	11630 11598,24505	11720 11687,99931	11810 11777,75357
11361 11329,97954	11451 11419,7338	11541 11509,48806	11631 11599,24232	11721 11688,99658	11811 11778,75084
11362 11330,97681	11452 11420,73107	11542 11510,48533	11632 11600,23959	11722 11689,99385	11812 11779,74811
11363 11331,97408	11453 11421,72834	11543 11511,4826	11633 11601,23686	11723 11690,99112	11813 11780,74538
11364 11332,97135	11454 11422,72561	11544 11512,47987	11634 11602,23413	11724 11691,98839	11814 11781,74265

TABLE TO FIND OUT THE POINT A IN EARTH RETURNS 179

11815	11782,73992	11905	11872,49418	11995	11962,24844	12085	12052,0027	12175	12141,75697	12265	12231,51123
11816	11783,73719	11906	11873,49145	11996	11963,24571	12086	12052,99997	12176	12142,75424	12266	12232,5085
11817	11784,73446	11907	11874,48872	11997	11964,24298	12087	12053,99724	12177	12143,7515	12267	12233,50577
11818	11785,73173	11908	11875,48599	11998	11965,24025	12088	12054,99451	12178	12144,74877	12268	12234,50304
11819	11786,729	11909	11876,48326	11999	11966,23752	12089	12055,99178	12179	12145,74604	12269	12235,5003
11820	11787,72627	11910	11877,48053	12000	11967,23479	12090	12056,98905	12180	12146,74331	12270	12236,49757
11821	11788,72354	11911	11878,4778	12001	11968,23206	12091	12057,98632	12181	12147,74058	12271	12237,49484
11822	11789,72081	11912	11879,47507	12002	11969,22933	12092	12058,98359	12182	12148,73785	12272	12238,49211
11823	11790,71808	11913	11880,47234	12003	11970,2266	12093	12059,98086	12183	12149,73512	12273	12239,48938
11824	11791,71535	11914	11881,46961	12004	11971,22387	12094	12060,97813	12184	12150,73239	12274	12240,48665
11825	11792,71262	11915	11882,46688	12005	11972,22114	12095	12061,9754	12185	12151,72966	12275	12241,48392
11826	11793,70989	11916	11883,46415	12006	11973,21841	12096	12062,97267	12186	12152,72693	12276	12242,48119
11827	11794,70716	11917	11884,46142	12007	11974,21568	12097	12063,96994	12187	12153,7242	12277	12243,47846
11828	11795,70443	11918	11885,45869	12008	11975,21295	12098	12064,96721	12188	12154,72147	12278	12244,47573
11829	11796,7017	11919	11886,45596	12009	11976,21022	12099	12065,96448	12189	12155,71874	12279	12245,473
11830	11797,69897	11920	11887,45323	12010	11977,20749	12100	12066,96175	12190	12156,71601	12280	12246,47027
11831	11798,69624	11921	11888,4505	12011	11978,20476	12101	12067,95902	12191	12157,71328	12281	12247,46754
11832	11799,6935	11922	11889,44777	12012	11979,20203	12102	12068,95629	12192	12158,71055	12282	12248,46481
11833	11800,69077	11923	11890,44504	12013	11980,1993	12103	12069,95356	12193	12159,70782	12283	12249,46208
11834	11801,68804	11924	11891,4423	12014	11981,19657	12104	12070,95083	12194	12160,70509	12284	12250,45935
11835	11802,68531	11925	11892,43957	12015	11982,19384	12105	12071,9481	12195	12161,70236	12285	12251,45662
11836	11803,68258	11926	11893,43684	12016	11983,1911	12106	12072,94537	12196	12162,69963	12286	12252,45389
11837	11804,67985	11927	11894,43411	12017	11984,18837	12107	12073,94264	12197	12163,6969	12287	12253,45116
11838	11805,67712	11928	11895,43138	12018	11985,18564	12108	12074,9399	12198	12164,69417	12288	12254,44843
11839	11806,67439	11929	11896,42865	12019	11986,18291	12109	12075,93717	12199	12165,69144	12289	12255,4457
11840	11807,67166	11930	11897,42592	12020	11987,18018	12110	12076,93444	12200	12166,6887	12290	12256,44297
11841	11808,66893	11931	11898,42319	12021	11988,17745	12111	12077,93171	12201	12167,68597	12291	12257,44024
11842	11809,6662	11932	11899,42046	12022	11989,17472	12112	12078,92898	12202	12168,68324	12292	12258,4375
11843	11810,66347	11933	11900,41773	12023	11990,17199	12113	12079,92625	12203	12169,68051	12293	12259,43477
11844	11811,66074	11934	11901,415	12024	11991,16926	12114	12080,92352	12204	12170,67778	12294	12260,43204
11845	11812,65801	11935	11902,41227	12025	11992,16653	12115	12081,92079	12205	12171,67505	12295	12261,42931
11846	11813,65528	11936	11903,40954	12026	11993,1638	12116	12082,91806	12206	12172,67232	12296	12262,42658
11847	11814,65255	11937	11904,40681	12027	11994,16107	12117	12083,91533	12207	12173,66959	12297	12263,42385
11848	11815,64982	11938	11905,40408	12028	11995,15834	12118	12084,9126	12208	12174,66686	12298	12264,42112
11849	11816,64709	11939	11906,40135	12029	11996,15561	12119	12085,90987	12209	12175,66413	12299	12265,41839
11850	11817,64436	11940	11907,39862	12030	11997,15288	12120	12086,90714	12210	12176,6614	12300	12266,41566
11851	11818,64163	11941	11908,39589	12031	11998,15015	12121	12087,90441	12211	12177,65867	12301	12267,41293
11852	11819,6389	11942	11909,39316	12032	11999,14742	12122	12088,90168	12212	12178,65594	12302	12268,4102
11853	11820,63617	11943	11910,39043	12033	12000,14469	12123	12089,89895	12213	12179,65321	12303	12269,40747
11854	11821,63344	11944	11911,3877	12034	12001,14196	12124	12090,89622	12214	12180,65048	12304	12270,40474
11855	11822,6307	11945	11912,38497	12035	12002,13923	12125	12091,89349	12215	12181,64775	12305	12271,40201
11856	11823,62797	11946	11913,38224	12036	12003,1365	12126	12092,89076	12216	12182,64502	12306	12272,39928
11857	11824,62524	11947	11914,3795	12037	12004,13377	12127	12093,88803	12217	12183,64229	12307	12273,39655
11858	11825,62251	11948	11915,37677	12038	12005,13104	12128	12094,8853	12218	12184,63956	12308	12274,39382
11859	11826,61978	11949	11916,37404	12039	12006,1283	12129	12095,88257	12219	12185,63683	12309	12275,39109
11860	11827,61705	11950	11917,37131	12040	12007,12557	12130	12096,87984	12220	12186,6341	12310	12276,38836
11861	11828,61432	11951	11918,36858	12041	12008,12284	12131	12097,8771	12221	12187,63137	12311	12277,38563
11862	11829,61159	11952	11919,36585	12042	12009,12011	12132	12098,87437	12222	12188,62864	12312	12278,3829
11863	11830,60886	11953	11920,36312	12043	12010,11738	12133	12099,87164	12223	12189,6259	12313	12279,38017
11864	11831,60613	11954	11921,36039	12044	12011,11465	12134	12100,86891	12224	12190,62317	12314	12280,37744
11865	11832,6034	11955	11922,35766	12045	12012,11192	12135	12101,86618	12225	12191,62044	12315	12281,3747
11866	11833,60067	11956	11923,35493	12046	12013,10919	12136	12102,86345	12226	12192,61771	12316	12282,37197
11867	11834,59794	11957	11924,3522	12047	12014,10646	12137	12103,86072	12227	12193,61498	12317	12283,36924
11868	11835,59521	11958	11925,34947	12048	12015,10373	12138	12104,85799	12228	12194,61225	12318	12284,36651
11869	11836,59248	11959	11926,34674	12049	12016,101	12139	12105,85526	12229	12195,60952	12319	12285,36378
11870	11837,58975	11960	11927,34401	12050	12017,09827	12140	12106,85253	12230	12196,60679	12320	12286,36105
11871	11838,58702	11961	11928,34128	12051	12018,09554	12141	12107,8498	12231	12197,60406	12321	12287,55832
11872	11839,58429	11962	11929,33855	12052	12019,09281	12142	12108,84707	12232	12198,60133	12322	12288,35559
11873	11840,58156	11963	11930,33582	12053	12020,09008	12143	12109,84434	12233	12199,5986	12323	12289,35286
11874	11841,57883	11964	11931,33309	12054	12021,08735	12144	12110,84161	12234	12200,59587	12324	12290,35013
11875	11842,5761	11965	11932,33036	12055	12022,08462	12145	12111,83888	12235	12201,59314	12325	12291,3474
11876	11843,57337	11966	11933,32763	12056	12023,08189	12146	12112,83615	12236	12202,59041	12326	12292,34467
11877	11844,57064	11967	11934,3249	12057	12024,07916	12147	12113,83342	12237	12203,58768	12327	12293,34194
11878	11845,5679	11968	11935,32217	12058	12025,07643	12148	12114,83069	12238	12204,58495	12328	12294,33921
11879	11846,56517	11969	11936,31944	12059	12026,0737	12149	12115,82796	12239	12205,58222	12329	12295,33648
11880	11847,56244	11970	11937,3167	12060	12027,07097	12150	12116,82523	12240	12206,57949	12330	12296,33375
11881	11848,55971	11971	11938,31397	12061	12028,06824	12151	12117,8225	12241	12207,57676	12331	12297,33102
11882	11849,55698	11972	11939,31124	12062	12029,0655	12152	12118,81977	12242	12208,57403	12332	12298,32829
11883	11850,55425	11973	11940,30851	12063	12030,06277	12153	12119,81704	12243	12209,5713	12333	12299,32556
11884	11851,55152	11974	11941,30578	12064	12031,06004	12154	12120,8143	12244	12210,56857	12334	12300,32283
11885	11852,54879	11975	11942,30305	12065	12032,05731	12155	12121,81157	12245	12211,56584	12335	12301,3201
11886	11853,54606	11976	11943,30032	12066	12033,05458	12156	12122,80884	12246	12212,5631	12336	12302,31737
11887	11854,54333	11977	11944,29759	12067	12034,05185	12157	12123,80611	12247	12213,56037	12337	12303,31464
11888	11855,5406	11978	11945,29486	12068	12035,04912	12158	12124,80338	12248	12214,55764	12338	12304,3119
11889	11856,53787	11979	11946,29213	12069	12036,04639	12159	12125,80065	12249	12215,55491	12339	12305,30917
11890	11857,53514	11980	11947,2894	12070	12037,04366	12160	12126,79792	12250	12216,55218	12340	12306,30644
11891	11858,53241	11981	11948,28667	12071	12038,04093	12161	12127,79519	12251	12217,54945	12341	12307,30371
11892	11859,52968	11982	11949,28394	12072	12039,0382	12162	12128,79246	12252	12218,54672	12342	12308,30098
11893	11860,52695	11983	11950,28121	12073	12040,03547	12163	12129,78973	12253	12219,54399	12343	12309,29825
11894	11861,52422	11984	11951,27848	12074	12041,03274	12164	12130,787	12254	12220,54126	12344	12310,29552
11895	11862,52149	11985	11952,27575	12075	12042,03001	12165	12131,78427	12255	12221,53853	12345	12311,29279
11896	11863,51876	11986	11953,27302	12076	12043,02728	12166	12132,78154	12256	12222,5358	12346	12312,29006
11897	11864,51603	11987	11954,27029	12077	12044,02455	12167	12133,77881	12257	12223,53307	12347	12313,28733
11898	11865,5133	11988	11955,26756	12078	12045,02182	12168	12134,77608	12258	12224,53034	12348	12314,2846
11899	11866,51057	11989	11956,26483	12079	12046,01909	12169	12135,77335	12259	12225,52761	12349	12315,28187
11900	11867,50784	11990	11957,2621	12080	12047,01636	12170	12136,77062	12260	12226,52488	12350	12316,27914
11901	11868,5051	11991	11958,25937	12081	12048,01363	12171	12137,76789	12261	12227,52215	12351	12317,27641
11902	11869,50237	11992	11959,25664	12082	12049,0109	12172	12138,76516	12262	12228,51942	12352	12318,27368
11903	11870,49964	11993	11960,2539	12083	12050,00817	12173	12139,76243	12263	12229,51669	12353	12319,27095
11904	11871,49691	11994	11961,25117	12084	12051,00544	12174	12140,7597	12264	12230,51396	12354	12320,26822

12355 12321,26549	12445 12411,01975	12535 12500,77401	12625 12590,52827	12715 12680,28253	12805 12770,03679
12356 12322,26276	12446 12412,01702	12536 12501,77128	12626 12591,52554	12716 12681,2798	12806 12771,03406
12357 12323,26003	12447 12413,01429	12537 12502,76855	12627 12592,52281	12717 12682,27707	12807 12772,03133
12358 12324,2573	12448 12414,01156	12538 12503,76582	12628 12593,52008	12718 12683,27434	12808 12773,0286
12359 12325,25457	12449 12415,00883	12539 12504,76309	12629 12594,51735	12719 12684,27161	12809 12774,02587
12360 12326,25184	12450 12416,0061	12540 12505,76036	12630 12595,51462	12720 12685,26888	12810 12775,02314
12361 12327,2491	12451 12417,00337	12541 12506,75763	12631 12596,51189	12721 12686,26615	12811 12776,02041
12362 12328,24637	12452 12418,00064	12542 12507,7549	12632 12597,50916	12722 12687,26342	12812 12777,01768
12363 12329,24364	12453 12418,99791	12543 12508,75217	12633 12598,50643	12723 12688,26069	12813 12778,01495
12364 12330,24091	12454 12419,99517	12544 12509,74944	12634 12599,5037	12724 12689,25796	12814 12779,01222
12365 12331,23818	12455 12420,99244	12545 12510,74671	12635 12600,50097	12725 12690,25523	12815 12780,00949
12366 12332,23545	12456 12421,98971	12546 12511,74397	12636 12601,49824	12726 12691,2525	12816 12781,00676
12367 12333,23272	12457 12422,98698	12547 12512,74124	12637 12602,49551	12727 12692,24977	12817 12782,00403
12368 12334,22999	12458 12423,98425	12548 12513,73851	12638 12603,49277	12728 12693,24704	12818 12783,0013
12369 12335,22726	12459 12424,98152	12549 12514,73578	12639 12604,49004	12729 12694,24431	12819 12783,99857
12370 12336,22453	12460 12425,97879	12550 12515,73305	12640 12605,48731	12730 12695,24157	12820 12784,99584
12371 12337,2218	12461 12426,97606	12551 12516,73032	12641 12606,48458	12731 12696,23884	12821 12785,99311
12372 12338,21907	12462 12427,97333	12552 12517,72759	12642 12607,48185	12732 12697,23611	12822 12786,99037
12373 12339,21634	12463 12428,9706	12553 12518,72486	12643 12608,47912	12733 12698,23338	12823 12787,98764
12374 12340,21361	12464 12429,96787	12554 12519,72213	12644 12609,47639	12734 12699,23065	12824 12788,98491
12375 12341,21088	12465 12430,96514	12555 12520,7194	12645 12610,47366	12735 12700,22792	12825 12789,98218
12376 12342,20815	12466 12431,96241	12556 12521,71667	12646 12611,47093	12736 12701,22519	12826 12790,97945
12377 12343,20542	12467 12432,95968	12557 12522,71394	12647 12612,4682	12737 12702,22246	12827 12791,97672
12378 12344,20269	12468 12433,95695	12558 12523,71121	12648 12613,46547	12738 12703,21973	12828 12792,97399
12379 12345,19996	12469 12434,95422	12559 12524,70848	12649 12614,46274	12739 12704,217	12829 12793,97126
12380 12346,19723	12470 12435,95149	12560 12525,70575	12650 12615,46001	12740 12705,21427	12830 12794,96853
12381 12347,1945	12471 12436,94876	12561 12526,70302	12651 12616,45728	12741 12706,21154	12831 12795,9658
12382 12348,19177	12472 12437,94603	12562 12527,70029	12652 12617,45455	12742 12707,20881	12832 12796,96307
12383 12349,18904	12473 12438,9433	12563 12528,69756	12653 12618,45182	12743 12708,20608	12833 12797,96034
12384 12350,18631	12474 12439,94057	12564 12529,69483	12654 12619,44909	12744 12709,20335	12834 12798,95761
12385 12351,18357	12475 12440,93784	12565 12530,6921	12655 12620,44636	12745 12710,20062	12835 12799,95488
12386 12352,18084	12476 12441,93511	12566 12531,68937	12656 12621,44363	12746 12711,19789	12836 12800,95215
12387 12353,17811	12477 12442,93237	12567 12532,68664	12657 12622,4409	12747 12712,19516	12837 12801,94942
12388 12354,17538	12478 12443,92964	12568 12533,68391	12658 12623,43817	12748 12713,19243	12838 12802,94669
12389 12355,17265	12479 12444,92691	12569 12534,68117	12659 12624,43544	12749 12714,1897	12839 12803,94396
12390 12356,16992	12480 12445,92418	12570 12535,67844	12660 12625,43271	12750 12715,18697	12840 12804,94123
12391 12357,16719	12481 12446,92145	12571 12536,67571	12661 12626,42997	12751 12716,18424	12841 12805,9385
12392 12358,16446	12482 12447,91872	12572 12537,67298	12662 12627,42724	12752 12717,18151	12842 12806,93577
12393 12359,16173	12483 12448,91599	12573 12538,67025	12663 12628,42451	12753 12718,17877	12843 12807,93304
12394 12360,159	12484 12449,91326	12574 12539,66752	12664 12629,42178	12754 12719,17604	12844 12808,93031
12395 12361,15627	12485 12450,91053	12575 12540,66479	12665 12630,41905	12755 12720,17331	12845 12809,92757
12396 12362,15354	12486 12451,9078	12576 12541,66206	12666 12631,41632	12756 12721,17058	12846 12810,92484
12397 12363,15081	12487 12452,90507	12577 12542,65933	12667 12632,41359	12757 12722,16785	12847 12811,92211
12398 12364,14808	12488 12453,90234	12578 12543,6566	12668 12633,41086	12758 12723,16512	12848 12812,91938
12399 12365,14535	12489 12454,89961	12579 12544,65387	12669 12634,40813	12759 12724,16239	12849 12813,91665
12400 12366,14262	12490 12455,89688	12580 12545,65114	12670 12635,4054	12760 12725,15966	12850 12814,91392
12401 12367,13989	12491 12456,89415	12581 12546,64841	12671 12636,40267	12761 12726,15693	12851 12815,91119
12402 12368,13716	12492 12457,89142	12582 12547,64568	12672 12637,39994	12762 12727,1542	12852 12816,90846
12403 12369,13443	12493 12458,88869	12583 12548,64295	12673 12638,39721	12763 12728,15147	12853 12817,90573
12404 12370,1317	12494 12459,88596	12584 12549,64022	12674 12639,39448	12764 12729,14874	12854 12818,903
12405 12371,12897	12495 12460,88323	12585 12550,63749	12675 12640,39175	12765 12730,14601	12855 12819,90027
12406 12372,12624	12496 12461,8805	12586 12551,63476	12676 12641,38902	12766 12731,14328	12856 12820,89754
12407 12373,12351	12497 12462,87777	12587 12552,63203	12677 12642,38629	12767 12732,14055	12857 12821,89481
12408 12374,12077	12498 12463,87504	12588 12553,6293	12678 12643,38356	12768 12733,13782	12858 12822,89208
12409 12375,11804	12499 12464,87231	12589 12554,62657	12679 12644,38083	12769 12734,13509	12859 12823,88935
12410 12376,11531	12500 12465,86957	12590 12555,62384	12680 12645,3781	12770 12735,13236	12860 12824,88662
12411 12377,11258	12501 12466,86684	12591 12556,62111	12681 12646,37537	12771 12736,12963	12861 12825,88389
12412 12378,10985	12502 12467,86411	12592 12557,61837	12682 12647,37264	12772 12737,1269	12862 12826,88116
12413 12379,10712	12503 12468,86138	12593 12558,61564	12683 12648,36991	12773 12738,12417	12863 12827,87843
12414 12380,10439	12504 12469,85865	12594 12559,61291	12684 12649,36717	12774 12739,12144	12864 12828,8757
12415 12381,10166	12505 12470,85592	12595 12560,61018	12685 12650,36444	12775 12740,11871	12865 12829,87297
12416 12382,09893	12506 12471,85319	12596 12561,60745	12686 12651,36171	12776 12741,11597	12866 12830,87024
12417 12383,0962	12507 12472,85046	12597 12562,60472	12687 12652,35898	12777 12742,11324	12867 12831,86751
12418 12384,09347	12508 12473,84773	12598 12563,60199	12688 12653,35625	12778 12743,11051	12868 12832,86477
12419 12385,09074	12509 12474,845	12599 12564,59926	12689 12654,35352	12779 12744,10778	12869 12833,86204
12420 12386,08801	12510 12475,84227	12600 12565,59653	12690 12655,35079	12780 12745,10505	12870 12834,85931
12421 12387,08528	12511 12476,83954	12601 12566,5938	12691 12656,34806	12781 12746,10232	12871 12835,85658
12422 12388,08255	12512 12477,83681	12602 12567,59107	12692 12657,34533	12782 12747,09959	12872 12836,85385
12423 12389,07982	12513 12478,83408	12603 12568,58834	12693 12658,3426	12783 12748,09686	12873 12837,85112
12424 12390,07709	12514 12479,83135	12604 12569,58561	12694 12659,33987	12784 12749,09413	12874 12838,84839
12425 12391,07436	12515 12480,82862	12605 12570,58288	12695 12660,33714	12785 12750,0914	12875 12839,84566
12426 12392,07163	12516 12481,82589	12606 12571,58015	12696 12661,33441	12786 12751,08867	12876 12840,84293
12427 12393,0689	12517 12482,82316	12607 12572,57742	12697 12662,33168	12787 12752,08594	12877 12841,8402
12428 12394,06617	12518 12483,82043	12608 12573,57469	12698 12663,32895	12788 12753,08321	12878 12842,83747
12429 12395,06344	12519 12484,8177	12609 12574,57196	12699 12664,32622	12789 12754,08048	12879 12843,83474
12430 12396,06071	12520 12485,81497	12610 12575,56923	12700 12665,32349	12790 12755,07775	12880 12844,83201
12431 12397,05797	12521 12486,81224	12611 12576,5665	12701 12666,32076	12791 12756,07502	12881 12845,82928
12432 12398,05524	12522 12487,80951	12612 12577,56377	12702 12667,31803	12792 12757,07229	12882 12846,82655
12433 12399,05251	12523 12488,80677	12613 12578,56104	12703 12668,3153	12793 12758,06956	12883 12847,82382
12434 12400,04978	12524 12489,80404	12614 12579,55831	12704 12669,31257	12794 12759,06683	12884 12848,82109
12435 12401,04705	12525 12490,80131	12615 12580,55557	12705 12670,30984	12795 12760,0641	12885 12849,81836
12436 12402,04432	12526 12491,79858	12616 12581,55284	12706 12671,30711	12796 12761,06137	12886 12850,81563
12437 12403,04159	12527 12492,79585	12617 12582,55011	12707 12672,30437	12797 12762,05864	12887 12851,8129
12438 12404,03886	12528 12493,79312	12618 12583,54738	12708 12673,30164	12798 12763,05591	12888 12852,81017
12439 12405,03613	12529 12494,79039	12619 12584,54465	12709 12674,29891	12799 12764,05317	12889 12853,80744
12440 12406,0334	12530 12495,78766	12620 12585,54192	12710 12675,29618	12800 12765,05044	12890 12854,80471
12441 12407,03067	12531 12496,78493	12621 12586,53919	12711 12676,29345	12801 12766,04771	12891 12855,80197
12442 12408,02794	12532 12497,7822	12622 12587,53646	12712 12677,29072	12802 12767,04498	12892 12856,79924
12443 12409,02521	12533 12498,77947	12623 12588,53373	12713 12678,28799	12803 12768,04225	12893 12857,79651
12444 12410,02248	12534 12499,77674	12624 12589,531	12714 12679,28526	12804 12769,03952	12894 12858,79378

TABLE TO FIND OUT THE POINT A IN EARTH RETURNS 181

12895	12859,79105	12985	12949,54531	13075	13039,29958	13165	13129,05384	13255	13218,8081	13345	13308,56236
12896	12860,78832	12986	12950,54258	13076	13040,29684	13166	13130,05111	13256	13219,80537	13346	13309,55963
12897	12861,78559	12987	12951,53985	13077	13041,29411	13167	13131,04838	13257	13220,80264	13347	13310,5569
12898	12862,78286	12988	12952,53712	13078	13042,29138	13168	13132,04564	13258	13221,79991	13348	13311,55417
12899	12863,78013	12989	12953,53439	13079	13043,28865	13169	13133,04291	13259	13222,79718	13349	13312,55144
12900	12864,7774	12990	12954,53166	13080	13044,28592	13170	13134,04018	13260	13223,79444	13350	13313,54871
12901	12865,77467	12991	12955,52893	13081	13045,28319	13171	13135,03745	13261	13224,79171	13351	13314,54598
12902	12866,77194	12992	12956,5262	13082	13046,28046	13172	13136,03472	13262	13225,78898	13352	13315,54324
12903	12867,76921	12993	12957,52347	13083	13047,27773	13173	13137,03199	13263	13226,78625	13353	13316,54051
12904	12868,76648	12994	12958,52074	13084	13048,275	13174	13138,02926	13264	13227,78352	13354	13317,53778
12905	12869,76375	12995	12959,51801	13085	13049,27227	13175	13139,02653	13265	13228,78079	13355	13318,53505
12906	12870,76102	12996	12960,51528	13086	13050,26954	13176	13140,0238	13266	13229,77806	13356	13319,53232
12907	12871,75829	12997	12961,51255	13087	13051,26681	13177	13141,02107	13267	13230,77533	13357	13320,52959
12908	12872,75556	12998	12962,50982	13088	13052,26408	13178	13142,01834	13268	13231,7726	13358	13321,52686
12909	12873,75283	12999	12963,50709	13089	13053,26135	13179	13143,01561	13269	13232,76987	13359	13322,52413
12910	12874,7501	13000	12964,50436	13090	13054,25862	13180	13144,01288	13270	13233,76714	13360	13323,5214
12911	12875,74737	13001	12965,50163	13091	13055,25589	13181	13145,01015	13271	13234,76441	13361	13324,51867
12912	12876,74464	13002	12966,4989	13092	13056,25316	13182	13146,00742	13272	13235,76168	13362	13325,51594
12913	12877,74191	13003	12967,49617	13093	13057,25043	13183	13147,00469	13273	13236,75895	13363	13326,51321
12914	12878,73917	13004	12968,49344	13094	13058,2477	13184	13148,00196	13274	13237,75622	13364	13327,51048
12915	12879,73644	13005	12969,49071	13095	13059,24497	13185	13148,99923	13275	13238,75349	13365	13328,50775
12916	12880,73371	13006	12970,48798	13096	13060,24224	13186	13149,9965	13276	13239,75076	13366	13329,50502
12917	12881,73098	13007	12971,48524	13097	13061,23951	13187	13150,99377	13277	13240,74803	13367	13330,50229
12918	12882,72825	13008	12972,48251	13098	13062,23678	13188	13151,99104	13278	13241,7453	13368	13331,49956
12919	12883,72552	13009	12973,47978	13099	13063,23404	13189	13152,98831	13279	13242,74257	13369	13332,49683
12920	12884,72279	13010	12974,47705	13100	13064,23131	13190	13153,98558	13280	13243,73984	13370	13333,4941
12921	12885,72006	13011	12975,47432	13101	13065,22858	13191	13154,98284	13281	13244,73711	13371	13334,49137
12922	12886,71733	13012	12976,47159	13102	13066,22585	13192	13155,98011	13282	13245,73438	13372	13335,48864
12923	12887,7146	13013	12977,46886	13103	13067,22312	13193	13156,97738	13283	13246,73164	13373	13336,48591
12924	12888,71187	13014	12978,46613	13104	13068,22039	13194	13157,97465	13284	13247,72891	13374	13337,48318
12925	12889,70914	13015	12979,4634	13105	13069,21766	13195	13158,97192	13285	13248,72618	13375	13338,48044
12926	12890,70641	13016	12980,46067	13106	13070,21493	13196	13159,96919	13286	13249,72345	13376	13339,47771
12927	12891,70368	13017	12981,45794	13107	13071,2122	13197	13160,96646	13287	13250,72072	13377	13340,47498
12928	12892,70095	13018	12982,45521	13108	13072,20947	13198	13161,96373	13288	13251,71799	13378	13341,47225
12929	12893,69822	13019	12983,45248	13109	13073,20674	13199	13162,961	13289	13252,71526	13379	13342,46952
12930	12894,69549	13020	12984,44975	13110	13074,20401	13200	13163,95827	13290	13253,71253	13380	13343,46679
12931	12895,69276	13021	12985,44702	13111	13075,20128	13201	13164,95554	13291	13254,7098	13381	13344,46406
12932	12896,69003	13022	12986,44429	13112	13076,19855	13202	13165,95281	13292	13255,70707	13382	13345,46133
12933	12897,6873	13023	12987,44156	13113	13077,19582	13203	13166,95008	13293	13256,70434	13383	13346,4586
12934	12898,68457	13024	12988,43883	13114	13078,19309	13204	13167,94735	13294	13257,70161	13384	13347,45587
12935	12899,68184	13025	12989,4361	13115	13079,19036	13205	13168,94462	13295	13258,69888	13385	13348,45314
12936	12900,67911	13026	12990,43337	13116	13080,18763	13206	13169,94189	13296	13259,69615	13386	13349,45041
12937	12901,67637	13027	12991,43064	13117	13081,1849	13207	13170,93916	13297	13260,69342	13387	13350,44768
12938	12902,67364	13028	12992,42791	13118	13082,18217	13208	13171,93643	13298	13261,69069	13388	13351,44495
12939	12903,67091	13029	12993,42518	13119	13083,17944	13209	13172,9337	13299	13262,68796	13389	13352,44222
12940	12904,66818	13030	12994,42244	13120	13084,17671	13210	13173,93097	13300	13263,68523	13390	13353,43949
12941	12905,66545	13031	12995,41971	13121	13085,17398	13211	13174,92824	13301	13264,6825	13391	13354,43676
12942	12906,66272	13032	12996,41698	13122	13086,17124	13212	13175,92551	13302	13265,67977	13392	13355,43403
12943	12907,65999	13033	12997,41425	13123	13087,16851	13213	13176,92278	13303	13266,67704	13393	13356,4313
12944	12908,65726	13034	12998,41152	13124	13088,16578	13214	13177,92004	13304	13267,67431	13394	13357,42857
12945	12909,65453	13035	12999,40879	13125	13089,16305	13215	13178,91731	13305	13268,67158	13395	13358,42584
12946	12910,6518	13036	13000,40606	13126	13090,16032	13216	13179,91458	13306	13269,66884	13396	13359,42311
12947	12911,64907	13037	13001,40333	13127	13091,15759	13217	13180,91185	13307	13270,66611	13397	13360,42038
12948	12912,64634	13038	13002,4006	13128	13092,15486	13218	13181,90912	13308	13271,66338	13398	13361,41764
12949	12913,64361	13039	13003,39787	13129	13093,15213	13219	13182,90639	13309	13272,66065	13399	13362,41491
12950	12914,64088	13040	13004,39514	13130	13094,1494	13220	13183,90366	13310	13273,65792	13400	13363,41218
12951	12915,63815	13041	13005,39241	13131	13095,14667	13221	13184,90093	13311	13274,65519	13401	13364,40945
12952	12916,63542	13042	13006,38968	13132	13096,14394	13222	13185,8982	13312	13275,65246	13402	13365,40672
12953	12917,63269	13043	13007,38695	13133	13097,14121	13223	13186,89547	13313	13276,64973	13403	13366,40399
12954	12918,62996	13044	13008,38422	13134	13098,13848	13224	13187,89274	13314	13277,647	13404	13367,40126
12955	12919,62723	13045	13009,38149	13135	13099,13575	13225	13188,89001	13315	13278,64427	13405	13368,39853
12956	12920,6245	13046	13010,37876	13136	13100,13302	13226	13189,88728	13316	13279,64154	13406	13369,3958
12957	12921,62177	13047	13011,37603	13137	13101,13029	13227	13190,88455	13317	13280,63881	13407	13370,39307
12958	12922,61904	13048	13012,3733	13138	13102,12756	13228	13191,88182	13318	13281,63608	13408	13371,39034
12959	12923,61631	13049	13013,37057	13139	13103,12483	13229	13192,87909	13319	13282,63335	13409	13372,38761
12960	12924,61358	13050	13014,36784	13140	13104,1221	13230	13193,87636	13320	13283,63062	13410	13373,38488
12961	12925,61084	13051	13015,36511	13141	13105,11937	13231	13194,87363	13321	13284,62789	13411	13374,38215
12962	12926,60811	13052	13016,36238	13142	13106,11664	13232	13195,8709	13322	13285,62516	13412	13375,37942
12963	12927,60538	13053	13017,35964	13143	13107,11391	13233	13196,86817	13323	13286,62243	13413	13376,37669
12964	12928,60265	13054	13018,35691	13144	13108,11118	13234	13197,86544	13324	13287,6197	13414	13377,37396
12965	12929,59992	13055	13019,35418	13145	13109,10844	13235	13198,86271	13325	13288,61697	13415	13378,37123
12966	12930,59719	13056	13020,35145	13146	13110,10571	13236	13199,85998	13326	13289,61424	13416	13379,3685
12967	12931,59446	13057	13021,34872	13147	13111,10298	13237	13200,85724	13327	13290,61151	13417	13380,36577
12968	12932,59173	13058	13022,34599	13148	13112,10025	13238	13201,85451	13328	13291,60878	13418	13381,36304
12969	12933,589	13059	13023,34326	13149	13113,09752	13239	13202,85178	13329	13292,60604	13419	13382,36031
12970	12934,58627	13060	13024,34053	13150	13114,09479	13240	13203,84905	13330	13293,60331	13420	13383,35758
12971	12935,58354	13061	13025,3378	13151	13115,09206	13241	13204,84632	13331	13294,60058	13421	13384,35484
12972	12936,58081	13062	13026,33507	13152	13116,08933	13242	13205,84359	13332	13295,59785	13422	13385,35211
12973	12937,57808	13063	13027,33234	13153	13117,0866	13243	13206,84086	13333	13296,59512	13423	13386,34938
12974	12938,57535	13064	13028,32961	13154	13118,08387	13244	13207,83813	13334	13297,59239	13424	13387,34665
12975	12939,57262	13065	13029,32688	13155	13119,08114	13245	13208,8354	13335	13298,58966	13425	13388,34392
12976	12940,56989	13066	13030,32415	13156	13120,07841	13246	13209,83267	13336	13299,58693	13426	13389,34119
12977	12941,56716	13067	13031,32142	13157	13121,07568	13247	13210,82994	13337	13300,5842	13427	13390,33846
12978	12942,56443	13068	13032,31869	13158	13122,07295	13248	13211,82721	13338	13301,58147	13428	13391,33573
12979	12943,5617	13069	13033,31596	13159	13123,07022	13249	13212,82448	13339	13302,57874	13429	13392,333
12980	12944,55897	13070	13034,31323	13160	13124,06749	13250	13213,82175	13340	13303,57601	13430	13393,33027
12981	12945,55624	13071	13035,3105	13161	13125,06476	13251	13214,81902	13341	13304,57328	13431	13394,32754
12982	12946,55351	13072	13036,30777	13162	13126,06203	13252	13215,81629	13342	13305,57055	13432	13395,32481
12983	12947,55078	13073	13037,30504	13163	13127,0593	13253	13216,81356	13343	13306,56782	13433	13396,32208
12984	12948,54804	13074	13038,30231	13164	13128,05657	13254	13217,81083	13344	13307,56509	13434	13397,31935

LUNAR RETURNS AND EARTH RETURNS

13435	13398,31662	13525	13488,07088	13615	13577,82514	13705	13667,5794	13795	13757,33366	13885	13847,08792
13436	13399,31389	13526	13489,06815	13616	13578,82241	13706	13668,57667	13796	13758,33093	13886	13848,08519
13437	13400,31116	13527	13490,06542	13617	13579,81968	13707	13669,57394	13797	13759,3282	13887	13849,08246
13438	13401,30843	13528	13491,06269	13618	13580,81695	13708	13670,57121	13798	13760,32547	13888	13850,07973
13439	13402,3057	13529	13492,05996	13619	13581,81422	13709	13671,56848	13799	13761,32274	13889	13851,077
13440	13403,30297	13530	13493,05723	13620	13582,81149	13710	13672,56575	13800	13762,32001	13890	13852,07427
13441	13404,30024	13531	13494,0545	13621	13583,80876	13711	13673,56302	13801	13763,31728	13891	13853,07154
13442	13405,29751	13532	13495,05177	13622	13584,80603	13712	13674,56029	13802	13764,31455	13892	13854,06881
13443	13406,29478	13533	13496,04904	13623	13585,8033	13713	13675,55756	13803	13765,31182	13893	13855,06608
13444	13407,29204	13534	13497,04631	13624	13586,80057	13714	13676,55483	13804	13766,30909	13894	13856,06335
13445	13408,28931	13535	13498,04358	13625	13587,79784	13715	13677,5521	13805	13767,30636	13895	13857,06062
13446	13409,28658	13536	13499,04085	13626	13588,79511	13716	13678,54937	13806	13768,30363	13896	13858,05789
13447	13410,28385	13537	13500,03811	13627	13589,79238	13717	13679,54664	13807	13769,3009	13897	13859,05516
13448	13411,28112	13538	13501,03538	13628	13590,78965	13718	13680,54391	13808	13770,29817	13898	13860,05243
13449	13412,27839	13539	13502,03265	13629	13591,78691	13719	13681,54118	13809	13771,29544	13899	13861,0497
13450	13413,27566	13540	13503,02992	13630	13592,78418	13720	13682,53845	13810	13772,29271	13900	13862,04697
13451	13414,27293	13541	13504,02719	13631	13593,78145	13721	13683,53571	13811	13773,28998	13901	13863,04424
13452	13415,2702	13542	13505,02446	13632	13594,77872	13722	13684,53298	13812	13774,28725	13902	13864,04151
13453	13416,26747	13543	13506,02173	13633	13595,77599	13723	13685,53025	13813	13775,28451	13903	13865,03878
13454	13417,26474	13544	13507,019	13634	13596,77326	13724	13686,52752	13814	13776,28178	13904	13866,03605
13455	13418,26201	13545	13508,01627	13635	13597,77053	13725	13687,52479	13815	13777,27905	13905	13867,03331
13456	13419,25928	13546	13509,01354	13636	13598,7678	13726	13688,52206	13816	13778,27632	13906	13868,03058
13457	13420,25655	13547	13510,01081	13637	13599,76507	13727	13689,51933	13817	13779,27359	13907	13869,02785
13458	13421,25382	13548	13511,00808	13638	13600,76234	13728	13690,5166	13818	13780,27086	13908	13870,02512
13459	13422,25109	13549	13512,00535	13639	13601,75961	13729	13691,51387	13819	13781,26813	13909	13871,02239
13460	13423,24836	13550	13513,00262	13640	13602,75688	13730	13692,51114	13820	13782,2654	13910	13872,01966
13461	13424,24563	13551	13513,99989	13641	13603,75415	13731	13693,50841	13821	13783,26267	13911	13873,01693
13462	13425,2429	13552	13514,99716	13642	13604,75142	13732	13694,50568	13822	13784,25994	13912	13874,0142
13463	13426,24017	13553	13515,99443	13643	13605,74869	13733	13695,50295	13823	13785,25721	13913	13875,01147
13464	13427,23744	13554	13516,9917	13644	13606,74596	13734	13696,50022	13824	13786,25448	13914	13876,00874
13465	13428,23471	13555	13517,98897	13645	13607,74323	13735	13697,49749	13825	13787,25175	13915	13877,00601
13466	13429,23198	13556	13518,98624	13646	13608,7405	13736	13698,49476	13826	13788,24902	13916	13878,00328
13467	13430,22924	13557	13519,98351	13647	13609,73777	13737	13699,49203	13827	13789,24629	13917	13879,00055
13468	13431,22651	13558	13520,98078	13648	13610,73504	13738	13700,4893	13828	13790,24356	13918	13879,99782
13469	13432,22378	13559	13521,97805	13649	13611,73231	13739	13701,48657	13829	13791,24083	13919	13880,99509
13470	13433,22105	13560	13522,97531	13650	13612,72958	13740	13702,48384	13830	13792,2381	13920	13881,99236
13471	13434,21832	13561	13523,97258	13651	13613,72685	13741	13703,48111	13831	13793,23537	13921	13882,98963
13472	13435,21559	13562	13524,96985	13652	13614,72411	13742	13704,47838	13832	13794,23264	13922	13883,9869
13473	13436,21286	13563	13525,96712	13653	13615,72138	13743	13705,47565	13833	13795,22991	13923	13884,98417
13474	13437,21013	13564	13526,96439	13654	13616,71865	13744	13706,47291	13834	13796,22718	13924	13885,98144
13475	13438,2074	13565	13527,96166	13655	13617,71592	13745	13707,47018	13835	13797,22445	13925	13886,97871
13476	13439,20467	13566	13528,95893	13656	13618,71319	13746	13708,46745	13836	13798,22171	13926	13887,97598
13477	13440,20194	13567	13529,9562	13657	13619,71046	13747	13709,46472	13837	13799,21898	13927	13888,97325
13478	13441,19921	13568	13530,95347	13658	13620,70773	13748	13710,46199	13838	13800,21625	13928	13889,97051
13479	13442,19648	13569	13531,95074	13659	13621,705	13749	13711,45926	13839	13801,21352	13929	13890,96778
13480	13443,19375	13570	13532,94801	13660	13622,70227	13750	13712,45653	13840	13802,21079	13930	13891,96505
13481	13444,19102	13571	13533,94528	13661	13623,69954	13751	13713,4538	13841	13803,20806	13931	13892,96232
13482	13445,18829	13572	13534,94255	13662	13624,69681	13752	13714,45107	13842	13804,20533	13932	13893,95959
13483	13446,18556	13573	13535,93982	13663	13625,69408	13753	13715,44834	13843	13805,2026	13933	13894,95686
13484	13447,18283	13574	13536,93709	13664	13626,69135	13754	13716,44561	13844	13806,19987	13934	13895,95413
13485	13448,1801	13575	13537,93436	13665	13627,68862	13755	13717,44288	13845	13807,19714	13935	13896,9514
13486	13449,17737	13576	13538,93163	13666	13628,68589	13756	13718,44015	13846	13808,19441	13936	13897,94867
13487	13450,17464	13577	13539,9289	13667	13629,68316	13757	13719,43742	13847	13809,19168	13937	13898,94594
13488	13451,17191	13578	13540,92617	13668	13630,68043	13758	13720,43469	13848	13810,18895	13938	13899,94321
13489	13452,16918	13579	13541,92344	13669	13631,6777	13759	13721,43196	13849	13811,18622	13939	13900,94048
13490	13453,16644	13580	13542,92071	13670	13632,67497	13760	13722,42923	13850	13812,18349	13940	13901,93775
13491	13454,16371	13581	13543,91798	13671	13633,67224	13761	13723,4265	13851	13813,18076	13941	13902,93502
13492	13455,16098	13582	13544,91525	13672	13634,66951	13762	13724,42377	13852	13814,17803	13942	13903,93229
13493	13456,15825	13583	13545,91251	13673	13635,66678	13763	13725,42104	13853	13815,1753	13943	13904,92956
13494	13457,15552	13584	13546,90978	13674	13636,66405	13764	13726,41831	13854	13816,17257	13944	13905,92683
13495	13458,15279	13585	13547,90705	13675	13637,66131	13765	13727,41558	13855	13817,16984	13945	13906,9241
13496	13459,15006	13586	13548,90432	13676	13638,65858	13766	13728,41285	13856	13818,16711	13946	13907,92137
13497	13460,14733	13587	13549,90159	13677	13639,65585	13767	13729,41011	13857	13819,16438	13947	13908,91864
13498	13461,1446	13588	13550,89886	13678	13640,65312	13768	13730,40738	13858	13820,16165	13948	13909,91591
13499	13462,14187	13589	13551,89613	13679	13641,65039	13769	13731,40465	13859	13821,15891	13949	13910,91318
13500	13463,13914	13590	13552,8934	13680	13642,64766	13770	13732,40192	13860	13822,15618	13950	13911,91045
13501	13464,13641	13591	13553,89067	13681	13643,64493	13771	13733,39919	13861	13823,15345	13951	13912,90771
13502	13465,13368	13592	13554,88794	13682	13644,6422	13772	13734,39646	13862	13824,15072	13952	13913,90498
13503	13466,13095	13593	13555,88521	13683	13645,63947	13773	13735,39373	13863	13825,14799	13953	13914,90225
13504	13467,12822	13594	13556,88248	13684	13646,63674	13774	13736,391	13864	13826,14526	13954	13915,89952
13505	13468,12549	13595	13557,87975	13685	13647,63401	13775	13737,38827	13865	13827,14253	13955	13916,89679
13506	13469,12276	13596	13558,87702	13686	13648,63128	13776	13738,38554	13866	13828,1398	13956	13917,89406
13507	13470,12003	13597	13559,87429	13687	13649,62855	13777	13739,38281	13867	13829,13707	13957	13918,89133
13508	13471,1173	13598	13560,87156	13688	13650,62582	13778	13740,38008	13868	13830,13434	13958	13919,8886
13509	13472,11457	13599	13561,86883	13689	13651,62309	13779	13741,37735	13869	13831,13161	13959	13920,88587
13510	13473,11184	13600	13562,8661	13690	13652,62036	13780	13742,37462	13870	13832,12888	13960	13921,88314
13511	13474,10911	13601	13563,86337	13691	13653,61763	13781	13743,37189	13871	13833,12615	13961	13922,88041
13512	13475,10638	13602	13564,86064	13692	13654,6149	13782	13744,36916	13872	13834,12342	13962	13923,87768
13513	13476,10364	13603	13565,85791	13693	13655,61217	13783	13745,36643	13873	13835,12069	13963	13924,87495
13514	13477,10091	13604	13566,85518	13694	13656,60944	13784	13746,3637	13874	13836,11796	13964	13925,87222
13515	13478,09818	13605	13567,85245	13695	13657,60671	13785	13747,36097	13875	13837,11523	13965	13926,86949
13516	13479,09545	13606	13568,84971	13696	13658,60398	13786	13748,35824	13876	13838,1125	13966	13927,86676
13517	13480,09272	13607	13569,84698	13697	13659,60125	13787	13749,35551	13877	13839,10977	13967	13928,86403
13518	13481,08999	13608	13570,84425	13698	13660,59851	13788	13750,35278	13878	13840,10704	13968	13929,8613
13519	13482,08726	13609	13571,84152	13699	13661,59578	13789	13751,35005	13879	13841,10431	13969	13930,85857
13520	13483,08453	13610	13572,83879	13700	13662,59305	13790	13752,34731	13880	13842,10158	13970	13931,85584
13521	13484,0818	13611	13573,83606	13701	13663,59032	13791	13753,34458	13881	13843,09885	13971	13932,85311
13522	13485,07907	13612	13574,83333	13702	13664,58759	13792	13754,34185	13882	13844,09611	13972	13933,85038
13523	13486,07634	13613	13575,8306	13703	13665,58486	13793	13755,33912	13883	13845,09338	13973	13934,84765
13524	13487,07361	13614	13576,82787	13704	13666,58213	13794	13756,33639	13884	13846,09065	13974	13935,84491

13975	13936,84218	14065	14026,59645	14155	14116,35071	14245	14206,10497	14335	14295,85923	14425	14385,61349
13976	13937,83945	14066	14027,59371	14156	14117,34798	14246	14207,10224	14336	14296,8565	14426	14386,61076
13977	13938,83672	14067	14028,59098	14157	14118,34525	14247	14208,09951	14337	14297,85377	14427	14387,60803
13978	13939,83399	14068	14029,58825	14158	14119,34252	14248	14209,09678	14338	14298,85104	14428	14388,6053
13979	13940,83126	14069	14030,58552	14159	14120,33978	14249	14210,09405	14339	14299,84831	14429	14389,60257
13980	13941,82853	14070	14031,58279	14160	14121,33705	14250	14211,09132	14340	14300,84558	14430	14390,59984
13981	13942,8258	14071	14032,58006	14161	14122,33432	14251	14212,08858	14341	14301,84285	14431	14391,59711
13982	13943,82307	14072	14033,57733	14162	14123,33159	14252	14213,08585	14342	14302,84012	14432	14392,59438
13983	13944,82034	14073	14034,5746	14163	14124,32886	14253	14214,08312	14343	14303,83738	14433	14393,59165
13984	13945,81761	14074	14035,57187	14164	14125,32613	14254	14215,08039	14344	14304,83465	14434	14394,58892
13985	13946,81488	14075	14036,56914	14165	14126,3234	14255	14216,07766	14345	14305,83192	14435	14395,58618
13986	13947,81215	14076	14037,56641	14166	14127,32067	14256	14217,07493	14346	14306,82919	14436	14396,58345
13987	13948,80942	14077	14038,56368	14167	14128,31794	14257	14218,0722	14347	14307,82646	14437	14397,58072
13988	13949,80669	14078	14039,56095	14168	14129,31521	14258	14219,06947	14348	14308,82373	14438	14398,57799
13989	13950,80396	14079	14040,55822	14169	14130,31248	14259	14220,06674	14349	14309,821	14439	14399,57526
13990	13951,80123	14080	14041,55549	14170	14131,30975	14260	14221,06401	14350	14310,81827	14440	14400,57253
13991	13952,7985	14081	14042,55276	14171	14132,30702	14261	14222,06128	14351	14311,81554	14441	14401,5698
13992	13953,79577	14082	14043,55003	14172	14133,30429	14262	14223,05855	14352	14312,81281	14442	14402,56707
13993	13954,79304	14083	14044,5473	14173	14134,30156	14263	14224,05582	14353	14313,81008	14443	14403,56434
13994	13955,79031	14084	14045,54457	14174	14135,29883	14264	14225,05309	14354	14314,80735	14444	14404,56161
13995	13956,78758	14085	14046,54184	14175	14136,2961	14265	14226,05036	14355	14315,80462	14445	14405,55888
13996	13957,78485	14086	14047,53911	14176	14137,29337	14266	14227,04763	14356	14316,80189	14446	14406,55615
13997	13958,78211	14087	14048,53638	14177	14138,29064	14267	14228,0449	14357	14317,79916	14447	14407,55342
13998	13959,77938	14088	14049,53365	14178	14139,28791	14268	14229,04217	14358	14318,79643	14448	14408,55069
13999	13960,77665	14089	14050,53091	14179	14140,28518	14269	14230,03944	14359	14319,7937	14449	14409,54796
14000	13961,77392	14090	14051,52818	14180	14141,28245	14270	14231,03671	14360	14320,79097	14450	14410,54523
14001	13962,77119	14091	14052,52545	14181	14142,27972	14271	14232,03398	14361	14321,78824	14451	14411,5425
14002	13963,76846	14092	14053,52272	14182	14143,27698	14272	14233,03125	14362	14322,78551	14452	14412,53977
14003	13964,76573	14093	14054,51999	14183	14144,27425	14273	14234,02852	14363	14323,78278	14453	14413,53704
14004	13965,763	14094	14055,51726	14184	14145,27152	14274	14235,02578	14364	14324,78005	14454	14414,53431
14005	13966,76027	14095	14056,51453	14185	14146,26879	14275	14236,02305	14365	14325,77732	14455	14415,53158
14006	13967,75754	14096	14057,5118	14186	14147,26606	14276	14237,02032	14366	14326,77458	14456	14416,52885
14007	13968,75481	14097	14058,50907	14187	14148,26333	14277	14238,01759	14367	14327,77185	14457	14417,52612
14008	13969,75208	14098	14059,50634	14188	14149,2606	14278	14239,01486	14368	14328,76912	14458	14418,52338
14009	13970,74935	14099	14060,50361	14189	14150,25787	14279	14240,01213	14369	14329,76639	14459	14419,52065
14010	13971,74662	14100	14061,50088	14190	14151,25514	14280	14241,0094	14370	14330,76366	14460	14420,51792
14011	13972,74389	14101	14062,49815	14191	14152,25241	14281	14242,00667	14371	14331,76093	14461	14421,51519
14012	13973,74116	14102	14063,49542	14192	14153,24968	14282	14243,00394	14372	14332,7582	14462	14422,51246
14013	13974,73843	14103	14064,49269	14193	14154,24695	14283	14244,00121	14373	14333,75547	14463	14423,50973
14014	13975,7357	14104	14065,48996	14194	14155,24422	14284	14244,99848	14374	14334,75274	14464	14424,507
14015	13976,73297	14105	14066,48723	14195	14156,24149	14285	14245,99575	14375	14335,75001	14465	14425,50427
14016	13977,73024	14106	14067,4845	14196	14157,23876	14286	14246,99302	14376	14336,74728	14466	14426,50154
14017	13978,72751	14107	14068,48177	14197	14158,23603	14287	14247,99029	14377	14337,74455	14467	14427,49881
14018	13979,72478	14108	14069,47904	14198	14159,2333	14288	14248,98756	14378	14338,74182	14468	14428,49608
14019	13980,72205	14109	14070,47631	14199	14160,23057	14289	14249,98483	14379	14339,73909	14469	14429,49335
14020	13981,71931	14110	14071,47358	14200	14161,22784	14290	14250,9821	14380	14340,73636	14470	14430,49062
14021	13982,71658	14111	14072,47085	14201	14162,22511	14291	14251,97937	14381	14341,73363	14471	14431,48789
14022	13983,71385	14112	14073,46812	14202	14163,22238	14292	14252,97664	14382	14342,7309	14472	14432,48516
14023	13984,71112	14113	14074,46538	14203	14164,21965	14293	14253,97391	14383	14343,72817	14473	14433,48243
14024	13985,70839	14114	14075,46265	14204	14165,21692	14294	14254,97118	14384	14344,72544	14474	14434,4797
14025	13986,70566	14115	14076,45992	14205	14166,21418	14295	14255,96845	14385	14345,72271	14475	14435,47697
14026	13987,70293	14116	14077,45719	14206	14167,21145	14296	14256,96572	14386	14346,71998	14476	14436,47424
14027	13988,7002	14117	14078,45446	14207	14168,20872	14297	14257,96298	14387	14347,71725	14477	14437,47151
14028	13989,69747	14118	14079,45173	14208	14169,20599	14298	14258,96025	14388	14348,71452	14478	14438,46878
14029	13990,69474	14119	14080,449	14209	14170,20326	14299	14259,95752	14389	14349,71178	14479	14439,46605
14030	13991,69201	14120	14081,44627	14210	14171,20053	14300	14260,95479	14390	14350,70905	14480	14440,46332
14031	13992,68928	14121	14082,44354	14211	14172,1978	14301	14261,95206	14391	14351,70632	14481	14441,46058
14032	13993,68655	14122	14083,44081	14212	14173,19507	14302	14262,94933	14392	14352,70359	14482	14442,45785
14033	13994,68382	14123	14084,43808	14213	14174,19234	14303	14263,9466	14393	14353,70086	14483	14443,45512
14034	13995,68109	14124	14085,43535	14214	14175,18961	14304	14264,94387	14394	14354,69813	14484	14444,45239
14035	13996,67836	14125	14086,43262	14215	14176,18688	14305	14265,94114	14395	14355,6954	14485	14445,44966
14036	13997,67563	14126	14087,42989	14216	14177,18415	14306	14266,93841	14396	14356,69267	14486	14446,44693
14037	13998,6729	14127	14088,42716	14217	14178,18142	14307	14267,93568	14397	14357,68994	14487	14447,4442
14038	13999,67017	14128	14089,42443	14218	14179,17869	14308	14268,93295	14398	14358,68721	14488	14448,44147
14039	14000,66744	14129	14090,4217	14219	14180,17596	14309	14269,93022	14399	14359,68448	14489	14449,43874
14040	14001,66471	14130	14091,41897	14220	14181,17323	14310	14270,92749	14400	14360,68175	14490	14450,43601
14041	14002,66198	14131	14092,41624	14221	14182,1705	14311	14271,92476	14401	14361,67902	14491	14451,43328
14042	14003,65925	14132	14093,41351	14222	14183,16777	14312	14272,92203	14402	14362,67629	14492	14452,43055
14043	14004,65651	14133	14094,41078	14223	14184,16504	14313	14273,9193	14403	14363,67356	14493	14453,42782
14044	14005,65378	14134	14095,40805	14224	14185,16231	14314	14274,91657	14404	14364,67083	14494	14454,42509
14045	14006,65105	14135	14096,40532	14225	14186,15958	14315	14275,91384	14405	14365,6681	14495	14455,42236
14046	14007,64832	14136	14097,40258	14226	14187,15685	14316	14276,91111	14406	14366,66537	14496	14456,41963
14047	14008,64559	14137	14098,39985	14227	14188,15412	14317	14277,90838	14407	14367,66264	14497	14457,4169
14048	14009,64286	14138	14099,39712	14228	14189,15138	14318	14278,90565	14408	14368,65991	14498	14458,41417
14049	14010,64013	14139	14100,39439	14229	14190,14865	14319	14279,90292	14409	14369,65718	14499	14459,41144
14050	14011,6374	14140	14101,39166	14230	14191,14592	14320	14280,90018	14410	14370,65445	14500	14460,40871
14051	14012,63467	14141	14102,38893	14231	14192,14319	14321	14281,89745	14411	14371,65172	14501	14461,40598
14052	14013,63194	14142	14103,3862	14232	14193,14046	14322	14282,89472	14412	14372,64898	14502	14462,40325
14053	14014,62921	14143	14104,38347	14233	14194,13773	14323	14283,89199	14413	14373,64625	14503	14463,40052
14054	14015,62648	14144	14105,38074	14234	14195,135	14324	14284,88926	14414	14374,64352	14504	14464,39778
14055	14016,62375	14145	14106,37801	14235	14196,13227	14325	14285,88653	14415	14375,64079	14505	14465,39505
14056	14017,62102	14146	14107,37528	14236	14197,12954	14326	14286,8838	14416	14376,63806	14506	14466,39232
14057	14018,61829	14147	14108,37255	14237	14198,12681	14327	14287,88107	14417	14377,63533	14507	14467,38959
14058	14019,61556	14148	14109,36982	14238	14199,12408	14328	14288,87834	14418	14378,6326	14508	14468,38686
14059	14020,61283	14149	14110,36709	14239	14200,12135	14329	14289,87561	14419	14379,62987	14509	14469,38413
14060	14021,6101	14150	14111,36436	14240	14201,11862	14330	14290,87288	14420	14380,62714	14510	14470,3814
14061	14022,60737	14151	14112,36163	14241	14202,11589	14331	14291,87015	14421	14381,62441	14511	14471,37867
14062	14023,60464	14152	14113,3589	14242	14203,11316	14332	14292,86742	14422	14382,62168	14512	14472,37594
14063	14024,60191	14153	14114,35617	14243	14204,11043	14333	14293,86469	14423	14383,61895	14513	14473,37321
14064	14025,59918	14154	14115,35344	14244	14205,1077	14334	14294,86196	14424	14384,61622	14514	14474,37048

14515 14475,36775	14605 14565,12201	14695 14654,87627	14785 14744,63053	14875 14834,38479	14965 14924,13905
14516 14476,36502	14606 14566,11928	14696 14655,87354	14786 14745,6278	14876 14835,38206	14966 14925,13632
14517 14477,36229	14607 14567,11655	14697 14656,87081	14787 14746,62507	14877 14836,37933	14967 14926,13359
14518 14478,35956	14608 14568,11382	14698 14657,86808	14788 14747,62234	14878 14837,3766	14968 14927,13086
14519 14479,35683	14609 14569,11109	14699 14658,86535	14789 14748,61961	14879 14838,37387	14969 14928,12813
14520 14480,3541	14610 14570,10836	14700 14659,86262	14790 14749,61688	14880 14839,37114	14970 14929,1254
14521 14481,35137	14611 14571,10563	14701 14660,85989	14791 14750,61415	14881 14840,36841	14971 14930,12267
14522 14482,34864	14612 14572,1029	14702 14661,85716	14792 14751,61142	14882 14841,36568	14972 14931,11994
14523 14483,34591	14613 14573,10017	14703 14662,85443	14793 14752,60869	14883 14842,36295	14973 14932,11721
14524 14484,34318	14614 14574,09744	14704 14663,8517	14794 14753,60596	14884 14843,36022	14974 14933,11448
14525 14485,34045	14615 14575,09471	14705 14664,84897	14795 14754,60323	14885 14844,35749	14975 14934,11175
14526 14486,33772	14616 14576,09198	14706 14665,84624	14796 14755,6005	14886 14845,35476	14976 14935,10902
14527 14487,33498	14617 14577,08925	14707 14666,84351	14797 14756,59777	14887 14846,35203	14977 14936,10629
14528 14488,33225	14618 14578,08652	14708 14667,84078	14798 14757,59504	14888 14847,3493	14978 14937,10356
14529 14489,32952	14619 14579,08378	14709 14668,83805	14799 14758,59231	14889 14848,34657	14979 14938,10083
14530 14490,32679	14620 14580,08105	14710 14669,83532	14800 14759,58958	14890 14849,34384	14980 14939,0981
14531 14491,32406	14621 14581,07832	14711 14670,83259	14801 14760,58685	14891 14850,34111	14981 14940,09537
14532 14492,32133	14622 14582,07559	14712 14671,82985	14802 14761,58412	14892 14851,33838	14982 14941,09264
14533 14493,3186	14623 14583,07286	14713 14672,82712	14803 14762,58139	14893 14852,33565	14983 14942,08991
14534 14494,31587	14624 14584,07013	14714 14673,82439	14804 14763,57865	14894 14853,33292	14984 14943,08718
14535 14495,31314	14625 14585,6174	14715 14674,82166	14805 14764,57592	14895 14854,33019	14985 14944,08445
14536 14496,31041	14626 14586,06467	14716 14675,81893	14806 14765,57319	14896 14855,32745	14986 14945,08172
14537 14497,30768	14627 14587,06194	14717 14676,8162	14807 14766,57046	14897 14856,32472	14987 14946,07899
14538 14498,30495	14628 14588,05921	14718 14677,81347	14808 14767,56773	14898 14857,32199	14988 14947,07625
14539 14499,30222	14629 14589,05648	14719 14678,81074	14809 14768,565	14899 14858,31926	14989 14948,07352
14540 14500,29949	14630 14590,05375	14720 14679,80801	14810 14769,56227	14900 14859,31653	14990 14949,07079
14541 14501,29676	14631 14591,05102	14721 14680,80528	14811 14770,55954	14901 14860,3138	14991 14950,06806
14542 14502,29403	14632 14592,04829	14722 14681,80255	14812 14771,55681	14902 14861,31107	14992 14951,06533
14543 14503,2913	14633 14593,04556	14723 14682,79982	14813 14772,55408	14903 14862,30834	14993 14952,0626
14544 14504,28857	14634 14594,04283	14724 14683,79709	14814 14773,55135	14904 14863,30561	14994 14953,05987
14545 14505,28584	14635 14595,0401	14725 14684,79436	14815 14774,54862	14905 14864,30288	14995 14954,05714
14546 14506,28311	14636 14596,03737	14726 14685,79163	14816 14775,54589	14906 14865,30015	14996 14955,05441
14547 14507,28038	14637 14597,03464	14727 14686,7889	14817 14776,54316	14907 14866,29742	14997 14956,05168
14548 14508,27765	14638 14598,03191	14728 14687,78617	14818 14777,54043	14908 14867,29469	14998 14957,04895
14549 14509,27492	14639 14599,02918	14729 14688,78344	14819 14778,5377	14909 14868,29196	14999 14958,04622
14550 14510,27218	14640 14600,02645	14730 14689,78071	14820 14779,53497	14910 14869,28923	15000 14959,04349
14551 14511,26945	14641 14601,02372	14731 14690,77798	14821 14780,53224	14911 14870,2865	15001 14960,04076
14552 14512,26672	14642 14602,02098	14732 14691,77525	14822 14781,52951	14912 14871,28377	15002 14961,03803
14553 14513,26399	14643 14603,01825	14733 14692,77252	14823 14782,52678	14913 14872,28104	15003 14962,0353
14554 14514,26126	14644 14604,01552	14734 14693,76979	14824 14783,52405	14914 14873,27831	15004 14963,03257
14555 14515,25853	14645 14605,01279	14735 14694,76705	14825 14784,52132	14915 14874,27558	15005 14964,02984
14556 14516,2558	14646 14606,01006	14736 14695,76432	14826 14785,51859	14916 14875,27285	15006 14965,02711
14557 14517,25307	14647 14607,00733	14737 14696,76159	14827 14786,51585	14917 14876,27012	15007 14966,02438
14558 14518,25034	14648 14608,0046	14738 14697,75886	14828 14787,51312	14918 14877,26739	15008 14967,02165
14559 14519,24761	14649 14609,00187	14739 14698,75613	14829 14788,51039	14919 14878,26465	15009 14968,01892
14560 14520,24488	14650 14609,99914	14740 14699,7534	14830 14789,50766	14920 14879,26192	15010 14969,01619
14561 14521,24215	14651 14610,99641	14741 14700,75067	14831 14790,50493	14921 14880,25919	15011 14970,01345
14562 14522,23942	14652 14611,99368	14742 14701,74794	14832 14791,5022	14922 14881,25646	15012 14971,01072
14563 14523,23669	14653 14612,99095	14743 14702,74521	14833 14792,49947	14923 14882,25373	15013 14972,00799
14564 14524,23396	14654 14613,98822	14744 14703,74248	14834 14793,49674	14924 14883,251	15014 14973,00526
14565 14525,23123	14655 14614,98549	14745 14704,73975	14835 14794,49401	14925 14884,24827	15015 14974,00253
14566 14526,2285	14656 14615,98276	14746 14705,73702	14836 14795,49128	14926 14885,24554	15016 14974,9998
14567 14527,22577	14657 14616,98003	14747 14706,73429	14837 14796,48855	14927 14886,24281	15017 14975,99707
14568 14528,22304	14658 14617,9773	14748 14707,73156	14838 14797,48582	14928 14887,24008	15018 14976,99434
14569 14529,22031	14659 14618,97457	14749 14708,72883	14839 14798,48309	14929 14888,23735	15019 14977,99161
14570 14530,21758	14660 14619,97184	14750 14709,7261	14840 14799,48036	14930 14889,23462	15020 14978,98888
14571 14531,21485	14661 14620,96911	14751 14710,72337	14841 14800,47763	14931 14890,23189	15021 14979,98615
14572 14532,21212	14662 14621,96638	14752 14711,72064	14842 14801,4749	14932 14891,22916	15022 14980,98342
14573 14533,20938	14663 14622,96365	14753 14712,71791	14843 14802,47217	14933 14892,22643	15023 14981,98069
14574 14534,20665	14664 14623,96092	14754 14713,71518	14844 14803,46944	14934 14893,2237	15024 14982,97796
14575 14535,20392	14665 14624,95818	14755 14714,71245	14845 14804,46671	14935 14894,22097	15025 14983,97523
14576 14536,20119	14666 14625,95545	14756 14715,70972	14846 14805,46398	14936 14895,21824	15026 14984,9725
14577 14537,19846	14667 14626,95272	14757 14716,70699	14847 14806,46125	14937 14896,21551	15027 14985,96977
14578 14538,19573	14668 14627,94999	14758 14717,70425	14848 14807,45852	14938 14897,21278	15028 14986,96704
14579 14539,193	14669 14628,94726	14759 14718,70152	14849 14808,45579	14939 14898,21005	15029 14987,96431
14580 14540,19027	14670 14629,94453	14760 14719,69879	14850 14809,45305	14940 14899,20732	15030 14988,96158
14581 14541,18754	14671 14630,9418	14761 14720,69606	14851 14810,45032	14941 14900,20459	15031 14989,95885
14582 14542,18481	14672 14631,93907	14762 14721,69333	14852 14811,44759	14942 14901,20185	15032 14990,95612
14583 14543,18208	14673 14632,93634	14763 14722,6906	14853 14812,44486	14943 14902,19912	15033 14991,95339
14584 14544,17935	14674 14633,93361	14764 14723,68787	14854 14813,44213	14944 14903,19639	15034 14992,95065
14585 14545,17662	14675 14634,93088	14765 14724,68514	14855 14814,4394	14945 14904,19366	15035 14993,94792
14586 14546,17389	14676 14635,92815	14766 14725,68241	14856 14815,43667	14946 14905,19093	15036 14994,94519
14587 14547,17116	14677 14636,92542	14767 14726,67968	14857 14816,43394	14947 14906,1882	15037 14995,94246
14588 14548,16843	14678 14637,92269	14768 14727,67695	14858 14817,43121	14948 14907,18547	15038 14996,93973
14589 14549,1657	14679 14638,91996	14769 14728,67422	14859 14818,42848	14949 14908,18274	15039 14997,937
14590 14550,16297	14680 14639,91723	14770 14729,67149	14860 14819,42575	14950 14909,18001	15040 14998,93427
14591 14551,16024	14681 14640,9145	14771 14730,66876	14861 14820,42302	14951 14910,17728	15041 14999,93154
14592 14552,15751	14682 14641,91177	14772 14731,66603	14862 14821,42029	14952 14911,17455	15042 15000,92881
14593 14553,15478	14683 14642,90904	14773 14732,6633	14863 14822,41756	14953 14912,17182	15043 15001,92608
14594 14554,15205	14684 14643,90631	14774 14733,66057	14864 14823,41483	14954 14913,16909	15044 15002,92335
14595 14555,14932	14685 14644,90358	14775 14734,65784	14865 14824,4121	14955 14914,16636	15045 15003,92062
14596 14556,14658	14686 14645,90085	14776 14735,65511	14866 14825,40937	14956 14915,16363	15046 15004,91789
14597 14557,14385	14687 14646,89812	14777 14736,65238	14867 14826,40664	14957 14916,1609	15047 15005,91516
14598 14558,14112	14688 14647,89539	14778 14737,64965	14868 14827,40391	14958 14917,15817	15048 15006,91243
14599 14559,13839	14689 14648,89265	14779 14738,64692	14869 14828,40118	14959 14918,15544	15049 15007,9097
14600 14560,13566	14690 14649,88992	14780 14739,64419	14870 14829,39845	14960 14919,15271	15050 15008,90697
14601 14561,13293	14691 14650,88719	14781 14740,64145	14871 14830,39572	14961 14920,14998	15051 15009,90424
14602 14562,1302	14692 14651,88446	14782 14741,63872	14872 14831,39299	14962 14921,14725	15052 15010,90151
14603 14563,12747	14693 14652,88173	14783 14742,63599	14873 14832,39025	14963 14922,14452	15053 15011,89878
14604 14564,12474	14694 14653,879	14784 14743,63326	14874 14833,38752	14964 14923,14179	15054 15012,89605

TABLE TO FIND OUT THE POINT A IN EARTH RETURNS 185

15055	15013,89332	15145	15103,64758	15235	15193,40184	15325	15283,1561	15415	15372,91036	15505	15462,66462
15056	15014,89059	15146	15104,64485	15236	15194,39911	15326	15284,15337	15416	15373,90763	15506	15463,66189
15057	15015,88785	15147	15105,64212	15237	15195,39638	15327	15285,15064	15417	15374,9049	15507	15464,65916
15058	15016,88512	15148	15106,63939	15238	15196,39365	15328	15286,14791	15418	15375,90217	15508	15465,65643
15059	15017,88239	15149	15107,63665	15239	15197,39092	15329	15287,14518	15419	15376,89944	15509	15466,6537
15060	15018,87966	15150	15108,63392	15240	15198,38819	15330	15288,14245	15420	15377,89671	15510	15467,65097
15061	15019,87693	15151	15109,63119	15241	15199,38545	15331	15289,13972	15421	15378,89398	15511	15468,64824
15062	15020,8742	15152	15110,62846	15242	15200,38272	15332	15290,13699	15422	15379,89125	15512	15469,64551
15063	15021,87147	15153	15111,62573	15243	15201,37999	15333	15291,13426	15423	15380,88852	15513	15470,64278
15064	15022,86874	15154	15112,623	15244	15202,37726	15334	15292,13152	15424	15381,88579	15514	15471,64005
15065	15023,86601	15155	15113,62027	15245	15203,37453	15335	15293,12879	15425	15382,88306	15515	15472,63732
15066	15024,86328	15156	15114,61754	15246	15204,3718	15336	15294,12606	15426	15383,88032	15516	15473,63459
15067	15025,86055	15157	15115,61481	15247	15205,36907	15337	15295,12333	15427	15384,87759	15517	15474,63186
15068	15026,85782	15158	15116,61208	15248	15206,36634	15338	15296,1206	15428	15385,87486	15518	15475,62912
15069	15027,85509	15159	15117,60935	15249	15207,36361	15339	15297,11787	15429	15386,87213	15519	15476,62639
15070	15028,85236	15160	15118,60662	15250	15208,36088	15340	15298,11514	15430	15387,8694	15520	15477,62366
15071	15029,84963	15161	15119,60389	15251	15209,35815	15341	15299,11241	15431	15388,86667	15521	15478,62093
15072	15030,8469	15162	15120,60116	15252	15210,35542	15342	15300,10968	15432	15389,86394	15522	15479,6182
15073	15031,84417	15163	15121,59843	15253	15211,35269	15343	15301,10695	15433	15390,86121	15523	15480,61547
15074	15032,84144	15164	15122,5957	15254	15212,34996	15344	15302,10422	15434	15391,85848	15524	15481,61274
15075	15033,83871	15165	15123,59297	15255	15213,34723	15345	15303,10149	15435	15392,85575	15525	15482,61001
15076	15034,83598	15166	15124,59024	15256	15214,3445	15346	15304,09876	15436	15393,85302	15526	15483,60728
15077	15035,83325	15167	15125,58751	15257	15215,34177	15347	15305,09603	15437	15394,85029	15527	15484,60455
15078	15036,83052	15168	15126,58478	15258	15216,33904	15348	15306,0933	15438	15395,84756	15528	15485,60182
15079	15037,82779	15169	15127,58205	15259	15217,33631	15349	15307,09057	15439	15396,84483	15529	15486,59909
15080	15038,82505	15170	15128,57932	15260	15218,33358	15350	15308,08784	15440	15397,8421	15530	15487,59636
15081	15039,82232	15171	15129,57659	15261	15219,33085	15351	15309,08511	15441	15398,83937	15531	15488,59363
15082	15040,81959	15172	15130,57385	15262	15220,32812	15352	15310,08238	15442	15399,83664	15532	15489,5909
15083	15041,81686	15173	15131,57112	15263	15221,32539	15353	15311,07965	15443	15400,83391	15533	15490,58817
15084	15042,81413	15174	15132,56839	15264	15222,32266	15354	15312,07692	15444	15401,83118	15534	15491,58544
15085	15043,8114	15175	15133,56566	15265	15223,31992	15355	15313,07419	15445	15402,82845	15535	15492,58271
15086	15044,80867	15176	15134,56293	15266	15224,31719	15356	15314,07146	15446	15403,82572	15536	15493,57998
15087	15045,80594	15177	15135,5602	15267	15225,31446	15357	15315,06872	15447	15404,82299	15537	15494,57725
15088	15046,80321	15178	15136,55747	15268	15226,31173	15358	15316,06599	15448	15405,82026	15538	15495,57452
15089	15047,80048	15179	15137,55474	15269	15227,309	15359	15317,06326	15449	15406,81752	15539	15496,57179
15090	15048,79775	15180	15138,55201	15270	15228,30627	15360	15318,06053	15450	15407,81479	15540	15497,56906
15091	15049,79502	15181	15139,54928	15271	15229,30354	15361	15319,0578	15451	15408,81206	15541	15498,56632
15092	15050,79229	15182	15140,54655	15272	15230,30081	15362	15320,05507	15452	15409,80933	15542	15499,56359
15093	15051,78956	15183	15141,54382	15273	15231,29808	15363	15321,05234	15453	15410,8066	15543	15500,56086
15094	15052,78683	15184	15142,54109	15274	15232,29535	15364	15322,04961	15454	15411,80387	15544	15501,55813
15095	15053,7841	15185	15143,53836	15275	15233,29262	15365	15323,04688	15455	15412,80114	15545	15502,5554
15096	15054,78137	15186	15144,53563	15276	15234,28989	15366	15324,04415	15456	15413,79841	15546	15503,55267
15097	15055,77864	15187	15145,5329	15277	15235,28716	15367	15325,04142	15457	15414,79568	15547	15504,54994
15098	15056,77591	15188	15146,53017	15278	15236,28443	15368	15326,03869	15458	15415,79295	15548	15505,54721
15099	15057,77318	15189	15147,52744	15279	15237,2817	15369	15327,03596	15459	15416,79022	15549	15506,54448
15100	15058,77045	15190	15148,52471	15280	15238,27897	15370	15328,03323	15460	15417,78749	15550	15507,54175
15101	15059,76772	15191	15149,52198	15281	15239,27624	15371	15329,0305	15461	15418,78476	15551	15508,53902
15102	15060,76499	15192	15150,51925	15282	15240,27351	15372	15330,02777	15462	15419,78203	15552	15509,53629
15103	15061,76225	15193	15151,51652	15283	15241,27078	15373	15331,02504	15463	15420,7793	15553	15510,53356
15104	15062,75952	15194	15152,51379	15284	15242,26805	15374	15332,02231	15464	15421,77657	15554	15511,53083
15105	15063,75679	15195	15153,51105	15285	15243,26532	15375	15333,01958	15465	15422,77384	15555	15512,5281
15106	15064,75406	15196	15154,50832	15286	15244,26259	15376	15334,01685	15466	15423,77111	15556	15513,52537
15107	15065,75133	15197	15155,50559	15287	15245,25986	15377	15335,01412	15467	15424,76838	15557	15514,52264
15108	15066,7486	15198	15156,50286	15288	15246,25712	15378	15336,01139	15468	15425,76565	15558	15515,51991
15109	15067,74587	15199	15157,50013	15289	15247,25439	15379	15337,00866	15469	15426,76292	15559	15516,51718
15110	15068,74314	15200	15158,4974	15290	15248,25166	15380	15338,00592	15470	15427,76019	15560	15517,51445
15111	15069,74041	15201	15159,49467	15291	15249,24893	15381	15339,00319	15471	15428,75746	15561	15518,51172
15112	15070,73768	15202	15160,49194	15292	15250,2462	15382	15340,00046	15472	15429,75472	15562	15519,50899
15113	15071,73495	15203	15161,48921	15293	15251,24347	15383	15340,99773	15473	15430,75199	15563	15520,50626
15114	15072,73222	15204	15162,48648	15294	15252,24074	15384	15341,995	15474	15431,74926	15564	15521,50352
15115	15073,72949	15205	15163,48375	15295	15253,23801	15385	15342,99227	15475	15432,74653	15565	15522,50079
15116	15074,72676	15206	15164,48102	15296	15254,23528	15386	15343,98954	15476	15433,7438	15566	15523,49806
15117	15075,72403	15207	15165,47829	15297	15255,23255	15387	15344,98681	15477	15434,74107	15567	15524,49533
15118	15076,7213	15208	15166,47556	15298	15256,22982	15388	15345,98408	15478	15435,73834	15568	15525,4926
15119	15077,71857	15209	15167,47283	15299	15257,22709	15389	15346,98135	15479	15436,73561	15569	15526,48987
15120	15078,71584	15210	15168,4701	15300	15258,22436	15390	15347,97862	15480	15437,73288	15570	15527,48714
15121	15079,7131	15211	15169,46737	15301	15259,22163	15391	15348,97589	15481	15438,73015	15571	15528,48441
15122	15080,71038	15212	15170,46464	15302	15260,2189	15392	15349,97316	15482	15439,72742	15572	15529,48168
15123	15081,70765	15213	15171,46191	15303	15261,21617	15393	15350,97043	15483	15440,72469	15573	15530,47895
15124	15082,70492	15214	15172,45918	15304	15262,21344	15394	15351,9677	15484	15441,72196	15574	15531,47622
15125	15083,70219	15215	15173,45645	15305	15263,21071	15395	15352,96497	15485	15442,71923	15575	15532,47349
15126	15084,69945	15216	15174,45372	15306	15264,20798	15396	15353,96224	15486	15443,7165	15576	15533,47076
15127	15085,69672	15217	15175,45099	15307	15265,20525	15397	15354,95951	15487	15444,71377	15577	15534,46803
15128	15086,69399	15218	15176,44825	15308	15266,20252	15398	15355,95678	15488	15445,71104	15578	15535,4653
15129	15087,69126	15219	15177,44552	15309	15267,19979	15399	15356,95405	15489	15446,70831	15579	15536,46257
15130	15088,68853	15220	15178,44279	15310	15268,19706	15400	15357,95132	15490	15447,70558	15580	15537,45984
15131	15089,6858	15221	15179,44006	15311	15269,19432	15401	15358,94859	15491	15448,70285	15581	15538,45711
15132	15090,68307	15222	15180,43733	15312	15270,19159	15402	15359,94586	15492	15449,70012	15582	15539,45438
15133	15091,68034	15223	15181,4346	15313	15271,18886	15403	15360,94312	15493	15450,69739	15583	15540,45165
15134	15092,67761	15224	15182,43187	15314	15272,18613	15404	15361,94039	15494	15451,69466	15584	15541,44892
15135	15093,67488	15225	15183,42914	15315	15273,1834	15405	15362,93766	15495	15452,69192	15585	15542,44619
15136	15094,67215	15226	15184,42641	15316	15274,18067	15406	15363,93493	15496	15453,68919	15586	15543,44346
15137	15095,66942	15227	15185,42368	15317	15275,17794	15407	15364,9322	15497	15454,68646	15587	15544,44072
15138	15096,66669	15228	15186,42095	15318	15276,17521	15408	15365,92947	15498	15455,68373	15588	15545,43799
15139	15097,66396	15229	15187,41822	15319	15277,17248	15409	15366,92674	15499	15456,681	15589	15546,43526
15140	15098,66123	15230	15188,41549	15320	15278,16975	15410	15367,92401	15500	15457,67827	15590	15547,43253
15141	15099,6585	15231	15189,41276	15321	15279,16702	15411	15368,92128	15501	15458,67554	15591	15548,4298
15142	15100,65577	15232	15190,41003	15322	15280,16429	15412	15369,91855	15502	15459,67281	15592	15549,42707
15143	15101,65304	15233	15191,4073	15323	15281,16156	15413	15370,91582	15503	15460,67008	15593	15550,42434
15144	15102,65031	15234	15192,40457	15324	15282,15883	15414	15371,91309	15504	15461,66735	15594	15551,42161

LUNAR RETURNS AND EARTH RETURNS

15595	15552,41888	15685	15642,17314	15775	15731,9274	15865	15821,68166	15955	15911,43593	16045	16001,19019
15596	15553,41615	15686	15643,17041	15776	15732,92467	15866	15822,67893	15956	15912,43319	16046	16002,18746
15597	15554,41342	15687	15644,16768	15777	15733,92194	15867	15823,6762	15957	15913,43046	16047	16003,18473
15598	15555,41069	15688	15645,16495	15778	15734,91921	15868	15824,67347	15958	15914,42773	16048	16004,18199
15599	15556,40796	15689	15646,16222	15779	15735,91648	15869	15825,67074	15959	15915,425	16049	16005,17926
15600	15557,40523	15690	15647,15949	15780	15736,91375	15870	15826,66801	15960	15916,42227	16050	16006,17653
15601	15558,4025	15691	15648,15676	15781	15737,91102	15871	15827,66528	15961	15917,41954	16051	16007,1738
15602	15559,39977	15692	15649,15403	15782	15738,90829	15872	15828,66255	15962	15918,41681	16052	16008,17107
15603	15560,39704	15693	15650,1513	15783	15739,90556	15873	15829,65982	15963	15919,41408	16053	16009,16834
15604	15561,39431	15694	15651,14857	15784	15740,90283	15874	15830,65709	15964	15920,41135	16054	16010,16561
15605	15562,39158	15695	15652,14584	15785	15741,9001	15875	15831,65436	15965	15921,40862	16055	16011,16288
15606	15563,38885	15696	15653,14311	15786	15742,89737	15876	15832,65163	15966	15922,40589	16056	16012,16015
15607	15564,38612	15697	15654,14038	15787	15743,89464	15877	15833,6489	15967	15923,40316	16057	16013,15742
15608	15565,38339	15698	15655,13765	15788	15744,89191	15878	15834,64617	15968	15924,40043	16058	16014,15469
15609	15566,38066	15699	15656,13492	15789	15745,88918	15879	15835,64344	15969	15925,3977	16059	16015,15196
15610	15567,37792	15700	15657,13219	15790	15746,88645	15880	15836,64071	15970	15926,39497	16060	16016,14923
15611	15568,37519	15701	15658,12946	15791	15747,88372	15881	15837,63798	15971	15927,39224	16061	16017,1465
15612	15569,37246	15702	15659,12672	15792	15748,88099	15882	15838,63525	15972	15928,38951	16062	16018,14377
15613	15570,36973	15703	15660,12399	15793	15749,87826	15883	15839,63252	15973	15929,38678	16063	16019,14104
15614	15571,367	15704	15661,12126	15794	15750,87552	15884	15840,62979	15974	15930,38405	16064	16020,13831
15615	15572,36427	15705	15662,11853	15795	15751,87279	15885	15841,62706	15975	15931,38132	16065	16021,13558
15616	15573,36154	15706	15663,1158	15796	15752,87006	15886	15842,62433	15976	15932,37859	16066	16022,13285
15617	15574,35881	15707	15664,11307	15797	15753,86733	15887	15843,62159	15977	15933,37586	16067	16023,13012
15618	15575,35608	15708	15665,11034	15798	15754,8646	15888	15844,61886	15978	15934,37313	16068	16024,12739
15619	15576,35335	15709	15666,10761	15799	15755,86187	15889	15845,61613	15979	15935,37039	16069	16025,12466
15620	15577,35062	15710	15667,10488	15800	15756,85914	15890	15846,6134	15980	15936,36766	16070	16026,12193
15621	15578,34789	15711	15668,10215	15801	15757,85641	15891	15847,61067	15981	15937,36493	16071	16027,11919
15622	15579,34516	15712	15669,09942	15802	15758,85368	15892	15848,60794	15982	15938,3622	16072	16028,11646
15623	15580,34243	15713	15670,09669	15803	15759,85095	15893	15849,60521	15983	15939,35947	16073	16029,11373
15624	15581,3397	15714	15671,09396	15804	15760,84822	15894	15850,60248	15984	15940,35674	16074	16030,111
15625	15582,33697	15715	15672,09123	15805	15761,84549	15895	15851,59975	15985	15941,35401	16075	16031,10827
15626	15583,33424	15716	15673,0885	15806	15762,84276	15896	15852,59702	15986	15942,35128	16076	16032,10554
15627	15584,33151	15717	15674,08577	15807	15763,84003	15897	15853,59429	15987	15943,34855	16077	16033,10281
15628	15585,32878	15718	15675,08304	15808	15764,8373	15898	15854,59156	15988	15944,34582	16078	16034,10008
15629	15586,32605	15719	15676,08031	15809	15765,83457	15899	15855,58883	15989	15945,34309	16079	16035,09735
15630	15587,32332	15720	15677,07758	15810	15766,83184	15900	15856,5861	15990	15946,34036	16080	16036,09462
15631	15588,32059	15721	15678,07485	15811	15767,82911	15901	15857,58337	15991	15947,33763	16081	16037,09189
15632	15589,31786	15722	15679,07212	15812	15768,82638	15902	15858,58064	15992	15948,3349	16082	16038,08916
15633	15590,31512	15723	15680,06939	15813	15769,82365	15903	15859,57791	15993	15949,33217	16083	16039,08643
15634	15591,31239	15724	15681,06666	15814	15770,82092	15904	15860,57518	15994	15950,32944	16084	16040,0837
15635	15592,30966	15725	15682,06392	15815	15771,81819	15905	15861,57245	15995	15951,32671	16085	16041,08097
15636	15593,30693	15726	15683,06119	15816	15772,81546	15906	15862,56972	15996	15952,32398	16086	16042,07824
15637	15594,3042	15727	15684,05846	15817	15773,81272	15907	15863,56699	15997	15953,32125	16087	16043,07551
15638	15595,30147	15728	15685,05573	15818	15774,80999	15908	15864,56426	15998	15954,31852	16088	16044,07278
15639	15596,29874	15729	15686,053	15819	15775,80726	15909	15865,56153	15999	15955,31579	16089	16045,07005
15640	15597,29601	15730	15687,05027	15820	15776,80453	15910	15866,55879	16000	15956,31306	16090	16046,06732
15641	15598,29328	15731	15688,04754	15821	15777,8018	15911	15867,55606	16001	15957,31033	16091	16047,06459
15642	15599,29055	15732	15689,04481	15822	15778,79907	15912	15868,55333	16002	15958,30759	16092	16048,06186
15643	15600,28782	15733	15690,04208	15823	15779,79634	15913	15869,5506	16003	15959,30486	16093	16049,05913
15644	15601,28509	15734	15691,03935	15824	15780,79361	15914	15870,54787	16004	15960,30213	16094	16050,05639
15645	15602,28236	15735	15692,03662	15825	15781,79088	15915	15871,54514	16005	15961,2994	16095	16051,05366
15646	15603,27963	15736	15693,03389	15826	15782,78815	15916	15872,54241	16006	15962,29667	16096	16052,05093
15647	15604,2769	15737	15694,03116	15827	15783,78542	15917	15873,53968	16007	15963,29394	16097	16053,0482
15648	15605,27417	15738	15695,02843	15828	15784,78269	15918	15874,53695	16008	15964,29121	16098	16054,04547
15649	15606,27144	15739	15696,0257	15829	15785,77996	15919	15875,53422	16009	15965,28848	16099	16055,04274
15650	15607,26871	15740	15697,02297	15830	15786,77723	15920	15876,53149	16010	15966,28575	16100	16056,04001
15651	15608,26598	15741	15698,02024	15831	15787,7745	15921	15877,52876	16011	15967,28302	16101	16057,03728
15652	15609,26325	15742	15699,01751	15832	15788,77177	15922	15878,52603	16012	15968,28029	16102	16058,03455
15653	15610,26052	15743	15700,01478	15833	15789,76904	15923	15879,5233	16013	15969,27756	16103	16059,03182
15654	15611,25779	15744	15701,01205	15834	15790,76631	15924	15880,52057	16014	15970,27483	16104	16060,02909
15655	15612,25506	15745	15702,00932	15835	15791,76358	15925	15881,51784	16015	15971,2721	16105	16061,02636
15656	15613,25232	15746	15703,00659	15836	15792,76085	15926	15882,51511	16016	15972,26937	16106	16062,02363
15657	15614,24959	15747	15704,00386	15837	15793,75812	15927	15883,51238	16017	15973,26664	16107	16063,0209
15658	15615,24686	15748	15705,00112	15838	15794,75539	15928	15884,50965	16018	15974,26391	16108	16064,01817
15659	15616,24413	15749	15705,99839	15839	15795,75266	15929	15885,50692	16019	15975,26118	16109	16065,01544
15660	15617,2414	15750	15706,99566	15840	15796,74993	15930	15886,50419	16020	15976,25845	16110	16066,01271
15661	15618,23867	15751	15707,99293	15841	15797,74719	15931	15887,50146	16021	15977,25572	16111	16067,00998
15662	15619,23594	15752	15708,9902	15842	15798,74446	15932	15888,49873	16022	15978,55299	16112	16068,00725
15663	15620,23321	15753	15709,98747	15843	15799,74173	15933	15889,49599	16023	15979,25026	16113	16069,00452
15664	15621,23048	15754	15710,98474	15844	15800,739	15934	15890,49326	16024	15980,24753	16114	16070,00179
15665	15622,22775	15755	15711,98201	15845	15801,73627	15935	15891,49053	16025	15981,24479	16115	16070,99906
15666	15623,22502	15756	15712,97928	15846	15802,73354	15936	15892,4878	16026	15982,24206	16116	16071,99633
15667	15624,22229	15757	15713,97655	15847	15803,73081	15937	15893,48507	16027	15983,23933	16117	16072,99359
15668	15625,21956	15758	15714,97382	15848	15804,72808	15938	15894,48234	16028	15984,2366	16118	16073,99086
15669	15626,21683	15759	15715,97109	15849	15805,72535	15939	15895,47961	16029	15985,23387	16119	16074,98813
15670	15627,2141	15760	15716,96836	15850	15806,72262	15940	15896,47688	16030	15986,23114	16120	16075,9854
15671	15628,21137	15761	15717,96563	15851	15807,71989	15941	15897,47415	16031	15987,22841	16121	16076,98267
15672	15629,20864	15762	15718,9629	15852	15808,71716	15942	15898,47142	16032	15988,22568	16122	16077,97994
15673	15630,20591	15763	15719,96017	15853	15809,71443	15943	15899,46869	16033	15989,22295	16123	16078,97721
15674	15631,20318	15764	15720,95744	15854	15810,7117	15944	15900,46596	16034	15990,22022	16124	16079,97448
15675	15632,20045	15765	15721,95471	15855	15811,70897	15945	15901,46323	16035	15991,21749	16125	16080,97175
15676	15633,19772	15766	15722,95198	15856	15812,70624	15946	15902,4605	16036	15992,21476	16126	16081,96902
15677	15634,19499	15767	15723,94925	15857	15813,70351	15947	15903,45777	16037	15993,21203	16127	16082,96629
15678	15635,19226	15768	15724,94652	15858	15814,70078	15948	15904,45504	16038	15994,2093	16128	16083,96356
15679	15636,18952	15769	15725,94379	15859	15815,69805	15949	15905,45231	16039	15995,20657	16129	16084,96083
15680	15637,18679	15770	15726,94106	15860	15816,69532	15950	15906,44958	16040	15996,20384	16130	16085,9581
15681	15638,18406	15771	15727,93832	15861	15817,69259	15951	15907,44685	16041	15997,20111	16131	16086,95537
15682	15639,18133	15772	15728,93559	15862	15818,68986	15952	15908,44412	16042	15998,19838	16132	16087,95264
15683	15640,1786	15773	15729,93286	15863	15819,68713	15953	15909,44139	16043	15999,19565	16133	16088,94991
15684	15641,17587	15774	15730,93013	15864	15820,68439	15954	15910,43866	16044	16000,19292	16134	16089,94718

TABLE TO FIND OUT THE POINT A IN EARTH RETURNS 187

16135	16090,94445	16225	16180,69871	16315	16270,45297	16405	16360,20723	16495	16449,96149	16585	16539,71575
16136	16091,94172	16226	16181,69598	16316	16271,45024	16406	16361,2045	16496	16450,95876	16586	16540,71302
16137	16092,93899	16227	16182,69325	16317	16272,44751	16407	16362,20177	16497	16451,95603	16587	16541,71029
16138	16093,93626	16228	16183,69052	16318	16273,44478	16408	16363,19904	16498	16452,9533	16588	16542,70756
16139	16094,93353	16229	16184,68779	16319	16274,44205	16409	16364,19631	16499	16453,95057	16589	16543,70483
16140	16095,93079	16230	16185,68506	16320	16275,43932	16410	16365,19358	16500	16454,94784	16590	16544,7021
16141	16096,92806	16231	16186,68233	16321	16276,43659	16411	16366,19085	16501	16455,94511	16591	16545,69937
16142	16097,92533	16232	16187,67959	16322	16277,43386	16412	16367,18812	16502	16456,94238	16592	16546,69664
16143	16098,9226	16233	16188,67686	16323	16278,43113	16413	16368,18539	16503	16457,93965	16593	16547,69391
16144	16099,91987	16234	16189,67413	16324	16279,42839	16414	16369,18266	16504	16458,93692	16594	16548,69118
16145	16100,91714	16235	16190,6714	16325	16280,42566	16415	16370,17993	16505	16459,93419	16595	16549,68845
16146	16101,91441	16236	16191,66867	16326	16281,42293	16416	16371,17719	16506	16460,93146	16596	16550,68572
16147	16102,91168	16237	16192,66594	16327	16282,4202	16417	16372,17446	16507	16461,92873	16597	16551,68299
16148	16103,90895	16238	16193,66321	16328	16283,41747	16418	16373,17173	16508	16462,926	16598	16552,68026
16149	16104,90622	16239	16194,66048	16329	16284,41474	16419	16374,169	16509	16463,92326	16599	16553,67753
16150	16105,90349	16240	16195,65775	16330	16285,41201	16420	16375,16627	16510	16464,92053	16600	16554,6748
16151	16106,90076	16241	16196,65502	16331	16286,40928	16421	16376,16354	16511	16465,9178	16601	16555,67206
16152	16107,89803	16242	16197,65229	16332	16287,40655	16422	16377,16081	16512	16466,91507	16602	16556,66933
16153	16108,8953	16243	16198,64956	16333	16288,40382	16423	16378,15808	16513	16467,91234	16603	16557,6666
16154	16109,89257	16244	16199,64683	16334	16289,40109	16424	16379,15535	16514	16468,90961	16604	16558,66387
16155	16110,88984	16245	16200,6441	16335	16290,39836	16425	16380,15262	16515	16469,90688	16605	16559,66114
16156	16111,88711	16246	16201,64137	16336	16291,39563	16426	16381,14989	16516	16470,90415	16606	16560,65841
16157	16112,88438	16247	16202,63864	16337	16292,3929	16427	16382,14716	16517	16471,90142	16607	16561,65568
16158	16113,88165	16248	16203,63591	16338	16293,39017	16428	16383,14443	16518	16472,89869	16608	16562,65295
16159	16114,87892	16249	16204,63318	16339	16294,38744	16429	16384,1417	16519	16473,89596	16609	16563,65022
16160	16115,87619	16250	16205,63045	16340	16295,38471	16430	16385,13897	16520	16474,89323	16610	16564,64749
16161	16116,87346	16251	16206,62772	16341	16296,38198	16431	16386,13624	16521	16475,8905	16611	16565,64476
16162	16117,87073	16252	16207,62499	16342	16297,37925	16432	16387,13351	16522	16476,88777	16612	16566,64203
16163	16118,86799	16253	16208,62226	16343	16298,37652	16433	16388,13078	16523	16477,88504	16613	16567,6393
16164	16119,86526	16254	16209,61953	16344	16299,37379	16434	16389,12805	16524	16478,88231	16614	16568,63657
16165	16120,86253	16255	16210,61679	16345	16300,37106	16435	16390,12532	16525	16479,87958	16615	16569,63384
16166	16121,8598	16256	16211,61406	16346	16301,36833	16436	16391,12259	16526	16480,87685	16616	16570,63111
16167	16122,85707	16257	16212,61133	16347	16302,36559	16437	16392,11986	16527	16481,87412	16617	16571,62838
16168	16123,85434	16258	16213,6086	16348	16303,36286	16438	16393,11713	16528	16482,87139	16618	16572,62565
16169	16124,85161	16259	16214,60587	16349	16304,36013	16439	16394,1144	16529	16483,86866	16619	16573,62292
16170	16125,84888	16260	16215,60314	16350	16305,3574	16440	16395,11166	16530	16484,86593	16620	16574,62019
16171	16126,84615	16261	16216,60041	16351	16306,35467	16441	16396,10893	16531	16485,8632	16621	16575,61746
16172	16127,84342	16262	16217,59768	16352	16307,35194	16442	16397,1062	16532	16486,86046	16622	16576,61473
16173	16128,84069	16263	16218,59495	16353	16308,34921	16443	16398,10347	16533	16487,85773	16623	16577,612
16174	16129,83796	16264	16219,59222	16354	16309,34648	16444	16399,10074	16534	16488,855	16624	16578,60926
16175	16130,83523	16265	16220,58949	16355	16310,34375	16445	16400,09801	16535	16489,85227	16625	16579,60653
16176	16131,8325	16266	16221,58676	16356	16311,34102	16446	16401,09528	16536	16490,84954	16626	16580,6038
16177	16132,82977	16267	16222,58403	16357	16312,33829	16447	16402,09255	16537	16491,84681	16627	16581,60107
16178	16133,82704	16268	16223,5813	16358	16313,33556	16448	16403,08982	16538	16492,84408	16628	16582,59834
16179	16134,82431	16269	16224,57857	16359	16314,33283	16449	16404,08709	16539	16493,84135	16629	16583,59561
16180	16135,82158	16270	16225,57584	16360	16315,3301	16450	16405,08436	16540	16494,83862	16630	16584,59288
16181	16136,81885	16271	16226,57311	16361	16316,32737	16451	16406,08163	16541	16495,83589	16631	16585,59015
16182	16137,81612	16272	16227,57038	16362	16317,32464	16452	16407,0789	16542	16496,83316	16632	16586,58742
16183	16138,81339	16273	16228,56765	16363	16318,32191	16453	16408,07617	16543	16497,83043	16633	16587,58469
16184	16139,81066	16274	16229,56492	16364	16319,31918	16454	16409,07344	16544	16498,8277	16634	16588,58196
16185	16140,80793	16275	16230,56219	16365	16320,31645	16455	16410,07071	16545	16499,82497	16635	16589,57923
16186	16141,80519	16276	16231,55946	16366	16321,31372	16456	16411,06798	16546	16500,82224	16636	16590,5765
16187	16142,80246	16277	16232,55673	16367	16322,31099	16457	16412,06525	16547	16501,81951	16637	16591,57377
16188	16143,79973	16278	16233,55399	16368	16323,30826	16458	16413,06252	16548	16502,81678	16638	16592,57104
16189	16144,797	16279	16234,55126	16369	16324,30553	16459	16414,05979	16549	16503,81405	16639	16593,56831
16190	16145,79427	16280	16235,54853	16370	16325,30279	16460	16415,05706	16550	16504,81132	16640	16594,56558
16191	16146,79154	16281	16236,5458	16371	16326,30006	16461	16416,05433	16551	16505,80859	16641	16595,56285
16192	16147,78881	16282	16237,54307	16372	16327,29733	16462	16417,0516	16552	16506,80586	16642	16596,56012
16193	16148,78608	16283	16238,54034	16373	16328,2946	16463	16418,04886	16553	16507,80313	16643	16597,55739
16194	16149,78335	16284	16239,53761	16374	16329,29187	16464	16419,04613	16554	16508,8004	16644	16598,55466
16195	16150,78062	16285	16240,53488	16375	16330,28914	16465	16420,0434	16555	16509,79766	16645	16599,55193
16196	16151,77789	16286	16241,53215	16376	16331,28641	16466	16421,04067	16556	16510,79493	16646	16600,5492
16197	16152,77516	16287	16242,52942	16377	16332,28368	16467	16422,03794	16557	16511,7922	16647	16601,54646
16198	16153,77243	16288	16243,52669	16378	16333,28095	16468	16423,03521	16558	16512,78947	16648	16602,54373
16199	16154,7697	16289	16244,52396	16379	16334,27822	16469	16424,03248	16559	16513,78674	16649	16603,541
16200	16155,76697	16290	16245,52123	16380	16335,27549	16470	16425,02975	16560	16514,78401	16650	16604,53827
16201	16156,76424	16291	16246,5185	16381	16336,27276	16471	16426,02702	16561	16515,78128	16651	16605,53554
16202	16157,76151	16292	16247,51577	16382	16337,27003	16472	16427,02429	16562	16516,77855	16652	16606,53281
16203	16158,75878	16293	16248,51304	16383	16338,2673	16473	16428,02156	16563	16517,77582	16653	16607,53008
16204	16159,75605	16294	16249,51031	16384	16339,26457	16474	16429,01883	16564	16518,77309	16654	16608,52735
16205	16160,75332	16295	16250,50758	16385	16340,26184	16475	16430,0161	16565	16519,77036	16655	16609,52462
16206	16161,75059	16296	16251,50485	16386	16341,25911	16476	16431,01337	16566	16520,76763	16656	16610,52189
16207	16162,74786	16297	16252,50212	16387	16342,25638	16477	16432,01064	16567	16521,7649	16657	16611,51916
16208	16163,74513	16298	16253,49939	16388	16343,25365	16478	16433,00791	16568	16522,76217	16658	16612,51643
16209	16164,74239	16299	16254,49666	16389	16344,25092	16479	16434,00518	16569	16523,75944	16659	16613,5137
16210	16165,73966	16300	16255,49393	16390	16345,24819	16480	16435,00245	16570	16524,75671	16660	16614,51097
16211	16166,73693	16301	16256,49119	16391	16346,24546	16481	16435,99972	16571	16525,75398	16661	16615,50824
16212	16167,7342	16302	16257,48846	16392	16347,24273	16482	16436,99699	16572	16526,75125	16662	16616,50551
16213	16168,73147	16303	16258,48573	16393	16348,23999	16483	16437,99426	16573	16527,74852	16663	16617,50278
16214	16169,72874	16304	16259,483	16394	16349,23726	16484	16438,99153	16574	16528,74579	16664	16618,50005
16215	16170,72601	16305	16260,48027	16395	16350,23453	16485	16439,9888	16575	16529,74306	16665	16619,49732
16216	16171,72328	16306	16261,47754	16396	16351,2318	16486	16440,98606	16576	16530,74033	16666	16620,49459
16217	16172,72055	16307	16262,47481	16397	16352,22907	16487	16441,98333	16577	16531,7376	16667	16621,49186
16218	16173,71782	16308	16263,47208	16398	16353,22634	16488	16442,9806	16578	16532,73486	16668	16622,48913
16219	16174,71509	16309	16264,46935	16399	16354,22361	16489	16443,97787	16579	16533,73213	16669	16623,4864
16220	16175,71236	16310	16265,46662	16400	16355,22088	16490	16444,97514	16580	16534,7294	16670	16624,48366
16221	16176,70963	16311	16266,46389	16401	16356,21815	16491	16445,97241	16581	16535,72667	16671	16625,48093
16222	16177,7069	16312	16267,46116	16402	16357,21542	16492	16446,96968	16582	16536,72394	16672	16626,4782
16223	16178,70417	16313	16268,45843	16403	16358,21269	16493	16447,96695	16583	16537,72121	16673	16627,47547
16224	16179,70144	16314	16269,4557	16404	16359,20996	16494	16448,96422	16584	16538,71848	16674	16628,47274

LUNAR RETURNS AND EARTH RETURNS

16675	16629,47001	16765	16719,22427	16855	16808,97853	16945	16898,7328	17035	16988,48706	17125	17078,24132
16676	16630,46728	16766	16720,22154	16856	16809,9758	16946	16899,73006	17036	16989,48433	17126	17079,23859
16677	16631,46455	16767	16721,21881	16857	16810,97307	16947	16900,72733	17037	16990,4816	17127	17080,23586
16678	16632,46182	16768	16722,21608	16858	16811,97034	16948	16901,7246	17038	16991,47887	17128	17081,23313
16679	16633,45909	16769	16723,21335	16859	16812,96761	16949	16902,72187	17039	16992,47613	17129	17082,2304
16680	16634,45636	16770	16724,21062	16860	16813,96488	16950	16903,71914	17040	16993,4734	17130	17083,22767
16681	16635,45363	16771	16725,20789	16861	16814,96215	16951	16904,71641	17041	16994,47067	17131	17084,22493
16682	16636,4509	16772	16726,20516	16862	16815,95942	16952	16905,71368	17042	16995,46794	17132	17085,2222
16683	16637,44817	16773	16727,20243	16863	16816,95669	16953	16906,71095	17043	16996,46521	17133	17086,21947
16684	16638,44544	16774	16728,1997	16864	16817,95396	16954	16907,70822	17044	16997,46248	17134	17087,21674
16685	16639,44271	16775	16729,19697	16865	16818,95123	16955	16908,70549	17045	16998,45975	17135	17088,21401
16686	16640,43998	16776	16730,19424	16866	16819,9485	16956	16909,70276	17046	16999,45702	17136	17089,21128
16687	16641,43725	16777	16731,19151	16867	16820,94577	16957	16910,70003	17047	17000,45429	17137	17090,20855
16688	16642,43452	16778	16732,18878	16868	16821,94304	16958	16911,6973	17048	17001,45156	17138	17091,20582
16689	16643,43179	16779	16733,18605	16869	16822,94031	16959	16912,69457	17049	17002,44883	17139	17092,20309
16690	16644,42906	16780	16734,18332	16870	16823,93758	16960	16913,69184	17050	17003,4461	17140	17093,20036
16691	16645,42633	16781	16735,18059	16871	16824,93485	16961	16914,68911	17051	17004,44337	17141	17094,19763
16692	16646,4236	16782	16736,17786	16872	16825,93212	16962	16915,68638	17052	17005,44064	17142	17095,1949
16693	16647,42086	16783	16737,17513	16873	16826,92939	16963	16916,68365	17053	17006,43791	17143	17096,19217
16694	16648,41813	16784	16738,1724	16874	16827,92666	16964	16917,68092	17054	17007,43518	17144	17097,18944
16695	16649,4154	16785	16739,16966	16875	16828,92393	16965	16918,67819	17055	17008,43245	17145	17098,18671
16696	16650,41267	16786	16740,16693	16876	16829,9212	16966	16919,67546	17056	17009,42972	17146	17099,18398
16697	16651,40994	16787	16741,1642	16877	16830,91846	16967	16920,67273	17057	17010,42699	17147	17100,18125
16698	16652,40721	16788	16742,16147	16878	16831,91573	16968	16921,67	17058	17011,42426	17148	17101,17852
16699	16653,40448	16789	16743,15874	16879	16832,913	16969	16922,66726	17059	17012,42153	17149	17102,17579
16700	16654,40175	16790	16744,15601	16880	16833,91027	16970	16923,66453	17060	17013,4188	17150	17103,17306
16701	16655,39902	16791	16745,15328	16881	16834,90754	16971	16924,6618	17061	17014,41607	17151	17104,17033
16702	16656,39629	16792	16746,15055	16882	16835,90481	16972	16925,65907	17062	17015,41333	17152	17105,1676
16703	16657,39356	16793	16747,14782	16883	16836,90208	16973	16926,65634	17063	17016,4106	17153	17106,16487
16704	16658,39083	16794	16748,14509	16884	16837,89935	16974	16927,65361	17064	17017,40787	17154	17107,16213
16705	16659,3881	16795	16749,14236	16885	16838,89662	16975	16928,65088	17065	17018,40514	17155	17108,1594
16706	16660,38537	16796	16750,13963	16886	16839,89389	16976	16929,64815	17066	17019,40241	17156	17109,15667
16707	16661,38264	16797	16751,1369	16887	16840,89116	16977	16930,64542	17067	17020,39968	17157	17110,15394
16708	16662,37991	16798	16752,13417	16888	16841,88843	16978	16931,64269	17068	17021,39695	17158	17111,15121
16709	16663,37718	16799	16753,13144	16889	16842,8857	16979	16932,63996	17069	17022,39422	17159	17112,14848
16710	16664,37445	16800	16754,12871	16890	16843,88297	16980	16933,63723	17070	17023,39149	17160	17113,14575
16711	16665,37172	16801	16755,12598	16891	16844,88024	16981	16934,6345	17071	17024,38876	17161	17114,14302
16712	16666,36899	16802	16756,12325	16892	16845,87751	16982	16935,63177	17072	17025,38603	17162	17115,14029
16713	16667,36626	16803	16757,12052	16893	16846,87478	16983	16936,62904	17073	17026,3833	17163	17116,13756
16714	16668,36353	16804	16758,11779	16894	16847,87205	16984	16937,62631	17074	17027,38057	17164	17117,13483
16715	16669,3608	16805	16759,11506	16895	16848,86932	16985	16938,62358	17075	17028,37784	17165	17118,1321
16716	16670,35806	16806	16760,11233	16896	16849,86659	16986	16939,62085	17076	17029,37511	17166	17119,12937
16717	16671,35533	16807	16761,1096	16897	16850,86386	16987	16940,61812	17077	17030,37238	17167	17120,12664
16718	16672,3526	16808	16762,10686	16898	16851,86113	16988	16941,61539	17078	17031,36965	17168	17121,12391
16719	16673,34987	16809	16763,10413	16899	16852,8584	16989	16942,61266	17079	17032,36692	17169	17122,12118
16720	16674,34714	16810	16764,1014	16900	16853,85566	16990	16943,60993	17080	17033,36419	17170	17123,11845
16721	16675,34441	16811	16765,09867	16901	16854,85293	16991	16944,6072	17081	17034,36146	17171	17124,11572
16722	16676,34168	16812	16766,09594	16902	16855,8502	16992	16945,60447	17082	17035,35873	17172	17125,11299
16723	16677,33895	16813	16767,09321	16903	16856,84747	16993	16946,60173	17083	17036,356	17173	17126,11026
16724	16678,33622	16814	16768,09048	16904	16857,84474	16994	16947,599	17084	17037,35327	17174	17127,10753
16725	16679,33349	16815	16769,08775	16905	16858,84201	16995	16948,59627	17085	17038,35053	17175	17128,1048
16726	16680,33076	16816	16770,08502	16906	16859,83928	16996	16949,59354	17086	17039,3478	17176	17129,10207
16727	16681,32803	16817	16771,08229	16907	16860,83655	16997	16950,59081	17087	17040,34507	17177	17130,09933
16728	16682,3253	16818	16772,07956	16908	16861,83382	16998	16951,58808	17088	17041,34234	17178	17131,0966
16729	16683,32257	16819	16773,07683	16909	16862,83109	16999	16952,58535	17089	17042,33961	17179	17132,09387
16730	16684,31984	16820	16774,0741	16910	16863,82836	17000	16953,58262	17090	17043,33688	17180	17133,09114
16731	16685,31711	16821	16775,07137	16911	16864,82563	17001	16954,57989	17091	17044,33415	17181	17134,08841
16732	16686,31438	16822	16776,06864	16912	16865,8229	17002	16955,57716	17092	17045,33142	17182	17135,08568
16733	16687,31165	16823	16777,06591	16913	16866,82017	17003	16956,57443	17093	17046,32869	17183	17136,08295
16734	16688,30892	16824	16778,06318	16914	16867,81744	17004	16957,5717	17094	17047,32596	17184	17137,08022
16735	16689,30619	16825	16779,06045	16915	16868,81471	17005	16958,56897	17095	17048,32323	17185	17138,07749
16736	16690,30346	16826	16780,05772	16916	16869,81198	17006	16959,56624	17096	17049,3205	17186	17139,07476
16737	16691,30073	16827	16781,05499	16917	16870,80925	17007	16960,56351	17097	17050,31777	17187	17140,07203
16738	16692,298	16828	16782,05226	16918	16871,80652	17008	16961,56078	17098	17051,31504	17188	17141,0693
16739	16693,29526	16829	16783,04953	16919	16872,80379	17009	16962,55805	17099	17052,31231	17189	17142,06657
16740	16694,29253	16830	16784,0468	16920	16873,80106	17010	16963,55532	17100	17053,30958	17190	17143,06384
16741	16695,2898	16831	16785,04406	16921	16874,79833	17011	16964,55259	17101	17054,30685	17191	17144,06111
16742	16696,28707	16832	16786,04133	16922	16875,7956	17012	16965,54986	17102	17055,30412	17192	17145,05838
16743	16697,28434	16833	16787,0386	16923	16876,79286	17013	16966,54713	17103	17056,30139	17193	17146,05565
16744	16698,28161	16834	16788,03587	16924	16877,79013	17014	16967,5444	17104	17057,29866	17194	17147,05292
16745	16699,27888	16835	16789,03314	16925	16878,7874	17015	16968,54167	17105	17058,29593	17195	17148,05019
16746	16700,27615	16836	16790,03041	16926	16879,78467	17016	16969,53893	17106	17059,2932	17196	17149,04746
16747	16701,27342	16837	16791,02768	16927	16880,78194	17017	16970,5362	17107	17060,29047	17197	17150,04473
16748	16702,27069	16838	16792,02495	16928	16881,77921	17018	16971,53347	17108	17061,28773	17198	17151,042
16749	16703,26796	16839	16793,02222	16929	16882,77648	17019	16972,53074	17109	17062,285	17199	17152,03927
16750	16704,26523	16840	16794,01949	16930	16883,77375	17020	16973,52801	17110	17063,28227	17200	17153,03653
16751	16705,2625	16841	16795,01676	16931	16884,77102	17021	16974,52528	17111	17064,27954	17201	17154,0338
16752	16706,25977	16842	16796,01403	16932	16885,76829	17022	16975,52255	17112	17065,27681	17202	17155,03107
16753	16707,25704	16843	16797,0113	16933	16886,76556	17023	16976,51982	17113	17066,27408	17203	17156,02834
16754	16708,25431	16844	16798,00857	16934	16887,76283	17024	16977,51709	17114	17067,27135	17204	17157,02561
16755	16709,25158	16845	16799,00584	16935	16888,7601	17025	16978,51436	17115	17068,26862	17205	17158,02288
16756	16710,24885	16846	16800,00311	16936	16889,75737	17026	16979,51163	17116	17069,26589	17206	17159,02015
16757	16711,24612	16847	16801,00038	16937	16890,75464	17027	16980,5089	17117	17070,26316	17207	17160,01742
16758	16712,24339	16848	16801,99765	16938	16891,75191	17028	16981,50617	17118	17071,26043	17208	17161,01469
16759	16713,24066	16849	16802,99492	16939	16892,74918	17029	16982,50344	17119	17072,2577	17209	17162,01196
16760	16714,23793	16850	16803,99219	16940	16893,74645	17030	16983,50071	17120	17073,25497	17210	17163,00923
16761	16715,2352	16851	16804,98946	16941	16894,74372	17031	16984,49798	17121	17074,25224	17211	17164,0065
16762	16716,23246	16852	16805,98673	16942	16895,74099	17032	16985,49525	17122	17075,24951	17212	17165,00377
16763	16717,22973	16853	16806,984	16943	16896,73826	17033	16986,49252	17123	17076,24678	17213	17166,00104
16764	16718,227	16854	16807,98126	16944	16897,73553	17034	16987,48979	17124	17077,24405	17214	17166,99831

TABLE TO FIND OUT THE POINT A IN EARTH RETURNS 189

17215 17167,99558	17305 17257,74984	17395 17347,5041	17485 17437,25836	17575 17527,01262	17665 17616,76688
17216 17168,99285	17306 17258,74711	17396 17348,50137	17486 17438,25563	17576 17528,00989	17666 17617,76415
17217 17169,99012	17307 17259,74438	17397 17349,49864	17487 17439,2529	17577 17529,00716	17667 17618,76142
17218 17170,98739	17308 17260,74165	17398 17350,49591	17488 17440,25017	17578 17530,00443	17668 17619,75869
17219 17171,98466	17309 17261,73892	17399 17351,49318	17489 17441,24744	17579 17531,0017	17669 17620,75596
17220 17172,98193	17310 17262,73619	17400 17352,49045	17490 17442,24471	17580 17531,99897	17670 17621,75323
17221 17173,9792	17311 17263,73346	17401 17353,48772	17491 17443,24198	17581 17532,99624	17671 17622,7505
17222 17174,97647	17312 17264,73073	17402 17354,48499	17492 17444,23925	17582 17533,99351	17672 17623,74777
17223 17175,97373	17313 17 2 6 5 ,7 2 8	17403 17355,48226	17493 17445,23652	17583 17534,99078	17673 17624,74504
17224 17 1 7 6 , 9 7 1	17314 17266,72527	17404 17356,47953	17494 17446,23379	17584 17535,98805	17674 17625,74231
17225 17177,96827	17315 17267,72253	17405 17357,4768	17495 17447,23106	17585 17536,98532	17675 17626,73958
17226 17178,96554	17316 17268,7198	17406 17358,47407	17496 17448,22833	17586 17537,98259	17676 17627,73685
17227 17179,96281	17317 17269,71707	17407 17359,47133	17497 17449,2256	17587 17538,97986	17677 17628,73412
17228 17180,96008	17318 17270,71434	17408 17 3 6 0 ,4 6 8 6	17498 17450,22287	17588 17539,97713	17678 17629,73139
17229 17181,95735	17319 17271,71161	17409 17361,46587	17499 17451,22013	17589 17540,9744	17679 17630,72866
17230 17182,95462	17320 17272,70888	17410 17362,46314	17500 17452,2174	17590 17541,97167	17680 17631,72593
17231 17183,95189	17321 17273,70615	17411 17363,46041	17501 17453,21467	17591 17542,96894	17681 17 6 3 2 ,7 2 3 2
17232 17184,94916	17322 17274,70342	17412 17364,45768	17502 17454,21194	17592 17543,9662	17682 17633,72047
17233 17185,94643	17323 17275,70069	17413 17365,45495	17503 17455,20921	17593 17544,96347	17683 17634,71774
17234 17186,9437	17324 17276,69796	17414 17366,45222	17504 17456,20648	17594 17545,96074	17684 17 6 3 5 , 7 1 5
17235 17187,94097	17325 17277,69523	17415 17367,44949	17505 17457,20375	17595 17546,95801	17685 17636,71227
17236 17188,93824	17326 17278,6925	17416 17368,44676	17506 17458,20102	17596 17547,95528	17686 17637,70954
17237 17189,93551	17327 17279,68977	17417 17369,44403	17507 17459,19829	17597 17548,95255	17687 17638,70681
17238 17190,93278	17328 17280,68704	17418 17370,4413	17508 17460,19556	17598 17549,94982	17688 17639,70408
17239 17191,93005	17329 17281,68431	17419 17371,43857	17509 17461,19283	17599 17550,94709	17689 17640,70135
17240 17192,92732	17330 17282,68158	17420 17372,43584	17510 17462,1901	17600 17551,94436	17690 17641,69862
17241 17193,92459	17331 17283,67885	17421 17373,43311	17511 17463,18737	17601 17552,94163	17691 17642,69589
17242 17194,92186	17332 17284,67612	17422 17374,43038	17512 17464,18464	17602 17553,9389	17692 17643,69316
17243 17195,91913	17333 17285,67339	17423 17375,42765	17513 17465,18191	17603 17554,93617	17693 17644,69043
17244 17196,9164	17334 17286,67066	17424 17376,42492	17514 17466,17918	17604 17555,93344	17694 17 6 4 5 ,6 8 7 7
17245 17197,91367	17335 17287,66793	17425 17377,42219	17515 17467,17645	17605 17556,93071	17695 17646,68497
17246 17198,91093	17336 17288,6652	17426 17378,41946	17516 17468,17372	17606 17557,92798	17696 17647,68224
17247 17199,9082	17337 17289,66247	17427 17379,41673	17517 17469,17099	17607 17558,92525	17697 17648,67951
17248 17200,90547	17338 17290,65973	17428 17 3 8 0 ,4 1 4	17518 17470,16826	17608 17559,92252	17698 17649,67678
17249 17201,90274	17339 17 2 9 1 , 6 5 7	17429 17381,41127	17519 17471,16553	17609 17560,91979	17699 17650,67405
17250 17202,90001	17340 17292,65427	17430 17382,40853	17520 17472,1628	17610 17561,91706	17700 17651,67132
17251 17203,89728	17341 17293,65154	17431 17 3 8 3 ,4 0 5 8	17521 17473,16007	17611 17562,91433	17701 17652,66859
17252 17204,89455	17342 17294,64881	17432 17384,40307	17522 17474,15733	17612 17563,9116	17702 17653,66586
17253 17205,89182	17343 17295,64608	17433 17385,40034	17523 17475,1546	17613 17564,90887	17703 17654,66313
17254 17206,88909	17344 17296,64335	17434 17386,39761	17524 17476,15187	17614 17565,90614	17704 17655,6604
17255 17207,88636	17345 17297,64062	17435 17387,39488	17525 17477,14914	17615 17566,9034	17705 17656,65767
17256 17208,88363	17346 17298,63789	17436 17388,39215	17526 17478,14641	17616 17567,90067	17706 17657,65494
17257 17 2 0 9 ,8 8 0 9	17347 17299,63516	17437 17389,38942	17527 17479,14368	17617 17568,89794	17707 17 6 5 8 ,6 5 2 2
17258 17210,87817	17348 17300,63243	17438 17390,38669	17528 17480,14095	17618 17569,89521	17708 17659,64947
17259 17211,87544	17349 17301,6297	17439 17391,38396	17529 17481,13822	17619 17570,89248	17709 17660,64674
17260 17212,87271	17350 17302,62697	17440 17392,38123	17530 17482,13549	17620 17571,88975	17710 17661,64401
17261 17213,86998	17351 17303,62424	17441 17 3 9 3 ,3 7 8 5	17531 17483,13276	17621 17572,88702	17711 17662,64128
17262 17214,86725	17352 17304,62151	17442 17394,37577	17532 17484,13003	17622 17573,88429	17712 17663,63855
17263 17215,86452	17353 17305,61878	17443 17395,37304	17533 17485,1273	17623 17574,88156	17713 17664,63582
17264 17216,86179	17354 17306,61605	17444 17396,37031	17534 17486,12457	17624 17575,87883	17714 17665,63309
17265 17217,85906	17355 17307,61332	17445 17397,36758	17535 17487,12184	17625 17576,8761	17715 17666,63036
17266 17218,85633	17356 17308,61059	17446 17398,36485	17536 17488,11911	17626 17577,87337	17716 17667,62763
17267 17219,8536	17357 17309,60786	17447 17399,36212	17537 17489,11638	17627 17578,87064	17717 17668,6249
17268 17220,85087	17358 17310,60513	17448 17400,35939	17538 17490,11365	17628 17579,86791	17718 17669,62217
17269 17221,84813	17359 17311,6024	17449 17401,35666	17539 17491,11092	17629 17580,86518	17719 17670,61944
17270 17 2 2 2 ,8 4 5 4	17360 17312,59967	17450 17402,35393	17540 17492,10819	17630 17581,86245	17720 17671,61671
17271 17223,84267	17361 17313,59693	17451 17 4 0 3 ,3 5 1 2	17541 17493,10546	17631 17582,85972	17721 17672,61398
17272 17224,83994	17362 17314,5942	17452 17404,34847	17542 17494,10273	17632 17583,85699	17722 17673,61125
17273 17225,83721	17363 17315,59147	17453 17405,34573	17543 17 4 9 5 , 1	17633 17584,85426	17723 17674,60852
17274 17226,83448	17364 17316,58874	17454 17 4 0 6 ,3 4 3	17544 17496,09727	17634 17585,85153	17724 17675,60579
17275 17227,83175	17365 17317,58601	17455 17407,34027	17545 17497,09453	17635 17586,8488	17725 17676,60306
17276 17228,82902	17366 17318,58328	17456 17408,33754	17546 17498,0918	17636 17587,84607	17726 17677,60033
17277 17229,82629	17367 17319,58055	17457 17409,33481	17547 17499,08907	17637 17588,84334	17727 17 6 7 8 ,5 9 7 6
17278 17230,82356	17368 17320,57782	17458 17410,33208	17548 17500,08634	17638 17589,8406	17728 17679,59487
17279 17231,82083	17369 17321,57509	17459 17411,32935	17549 17501,08361	17639 17590,83787	17729 17680,59214
17280 17 2 3 2 ,8 1 8 1	17370 17322,57236	17460 17412,32662	17550 17502,02088	17640 17591,83514	17730 17681,5894
17281 17233,81537	17371 17323,56963	17461 17413,32389	17551 17503,07815	17641 17592,83241	17731 17682,58667
17282 17234,81264	17372 17324,5669	17462 17414,32116	17552 17504,07542	17642 17593,82968	17732 17683,58394
17283 17235,80991	17373 17325,66417	17463 17415,31843	17553 17505,07269	17643 17594,82695	17733 17684,58121
17284 17236,80718	17374 17326,56144	17464 17416,3157	17554 17506,06996	17644 17595,82422	17734 17685,57848
17285 17237,80445	17375 17327,55871	17465 17417,31297	17555 17507,06723	17645 17596,82149	17735 17686,57575
17286 17238,80172	17376 17328,55598	17466 17418,31024	17556 17508,0645	17646 17597,81876	17736 17687,57302
17287 17239,79899	17377 17329,55325	17467 17419,30751	17557 17509,06177	17647 17598,81603	17737 17688,57029
17288 17240,79626	17378 17330,55052	17468 17420,30478	17558 17510,05904	17648 17599,8133	17738 17689,56756
17289 17241,79353	17379 17331,54779	17469 17421,30205	17559 17511,05631	17649 17600,81057	17739 17690,56483
17290 17 2 4 2 ,7 9 0 8	17380 17332,54506	17470 17422,29932	17560 17512,05358	17650 17601,80784	17740 17691,5621
17291 17243,78807	17381 17333,54233	17471 17423,29659	17561 17513,05085	17651 17602,80511	17741 17692,55937
17292 17244,78533	17382 17 3 3 4 ,5 3 9 6	17472 17424,29386	17562 17514,04812	17652 17603,80238	17742 17693,55664
17293 17245,7826	17383 17335,53687	17473 17425,29113	17563 17515,04539	17653 17604,79965	17743 17694,55391
17294 17246,77987	17384 17336,53413	17474 17426,2884	17564 17516,04266	17654 17605,79692	17744 17695,55118
17295 17247,77714	17385 17 3 3 7 ,5 3 1 4	17475 17427,28567	17565 17517,03993	17655 17606,79419	17745 17696,54845
17296 17248,77441	17386 17338,52867	17476 17428,28293	17566 17518,0372	17656 17607,79146	17746 17697,54572
17297 17249,77168	17387 17339,52594	17477 17429,2802	17567 17519,03447	17657 17608,78873	17747 17698,54299
17298 17250,76895	17388 17340,52321	17478 17430,27747	17568 17520,03174	17658 17 6 0 9 ,7 8 6	17748 17699,54026
17299 17251,76622	17389 17341,52048	17479 17431,27474	17569 17 5 2 1 , 0 2 9	17659 17610,78327	17749 17700,53753
17300 17252,76349	17390 17342,51775	17480 17432,27201	17570 17522,02627	17660 17611,78054	17750 17 7 0 1 ,5 3 4 8
17301 17253,76076	17391 17343,51502	17481 17433,26928	17571 17523,02354	17661 17612,7778	17751 17702,53207
17302 17254,75803	17392 17344,51229	17482 17434,26655	17572 17524,02081	17662 17613,77507	17752 17703,52934
17303 17255,7553	17393 17345,50956	17483 17435,26382	17573 17525,01808	17663 17614,77234	17753 17 7 0 4 ,5 2 6 6
17304 17256,75257	17394 17346,50683	17484 17436,26109	17574 17526,01535	17664 17615,76961	17754 17705,52387

LUNAR RETURNS AND EARTH RETURNS

17755	17706,52114	17845	17796,2754	17935	17886,02967	18025	17975,78393	18115	18065,53819	18205	18155,29245
17756	17707,51841	17846	17797,27267	17936	17887,02694	18026	17976,7812	18116	18066,53546	18206	18156,28972
17757	17708,51568	17847	17798,26994	17937	17888,0242	18027	17977,77847	18117	18067,53273	18207	18157,28699
17758	17709,51295	17848	17799,26721	17938	17889,02147	18028	17978,77574	18118	18068,53	18208	18158,28426
17759	17710,51022	17849	17800,26448	17939	17890,01874	18029	17979,773	18119	18069,52727	18209	18159,28153
17760	17711,50749	17850	17801,26175	17940	17891,01601	18030	17980,77027	18120	18070,52454	18210	18160,2788
17761	17712,50476	17851	17802,25902	17941	17892,01328	18031	17981,76754	18121	18071,5218	18211	18161,27607
17762	17713,50203	17852	17803,25629	17942	17893,01055	18032	17982,76481	18122	18072,51907	18212	18162,27334
17763	17714,4993	17853	17804,25356	17943	17894,00782	18033	17983,76208	18123	18073,51634	18213	18163,27061
17764	17715,49657	17854	17805,25083	17944	17895,00509	18034	17984,75935	18124	18074,51361	18214	18164,26787
17765	17716,49384	17855	17806,2481	17945	17896,00236	18035	17985,75662	18125	18075,51088	18215	18165,26514
17766	17717,49111	17856	17807,24537	17946	17896,99963	18036	17986,75389	18126	18076,50815	18216	18166,26241
17767	17718,48838	17857	17808,24264	17947	17897,9969	18037	17987,75116	18127	18077,50542	18217	18167,25968
17768	17719,48565	17858	17809,23991	17948	17898,99417	18038	17988,74843	18128	18078,50269	18218	18168,25695
17769	17720,48292	17859	17810,23718	17949	17899,99144	18039	17989,7457	18129	18079,49996	18219	18169,25422
17770	17721,48019	17860	17811,23445	17950	17900,98871	18040	17990,74297	18130	18080,49723	18220	18170,25149
17771	17722,47746	17861	17812,23172	17951	17901,98598	18041	17991,74024	18131	18081,4945	18221	18171,24876
17772	17723,47473	17862	17813,22899	17952	17902,98325	18042	17992,73751	18132	18082,49177	18222	18172,24603
17773	17724,472	17863	17814,22626	17953	17903,98052	18043	17993,73478	18133	18083,48904	18223	18173,2433
17774	17725,46927	17864	17815,22353	17954	17904,97779	18044	17994,73205	18134	18084,48631	18224	18174,24057
17775	17726,46654	17865	17816,2208	17955	17905,97506	18045	17995,72932	18135	18085,48358	18225	18175,23784
17776	17727,4638	17866	17817,21807	17956	17906,97233	18046	17996,72659	18136	18086,48085	18226	18176,23511
17777	17728,46107	17867	17818,21534	17957	17907,9696	18047	17997,72386	18137	18087,47812	18227	18177,23238
17778	17729,45834	17868	17819,2126	17958	17908,96687	18048	17998,72113	18138	18088,47539	18228	18178,22965
17779	17730,45561	17869	17820,20987	17959	17909,96414	18049	17999,7184	18139	18089,47266	18229	18179,22692
17780	17731,45288	17870	17821,20714	17960	17910,9614	18050	18000,71567	18140	18090,46993	18230	18180,22419
17781	17732,45015	17871	17822,20441	17961	17911,95867	18051	18001,71294	18141	18091,4672	18231	18181,22146
17782	17733,44742	17872	17823,20168	17962	17912,95594	18052	18002,7102	18142	18092,46447	18232	18182,21873
17783	17734,44469	17873	17824,19895	17963	17913,95321	18053	18003,70747	18143	18093,46174	18233	18183,216
17784	17735,44196	17874	17825,19622	17964	17914,95048	18054	18004,70474	18144	18094,45901	18234	18184,21327
17785	17736,43923	17875	17826,19349	17965	17915,94775	18055	18005,70201	18145	18095,45627	18235	18185,21054
17786	17737,4365	17876	17827,19076	17966	17916,94502	18056	18006,69928	18146	18096,45354	18236	18186,20781
17787	17738,43377	17877	17828,18803	17967	17917,94229	18057	18007,69655	18147	18097,45081	18237	18187,20507
17788	17739,43104	17878	17829,1853	17968	17918,93956	18058	18008,69382	18148	18098,44808	18238	18188,20234
17789	17740,42831	17879	17830,18257	17969	17919,93683	18059	18009,69109	18149	18099,44535	18239	18189,19961
17790	17741,42558	17880	17831,17984	17970	17920,9341	18060	18010,68836	18150	18100,44262	18240	18190,19688
17791	17742,42285	17881	17832,17711	17971	17921,93137	18061	18011,68563	18151	18101,43989	18241	18191,19415
17792	17743,42012	17882	17833,17438	17972	17922,92864	18062	18012,6829	18152	18102,43716	18242	18192,19142
17793	17744,41739	17883	17834,17165	17973	17923,92591	18063	18013,68017	18153	18103,43443	18243	18193,18869
17794	17745,41466	17884	17835,16892	17974	17924,92318	18064	18014,67744	18154	18104,4317	18244	18194,18596
17795	17746,41193	17885	17836,16619	17975	17925,92045	18065	18015,67471	18155	18105,42897	18245	18195,18323
17796	17747,4092	17886	17837,16346	17976	17926,91772	18066	18016,67198	18156	18106,42624	18246	18196,1805
17797	17748,40647	17887	17838,16073	17977	17927,91499	18067	18017,66925	18157	18107,42351	18247	18197,17777
17798	17749,40374	17888	17839,158	17978	17928,91226	18068	18018,66652	18158	18108,42078	18248	18198,17504
17799	17750,401	17889	17840,15527	17979	17929,90953	18069	18019,66379	18159	18109,41805	18249	18199,17231
17800	17751,39827	17890	17841,15254	17980	17930,9068	18070	18020,66106	18160	18110,41532	18250	18200,16958
17801	17752,39554	17891	17842,1498	17981	17931,90407	18071	18021,65833	18161	18111,41259	18251	18201,16685
17802	17753,39281	17892	17843,14707	17982	17932,90134	18072	18022,6556	18162	18112,40986	18252	18202,16412
17803	17754,39008	17893	17844,14434	17983	17933,8986	18073	18023,65287	18163	18113,40713	18253	18203,16139
17804	17755,38735	17894	17845,14161	17984	17934,89587	18074	18024,65014	18164	18114,4044	18254	18204,15866
17805	17756,38462	17895	17846,13888	17985	17935,89314	18075	18025,6474	18165	18115,40167	18255	18205,15593
17806	17757,38189	17896	17847,13615	17986	17936,89041	18076	18026,64467	18166	18116,39894	18256	18206,1532
17807	17758,37916	17897	17848,13342	17987	17937,88768	18077	18027,64194	18167	18117,39621	18257	18207,15047
17808	17759,37643	17898	17849,13069	17988	17938,88495	18078	18028,63921	18168	18118,39347	18258	18208,14774
17809	17760,3737	17899	17850,12796	17989	17939,88222	18079	18029,63648	18169	18119,39074	18259	18209,14501
17810	17761,37097	17900	17851,12523	17990	17940,87949	18080	18030,63375	18170	18120,38801	18260	18210,14227
17811	17762,36824	17901	17852,1225	17991	17941,87676	18081	18031,63102	18171	18121,38528	18261	18211,13954
17812	17763,36551	17902	17853,11977	17992	17942,87403	18082	18032,62829	18172	18122,38255	18262	18212,13681
17813	17764,36278	17903	17854,11704	17993	17943,8713	18083	18033,62556	18173	18123,37982	18263	18213,13408
17814	17765,36005	17904	17855,11431	17994	17944,86857	18084	18034,62283	18174	18124,37709	18264	18214,13135
17815	17766,35732	17905	17856,11158	17995	17945,86584	18085	18035,6201	18175	18125,37436	18265	18215,12862
17816	17767,35459	17906	17857,10885	17996	17946,86311	18086	18036,61737	18176	18126,37163	18266	18216,12589
17817	17768,35186	17907	17858,10612	17997	17947,86038	18087	18037,61464	18177	18127,3689	18267	18217,12316
17818	17769,34913	17908	17859,10339	17998	17948,85765	18088	18038,61191	18178	18128,36617	18268	18218,12043
17819	17770,3464	17909	17860,10066	17999	17949,85492	18089	18039,60918	18179	18129,36344	18269	18219,1177
17820	17771,34367	17910	17861,09793	18000	17950,85219	18090	18040,60645	18180	18130,36071	18270	18220,11497
17821	17772,34094	17911	17862,0952	18001	17951,84946	18091	18041,60372	18181	18131,35798	18271	18221,11224
17822	17773,3382	17912	17863,09247	18002	17952,84673	18092	18042,60099	18182	18132,35525	18272	18222,10951
17823	17774,33547	17913	17864,08974	18003	17953,844	18093	18043,59826	18183	18133,35252	18273	18223,10678
17824	17775,33274	17914	17865,087	18004	17954,84127	18094	18044,59553	18184	18134,34979	18274	18224,10405
17825	17776,33001	17915	17866,08427	18005	17955,83854	18095	18045,5928	18185	18135,34706	18275	18225,10132
17826	17777,32728	17916	17867,08154	18006	17956,8358	18096	18046,59007	18186	18136,34433	18276	18226,09859
17827	17778,32455	17917	17868,07881	18007	17957,83307	18097	18047,58734	18187	18137,3416	18277	18227,09586
17828	17779,32182	17918	17869,07608	18008	17958,83034	18098	18048,5846	18188	18138,33887	18278	18228,09313
17829	17780,31909	17919	17870,07335	18009	17959,82761	18099	18049,58187	18189	18139,33614	18279	18229,0904
17830	17781,31636	17920	17871,07062	18010	17960,62488	18100	18050,57914	18190	18140,33341	18280	18230,08767
17831	17782,31363	17921	17872,06789	18011	17961,82215	18101	18051,57641	18191	18141,33067	18281	18231,08494
17832	17783,3109	17922	17873,06516	18012	17962,81942	18102	18052,57368	18192	18142,32794	18282	18232,08221
17833	17784,30817	17923	17874,06243	18013	17963,81669	18103	18053,57095	18193	18143,32521	18283	18233,07947
17834	17785,30544	17924	17875,0597	18014	17964,81396	18104	18054,56822	18194	18144,32248	18284	18234,07674
17835	17786,30271	17925	17876,05697	18015	17965,81123	18105	18055,56549	18195	18145,31975	18285	18235,07401
17836	17787,29998	17926	17877,05424	18016	17966,8085	18106	18056,56276	18196	18146,31702	18286	18236,07128
17837	17788,29725	17927	17878,05151	18017	17967,80577	18107	18057,56003	18197	18147,31429	18287	18237,06855
17838	17789,29452	17928	17879,04878	18018	17968,80304	18108	18058,5573	18198	18148,31156	18288	18238,06582
17839	17790,29179	17929	17880,04605	18019	17969,80031	18109	18059,55457	18199	18149,30883	18289	18239,06309
17840	17791,28906	17930	17881,04332	18020	17970,79758	18110	18060,55184	18200	18150,3061	18290	18240,06036
17841	17792,28633	17931	17882,04059	18021	17971,79485	18111	18061,54911	18201	18151,30337	18291	18241,05763
17842	17793,2836	17932	17883,03786	18022	17972,79212	18112	18062,54638	18202	18152,30064	18292	18242,0549
17843	17794,28087	17933	17884,03513	18023	17973,78939	18113	18063,54365	18203	18153,29791	18293	18243,05217
17844	17795,27814	17934	17885,0324	18024	17974,78666	18114	18064,54092	18204	18154,29518	18294	18244,04944

TABLE TO FIND OUT THE POINT A IN EARTH RETURNS 191

18295	18245,04671	18385	18334,80097	18475	18424,55523	18565	18514,30949	18655	18604,06375	18745	18693,81801
18296	18246,04398	18386	18335,79824	18476	18425,5525	18566	18515,30676	18656	18605,06102	18746	18694,81528
18297	18247,04125	18387	18336,79551	18477	18426,54977	18567	18516,30403	18657	18606,05829	18747	18695,81255
18298	18248,03852	18388	18337,79278	18478	18427,54704	18568	18517,3013	18658	18607,05556	18748	18696,80982
18299	18249,03579	18389	18338,79005	18479	18428,54431	18569	18518,29857	18659	18608,05283	18749	18697,80709
18300	18250,03306	18390	18339,78732	18480	18429,54158	18570	18519,29584	18660	18609,0501	18750	18698,80436
18301	18251,03033	18391	18340,78459	18481	18430,53885	18571	18520,29311	18661	18610,04737	18751	18699,80163
18302	18252,0276	18392	18341,78186	18482	18431,53612	18572	18521,29038	18662	18611,04464	18752	18700,7989
18303	18253,02487	18393	18342,77913	18483	18432,53339	18573	18522,28765	18663	18612,04191	18753	18701,79617
18304	18254,02214	18394	18343,7764	18484	18433,53066	18574	18523,28492	18664	18613,03918	18754	18702,79344
18305	18255,01941	18395	18344,77367	18485	18434,52793	18575	18524,28219	18665	18614,03645	18755	18703,79071
18306	18256,01667	18396	18345,77094	18486	18435,5252	18576	18525,27946	18666	18615,03372	18756	18704,78798
18307	18257,01394	18397	18346,76821	18487	18436,52247	18577	18526,27673	18667	18616,03099	18757	18705,78525
18308	18258,01121	18398	18347,76547	18488	18437,51974	18578	18527,274	18668	18617,02826	18758	18706,78252
18309	18259,00848	18399	18348,76274	18489	18438,51701	18579	18528,27127	18669	18618,02553	18759	18707,77979
18310	18260,00575	18400	18349,76001	18490	18439,51427	18580	18529,26854	18670	18619,0228	18760	18708,77706
18311	18261,00302	18401	18350,75728	18491	18440,51154	18581	18530,26581	18671	18620,02007	18761	18709,77433
18312	18262,00029	18402	18351,75455	18492	18441,50881	18582	18531,26307	18672	18621,01734	18762	18710,7716
18313	18262,99756	18403	18352,75182	18493	18442,50608	18583	18532,26034	18673	18622,01461	18763	18711,76887
18314	18263,99483	18404	18353,74909	18494	18443,50335	18584	18533,25761	18674	18623,01187	18764	18712,76614
18315	18264,9921	18405	18354,74636	18495	18444,50062	18585	18534,25488	18675	18624,00914	18765	18713,76341
18316	18265,98937	18406	18355,74363	18496	18445,49789	18586	18535,25215	18676	18625,00641	18766	18714,76068
18317	18266,98664	18407	18356,7409	18497	18446,49516	18587	18536,24942	18677	18626,00368	18767	18715,75794
18318	18267,98391	18408	18357,73817	18498	18447,49243	18588	18537,24669	18678	18627,00095	18768	18716,75521
18319	18268,98118	18409	18358,73544	18499	18448,4897	18589	18538,24396	18679	18627,99822	18769	18717,75248
18320	18269,97845	18410	18359,73271	18500	18449,48697	18590	18539,24123	18680	18628,99549	18770	18718,74975
18321	18270,97572	18411	18360,72998	18501	18450,48424	18591	18540,2385	18681	18629,99276	18771	18719,74702
18322	18271,97299	18412	18361,72725	18502	18451,48151	18592	18541,23577	18682	18630,99003	18772	18720,74429
18323	18272,97026	18413	18362,72452	18503	18452,47878	18593	18542,23304	18683	18631,9873	18773	18721,74156
18324	18273,96753	18414	18363,72179	18504	18453,47605	18594	18543,23031	18684	18632,98457	18774	18722,73883
18325	18274,9648	18415	18364,71906	18505	18454,47332	18595	18544,22758	18685	18633,98184	18775	18723,7361
18326	18275,96207	18416	18365,71633	18506	18455,47059	18596	18545,22485	18686	18634,97911	18776	18724,73337
18327	18276,95934	18417	18366,7136	18507	18456,46786	18597	18546,22212	18687	18635,97638	18777	18725,73064
18328	18277,95661	18418	18367,71087	18508	18457,46513	18598	18547,21939	18688	18636,97365	18778	18726,72791
18329	18278,95387	18419	18368,70814	18509	18458,4624	18599	18548,21666	18689	18637,97092	18779	18727,72518
18330	18279,95114	18420	18369,70541	18510	18459,45967	18600	18549,21393	18690	18638,96819	18780	18728,72245
18331	18280,94841	18421	18370,70267	18511	18460,45694	18601	18550,2112	18691	18639,96546	18781	18729,71972
18332	18281,94568	18422	18371,69994	18512	18461,45421	18602	18551,20847	18692	18640,96273	18782	18730,71699
18333	18282,94295	18423	18372,69721	18513	18462,45147	18603	18552,20574	18693	18641,96	18783	18731,71426
18334	18283,94022	18424	18373,69448	18514	18463,44874	18604	18553,20301	18694	18642,95727	18784	18732,71153
18335	18284,93749	18425	18374,69175	18515	18464,44601	18605	18554,20027	18695	18643,95454	18785	18733,7088
18336	18285,93476	18426	18375,68902	18516	18465,44328	18606	18555,19754	18696	18644,95181	18786	18734,70607
18337	18286,93203	18427	18376,68629	18517	18466,44055	18607	18556,19481	18697	18645,94907	18787	18735,70334
18338	18287,9293	18428	18377,68356	18518	18467,43782	18608	18557,19208	18698	18646,94634	18788	18736,70061
18339	18288,92657	18429	18378,68083	18519	18468,43509	18609	18558,18935	18699	18647,94361	18789	18737,69788
18340	18289,92384	18430	18379,6781	18520	18469,43236	18610	18559,18662	18700	18648,94088	18790	18738,69514
18341	18290,92111	18431	18380,67537	18521	18470,42963	18611	18560,18389	18701	18649,93815	18791	18739,69241
18342	18291,91838	18432	18381,67264	18522	18471,4269	18612	18561,18116	18702	18650,93542	18792	18740,68968
18343	18292,91565	18433	18382,66991	18523	18472,42417	18613	18562,17843	18703	18651,93269	18793	18741,68695
18344	18293,91292	18434	18383,66718	18524	18473,42144	18614	18563,1757	18704	18652,92996	18794	18742,68422
18345	18294,91019	18435	18384,66445	18525	18474,41871	18615	18564,17297	18705	18653,92723	18795	18743,68149
18346	18295,90746	18436	18385,66172	18526	18475,41598	18616	18565,17024	18706	18654,9245	18796	18744,67876
18347	18296,90473	18437	18386,65899	18527	18476,41325	18617	18566,16751	18707	18655,92177	18797	18745,67603
18348	18297,902	18438	18387,65626	18528	18477,41052	18618	18567,16478	18708	18656,91904	18798	18746,6733
18349	18298,89927	18439	18388,65353	18529	18478,40779	18619	18568,16205	18709	18657,91631	18799	18747,67057
18350	18299,89654	18440	18389,6508	18530	18479,40506	18620	18569,15932	18710	18658,91358	18800	18748,66784
18351	18300,89381	18441	18390,64807	18531	18480,40233	18621	18570,15659	18711	18659,91085	18801	18749,66511
18352	18301,89107	18442	18391,64534	18532	18481,3996	18622	18571,15386	18712	18660,90812	18802	18750,66238
18353	18302,88834	18443	18392,64261	18533	18482,39687	18623	18572,15113	18713	18661,90539	18803	18751,65965
18354	18303,88561	18444	18393,63987	18534	18483,39414	18624	18573,1484	18714	18662,90266	18804	18752,65692
18355	18304,88288	18445	18394,63714	18535	18484,39141	18625	18574,14567	18715	18663,89993	18805	18753,65419
18356	18305,88015	18446	18395,63441	18536	18485,38867	18626	18575,14294	18716	18664,8972	18806	18754,65146
18357	18306,87742	18447	18396,63168	18537	18486,38594	18627	18576,14021	18717	18665,89447	18807	18755,64873
18358	18307,87469	18448	18397,62895	18538	18487,38321	18628	18577,13747	18718	18666,89174	18808	18756,646
18359	18308,87196	18449	18398,62622	18539	18488,38048	18629	18578,13474	18719	18667,88901	18809	18757,64327
18360	18309,86923	18450	18399,62349	18540	18489,37775	18630	18579,13201	18720	18668,88628	18810	18758,64054
18361	18310,8665	18451	18400,62076	18541	18490,37502	18631	18580,12928	18721	18669,88354	18811	18759,63781
18362	18311,86377	18452	18401,61803	18542	18491,37229	18632	18581,12655	18722	18670,88081	18812	18760,63508
18363	18312,86104	18453	18402,6153	18543	18492,36956	18633	18582,12382	18723	18671,87808	18813	18761,63234
18364	18313,85831	18454	18403,61257	18544	18493,36683	18634	18583,12109	18724	18672,87535	18814	18762,62961
18365	18314,85558	18455	18404,60984	18545	18494,3641	18635	18584,11836	18725	18673,87262	18815	18763,62688
18366	18315,85285	18456	18405,60711	18546	18495,36137	18636	18585,11563	18726	18674,86989	18816	18764,62415
18367	18316,85012	18457	18406,60438	18547	18496,35864	18637	18586,1129	18727	18675,86716	18817	18765,62142
18368	18317,84739	18458	18407,60165	18548	18497,35591	18638	18587,11017	18728	18676,86443	18818	18766,61869
18369	18318,84466	18459	18408,59892	18549	18498,35318	18639	18588,10744	18729	18677,8617	18819	18767,61596
18370	18319,84193	18460	18409,59619	18550	18499,35045	18640	18589,10471	18730	18678,85897	18820	18768,61323
18371	18320,8392	18461	18410,59346	18551	18500,34772	18641	18590,10198	18731	18679,85624	18821	18769,6105
18372	18321,83647	18462	18411,59073	18552	18501,34499	18642	18591,09925	18732	18680,85351	18822	18770,60777
18373	18322,83374	18463	18412,588	18553	18502,34226	18643	18592,09652	18733	18681,85078	18823	18771,60504
18374	18323,83101	18464	18413,58527	18554	18503,33953	18644	18593,09379	18734	18682,84805	18824	18772,60231
18375	18324,82827	18465	18414,58254	18555	18504,3368	18645	18594,09106	18735	18683,84532	18825	18773,59958
18376	18325,82554	18466	18415,57981	18556	18505,33407	18646	18595,08833	18736	18684,84259	18826	18774,59685
18377	18326,82281	18467	18416,57707	18557	18506,33134	18647	18596,0856	18737	18685,83986	18827	18775,59412
18378	18327,82008	18468	18417,57434	18558	18507,32861	18648	18597,08287	18738	18686,83713	18828	18776,59139
18379	18328,81735	18469	18418,57161	18559	18508,32587	18649	18598,08014	18739	18687,8344	18829	18777,58866
18380	18329,81462	18470	18419,56888	18560	18509,32314	18650	18599,07741	18740	18688,83167	18830	18778,58593
18381	18330,81189	18471	18420,56615	18561	18510,32041	18651	18600,07467	18741	18689,82894	18831	18779,5832
18382	18331,80916	18472	18421,56342	18562	18511,31768	18652	18601,07194	18742	18690,82621	18832	18780,58047
18383	18332,80643	18473	18422,56069	18563	18512,31495	18653	18602,06921	18743	18691,82348	18833	18781,57774
18384	18333,8037	18474	18423,55796	18564	18513,31222	18654	18603,06648	18744	18692,82074	18834	18782,57501

LUNAR RETURNS AND EARTH RETURNS

18835	18783,57228	18925	18873,32654	19015	18963,0808	19105	19052,83506	19195	19142,58932	19285	19232,34358
18836	18784,56954	18926	18874,32381	19016	18964,07807	19106	19053,83233	19196	19143,58659	19286	19233,34085
18837	18785,56681	18927	18875,32108	19017	18965,07534	19107	19054,8296	19197	19144,58386	19287	19234,33812
18838	18786,56408	18928	18876,31834	19018	18966,07261	19108	19055,82687	19198	19145,58113	19288	19235,33539
18839	18787,56135	18929	18877,31561	19019	18967,06988	19109	19056,82414	19199	19146,5784	19289	19236,33266
18840	18788,55862	18930	18878,31288	19020	18968,06714	19110	19057,82141	19200	19147,57567	19290	19237,32993
18841	18789,55589	18931	18879,31015	19021	18969,06441	19111	19058,81868	19201	19148,57294	19291	19238,3272
18842	18790,55316	18932	18880,30742	19022	18970,06168	19112	19059,81594	19202	19149,57021	19292	19239,32447
18843	18791,55043	18933	18881,30469	19023	18971,05895	19113	19060,81321	19203	19150,56748	19293	19240,32174
18844	18792,5477	18934	18882,30196	19024	18972,05622	19114	19061,81048	19204	19151,56474	19294	19241,31901
18845	18793,54497	18935	18883,29923	19025	18973,05349	19115	19062,80775	19205	19152,56201	19295	19242,31628
18846	18794,54224	18936	18884,2965	19026	18974,05076	19116	19063,80502	19206	19153,55928	19296	19243,31355
18847	18795,53951	18937	18885,29377	19027	18975,04803	19117	19064,80229	19207	19154,55655	19297	19244,31081
18848	18796,53678	18938	18886,29104	19028	18976,0453	19118	19065,79956	19208	19155,55382	19298	19245,30808
18849	18797,53405	18939	18887,28831	19029	18977,04257	19119	19066,79683	19209	19156,55109	19299	19246,30535
18850	18798,53132	18940	18888,28558	19030	18978,03984	19120	19067,7941	19210	19157,54836	19300	19247,30262
18851	18799,52859	18941	18889,28285	19031	18979,03711	19121	19068,79137	19211	19158,54563	19301	19248,29989
18852	18800,52586	18942	18890,28012	19032	18980,03438	19122	19069,78864	19212	19159,5429	19302	19249,29716
18853	18801,52313	18943	18891,27739	19033	18981,03165	19123	19070,78591	19213	19160,54017	19303	19250,29443
18854	18802,5204	18944	18892,27466	19034	18982,02892	19124	19071,78318	19214	19161,53744	19304	19251,2917
18855	18803,51767	18945	18893,27193	19035	18983,02619	19125	19072,78045	19215	19162,53471	19305	19252,28897
18856	18804,51494	18946	18894,2692	19036	18984,02346	19126	19073,77772	19216	19163,53198	19306	19253,28624
18857	18805,51221	18947	18895,26647	19037	18985,02073	19127	19074,77499	19217	19164,52925	19307	19254,28351
18858	18806,50948	18948	18896,26374	19038	18986,018	19128	19075,77226	19218	19165,52652	19308	19255,28078
18859	18807,50674	18949	18897,26101	19039	18987,01527	19129	19076,76953	19219	19166,52379	19309	19256,27805
18860	18808,50401	18950	18898,25828	19040	18988,01254	19130	19077,7668	19220	19167,52106	19310	19257,27532
18861	18809,50128	18951	18899,25554	19041	18989,00981	19131	19078,76407	19221	19168,51833	19311	19258,27259
18862	18810,49855	18952	18900,25281	19042	18990,00708	19132	19079,76134	19222	19169,5156	19312	19259,26986
18863	18811,49582	18953	18901,25008	19043	18991,00434	19133	19080,75861	19223	19170,51287	19313	19260,26713
18864	18812,49309	18954	18902,24735	19044	18992,00161	19134	19081,75588	19224	19171,51014	19314	19261,2644
18865	18813,49036	18955	18903,24462	19045	18992,99888	19135	19082,75314	19225	19172,50741	19315	19262,26167
18866	18814,48763	18956	18904,24189	19046	18993,99615	19136	19083,75041	19226	19173,50468	19316	19263,25894
18867	18815,4849	18957	18905,23916	19047	18994,99342	19137	19084,74768	19227	19174,50194	19317	19264,25621
18868	18816,48217	18958	18906,23643	19048	18995,99069	19138	19085,74495	19228	19175,49921	19318	19265,25348
18869	18817,47944	18959	18907,2337	19049	18996,98796	19139	19086,74222	19229	19176,49648	19319	19266,25075
18870	18818,47671	18960	18908,23097	19050	18997,98523	19140	19087,73949	19230	19177,49375	19320	19267,24801
18871	18819,47398	18961	18909,22824	19051	18998,9825	19141	19088,73676	19231	19178,49102	19321	19268,24528
18872	18820,47125	18962	18910,22551	19052	18999,97977	19142	19089,73403	19232	19179,48829	19322	19269,24255
18873	18821,46852	18963	18911,22278	19053	19000,97704	19143	19090,7313	19233	19180,48556	19323	19270,23982
18874	18822,46579	18964	18912,22005	19054	19001,97431	19144	19091,72857	19234	19181,48283	19324	19271,23709
18875	18823,46306	18965	18913,21732	19055	19002,97158	19145	19092,72584	19235	19182,4801	19325	19272,23436
18876	18824,46033	18966	18914,21459	19056	19003,96885	19146	19093,72311	19236	19183,47737	19326	19273,23163
18877	18825,4576	18967	18915,21186	19057	19004,96612	19147	19094,72038	19237	19184,47464	19327	19274,2289
18878	18826,45487	18968	18916,20913	19058	19005,96339	19148	19095,71765	19238	19185,47191	19328	19275,22617
18879	18827,45214	18969	18917,2064	19059	19006,96066	19149	19096,71492	19239	19186,46918	19329	19276,22344
18880	18828,44941	18970	18918,20367	19060	19007,95793	19150	19097,71219	19240	19187,46645	19330	19277,22071
18881	18829,44668	18971	18919,20094	19061	19008,9552	19151	19098,70946	19241	19188,46372	19331	19278,21798
18882	18830,44394	18972	18920,19821	19062	19009,95247	19152	19099,70673	19242	19189,46099	19332	19279,21525
18883	18831,44121	18973	18921,19548	19063	19010,94974	19153	19100,704	19243	19190,45826	19333	19280,21252
18884	18832,43848	18974	18922,19274	19064	19011,94701	19154	19101,70127	19244	19191,45553	19334	19281,20979
18885	18833,43575	18975	18923,19001	19065	19012,94428	19155	19102,69854	19245	19192,4528	19335	19282,20706
18886	18834,43302	18976	18924,18728	19066	19013,94154	19156	19103,69581	19246	19193,45007	19336	19283,20433
18887	18835,43029	18977	18925,18455	19067	19014,93881	19157	19104,69308	19247	19194,44734	19337	19284,2016
18888	18836,42756	18978	18926,18182	19068	19015,93608	19158	19105,69034	19248	19195,44461	19338	19285,19887
18889	18837,42483	18979	18927,17909	19069	19016,93335	19159	19106,68761	19249	19196,44188	19339	19286,19614
18890	18838,4221	18980	18928,17636	19070	19017,93062	19160	19107,68488	19250	19197,43914	19340	19287,19341
18891	18839,41937	18981	18929,17363	19071	19018,92789	19161	19108,68215	19251	19198,43641	19341	19288,19068
18892	18840,41664	18982	18930,1709	19072	19019,92516	19162	19109,67942	19252	19199,43368	19342	19289,18795
18893	18841,41391	18983	18931,16817	19073	19020,92243	19163	19110,67669	19253	19200,43095	19343	19290,18521
18894	18842,41118	18984	18932,16544	19074	19021,9197	19164	19111,67396	19254	19201,42822	19344	19291,18248
18895	18843,40845	18985	18933,16271	19075	19022,91697	19165	19112,67123	19255	19202,42549	19345	19292,17975
18896	18844,40572	18986	18934,15998	19076	19023,91424	19166	19113,6685	19256	19203,42276	19346	19293,17702
18897	18845,40299	18987	18935,15725	19077	19024,91151	19167	19114,66577	19257	19204,42003	19347	19294,17429
18898	18846,40026	18988	18936,15452	19078	19025,90878	19168	19115,66304	19258	19205,4173	19348	19295,17156
18899	18847,39753	18989	18937,15179	19079	19026,90605	19169	19116,66031	19259	19206,41457	19349	19296,16883
18900	18848,3948	18990	18938,14906	19080	19027,90332	19170	19117,65758	19260	19207,41184	19350	19297,1661
18901	18849,39207	18991	18939,14633	19081	19028,90059	19171	19118,65485	19261	19208,40911	19351	19298,16337
18902	18850,38934	18992	18940,1436	19082	19029,89786	19172	19119,65212	19262	19209,40638	19352	19299,16064
18903	18851,38661	18993	18941,14087	19083	19030,89513	19173	19120,64939	19263	19210,40365	19353	19300,15791
18904	18852,38388	18994	18942,13814	19084	19031,8924	19174	19121,64666	19264	19211,40092	19354	19301,15518
18905	18853,38114	18995	18943,13541	19085	19032,88967	19175	19122,64393	19265	19212,39819	19355	19302,15245
18906	18854,37841	18996	18944,13268	19086	19033,88694	19176	19123,6412	19266	19213,39546	19356	19303,14972
18907	18855,37568	18997	18945,12994	19087	19034,88421	19177	19124,63847	19267	19214,39273	19357	19304,14699
18908	18856,37295	18998	18946,12721	19088	19035,88148	19178	19125,63574	19268	19215,39	19358	19305,14426
18909	18857,37022	18999	18947,12448	19089	19036,87874	19179	19126,63301	19269	19216,38727	19359	19306,14153
18910	18858,36749	19000	18948,12175	19090	19037,87601	19180	19127,63028	19270	19217,38454	19360	19307,1388
18911	18859,36476	19001	18949,11902	19091	19038,87328	19181	19128,62754	19271	19218,38181	19361	19308,13607
18912	18860,36203	19002	18950,11629	19092	19039,87055	19182	19129,62481	19272	19219,37908	19362	19309,13334
18913	18861,3593	19003	18951,11356	19093	19040,86782	19183	19130,62208	19273	19220,37634	19363	19310,13061
18914	18862,35657	19004	18952,11083	19094	19041,86509	19184	19131,61935	19274	19221,37361	19364	19311,12788
18915	18863,35384	19005	18953,1081	19095	19042,86236	19185	19132,61662	19275	19222,37088	19365	19312,12515
18916	18864,35111	19006	18954,10537	19096	19043,85963	19186	19133,61389	19276	19223,36815	19366	19313,12241
18917	18865,34838	19007	18955,10264	19097	19044,8569	19187	19134,61116	19277	19224,36542	19367	19314,11968
18918	18866,34565	19008	18956,09991	19098	19045,85417	19188	19135,60843	19278	19225,36269	19368	19315,11695
18919	18867,34292	19009	18957,09718	19099	19046,85144	19189	19136,6057	19279	19226,35996	19369	19316,11422
18920	18868,34019	19010	18958,09445	19100	19047,84871	19190	19137,60297	19280	19227,35723	19370	19317,11149
18921	18869,33746	19011	18959,09172	19101	19048,84598	19191	19138,60024	19281	19228,3545	19371	19318,10876
18922	18870,33473	19012	18960,08899	19102	19049,84325	19192	19139,59751	19282	19229,35177	19372	19319,10603
18923	18871,332	19013	18961,08626	19103	19050,84052	19193	19140,59478	19283	19230,34904	19373	19320,1033
18924	18872,32927	19014	18962,08353	19104	19051,83779	19194	19141,59205	19284	19231,34631	19374	19321,10057

TABLE TO FIND OUT THE POINT A IN EARTH RETURNS 193

19375	19322,09784	19465	19411,8521	19555	19501,60636	19645	19591,36062	19735	19681,11488	19825	19770,86915
19376	19323,09511	19466	19412,84937	19556	19502,60363	19646	19592,35789	19736	19682,11215	19826	19771,86641
19377	19324,09238	19467	19413,84664	19557	19503,6009	19647	19593,35516	19737	19683,10942	19827	19772,86368
19378	19325,08965	19468	19414,84391	19558	19504,59817	19648	19594,35243	19738	19684,10669	19828	19773,86095
19379	19326,08692	19469	19415,84118	19559	19505,59544	19649	19595,3497	19739	19685,10396	19829	19774,85822
19380	19327,08419	19470	19416,83845	19560	19506,59271	19650	19596,34697	19740	19686,10123	19830	19775,85549
19381	19328,08146	19471	19417,83572	19561	19507,58998	19651	19597,34424	19741	19687,0985	19831	19776,85276
19382	19329,07873	19472	19418,83299	19562	19508,58725	19652	19598,34151	19742	19688,09577	19832	19777,85003
19383	19330,076	19473	19419,83026	19563	19509,58452	19653	19599,33878	19743	19689,09304	19833	19778,8473
19384	19331,07327	19474	19420,82753	19564	19510,58179	19654	19600,33605	19744	19690,09031	19834	19779,84457
19385	19332,07054	19475	19421,8248	19565	19511,57906	19655	19601,33332	19745	19691,08758	19835	19780,84184
19386	19333,06781	19476	19422,82207	19566	19512,57633	19656	19602,33059	19746	19692,08485	19836	19781,83911
19387	19334,06508	19477	19423,81934	19567	19513,5736	19657	19603,32786	19747	19693,08212	19837	19782,83638
19388	19335,06235	19478	19424,81661	19568	19514,57087	19658	19604,32513	19748	19694,07939	19838	19783,83365
19389	19336,05961	19479	19425,81388	19569	19515,56814	19659	19605,3224	19749	19695,07666	19839	19784,83092
19390	19337,05688	19480	19426,81115	19570	19516,56541	19660	19606,31967	19750	19696,07393	19840	19785,82819
19391	19338,05415	19481	19427,80841	19571	19517,56268	19661	19607,31694	19751	19697,0712	19841	19786,82546
19392	19339,05142	19482	19428,80568	19572	19518,55995	19662	19608,31421	19752	19698,06847	19842	19787,82273
19393	19340,04869	19483	19429,80295	19573	19519,55721	19663	19609,31148	19753	19699,06574	19843	19788,82
19394	19341,04596	19484	19430,80022	19574	19520,55448	19664	19610,30875	19754	19700,06301	19844	19789,81727
19395	19342,04323	19485	19431,79749	19575	19521,55175	19665	19611,30601	19755	19701,06028	19845	19790,81454
19396	19343,0405	19486	19432,79476	19576	19522,54902	19666	19612,30328	19756	19702,05755	19846	19791,81181
19397	19344,03777	19487	19433,79203	19577	19523,54629	19667	19613,30055	19757	19703,05481	19847	19792,80908
19398	19345,03504	19488	19434,7893	19578	19524,54356	19668	19614,29782	19758	19704,05208	19848	19793,80635
19399	19346,03231	19489	19435,78657	19579	19525,54083	19669	19615,29509	19759	19705,04935	19849	19794,80361
19400	19347,02958	19490	19436,78384	19580	19526,5381	19670	19616,29236	19760	19706,04662	19850	19795,80088
19401	19348,02685	19491	19437,78111	19581	19527,53537	19671	19617,28963	19761	19707,04389	19851	19796,79815
19402	19349,02412	19492	19438,77838	19582	19528,53264	19672	19618,2869	19762	19708,04116	19852	19797,79542
19403	19350,02139	19493	19439,77565	19583	19529,52991	19673	19619,28417	19763	19709,03843	19853	19798,79269
19404	19351,01866	19494	19440,77292	19584	19530,52718	19674	19620,28144	19764	19710,0357	19854	19799,78996
19405	19352,01593	19495	19441,77019	19585	19531,52445	19675	19621,27871	19765	19711,03297	19855	19800,78723
19406	19353,0132	19496	19442,76746	19586	19532,52172	19676	19622,27598	19766	19712,03024	19856	19801,7845
19407	19354,01047	19497	19443,76473	19587	19533,51899	19677	19623,27325	19767	19713,02751	19857	19802,78177
19408	19355,00774	19498	19444,762	19588	19534,51626	19678	19624,27052	19768	19714,02478	19858	19803,77904
19409	19356,00501	19499	19445,75927	19589	19535,51353	19679	19625,26779	19769	19715,02205	19859	19804,77631
19410	19357,00228	19500	19446,75654	19590	19536,5108	19680	19626,26506	19770	19716,01932	19860	19805,77358
19411	19357,99955	19501	19447,75381	19591	19537,50807	19681	19627,26233	19771	19717,01659	19861	19806,77085
19412	19358,99681	19502	19448,75108	19592	19538,50534	19682	19628,2596	19772	19718,01386	19862	19807,76812
19413	19359,99408	19503	19449,74835	19593	19539,50261	19683	19629,25687	19773	19719,01113	19863	19808,76539
19414	19360,99135	19504	19450,74561	19594	19540,49988	19684	19630,25414	19774	19720,0084	19864	19809,76266
19415	19361,98862	19505	19451,74288	19595	19541,49715	19685	19631,25141	19775	19721,00567	19865	19810,75993
19416	19362,98589	19506	19452,74015	19596	19542,49441	19686	19632,24868	19776	19722,00294	19866	19811,7572
19417	19363,98316	19507	19453,73742	19597	19543,49168	19687	19633,24595	19777	19723,00021	19867	19812,75447
19418	19364,98043	19508	19454,73469	19598	19544,48895	19688	19634,24321	19778	19723,99748	19868	19813,75174
19419	19365,9777	19509	19455,73196	19599	19545,48622	19689	19635,24048	19779	19724,99475	19869	19814,74901
19420	19366,97497	19510	19456,72923	19600	19546,48349	19690	19636,23775	19780	19725,99201	19870	19815,74628
19421	19367,97224	19511	19457,7265	19601	19547,48076	19691	19637,23502	19781	19726,98928	19871	19816,74355
19422	19368,96951	19512	19458,72377	19602	19548,47803	19692	19638,23229	19782	19727,98655	19872	19817,74082
19423	19369,96678	19513	19459,72104	19603	19549,4753	19693	19639,22956	19783	19728,98382	19873	19818,73808
19424	19370,96405	19514	19460,71831	19604	19550,47257	19694	19640,22683	19784	19729,98109	19874	19819,73535
19425	19371,96132	19515	19461,71558	19605	19551,46984	19695	19641,2241	19785	19730,97836	19875	19820,73262
19426	19372,95859	19516	19462,71285	19606	19552,46711	19696	19642,22137	19786	19731,97563	19876	19821,72989
19427	19373,95586	19517	19463,71012	19607	19553,46438	19697	19643,21864	19787	19732,9729	19877	19822,72716
19428	19374,95313	19518	19464,70739	19608	19554,46165	19698	19644,21591	19788	19733,97017	19878	19823,72443
19429	19375,9504	19519	19465,70466	19609	19555,45892	19699	19645,21318	19789	19734,96744	19879	19824,7217
19430	19376,94767	19520	19466,70193	19610	19556,45619	19700	19646,21045	19790	19735,96471	19880	19825,71897
19431	19377,94494	19521	19467,6992	19611	19557,45346	19701	19647,20772	19791	19736,96198	19881	19826,71624
19432	19378,94221	19522	19468,69647	19612	19558,45073	19702	19648,20499	19792	19737,95925	19882	19827,71351
19433	19379,93948	19523	19469,69374	19613	19559,448	19703	19649,20226	19793	19738,95652	19883	19828,71078
19434	19380,93675	19524	19470,69101	19614	19560,44527	19704	19650,19953	19794	19739,95379	19884	19829,70805
19435	19381,93401	19525	19471,68828	19615	19561,44254	19705	19651,1968	19795	19740,95106	19885	19830,70532
19436	19382,93128	19526	19472,68555	19616	19562,43981	19706	19652,19407	19796	19741,94833	19886	19831,70259
19437	19383,92855	19527	19473,68281	19617	19563,43708	19707	19653,19134	19797	19742,9456	19887	19832,69986
19438	19384,92582	19528	19474,68008	19618	19564,43435	19708	19654,18861	19798	19743,94287	19888	19833,69713
19439	19385,92309	19529	19475,67735	19619	19565,43161	19709	19655,18588	19799	19744,94014	19889	19834,6944
19440	19386,92036	19530	19476,67462	19620	19566,42888	19710	19656,18315	19800	19745,93741	19890	19835,69167
19441	19387,91763	19531	19477,67189	19621	19567,42615	19711	19657,18041	19801	19746,93468	19891	19836,68894
19442	19388,9149	19532	19478,66916	19622	19568,42342	19712	19658,17768	19802	19747,93195	19892	19837,68621
19443	19389,91217	19533	19479,66643	19623	19569,42069	19713	19659,17495	19803	19748,92921	19893	19838,68348
19444	19390,90944	19534	19480,6637	19624	19570,41796	19714	19660,17222	19804	19749,92648	19894	19839,68075
19445	19391,90671	19535	19481,66097	19625	19571,41523	19715	19661,16949	19805	19750,92375	19895	19840,67802
19446	19392,90398	19536	19482,65824	19626	19572,4125	19716	19662,16676	19806	19751,92102	19896	19841,67528
19447	19393,90125	19537	19483,65551	19627	19573,40977	19717	19663,16403	19807	19752,91829	19897	19842,67255
19448	19394,89852	19538	19484,65278	19628	19574,40704	19718	19664,1613	19808	19753,91556	19898	19843,66982
19449	19395,89579	19539	19485,65005	19629	19575,40431	19719	19665,15857	19809	19754,91283	19899	19844,66709
19450	19396,89306	19540	19486,64732	19630	19576,40158	19720	19666,15584	19810	19755,9101	19900	19845,66436
19451	19397,89033	19541	19487,64459	19631	19577,39885	19721	19667,15311	19811	19756,90737	19901	19846,66163
19452	19398,8876	19542	19488,64186	19632	19578,39612	19722	19668,15038	19812	19757,90464	19902	19847,6589
19453	19399,88487	19543	19489,63913	19633	19579,39339	19723	19669,14765	19813	19758,90191	19903	19848,65617
19454	19400,88214	19544	19490,6364	19634	19580,39066	19724	19670,14492	19814	19759,89918	19904	19849,65344
19455	19401,87941	19545	19491,63367	19635	19581,38793	19725	19671,14219	19815	19760,89645	19905	19850,65071
19456	19402,87668	19546	19492,63094	19636	19582,3852	19726	19672,13946	19816	19761,89372	19906	19851,64798
19457	19403,87395	19547	19493,62821	19637	19583,38247	19727	19673,13673	19817	19762,89099	19907	19852,64525
19458	19404,87121	19548	19494,62548	19638	19584,37974	19728	19674,134	19818	19763,88826	19908	19853,64252
19459	19405,86848	19549	19495,62275	19639	19585,37701	19729	19675,13127	19819	19764,88553	19909	19854,63979
19460	19406,86575	19550	19496,62001	19640	19586,37428	19730	19676,12854	19820	19765,8828	19910	19855,63706
19461	19407,86302	19551	19497,61728	19641	19587,37155	19731	19677,12581	19821	19766,88007	19911	19856,63433
19462	19408,86029	19552	19498,61455	19642	19588,36881	19732	19678,12308	19822	19767,87734	19912	19857,6316
19463	19409,85756	19553	19499,61182	19643	19589,36608	19733	19679,12035	19823	19768,87461	19913	19858,62887
19464	19410,85483	19554	19500,60909	19644	19590,36335	19734	19680,11761	19824	19769,87188	19914	19859,62614

LUNAR RETURNS AND EARTH RETURNS

19915	19860,62341	20005	19950,37767	20095	20040,13193	20185	20129,88619	20275	20219,64045	20365	20309,39471
19916	19861,62068	20006	19951,37494	20096	20041,1292	20186	20130,88346	20276	20220,63772	20366	20310,39198
19917	19862,61795	20007	19952,37221	20097	20042,12647	20187	20131,88073	20277	20221,63499	20367	20311,38925
19918	19863,61522	20008	19953,36948	20098	20043,12374	20188	20132,878	20278	20222,63226	20368	20312,38652
19919	19864,61248	20009	19954,36675	20099	20044,12101	20189	20133,87527	20279	20223,62953	20369	20313,38379
19920	19865,60975	20010	19955,36402	20100	20045,11828	20190	20134,87254	20280	20224,6268	20370	20314,38106
19921	19866,60702	20011	19956,36128	20101	20046,11555	20191	20135,86981	20281	20225,62407	20371	20315,37833
19922	19867,60429	20012	19957,35855	20102	20047,11282	20192	20136,86708	20282	20226,62134	20372	20316,3756
19923	19868,60156	20013	19958,35582	20103	20048,11008	20193	20137,86435	20283	20227,61861	20373	20317,37287
19924	19869,59883	20014	19959,35309	20104	20049,10735	20194	20138,86162	20284	20228,61588	20374	20318,37014
19925	19870,5961	20015	19960,35036	20105	20050,10462	20195	20139,85888	20285	20229,61315	20375	20319,36741
19926	19871,59337	20016	19961,34763	20106	20051,10189	20196	20140,85615	20286	20230,61042	20376	20320,36468
19927	19872,59064	20017	19962,3449	20107	20052,09916	20197	20141,85342	20287	20231,60768	20377	20321,36195
19928	19873,58791	20018	19963,34217	20108	20053,09643	20198	20142,85069	20288	20232,60495	20378	20322,35922
19929	19874,58518	20019	19964,33944	20109	20054,0937	20199	20143,84796	20289	20233,60222	20379	20323,35648
19930	19875,58245	20020	19965,33671	20110	20055,09097	20200	20144,84523	20290	20234,59949	20380	20324,35375
19931	19876,57972	20021	19966,33398	20111	20056,08824	20201	20145,8425	20291	20235,59676	20381	20325,35102
19932	19877,57699	20022	19967,33125	20112	20057,08551	20202	20146,83977	20292	20236,59403	20382	20326,34829
19933	19878,57426	20023	19968,32852	20113	20058,08278	20203	20147,83704	20293	20237,5913	20383	20327,34556
19934	19879,57153	20024	19969,32579	20114	20059,08005	20204	20148,83431	20294	20238,58857	20384	20328,34283
19935	19880,5688	20025	19970,32306	20115	20060,07732	20205	20149,83158	20295	20239,58584	20385	20329,3401
19936	19881,56607	20026	19971,32033	20116	20061,07459	20206	20150,82885	20296	20240,58311	20386	20330,33737
19937	19882,56334	20027	19972,3176	20117	20062,07186	20207	20151,82612	20297	20241,58038	20387	20331,33464
19938	19883,56061	20028	19973,31487	20118	20063,06913	20208	20152,82339	20298	20242,57765	20388	20332,33191
19939	19884,55788	20029	19974,31214	20119	20064,0664	20209	20153,82066	20299	20243,57492	20389	20333,32918
19940	19885,55515	20030	19975,30941	20120	20065,06367	20210	20154,81793	20300	20244,57219	20390	20334,32645
19941	19886,55242	20031	19976,30668	20121	20066,06094	20211	20155,8152	20301	20245,56946	20391	20335,32372
19942	19887,54968	20032	19977,30395	20122	20067,05821	20212	20156,81247	20302	20246,56673	20392	20336,32099
19943	19888,54695	20033	19978,30122	20123	20068,05548	20213	20157,80974	20303	20247,564	20393	20337,31826
19944	19889,54422	20034	19979,29848	20124	20069,05275	20214	20158,80701	20304	20248,56127	20394	20338,31553
19945	19890,54149	20035	19980,29575	20125	20070,05002	20215	20159,80428	20305	20249,55854	20395	20339,3128
19946	19891,53876	20036	19981,29302	20126	20071,04728	20216	20160,80155	20306	20250,55581	20396	20340,31007
19947	19892,53603	20037	19982,29029	20127	20072,04455	20217	20161,79882	20307	20251,55308	20397	20341,30734
19948	19893,5333	20038	19983,28756	20128	20073,04182	20218	20162,79608	20308	20252,55035	20398	20342,30461
19949	19894,53057	20039	19984,28483	20129	20074,03909	20219	20163,79335	20309	20253,54762	20399	20343,30188
19950	19895,52784	20040	19985,2821	20130	20075,03636	20220	20164,79062	20310	20254,54488	20400	20344,29915
19951	19896,52511	20041	19986,27937	20131	20076,03363	20221	20165,78789	20311	20255,54215	20401	20345,29642
19952	19897,52238	20042	19987,27664	20132	20077,0309	20222	20166,78516	20312	20256,53942	20402	20346,29368
19953	19898,51965	20043	19988,27391	20133	20078,02817	20223	20167,78243	20313	20257,53669	20403	20347,29095
19954	19899,51692	20044	19989,27118	20134	20079,02544	20224	20168,7797	20314	20258,53396	20404	20348,28822
19955	19900,51419	20045	19990,26845	20135	20080,02271	20225	20169,77697	20315	20259,53123	20405	20349,28549
19956	19901,51146	20046	19991,26572	20136	20081,01998	20226	20170,77424	20316	20260,5285	20406	20350,28276
19957	19902,50873	20047	19992,26299	20137	20082,01725	20227	20171,77151	20317	20261,52577	20407	20351,28003
19958	19903,506	20048	19993,26026	20138	20083,01452	20228	20172,76878	20318	20262,52304	20408	20352,2773
19959	19904,50327	20049	19994,25753	20139	20084,01179	20229	20173,76605	20319	20263,52031	20409	20353,27457
19960	19905,50054	20050	19995,2548	20140	20085,00906	20230	20174,76332	20320	20264,51758	20410	20354,27184
19961	19906,49781	20051	19996,25207	20141	20086,00633	20231	20175,76059	20321	20265,51485	20411	20355,26911
19962	19907,49508	20052	19997,24934	20142	20087,0036	20232	20176,75786	20322	20266,51212	20412	20356,26638
19963	19908,49235	20053	19998,24661	20143	20088,00087	20233	20177,75513	20323	20267,50939	20413	20357,26365
19964	19909,48962	20054	19999,24388	20144	20088,99814	20234	20178,7524	20324	20268,50666	20414	20358,26092
19965	19910,48688	20055	20000,24115	20145	20089,99541	20235	20179,74967	20325	20269,50393	20415	20359,25819
19966	19911,48415	20056	20001,23842	20146	20090,99268	20236	20180,74694	20326	20270,5012	20416	20360,25546
19967	19912,48142	20057	20002,23568	20147	20091,98995	20237	20181,74421	20327	20271,49847	20417	20361,25273
19968	19913,47869	20058	20003,23295	20148	20092,98722	20238	20182,74148	20328	20272,49574	20418	20362,25
19969	19914,47596	20059	20004,23022	20149	20093,98448	20239	20183,73875	20329	20273,49301	20419	20363,24727
19970	19915,47323	20060	20005,22749	20150	20094,98175	20240	20184,73602	20330	20274,49028	20420	20364,24454
19971	19916,4705	20061	20006,22476	20151	20095,97902	20241	20185,73328	20331	20275,48755	20421	20365,24181
19972	19917,46777	20062	20007,22203	20152	20096,97629	20242	20186,73055	20332	20276,48482	20422	20366,23908
19973	19918,46504	20063	20008,2193	20153	20097,97356	20243	20187,72782	20333	20277,48208	20423	20367,23635
19974	19919,46231	20064	20009,21657	20154	20098,97083	20244	20188,72509	20334	20278,47935	20424	20368,23362
19975	19920,45958	20065	20010,21384	20155	20099,9681	20245	20189,72236	20335	20279,47662	20425	20369,23088
19976	19921,45685	20066	20011,21111	20156	20100,96537	20246	20190,71963	20336	20280,47389	20426	20370,22815
19977	19922,45412	20067	20012,20838	20157	20101,96264	20247	20191,7169	20337	20281,47116	20427	20371,22542
19978	19923,45139	20068	20013,20565	20158	20102,95991	20248	20192,71417	20338	20282,46843	20428	20372,22269
19979	19924,44866	20069	20014,20292	20159	20103,95718	20249	20193,71144	20339	20283,4657	20429	20373,21996
19980	19925,44593	20070	20015,20019	20160	20104,95445	20250	20194,70871	20340	20284,46297	20430	20374,21723
19981	19926,4432	20071	20016,19746	20161	20105,95172	20251	20195,70598	20341	20285,46024	20431	20375,2145
19982	19927,44047	20072	20017,19473	20162	20106,94899	20252	20196,70325	20342	20286,45751	20432	20376,21177
19983	19928,43774	20073	20018,192	20163	20107,94626	20253	20197,70052	20343	20287,45478	20433	20377,20904
19984	19929,43501	20074	20019,18927	20164	20108,94353	20254	20198,69779	20344	20288,45205	20434	20378,20631
19985	19930,43228	20075	20020,18654	20165	20109,9408	20255	20199,69506	20345	20289,44932	20435	20379,20358
19986	19931,42955	20076	20021,18381	20166	20110,93807	20256	20200,69233	20346	20290,44659	20436	20380,20085
19987	19932,42682	20077	20022,18108	20167	20111,93534	20257	20201,6896	20347	20291,44386	20437	20381,19812
19988	19933,42408	20078	20023,17835	20168	20112,93261	20258	20202,68687	20348	20292,44113	20438	20382,19539
19989	19934,42135	20079	20024,17562	20169	20113,92988	20259	20203,68414	20349	20293,4384	20439	20383,19266
19990	19935,41862	20080	20025,17288	20170	20114,92715	20260	20204,68141	20350	20294,43567	20440	20384,18993
19991	19936,41589	20081	20026,17015	20171	20115,92442	20261	20205,67868	20351	20295,43294	20441	20385,1872
19992	19937,41316	20082	20027,16742	20172	20116,92168	20262	20206,67595	20352	20296,43021	20442	20386,18447
19993	19938,41043	20083	20028,16469	20173	20117,91895	20263	20207,67322	20353	20297,42748	20443	20387,18174
19994	19939,4077	20084	20029,16196	20174	20118,91622	20264	20208,67048	20354	20298,42475	20444	20388,17901
19995	19940,40497	20085	20030,15923	20175	20119,91349	20265	20209,66775	20355	20299,42202	20445	20389,17628
19996	19941,40224	20086	20031,1565	20176	20120,91076	20266	20210,66502	20356	20300,41928	20446	20390,17355
19997	19942,39951	20087	20032,15377	20177	20121,90803	20267	20211,66229	20357	20301,41655	20447	20391,17082
19998	19943,39678	20088	20033,15104	20178	20122,9053	20268	20212,65956	20358	20302,41382	20448	20392,16809
19999	19944,39405	20089	20034,14831	20179	20123,90257	20269	20213,65683	20359	20303,41109	20449	20393,16535
20000	19945,39132	20090	20035,14558	20180	20124,89984	20270	20214,6541	20360	20304,40836	20450	20394,16262
20001	19946,38859	20091	20036,14285	20181	20125,89711	20271	20215,65137	20361	20305,40563	20451	20395,15989
20002	19947,38586	20092	20037,14012	20182	20126,89438	20272	20216,64864	20362	20306,4029	20452	20396,15716
20003	19948,38313	20093	20038,13739	20183	20127,89165	20273	20217,64591	20363	20307,40017	20453	20397,15443
20004	19949,3804	20094	20039,13466	20184	20128,88892	20274	20218,64318	20364	20308,39744	20454	20398,1517

TABLE TO FIND OUT THE POINT A IN EARTH RETURNS 195

20455	20399,14897	20545	20488,90323	20635	20578,65749	20725	20668,41175	20815	20758,16602	20905	20847,92028
20456	20400,14624	20546	20489,9005	20636	20579,65476	20726	20669,40902	20816	20759,16329	20906	20848,91755
20457	20401,14351	20547	20490,89777	20637	20580,65203	20727	20670,40629	20817	20760,16055	20907	20849,91482
20458	20402,14078	20548	20491,89504	20638	20581,6493	20728	20671,40356	20818	20761,15782	20908	20850,91209
20459	20403,13805	20549	20492,89231	20639	20582,64657	20729	20672,40083	20819	20762,15509	20909	20851,90935
20460	20404,13532	20550	20493,88958	20640	20583,64384	20730	20673,3981	20820	20763,15236	20910	20852,90662
20461	20405,13259	20551	20494,88685	20641	20584,64111	20731	20674,39537	20821	20764,14963	20911	20853,90389
20462	20406,12986	20552	20495,88412	20642	20585,63838	20732	20675,39264	20822	20765,1469	20912	20854,90116
20463	20407,12713	20553	20496,88139	20643	20586,63565	20733	20676,38991	20823	20766,14417	20913	20855,89843
20464	20408,1244	20554	20497,87866	20644	20587,63292	20734	20677,38718	20824	20767,14144	20914	20856,8957
20465	20409,12167	20555	20498,87593	20645	20588,63019	20735	20678,38445	20825	20768,13871	20915	20857,89297
20466	20410,11894	20556	20499,8732	20646	20589,62746	20736	20679,38172	20826	20769,13598	20916	20858,89024
20467	20411,11621	20557	20500,87047	20647	20590,62473	20737	20680,37899	20827	20770,13325	20917	20859,88751
20468	20412,11348	20558	20501,86774	20648	20591,622	20738	20681,37626	20828	20771,13052	20918	20860,88478
20469	20413,11075	20559	20502,86501	20649	20592,61927	20739	20682,37353	20829	20772,12779	20919	20861,88205
20470	20414,10802	20560	20503,86228	20650	20593,61654	20740	20683,3708	20830	20773,12506	20920	20862,87932
20471	20415,10529	20561	20504,85955	20651	20594,61381	20741	20684,36807	20831	20774,12233	20921	20863,87659
20472	20416,10255	20562	20505,85682	20652	20595,61108	20742	20685,36534	20832	20775,1196	20922	20864,87386
20473	20417,09982	20563	20506,85409	20653	20596,60835	20743	20686,36261	20833	20776,11687	20923	20865,87113
20474	20418,09709	20564	20507,85135	20654	20597,60562	20744	20687,35988	20834	20777,11414	20924	20866,8684
20475	20419,09436	20565	20508,84862	20655	20598,60289	20745	20688,35715	20835	20778,11141	20925	20867,86567
20476	20420,09163	20566	20509,84589	20656	20599,60015	20746	20689,35442	20836	20779,10868	20926	20868,86294
20477	20421,0889	20567	20510,84316	20657	20600,59742	20747	20690,35169	20837	20780,10595	20927	20869,86021
20478	20422,08617	20568	20511,84043	20658	20601,59469	20748	20691,34895	20838	20781,10322	20928	20870,85748
20479	20423,08344	20569	20512,8377	20659	20602,59196	20749	20692,34622	20839	20782,10049	20929	20871,85475
20480	20424,08071	20570	20513,83497	20660	20603,58923	20750	20693,34349	20840	20783,09775	20930	20872,85202
20481	20425,07798	20571	20514,83224	20661	20604,5865	20751	20694,34076	20841	20784,09502	20931	20873,84929
20482	20426,07525	20572	20515,82951	20662	20605,58377	20752	20695,33803	20842	20785,09229	20932	20874,84655
20483	20427,07252	20573	20516,82678	20663	20606,58104	20753	20696,3353	20843	20786,08956	20933	20875,84382
20484	20428,06979	20574	20517,82405	20664	20607,57831	20754	20697,33257	20844	20787,08683	20934	20876,84109
20485	20429,06706	20575	20518,82132	20665	20608,57558	20755	20698,32984	20845	20788,0841	20935	20877,83836
20486	20430,06433	20576	20519,81859	20666	20609,57285	20756	20699,32711	20846	20789,08137	20936	20878,83563
20487	20431,0616	20577	20520,81586	20667	20610,57012	20757	20700,32438	20847	20790,07864	20937	20879,8329
20488	20432,05887	20578	20521,81313	20668	20611,56739	20758	20701,32165	20848	20791,07591	20938	20880,83017
20489	20433,05614	20579	20522,8104	20669	20612,56466	20759	20702,31892	20849	20792,07318	20939	20881,82744
20490	20434,05341	20580	20523,80767	20670	20613,56193	20760	20703,31619	20850	20793,07045	20940	20882,82471
20491	20435,05068	20581	20524,80494	20671	20614,5592	20761	20704,31346	20851	20794,06772	20941	20883,82198
20492	20436,04795	20582	20525,80221	20672	20615,55647	20762	20705,31073	20852	20795,06499	20942	20884,81925
20493	20437,04522	20583	20526,79948	20673	20616,55374	20763	20706,308	20853	20796,06226	20943	20885,81652
20494	20438,04249	20584	20527,79675	20674	20617,55101	20764	20707,30527	20854	20797,05953	20944	20886,81379
20495	20439,03975	20585	20528,79402	20675	20618,54828	20765	20708,30254	20855	20798,0568	20945	20887,81106
20496	20440,03702	20586	20529,79129	20676	20619,54555	20766	20709,29981	20856	20799,05407	20946	20888,80833
20497	20441,03429	20587	20530,78855	20677	20620,54282	20767	20710,29708	20857	20800,05134	20947	20889,8056
20498	20442,03156	20588	20531,78582	20678	20621,54009	20768	20711,29435	20858	20801,04861	20948	20890,80287
20499	20443,02883	20589	20532,78309	20679	20622,53735	20769	20712,29162	20859	20802,04588	20949	20891,80014
20500	20444,0261	20590	20533,78036	20680	20623,53462	20770	20713,28889	20860	20803,04315	20950	20892,79741
20501	20445,02337	20591	20534,77763	20681	20624,53189	20771	20714,28615	20861	20804,04042	20951	20893,79468
20502	20446,02064	20592	20535,7749	20682	20625,52916	20772	20715,28342	20862	20805,03769	20952	20894,79195
20503	20447,01791	20593	20536,77217	20683	20626,52643	20773	20716,28069	20863	20806,03495	20953	20895,78922
20504	20448,01518	20594	20537,76944	20684	20627,5237	20774	20717,27796	20864	20807,03222	20954	20896,78649
20505	20449,01245	20595	20538,76671	20685	20628,52097	20775	20718,27523	20865	20808,02949	20955	20897,78375
20506	20450,00972	20596	20539,76398	20686	20629,51824	20776	20719,2725	20866	20809,02676	20956	20898,78102
20507	20451,00699	20597	20540,76125	20687	20630,51551	20777	20720,26977	20867	20810,02403	20957	20899,77829
20508	20452,00426	20598	20541,75852	20688	20631,51278	20778	20721,26704	20868	20811,0213	20958	20900,77556
20509	20453,00153	20599	20542,75579	20689	20632,51005	20779	20722,26431	20869	20812,01857	20959	20901,77283
20510	20453,9988	20600	20543,75306	20690	20633,50732	20780	20723,26158	20870	20813,01584	20960	20902,7701
20511	20454,99607	20601	20544,75033	20691	20634,50459	20781	20724,25885	20871	20814,01311	20961	20903,76737
20512	20455,99334	20602	20545,7476	20692	20635,50186	20782	20725,25612	20872	20815,01038	20962	20904,76464
20513	20456,99061	20603	20546,74487	20693	20636,49913	20783	20726,25339	20873	20816,00765	20963	20905,76191
20514	20457,98788	20604	20547,74214	20694	20637,4964	20784	20727,25066	20874	20817,00492	20964	20906,75918
20515	20458,98515	20605	20548,73941	20695	20638,49367	20785	20728,24793	20875	20818,00219	20965	20907,75645
20516	20459,98242	20606	20549,73668	20696	20639,49094	20786	20729,2452	20876	20818,99946	20966	20908,75372
20517	20460,97969	20607	20550,73395	20697	20640,48821	20787	20730,24247	20877	20819,99673	20967	20909,75099
20518	20461,97695	20608	20551,73122	20698	20641,48548	20788	20731,23974	20878	20820,994	20968	20910,74826
20519	20462,97422	20609	20552,72849	20699	20642,48275	20789	20732,23701	20879	20821,99127	20969	20911,74553
20520	20463,97149	20610	20553,72575	20700	20643,48002	20790	20733,23428	20880	20822,98854	20970	20912,7428
20521	20464,96876	20611	20554,72302	20701	20644,47729	20791	20734,23155	20881	20823,98581	20971	20913,74007
20522	20465,96603	20612	20555,72029	20702	20645,47455	20792	20735,22882	20882	20824,98308	20972	20914,73734
20523	20466,9633	20613	20556,71756	20703	20646,47182	20793	20736,22609	20883	20825,98035	20973	20915,73461
20524	20467,96057	20614	20557,71483	20704	20647,46909	20794	20737,22335	20884	20826,97762	20974	20916,73188
20525	20468,95784	20615	20558,7121	20705	20648,46636	20795	20738,22062	20885	20827,97489	20975	20917,72915
20526	20469,95511	20616	20559,70937	20706	20649,46363	20796	20739,21789	20886	20828,97215	20976	20918,72642
20527	20470,95238	20617	20560,70664	20707	20650,4609	20797	20740,21516	20887	20829,96942	20977	20919,72369
20528	20471,94965	20618	20561,70391	20708	20651,45817	20798	20741,21243	20888	20830,96669	20978	20920,72095
20529	20472,94692	20619	20562,70118	20709	20652,45544	20799	20742,2097	20889	20831,96396	20979	20921,71822
20530	20473,94419	20620	20563,69845	20710	20653,45271	20800	20743,20697	20890	20832,96123	20980	20922,71549
20531	20474,94146	20621	20564,69572	20711	20654,44998	20801	20744,20424	20891	20833,9585	20981	20923,71276
20532	20475,93873	20622	20565,69299	20712	20655,44725	20802	20745,20151	20892	20834,95577	20982	20924,71003
20533	20476,936	20623	20566,69026	20713	20656,44452	20803	20746,19878	20893	20835,95304	20983	20925,7073
20534	20477,93327	20624	20567,68753	20714	20657,44179	20804	20747,19605	20894	20836,95031	20984	20926,70457
20535	20478,93054	20625	20568,6848	20715	20658,43906	20805	20748,19332	20895	20837,94758	20985	20927,70184
20536	20479,92781	20626	20569,68207	20716	20659,43633	20806	20749,19059	20896	20838,94485	20986	20928,69911
20537	20480,92508	20627	20570,67934	20717	20660,4336	20807	20750,18786	20897	20839,94212	20987	20929,69638
20538	20481,92235	20628	20571,67661	20718	20661,43087	20808	20751,18513	20898	20840,93939	20988	20930,69365
20539	20482,81962	20629	20572,67388	20719	20662,42814	20809	20752,1824	20899	20841,93666	20989	20931,69092
20540	20483,91689	20630	20573,67115	20720	20663,42541	20810	20753,17967	20900	20842,93393	20990	20932,68819
20541	20484,91415	20631	20574,66842	20721	20664,42268	20811	20754,17694	20901	20843,9312	20991	20933,68546
20542	20485,91142	20632	20575,66569	20722	20665,41995	20812	20755,17421	20902	20844,92847	20992	20934,68273
20543	20486,90869	20633	20576,66295	20723	20666,41722	20813	20756,17148	20903	20845,92574	20993	20935,68
20544	20487,90596	20634	20577,66022	20724	20667,41449	20814	20757,16875	20904	20846,92301	20994	20936,67727

LUNAR RETURNS AND EARTH RETURNS

20995	20937,67454	21085	21027,4288	21175	21117,18306	21265	21206,93732	21355	21296,69158	21445	21386,44584
20996	20938,67181	21086	21028,42607	21176	21118,18033	21266	21207,93459	21356	21297,68885	21446	21387,44311
20997	20939,66908	21087	21029,42334	21177	21119,1776	21267	21208,93186	21357	21298,68612	21447	21388,44038
20998	20940,66635	21088	21030,42061	21178	21120,17487	21268	21209,92913	21358	21299,68339	21448	21389,43765
20999	20941,66362	21089	21031,41788	21179	21121,17214	21269	21210,9264	21359	21300,68066	21449	21390,43492
21000	20942,66089	21090	21032,41515	21180	21122,16941	21270	21211,92367	21360	21301,67793	21450	21391,43219
21001	20943,65815	21091	21033,41242	21181	21123,16668	21271	21212,92094	21361	21302,6752	21451	21392,42946
21002	20944,65542	21092	21034,40969	21182	21124,16395	21272	21213,91821	21362	21303,67247	21452	21393,42673
21003	20945,65269	21093	21035,40696	21183	21125,16122	21273	21214,91548	21363	21304,66974	21453	21394,424
21004	20946,64996	21094	21036,40422	21184	21126,15849	21274	21215,91275	21364	21305,66701	21454	21395,42127
21005	20947,64723	21095	21037,40149	21185	21127,15576	21275	21216,91002	21365	21306,66428	21455	21396,41854
21006	20948,6445	21096	21038,39876	21186	21128,15302	21276	21217,90729	21366	21307,66155	21456	21397,41581
21007	20949,64177	21097	21039,39603	21187	21129,15029	21277	21218,90456	21367	21308,65882	21457	21398,41308
21008	20950,63904	21098	21040,3933	21188	21130,14756	21278	21219,90182	21368	21309,65609	21458	21399,41035
21009	20951,63631	21099	21041,39057	21189	21131,14483	21279	21220,89909	21369	21310,65336	21459	21400,40762
21010	20952,63358	21100	21042,38784	21190	21132,1421	21280	21221,89636	21370	21311,65062	21460	21401,40489
21011	20953,63085	21101	21043,38511	21191	21133,13937	21281	21222,89363	21371	21312,64789	21461	21402,40216
21012	20954,62812	21102	21044,38238	21192	21134,13664	21282	21223,8909	21372	21313,64516	21462	21403,39942
21013	20955,62539	21103	21045,37965	21193	21135,13391	21283	21224,88817	21373	21314,64243	21463	21404,39669
21014	20956,62266	21104	21046,37692	21194	21136,13118	21284	21225,88544	21374	21315,6397	21464	21405,39396
21015	20957,61993	21105	21047,37419	21195	21137,12845	21285	21226,88271	21375	21316,63697	21465	21406,39123
21016	20958,6172	21106	21048,37146	21196	21138,12572	21286	21227,87998	21376	21317,63424	21466	21407,3885
21017	20959,61447	21107	21049,36873	21197	21139,12299	21287	21228,87725	21377	21318,63151	21467	21408,38577
21018	20960,61174	21108	21050,366	21198	21140,12026	21288	21229,87452	21378	21319,62878	21468	21409,38304
21019	20961,60901	21109	21051,36327	21199	21141,11753	21289	21230,87179	21379	21320,62605	21469	21410,38031
21020	20962,60628	21110	21052,36054	21200	21142,1148	21290	21231,86906	21380	21321,62332	21470	21411,37758
21021	20963,60355	21111	21053,35781	21201	21143,11207	21291	21232,86633	21381	21322,62059	21471	21412,37485
21022	20964,60082	21112	21054,35508	21202	21144,10934	21292	21233,8636	21382	21323,61786	21472	21413,37212
21023	20965,59809	21113	21055,35235	21203	21145,10661	21293	21234,86087	21383	21324,61513	21473	21414,36939
21024	20966,59536	21114	21056,34962	21204	21146,10388	21294	21235,85814	21384	21325,6124	21474	21415,36666
21025	20967,59262	21115	21057,34689	21205	21147,10115	21295	21236,85541	21385	21326,60967	21475	21416,36393
21026	20968,58989	21116	21058,34416	21206	21148,09842	21296	21237,85268	21386	21327,60694	21476	21417,3612
21027	20969,58716	21117	21059,34142	21207	21149,09569	21297	21238,84995	21387	21328,60421	21477	21418,35847
21028	20970,58443	21118	21060,33869	21208	21150,09296	21298	21239,84722	21388	21329,60148	21478	21419,35574
21029	20971,5817	21119	21061,33596	21209	21151,09022	21299	21240,84449	21389	21330,59875	21479	21420,35301
21030	20972,57897	21120	21062,33323	21210	21152,08749	21300	21241,84176	21390	21331,59602	21480	21421,35028
21031	20973,57624	21121	21063,3305	21211	21153,08476	21301	21242,83902	21391	21332,59329	21481	21422,34755
21032	20974,57351	21122	21064,32777	21212	21154,08203	21302	21243,83629	21392	21333,59056	21482	21423,34482
21033	20975,57078	21123	21065,32504	21213	21155,0793	21303	21244,83356	21393	21334,58782	21483	21424,34209
21034	20976,56805	21124	21066,32231	21214	21156,07657	21304	21245,83083	21394	21335,58509	21484	21425,33936
21035	20977,56532	21125	21067,31958	21215	21157,07384	21305	21246,8281	21395	21336,58236	21485	21426,33662
21036	20978,56259	21126	21068,31685	21216	21158,07111	21306	21247,82537	21396	21337,57963	21486	21427,33389
21037	20979,55986	21127	21069,31412	21217	21159,06838	21307	21248,82264	21397	21338,5769	21487	21428,33116
21038	20980,55713	21128	21070,31139	21218	21160,06565	21308	21249,81991	21398	21339,57417	21488	21429,32843
21039	20981,5544	21129	21071,30866	21219	21161,06292	21309	21250,81718	21399	21340,57144	21489	21430,3257
21040	20982,55167	21130	21072,30593	21220	21162,06019	21310	21251,81445	21400	21341,56871	21490	21431,32297
21041	20983,54894	21131	21073,3032	21221	21163,05746	21311	21252,81172	21401	21342,56598	21491	21432,32024
21042	20984,54621	21132	21074,30047	21222	21164,05473	21312	21253,80899	21402	21343,56325	21492	21433,31751
21043	20985,54348	21133	21075,29774	21223	21165,052	21313	21254,80626	21403	21344,56052	21493	21434,31478
21044	20986,54075	21134	21076,29501	21224	21166,04927	21314	21255,80353	21404	21345,55779	21494	21435,31205
21045	20987,53802	21135	21077,29228	21225	21167,04654	21315	21256,8008	21405	21346,55506	21495	21436,30932
21046	20988,53529	21136	21078,28955	21226	21168,04381	21316	21257,79807	21406	21347,55233	21496	21437,30659
21047	20989,53256	21137	21079,28682	21227	21169,04108	21317	21258,79534	21407	21348,5496	21497	21438,30386
21048	20990,52982	21138	21080,28409	21228	21170,03835	21318	21259,79261	21408	21349,54687	21498	21439,30113
21049	20991,52709	21139	21081,28136	21229	21171,03562	21319	21260,78988	21409	21350,54414	21499	21440,2984
21050	20992,52436	21140	21082,27862	21230	21172,03289	21320	21261,78715	21410	21351,54141	21500	21441,29567
21051	20993,52163	21141	21083,27589	21231	21173,03016	21321	21262,78442	21411	21352,53868	21501	21442,29294
21052	20994,5189	21142	21084,27316	21232	21174,02742	21322	21263,78169	21412	21353,53595	21502	21443,29021
21053	20995,51617	21143	21085,27043	21233	21175,02469	21323	21264,77896	21413	21354,53322	21503	21444,28748
21054	20996,51344	21144	21086,2677	21234	21176,02196	21324	21265,77622	21414	21355,53049	21504	21445,28475
21055	20997,51071	21145	21087,26497	21235	21177,01923	21325	21266,77349	21415	21356,52776	21505	21446,28202
21056	20998,50798	21146	21088,26224	21236	21178,0165	21326	21267,77076	21416	21357,52502	21506	21447,27929
21057	20999,50525	21147	21089,25951	21237	21179,01377	21327	21268,76803	21417	21358,52229	21507	21448,27656
21058	21000,50252	21148	21090,25678	21238	21180,01104	21328	21269,7653	21418	21359,51956	21508	21449,27382
21059	21001,49979	21149	21091,25405	21239	21181,00831	21329	21270,76257	21419	21360,51683	21509	21450,27109
21060	21002,49706	21150	21092,25132	21240	21182,00558	21330	21271,75984	21420	21361,5141	21510	21451,26836
21061	21003,49433	21151	21093,24859	21241	21183,00285	21331	21272,75711	21421	21362,51137	21511	21452,26563
21062	21004,4916	21152	21094,24586	21242	21184,00012	21332	21273,75438	21422	21363,50864	21512	21453,2629
21063	21005,48887	21153	21095,24313	21243	21184,99739	21333	21274,75165	21423	21364,50591	21513	21454,26017
21064	21006,48614	21154	21096,2404	21244	21185,99466	21334	21275,74892	21424	21365,50318	21514	21455,25744
21065	21007,48341	21155	21097,23767	21245	21186,99193	21335	21276,74619	21425	21366,50045	21515	21456,25471
21066	21008,48068	21156	21098,23494	21246	21187,9892	21336	21277,74346	21426	21367,49772	21516	21457,25198
21067	21009,47795	21157	21099,23221	21247	21188,98647	21337	21278,74073	21427	21368,49499	21517	21458,24925
21068	21010,47522	21158	21100,22948	21248	21189,98374	21338	21279,738	21428	21369,49226	21518	21459,24652
21069	21011,47249	21159	21101,22675	21249	21190,98101	21339	21280,73527	21429	21370,48953	21519	21460,24379
21070	21012,46976	21160	21102,22402	21250	21191,97828	21340	21281,73254	21430	21371,4868	21520	21461,24106
21071	21013,46702	21161	21103,22129	21251	21192,97555	21341	21282,72981	21431	21372,48407	21521	21462,23833
21072	21014,46429	21162	21104,21856	21252	21193,97282	21342	21283,72708	21432	21373,48134	21522	21463,2356
21073	21015,46156	21163	21105,21582	21253	21194,97009	21343	21284,72435	21433	21374,47861	21523	21464,23287
21074	21016,45883	21164	21106,21309	21254	21195,96736	21344	21285,72162	21434	21375,47588	21524	21465,23014
21075	21017,4561	21165	21107,21036	21255	21196,96462	21345	21286,71889	21435	21376,47315	21525	21466,22741
21076	21018,45337	21166	21108,20763	21256	21197,96189	21346	21287,71616	21436	21377,47042	21526	21467,22468
21077	21019,45064	21167	21109,2049	21257	21198,95916	21347	21288,71342	21437	21378,46769	21527	21468,22195
21078	21020,44791	21168	21110,20217	21258	21199,95643	21348	21289,71069	21438	21379,46496	21528	21469,21922
21079	21021,44518	21169	21111,19944	21259	21200,9537	21349	21290,70796	21439	21380,46222	21529	21470,21649
21080	21022,44245	21170	21112,19671	21260	21201,95097	21350	21291,70523	21440	21381,45949	21530	21471,21376
21081	21023,43972	21171	21113,19398	21261	21202,94824	21351	21292,7025	21441	21382,45676	21531	21472,21102
21082	21024,43699	21172	21114,19125	21262	21203,94551	21352	21293,69977	21442	21383,45403	21532	21473,20829
21083	21025,43426	21173	21115,18852	21263	21204,94278	21353	21294,69704	21443	21384,4513	21533	21474,20556
21084	21026,43153	21174	21116,18579	21264	21205,94005	21354	21295,69431	21444	21385,44857	21534	21475,20283

TABLE TO FIND OUT THE POINT A IN EARTH RETURNS 197

21535	21476,2001	21625	21565,95436	21715	21655,70863	21805	21745,46289	21895	21835,21715	21985	21924,97141
21536	21477,19737	21626	21566,95163	21716	21656,70589	21806	21746,46016	21896	21836,21442	21986	21925,96868
21537	21478,19464	21627	21567,9489	21717	21657,70316	21807	21747,45743	21897	21837,21169	21987	21926,96595
21538	21479,19191	21628	21568,94617	21718	21658,70043	21808	21748,45469	21898	21838,20896	21988	21927,96322
21539	21480,18918	21629	21569,94344	21719	21659,6977	21809	21749,45196	21899	21839,20623	21989	21928,96049
21540	21481,18645	21630	21570,94071	21720	21660,69497	21810	21750,44923	21900	21840,20349	21990	21929,95776
21541	21482,18372	21631	21571,93798	21721	21661,69224	21811	21751,4465	21901	21841,20076	21991	21930,95503
21542	21483,18099	21632	21572,93525	21722	21662,68951	21812	21752,44377	21902	21842,19803	21992	21931,95229
21543	21484,17826	21633	21573,93252	21723	21663,68678	21813	21753,44104	21903	21843,1953	21993	21932,94956
21544	21485,17553	21634	21574,92979	21724	21664,68405	21814	21754,43831	21904	21844,19257	21994	21933,94683
21545	21486,1728	21635	21575,92706	21725	21665,68132	21815	21755,43558	21905	21845,18984	21995	21934,9441
21546	21487,17007	21636	21576,92433	21726	21666,67859	21816	21756,43285	21906	21846,18711	21996	21935,94137
21547	21488,16734	21637	21577,9216	21727	21667,67586	21817	21757,43012	21907	21847,18438	21997	21936,93864
21548	21489,16461	21638	21578,91887	21728	21668,67313	21818	21758,42739	21908	21848,18165	21998	21937,93591
21549	21490,16188	21639	21579,91614	21729	21669,6704	21819	21759,42466	21909	21849,17892	21999	21938,93318
21550	21491,15915	21640	21580,91341	21730	21670,66767	21820	21760,42193	21910	21850,17619	22000	21939,93045
21551	21492,15642	21641	21581,91068	21731	21671,66494	21821	21761,4192	21911	21851,17346	22001	21940,92772
21552	21493,15369	21642	21582,90795	21732	21672,66221	21822	21762,41647	21912	21852,17073	22002	21941,92499
21553	21494,15096	21643	21583,90522	21733	21673,65948	21823	21763,41374	21913	21853,168	22003	21942,92226
21554	21495,14822	21644	21584,90249	21734	21674,65675	21824	21764,41101	21914	21854,16527	22004	21943,91953
21555	21496,14549	21645	21585,89976	21735	21675,65402	21825	21765,40828	21915	21855,16254	22005	21944,9168
21556	21497,14276	21646	21586,89703	21736	21676,65129	21826	21766,40555	21916	21856,15981	22006	21945,91407
21557	21498,14003	21647	21587,89429	21737	21677,64856	21827	21767,40282	21917	21857,15708	22007	21946,91134
21558	21499,1373	21648	21588,89156	21738	21678,64583	21828	21768,40009	21918	21858,15435	22008	21947,90861
21559	21500,13457	21649	21589,88883	21739	21679,64309	21829	21769,39736	21919	21859,15162	22009	21948,90588
21560	21501,13184	21650	21590,8861	21740	21680,64036	21830	21770,39463	21920	21860,14889	22010	21949,90315
21561	21502,12911	21651	21591,88337	21741	21681,63763	21831	21771,39189	21921	21861,14616	22011	21950,90042
21562	21503,12638	21652	21592,88064	21742	21682,6349	21832	21772,38916	21922	21862,14343	22012	21951,89769
21563	21504,12365	21653	21593,87791	21743	21683,63217	21833	21773,38643	21923	21863,14069	22013	21952,89496
21564	21505,12092	21654	21594,87518	21744	21684,62944	21834	21774,3837	21924	21864,13796	22014	21953,89223
21565	21506,11819	21655	21595,87245	21745	21685,62671	21835	21775,38097	21925	21865,13523	22015	21954,88949
21566	21507,11546	21656	21596,86972	21746	21686,62398	21836	21776,37824	21926	21866,1325	22016	21955,88676
21567	21508,11273	21657	21597,86699	21747	21687,62125	21837	21777,37551	21927	21867,12977	22017	21956,88403
21568	21509,11	21658	21598,86426	21748	21688,61852	21838	21778,37278	21928	21868,12704	22018	21957,8813
21569	21510,10727	21659	21599,86153	21749	21689,61579	21839	21779,37005	21929	21869,12431	22019	21958,87857
21570	21511,10454	21660	21600,8588	21750	21690,61306	21840	21780,36732	21930	21870,12158	22020	21959,87584
21571	21512,10181	21661	21601,85607	21751	21691,61033	21841	21781,36459	21931	21871,11885	22021	21960,87311
21572	21513,09908	21662	21602,85334	21752	21692,6076	21842	21782,36186	21932	21872,11612	22022	21961,87038
21573	21514,09635	21663	21603,85061	21753	21693,60487	21843	21783,35913	21933	21873,11339	22023	21962,86765
21574	21515,09362	21664	21604,84788	21754	21694,60214	21844	21784,3564	21934	21874,11066	22024	21963,86492
21575	21516,09089	21665	21605,84515	21755	21695,59941	21845	21785,35367	21935	21875,10793	22025	21964,86219
21576	21517,08816	21666	21606,84242	21756	21696,59668	21846	21786,35094	21936	21876,1052	22026	21965,85946
21577	21518,08542	21667	21607,83969	21757	21697,59395	21847	21787,34821	21937	21877,10247	22027	21966,85673
21578	21519,08269	21668	21608,83696	21758	21698,59122	21848	21788,34548	21938	21878,09974	22028	21967,854
21579	21520,07996	21669	21609,83423	21759	21699,58849	21849	21789,34275	21939	21879,09701	22029	21968,85127
21580	21521,07723	21670	21610,83149	21760	21700,58576	21850	21790,34002	21940	21880,09428	22030	21969,84854
21581	21522,0745	21671	21611,82876	21761	21701,58303	21851	21791,33729	21941	21881,09155	22031	21970,84581
21582	21523,07177	21672	21612,82603	21762	21702,58029	21852	21792,33456	21942	21882,08882	22032	21971,84308
21583	21524,06904	21673	21613,8233	21763	21703,57756	21853	21793,33183	21943	21883,08609	22033	21972,84035
21584	21525,06631	21674	21614,82057	21764	21704,57483	21854	21794,32909	21944	21884,08336	22034	21973,83762
21585	21526,06358	21675	21615,81784	21765	21705,5721	21855	21795,32636	21945	21885,08063	22035	21974,83489
21586	21527,06085	21676	21616,81511	21766	21706,56937	21856	21796,32363	21946	21886,07789	22036	21975,83216
21587	21528,05812	21677	21617,81238	21767	21707,56664	21857	21797,3209	21947	21887,07516	22037	21976,82943
21588	21529,05539	21678	21618,80965	21768	21708,56391	21858	21798,31817	21948	21888,07243	22038	21977,82669
21589	21530,05266	21679	21619,80692	21769	21709,56118	21859	21799,31544	21949	21889,0697	22039	21978,82396
21590	21531,04993	21680	21620,80419	21770	21710,55845	21860	21800,31271	21950	21890,06697	22040	21979,82123
21591	21532,0472	21681	21621,80146	21771	21711,55572	21861	21801,30998	21951	21891,06424	22041	21980,8185
21592	21533,04447	21682	21622,79873	21772	21712,55299	21862	21802,30725	21952	21892,06151	22042	21981,81577
21593	21534,04174	21683	21623,796	21773	21713,55026	21863	21803,30452	21953	21893,05878	22043	21982,81304
21594	21535,03901	21684	21624,79327	21774	21714,54753	21864	21804,30179	21954	21894,05605	22044	21983,81031
21595	21536,03628	21685	21625,79054	21775	21715,5448	21865	21805,29906	21955	21895,05332	22045	21984,80758
21596	21537,03355	21686	21626,78781	21776	21716,54207	21866	21806,29633	21956	21896,05059	22046	21985,80485
21597	21538,03082	21687	21627,78508	21777	21717,53934	21867	21807,2936	21957	21897,04786	22047	21986,80212
21598	21539,02809	21688	21628,78235	21778	21718,53661	21868	21808,29087	21958	21898,04513	22048	21987,79939
21599	21540,02536	21689	21629,77962	21779	21719,53388	21869	21809,28814	21959	21899,0424	22049	21988,79666
21600	21541,02263	21690	21630,77689	21780	21720,53115	21870	21810,28541	21960	21900,03967	22050	21989,79393
21601	21542,01989	21691	21631,77416	21781	21721,52842	21871	21811,28268	21961	21901,03694	22051	21990,7912
21602	21543,01716	21692	21632,77143	21782	21722,52569	21872	21812,27995	21962	21902,03421	22052	21991,78847
21603	21544,01443	21693	21633,76869	21783	21723,52296	21873	21813,27722	21963	21903,03148	22053	21992,78574
21604	21545,0117	21694	21634,66596	21784	21724,52023	21874	21814,27449	21964	21904,02875	22054	21993,78301
21605	21546,00897	21695	21635,76323	21785	21725,51749	21875	21815,27176	21965	21905,02602	22055	21994,78028
21606	21547,00624	21696	21636,7605	21786	21726,51476	21876	21816,26903	21966	21906,02329	22056	21995,77755
21607	21548,00351	21697	21637,75777	21787	21727,51203	21877	21817,26629	21967	21907,02056	22057	21996,77482
21608	21549,00078	21698	21638,75504	21788	21728,5093	21878	21818,26356	21968	21908,01783	22058	21997,77209
21609	21549,99805	21699	21639,75231	21789	21729,50657	21879	21819,26083	21969	21909,01509	22059	21998,76936
21610	21550,99532	21700	21640,74958	21790	21730,50384	21880	21820,2581	21970	21910,01236	22060	21999,76663
21611	21551,99259	21701	21641,74685	21791	21731,50111	21881	21821,25537	21971	21911,00963	22061	22000,76389
21612	21552,98986	21702	21642,74412	21792	21732,49838	21882	21822,25264	21972	21912,0069	22062	22001,76116
21613	21553,98713	21703	21643,74139	21793	21733,49565	21883	21823,24991	21973	21913,00417	22063	22002,75843
21614	21554,9844	21704	21644,73866	21794	21734,49292	21884	21824,24718	21974	21914,00144	22064	22003,7557
21615	21555,98167	21705	21645,73593	21795	21735,49019	21885	21825,24445	21975	21914,99871	22065	22004,75297
21616	21556,97894	21706	21646,7332	21796	21736,48746	21886	21826,24172	21976	21915,99598	22066	22005,75024
21617	21557,97621	21707	21647,73047	21797	21737,48473	21887	21827,23899	21977	21916,99325	22067	22006,74751
21618	21558,97348	21708	21648,72774	21798	21738,482	21888	21828,23626	21978	21917,99052	22068	22007,74478
21619	21559,97075	21709	21649,72501	21799	21739,47927	21889	21829,23353	21979	21918,98779	22069	22008,74205
21620	21560,96802	21710	21650,72228	21800	21740,47654	21890	21830,2308	21980	21919,98506	22070	22009,73932
21621	21561,96529	21711	21651,71955	21801	21741,47381	21891	21831,22807	21981	21920,98233	22071	22010,73659
21622	21562,96256	21712	21652,71682	21802	21742,47108	21892	21832,22534	21982	21921,9796	22072	22011,73386
21623	21563,95983	21713	21653,71409	21803	21743,46835	21893	21833,22261	21983	21922,97687	22073	22012,73113
21624	21564,95709	21714	21654,71136	21804	21744,46562	21894	21834,21988	21984	21923,97414	22074	22013,7284

22075 22014,72567	22165 22104,47993	22255 22194,23419	22345 22283,98845	22435 22373,74271	22525 22463,49697
22076 22015,72294	22166 22105,4772	22256 22195,23146	22346 22284,98572	22436 22374,73998	22526 22464,49424
22077 22016,72021	22167 22106,47447	22257 22196,22873	22347 22285,98299	22437 22375,73725	22527 22465,49151
22078 22017,71748	22168 22107,47174	22258 22197,226	22348 22286,98026	22438 22376,73452	22528 22466,48878
22079 22018,71475	22169 22108,46901	22259 22198,22327	22349 22287,97753	22439 22377,73179	22529 22467,48605
22080 22019,71202	22170 22109,46628	22260 22199,22054	22350 22288,9748	22440 22378,72906	22530 22468,48332
22081 22020,70929	22171 22110,46355	22261 22200,21781	22351 22289,97207	22441 22379,72633	22531 22469,48059
22082 22021,70656	22172 22111,46082	22262 22201,21508	22352 22290,96934	22442 22380,7236	22532 22470,47786
22083 22022,70383	22173 22112,45809	22263 22202,21235	22353 22291,96661	22443 22381,72087	22533 22471,47513
22084 22023,70109	22174 22113,45536	22264 22203,20962	22354 22292,96388	22444 22382,71814	22534 22472,4724
22085 22024,69836	22175 22114,45263	22265 22204,20689	22355 22293,96115	22445 22383,71541	22535 22473,46967
22086 22025,69563	22176 22115,4499	22266 22205,20416	22356 22294,95842	22446 22384,71268	22536 22474,46694
22087 22026,6929	22177 22116,44716	22267 22206,20143	22357 22295,95569	22447 22385,70995	22537 22475,46421
22088 22027,69017	22178 22117,44443	22268 22207,1987	22358 22296,95296	22448 22386,70722	22538 22476,46148
22089 22028,68744	22179 22118,4417	22269 22208,19596	22359 22297,95023	22449 22387,70449	22539 22477,45875
22090 22029,68471	22180 22119,43897	22270 22209,19323	22360 22298,9475	22450 22388,70176	22540 22478,45602
22091 22030,68198	22181 22120,43624	22271 22210,1905	22361 22299,94476	22451 22389,69903	22541 22479,45329
22092 22031,67925	22182 22121,43351	22272 22211,18777	22362 22300,94203	22452 22390,6963	22542 22480,45056
22093 22032,67652	22183 22122,43078	22273 22212,18504	22363 22301,9393	22453 22391,69356	22543 22481,44783
22094 22033,67379	22184 22123,42805	22274 22213,18231	22364 22302,93657	22454 22392,69083	22544 22482,4451
22095 22034,67106	22185 22124,42532	22275 22214,17958	22365 22303,93384	22455 22393,6881	22545 22483,44236
22096 22035,66833	22186 22125,42259	22276 22215,17685	22366 22304,93111	22456 22394,68537	22546 22484,43963
22097 22036,6656	22187 22126,41986	22277 22216,17412	22367 22305,92838	22457 22395,68264	22547 22485,4369
22098 22037,66287	22188 22127,41713	22278 22217,17139	22368 22306,92565	22458 22396,67991	22548 22486,43417
22099 22038,66014	22189 22128,4144	22279 22218,16866	22369 22307,92292	22459 22397,67718	22549 22487,43144
22100 22039,65741	22190 22129,41167	22280 22219,16593	22370 22308,92019	22460 22398,67445	22550 22488,42871
22101 22040,65468	22191 22130,40894	22281 22220,1632	22371 22309,91746	22461 22399,67172	22551 22489,42598
22102 22041,65195	22192 22131,40621	22282 22221,16047	22372 22310,91473	22462 22400,66899	22552 22490,42325
22103 22042,64922	22193 22132,40348	22283 22222,15774	22373 22311,912	22463 22401,66626	22553 22491,42052
22104 22043,64649	22194 22133,40075	22284 22223,15501	22374 22312,90927	22464 22402,66353	22554 22492,41779
22105 22044,64376	22195 22134,39802	22285 22224,15228	22375 22313,90654	22465 22403,6608	22555 22493,41506
22106 22045,64103	22196 22135,39529	22286 22225,14955	22376 22314,90381	22466 22404,65807	22556 22494,41233
22107 22046,63829	22197 22136,39256	22287 22226,14682	22377 22315,90108	22467 22405,65534	22557 22495,4096
22108 22047,63556	22198 22137,38983	22288 22227,14409	22378 22316,89835	22468 22406,65261	22558 22496,40687
22109 22048,63283	22199 22138,3871	22289 22228,14136	22379 22317,89562	22469 22407,64988	22559 22497,40414
22110 22049,6301	22200 22139,38436	22290 22229,13863	22380 22318,89289	22470 22408,64715	22560 22498,40141
22111 22050,62737	22201 22140,38163	22291 22230,1359	22381 22319,89016	22471 22409,64442	22561 22499,39868
22112 22051,62464	22202 22141,3789	22292 22231,13316	22382 22320,88743	22472 22410,64169	22562 22500,39595
22113 22052,62191	22203 22142,37617	22293 22232,13043	22383 22321,8847	22473 22411,63896	22563 22501,39322
22114 22053,61918	22204 22143,37344	22294 22233,1277	22384 22322,88196	22474 22412,63623	22564 22502,39049
22115 22054,61645	22205 22144,37071	22295 22234,12497	22385 22323,87923	22475 22413,6335	22565 22503,38776
22116 22055,61372	22206 22145,36798	22296 22235,12224	22386 22324,8765	22476 22414,63076	22566 22504,38503
22117 22056,61099	22207 22146,36525	22297 22236,11951	22387 22325,87377	22477 22415,62803	22567 22505,3823
22118 22057,60826	22208 22147,36252	22298 22237,11678	22388 22326,87104	22478 22416,6253	22568 22506,37956
22119 22058,60553	22209 22148,35979	22299 22238,11405	22389 22327,86831	22479 22417,62257	22569 22507,37683
22120 22059,6028	22210 22149,35706	22300 22239,11132	22390 22328,86558	22480 22418,61984	22570 22508,3741
22121 22060,60007	22211 22150,35433	22301 22240,10859	22391 22329,86285	22481 22419,61711	22571 22509,37137
22122 22061,59734	22212 22151,3516	22302 22241,10586	22392 22330,86012	22482 22420,61438	22572 22510,36864
22123 22062,59461	22213 22152,34887	22303 22242,10313	22393 22331,85739	22483 22421,61165	22573 22511,36591
22124 22063,59188	22214 22153,34614	22304 22243,1004	22394 22332,85466	22484 22422,60892	22574 22512,36318
22125 22064,58915	22215 22154,34341	22305 22244,09767	22395 22333,85193	22485 22423,60619	22575 22513,36045
22126 22065,58642	22216 22155,34068	22306 22245,09494	22396 22334,8492	22486 22424,60346	22576 22514,35772
22127 22066,58369	22217 22156,33795	22307 22246,09221	22397 22335,84647	22487 22425,60073	22577 22515,35499
22128 22067,58096	22218 22157,33522	22308 22247,08948	22398 22336,84374	22488 22426,598	22578 22516,35226
22129 22068,57823	22219 22158,33249	22309 22248,08675	22399 22337,84101	22489 22427,59527	22579 22517,34953
22130 22069,57549	22220 22159,32976	22310 22249,08402	22400 22338,83828	22490 22428,59254	22580 22518,3468
22131 22070,57276	22221 22160,32703	22311 22250,08129	22401 22339,83555	22491 22429,58981	22581 22519,34407
22132 22071,57003	22222 22161,3243	22312 22251,07856	22402 22340,83282	22492 22430,58708	22582 22520,34134
22133 22072,5673	22223 22162,32156	22313 22252,07583	22403 22341,83009	22493 22431,58435	22583 22521,33861
22134 22073,56457	22224 22163,31883	22314 22253,0731	22404 22342,82736	22494 22432,58162	22584 22522,33588
22135 22074,56184	22225 22164,3161	22315 22254,07036	22405 22343,82463	22495 22433,57889	22585 22523,33315
22136 22075,55911	22226 22165,31337	22316 22255,06763	22406 22344,8219	22496 22434,57616	22586 22524,33042
22137 22076,55638	22227 22166,31064	22317 22256,0649	22407 22345,81916	22497 22435,57343	22587 22525,32769
22138 22077,55365	22228 22167,30791	22318 22257,06217	22408 22346,81643	22498 22436,5707	22588 22526,32496
22139 22078,55092	22229 22168,30518	22319 22258,05944	22409 22347,8137	22499 22437,56796	22589 22527,32223
22140 22079,54819	22230 22169,30245	22320 22259,05671	22410 22348,81097	22500 22438,56523	22590 22528,3195
22141 22080,54546	22231 22170,29972	22321 22260,05398	22411 22349,80824	22501 22439,5625	22591 22529,31676
22142 22081,54273	22232 22171,29699	22322 22261,05125	22412 22350,80551	22502 22440,55977	22592 22530,31403
22143 22082,54	22233 22172,29426	22323 22262,04852	22413 22351,80278	22503 22441,55704	22593 22531,3113
22144 22083,53727	22234 22173,29153	22324 22263,04579	22414 22352,80005	22504 22442,55431	22594 22532,30857
22145 22084,53454	22235 22174,2888	22325 22264,04306	22415 22353,79732	22505 22443,55158	22595 22533,30584
22146 22085,53181	22236 22175,28607	22326 22265,04033	22416 22354,79459	22506 22444,54885	22596 22534,30311
22147 22086,52908	22237 22176,28334	22327 22266,0376	22417 22355,79186	22507 22445,54612	22597 22535,30038
22148 22087,52635	22238 22177,28061	22328 22267,03487	22418 22356,78913	22508 22446,54339	22598 22536,29765
22149 22088,52362	22239 22178,27788	22329 22268,03214	22419 22357,7864	22509 22447,54066	22599 22537,29492
22150 22089,52089	22240 22179,27515	22330 22269,02941	22420 22358,78367	22510 22448,53793	22600 22538,29219
22151 22090,51816	22241 22180,27242	22331 22270,02668	22421 22359,78094	22511 22449,5352	22601 22539,28946
22152 22091,51543	22242 22181,26969	22332 22271,02395	22422 22360,77821	22512 22450,53247	22602 22540,28673
22153 22092,51269	22243 22182,26696	22333 22272,02122	22423 22361,77548	22513 22451,52974	22603 22541,284
22154 22093,50996	22244 22183,26423	22334 22273,01849	22424 22362,77275	22514 22452,52701	22604 22542,28127
22155 22094,50723	22245 22184,2615	22335 22274,01576	22425 22363,77002	22515 22453,52428	22605 22543,27854
22156 22095,5045	22246 22185,25876	22336 22275,01303	22426 22364,76729	22516 22454,52155	22606 22544,27581
22157 22096,50177	22247 22186,25603	22337 22276,0103	22427 22365,76456	22517 22455,51882	22607 22545,27308
22158 22097,49904	22248 22187,2533	22338 22277,00756	22428 22366,76183	22518 22456,51609	22608 22546,27035
22159 22098,49631	22249 22188,25057	22339 22278,00483	22429 22367,7591	22519 22457,51336	22609 22547,26762
22160 22099,49358	22250 22189,24784	22340 22279,0021	22430 22368,75636	22520 22458,51063	22610 22548,26489
22161 22100,49085	22251 22190,24511	22341 22279,99937	22431 22369,75363	22521 22459,5079	22611 22549,26216
22162 22101,48812	22252 22191,24238	22342 22280,99664	22432 22370,7509	22522 22460,50516	22612 22550,25943
22163 22102,48539	22253 22192,23965	22343 22281,99391	22433 22371,74817	22523 22461,50243	22613 22551,2567
22164 22103,48266	22254 22193,23692	22344 22282,99118	22434 22372,74544	22524 22462,4997	22614 22552,25396

TABLE TO FIND OUT THE POINT A IN EARTH RETURNS 199

22615 22553,25123	22705 22643,0055	22795 22732,75976	22885 22822,51402	22975 22912,26828	23065 23002,02254
22616 22554,2485	22706 22644,00276	22796 22733,75703	22886 22823,51129	22976 22913,26555	23066 23003,01981
22617 22555,24577	22707 22645,00003	22797 22734,7543	22887 22824,50856	22977 22914,26282	23067 23004,01708
22618 22556,24304	22708 22645,9973	22798 22735,75157	22888 22825,50583	22978 22915,26009	23068 23005,01435
22619 22557,24031	22709 22646,99457	22799 22736,74883	22889 22826,5031	22979 22916,25736	23069 23006,01162
22620 22558,23758	22710 22647,99184	22800 22737,7461	22890 22827,50037	22980 22917,25463	23070 23007,00889
22621 22559,23485	22711 22648,98911	22801 22738,74337	22891 22828,49763	22981 22918,2519	23071 23008,00616
22622 22560,23212	22712 22649,98638	22802 22739,74064	22892 22829,4949	22982 22919,24917	23072 23009,00343
22623 22561,22939	22713 22650,98365	22803 22740,73791	22893 22830,49217	22983 22920,24643	23073 23010,0007
22624 22562,22666	22714 22651,98092	22804 22741,73518	22894 22831,48944	22984 22921,2437	23074 23010,99797
22625 22563,22393	22715 22652,97819	22805 22742,73245	22895 22832,48671	22985 22922,24097	23075 23011,99523
22626 22564,2212	22716 22653,97546	22806 22743,72972	22896 22833,48398	22986 22923,23824	23076 23012,9925
22627 22565,21847	22717 22654,97273	22807 22744,72699	22897 22834,48125	22987 22924,23551	23077 23013,98977
22628 22566,21574	22718 22655,97	22808 22745,72426	22898 22835,47852	22988 22925,23278	23078 23014,98704
22629 22567,21301	22719 22656,96727	22809 22746,72153	22899 22836,47579	22989 22926,23005	23079 23015,98431
22630 22568,21028	22720 22657,96454	22810 22747,7188	22900 22837,47306	22990 22927,22732	23080 23016,98158
22631 22569,20755	22721 22658,96181	22811 22748,71607	22901 22838,47033	22991 22928,22459	23081 23017,97885
22632 22570,20482	22722 22659,95908	22812 22749,71334	22902 22839,4676	22992 22929,22186	23082 23018,97612
22633 22571,20209	22723 22660,95635	22813 22750,71061	22903 22840,46487	22993 22930,21913	23083 23019,97339
22634 22572,19936	22724 22661,95362	22814 22751,70788	22904 22841,46214	22994 22931,2164	23084 23020,97066
22635 22573,19663	22725 22662,95089	22815 22752,70515	22905 22842,45941	22995 22932,21367	23085 23021,96793
22636 22574,1939	22726 22663,94816	22816 22753,70242	22906 22843,45668	22996 22933,21094	23086 23022,9652
22637 22575,19116	22727 22664,94543	22817 22754,69969	22907 22844,45395	22997 22934,20821	23087 23023,96247
22638 22576,18843	22728 22665,9427	22818 22755,69696	22908 22845,45122	22998 22935,20548	23088 23024,95974
22639 22577,1857	22729 22666,93996	22819 22756,69423	22909 22846,44849	22999 22936,20275	23089 23025,95701
22640 22578,18297	22730 22667,93723	22820 22757,6915	22910 22847,44576	23000 22937,20002	23090 23026,95428
22641 22579,18024	22731 22668,9345	22821 22758,68877	22911 22848,44303	23001 22938,19729	23091 23027,95155
22642 22580,17751	22732 22669,93177	22822 22759,68603	22912 22849,4403	23002 22939,19456	23092 23028,94882
22643 22581,17478	22733 22670,92904	22823 22760,6833	22913 22850,43757	23003 22940,19183	23093 23029,94609
22644 22582,17205	22734 22671,92631	22824 22761,68057	22914 22851,43483	23004 22941,1891	23094 23030,94336
22645 22583,16932	22735 22672,92358	22825 22762,67784	22915 22852,4321	23005 22942,18637	23095 23031,94063
22646 22584,16659	22736 22673,92085	22826 22763,67511	22916 22853,42937	23006 22943,18363	23096 23032,9379
22647 22585,16386	22737 22674,91812	22827 22764,67238	22917 22854,42664	23007 22944,1809	23097 23033,93517
22648 22586,16113	22738 22675,91539	22828 22765,66965	22918 22855,42391	23008 22945,17817	23098 23034,93243
22649 22587,1584	22739 22676,91266	22829 22766,66692	22919 22856,42118	23009 22946,17544	23099 23035,9297
22650 22588,15567	22740 22677,90993	22830 22767,66419	22920 22857,41845	23010 22947,17271	23100 23036,92697
22651 22589,15294	22741 22678,9072	22831 22768,66146	22921 22858,41572	23011 22948,16998	23101 23037,92424
22652 22590,15021	22742 22679,90447	22832 22769,65873	22922 22859,41299	23012 22949,16725	23102 23038,92151
22653 22591,14748	22743 22680,90174	22833 22770,656	22923 22860,41026	23013 22950,16452	23103 23039,91878
22654 22592,14475	22744 22681,89901	22834 22771,65327	22924 22861,40753	23014 22951,16179	23104 23040,91605
22655 22593,14202	22745 22682,89628	22835 22772,65054	22925 22862,4048	23015 22952,15906	23105 23041,91332
22656 22594,13929	22746 22683,89355	22836 22773,64781	22926 22863,40207	23016 22953,15633	23106 23042,91059
22657 22595,13656	22747 22684,89082	22837 22774,64508	22927 22864,39934	23017 22954,1536	23107 23043,90786
22658 22596,13383	22748 22685,88809	22838 22775,64235	22928 22865,39661	23018 22955,15087	23108 23044,90513
22659 22597,1311	22749 22686,88536	22839 22776,63962	22929 22866,39388	23019 22956,14814	23109 23045,9024
22660 22598,12836	22750 22687,88263	22840 22777,63689	22930 22867,39115	23020 22957,14541	23110 23046,89967
22661 22599,12563	22751 22688,8799	22841 22778,63416	22931 22868,38842	23021 22958,14268	23111 23047,89694
22662 22600,1229	22752 22689,87717	22842 22779,63143	22932 22869,38569	23022 22959,13995	23112 23048,89421
22663 22601,12017	22753 22690,87443	22843 22780,6287	22933 22870,38296	23023 22960,13722	23113 23049,89148
22664 22602,11744	22754 22691,8717	22844 22781,62597	22934 22871,38023	23024 22961,13449	23114 23050,88875
22665 22603,11471	22755 22692,86897	22845 22782,62323	22935 22872,3775	23025 22962,13176	23115 23051,88602
22666 22604,11198	22756 22693,86624	22846 22783,6205	22936 22873,37477	23026 22963,12903	23116 23052,88329
22667 22605,10925	22757 22694,86351	22847 22784,61777	22937 22874,37203	23027 22964,1263	23117 23053,88056
22668 22606,10652	22758 22695,86078	22848 22785,61504	22938 22875,3693	23028 22965,12357	23118 23054,87783
22669 22607,10379	22759 22696,85805	22849 22786,61231	22939 22876,86657	23029 22966,12083	23119 23055,8751
22670 22608,10106	22760 22697,85532	22850 22787,60958	22940 22877,36384	23030 22967,1181	23120 23056,87237
22671 22609,09833	22761 22698,85259	22851 22788,60685	22941 22878,36111	23031 22968,11537	23121 23057,86963
22672 22610,0956	22762 22699,84986	22852 22789,60412	22942 22879,35838	23032 22969,11264	23122 23058,8669
22673 22611,09287	22763 22700,84713	22853 22790,60139	22943 22880,35565	23033 22970,10991	23123 23059,86417
22674 22612,09014	22764 22701,8444	22854 22791,59866	22944 22881,35292	23034 22971,10718	23124 23060,86144
22675 22613,08741	22765 22702,84167	22855 22792,59593	22945 22882,35019	23035 22972,10445	23125 23061,85871
22676 22614,08468	22766 22703,83894	22856 22793,5932	22946 22883,34746	23036 22973,10172	23126 23062,85598
22677 22615,08195	22767 22704,83621	22857 22794,59047	22947 22884,34473	23037 22974,09899	23127 23063,85325
22678 22616,07922	22768 22705,83348	22858 22795,58774	22948 22885,342	23038 22975,09626	23128 23064,85052
22679 22617,07649	22769 22706,83075	22859 22796,58501	22949 22886,33927	23039 22976,09353	23129 23065,84779
22680 22618,07376	22770 22707,82802	22860 22797,58228	22950 22887,33654	23040 22977,0908	23130 23066,84506
22681 22619,07103	22771 22708,82529	22861 22798,57955	22951 22888,33381	23041 22978,08807	23131 23067,84233
22682 22620,0683	22772 22709,82256	22862 22799,57682	22952 22889,33108	23042 22979,08534	23132 23068,8396
22683 22621,06556	22773 22710,81983	22863 22800,57409	22953 22890,32835	23043 22980,08261	23133 23069,83687
22684 22622,06283	22774 22711,8171	22864 22801,57136	22954 22891,32562	23044 22981,07988	23134 23070,83414
22685 22623,0601	22775 22712,81437	22865 22802,56863	22955 22892,32289	23045 22982,07715	23135 23071,83141
22686 22624,05737	22776 22713,81163	22866 22803,5659	22956 22893,32016	23046 22983,07442	23136 23072,82868
22687 22625,05464	22777 22714,8089	22867 22804,56317	22957 22894,31743	23047 22984,07169	23137 23073,82595
22688 22626,05191	22778 22715,80617	22868 22805,56043	22958 22895,3147	23048 22985,06896	23138 23074,82322
22689 22627,04918	22779 22716,80344	22869 22806,5577	22959 22896,31197	23049 22986,06623	23139 23075,82049
22690 22628,04645	22780 22717,80071	22870 22807,55497	22960 22897,30923	23050 22987,0635	23140 23076,81776
22691 22629,04372	22781 22718,79798	22871 22808,55224	22961 22898,3065	23051 22988,06077	23141 23077,81503
22692 22630,04099	22782 22719,79525	22872 22809,54951	22962 22899,30377	23052 22989,05803	23142 23078,8123
22693 22631,03826	22783 22720,79252	22873 22810,54678	22963 22900,30104	23053 22990,0553	23143 23079,80957
22694 22632,03553	22784 22721,78979	22874 22811,54405	22964 22901,29831	23054 22991,05257	23144 23080,80683
22695 22633,0328	22785 22722,78706	22875 22812,54132	22965 22902,29558	23055 22992,04984	23145 23081,8041
22696 22634,03007	22786 22723,78433	22876 22813,53859	22966 22903,29285	23056 22993,04711	23146 23082,80137
22697 22635,02734	22787 22724,7816	22877 22814,53586	22967 22904,29012	23057 22994,04438	23147 23083,79864
22698 22636,02461	22788 22725,77887	22878 22815,53313	22968 22905,28739	23058 22995,04165	23148 23084,79591
22699 22637,02188	22789 22726,77614	22879 22816,5304	22969 22906,28466	23059 22996,03892	23149 23085,79318
22700 22638,01915	22790 22727,77341	22880 22817,52767	22970 22907,28193	23060 22997,03619	23150 23086,79045
22701 22639,01642	22791 22728,77068	22881 22818,52494	22971 22908,2792	23061 22998,03346	23151 23087,78772
22702 22640,01369	22792 22729,76795	22882 22819,52221	22972 22909,27647	23062 22999,03073	23152 23088,78499
22703 22641,01096	22793 22730,76522	22883 22820,51948	22973 22910,27374	23063 23000,028	23153 23089,78226
22704 22642,00823	22794 22731,76249	22884 22821,51675	22974 22911,27101	23064 23001,02527	23154 23090,77953

23155	23091,7768	23245	23181,53106	23335	23271,28532	23425	23361,03958	23515	23450,79384	23605	23540,5481
23156	23092,77407	23246	23182,52833	23336	23272,28259	23426	23362,03685	23516	23451,79111	23606	23541,54537
23157	23093,77134	23247	23183,5256	23337	23273,27986	23427	23363,03412	23517	23452,78838	23607	23542,54264
23158	23094,76861	23248	23184,52287	23338	23274,27713	23428	23364,03139	23518	23453,78565	23608	23543,53991
23159	23095,76588	23249	23185,52014	23339	23275,2744	23429	23365,02866	23519	23454,78292	23609	23544,53718
23160	23096,76315	23250	23186,51741	23340	23276,27167	23430	23366,02593	23520	23455,78019	23610	23545,53445
23161	23097,76042	23251	23187,51468	23341	23277,26894	23431	23367,0232	23521	23456,77746	23611	23546,53172
23162	23098,75769	23252	23188,51195	23342	23278,26621	23432	23368,02047	23522	23457,77473	23612	23547,52899
23163	23099,75496	23253	23189,50922	23343	23279,26348	23433	23369,01774	23523	23458,772	23613	23548,52626
23164	23100,75223	23254	23190,50649	23344	23280,26075	23434	23370,01501	23524	23459,76927	23614	23549,52353
23165	23101,7495	23255	23191,50376	23345	23281,25802	23435	23371,01228	23525	23460,76654	23615	23550,5208
23166	23102,74677	23256	23192,50103	23346	23282,25529	23436	23372,00955	23526	23461,76381	23616	23551,51807
23167	23103,74403	23257	23193,4983	23347	23283,25256	23437	23373,00682	23527	23462,76108	23617	23552,51534
23168	23104,7413	23258	23194,49557	23348	23284,24983	23438	23374,00409	23528	23463,75835	23618	23553,51261
23169	23105,73857	23259	23195,49283	23349	23285,2471	23439	23375,00136	23529	23464,75562	23619	23554,50988
23170	23106,73584	23260	23196,4901	23350	23286,24437	23440	23375,99863	23530	23465,75289	23620	23555,50715
23171	23107,73311	23261	23197,48737	23351	23287,24164	23441	23376,9959	23531	23466,75016	23621	23556,50442
23172	23108,73038	23262	23198,48464	23352	23288,2389	23442	23377,99317	23532	23467,74743	23622	23557,50169
23173	23109,72765	23263	23199,48191	23353	23289,23617	23443	23378,99044	23533	23468,7447	23623	23558,49896
23174	23110,72492	23264	23200,47918	23354	23290,23344	23444	23379,9877	23534	23469,74197	23624	23559,49623
23175	23111,72219	23265	23201,47645	23355	23291,23071	23445	23380,98497	23535	23470,73924	23625	23560,4935
23176	23112,71946	23266	23202,47372	23356	23292,22798	23446	23381,98224	23536	23471,7365	23626	23561,49077
23177	23113,71673	23267	23203,47099	23357	23293,22525	23447	23382,97951	23537	23472,73377	23627	23562,48804
23178	23114,714	23268	23204,46826	23358	23294,22252	23448	23383,97678	23538	23473,73104	23628	23563,4853
23179	23115,71127	23269	23205,46553	23359	23295,21979	23449	23384,97405	23539	23474,72831	23629	23564,48257
23180	23116,70854	23270	23206,4628	23360	23296,21706	23450	23385,97132	23540	23475,72558	23630	23565,47984
23181	23117,70581	23271	23207,46007	23361	23297,21433	23451	23386,96859	23541	23476,72285	23631	23566,47711
23182	23118,70308	23272	23208,45734	23362	23298,2116	23452	23387,96586	23542	23477,72012	23632	23567,47438
23183	23119,70035	23273	23209,45461	23363	23299,20887	23453	23388,96313	23543	23478,71739	23633	23568,47165
23184	23120,69762	23274	23210,45188	23364	23300,20614	23454	23389,9604	23544	23479,71466	23634	23569,46892
23185	23121,69489	23275	23211,44915	23365	23301,20341	23455	23390,95767	23545	23480,71193	23635	23570,46619
23186	23122,69216	23276	23212,44642	23366	23302,20068	23456	23391,95494	23546	23481,7092	23636	23571,46346
23187	23123,68943	23277	23213,44369	23367	23303,19795	23457	23392,95221	23547	23482,70647	23637	23572,46073
23188	23124,6867	23278	23214,44096	23368	23304,19522	23458	23393,94948	23548	23483,70374	23638	23573,458
23189	23125,68397	23279	23215,43823	23369	23305,19249	23459	23394,94675	23549	23484,70101	23639	23574,45527
23190	23126,68123	23280	23216,4355	23370	23306,18976	23460	23395,94402	23550	23485,69828	23640	23575,45254
23191	23127,6785	23281	23217,43277	23371	23307,18703	23461	23396,94129	23551	23486,69555	23641	23576,44981
23192	23128,67577	23282	23218,43003	23372	23308,1843	23462	23397,93856	23552	23487,69282	23642	23577,44708
23193	23129,67304	23283	23219,4273	23373	23309,18157	23463	23398,93583	23553	23488,69009	23643	23578,44435
23194	23130,67031	23284	23220,42457	23374	23310,17884	23464	23399,9331	23554	23489,68736	23644	23579,44162
23195	23131,66758	23285	23221,42184	23375	23311,1761	23465	23400,93037	23555	23490,68463	23645	23580,43889
23196	23132,66485	23286	23222,41911	23376	23312,17337	23466	23401,92764	23556	23491,6819	23646	23581,43616
23197	23133,66212	23287	23223,41638	23377	23313,17064	23467	23402,9249	23557	23492,67917	23647	23582,43343
23198	23134,65939	23288	23224,41365	23378	23314,16791	23468	23403,92217	23558	23493,67644	23648	23583,4307
23199	23135,65666	23289	23225,41092	23379	23315,16518	23469	23404,91944	23559	23494,6737	23649	23584,42797
23200	23136,65393	23290	23226,40819	23380	23316,16245	23470	23405,91671	23560	23495,67097	23650	23585,42524
23201	23137,6512	23291	23227,40546	23381	23317,15972	23471	23406,91398	23561	23496,66824	23651	23586,4225
23202	23138,64847	23292	23228,40273	23382	23318,15699	23472	23407,91125	23562	23497,66551	23652	23587,41977
23203	23139,64574	23293	23229,4	23383	23319,15426	23473	23408,90852	23563	23498,66278	23653	23588,41704
23204	23140,64301	23294	23230,39727	23384	23320,15153	23474	23409,90579	23564	23499,66005	23654	23589,41431
23205	23141,64028	23295	23231,39454	23385	23321,1488	23475	23410,90306	23565	23500,65732	23655	23590,41158
23206	23142,63755	23296	23232,39181	23386	23322,14607	23476	23411,90033	23566	23501,65459	23656	23591,40885
23207	23143,63482	23297	23233,38908	23387	23323,14334	23477	23412,8976	23567	23502,65186	23657	23592,40612
23208	23144,63209	23298	23234,38635	23388	23324,14061	23478	23413,89487	23568	23503,64913	23658	23593,40339
23209	23145,62936	23299	23235,38362	23389	23325,13788	23479	23414,89214	23569	23504,6464	23659	23594,40066
23210	23146,62663	23300	23236,38089	23390	23326,13515	23480	23415,88941	23570	23505,64367	23660	23595,39793
23211	23147,6239	23301	23237,37816	23391	23327,13242	23481	23416,88668	23571	23506,64094	23661	23596,3952
23212	23148,62117	23302	23238,37543	23392	23328,12969	23482	23417,88395	23572	23507,63821	23662	23597,39247
23213	23149,61843	23303	23239,3727	23393	23329,12696	23483	23418,88122	23573	23508,63548	23663	23598,38974
23214	23150,6157	23304	23240,36997	23394	23330,12423	23484	23419,87849	23574	23509,63275	23664	23599,38701
23215	23151,61297	23305	23241,36723	23395	23331,1215	23485	23420,87576	23575	23510,63002	23665	23600,38428
23216	23152,61024	23306	23242,3645	23396	23332,11877	23486	23421,87303	23576	23511,62729	23666	23601,38155
23217	23153,60751	23307	23243,36177	23397	23333,11604	23487	23422,8703	23577	23512,62456	23667	23602,37882
23218	23154,60478	23308	23244,35904	23398	23334,1133	23488	23423,86757	23578	23513,62183	23668	23603,37609
23219	23155,60205	23309	23245,35631	23399	23335,11057	23489	23424,86484	23579	23514,6191	23669	23604,37336
23220	23156,59932	23310	23246,35358	23400	23336,10784	23490	23425,8621	23580	23515,61637	23670	23605,37063
23221	23157,59659	23311	23247,35085	23401	23337,10511	23491	23426,85937	23581	23516,61364	23671	23606,3679
23222	23158,59386	23312	23248,34812	23402	23338,10238	23492	23427,85664	23582	23517,6109	23672	23607,36517
23223	23159,59113	23313	23249,34539	23403	23339,09965	23493	23428,85391	23583	23518,60817	23673	23608,36244
23224	23160,5884	23314	23250,34266	23404	23340,09692	23494	23429,85118	23584	23519,60544	23674	23609,3597
23225	23161,58567	23315	23251,33993	23405	23341,09419	23495	23430,84845	23585	23520,60271	23675	23610,35697
23226	23162,58294	23316	23252,3372	23406	23342,09146	23496	23431,84572	23586	23521,59998	23676	23611,35424
23227	23163,58021	23317	23253,33447	23407	23343,08873	23497	23432,84299	23587	23522,59725	23677	23612,35151
23228	23164,57748	23318	23254,33174	23408	23344,086	23498	23433,84026	23588	23523,59452	23678	23613,34878
23229	23165,57475	23319	23255,32901	23409	23345,08327	23499	23434,83753	23589	23524,59179	23679	23614,34605
23230	23166,57202	23320	23256,32628	23410	23346,08054	23500	23435,8348	23590	23525,58906	23680	23615,34332
23231	23167,56929	23321	23257,32355	23411	23347,07781	23501	23436,83207	23591	23526,58633	23681	23616,34059
23232	23168,56656	23322	23258,32082	23412	23348,07508	23502	23437,82934	23592	23527,5836	23682	23617,33786
23233	23169,56383	23323	23259,31809	23413	23349,07235	23503	23438,82661	23593	23528,58087	23683	23618,33513
23234	23170,5611	23324	23260,31536	23414	23350,06962	23504	23439,82388	23594	23529,57814	23684	23619,3324
23235	23171,55837	23325	23261,31263	23415	23351,06689	23505	23440,82115	23595	23530,57541	23685	23620,32967
23236	23172,55563	23326	23262,3099	23416	23352,06416	23506	23441,81842	23596	23531,57268	23686	23621,32694
23237	23173,5529	23327	23263,30717	23417	23353,06143	23507	23442,81569	23597	23532,56995	23687	23622,32421
23238	23174,55017	23328	23264,30444	23418	23354,0587	23508	23443,81296	23598	23533,56722	23688	23623,32148
23239	23175,54744	23329	23265,3017	23419	23355,05597	23509	23444,81023	23599	23534,56449	23689	23624,31875
23240	23176,54471	23330	23266,29897	23420	23356,05324	23510	23445,8075	23600	23535,56176	23690	23625,31602
23241	23177,54198	23331	23267,29624	23421	23357,0505	23511	23446,80477	23601	23536,55903	23691	23626,31329
23242	23178,53925	23332	23268,29351	23422	23358,04777	23512	23447,80204	23602	23537,5563	23692	23627,31056
23243	23179,53652	23333	23269,29078	23423	23359,04504	23513	23448,7993	23603	23538,55357	23693	23628,30783
23244	23180,53379	23334	23270,28805	23424	23360,04231	23514	23449,79657	23604	23539,55084	23694	23629,3051

TABLE TO FIND OUT THE POINT A IN EARTH RETURNS

23695	23630,30237	23785	23720,05663	23875	23809,81089	23965	23899,56515	24055	23989,31941	24145	24079,07367
23696	23631,29964	23786	23721,0539	23876	23810,80816	23966	23900,56242	24056	23990,31668	24146	24080,07094
23697	23632,2969	23787	23722,05117	23877	23811,80543	23967	23901,55969	24057	23991,31395	24147	24081,06821
23698	23633,29417	23788	23723,04844	23878	23812,8027	23968	23902,55696	24058	23992,31122	24148	24082,06548
23699	23634,29144	23789	23724,0457	23879	23813,79997	23969	23903,55423	24059	23993,30849	24149	24083,06275
23700	23635,28871	23790	23725,04297	23880	23814,79724	23970	23904,5515	24060	23994,30576	24150	24084,06002
23701	23636,28598	23791	23726,44024	23881	23815,7945	23971	23905,54877	24061	23995,30303	24151	24085,05729
23702	23637,28325	23792	23727,03751	23882	23816,79177	23972	23906,54604	24062	23996,3003	24152	24086,05456
23703	23638,28052	23793	23728,03478	23883	23817,78904	23973	23907,54331	24063	23997,29757	24153	24087,05183
23704	23639,27779	23794	23729,03205	23884	23818,78631	23974	23908,54057	24064	23998,29484	24154	24088,0491
23705	23640,27506	23795	23730,02932	23885	23819,78358	23975	23909,53784	24065	23999,29211	24155	24089,04637
23706	23641,27233	23796	23731,02659	23886	23820,78085	23976	23910,53511	24066	24000,28937	24156	24090,04364
23707	23642,2696	23797	23732,02386	23887	23821,77812	23977	23911,53238	24067	24001,28664	24157	24091,04091
23708	23643,26687	23798	23733,02113	23888	23822,77539	23978	23912,52965	24068	24002,28391	24158	24092,03817
23709	23644,26414	23799	23734,0184	23889	23823,77266	23979	23913,52692	24069	24003,28118	24159	24093,03544
23710	23645,26141	23800	23735,01567	23890	23824,76993	23980	23914,52419	24070	24004,27845	24160	24094,03271
23711	23646,25868	23801	23736,01294	23891	23825,7672	23981	23915,52146	24071	24005,27572	24161	24095,02998
23712	23647,25595	23802	23737,01021	23892	23826,76447	23982	23916,51873	24072	24006,27299	24162	24096,02725
23713	23648,25322	23803	23738,00748	23893	23827,76174	23983	23917,516	24073	24007,27026	24163	24097,02452
23714	23649,25049	23804	23739,00475	23894	23828,75901	23984	23918,51327	24074	24008,26753	24164	24098,02179
23715	23650,24776	23805	23740,00202	23895	23829,75628	23985	23919,51054	24075	24009,2648	24165	24099,01906
23716	23651,24503	23806	23740,99929	23896	23830,75355	23986	23920,50781	24076	24010,26207	24166	24100,01633
23717	23652,2423	23807	23741,99656	23897	23831,75082	23987	23921,50508	24077	24011,25934	24167	24101,0136
23718	23653,23957	23808	23742,99383	23898	23832,74809	23988	23922,50235	24078	24012,25661	24168	24102,01087
23719	23654,23684	23809	23743,9911	23899	23833,74536	23989	23923,49962	24079	24013,25388	24169	24103,00814
23720	23655,2341	23810	23744,98837	23900	23834,74263	23990	23924,49689	24080	24014,25115	24170	24104,00541
23721	23656,23137	23811	23745,98564	23901	23835,7399	23991	23925,49416	24081	24015,24842	24171	24105,00268
23722	23657,22864	23812	23746,9829	23902	23836,73717	23992	23926,49143	24082	24016,24569	24172	24105,99995
23723	23658,22591	23813	23747,98017	23903	23837,73444	23993	23927,4887	24083	24017,24296	24173	24106,99722
23724	23659,22318	23814	23748,97744	23904	23838,73171	23994	23928,48597	24084	24018,24023	24174	24107,99449
23725	23660,22045	23815	23749,97471	23905	23839,72897	23995	23929,48324	24085	24019,2375	24175	24108,99176
23726	23661,21772	23816	23750,97198	23906	23840,72624	23996	23930,48051	24086	24020,23477	24176	24109,98903
23727	23662,21499	23817	23751,96925	23907	23841,72351	23997	23931,47777	24087	24021,23204	24177	24110,9863
23728	23663,21226	23818	23752,96652	23908	23842,72078	23998	23932,47504	24088	24022,22931	24178	24111,98357
23729	23664,20953	23819	23753,96379	23909	23843,71805	23999	23933,47231	24089	24023,22657	24179	24112,98084
23730	23665,2068	23820	23754,96106	23910	23844,71532	24000	23934,46958	24090	24024,22384	24180	24113,97811
23731	23666,20407	23821	23755,95833	23911	23845,71259	24001	23935,46685	24091	24025,22111	24181	24114,97537
23732	23667,20134	23822	23756,9556	23912	23846,70986	24002	23936,46412	24092	24026,21838	24182	24115,97264
23733	23668,19861	23823	23757,95287	23913	23847,70713	24003	23937,46139	24093	24027,21565	24183	24116,96991
23734	23669,19588	23824	23758,95014	23914	23848,7044	24004	23938,45866	24094	24028,21292	24184	24117,96718
23735	23670,19315	23825	23759,94741	23915	23849,70167	24005	23939,45593	24095	24029,21019	24185	24118,96445
23736	23671,19042	23826	23760,94468	23916	23850,69894	24006	23940,4532	24096	24030,20746	24186	24119,96172
23737	23672,18769	23827	23761,94195	23917	23851,69621	24007	23941,45047	24097	24031,20473	24187	24120,95899
23738	23673,18496	23828	23762,93922	23918	23852,69348	24008	23942,44774	24098	24032,202	24188	24121,95626
23739	23674,18223	23829	23763,93649	23919	23853,69075	24009	23943,44501	24099	24033,19927	24189	24122,95353
23740	23675,1795	23830	23764,93376	23920	23854,68802	24010	23944,44228	24100	24034,19654	24190	24123,9508
23741	23676,17677	23831	23765,93103	23921	23855,68529	24011	23945,43955	24101	24035,19381	24191	24124,94807
23742	23677,17404	23832	23766,9283	23922	23856,68256	24012	23946,43682	24102	24036,19108	24192	24125,94534
23743	23678,1713	23833	23767,92557	23923	23857,67983	24013	23947,43409	24103	24037,18835	24193	24126,94261
23744	23679,16857	23834	23768,92284	23924	23858,6771	24014	23948,43136	24104	24038,18562	24194	24127,93988
23745	23680,16584	23835	23769,9201	23925	23859,67437	24015	23949,42863	24105	24039,18289	24195	24128,93715
23746	23681,16311	23836	23770,91737	23926	23860,67164	24016	23950,4259	24106	24040,18016	24196	24129,93442
23747	23682,16038	23837	23771,91464	23927	23861,66891	24017	23951,42317	24107	24041,17743	24197	24130,93169
23748	23683,15765	23838	23772,91191	23928	23862,66617	24018	23952,42044	24108	24042,1747	24198	24131,92896
23749	23684,15492	23839	23773,90918	23929	23863,66344	24019	23953,41771	24109	24043,17197	24199	24132,92623
23750	23685,15219	23840	23774,90645	23930	23864,66071	24020	23954,41497	24110	24044,16924	24200	24133,9235
23751	23686,14946	23841	23775,90372	23931	23865,65798	24021	23955,41224	24111	24045,16651	24201	24134,92077
23752	23687,14673	23842	23776,90099	23932	23866,65525	24022	23956,40951	24112	24046,16377	24202	24135,91804
23753	23688,144	23843	23777,89826	23933	23867,65252	24023	23957,40678	24113	24047,16104	24203	24136,91531
23754	23689,14127	23844	23778,89553	23934	23868,64979	24024	23958,40405	24114	24048,15831	24204	24137,91257
23755	23690,13854	23845	23779,8928	23935	23869,64706	24025	23959,40132	24115	24049,15558	24205	24138,90984
23756	23691,13581	23846	23780,89007	23936	23870,64433	24026	23960,39859	24116	24050,15285	24206	24139,90711
23757	23692,13308	23847	23781,88734	23937	23871,6416	24027	23961,39586	24117	24051,15012	24207	24140,90438
23758	23693,13035	23848	23782,88461	23938	23872,63887	24028	23962,39313	24118	24052,14739	24208	24141,90165
23759	23694,12762	23849	23783,88188	23939	23873,63614	24029	23963,3904	24119	24053,14466	24209	24142,89892
23760	23695,12489	23850	23784,87915	23940	23874,63341	24030	23964,38767	24120	24054,14193	24210	24143,89619
23761	23696,12216	23851	23785,87642	23941	23875,63068	24031	23965,38494	24121	24055,1392	24211	24144,89346
23762	23697,11943	23852	23786,87369	23942	23876,62795	24032	23966,38221	24122	24056,13647	24212	24145,89073
23763	23698,1167	23853	23787,87096	23943	23877,62522	24033	23967,37948	24123	24057,13374	24213	24146,888
23764	23699,11397	23854	23788,86823	23944	23878,62249	24034	23968,37675	24124	24058,13101	24214	24147,88527
23765	23700,11124	23855	23789,8655	23945	23879,61976	24035	23969,37402	24125	24059,12828	24215	24148,88254
23766	23701,1085	23856	23790,86277	23946	23880,61703	24036	23970,37129	24126	24060,12555	24216	24149,87981
23767	23702,10577	23857	23791,86004	23947	23881,6143	24037	23971,36856	24127	24061,12282	24217	24150,87708
23768	23703,10304	23858	23792,8573	23948	23882,61157	24038	23972,36583	24128	24062,12009	24218	24151,87435
23769	23704,10031	23859	23793,85457	23949	23883,60884	24039	23973,3631	24129	24063,11736	24219	24152,87162
23770	23705,09758	23860	23794,85184	23950	23884,60611	24040	23974,36037	24130	24064,11463	24220	24153,86889
23771	23706,09485	23861	23795,84911	23951	23885,60337	24041	23975,35764	24131	24065,1119	24221	24154,86616
23772	23707,09212	23862	23796,84638	23952	23886,60064	24042	23976,35491	24132	24066,10917	24222	24155,86343
23773	23708,08939	23863	23797,84365	23953	23887,59791	24043	23977,35217	24133	24067,10644	24223	24156,8607
23774	23709,08666	23864	23798,84092	23954	23888,59518	24044	23978,34944	24134	24068,10371	24224	24157,85797
23775	23710,08393	23865	23799,83819	23955	23889,59245	24045	23979,34671	24135	24069,10097	24225	24158,85524
23776	23711,0812	23866	23800,83546	23956	23890,58972	24046	23980,34398	24136	24070,09824	24226	24159,85251
23777	23712,07847	23867	23801,83273	23957	23891,58699	24047	23981,34125	24137	24071,09551	24227	24160,84977
23778	23713,07574	23868	23802,83	23958	23892,58426	24048	23982,33852	24138	24072,09278	24228	24161,84704
23779	23714,07301	23869	23803,82727	23959	23893,58153	24049	23983,33579	24139	24073,09005	24229	24162,84431
23780	23715,07028	23870	23804,82454	23960	23894,5788	24050	23984,33306	24140	24074,08732	24230	24163,84158
23781	23716,06755	23871	23805,82181	23961	23895,57607	24051	23985,33033	24141	24075,08459	24231	24164,83885
23782	23717,06482	23872	23806,81908	23962	23896,57334	24052	23986,3276	24142	24076,08186	24232	24165,83612
23783	23718,06209	23873	23807,81635	23963	23897,57061	24053	23987,32487	24143	24077,07913	24233	24166,83339
23784	23719,05936	23874	23808,81362	23964	23898,56788	24054	23988,32214	24144	24078,0764	24234	24167,83066

24235	24168,82793	24325	24258,58219	24415	24348,33645	24505	24438,09071	24595	24527,84498	24685	24617,59924
24236	24169,8252	24326	24259,57946	24416	24349,33372	24506	24439,08798	24596	24528,84224	24686	24618,59651
24237	24170,82247	24327	24260,57673	24417	24350,33099	24507	24440,08525	24597	24529,83951	24687	24619,59378
24238	24171,81974	24328	24261,574	24418	24351,32826	24508	24441,08252	24598	24530,83678	24688	24620,59104
24239	24172,81701	24329	24262,57127	24419	24352,32553	24509	24442,07979	24599	24531,83405	24689	24621,58831
24240	24173,81428	24330	24263,56854	24420	24353,3228	24510	24443,07706	24600	24532,83132	24690	24622,58558
24241	24174,81155	24331	24264,56581	24421	24354,32007	24511	24444,07433	24601	24533,82859	24691	24623,58285
24242	24175,80882	24332	24265,56308	24422	24355,31734	24512	24445,0716	24602	24534,82586	24692	24624,58012
24243	24176,80609	24333	24266,56035	24423	24356,31461	24513	24446,06887	24603	24535,82313	24693	24625,57739
24244	24177,80336	24334	24267,55762	24424	24357,31188	24514	24447,06614	24604	24536,8204	24694	24626,57466
24245	24178,80063	24335	24268,55489	24425	24358,30915	24515	24448,06341	24605	24537,81767	24695	24627,57193
24246	24179,7979	24336	24269,55216	24426	24359,30642	24516	24449,06068	24606	24538,81494	24696	24628,5692
24247	24180,79517	24337	24270,54943	24427	24360,30369	24517	24450,05795	24607	24539,81221	24697	24629,56647
24248	24181,79244	24338	24271,5467	24428	24361,30096	24518	24451,05522	24608	24540,80948	24698	24630,56374
24249	24182,78971	24339	24272,54397	24429	24362,29823	24519	24452,05249	24609	24541,80675	24699	24631,56101
24250	24183,78697	24340	24273,54124	24430	24363,2955	24520	24453,04976	24610	24542,80402	24700	24632,55828
24251	24184,78424	24341	24274,53851	24431	24364,29277	24521	24454,04703	24611	24543,80129	24701	24633,55555
24252	24185,78151	24342	24275,53577	24432	24365,29004	24522	24455,0443	24612	24544,79856	24702	24634,55282
24253	24186,77878	24343	24276,53304	24433	24366,28731	24523	24456,04157	24613	24545,79583	24703	24635,55009
24254	24187,77605	24344	24277,53031	24434	24367,28457	24524	24457,03884	24614	24546,7931	24704	24636,54736
24255	24188,77332	24345	24278,52758	24435	24368,28184	24525	24458,03611	24615	24547,79037	24705	24637,54463
24256	24189,77059	24346	24279,52485	24436	24369,27911	24526	24459,03338	24616	24548,78764	24706	24638,5419
24257	24190,76786	24347	24280,52212	24437	24370,27638	24527	24460,03064	24617	24549,78491	24707	24639,53917
24258	24191,76513	24348	24281,51939	24438	24371,27365	24528	24461,02791	24618	24550,78218	24708	24640,53644
24259	24192,7624	24349	24282,51666	24439	24372,27092	24529	24462,02518	24619	24551,77944	24709	24641,53371
24260	24193,75967	24350	24283,51393	24440	24373,26819	24530	24463,02245	24620	24552,77671	24710	24642,53098
24261	24194,75694	24351	24284,5112	24441	24374,26546	24531	24464,01972	24621	24553,77398	24711	24643,52824
24262	24195,75421	24352	24285,50847	24442	24375,26273	24532	24465,01699	24622	24554,77125	24712	24644,52551
24263	24196,75148	24353	24286,50574	24443	24376,26	24533	24466,01426	24623	24555,76852	24713	24645,52278
24264	24197,74875	24354	24287,50301	24444	24377,25727	24534	24467,01153	24624	24556,76579	24714	24646,52005
24265	24198,74602	24355	24288,50028	24445	24378,25454	24535	24468,0088	24625	24557,76306	24715	24647,51732
24266	24199,74329	24356	24289,49755	24446	24379,25181	24536	24469,00607	24626	24558,76033	24716	24648,51459
24267	24200,74056	24357	24290,49482	24447	24380,24908	24537	24470,00334	24627	24559,7576	24717	24649,51186
24268	24201,73783	24358	24291,49209	24448	24381,24635	24538	24471,00061	24628	24560,75487	24718	24650,50913
24269	24202,7351	24359	24292,48936	24449	24382,24362	24539	24471,99788	24629	24561,75214	24719	24651,5064
24270	24203,73237	24360	24293,48663	24450	24383,24089	24540	24472,99515	24630	24562,74941	24720	24652,50367
24271	24204,72964	24361	24294,4839	24451	24384,23816	24541	24473,99242	24631	24563,74668	24721	24653,50094
24272	24205,72691	24362	24295,48117	24452	24385,23543	24542	24474,98969	24632	24564,74395	24722	24654,49821
24273	24206,72417	24363	24296,47844	24453	24386,2327	24543	24475,98696	24633	24565,74122	24723	24655,49548
24274	24207,72144	24364	24297,47571	24454	24387,22997	24544	24476,98423	24634	24566,73849	24724	24656,49275
24275	24208,71871	24365	24298,47297	24455	24388,22724	24545	24477,9815	24635	24567,73576	24725	24657,49002
24276	24209,71598	24366	24299,47024	24456	24389,22451	24546	24478,97877	24636	24568,73303	24726	24658,48729
24277	24210,71325	24367	24300,46751	24457	24390,22177	24547	24479,97604	24637	24569,7303	24727	24659,48456
24278	24211,71052	24368	24301,46478	24458	24391,21904	24548	24480,97331	24638	24570,72757	24728	24660,48183
24279	24212,70779	24369	24302,46205	24459	24392,21631	24549	24481,97058	24639	24571,72484	24729	24661,4791
24280	24213,70506	24370	24303,45932	24460	24393,21358	24550	24482,96784	24640	24572,72211	24730	24662,47637
24281	24214,70233	24371	24304,45659	24461	24394,21085	24551	24483,96511	24641	24573,71938	24731	24663,47364
24282	24215,6996	24372	24305,45386	24462	24395,20812	24552	24484,96238	24642	24574,71664	24732	24664,47091
24283	24216,69687	24373	24306,45113	24463	24396,20539	24553	24485,95965	24643	24575,71391	24733	24665,46818
24284	24217,69414	24374	24307,4484	24464	24397,20266	24554	24486,95692	24644	24576,71118	24734	24666,46544
24285	24218,69141	24375	24308,44567	24465	24398,19993	24555	24487,95419	24645	24577,70845	24735	24667,46271
24286	24219,68868	24376	24309,44294	24466	24399,1972	24556	24488,95146	24646	24578,70572	24736	24668,45998
24287	24220,68595	24377	24310,44021	24467	24400,19447	24557	24489,94873	24647	24579,70299	24737	24669,45725
24288	24221,68322	24378	24311,43748	24468	24401,19174	24558	24490,946	24648	24580,70026	24738	24670,45452
24289	24222,68049	24379	24312,43475	24469	24402,18901	24559	24491,94327	24649	24581,69753	24739	24671,45179
24290	24223,67776	24380	24313,43202	24470	24403,18628	24560	24492,94054	24650	24582,6948	24740	24672,44906
24291	24224,67503	24381	24314,42929	24471	24404,18355	24561	24493,93781	24651	24583,69207	24741	24673,44633
24292	24225,6723	24382	24315,42656	24472	24405,18082	24562	24494,93508	24652	24584,68934	24742	24674,4436
24293	24226,66957	24383	24316,42383	24473	24406,17809	24563	24495,93235	24653	24585,68661	24743	24675,44087
24294	24227,66684	24384	24317,4211	24474	24407,17536	24564	24496,92962	24654	24586,68388	24744	24676,43814
24295	24228,66411	24385	24318,41837	24475	24408,17263	24565	24497,92689	24655	24587,68115	24745	24677,43541
24296	24229,66137	24386	24319,41564	24476	24409,1699	24566	24498,92416	24656	24588,67842	24746	24678,43268
24297	24230,65864	24387	24320,41291	24477	24410,16717	24567	24499,92143	24657	24589,67569	24747	24679,42995
24298	24231,65591	24388	24321,41017	24478	24411,16444	24568	24500,9187	24658	24590,67296	24748	24680,42722
24299	24232,65318	24389	24322,40744	24479	24412,16171	24569	24501,91597	24659	24591,67023	24749	24681,42449
24300	24233,65045	24390	24323,40471	24480	24413,15898	24570	24502,91324	24660	24592,6675	24750	24682,42176
24301	24234,64772	24391	24324,40198	24481	24414,15625	24571	24503,91051	24661	24593,66477	24751	24683,41903
24302	24235,64499	24392	24325,39925	24482	24415,15351	24572	24504,90778	24662	24594,66204	24752	24684,4163
24303	24236,64226	24393	24326,39652	24483	24416,15078	24573	24505,90504	24663	24595,65931	24753	24685,41357
24304	24237,63953	24394	24327,39379	24484	24417,14805	24574	24506,90231	24664	24596,65658	24754	24686,41084
24305	24238,6368	24395	24328,39106	24485	24418,14532	24575	24507,89958	24665	24597,65384	24755	24687,40811
24306	24239,63407	24396	24329,38833	24486	24419,14259	24576	24508,89685	24666	24598,65111	24756	24688,40538
24307	24240,63134	24397	24330,3856	24487	24420,13986	24577	24509,89412	24667	24599,64838	24757	24689,40264
24308	24241,62861	24398	24331,38287	24488	24421,13713	24578	24510,89139	24668	24600,64565	24758	24690,39991
24309	24242,62588	24399	24332,38014	24489	24422,1344	24579	24511,88866	24669	24601,64292	24759	24691,39718
24310	24243,62315	24400	24333,37741	24490	24423,13167	24580	24512,88593	24670	24602,64019	24760	24692,39445
24311	24244,62042	24401	24334,37468	24491	24424,12894	24581	24513,8832	24671	24603,63746	24761	24693,39172
24312	24245,61769	24402	24335,37195	24492	24425,12621	24582	24514,88047	24672	24604,63473	24762	24694,38899
24313	24246,61496	24403	24336,36922	24493	24426,12348	24583	24515,87774	24673	24605,632	24763	24695,38626
24314	24247,61223	24404	24337,36649	24494	24427,12075	24584	24516,87501	24674	24606,62927	24764	24696,38353
24315	24248,6095	24405	24338,36376	24495	24428,11802	24585	24517,87228	24675	24607,62654	24765	24697,3808
24316	24249,60677	24406	24339,36103	24496	24429,11529	24586	24518,86955	24676	24608,62381	24766	24698,37807
24317	24250,60404	24407	24340,3583	24497	24430,11256	24587	24519,86682	24677	24609,62108	24767	24699,37534
24318	24251,60131	24408	24341,35557	24498	24431,10983	24588	24520,86409	24678	24610,61835	24768	24700,37261
24319	24252,59857	24409	24342,35284	24499	24432,1071	24589	24521,86136	24679	24611,61562	24769	24701,36988
24320	24253,59584	24410	24343,35011	24500	24433,10437	24590	24522,85863	24680	24612,61289	24770	24702,36715
24321	24254,59311	24411	24344,34737	24501	24434,10164	24591	24523,8559	24681	24613,61016	24771	24703,36442
24322	24255,59038	24412	24345,34464	24502	24435,09891	24592	24524,85317	24682	24614,60743	24772	24704,36169
24323	24256,58765	24413	24346,34191	24503	24436,09618	24593	24525,85044	24683	24615,6047	24773	24705,35896
24324	24257,58492	24414	24347,33918	24504	24437,09344	24594	24526,84771	24684	24616,60197	24774	24706,35623

TABLE TO FIND OUT THE POINT A IN EARTH RETURNS 203

24775	24707,3535	24865	24797,10776	24955	24886,86202	25045	24976,61628	25135	25066,37054	25225	25156,1248
24776	24708,35077	24866	24798,10503	24956	24887,85929	25046	24977,61355	25136	25067,36781	25226	25157,12207
24777	24709,34804	24867	24799,1023	24957	24888,85656	25047	24978,61082	25137	25068,36508	25227	25158,11934
24778	24710,34531	24868	24800,09957	24958	24889,85383	25048	24979,60809	25138	25069,36235	25228	25159,11661
24779	24711,34258	24869	24801,09684	24959	24890,8511	25049	24980,60536	25139	25070,35962	25229	25160,11388
24780	24712,33984	24870	24802,09411	24960	24891,84837	25050	24981,60263	25140	25071,35689	25230	25161,11115
24781	24713,33711	24871	24803,09138	24961	24892,84564	25051	24982,5999	25141	25072,35416	25231	25162,10842
24782	24714,33438	24872	24804,08864	24962	24893,84291	25052	24983,59717	25142	25073,35143	25232	25163,10569
24783	24715,33165	24873	24805,08591	24963	24894,84018	25053	24984,59444	25143	25074,3487	25233	25164,10296
24784	24716,32892	24874	24806,08318	24964	24895,83744	25054	24985,59171	25144	25075,34597	25234	25165,10023
24785	24717,32619	24875	24807,08045	24965	24896,83471	25055	24986,58898	25145	25076,34324	25235	25166,0975
24786	24718,32346	24876	24808,07772	24966	24897,83198	25056	24987,58625	25146	25077,34051	25236	25167,09477
24787	24719,32073	24877	24809,07499	24967	24898,82925	25057	24988,58351	25147	25078,33778	25237	25168,09204
24788	24720,318	24878	24810,07226	24968	24899,82652	25058	24989,58078	25148	25079,33505	25238	25169,08931
24789	24721,31527	24879	24811,06953	24969	24900,82379	25059	24990,57805	25149	25080,33231	25239	25170,08658
24790	24722,31254	24880	24812,0668	24970	24901,82106	25060	24991,57532	25150	25081,32958	25240	25171,08385
24791	24723,30981	24881	24813,06407	24971	24902,81833	25061	24992,57259	25151	25082,32685	25241	25172,08111
24792	24724,30708	24882	24814,06134	24972	24903,8156	25062	24993,56986	25152	25083,32412	25242	25173,07838
24793	24725,30435	24883	24815,05861	24973	24904,81287	25063	24994,56713	25153	25084,32139	25243	25174,07565
24794	24726,30162	24884	24816,05588	24974	24905,81014	25064	24995,5644	25154	25085,31866	25244	25175,07292
24795	24727,29889	24885	24817,05315	24975	24906,80741	25065	24996,56167	25155	25086,31593	25245	25176,07019
24796	24728,29616	24886	24818,05042	24976	24907,80468	25066	24997,55894	25156	25087,3132	25246	25177,06746
24797	24729,29343	24887	24819,04769	24977	24908,80195	25067	24998,55621	25157	25088,31047	25247	25178,06473
24798	24730,2907	24888	24820,04496	24978	24909,79922	25068	24999,55348	25158	25089,30774	25248	25179,062
24799	24731,28797	24889	24821,04223	24979	24910,79649	25069	25000,55075	25159	25090,30501	25249	25180,05927
24800	24732,28524	24890	24822,0395	24980	24911,79376	25070	25001,54802	25160	25091,30228	25250	25181,05654
24801	24733,28251	24891	24823,03677	24981	24912,79103	25071	25002,54529	25161	25092,29955	25251	25182,05381
24802	24734,27978	24892	24824,03404	24982	24913,7883	25072	25003,54256	25162	25093,29682	25252	25183,05108
24803	24735,27704	24893	24825,03131	24983	24914,78557	25073	25004,53983	25163	25094,29409	25253	25184,04835
24804	24736,27431	24894	24826,02858	24984	24915,78284	25074	25005,5371	25164	25095,29136	25254	25185,04562
24805	24737,27158	24895	24827,02584	24985	24916,78011	25075	25006,53437	25165	25096,28863	25255	25186,04289
24806	24738,26885	24896	24828,02311	24986	24917,77738	25076	25007,53164	25166	25097,2859	25256	25187,04016
24807	24739,26612	24897	24829,02038	24987	24918,77464	25077	25008,52891	25167	25098,28317	25257	25188,03743
24808	24740,26339	24898	24830,01765	24988	24919,77191	25078	25009,52618	25168	25099,28044	25258	25189,0347
24809	24741,26066	24899	24831,01492	24989	24920,76918	25079	25010,52345	25169	25100,27771	25259	25190,03197
24810	24742,25793	24900	24832,01219	24990	24921,76645	25080	25011,52071	25170	25101,27498	25260	25191,02924
24811	24743,2552	24901	24833,00946	24991	24922,76372	25081	25012,51798	25171	25102,27225	25261	25192,02651
24812	24744,25247	24902	24834,00673	24992	24923,76099	25082	25013,51525	25172	25103,26951	25262	25193,02378
24813	24745,24974	24903	24835,004	24993	24924,75826	25083	25014,51252	25173	25104,26678	25263	25194,02105
24814	24746,24701	24904	24836,00127	24994	24925,75553	25084	25015,50979	25174	25105,26405	25264	25195,01831
24815	24747,24428	24905	24836,99854	24995	24926,7528	25085	25016,50706	25175	25106,26132	25265	25196,01558
24816	24748,24155	24906	24837,99581	24996	24927,75007	25086	25017,50433	25176	25107,25859	25266	25197,01285
24817	24749,23882	24907	24838,99308	24997	24928,74734	25087	25018,5016	25177	25108,25586	25267	25198,01012
24818	24750,23609	24908	24839,99035	24998	24929,74461	25088	25019,49887	25178	25109,25313	25268	25199,00739
24819	24751,23336	24909	24840,98762	24999	24930,74188	25089	25020,49614	25179	25110,2504	25269	25200,00466
24820	24752,23063	24910	24841,98489	25000	24931,73915	25090	25021,49341	25180	25111,24767	25270	25201,00193
24821	24753,2279	24911	24842,98216	25001	24932,73642	25091	25022,49068	25181	25112,24494	25271	25201,9992
24822	24754,22517	24912	24843,97943	25002	24933,73369	25092	25023,48795	25182	25113,24221	25272	25202,99647
24823	24755,22244	24913	24844,9767	25003	24934,73096	25093	25024,48522	25183	25114,23948	25273	25203,99374
24824	24756,21971	24914	24845,97397	25004	24935,72823	25094	25025,48249	25184	25115,23675	25274	25204,99101
24825	24757,21698	24915	24846,97124	25005	24936,7255	25095	25026,47976	25185	25116,23402	25275	25205,98828
24826	24758,21424	24916	24847,96851	25006	24937,72277	25096	25027,47703	25186	25117,23129	25276	25206,98555
24827	24759,21151	24917	24848,96578	25007	24938,72004	25097	25028,4743	25187	25118,22856	25277	25207,98282
24828	24760,20878	24918	24849,96304	25008	24939,71731	25098	25029,47157	25188	25119,22583	25278	25208,98009
24829	24761,20605	24919	24850,96031	25009	24940,71458	25099	25030,46884	25189	25120,2231	25279	25209,97736
24830	24762,20332	24920	24851,95758	25010	24941,71184	25100	25031,46611	25190	25121,22037	25280	25210,97463
24831	24763,20059	24921	24852,95485	25011	24942,70911	25101	25032,46338	25191	25122,21764	25281	25211,9719
24832	24764,19786	24922	24853,95212	25012	24943,70638	25102	25033,46065	25192	25123,21491	25282	25212,96917
24833	24765,19513	24923	24854,94939	25013	24944,70365	25103	25034,45791	25193	25124,21218	25283	25213,96644
24834	24766,1924	24924	24855,94666	25014	24945,70092	25104	25035,45518	25194	25125,20945	25284	25214,96371
24835	24767,18967	24925	24856,94393	25015	24946,69819	25105	25036,45245	25195	25126,20671	25285	25215,96098
24836	24768,18694	24926	24857,9412	25016	24947,69546	25106	25037,44972	25196	25127,20398	25286	25216,95825
24837	24769,18421	24927	24858,93847	25017	24948,69273	25107	25038,44699	25197	25128,20125	25287	25217,95551
24838	24770,18148	24928	24859,93574	25018	24949,69	25108	25039,44426	25198	25129,19852	25288	25218,95278
24839	24771,17875	24929	24860,93301	25019	24950,68727	25109	25040,44153	25199	25130,19579	25289	25219,95005
24840	24772,17602	24930	24861,93028	25020	24951,68454	25110	25041,4388	25200	25131,19306	25290	25220,94732
24841	24773,17329	24931	24862,92755	25021	24952,68181	25111	25042,43607	25201	25132,19033	25291	25221,94459
24842	24774,17056	24932	24863,92482	25022	24953,67908	25112	25043,43334	25202	25133,1876	25292	25222,94186
24843	24775,16783	24933	24864,92209	25023	24954,67635	25113	25044,43061	25203	25134,18487	25293	25223,93913
24844	24776,1651	24934	24865,91936	25024	24955,67362	25114	25045,42788	25204	25135,18214	25294	25224,9364
24845	24777,16237	24935	24866,91663	25025	24956,67089	25115	25046,42515	25205	25136,17941	25295	25225,93367
24846	24778,15964	24936	24867,9139	25026	24957,66816	25116	25047,42242	25206	25137,17668	25296	25226,93094
24847	24779,15691	24937	24868,91117	25027	24958,66543	25117	25048,41969	25207	25138,17395	25297	25227,92821
24848	24780,15418	24938	24869,90844	25028	24959,6627	25118	25049,41696	25208	25139,17122	25298	25228,92548
24849	24781,15144	24939	24870,90571	25029	24960,65997	25119	25050,41423	25209	25140,16849	25299	25229,92275
24850	24782,14871	24940	24871,90298	25030	24961,65724	25120	25051,4115	25210	25141,16576	25300	25230,92002
24851	24783,14598	24941	24872,90024	25031	24962,65451	25121	25052,40877	25211	25142,16303	25301	25231,91729
24852	24784,14325	24942	24873,89751	25032	24963,65178	25122	25053,40604	25212	25143,1603	25302	25232,91456
24853	24785,14052	24943	24874,89478	25033	24964,64904	25123	25054,40331	25213	25144,15757	25303	25233,91183
24854	24786,13779	24944	24875,89205	25034	24965,64631	25124	25055,40058	25214	25145,15484	25304	25234,9091
24855	24787,13506	24945	24876,88932	25035	24966,64358	25125	25056,39785	25215	25146,15211	25305	25235,90637
24856	24788,13233	24946	24877,88659	25036	24967,64085	25126	25057,39511	25216	25147,14938	25306	25236,90364
24857	24789,1296	24947	24878,88386	25037	24968,63812	25127	25058,39238	25217	25148,14665	25307	25237,90091
24858	24790,12687	24948	24879,88113	25038	24969,63539	25128	25059,38965	25218	25149,14391	25308	25238,89818
24859	24791,12414	24949	24880,8784	25039	24970,63266	25129	25060,38692	25219	25150,14118	25309	25239,89545
24860	24792,12141	24950	24881,87567	25040	24971,62993	25130	25061,38419	25220	25151,13845	25310	25240,89272
24861	24793,11868	24951	24882,87294	25041	24972,6272	25131	25062,38146	25221	25152,13572	25311	25241,88998
24862	24794,11595	24952	24883,87021	25042	24973,62447	25132	25063,37873	25222	25153,13299	25312	25242,88725
24863	24795,11322	24953	24884,86748	25043	24974,62174	25133	25064,376	25223	25154,13026	25313	25243,88452
24864	24796,11049	24954	24885,86475	25044	24975,61901	25134	25065,37327	25224	25155,12753	25314	25244,88179

25315 25245,87906	25405 25335,63332	25495 25425,38758	25585 25515,14185	25675 25604,89611	25765 25694,65037		
25316 25246,87633	25406 25336,63059	25496 25426,38485	25586 25516,13911	25676 25605,89338	25766 25695,64764		
25317 25247,8736	25407 25337,62786	25497 25427,38212	25587 25517,13638	25677 25606,89065	25767 25696,64491		
25318 25248,87087	25408 25338,62513	25498 25428,37939	25588 25518,13365	25678 25607,88792	25768 25697,64218		
25319 25249,86814	25409 25339,6224	25499 25429,37666	25589 25519,13092	25679 25608,88518	25769 25698,63945		
25320 25250,86541	25410 25340,61967	25500 25430,37393	25590 25520,12819	25680 25609,88245	25770 25699,63672		
25321 25251,86268	25411 25341,61694	25501 25431,3712	25591 25521,12546	25681 25610,87972	25771 25700,63398		
25322 25252,85995	25412 25342,61421	25502 25432,36847	25592 25522,12273	25682 25611,87699	25772 25701,63125		
25323 25253,85722	25413 25343,61148	25503 25433,36574	25593 2 5 5 2 3 , 1 2	25683 25612,87426	25773 25702,62852		
25324 25254,85449	25414 25344,60875	25504 25434,36301	25594 25524,11727	25684 25613,87153	25774 25703,62579		
25325 25255,85176	25415 25345,60602	25505 25435,36028	25595 25525,11454	25685 25614,8688	25775 25704,62306		
25326 25256,84903	25416 25346,60329	25506 25436,35755	25596 25526,11181	25686 25615,86607	25776 25705,62033		
25327 25257,8463	25417 25347,60056	25507 25437,35482	25597 25527,10908	25687 25616,86334	25777 25706,6176		
25328 25258,84357	25418 25348,59783	25508 25438,35209	25598 25528,10635	25688 25617,86061	25778 25707,61487		
25329 25259,84084	25419 25349,5951	25509 25439,34936	25599 25529,10362	25689 25618,85788	25779 25708,61214		
25330 25260,83811	25420 25350,59237	25510 25440,34663	25600 25530,10089	25690 25619,85515	25780 25709,60941		
25331 25261,83538	25421 25351,58964	25511 25441,3439	25601 25531,09816	25691 25620,85242	25781 25710,60668		
25332 25262,83265	25422 25352,58691	25512 25442,34117	25602 25532,09543	25692 25621,84969	25782 25711,60395		
25333 25263,82991	25423 25353,58418	25513 25443,33844	25603 25533,0927	25693 25622,84696	25783 25712,60122		
25334 25264,82718	25424 25354,58145	25514 25444,33571	25604 25534,08997	25694 25623,84423	25784 25713,59849		
25335 25265,82445	25425 25355,57871	25515 25445,33298	25605 25535,08724	25695 25624,8415	25785 25714,59576		
25336 25266,82172	25426 25356,57598	25516 25446,33025	25606 25536,08451	25696 25625,83877	25786 25715,59303		
25337 25267,81899	25427 25357,57325	25517 25447,32751	25607 25537,08178	25697 25626,83604	25787 25716,5903		
25338 25268,81626	25428 25358,57052	25518 25448,32478	25608 25538,07905	25698 25627,83331	25788 25717,58757		
25339 25269,81353	25429 25359,56779	25519 25449,32205	25609 25539,07631	25699 25628,83058	25789 25718,58484		
25340 25270,8108	25430 25360,56506	25520 25450,31932	25610 25540,07358	25700 25629,82785	25790 25719,58211		
25341 25271,80807	25431 25361,56233	25521 25451,31659	25611 25541,07085	25701 25630,82512	25791 25720,57938		
25342 25272,80534	25432 25362,5596	25522 25452,31386	25612 25542,06812	25702 25631,82238	25792 25721,57665		
25343 25273,80261	25433 25363,55687	25523 25453,31113	25613 25543,06539	25703 25632,81965	25793 25722,57392		
25344 25274,79988	25434 25364,55414	25524 25454,3084	25614 25544,06266	25704 25633,81692	25794 25723,57118		
25345 25275,79715	25435 25365,55141	25525 25455,30567	25615 25545,05993	25705 25634,81419	25795 25724,56845		
25346 25276,79442	25436 25366,54868	25526 25456,30294	25616 25546,0572	25706 25635,81146	25796 25725,56572		
25347 25277,79169	25437 25367,54595	25527 25457,30021	25617 25547,05447	25707 25636,80873	25797 25726,56299		
25348 25278,78896	25438 25368,54322	25528 25458,29748	25618 25548,05174	25708 2 5 6 3 7 , 8 0 6	25798 25727,56026		
25349 25279,78623	25439 25369,54049	25529 25459,29475	25619 25549,04901	25709 25638,80327	25799 25728,55753		
25350 25280,7835	25440 25370,53776	25530 25460,29202	25620 25550,04628	25710 25639,80054	25800 25729,5548		
25351 25281,78077	25441 25371,53503	25531 25461,28929	25621 25551,04355	25711 25640,79781	25801 25730,55207		
25352 25282,77804	25442 25372,5323	25532 25462,28656	25622 25552,04082	25712 25641,79508	25802 25731,54934		
25353 25283,77531	25443 25373,52957	25533 25463,28383	25623 25553,03809	25713 25642,79235	25803 25732,54661		
25354 25284,77258	25444 25374,52684	25534 25464,2811	25624 25554,03536	25714 25643,78962	25804 25733,54388		
25355 25285,76985	25445 25375,52411	25535 25465,27837	25625 25555,03263	25715 25644,78689	25805 25734,54115		
25356 25286,76711	25446 25376,52138	25536 25466,27564	25626 25556,0299	25716 25645,78416	25806 25735,53842		
25357 25287,76438	25447 25377,51865	25537 25467,27291	25627 25557,02717	25717 25646,78143	25807 25736,53569		
25358 25288,76165	25448 25378,51591	25538 25468,27018	25628 25558,02444	25718 25647,7787	25808 25737,53296		
25359 25289,75892	25449 25379,51318	25539 25469,26745	25629 25559,02171	25719 25648,77597	25809 25738,53023		
25360 25290,75619	25450 25380,51045	25540 25470,26471	25630 25560,01898	25720 25649,77324	25810 25739,5275		
25361 25291,75346	25451 25381,50772	25541 25471,26198	25631 25561,01625	25721 25650,77051	25811 25740,52477		
25362 25292,75073	25452 25382,50499	25542 25472,25925	25632 25562,01352	25722 25651,76778	25812 25741,52204		
25363 2 5 2 9 3 , 7 4 8	25453 25383,50226	25543 25473,25652	25633 25563,01078	25723 25652,76505	25813 25742,51931		
25364 25294,74527	25454 25384,49953	25544 25474,25379	25634 25564,00805	25724 25653,76232	25814 25743,51658		
25365 25295,74254	25455 25385,4968	25545 25475,25106	25635 25565,00532	25725 25654,75958	25815 25744,51385		
25366 25296,73981	25456 25386,49407	25546 25476,24833	25636 25566,00259	25726 25655,75685	25816 25745,51112		
25367 25297,73708	25457 25387,49134	25547 25477,2456	25637 25566,99986	25727 25656,75412	25817 25746,50838		
25368 25298,73435	25458 25388,48861	25548 25478,24287	25638 25567,99713	25728 25657,75139	25818 25747,50565		
25369 25299,73162	25459 25389,48588	25549 25479,24014	25639 25568,9944	25729 25658,74866	25819 25748,50292		
25370 25300,72889	25460 25390,48315	25550 25480,23741	25640 25569,99167	25730 25659,74593	25820 25749,50019		
25371 25301,72616	25461 25391,48042	25551 25481,23468	25641 25570,98894	25731 25660,7432	25821 25750,49746		
25372 25302,72343	25462 25392,47769	25552 25482,23195	25642 25571,98621	25732 25661,74047	25822 25751,49473		
25373 25303,7207	25463 25393,47496	25553 25483,22922	25643 25572,98348	25733 25662,73774	25823 2 5 7 5 2 , 4 9 2		
25374 25304,71797	25464 25394,47223	25554 25484,22649	25644 25573,98075	25734 25663,73501	25824 25753,48927		
25375 25305,71524	25465 25395,4695	25555 25485,22376	25645 25574,97802	25735 25664,73228	25825 25754,48654		
25376 25306,71251	25466 25396,46677	25556 25486,22103	25646 25575,97529	25736 25665,72955	25826 25755,48381		
25377 25307,70978	25467 25397,46404	25557 25487,2183	25647 25576,97256	25737 25666,72682	25827 25756,48108		
25378 25308,70705	25468 25398,46131	25558 25488,21557	25648 25577,96983	25738 25667,72409	25828 25757,47835		
25379 25309,70431	25469 25399,45858	25559 25489,21284	25649 25578,9671	25739 25668,72136	25829 25758,47562		
25380 25310,70158	25470 25400,45585	25560 25490,21011	25650 25579,96437	25740 25669,71863	25830 25759,47289		
25381 25311,69885	25471 25401,45311	25561 25491,20738	25651 25580,96164	25741 25670,7159	25831 25760,47016		
25382 25312,69612	25472 25402,45038	25562 25492,20465	25652 25581,95891	25742 25671,71317	25832 25761,46743		
25383 25313,69339	25473 25403,44765	25563 25493,20191	25653 25582,95618	25743 25672,71044	25833 25762,4647		
25384 25314,69066	25474 25404,44492	25564 25494,19918	25654 25583,95345	25744 25673,70771	25834 25763,46197		
25385 25315,68793	25475 25405,44219	25565 25495,19645	25655 25584,95072	25745 25674,70498	25835 25764,45924		
25386 25316,6852	25476 25406,43946	25566 25496,19372	25656 25585,94798	25746 25675,70225	25836 25765,45651		
25387 25317,68247	25477 25407,43673	25567 25497,19099	25657 25586,94525	25747 25676,69952	25837 25766,45378		
25388 25318,67974	25478 25408,434	25568 25498,18826	25658 25587,94252	25748 25677,69678	25838 25767,45105		
25389 25319,67701	25479 25409,43127	25569 25499,18553	25659 25588,93979	25749 25678,69405	25839 25768,44832		
25390 25320,67428	25480 25410,42854	25570 25500,1828	25660 25589,93706	25750 25679,69132	25840 25769,44558		
25391 25321,67155	25481 25411,42581	25571 25501,18007	25661 25590,93433	25751 25680,68859	25841 25770,44285		
25392 25322,66882	25482 25412,42308	25572 25502,17734	25662 25591,9316	25752 25681,68586	25842 25771,44012		
25393 25323,66609	25483 25413,42035	25573 25503,17461	25663 25592,92887	25753 25682,68313	25843 25772,43739		
25394 25324,66336	25484 25414,41762	25574 25504,17188	25664 25593,92614	25754 25683,6804	25844 25773,43466		
25395 25325,66063	25485 25415,41489	25575 25505,16915	25665 25594,92341	25755 25684,67767	25845 25774,43193		
25396 25326,6579	25486 25416,41216	25576 25506,16642	25666 25595,92068	25756 25685,67494	25846 25775,4292		
25397 25327,65517	25487 25417,40943	25577 25507,16369	25667 25596,91795	25757 25686,67221	25847 25776,42647		
25398 25328,65244	25488 25418,4067	25578 25508,16096	25668 25597,91522	25758 25687,66948	25848 25777,42374		
25399 25329,64971	25489 25419,40397	25579 25509,15823	25669 25598,91249	25759 25688,66675	25849 25778,42101		
25400 25330,64698	25490 25420,40124	25580 25510,1555	25670 25599,90976	25760 25689,66402	25850 25779,41828		
25401 25331,64425	25491 25421,39851	25581 25511,15277	25671 25600,90703	25761 25690,66129	25851 25780,41555		
25402 25332,64151	25492 25422,39578	25582 25512,15004	25672 25601,9043	25762 25691,65856	25852 25781,41282		
25403 25333,63878	25493 25423,39305	25583 25513,14731	25673 25602,90157	25763 25692,65583	25853 25782,41009		
25404 25334,63605	25494 25424,39031	25584 25514,14458	25674 25603,89884	25764 25693,6531	25854 25783,40736		

TABLE TO FIND OUT THE POINT A IN EARTH RETURNS 205

25855	25784,40463	25945	25874,15889	26035	25963,91315	26125	26053,66741	26215	26143,42167	26305	26233,17593
25856	25785,4019	25946	25875,15616	26036	25964,91042	26126	26054,66468	26216	26144,41894	26306	26234,1732
25857	25786,39917	25947	25876,15343	26037	25965,90769	26127	26055,66195	26217	26145,41621	26307	26235,17047
25858	25787,39644	25948	25877,1507	26038	25966,90496	26128	26056,65922	26218	26146,41348	26308	26236,16774
25859	25788,39371	25949	25878,14797	26039	25967,90223	26129	26057,65649	26219	26147,41075	26309	26237,16501
25860	25789,39098	25950	25879,14524	26040	25968,8995	26130	26058,65376	26220	26148,40802	26310	26238,16228
25861	25790,38825	25951	25880,14251	26041	25969,89677	26131	26059,65103	26221	26149,40529	26311	26239,15955
25862	25791,38552	25952	25881,13978	26042	25970,89404	26132	26060,6483	26222	26150,40256	26312	26240,15682
25863	25792,38278	25953	25882,13705	26043	25971,89131	26133	26061,64557	26223	26151,39983	26313	26241,15409
25864	25793,38005	25954	25883,13432	26044	25972,88858	26134	26062,64284	26224	26152,3971	26314	26242,15136
25865	25794,37732	25955	25884,13158	26045	25973,88585	26135	26063,64011	26225	26153,39437	26315	26243,14863
25866	25795,37459	25956	25885,12885	26046	25974,88312	26136	26064,63738	26226	26154,39164	26316	26244,1459
25867	25796,37186	25957	25886,12612	26047	25975,88038	26137	26065,63465	26227	26155,38891	26317	26245,14317
25868	25797,36913	25958	25887,12339	26048	25976,87765	26138	26066,63192	26228	26156,38618	26318	26246,14044
25869	25798,3664	25959	25888,12066	26049	25977,87492	26139	26067,62918	26229	26157,38345	26319	26247,13771
25870	25799,36367	25960	25889,11793	26050	25978,87219	26140	26068,62645	26230	26158,38072	26320	26248,13498
25871	25800,36094	25961	25890,1152	26051	25979,86946	26141	26069,62372	26231	26159,37799	26321	26249,13225
25872	25801,35821	25962	25891,11247	26052	25980,86673	26142	26070,62099	26232	26160,37525	26322	26250,12952
25873	25802,35548	25963	25892,10974	26053	25981,864	26143	26071,61826	26233	26161,37252	26323	26251,12679
25874	25803,35275	25964	25893,10701	26054	25982,86127	26144	26072,61553	26234	26162,36979	26324	26252,12405
25875	25804,35002	25965	25894,10428	26055	25983,85854	26145	26073,6128	26235	26163,36706	26325	26253,12132
25876	25805,34729	25966	25895,10155	26056	25984,85581	26146	26074,61007	26236	26164,36433	26326	26254,11859
25877	25806,34456	25967	25896,09882	26057	25985,85308	26147	26075,60734	26237	26165,3616	26327	26255,11586
25878	25807,34183	25968	25897,09609	26058	25986,85035	26148	26076,60461	26238	26166,35887	26328	26256,11313
25879	25808,3391	25969	25898,09336	26059	25987,84762	26149	26077,60188	26239	26167,35614	26329	26257,1104
25880	25809,33637	25970	25899,09063	26060	25988,84489	26150	26078,59915	26240	26168,35341	26330	26258,10767
25881	25810,33364	25971	25900,0879	26061	25989,84216	26151	26079,59642	26241	26169,35068	26331	26259,10494
25882	25811,33091	25972	25901,08517	26062	25990,83943	26152	26080,59369	26242	26170,34795	26332	26260,10221
25883	25812,32818	25973	25902,08244	26063	25991,8367	26153	26081,59096	26243	26171,34522	26333	26261,09948
25884	25813,32545	25974	25903,07971	26064	25992,83397	26154	26082,58823	26244	26172,34249	26334	26262,09675
25885	25814,32272	25975	25904,07698	26065	25993,83124	26155	26083,5855	26245	26173,33976	26335	26263,09402
25886	25815,31998	25976	25905,07425	26066	25994,82851	26156	26084,58277	26246	26174,33703	26336	26264,09129
25887	25816,31725	25977	25906,07152	26067	25995,82578	26157	26085,58004	26247	26175,3343	26337	26265,08856
25888	25817,31452	25978	25907,06878	26068	25996,82305	26158	26086,57731	26248	26176,33157	26338	26266,08583
25889	25818,31179	25979	25908,06605	26069	25997,82032	26159	26087,57458	26249	26177,32884	26339	26267,0831
25890	25819,30906	25980	25909,06332	26070	25998,81758	26160	26088,57185	26250	26178,32611	26340	26268,08037
25891	25820,30633	25981	25910,06059	26071	25999,81485	26161	26089,56912	26251	26179,32338	26341	26269,07764
25892	25821,3036	25982	25911,05786	26072	26000,81212	26162	26090,56638	26252	26180,32065	26342	26270,07491
25893	25822,30087	25983	25912,05513	26073	26001,80939	26163	26091,56365	26253	26181,31792	26343	26271,07218
25894	25823,29814	25984	25913,0524	26074	26002,80666	26164	26092,56092	26254	26182,31519	26344	26272,06945
25895	25824,29541	25985	25914,04967	26075	26003,80393	26165	26093,55819	26255	26183,31245	26345	26273,06672
25896	25825,29268	25986	25915,04694	26076	26004,8012	26166	26094,55546	26256	26184,30972	26346	26274,06399
25897	25826,28995	25987	25916,04421	26077	26005,79847	26167	26095,55273	26257	26185,30699	26347	26275,06125
25898	25827,28722	25988	25917,04148	26078	26006,79574	26168	2 6 0 9 6 , 5 5	26258	26186,30426	26348	26276,05852
25899	25828,28449	25989	25918,03875	26079	26007,79301	26169	26097,54727	26259	26187,30153	26349	26277,05579
25900	25829,28176	25990	25919,03602	26080	26008,79028	26170	26098,54454	26260	26188,2988	26350	26278,05306
25901	25830,27903	25991	25920,03329	26081	26009,78755	26171	26099,54181	26261	26189,29607	26351	26279,05033
25902	25831,2763	25992	25921,03056	26082	26010,78482	26172	26100,53908	26262	26190,29334	26352	26280,0476
25903	25832,27357	25993	25922,02783	26083	26011,78209	26173	26101,53635	26263	26191,29061	26353	26281,04487
25904	25833,27084	25994	2 5 9 2 3 , 0 2 5 1	26084	26012,77936	26174	26102,53362	26264	26192,28788	26354	26282,04214
25905	25834,26811	25995	25924,02237	26085	26013,77663	26175	26103,53089	26265	26193,28515	26355	26283,03941
25906	25835,26538	25996	25925,01964	26086	26014,7739	26176	26104,52816	26266	26194,28242	26356	26284,03668
25907	25836,26265	25997	25926,01691	26087	26015,77117	26177	26105,52543	26267	26195,27969	26357	26285,03395
25908	25837,25992	25998	25927,01418	26088	26016,76844	26178	26106,5227	26268	26196,27696	26358	26286,03122
25909	25838,25718	25999	25928,01145	26089	26017,76571	26179	26107,51997	26269	26197,27423	26359	26287,02849
25910	25839,25445	26000	25929,00872	26090	26018,76298	26180	26108,51724	26270	26198,2715	26360	26288,02576
25911	25840,25172	26001	25930,00598	26091	26019,76025	26181	26109,51451	26271	26199,26877	26361	26289,02303
25912	25841,24899	26002	25931,00325	26092	26020,75752	26182	26110,51178	26272	26200,26604	26362	26290,0203
25913	25842,24626	26003	25932,00052	26093	26021,75478	26183	26111,50905	26273	26201,26331	26363	26291,01757
25914	25843,24353	26004	25932,99779	26094	26022,75205	26184	26112,50632	26274	26202,26058	26364	26292,01484
25915	25844,2408	26005	25933,99506	26095	26023,74932	26185	26113,50358	26275	26203,25785	26365	26293,01211
25916	25845,23807	26006	25934,99233	26096	26024,74659	26186	26114,50085	26276	26204,25512	26366	26294,00938
25917	25846,23534	26007	25935,9896	26097	26025,74386	26187	26115,49812	26277	26205,25239	26367	26295,00665
25918	25847,23261	26008	25936,98687	26098	26026,74113	26188	26116,49539	26278	26206,24965	26368	26296,00392
25919	25848,22988	26009	25937,98414	26099	26027,7384	26189	26117,49266	26279	26207,24692	26369	26297,00119
25920	25849,22715	26010	25938,98141	26100	26028,73567	26190	26118,48993	26280	26208,24419	26370	26297,99845
25921	25850,22442	26011	25939,97868	26101	26029,73294	26191	26119,4872	26281	26209,24146	26371	26298,99572
25922	25851,22169	26012	25940,97595	26102	26030,73021	26192	26120,48447	26282	26210,23873	26372	26299,99299
25923	25852,21896	26013	25941,97322	26103	26031,72748	26193	26121,48174	26283	2 6 2 1 1 , 2 3 6	26373	26300,99026
25924	25853,21623	26014	25942,97049	26104	26032,72475	26194	26122,47901	26284	26212,23327	26374	26301,98753
25925	25854,2135	26015	25943,96776	26105	26033,72202	26195	26123,47628	26285	26213,23054	26375	26302,9848
25926	25855,21077	26016	25944,96503	26106	26034,71929	26196	26124,47355	26286	26214,22781	26376	26303,98207
25927	25856,20804	26017	25945,9623	26107	26035,71656	26197	26125,47082	26287	26215,22508	26377	26304,97934
25928	25857,20531	26018	25946,95957	26108	26036,71383	26198	26126,46809	26288	26216,22235	26378	26305,97661
25929	25858,20258	26019	25947,95684	26109	26037,7111	26199	26127,46536	26289	26217,21962	26379	26306,97388
25930	25859,19985	26020	25948,95411	26110	26038,70837	26200	26128,46263	26290	26218,21689	26380	26307,97115
25931	25860,19712	26021	25949,95138	26111	26039,70564	26201	26129,4599	26291	26219,21416	26381	26308,96842
25932	25861,19438	26022	25950,94865	26112	26040,70291	26202	26130,45717	26292	26220,21143	26382	26309,96569
25933	25862,19165	26023	25951,94592	26113	26041,70018	26203	26131,45444	26293	26221,2087	26383	26310,96296
25934	25863,18892	26024	25952,94318	26114	26042,69745	26204	26132,45171	26294	26222,20597	26384	26311,96023
25935	25864,18619	26025	25953,94045	26115	26043,69472	26205	26133,44898	26295	26223,20324	26385	26312,9575
25936	25865,18346	26026	25954,93772	26116	26044,69198	26206	26134,44625	26296	26224,20051	26386	26313,95477
25937	25866,18073	26027	25955,93499	26117	26045,68925	26207	26135,44352	26297	26225,19778	26387	26314,95204
25938	2 5 8 6 7 , 1 7 8	26028	25956,93226	26118	26046,68652	26208	26136,44079	26298	26226,19505	26388	26315,94931
25939	25868,17527	26029	25957,92953	26119	26047,68379	26209	26137,43805	26299	26227,19232	26389	26316,94658
25940	25869,17254	26030	25958,9268	26120	26048,68106	26210	26138,43532	26300	26228,18959	26390	26317,94385
25941	25870,16981	26031	25959,92407	26121	26049,67833	26211	26139,43259	26301	26229,18685	26391	26318,94112
25942	25871,16708	26032	25960,92134	26122	26050,6756	26212	26140,42986	26302	26230,18412	26392	26319,93839
25943	25872,16435	26033	25961,91861	26123	26051,67287	26213	26141,42713	26303	26231,18139	26393	26320,93565
25944	25873,16162	26034	25962,91588	26124	26052,67014	26214	26142,4244	26304	26232,17866	26394	26321,93292

26395	26322,93019	26485	26412,68445	26575	26502,43872	26665	26592,19298	26755	26681,94724	26845	26771,7015
26396	26323,92746	26486	26413,68172	26576	26503,43599	26666	26593,19025	26756	26682,94451	26846	26772,69877
26397	26324,92473	26487	26414,67899	26577	26504,43325	26667	26594,18752	26757	26683,94178	26847	26773,69604
26398	26325,922	26488	26415,67626	26578	26505,43052	26668	26595,18479	26758	26684,93905	26848	26774,69331
26399	26326,91927	26489	26416,67353	26579	26506,42779	26669	26596,18205	26759	26685,93632	26849	26775,69058
26400	26327,91654	26490	26417,6708	26580	26507,42506	26670	26597,17932	26760	26686,93359	26850	26776,68785
26401	26328,91381	26491	26418,66807	26581	26508,42233	26671	26598,17659	26761	26687,93085	26851	26777,68512
26402	26329,91108	26492	26419,66534	26582	26509,4196	26672	26599,17386	26762	26688,92812	26852	26778,68239
26403	26330,90835	26493	26420,66261	26583	26510,41687	26673	26600,17113	26763	26689,92539	26853	26779,67966
26404	26331,90562	26494	26421,65988	26584	26511,41414	26674	26601,1684	26764	26690,92266	26854	26780,67692
26405	26332,90289	26495	26422,65715	26585	26512,41141	26675	26602,16567	26765	26691,91993	26855	26781,67419
26406	26333,90016	26496	26423,65442	26586	26513,40868	26676	26603,16294	26766	26692,9172	26856	26782,67146
26407	26334,89743	26497	26424,65169	26587	26514,40595	26677	26604,16021	26767	26693,91447	26857	26783,66873
26408	26335,8947	26498	26425,64896	26588	26515,40322	26678	26605,15748	26768	26694,91174	26858	26784,666
26409	26336,89197	26499	26426,64623	26589	26516,40049	26679	26606,15475	26769	26695,90901	26859	26785,66327
26410	26337,88924	26500	26427,6435	26590	26517,39776	26680	26607,15202	26770	26696,90628	26860	26786,66054
26411	26338,88651	26501	26428,64077	26591	26518,39503	26681	26608,14929	26771	26697,90355	26861	26787,65781
26412	26339,88378	26502	26429,63804	26592	26519,3923	26682	26609,14656	26772	26698,90082	26862	26788,65508
26413	26340,88105	26503	26430,63531	26593	26520,38957	26683	26610,14383	26773	26699,89809	26863	26789,65235
26414	26341,87832	26504	26431,63258	26594	26521,38684	26684	26611,1411	26774	26700,89536	26864	26790,64962
26415	26342,87559	26505	26432,62985	26595	26522,38411	26685	26612,13837	26775	26701,89263	26865	26791,64689
26416	26343,87285	26506	26433,62712	26596	26523,38138	26686	26613,13564	26776	26702,8899	26866	26792,64416
26417	26344,87012	26507	26434,62439	26597	26524,37865	26687	26614,13291	26777	26703,88717	26867	26793,64143
26418	26345,86739	26508	26435,62165	26598	26525,37592	26688	26615,13018	26778	26704,88444	26868	26794,6387
26419	26346,86466	26509	26436,61892	26599	26526,37319	26689	26616,12745	26779	26705,88171	26869	26795,63597
26420	26347,86193	26510	26437,61619	26600	26527,37045	26690	26617,12472	26780	26706,87898	26870	26796,63324
26421	26348,8592	26511	26438,61346	26601	26528,36772	26691	26618,12199	26781	26707,87625	26871	26797,63051
26422	26349,85647	26512	26439,61073	26602	26529,36499	26692	26619,11925	26782	26708,87352	26872	26798,62778
26423	26350,85374	26513	26440,608	26603	26530,36226	26693	26620,11652	26783	26709,87079	26873	26799,62505
26424	26351,85101	26514	26441,60527	26604	26531,35953	26694	26621,11379	26784	26710,86806	26874	26800,62232
26425	26352,84828	26515	26442,60254	26605	26532,3568	26695	26622,11106	26785	26711,86532	26875	26801,61959
26426	26353,84555	26516	26443,59981	26606	26533,35407	26696	26623,10833	26786	26712,86259	26876	26802,61686
26427	26354,84282	26517	26444,59708	26607	26534,35134	26697	26624,1056	26787	26713,85986	26877	26803,61412
26428	26355,84009	26518	26445,59435	26608	26535,34861	26698	26625,10287	26788	26714,85713	26878	26804,61139
26429	26356,83736	26519	26446,59162	26609	26536,34588	26699	26626,10014	26789	26715,8544	26879	26805,60866
26430	26357,83463	26520	26447,58889	26610	26537,34315	26700	26627,09741	26790	26716,85167	26880	26806,60593
26431	26358,8319	26521	26448,58616	26611	26538,34042	26701	26628,09468	26791	26717,84894	26881	26807,6032
26432	26359,82917	26522	26449,58343	26612	26539,33769	26702	26629,09195	26792	26718,84621	26882	26808,60047
26433	26360,82644	26523	26450,5807	26613	26540,33496	26703	26630,08922	26793	26719,84348	26883	26809,59774
26434	26361,82371	26524	26451,57797	26614	26541,33223	26704	26631,08649	26794	26720,84075	26884	26810,59501
26435	26362,82098	26525	26452,57524	26615	26542,3295	26705	26632,08376	26795	26721,83802	26885	26811,59228
26436	26363,81825	26526	26453,57251	26616	26543,32677	26706	26633,08103	26796	26722,83529	26886	26812,58955
26437	26364,81552	26527	26454,56978	26617	26544,32404	26707	26634,0783	26797	26723,83256	26887	26813,58682
26438	26365,81279	26528	26455,56705	26618	26545,32131	26708	26635,07557	26798	26724,82983	26888	26814,58409
26439	26366,81005	26529	26456,56432	26619	26546,31858	26709	26636,07284	26799	26725,8271	26889	26815,58136
26440	26367,80732	26530	26457,56159	26620	26547,31585	26710	26637,07011	26800	26726,82437	26890	26816,57863
26441	26368,80459	26531	26458,55885	26621	26548,31312	26711	26638,06738	26801	26727,82164	26891	26817,5759
26442	26369,80186	26532	26459,55612	26622	26549,31039	26712	26639,06465	26802	26728,81891	26892	26818,57317
26443	26370,79913	26533	26460,55339	26623	26550,30765	26713	26640,06192	26803	26729,81618	26893	26819,57044
26444	26371,7964	26534	26461,55066	26624	26551,30492	26714	26641,05919	26804	26730,81345	26894	26820,56771
26445	26372,79367	26535	26462,54793	26625	26552,30219	26715	26642,05645	26805	26731,81072	26895	26821,56498
26446	26373,79094	26536	26463,5452	26626	26553,29946	26716	26643,05372	26806	26732,80799	26896	26822,56225
26447	26374,78821	26537	26464,54247	26627	26554,29673	26717	26644,05099	26807	26733,80526	26897	26823,55952
26448	26375,78548	26538	26465,53974	26628	26555,294	26718	26645,04826	26808	26734,80252	26898	26824,55679
26449	26376,78275	26539	26466,53701	26629	26556,29127	26719	26646,04553	26809	26735,79979	26899	26825,55406
26450	26377,78002	26540	26467,53428	26630	26557,28854	26720	26647,0428	26810	26736,79706	26900	26826,55132
26451	26378,77729	26541	26468,53155	26631	26558,28581	26721	26648,04007	26811	26737,79433	26901	26827,54859
26452	26379,77456	26542	26469,52882	26632	26559,28308	26722	26649,03734	26812	26738,7916	26902	26828,54586
26453	26380,77183	26543	26470,52609	26633	26560,28035	26723	26650,03461	26813	26739,78887	26903	26829,54313
26454	26381,7691	26544	26471,52336	26634	26561,27762	26724	26651,03188	26814	26740,78614	26904	26830,5404
26455	26382,76637	26545	26472,52063	26635	26562,27489	26725	26652,02915	26815	26741,78341	26905	26831,53767
26456	26383,76364	26546	26473,5179	26636	26563,27216	26726	26653,02642	26816	26742,78068	26906	26832,53494
26457	26384,76091	26547	26474,51517	26637	26564,26943	26727	26654,02369	26817	26743,77795	26907	26833,53221
26458	26385,75818	26548	26475,51244	26638	26565,2667	26728	26655,02096	26818	26744,77522	26908	26834,52948
26459	26386,75545	26549	26476,50971	26639	26566,26397	26729	26656,01823	26819	26745,77249	26909	26835,52675
26460	26387,75272	26550	26477,50698	26640	26567,26124	26730	26657,0155	26820	26746,76976	26910	26836,52402
26461	26388,74999	26551	26478,50425	26641	26568,25851	26731	26658,01277	26821	26747,76703	26911	26837,52129
26462	26389,74725	26552	26479,50152	26642	26569,25578	26732	26659,01004	26822	26748,7643	26912	26838,51856
26463	26390,74452	26553	26480,49879	26643	26570,25305	26733	26660,00731	26823	26749,76157	26913	26839,51583
26464	26391,74179	26554	26481,49605	26644	26571,25032	26734	26661,00458	26824	26750,75884	26914	26840,5131
26465	26392,73906	26555	26482,49332	26645	26572,24759	26735	26662,00185	26825	26751,75611	26915	26841,51037
26466	26393,73633	26556	26483,49059	26646	26573,24485	26736	26662,99912	26826	26752,75338	26916	26842,50764
26467	26394,7336	26557	26484,48786	26647	26574,24212	26737	26663,99639	26827	26753,75065	26917	26843,50491
26468	26395,73087	26558	26485,48513	26648	26575,23939	26738	26664,99365	26828	26754,74792	26918	26844,50218
26469	26396,72814	26559	26486,4824	26649	26576,23666	26739	26665,99092	26829	26755,74519	26919	26845,49945
26470	26397,72541	26560	26487,47967	26650	26577,23393	26740	26666,98819	26830	26756,74246	26920	26846,49672
26471	26398,72268	26561	26488,47694	26651	26578,2312	26741	26667,98546	26831	26757,73972	26921	26847,49399
26472	26399,71995	26562	26489,47421	26652	26579,22847	26742	26668,98273	26832	26758,73699	26922	26848,49126
26473	26400,71722	26563	26490,47148	26653	26580,22574	26743	26669,98	26833	26759,73426	26923	26849,48852
26474	26401,71449	26564	26491,46875	26654	26581,22301	26744	26670,97727	26834	26760,73153	26924	26850,48579
26475	26402,71176	26565	26492,46602	26655	26582,22028	26745	26671,97454	26835	26761,7288	26925	26851,48306
26476	26403,70903	26566	26493,46329	26656	26583,21755	26746	26672,97181	26836	26762,72607	26926	26852,48033
26477	26404,7063	26567	26494,46056	26657	26584,21482	26747	26673,96908	26837	26763,72334	26927	26853,4776
26478	26405,70357	26568	26495,45783	26658	26585,21209	26748	26674,96635	26838	26764,72061	26928	26854,47487
26479	26406,70084	26569	26496,4551	26659	26586,20936	26749	26675,96362	26839	26765,71788	26929	26855,47214
26480	26407,69811	26570	26497,45237	26660	26587,20663	26750	26676,96089	26840	26766,71515	26930	26856,46941
26481	26408,69538	26571	26498,44964	26661	26588,2039	26751	26677,95816	26841	26767,71242	26931	26857,46668
26482	26409,69265	26572	26499,44691	26662	26589,20117	26752	26678,95543	26842	26768,70969	26932	26858,46395
26483	26410,68992	26573	26500,44418	26663	26590,19844	26753	26679,9527	26843	26769,70696	26933	26859,46122
26484	26411,68719	26574	26501,44145	26664	26591,19571	26754	26680,94997	26844	26770,70423	26934	26860,45849

TABLE TO FIND OUT THE POINT A IN EARTH RETURNS

26935	26861,45576	27025	26951,21002	27115	27040,96428	27205	27130,71854	27295	27220,4728	27385	27310,22706
26936	26862,45303	27026	26952,20729	27116	27041,96155	27206	27131,71581	27296	27221,47007	27386	27311,22433
26937	26863,4503	27027	26953,20456	27117	27042,95882	27207	27132,71308	27297	27222,46734	27387	27312,2216
26938	26864,44757	27028	26954,20183	27118	27043,95609	27208	27133,71035	27298	27223,46461	27388	27313,21887
26939	26865,44484	27029	26955,1991	27119	27044,95336	27209	27134,70762	27299	27224,46188	27389	27314,21614
26940	26866,44211	27030	26956,19637	27120	27045,95063	27210	27135,70489	27300	27225,45915	27390	27315,21341
26941	26867,43938	27031	26957,19364	27121	27046,9479	27211	27136,70216	27301	27226,45642	27391	27316,21068
26942	26868,43665	27032	26958,19091	27122	27047,94517	27212	27137,69943	27302	27227,45369	27392	27317,20795
26943	26869,43392	27033	26959,18818	27123	27048,94244	27213	27138,6967	27303	27228,45096	27393	27318,20522
26944	26870,43119	27034	26960,18545	27124	27049,93971	27214	27139,69397	27304	27229,44823	27394	27319,20249
26945	26871,42846	27035	26961,18272	27125	27050,93698	27215	27140,69124	27305	27230,4455	27395	27320,19976
26946	26872,42572	27036	26962,17999	27126	27051,93425	27216	27141,68851	27306	27231,44277	27396	27321,19703
26947	26873,42299	27037	26963,17726	27127	27052,93152	27217	27142,68578	27307	27232,44004	27397	27322,1943
26948	26874,42026	27038	26964,17452	27128	27053,92879	27218	27143,68305	27308	27233,43731	27398	27323,19157
26949	26875,41753	27039	26965,17179	27129	27054,92606	27219	27144,68032	27309	27234,43458	27399	27324,18884
26950	26876,4148	27040	26966,16906	27130	27055,92332	27220	27145,67759	27310	27235,43185	27400	27325,18611
26951	26877,41207	27041	26967,16633	27131	27056,92059	27221	27146,67486	27311	27236,42912	27401	27326,18338
26952	26878,40934	27042	26968,1636	27132	27057,91786	27222	27147,67212	27312	27237,42639	27402	27327,18065
26953	26879,40661	27043	26969,16087	27133	27058,91513	27223	27148,66939	27313	27238,42366	27403	27328,17792
26954	26880,40388	27044	26970,15814	27134	27059,9124	27224	27149,66666	27314	27239,42092	27404	27329,17519
26955	26881,40115	27045	26971,15541	27135	27060,90967	27225	27150,66393	27315	27240,41819	27405	27330,17246
26956	26882,39842	27046	26972,15268	27136	27061,90694	27226	27151,6612	27316	27241,41546	27406	27331,16973
26957	26883,39569	27047	26973,14995	27137	27062,90421	27227	27152,65847	27317	27242,41273	27407	27332,16699
26958	26884,39296	27048	26974,14722	27138	27063,90148	27228	27153,65574	27318	2 7 2 4 3 , 4 1	27408	27333,16426
26959	26885,39023	27049	26975,14449	27139	27064,89875	27229	27154,65301	27319	27244,40727	27409	27334,16153
26960	26886,3875	27050	26976,14176	27140	27065,89602	27230	27155,65028	27320	27245,40454	27410	27335,1588
26961	26887,38477	27051	26977,13903	27141	27066,89329	27231	27156,64755	27321	27246,40181	27411	27336,15607
26962	26888,38204	27052	26978,1363	27142	27067,89056	27232	27157,64482	27322	27247,39908	27412	27337,15334
26963	26889,37931	27053	26979,13357	27143	27068,88783	27233	27158,64209	27323	27248,39635	27413	27338,15061
26964	26890,37658	27054	26980,13084	27144	27069,8851	27234	27159,63936	27324	27249,39362	27414	27339,14788
26965	26891,37385	27055	26981,12811	27145	27070,88237	27235	27160,63663	27325	27250,39089	27415	27340,14515
26966	26892,37112	27056	26982,12538	27146	27071,87964	27236	27161,6339	27326	27251,38816	27416	27341,14242
26967	26893,36839	27057	26983,12265	27147	27072,87691	27237	27162,63117	27327	27252,38543	27417	27342,13969
26968	26894,36566	27058	26984,11992	27148	27073,87418	27238	27163,62844	27328	27253,3827	27418	27343,13696
26969	26895,36292	27059	26985,11719	27149	27074,87145	27239	27164,62571	27329	27254,37997	27419	27344,13423
26970	26896,36019	27060	26986,11446	27150	27075,86872	27240	27165,62298	27330	27255,37724	27420	27345,1315
26971	26897,35746	27061	26987,11172	27151	27076,86599	27241	27166,62025	27331	27256,37451	27421	27346,12877
26972	26898,35473	27062	26988,10899	27152	27077,86326	27242	27167,61752	27332	27257,37178	27422	27347,12604
26973	2 6 8 9 9 , 3 5 2	27063	26989,10626	27153	27078,86052	27243	27168,61479	27333	27258,36905	27423	27348,12331
26974	26900,34927	27064	26990,10353	27154	27079,85779	27244	27169,61206	27334	27259,36632	27424	27349,12058
26975	26901,34654	27065	26991,1008	27155	27080,85506	27245	27170,60932	27335	27260,36359	27425	27350,11785
26976	26902,34381	27066	26992,09807	27156	27081,85233	27246	27171,60659	27336	27261,36086	27426	27351,11512
26977	26903,34108	27067	26993,09534	27157	27082,8496	27247	27172,60386	27337	27262,35812	27427	27352,11239
26978	26904,33835	27068	26994,09261	27158	27083,84687	27248	27173,60113	27338	27263,35539	27428	27353,10966
26979	26905,33562	27069	26995,08988	27159	27084,84414	27249	27174,5984	27339	27264,35266	27429	27354,10693
26980	26906,33289	27070	26996,08715	27160	27085,84141	27250	27175,59567	27340	27265,34993	27430	27355,10419
26981	26907,33016	27071	26997,08442	27161	27086,83868	27251	27176,59294	27341	27266,3472	27431	27356,10146
26982	26908,32743	27072	26998,08169	27162	27087,83595	27252	27177,59021	27342	27267,34447	27432	27357,09873
26983	26909,3247	27073	26999,07896	27163	27088,83322	27253	27178,58748	27343	27268,34174	27433	2 7 3 5 8 , 0 9 6
26984	26910,32197	27074	27000,07623	27164	27089,83049	27254	27179,58475	27344	27269,33901	27434	27359,09327
26985	26911,31924	27075	27001,0735	27165	27090,82776	27255	27180,58202	27345	27270,33628	27435	27360,09054
26986	26912,31651	27076	27002,07077	27166	27091,82503	27256	27181,57929	27346	27271,33355	27436	27361,08781
26987	26913,31378	27077	27003,06804	27167	27092,8223	27257	27182,57656	27347	27272,33082	27437	27362,08508
26988	26914,31105	27078	27004,06531	27168	27093,81957	27258	27183,57383	27348	27273,32809	27438	27363,08235
26989	26915,30832	27079	27005,06258	27169	27094,81684	27259	27184,5711	27349	27274,32536	27439	27364,07962
26990	26916,30559	27080	27006,05985	27170	27095,81411	27260	27185,56837	27350	27275,32263	27440	27365,07689
26991	26917,30286	27081	27007,05712	27171	27096,81138	27261	27186,56564	27351	27276,3199	27441	27366,07416
26992	26918,30012	27082	27008,05439	27172	27097,80865	27262	27187,56291	27352	27277,31717	27442	27367,07143
26993	26919,29739	27083	27009,05166	27173	27098,80592	27263	27188,56018	27353	27278,31444	27443	27368,0687
26994	26920,29466	27084	27010,04892	27174	27099,80319	27264	27189,55745	27354	27279,31171	27444	27369,06597
26995	26921,29193	27085	27011,04619	27175	27100,80046	27265	27190,55472	27355	27280,30898	27445	27370,06324
26996	26922,2892	27086	27012,04346	27176	27101,79772	27266	27191,55199	27356	27281,30625	27446	27371,06051
26997	26923,28647	27087	27013,04073	27177	27102,79499	27267	27192,54926	27357	27282,30352	27447	27372,05778
26998	26924,28374	27088	2 7 0 1 4 , 0 3 8	27178	27103,79226	27268	27193,54652	27358	27283,30079	27448	27373,05505
26999	26925,28101	27089	27015,03527	27179	27104,78953	27269	27194,54379	27359	27284,29806	27449	27374,05232
27000	26926,27828	27090	27016,03254	27180	27105,7868	27270	27195,54106	27360	27285,29533	27450	27375,04959
27001	26927,27555	27091	27017,02981	27181	27106,78407	27271	27196,53833	27361	27286,29259	27451	27376,04686
27002	26928,27282	27092	27018,02708	27182	27107,78134	27272	27197,5356	27362	27287,28986	27452	27377,04413
27003	26929,27009	27093	27019,02435	27183	27108,77861	27273	27198,53287	27363	27288,28713	27453	27378,04139
27004	26930,26736	27094	27020,02162	27184	27109,77588	27274	27199,53014	27364	27289,2844	27454	27379,03866
27005	26931,26463	27095	27021,01889	27185	27110,77315	27275	27200,52741	27365	27290,28167	27455	27380,03593
27006	26932,2619	27096	27022,01616	27186	27111,77042	27276	27201,52468	27366	27291,27894	27456	27381,0332
27007	26933,25917	27097	27023,01343	27187	27112,76769	27277	27202,52195	27367	27292,27621	27457	27382,03047
27008	26934,25644	27098	27024,0107	27188	27113,76496	27278	27203,51922	27368	27293,27348	27458	27383,02774
27009	26935,25371	27099	27025,00797	27189	27114,76223	27279	27204,51649	27369	27294,27075	27459	27384,02501
27010	26936,25098	27100	27026,00524	27190	27115,7595	27280	27205,51376	27370	27295,26802	27460	27385,02228
27011	26937,24825	27101	27027,00251	27191	27116,75677	27281	27206,51103	27371	27296,26529	27461	27386,01955
27012	26938,24552	27102	27027,99978	27192	27117,75404	27282	27207,5083	27372	27297,26256	27462	27387,01682
27013	26939,24279	27103	27028,99705	27193	27118,75131	27283	27208,50557	27373	27298,25983	27463	27388,01409
27014	26940,24006	27104	27029,99432	27194	27119,74858	27284	27209,50284	27374	27299,2571	27464	27389,01136
27015	26941,23732	27105	27030,99159	27195	27120,74585	27285	27210,50011	27375	27300,25437	27465	27390,00863
27016	26942,23459	27106	27031,98886	27196	27121,74312	27286	27211,49738	27376	27301,25164	27466	27391,0059
27017	26943,23186	27107	27032,98612	27197	27122,74039	27287	27212,49465	27377	27302,24891	27467	27392,00317
27018	26944,22913	27108	27033,98339	27198	27123,73766	27288	27213,49192	27378	27303,24618	27468	27393,00044
27019	26945,2264	27109	27034,98066	27199	27124,73492	27289	27214,48919	27379	27304,24345	27469	27393,99771
27020	26946,22367	27110	27035,97793	27200	27125,73219	27290	27215,48646	27380	27305,24072	27470	27394,99498
27021	26947,22094	27111	27036,9752	27201	27126,72946	27291	27216,48372	27381	27306,23799	27471	27395,99225
27022	26948,21821	27112	27037,97247	27202	27127,72673	27292	27217,48099	27382	27307,23526	27472	27396,98952
27023	26949,21548	27113	27038,96974	27203	2 7 1 2 8 , 7 2 4	27293	27218,47826	27383	27308,23253	27473	27397,98679
27024	26950,21275	27114	27039,96701	27204	27129,72127	27294	27219,47553	27384	27309,22979	27474	27398,98406

27475	27399,98133	27565	27489,73559	27655	27579,48985	27745	27669,24411	27835	27758,99837	27925	27848,75263
27476	27400,97859	27566	27490,73286	27656	27580,48712	27746	27670,24138	27836	27759,99564	27926	27849,7499
27477	27401,97586	27567	27491,73013	27657	27581,48439	27747	27671,23865	27837	27760,99291	27927	27850,74717
27478	27402,97313	27568	27492,72739	27658	27582,48166	27748	27672,23592	27838	27761,99018	27928	27851,74444
27479	27403,9704	27569	27493,72466	27659	27583,47893	27749	27673,23319	27839	27762,98745	27929	27852,74171
27480	27404,96767	27570	27494,72193	27660	27584,47619	27750	27674,23046	27840	27763,98472	27930	27853,73898
27481	27405,96494	27571	27495,7192	27661	27585,47346	27751	27675,22773	27841	27764,98199	27931	27854,73625
27482	27406,96221	27572	27496,71647	27662	27586,47073	27752	27676,22499	27842	27765,97926	27932	27855,73352
27483	27407,95948	27573	27497,71374	27663	27587,468	27753	27677,22226	27843	27766,97653	27933	27856,73079
27484	27408,95675	27574	27498,71101	27664	27588,46527	27754	27678,21953	27844	27767,97379	27934	27857,72806
27485	27409,95402	27575	27499,70828	27665	27589,46254	27755	27679,2168	27845	27768,97106	27935	27858,72533
27486	27410,95129	27576	27500,70555	27666	27590,45981	27756	27680,21407	27846	27769,96833	27936	27859,7226
27487	27411,94856	27577	27501,70282	27667	27591,45708	27757	27681,21134	27847	27770,9656	27937	27860,71986
27488	27412,94583	27578	27502,70009	27668	27592,45435	27758	27682,20861	27848	27771,96287	27938	27861,71713
27489	27413,9431	27579	27503,69736	27669	27593,45162	27759	27683,20588	27849	27772,96014	27939	27862,7144
27490	27414,94037	27580	27504,69463	27670	27594,44889	27760	27684,20315	27850	27773,95741	27940	27863,71167
27491	27415,93764	27581	27505,6919	27671	27595,44616	27761	27685,20042	27851	27774,95468	27941	27864,70894
27492	27416,93491	27582	27506,68917	27672	27596,44343	27762	27686,19769	27852	27775,95195	27942	27865,70621
27493	27417,93218	27583	27507,68644	27673	27597,4407	27763	27687,19496	27853	27776,94922	27943	27866,70348
27494	27418,92945	27584	27508,68371	27674	27598,43797	27764	27688,19223	27854	27777,94649	27944	27867,70075
27495	27419,92672	27585	27509,68098	27675	27599,43524	27765	27689,1895	27855	27778,94376	27945	27868,69802
27496	27420,92399	27586	27510,67825	27676	27600,43251	27766	27690,18677	27856	27779,94103	27946	27869,69529
27497	27421,92126	27587	27511,67552	27677	27601,42978	27767	27691,18404	27857	27780,9383	27947	27870,69256
27498	27422,91853	27588	27512,67279	27678	27602,42705	27768	27692,18131	27858	27781,93557	27948	27871,68983
27499	27423,91579	27589	27513,67006	27679	27603,42432	27769	27693,17858	27859	27782,93284	27949	27872,6871
27500	27424,91306	27590	27514,66733	27680	27604,42159	27770	27694,17585	27860	27783,93011	27950	27873,68437
27501	27425,91033	27591	27515,66459	27681	27605,41886	27771	27695,17312	27861	27784,92738	27951	27874,68164
27502	27426,9076	27592	27516,66186	27682	27606,41613	27772	27696,17039	27862	27785,92465	27952	27875,67891
27503	27427,90487	27593	27517,65913	27683	27607,41339	27773	27697,16766	27863	27786,92192	27953	27876,67618
27504	27428,90214	27594	27518,6564	27684	27608,41066	27774	27698,16493	27864	27787,91919	27954	27877,67345
27505	27429,89941	27595	27519,65367	27685	27609,40793	27775	27699,16219	27865	27788,91646	27955	27878,67072
27506	27430,89668	27596	27520,65094	27686	27610,4052	27776	27700,15946	27866	27789,91373	27956	27879,66799
27507	27431,89395	27597	27521,64821	27687	27611,40247	27777	27701,15673	27867	27790,91099	27957	27880,66526
27508	27432,89122	27598	27522,64548	27688	27612,39974	27778	2 7702,154	27868	27791,90826	27958	27881,66253
27509	27433,88849	27599	27523,64275	27689	27613,39701	27779	27703,15127	27869	27792,90553	27959	27882,6598
27510	27434,88576	27600	27524,64002	27690	27614,39428	27780	27704,14854	27870	27793,9028	27960	27883,65706
27511	27435,88303	27601	27525,63729	27691	27615,39155	27781	27705,14581	27871	27794,90007	27961	27884,65433
27512	27436,8803	27602	27526,63456	27692	27616,38882	27782	27706,14308	27872	27795,89734	27962	27885,6516
27513	27437,87757	27603	27527,63183	27693	27617,38609	27783	27707,14035	27873	27796,89461	27963	27886,64887
27514	27438,87484	27604	27528,6291	27694	27618,38336	27784	27708,13762	27874	27797,89188	27964	27887,64614
27515	27439,87211	27605	27529,62637	27695	27619,38063	27785	27709,13489	27875	27798,88915	27965	27888,64341
27516	27440,86938	27606	27530,62364	27696	27620,3779	27786	27710,13216	27876	27799,88642	27966	27889,64068
27517	27441,86665	27607	27531,62091	27697	27621,37517	27787	27711,12943	27877	27800,88369	27967	27890,63795
27518	27442,86392	27608	27532,61818	27698	27622,37244	27788	27712,1267	27878	27801,88096	27968	27891,63522
27519	27443,86119	27609	27533,61545	27699	27623,36971	27789	27713,12397	27879	27802,87823	27969	27892,63249
27520	27444,85846	27610	27534,61272	27700	27624,36698	27790	27714,12124	27880	27803,8755	27970	27893,62976
27521	27445,85573	27611	27535,60999	27701	27625,36425	27791	27715,11851	27881	27804,87277	27971	27894,62703
27522	27446,85299	27612	27536,60726	27702	27626,36152	27792	27716,11578	27882	27805,87004	27972	27895,6243
27523	27447,85026	27613	27537,60453	27703	27627,35879	27793	27717,11305	27883	27806,86731	27973	27896,62157
27524	27448,84753	27614	27538,6018	27704	27628,35606	27794	27718,11032	27884	27807,86458	27974	27897,61884
27525	27449,8448	27615	27539,59906	27705	27629,35333	27795	27719,10759	27885	27808,86185	27975	27898,61611
27526	27450,84207	27616	27540,59633	27706	27630,35059	27796	27720,10486	27886	27809,85912	27976	27899,61338
27527	27451,83934	27617	27541,5936	27707	27631,34786	27797	27721,10213	27887	27810,85639	27977	27900,61065
27528	27452,83661	27618	27542,59087	27708	27632,34513	27798	27722,09939	27888	27811,85366	27978	27901,60792
27529	27453,83388	27619	27543,58814	27709	27633,3424	27799	27723,09666	27889	27812,85093	27979	27902,60519
27530	27454,83115	27620	27544,58541	27710	27634,33967	27800	27724,09393	27890	27813,84819	27980	27903,60246
27531	27455,82842	27621	27545,58268	27711	27635,33694	27801	27725,0912	27891	27814,84546	27981	27904,59973
27532	27456,82569	27622	27546,57995	27712	27636,33421	27802	27726,08847	27892	27815,84273	27982	27905,597
27533	27457,82296	27623	27547,57722	27713	27637,33148	27803	27727,08574	27893	2 7816,84	27983	27906,59426
27534	27458,82023	27624	27548,57449	27714	27638,32875	27804	27728,08301	27894	27817,83727	27984	27907,59153
27535	27459,8175	27625	27549,57176	27715	27639,32602	27805	27729,08028	27895	27818,83454	27985	27908,5888
27536	27460,81477	27626	27550,56903	27716	27640,32329	27806	27730,07755	27896	27819,83181	27986	27909,58607
27537	27461,81204	27627	27551,5663	27717	27641,32056	27807	27731,07482	27897	27820,82908	27987	27910,58334
27538	27462,80931	27628	27552,56357	27718	27642,31783	27808	27732,07209	27898	27821,82635	27988	27911,58061
27539	27463,80658	27629	27553,56084	27719	27643,3151	27809	27733,06936	27899	27822,82362	27989	27912,57788
27540	27464,80385	27630	27554,55811	27720	27644,31237	27810	27734,06663	27900	27823,82089	27990	27913,57515
27541	27465,80112	27631	27555,55538	27721	27645,30964	27811	27735,0639	27901	27824,81816	27991	27914,57242
27542	27466,79839	27632	27556,55265	27722	27646,30691	27812	27736,06117	27902	27825,81543	27992	27915,56969
27543	27467,79566	27633	27557,54992	27723	27647,30418	27813	27737,05844	27903	27826,8127	27993	27916,56696
27544	27468,79293	27634	27558,54719	27724	27648,30145	27814	27738,05571	27904	27827,80997	27994	27917,56423
27545	27469,79019	27635	27559,54446	27725	27649,29872	27815	27739,05298	27905	27828,80724	27995	27918,5615
27546	27470,78746	27636	27560,54173	27726	27650,29599	27816	27740,05025	27906	27829,80451	27996	27919,55877
27547	27471,78473	27637	27561,53899	27727	27651,29326	27817	27741,04752	27907	27830,80178	27997	27920,55604
27548	2 7472,782	27638	27562,53626	27728	27652,29053	27818	27742,04479	27908	27831,79905	27998	27921,55331
27549	27473,77927	27639	27563,53353	27729	27653,28779	27819	27743,04206	27909	27832,79632	27999	27922,55058
27550	27474,77654	27640	27564,5308	27730	27654,28506	27820	27744,03933	27910	27833,79359	28000	27923,54785
27551	27475,77381	27641	27565,52807	27731	27655,28233	27821	27745,03659	27911	27834,79086	28001	27924,54512
27552	27476,77108	27642	27566,52534	27732	27656,2796	27822	27746,03386	27912	27835,78813	28002	27925,54239
27553	27477,76835	27643	27567,52261	27733	27657,27687	27823	27747,03113	27913	27836,7854	28003	27926,53966
27554	27478,76562	27644	27568,51988	27734	27658,27414	27824	27748,0284	27914	27837,78266	28004	27927,53693
27555	27479,76289	27645	27569,51715	27735	27659,27141	27825	27749,02567	27915	27838,77993	28005	27928,5342
27556	27480,76016	27646	27570,51442	27736	27660,26868	27826	27750,02294	27916	27839,7772	28006	27929,53146
27557	27481,75743	27647	27571,51169	27737	27661,26595	27827	27751,02021	27917	27840,77447	28007	27930,52873
27558	2 7482,7547	27648	27572,50896	27738	27662,26322	27828	27752,01748	27918	27841,77174	28008	27931,526
27559	27483,75197	27649	27573,50623	27739	27663,26049	27829	27753,01475	27919	27842,76901	28009	27932,52327
27560	27484,74924	27650	27574,5035	27740	27664,25776	27830	27754,01202	27920	27843,76628	28010	27933,52054
27561	27485,74651	27651	27575,50077	27741	27665,25503	27831	27755,00929	27921	27844,76355	28011	27934,51781
27562	27486,74378	27652	27576,49804	27742	27666,2523	27832	27756,00656	27922	27845,76082	28012	27935,51508
27563	27487,74105	27653	27577,49531	27743	27667,24957	27833	27757,00383	27923	27846,75809	28013	27936,51235
27564	27488,73832	27654	27578,49258	27744	27668,24684	27834	27758,0011	27924	27847,75536	28014	27937,50962

TABLE TO FIND OUT THE POINT A IN EARTH RETURNS 209

28015 27938,50689	28105 28028,26115	28195 28118,01541	28285 28207,76967	28375 28297,52393	28465 28387,2782
28016 27939,50416	28106 28029,25842	28196 28119,01268	28286 28208,76694	28376 28298,5212	28466 28388,27546
28017 27940,50143	28107 28030,25569	28197 28120,00995	28287 28209,76421	28377 28299,51847	28467 28389,27273
28018 27941,4987	28108 28031,25296	28198 28121,00722	28288 28210,76148	28378 28300,51574	28468 28390,27
28019 27942,49597	28109 28032,25023	28199 28122,00449	28289 28211,75875	28379 28301,51301	28469 28391,26727
28020 27943,49324	28110 28033,2475	28200 28123,00176	28290 28212,75602	28380 28302,51028	28470 28392,26454
28021 27944,49051	28111 28034,24477	28201 28123,99903	28291 28213,75329	28381 28303,50755	28471 28393,26181
28022 27945,48778	28112 28035,24204	28202 28124,9963	28292 28214,75056	28382 28304,50482	28472 28394,25908
28023 27946,48505	28113 28036,23931	28203 28125,99357	28293 28215,74783	28383 28305,50209	28473 28395,25635
28024 27947,48232	28114 28037,23658	28204 28126,99084	28294 28216,7451	28384 28306,49936	28474 28396,25362
28025 27948,47959	28115 28038,23385	28205 28127,98811	28295 28217,74237	28385 28307,49663	28475 28397,25089
28026 27949,47686	28116 28039,23112	28206 28128,98538	28296 28218,73964	28386 28308,4939	28476 28398,24816
28027 27950,47413	28117 28040,22839	28207 28129,98265	28297 28219,73691	28387 28309,49117	28477 28399,24543
28028 27951,4714	28118 28041,22566	28208 28130,97992	28298 28220,73418	28388 28310,48844	28478 28400,2427
28029 27952,46866	28119 28042,22293	28209 28131,97719	28299 28221,73145	28389 28311,48571	28479 28401,23997
28030 27953,46593	28120 28043,2202	28210 28132,97446	28300 28222,72872	28390 28312,48298	28480 28402,23724
28031 27954,4632	28121 28044,21746	28211 28133,97173	28301 28223,72599	28391 28313,48025	28481 28403,23451
28032 27955,46047	28122 28045,21473	28212 28134,969	28302 28224,72326	28392 28314,47752	28482 28404,23178
28033 27956,45774	28123 28046,212	28213 28135,96626	28303 28225,72053	28393 28315,47479	28483 28405,22905
28034 27957,45501	28124 28047,20927	28214 28136,96353	28304 28226,7178	28394 28316,47206	28484 28406,22632
28035 27958,45228	28125 28048,20654	28215 28137,9608	28305 28227,71506	28395 28317,46933	28485 28407,22359
28036 27959,44955	28126 28049,20381	28216 28138,95807	28306 28228,71233	28396 28318,4666	28486 28408,22086
28037 27960,44682	28127 28050,20108	28217 28139,95534	28307 28229,7096	28397 28319,46386	28487 28409,21813
28038 27961,44409	28128 28051,19835	28218 28140,95261	28308 28230,70687	28398 28320,46113	28488 28410,2154
28039 27962,44136	28129 28052,19562	28219 28141,94988	28309 28231,70414	28399 28321,4584	28489 28411,21266
28040 27963,43863	28130 28053,19289	28220 28142,94715	28310 28232,70141	28400 28322,45567	28490 28412,20993
28041 27964,4359	28131 28054,19016	28221 28143,94442	28311 28233,69868	28401 28323,45294	28491 28413,2072
28042 27965,43317	28132 28055,18743	28222 28144,94169	28312 28234,69595	28402 28324,45021	28492 28414,20447
28043 27966,43044	28133 28056,1847	28223 28145,93896	28313 28235,69322	28403 28325,44748	28493 28415,20174
28044 27967,42771	28134 28057,18197	28224 28146,93623	28314 28236,69049	28404 28326,44475	28494 28416,19901
28045 27968,42498	28135 28058,17924	28225 28147,9335	28315 28237,68776	28405 28327,44202	28495 28417,19628
28046 27969,42225	28136 28059,17651	28226 28148,93077	28316 28238,68503	28406 28328,43929	28496 28418,19355
28047 27970,41952	28137 28060,17378	28227 28149,92804	28317 28239,6823	28407 28329,43656	28497 28419,19082
28048 27971,41679	28138 28061,17105	28228 28150,92531	28318 28240,67957	28408 28330,43383	28498 28420,18809
28049 27972,41406	28139 28062,16832	28229 28151,92258	28319 28241,67684	28409 28331,4311	28499 28421,18536
28050 27973,41133	28140 28063,16559	28230 28152,91985	28320 28242,67411	28410 28332,42837	28500 28422,18263
28051 27974,4086	28141 28064,16286	28231 28153,91712	28321 28243,67138	28411 28333,42564	28501 28423,1799
28052 27975,40586	28142 28065,16013	28232 28154,91439	28322 28244,66865	28412 28334,42291	28502 28424,17717
28053 27976,40313	28143 28066,1574	28233 28155,91166	28323 28245,66592	28413 28335,42018	28503 28425,17444
28054 27977,4004	28144 28067,15466	28234 28156,90893	28324 28246,66319	28414 28336,41745	28504 28426,17171
28055 27978,39767	28145 28068,15193	28235 28157,9062	28325 28247,66046	28415 28337,41472	28505 28427,16898
28056 27979,39494	28146 28069,1492	28236 28158,90346	28326 28248,65773	28416 28338,41199	28506 28428,16625
28057 27980,39221	28147 28070,14647	28237 28159,90073	28327 28249,655	28417 28339,40926	28507 28429,16352
28058 27981,38948	28148 28071,14374	28238 28160,898	28328 28250,65226	28418 28340,40653	28508 28430,16079
28059 27982,38675	28149 28072,14101	28239 28161,89527	28329 28251,64953	28419 28341,4038	28509 28431,15806
28060 27983,38402	28150 28073,13828	28240 28162,89254	28330 28252,6468	28420 28342,40106	28510 28432,15533
28061 27984,38129	28151 28074,13555	28241 28163,88981	28331 28253,64407	28421 28343,39833	28511 28433,1526
28062 27985,37856	28152 28075,13282	28242 28164,88708	28332 28254,64134	28422 28344,3956	28512 28434,14987
28063 27986,37583	28153 28076,13009	28243 28165,88435	28333 28255,63861	28423 28345,39287	28513 28435,14713
28064 27987,3731	28154 28077,12736	28244 28166,88162	28334 28256,63588	28424 28346,39014	28514 28436,1444
28065 27988,37037	28155 28078,12463	28245 28167,87889	28335 28257,63315	28425 28347,38741	28515 28437,14167
28066 27989,36764	28156 28079,1219	28246 28168,87616	28336 28258,63042	28426 28348,38468	28516 28438,13894
28067 27990,36491	28157 28080,11917	28247 28169,87343	28337 28259,62769	28427 28349,38195	28517 28439,13621
28068 27991,36218	28158 28081,11644	28248 28170,8707	28338 28260,62496	28428 28350,37922	28518 28440,13348
28069 27992,35945	28159 28082,11371	28249 28171,86797	28339 28261,62223	28429 28351,37649	28519 28441,13075
28070 27993,35672	28160 28083,11098	28250 28172,86524	28340 28262,6195	28430 28352,37376	28520 28442,12802
28071 27994,35399	28161 28084,10825	28251 28173,86251	28341 28263,61677	28431 28353,37103	28521 28443,12529
28072 27995,35126	28162 28085,10552	28252 28174,85978	28342 28264,61404	28432 28354,3683	28522 28444,12256
28073 27996,34853	28163 28086,10279	28253 28175,85705	28343 28265,61131	28433 28355,36557	28523 28445,11983
28074 27997,3458	28164 28087,10006	28254 28176,85432	28344 28266,60858	28434 28356,36284	28524 28446,1171
28075 27998,34306	28165 28088,09733	28255 28177,85159	28345 28267,60585	28435 28357,36011	28525 28447,11437
28076 27999,34033	28166 28089,0946	28256 28178,84886	28346 28268,60312	28436 28358,35738	28526 28448,11164
28077 28000,3376	28167 28090,09186	28257 28179,84613	28347 28269,60039	28437 28359,35465	28527 28449,10891
28078 28001,33487	28168 28091,08913	28258 28180,8434	28348 28270,59766	28438 28360,35192	28528 28450,10618
28079 28002,33214	28169 28092,0864	28259 28181,84066	28349 28271,59493	28439 28361,34919	28529 28451,10345
28080 28003,32941	28170 28093,08367	28260 28182,83793	28350 28272,5922	28440 28362,34646	28530 28452,10072
28081 28004,32668	28171 28094,08094	28261 28183,8352	28351 28273,58946	28441 28363,34373	28531 28453,09799
28082 28005,32395	28172 28095,07821	28262 28184,83247	28352 28274,58673	28442 28364,341	28532 28454,09526
28083 28006,32122	28173 28096,07548	28263 28185,82974	28353 28275,584	28443 28365,33826	28533 28455,09253
28084 28007,31849	28174 28097,07275	28264 28186,82701	28354 28276,58127	28444 28366,33553	28534 28456,0898
28085 28008,31576	28175 28098,07002	28265 28187,82428	28355 28277,57854	28445 28367,3328	28535 28457,08707
28086 28009,31303	28176 28099,06729	28266 28188,82155	28356 28278,57581	28446 28368,33007	28536 28458,08433
28087 28010,3103	28177 28100,06456	28267 28189,81882	28357 28279,57308	28447 28369,32734	28537 28459,0816
28088 28011,30757	28178 28101,06183	28268 28190,81609	28358 28280,57035	28448 28370,32461	28538 28460,07887
28089 28012,30484	28179 28102,0591	28269 28191,81336	28359 28281,56762	28449 28371,32188	28539 28461,07614
28090 28013,30211	28180 28103,05637	28270 28192,81063	28360 28282,56489	28450 28372,31915	28540 28462,07341
28091 28014,29938	28181 28104,05364	28271 28193,8079	28361 28283,56216	28451 28373,31642	28541 28463,07068
28092 28015,29665	28182 28105,05091	28272 28194,80517	28362 28284,55943	28452 28374,31369	28542 28464,06795
28093 28016,29392	28183 28106,04818	28273 28195,80244	28363 28285,5567	28453 28375,31096	28543 28465,06522
28094 28017,29119	28184 28107,04545	28274 28196,79971	28364 28286,55397	28454 28376,30823	28544 28466,06249
28095 28018,28846	28185 28108,04272	28275 28197,79698	28365 28287,55124	28455 28377,3055	28545 28467,05976
28096 28019,28573	28186 28109,03999	28276 28198,79425	28366 28288,54851	28456 28378,30277	28546 28468,05703
28097 28020,283	28187 28110,03726	28277 28199,79152	28367 28289,54578	28457 28379,30004	28547 28469,0543
28098 28021,28026	28188 28111,03453	28278 28200,78879	28368 28290,54305	28458 28380,29731	28548 28470,05157
28099 28022,27753	28189 28112,0318	28279 28201,78606	28369 28291,54032	28459 28381,29458	28549 28471,04884
28100 28023,2748	28190 28113,02906	28280 28202,78333	28370 28292,53759	28460 28382,29185	28550 28472,04611
28101 28024,27207	28191 28114,02633	28281 28203,7806	28371 28293,53486	28461 28383,28912	28551 28473,04338
28102 28025,26934	28192 28115,0236	28282 28204,77786	28372 28294,53213	28462 28384,28639	28552 28474,04065
28103 28026,26661	28193 28116,02087	28283 28205,77513	28373 28295,5294	28463 28385,28366	28553 28475,03792
28104 28027,26388	28194 28117,01814	28284 28206,7724	28374 28296,52666	28464 28386,28093	28554 28476,03519

28555 28477,03246	28645 28566,78672	28735 28656,54098	28825 28746,29524	28915 28836,0495	29005 28925,80376
28556 28478,02973	28646 28567,78399	28736 28657,53825	28826 28747,29251	28916 28837,04677	29006 28926,80103
28557 28479,027	28647 28568,78126	28737 28658,53552	28827 28748,28978	28917 28838,04404	29007 28927,7983
28558 28480,02427	28648 28569,77853	28738 28659,53279	28828 28749,28705	28918 28839,04131	29008 28928,79557
28559 28481,02153	28649 28570,7758	28739 28660,53006	28829 28750,28432	28919 28840,03858	29009 28929,79284
28560 28482,0188	28650 28571,77307	28740 28661,52733	28830 28751,28159	28920 28841,03585	29010 28930,79011
28561 28483,01607	28651 28572,77033	28741 28662,5246	28831 28752,27886	28921 28842,03312	29011 28931,78738
28562 28484,01334	28652 28573,7676	28742 28663,52187	28832 28753,27613	28922 28843,03039	29012 28932,78465
28563 28485,01061	28653 28574,76487	28743 28664,51913	28833 28754,2734	28923 28844,02766	29013 28933,78192
28564 28486,00788	28654 28575,76214	28744 28665,5164	28834 28755,27067	28924 28845,02493	29014 28934,77919
28565 28487,00515	28655 28576,75941	28745 28666,51367	28835 28756,26793	28925 28846,0222	29015 28935,77646
28566 28488,00242	28656 28577,75668	28746 28667,51094	28836 28757,2652	28926 28847,01947	29016 28936,77373
28567 28488,99969	28657 28578,75395	28747 28668,50821	28837 28758,26247	28927 28848,01673	29017 28937,771
28568 28489,99696	28658 28579,75122	28748 28669,50548	28838 28759,25974	28928 28849,014	29018 28938,76827
28569 28490,99423	28659 28580,74849	28749 28670,50275	28839 28760,25701	28929 28850,01127	29019 28939,76553
28570 28491,9915	28660 28581,74576	28750 28671,50002	28840 28761,25428	28930 28851,00854	29020 28940,7628
28571 28492,98877	28661 28582,74303	28751 28672,49729	28841 28762,25155	28931 28852,00581	29021 28941,76007
28572 28493,98604	28662 28583,7403	28752 28673,49456	28842 28763,24882	28932 28853,00308	29022 28942,75734
28573 28494,98331	28663 28584,73757	28753 28674,49183	28843 28764,24609	28933 28854,00035	29023 28943,75461
28574 28495,98058	28664 28585,73484	28754 28675,4891	28844 28765,24336	28934 28854,99762	29024 28944,75188
28575 28496,97785	28665 28586,73211	28755 28676,48637	28845 28766,24063	28935 28855,99489	29025 28945,74915
28576 28497,97512	28666 28587,72938	28756 28677,48364	28846 28767,2379	28936 28856,99216	29026 28946,74642
28577 28498,97239	28667 28588,72665	28757 28678,48091	28847 28768,23517	28937 28857,98943	29027 28947,74369
28578 28499,96966	28668 28589,72392	28758 28679,47818	28848 28769,23244	28938 28858,9867	29028 28948,74096
28579 28500,96693	28669 28590,72119	28759 28680,47545	28849 28770,22971	28939 28859,98397	29029 28949,73823
28580 28501,9642	28670 28591,71846	28760 28681,47272	28850 28771,22698	28940 28860,98124	29030 28950,7355
28581 28502,96147	28671 28592,71573	28761 28682,46999	28851 28772,22425	28941 28861,97851	29031 28951,73277
28582 28503,95873	28672 28593,713	28762 28683,46726	28852 28773,22152	28942 28862,97578	29032 28952,73004
28583 28504,956	28673 28594,71027	28763 28684,46453	28853 28774,21879	28943 28863,97305	29033 28953,72731
28584 28505,95327	28674 28595,70753	28764 28685,4618	28854 28775,21606	28944 28864,97032	29034 28954,72458
28585 28506,95054	28675 28596,7048	28765 28686,45907	28855 28776,21333	28945 28865,96759	29035 28955,72185
28586 28507,94781	28676 28597,70207	28766 28687,45633	28856 28777,2106	28946 28866,96486	29036 28956,71912
28587 28508,94508	28677 28598,69934	28767 28688,4536	28857 28778,20787	28947 28867,96213	29037 28957,71639
28588 28509,94235	28678 28599,69661	28768 28689,45087	28858 28779,20513	28948 28868,9594	29038 28958,71366
28589 28510,93962	28679 28600,69388	28769 28690,44814	28859 28780,2024	28949 28869,95667	29039 28959,71093
28590 28511,93689	28680 28601,69115	28770 28691,44541	28860 28781,19967	28950 28870,95393	29040 28960,7082
28591 28512,93416	28681 28602,68842	28771 28692,44268	28861 28782,19694	28951 28871,9512	29041 28961,70547
28592 28513,93143	28682 28603,68569	28772 28693,43995	28862 28783,19421	28952 28872,94847	29042 28962,70273
28593 28514,9287	28683 28604,68296	28773 28694,43722	28863 28784,19148	28953 28873,94574	29043 28963,7
28594 28515,92597	28684 28605,68023	28774 28695,43449	28864 28785,18875	28954 28874,94301	29044 28964,69727
28595 28516,92324	28685 28606,6775	28775 28696,43176	28865 28786,18602	28955 28875,94028	29045 28965,69454
28596 28517,92051	28686 28607,67477	28776 28697,42903	28866 28787,18329	28956 28876,93755	29046 28966,69181
28597 28518,91778	28687 28608,67204	28777 28698,4263	28867 28788,18056	28957 28877,93482	29047 28967,68908
28598 28519,91505	28688 28609,66931	28778 28699,42357	28868 28789,17783	28958 28878,93209	29048 28968,68635
28599 28520,91232	28689 28610,66658	28779 28700,42084	28869 28790,1751	28959 28879,92936	29049 28969,68362
28600 28521,90959	28690 28611,66385	28780 28701,41811	28870 28791,17237	28960 28880,92663	29050 28970,68089
28601 28522,90686	28691 28612,66112	28781 28702,41538	28871 28792,16964	28961 28881,9239	29051 28971,67816
28602 28523,90413	28692 28613,65839	28782 28703,41265	28872 28793,16691	28962 28882,92117	29052 28972,67543
28603 28524,9014	28693 28614,65566	28783 28704,40992	28873 28794,16418	28963 28883,91844	29053 28973,6727
28604 28525,89867	28694 28615,65293	28784 28705,40719	28874 28795,16145	28964 28884,91571	29054 28974,66997
28605 28526,89593	28695 28616,6502	28785 28706,40446	28875 28796,15872	28965 28885,91298	29055 28975,66724
28606 28527,8932	28696 28617,64747	28786 28707,40173	28876 28797,15599	28966 28886,91025	29056 28976,66451
28607 28528,89047	28697 28618,64473	28787 28708,399	28877 28798,15326	28967 28887,90752	29057 28977,66178
28608 28529,88774	28698 28619,642	28788 28709,39627	28878 28799,15053	28968 28888,90479	29058 28978,65905
28609 28530,88501	28699 28620,63927	28789 28710,39353	28879 28800,1478	28969 28889,90206	29059 28979,65632
28610 28531,88228	28700 28621,63654	28790 28711,3908	28880 28801,14507	28970 28890,89933	29060 28980,65359
28611 28532,87955	28701 28622,63381	28791 28712,38807	28881 28802,14233	28971 28891,8966	29061 28981,65086
28612 28533,87682	28702 28623,63108	28792 28713,38534	28882 28803,1396	28972 28892,89387	29062 28982,64813
28613 28534,87409	28703 28624,62835	28793 28714,38261	28883 28804,13687	28973 28893,89113	29063 28983,6454
28614 28535,87136	28704 28625,62562	28794 28715,37988	28884 28805,13414	28974 28894,8884	29064 28984,64267
28615 28536,86863	28705 28626,62289	28795 28716,37715	28885 28806,13141	28975 28895,88567	29065 28985,63993
28616 28537,8659	28706 28627,62016	28796 28717,37442	28886 28807,12868	28976 28896,88294	29066 28986,6372
28617 28538,86317	28707 28628,61743	28797 28718,37169	28887 28808,12595	28977 28897,88021	29067 28987,63447
28618 28539,86044	28708 28629,6147	28798 28719,36896	28888 28809,12322	28978 28898,87748	29068 28988,63174
28619 28540,85771	28709 28630,61197	28799 28720,36623	28889 28810,12049	28979 28899,87475	29069 28989,62901
28620 28541,85498	28710 28631,60924	28800 28721,3635	28890 28811,11776	28980 28900,87202	29070 28990,62628
28621 28542,85225	28711 28632,60651	28801 28722,36077	28891 28812,11503	28981 28901,86929	29071 28991,62355
28622 28543,84952	28712 28633,60378	28802 28723,35804	28892 28813,1123	28982 28902,86656	29072 28992,62082
28623 28544,84679	28713 28634,60105	28803 28724,35531	28893 28814,10957	28983 28903,86383	29073 28993,61809
28624 28545,84406	28714 28635,59832	28804 28725,35258	28894 28815,10684	28984 28904,8611	29074 28994,61536
28625 28546,84133	28715 28636,59559	28805 28726,34985	28895 28816,10411	28985 28905,85837	29075 28995,61263
28626 28547,8386	28716 28637,59286	28806 28727,34712	28896 28817,10138	28986 28906,85564	29076 28996,6099
28627 28548,83587	28717 28638,59013	28807 28728,34439	28897 28818,09865	28987 28907,85291	29077 28997,60717
28628 28549,83313	28718 28639,5874	28808 28729,34166	28898 28819,09592	28988 28908,85018	29078 28998,60444
28629 28550,8304	28719 28640,58467	28809 28730,33893	28899 28820,09319	28989 28909,84745	29079 28999,60171
28630 28551,82767	28720 28641,58193	28810 28731,3362	28900 28821,09046	28990 28910,84472	29080 29000,59898
28631 28552,82494	28721 28642,5792	28811 28732,33347	28901 28822,08773	28991 28911,84199	29081 29001,59625
28632 28553,82221	28722 28643,57647	28812 28733,33073	28902 28823,085	28992 28912,83926	29082 29002,59352
28633 28554,81948	28723 28644,57374	28813 28734,328	28903 28824,08227	28993 28913,83653	29083 29003,59079
28634 28555,81675	28724 28645,57101	28814 28735,32527	28904 28825,07953	28994 28914,8338	29084 29004,58806
28635 28556,81402	28725 28646,56828	28815 28736,32254	28905 28826,0768	28995 28915,83107	29085 29005,58533
28636 28557,81129	28726 28647,56555	28816 28737,31981	28906 28827,07407	28996 28916,82833	29086 29006,5826
28637 28558,80856	28727 28648,56282	28817 28738,31708	28907 28828,07134	28997 28917,8256	29087 29007,57987
28638 28559,80583	28728 28649,56009	28818 28739,31435	28908 28829,06861	28998 28918,82287	29088 29008,57714
28639 28560,8031	28729 28650,55736	28819 28740,31162	28909 28830,06588	28999 28919,82014	29089 29009,5744
28640 28561,80037	28730 28651,55463	28820 28741,30889	28910 28831,06315	29000 28920,81741	29090 29010,57167
28641 28562,79764	28731 28652,5519	28821 28742,30616	28911 28832,06042	29001 28921,81468	29091 29011,56894
28642 28563,79491	28732 28653,54917	28822 28743,30343	28912 28833,05769	29002 28922,81195	29092 29012,56621
28643 28564,79218	28733 28654,54644	28823 28744,3007	28913 28834,05496	29003 28923,80922	29093 29013,56348
28644 28565,78945	28734 28655,54371	28824 28745,29797	28914 28835,05223	29004 28924,80649	29094 29014,56075

TABLE TO FIND OUT THE POINT A IN EARTH RETURNS 211

29095	29015,55802	29185	29105,31228	29275	29195,06654	29365	29284,8208	29455	29374,57507	29545	29464,32933
29096	29016,55529	29186	29106,30955	29276	29196,06381	29366	29285,81807	29456	29375,57234	29546	29465,3266
29097	29017,55256	29187	29107,30682	29277	29197,06108	29367	29286,81534	29457	29376,5696	29547	29466,32387
29098	29018,54983	29188	29108,30409	29278	29198,05835	29368	29287,81261	29458	29377,56687	29548	29467,32114
29099	29019,5471	29189	29109,30136	29279	29199,05562	29369	29288,80988	29459	29378,56414	29549	29468,3184
29100	29020,54437	29190	29110,29863	29280	29200,05289	29370	29289,80715	29460	29379,56141	29550	29469,31567
29101	29021,54164	29191	29111,2959	29281	29201,05016	29371	29290,80442	29461	29380,55868	29551	29470,31294
29102	29022,53891	29192	29112,29317	29282	29202,04743	29372	29291,80169	29462	29381,55595	29552	29471,31021
29103	29023,53618	29193	29113,29044	29283	29203,0447	29373	29292,79896	29463	29382,55322	29553	29472,30748
29104	29024,53345	29194	29114,28771	29284	29204,04197	29374	29293,79623	29464	29383,55049	29554	29473,30475
29105	29025,53072	29195	29115,28498	29285	29205,03924	29375	29294,7935	29465	29384,54776	29555	29474,30202
29106	29026,52799	29196	29116,28225	29286	29206,03651	29376	29295,79077	29466	29385,54503	29556	29475,29929
29107	29027,52526	29197	29117,27952	29287	29207,03378	29377	29296,78804	29467	29386,5423	29557	29476,29656
29108	29028,52253	29198	29118,27679	29288	29208,03105	29378	29297,78531	29468	29387,53957	29558	29477,29383
29109	29029,5198	29199	29119,27406	29289	29209,02832	29379	29298,78258	29469	29388,53684	29559	29478,2911
29110	29030,51707	29200	29120,27133	29290	29210,02559	29380	29299,77985	29470	29389,53411	29560	29479,28837
29111	29031,51434	29201	29121,2686	29291	29211,02286	29381	29300,77712	29471	29390,53138	29561	29480,28564
29112	29032,5116	29202	29122,26587	29292	29212,02013	29382	29301,77439	29472	29391,52865	29562	29481,28291
29113	29033,50887	29203	29123,26314	29293	29213,0174	29383	29302,77166	29473	29392,52592	29563	29482,28018
29114	29034,50614	29204	29124,2604	29294	29214,01467	29384	29303,76893	29474	29393,52319	29564	29483,27745
29115	29035,50341	29205	29125,25767	29295	29215,01194	29385	29304,7662	29475	29394,52046	29565	29484,27472
29116	29036,50068	29206	29126,25494	29296	29216,0092	29386	29305,76347	29476	29395,51773	29566	29485,27199
29117	29037,49795	29207	29127,25221	29297	29217,00647	29387	29306,76074	29477	29396,515	29567	29486,26926
29118	29038,49522	29208	29128,24948	29298	29218,00374	29388	29307,758	29478	29397,51227	29568	29487,26653
29119	29039,49249	29209	29129,24675	29299	29219,00101	29389	29308,75527	29479	29398,50954	29569	29488,2638
29120	29040,48976	29210	29130,24402	29300	29219,99828	29390	29309,75254	29480	29399,5068	29570	29489,26107
29121	29041,48703	29211	29131,24129	29301	29220,99555	29391	29310,74981	29481	29400,50407	29571	29490,25834
29122	29042,4843	29212	29132,23856	29302	29221,99282	29392	29311,74708	29482	29401,50134	29572	29491,2556
29123	29043,48157	29213	29133,23583	29303	29222,99009	29393	29312,74435	29483	29402,49861	29573	29492,25287
29124	29044,47884	29214	29134,2331	29304	29223,98736	29394	29313,74162	29484	29403,49588	29574	29493,25014
29125	29045,47611	29215	29135,23037	29305	29224,98463	29395	29314,73889	29485	29404,49315	29575	29494,24741
29126	29046,47338	29216	29136,22764	29306	29225,9819	29396	29315,73616	29486	29405,49042	29576	29495,24468
29127	29047,47065	29217	29137,22491	29307	29226,97917	29397	29316,73343	29487	29406,48769	29577	29496,24195
29128	29048,46792	29218	29138,22218	29308	29227,97644	29398	29317,7307	29488	29407,48496	29578	29497,23922
29129	29049,46519	29219	29139,21945	29309	29228,97371	29399	29318,72797	29489	29408,48223	29579	29498,23649
29130	29050,46246	29220	29140,21672	29310	29229,97098	29400	29319,72524	29490	29409,4795	29580	29499,23376
29131	29051,45973	29221	29141,21399	29311	29230,96825	29401	29320,72251	29491	29410,47677	29581	29500,23103
29132	29052,457	29222	29142,21126	29312	29231,96552	29402	29321,71978	29492	29411,47404	29582	29501,2283
29133	29053,45427	29223	29143,20853	29313	29232,96279	29403	29322,71705	29493	29412,47131	29583	29502,22557
29134	29054,45154	29224	29144,2058	29314	29233,96006	29404	29323,71432	29494	29413,46858	29584	29503,22284
29135	29055,4488	29225	29145,20307	29315	29234,95733	29405	29324,71159	29495	29414,46585	29585	29504,22011
29136	29056,44607	29226	29146,20034	29316	29235,9546	29406	29325,70886	29496	29415,46312	29586	29505,21738
29137	29057,44334	29227	29147,1976	29317	29236,95187	29407	29326,70613	29497	29416,46039	29587	29506,21465
29138	29058,44061	29228	29148,19487	29318	29237,94914	29408	29327,7034	29498	29417,45766	29588	29507,21192
29139	29059,43788	29229	29149,19214	29319	29238,9464	29409	29328,70067	29499	29418,45493	29589	29508,20919
29140	29060,43515	29230	29150,18941	29320	29239,94367	29410	29329,69794	29500	29419,4522	29590	29509,20646
29141	29061,43242	29231	29151,18668	29321	29240,94094	29411	29330,6952	29501	29420,44947	29591	29510,20373
29142	29062,42969	29232	29152,18395	29322	29241,93821	29412	29331,69247	29502	29421,44674	29592	29511,201
29143	29063,42696	29233	29153,18122	29323	29242,93548	29413	29332,68974	29503	29422,4444	29593	29512,19827
29144	29064,42423	29234	29154,17849	29324	29243,93275	29414	29333,68701	29504	29423,44127	29594	29513,19554
29145	29065,4215	29235	29155,17576	29325	29244,93002	29415	29334,68428	29505	29424,43854	29595	29514,1928
29146	29066,41877	29236	29156,17303	29326	29245,92729	29416	29335,68155	29506	29425,43581	29596	29515,19007
29147	29067,41604	29237	29157,1703	29327	29246,92456	29417	29336,67882	29507	29426,43308	29597	29516,18734
29148	29068,41331	29238	29158,16757	29328	29247,92183	29418	29337,67609	29508	29427,43035	29598	29517,18461
29149	29069,41058	29239	29159,16484	29329	29248,9191	29419	29338,67336	29509	29428,42762	29599	29518,18188
29150	29070,40785	29240	29160,16211	29330	29249,91637	29420	29339,67063	29510	29429,42489	29600	29519,17915
29151	29071,40512	29241	29161,15938	29331	29250,91364	29421	29340,6679	29511	29430,42216	29601	29520,17642
29152	29072,40239	29242	29162,15665	29332	29251,91091	29422	29341,66517	29512	29431,41943	29602	29521,17369
29153	29073,39966	29243	29163,15392	29333	29252,90818	29423	29342,66244	29513	29432,4167	29603	29522,17096
29154	29074,39693	29244	29164,15119	29334	29253,90545	29424	29343,65971	29514	29433,41397	29604	29523,16823
29155	29075,3942	29245	29165,14846	29335	29254,90272	29425	29344,65698	29515	29434,41124	29605	29524,1655
29156	29076,39147	29246	29166,14573	29336	29255,89999	29426	29345,65425	29516	29435,40851	29606	29525,16277
29157	29077,38874	29247	29167,143	29337	29256,89726	29427	29346,65152	29517	29436,40578	29607	29526,16004
29158	29078,386	29248	29168,14027	29338	29257,89453	29428	29347,64879	29518	29437,40305	29608	29527,15731
29159	29079,38327	29249	29169,13754	29339	29258,8918	29429	29348,64606	29519	29438,40032	29609	29528,15458
29160	29080,38054	29250	29170,1348	29340	29259,88907	29430	29349,64333	29520	29439,39759	29610	29529,15185
29161	29081,37781	29251	29171,13207	29341	29260,88634	29431	29350,6406	29521	29440,39486	29611	29530,14912
29162	29082,37508	29252	29172,12934	29342	29261,8836	29432	29351,63787	29522	29441,39213	29612	29531,14639
29163	29083,37235	29253	29173,12661	29343	29262,88087	29433	29352,63514	29523	29442,3894	29613	29532,14366
29164	29084,36962	29254	29174,12388	29344	29263,87814	29434	29353,6324	29524	29443,38667	29614	29533,14093
29165	29085,36689	29255	29175,12115	29345	29264,87541	29435	29354,62967	29525	29444,38394	29615	29534,1382
29166	29086,36416	29256	29176,11842	29346	29265,87268	29436	29355,62694	29526	29445,3812	29616	29535,13547
29167	29087,36143	29257	29177,11569	29347	29266,86995	29437	29356,62421	29527	29446,37847	29617	29536,13274
29168	29088,3587	29258	29178,11296	29348	29267,86722	29438	29357,62148	29528	29447,37574	29618	29537,13
29169	29089,35597	29259	29179,11023	29349	29268,86449	29439	29358,61875	29529	29448,37301	29619	29538,12727
29170	29090,35324	29260	29180,1075	29350	29269,86176	29440	29359,61602	29530	29449,37028	29620	29539,12454
29171	29091,35051	29261	29181,10477	29351	29270,85903	29441	29360,61329	29531	29450,36755	29621	29540,12181
29172	29092,34778	29262	29182,10204	29352	29271,8563	29442	29361,61056	29532	29451,36482	29622	29541,11908
29173	29093,34505	29263	29183,09931	29353	29272,85357	29443	29362,60783	29533	29452,36209	29623	29542,11635
29174	29094,34232	29264	29184,09658	29354	29273,85084	29444	29363,6051	29534	29453,35936	29624	29543,11362
29175	29095,33959	29265	29185,09385	29355	29274,84811	29445	29364,60237	29535	29454,35663	29625	29544,11089
29176	29096,33686	29266	29186,09112	29356	29275,84538	29446	29365,59964	29536	29455,3539	29626	29545,10816
29177	29097,33413	29267	29187,08839	29357	29276,84265	29447	29366,59691	29537	29456,35117	29627	29546,10543
29178	29098,3314	29268	29188,08566	29358	29277,83992	29448	29367,59418	29538	29457,34844	29628	29547,1027
29179	29099,32867	29269	29189,08293	29359	29278,83719	29449	29368,59145	29539	29458,34571	29629	29548,09997
29180	29100,32594	29270	29190,0802	29360	29279,83446	29450	29369,58872	29540	29459,34298	29630	29549,09724
29181	29101,3232	29271	29191,07747	29361	29280,83173	29451	29370,58599	29541	29460,34025	29631	29550,09451
29182	29102,32047	29272	29192,07474	29362	29281,829	29452	29371,58326	29542	29461,33752	29632	29551,09178
29183	29103,31774	29273	29193,072	29363	29282,82627	29453	29372,58053	29543	29462,33479	29633	29552,08905
29184	29104,31501	29274	29194,06927	29364	29283,82354	29454	29373,5778	29544	29463,33206	29634	29553,08632

PART III

MISCELLANY AND NEW RESEARCHES ON SOLAR RETURNS

19.
The significant value of synergy in the aimed birthdays of a whole family

An ASR is always striking[1].

The synergic effect on the aimed birthdays of a whole family is even more striking, either on the negative or on the positive meaning of the term.

Let us consider three examples.

First example: The arrest of Benito Mussolini

This is the story of his arrest in brief.

Benito Mussolini was arrested on the 25th of July of 1943 by an order of the King of Italy. Besides splitting our country in two from a moral, political, and social point of view, this event also caused a catastrophe of huge proportions inside the Duce's family – of course if you consider the event from the point of view of *that* specific family. This is even more evident if you consider that to the leader of Fascism, his own arrest meant dishonour even worse than being attempted to be killed by a terrorist or being shot by political enemies. It all happened above within the frame of a huge scandal (this is why we can see that the transits of Jupiter play a major role in this event) as well as the collapse of a position of absolute power. Today, as we try to read that event under the light of History, we are probably unable to perceive the intensity of that tragedy

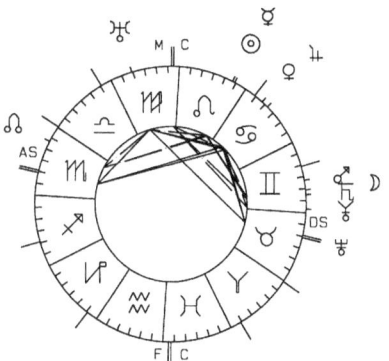

Benito Mussolini's natal

(as seen from Mussolini's family), which in my opinion represented an important milestone for the emancipation for Italy.

His previous SR (i.e. the current one)

To be noted the stellium and the Sun in the 6th House of SR: two of the most negative values of a SR. Please also note Mars in the 7th House corresponding to arrests, assasination attempts and attacks on several occasions.

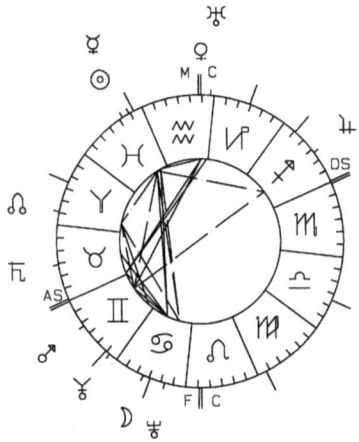

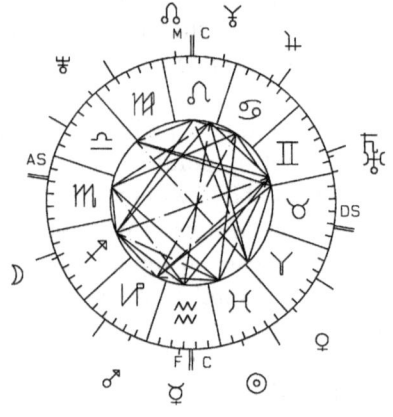

Left, Claretta Petacci's natal and right, her SR. The Ascendant of her SR lies in her 6th natal House. Is there any need for further explanation? As a gift pack, Saturn and Uranus in the 7th House.

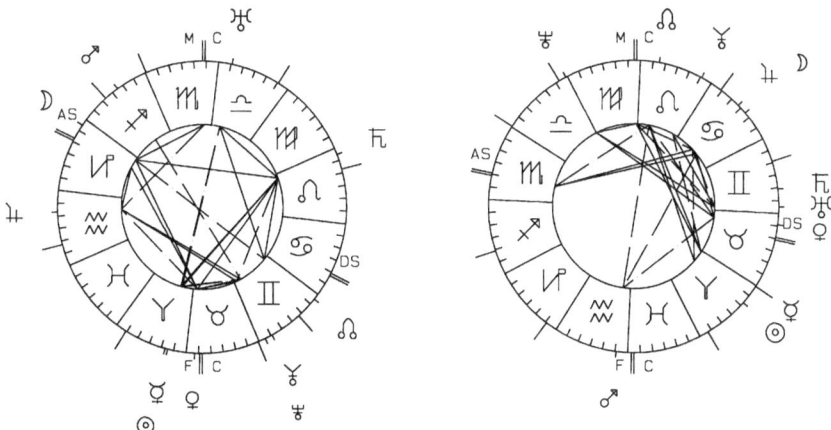

Left, Rachele Mussolini's natal and right, her SR. The Ascendant of her SR lies in her 10th natal House: the upsetting of her social position. As a gift pack, Saturn, Uranus, and Venus in the 7th House.

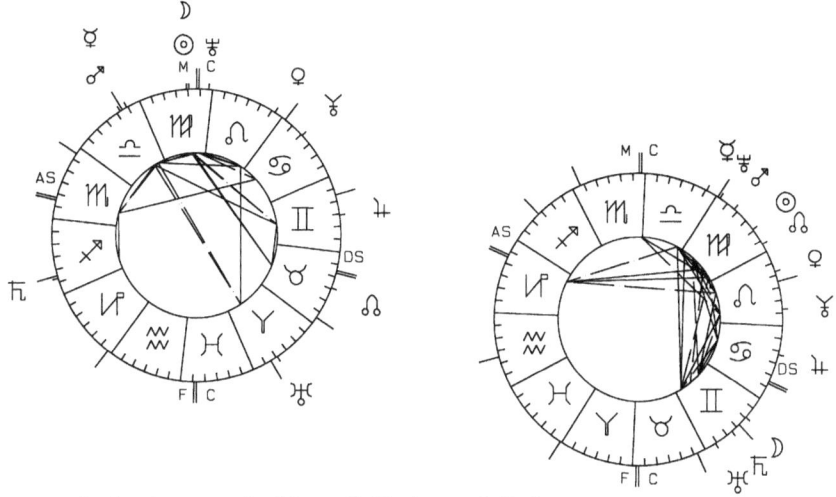

Left, Annamaria Mussolini's (one of their daughters) natal and right, her SR. The Sun and a powerful stellium in the 8th House of SR may be compared to an Ascendant of SR in the 12th natal House. Moreover, do not forget that the 8th House often corresponds to the end of the things and to jail. Jupiter and Pluto in the 7th House of SR: see the 'bistable relay' effect of Jupiter in the 7th House explained in my volume *Transits and Solar Returns*.

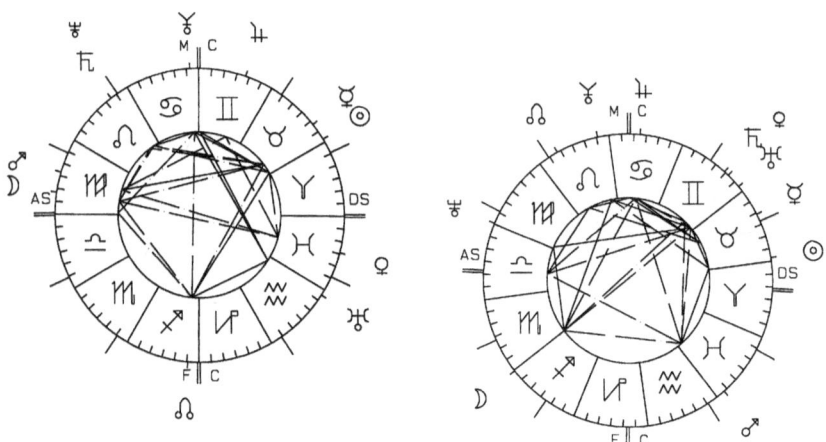

Left, Bruno Mussolini's (Benito's second son) natal and right, his SR. The Ascendant of his SR lies in his 1st natal House – do you need anything else? If you do, there's also a powerful stellium in the 8th House and the Sun in the 7th House of SR – the latter meaning possible troubles with law for the subject or a member of his family.

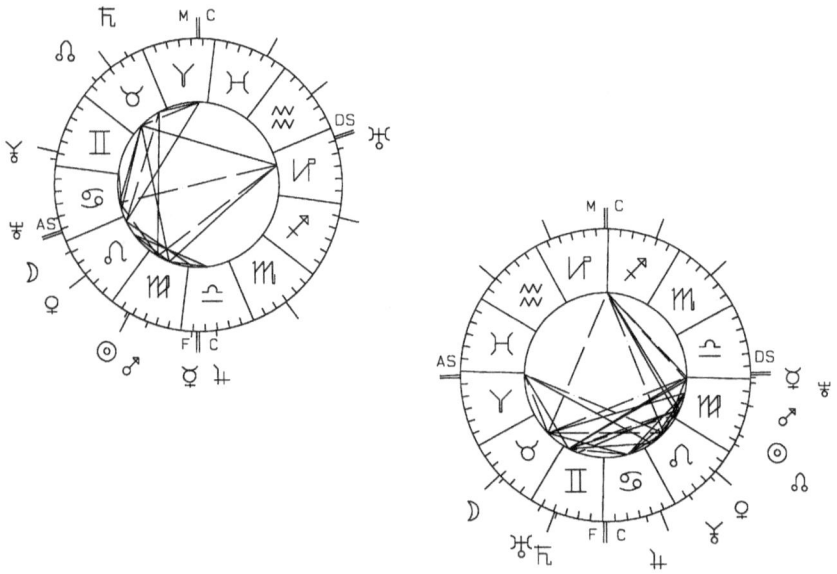

Left, Edda Mussolini's (Benito's daughter and Galeazzo Ciano's wife) natal and right, her SR. The Sun is in the 6th House of SR – isn't it enough? There is also Mars is in the 6th House of SR. Further there is a stellium in the 6th House. In fact even one of these elements would have been enough.

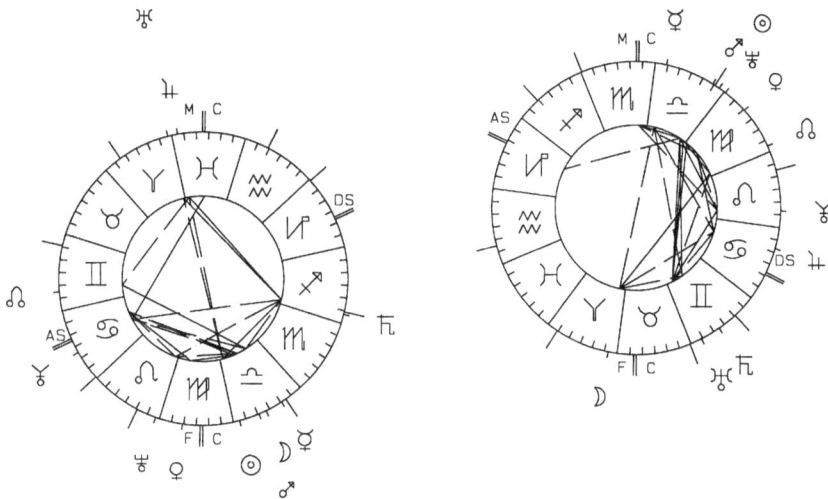

Left, Romano Mussolini's (Benito's son and a talented musician) natal and right, his SR. The Ascendant of SR lies both in the 6th and in the 7th natal House – isn't it enough? Added to it is a powerful stellium in the 8th House as well as Jupiter and Pluto in the 7th House of SR.

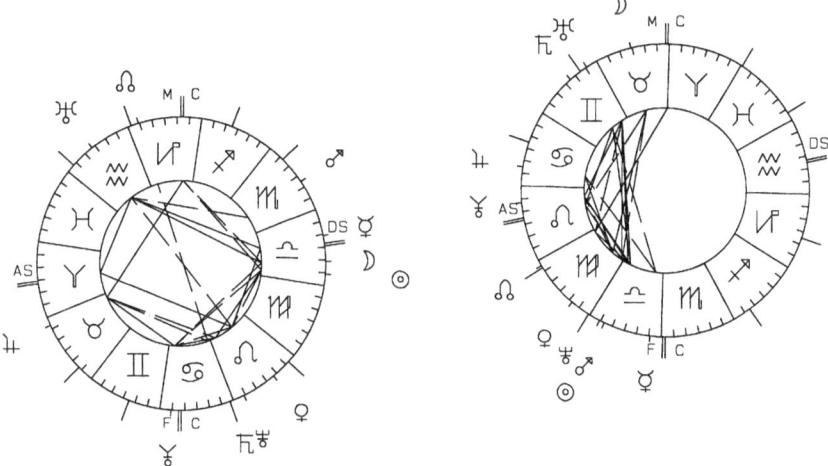

Left, Vittorio Mussolini's (Benito's son) natal and right, his SR. I have already written on the apparent anomaly of this SR in my volume *Nuovo Trattato di Astrologia*, Armenia ed., so I had better not repeat myself. May I add that probably his time of birth should be rectified by a very few minutes, which would place Saturn, Uranus, and the Moon in the 10th House of SR – an extremely eloquent position for such an event. To summarize it, everybody – perhaps with the exception of the mentally blind, who are much more handicapped than any other blind – could see that all the SRs of the Mussolini's family sang the song of the tragedy of their Duce.

Second example: a positive synergy of all the members of the family

Many of you know that last year (I am writing these lines in the middle of June, 2004) the front page of all Italian newspapers talked about my wife and myself because we went to spend her birthday in Hong Kong on the 11th and the 12th of April – i.e. during the possibly most mortal week of that epidemic of SARS. The papers got to know it and they prepared the 'scoop'. Many popular Italian TV show such as *Domenica in...* wanted us to be their guest, but we declined. We only accepted to grant an interview to the daily paper of Naples, for which I work, *IL MATTINO*; and another one for the TV show *La vita in diretta*. They sent a troupe to our place and the interview was filmed and broadcast at the end of April 2003. The reporter asked my wife, not without sarcasm, «Mrs Discepolo, you're a lawyer – in order to protect you on the ground of health, your husband led you straight to Hong Kong on the day of your birthday and in the period in which people were dying there at every street corner?» This is how my wife calmly replied: «You're a journalist and you are a layman. My husband also is a journalist but he's above all an astrologer of great experience in the field. So if he tells me to go to Hong Kong, I trust him and I go.»

In April 2004 we also went to Eastern Siberia for my wife's following birthday, so we can take stock. Perhaps we'll get a disease or we'll have a car accident, but for the time being the past year has been the best year of our life. It has also been a very positive year – in my opinion – for the life of our daughters.

Before leaving for Hong Kong many friends and close relatives made attempts to convince us not to leave. Some of them even reached the point of threatening and insulting us.

My wife (not me) got a little bit upset and asked me, «Are you sure that nothing dangerous would happen to us there?»

Then I made her sit down beside me and I showed her some astral charts on my PC monitor. I showed her that in both the ASRs of our two daughters of that period there was Jupiter in their 4th House (the House of parents) and I asked her,»Do you find it plausible that in the same year when our two daughters have their Jupiter of SR in the 4th House of SR, their parents would die of SARS in China?»

And in fact, as I told you, those were our best years since we were married. My wife had been suffering from thyroid cold nodules; she knew that in March 2004 she would have to make arrangements for a surgical intervention because her nodules had grown too much, she had already resigned to her fate. When we went to her doctor (who knew nothing of our aimed birthdays) he examined the results of my wife's ultrasound scans and he compared them with those of the previous year. He watched them carefully also without glasses, and once again with his glasses on. He observed them with a magnifier. He read the attached medical report and it was clear that he was puzzled. Eventually he declared, «Milady, I am not able to explain it – but the volume and the size of your nodules have significantly decreased. This means that you don't need to be operated this year – you don't need to be operated ever!»

A second important event for my wife was winning a case against her Municipal Bar (where she works). Several lawyers had tried to bring such a suit elsewhere in Italy without success, with the exception of my wife and seven colleagues of hers who appealed against the same Bar.

As far as I am concerned, I published two new books: among my fifty volumes, perhaps they'll be the most appreciated or the most read ones. One of them is quite 'monumental', with its 800 pages. Furthermore, following three and a half year of indescribable suffering, I have eventually released a marvellous piece of software to calculate the Automatic Aimed Solar Returns, and I'm having enormous satisfaction from it.

When I projected the ASRs of my two daughters with their Jupiter in the 4th House of SR I didn't intend to gain personal advantages from it. In my daughter Laura's ASR Jupiter was on the cusp 4th-5th House because I aimed to help her find a house on lease; at the same time I hoped to strengthen her relationship with her husband – thank God their relationship is alright now. Talking about my daughter Luna, I meant to tune up her Base SR of Naples: in fact I suggested her to spend her birthday in Palermo simply in order to avoid a Moon in the 12th House of SR, while Jupiter would have been in the 4th House also in Naples.

To make a long story short, I believe that – using a paradox – no wife could kill a rival in love by simply placing Mars in the 7th House of her husband's SR. On the other hand if, say, my son has to pass an important exam and I can 'set' a very good Jupiter in the 5th House of my own SR, well I am convinced that my son would surely benefit from it.

In other words, for years I have been trying to enhance the SRs of single members of a family. At the same time, if studying their single SRs I realize that I can also 'throw some rays of positivity' on the House of another member of the same family who particularly needs it that year – for example by properly placing Venus or Jupiter – well I do so.

If any of you ask me how this can be explained, I answer with my usual example of the 'radio repairer' who knows how to change a valve to fix a radio set, although he may ignore its 'scientific' explanation. I am satisfied with leaving the explanation to philosophers and all those people who have been able to fully penetrate the mysteries of life, death, faith, reincarnation, and other deep truths.

Third example: an exceptional year for a whole family whose members (each of them) had a gorgeous ASR in process.

Those, who carefully study my ASRs for themselves or for others who consult them, know that since years I have been trying to focus on two fundamental hinges of such a technique which, I believe, I have lately succeeded in elaborating quite well, as you can read in my works on the subject.

The cusp is a really exceptional point of strength in a map of SR. I have written more extensively on its value in my volume *Nuovo Trattato di Astrologia*, Armenia ed. The other one is the attempt to achieve the utmost synergy in the correct application of Active Astrology, using a particular approach when relocating the ASRs of a whole family.

The basic concept in this type of research consists fundamentally in trying to protect any single element of the family; trying to achieve the best performance – in a broad sense – for each of them; and studying the possibility of protecting further the weakest link(s) also through the Aimed Solar Returns of the other members of the family. Still sticking to theory we might then say that generally speaking, it will be a good thing trying to protect children –who perhaps haven't huge problems to solve – and at the same time trying to give a hand to one or both parents – who usually need it more – also by enhancing the celestial positions of the SRs of their children. Every time I had the chance of acting this way, I attained almost extraordinary results – surely, often the results went much beyond the aimed ones. What if one member of the family, willingly or unwillingly, moves against the family? In this case, if the other members are astrologically protected, the damage would be marginal; but the overall strategy – studied for a family in which each of the members would have his/her own ASR – may lead to lesser results than the ones that might have been originally attained if all the members had acted following an astrologically winning group strategy. As far as my family is concerned, I have applied this rule as many times as I could, that's to say up to our birthdays of 2004 – and the results have been magnificent.

Let us consider then another practical example. Let us examine the aimed birthdays of a whole family of Veneto: father, mother, and two sons.

The mother used to have serious health problems. Now she's perfectly recovered but – for the sake of caution – with her consent whenever we project a new ASR we always consider protecting health above any other thing. The parents are separated. The husband has been abandoning himself, especially to despair, and with significant professional and financial falls.

The mother's ASR has been conceived in order to protect her health as much as possible (Venus in the 6th House). Her time of birth is not certain – we consider that it may be thirty minutes before the officially recorded time. In such a circumstance, after years of attempts, she appears to be born 5 or 10 minutes after the rectified time of birth; if so, her Venus would fall over the cusp between the 5th and the 6th House: a wonderful position for this planet.

Their first son would have had the Ascendant of SR in his 1st natal House and Mars in the 4th House of SR – the House of parents. By carefully relocating his SR – with the aforementioned goals – I have placed his Venus over the cusp between the 5th and the 6th House. This changed radically the elder son's year in a positive direction. Another result attained was placing the wonderful conjunction of Sun and Jupiter in the 4th House – the parents!

Considering a suitable place for the relocation of the younger son's SR I have followed the same approach. Had he celebrated his birthday at home, he would have had the Sun in the 6th House and Mars in the 1st House. Relocating, he eventually had the Sun in the 3rd House of SR (fairly good for his education) and, above all, the same conjunction Sun-Jupiter as his brother, in the 4th House – still the parents!

As for their father, his BSR (i.e. the one cast for his place of residence) was so good that there was no need for relocation. In fact Venus in the 8th House of SR forecast a net improvement in his financial situation, while Jupiter on the cusp 7th-8th House of SR announced the chance of significant enhancement in his marriage.

I judge the results of this strategy to be transparent: all four members of the family had gorgeous health; the father has a sort of shake-up from life: thanks to Uranus at the Ascendant and also thanks to other 'chance' events his professional activity and his income had a significant growth. I have been in touch with this family since years and I like to 'support' them: so from my point of view the most wonderful event which has taken place is the pacification between the parents. Of course it may be a temporary state, but it is a little miracle, knowing the past story of this family.

I must underline one other thing, concerning how well did Venus work in the aimed SR of the mother. As I proceed year after year in my practice and my researches, I am becoming more and more demanding. Each time I try to obtain more and more ambitious goals. Why stick to one goal only if you can achieve two?

Of course, even if I have known and astrologically dealt with certain people for several years, I can never swear to know their time of birth with a precision higher than five minutes, so I always consider a wider range.

In the case of the mother I intended to place that wonderful Venus exactly on the cusp of the 5th and 6th House of SR, but I obviously could not be sure of the result. Nevertheless I had taken certain precautions, so that if I had missed one of the two goals (health, or love & sons) I would have kept the more important one in this specific case – health.

Similarly, when I try to place Venus of SR on the cusp between the 7th and the 6th House, I always consider the possibility that the time of birth may be different; and if so, Venus would fall in the 6th rather than in the 7th House of SR.

Somebody would argue, «How come you still have doubts on someone's time of birth if you have been dealing for ages with him or her?» The answer is easy. Ages ago I was satisfied with placing Venus of SR right in the middle of the 6th, or 7th, or 5th House of SR. Now, as I have underlined, I wish to attain more and I place celestials on the cusps. In order to achieve this goal I must 'centre' one's time of birth with much more precision than I used to, when I could even consider it 'uncertain'.

The mother's BSR

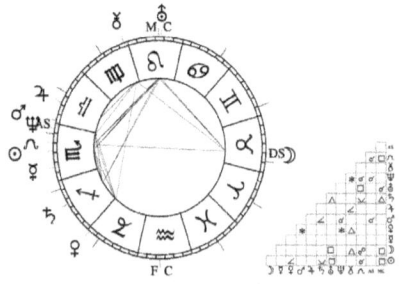
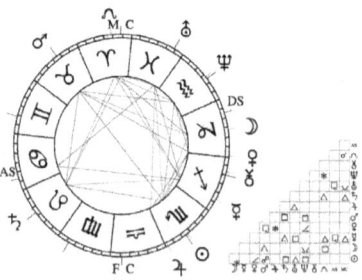

SYNERGY IN THE AIMED BIRTHDAYS OF A WHOLE FAMILY 225

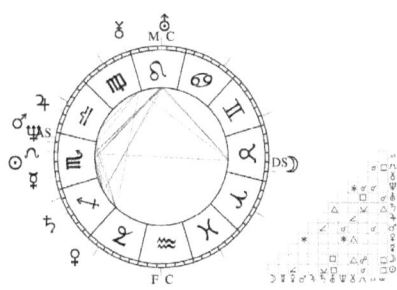

The mother's ASR

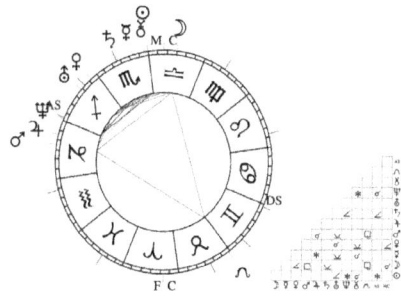

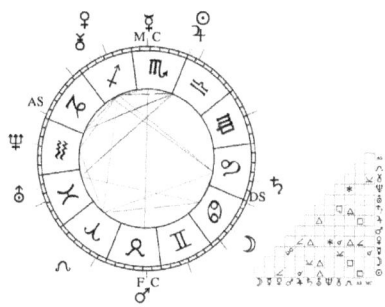

The first son's BSR

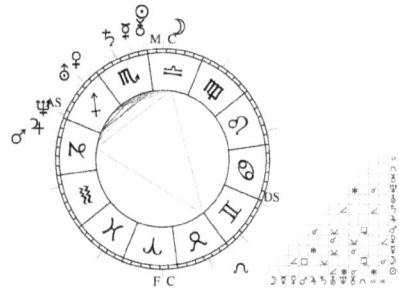

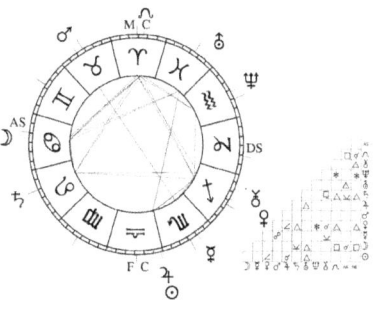

The first son's ASR

The second son's BSR

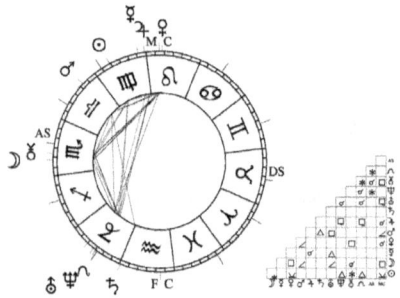
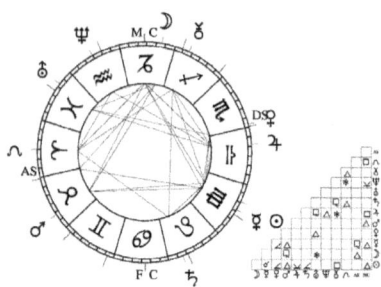

The second son's ASR

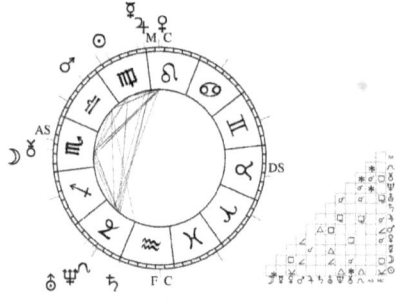
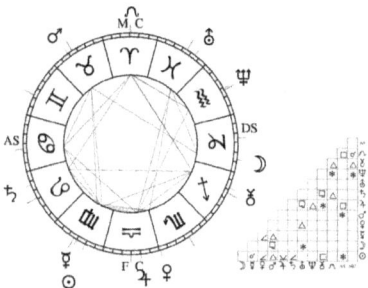

The father's BSR

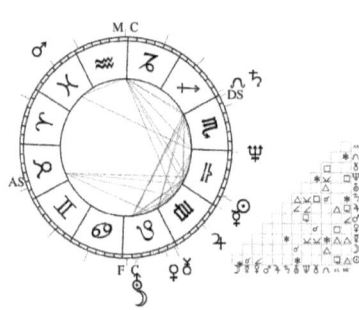
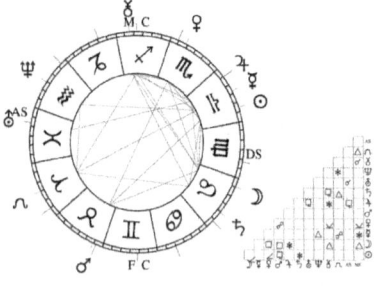

Notes
1) In a way, a **Solar Return is always 'aimed'** if you intentionally decide to spend it in your usual place of residence. *This way it is aimed to stay there, still it's 'aimed'.*

20.
An attempt to get pregnant in advanced years

In my opinion any exercise concerning ASRs is, in some way, like studying the plan of a battle: the final result being given both by one's specific technical know-how and by the learned integration of an excellent strategy.

The first point from which one should start with is detaching as much as possible from such an elementary logic as 'the subject needs money, so I place the Ascendant of his/her SR in his/her 2nd natal House.' – This is what I've seen performed by many colleagues of mine, even if the subject was a worker in temporary layoff so that the final result was him losing his job definitely. Apparently, at a higher level one could follow a leit-motiv-like way of reasoning like this: «The subject wants to graduate, so I place Jupiter in his/her 3rd House of SR.»

No: in my opinion, in the majority of cases what you need is trying to put three or four elements in synergy.

The following example will probably clear this notion very well.

Before us there's the case of a Brazilian woman of about forty-five years. She hasn't presently a partner in love. She would like to aim her birthday hoping to find love and, hopefully, to get eventually pregnant.

It is a quite complex problem, for different reasons, starting from the fact that she hasn't got a steady partner at present, and she would not like to become pregnant with the contribution of a 'borrowed' partner.

So what you should do before anything else is having a look at her natal map, to see whether her project is feasible at all.

Her natal shows the rather strict conjunction of Jupiter and Saturn in the 5th House, creating many different aspects with other elements of her natal sky.

Saturn would resolutely oppose this project, but it might also announce a baby born late, very late in her life. Jupiter on the other hand favours the projects and it might even help Saturn expressing its own symbolism in full.

Furthermore we have two really exceptional transits that may act as a background to such a project: namely, Uranus trine to her natal Moon and Uranus proceeding (during the days in which I am studying her request) to become conjunct to her Descendant. I have explained several times that, according to my experience based on thousands of aimed birthdays verified in practice – not only in theory – over decades, compared to the elements of the map of SR, transits have a really low influence as far as the events of the year are concerned. This is true unless transits receive the direct support of the elements of a SR: if so, those transits may even 'explode' with all their power.

In the present case, as I told you, we have two transits of such a primary importance that they can justify the attempt of making the lady's ambition true.

At this point what you need is developing a strategy.

If I could have two *Jupiters* and two *Venuses* at disposition, well – there would be no doubt: I'd place any of those four 'chessmen' in her 5th House (sons & daughters, the native's partner in love); in the 7th House (the subject's partner); in the 10th House (the native's social growth – for a lady over 45 years, having a baby after having desired it for decades certainly means social growth); and in her 6th House or 1st House of SR (as a strong defence to her health, surely required to have a safe pregnancy).

Unluckily God had provided us with only one Venus and one Jupiter, so we must try to achieve the best possible synergy not only among the celestials in the sky, but also with the celestials forming precise angles on the very day of the subject's coming birthday. These are my choices and the relevant pieces of advice which I gave to her, explaining them up to their smallest details.

First proposal. Sun and Mercury in the 5th House. Just think to it: the Sun in a House of SR cannot be defined either positive or negative – it is simply a front page, the nine-column headline of that year, focusing on a given field of the subject's life. It does not guarantee anything about the final result that we wish to achieve by aiming that SR. It guarantees that the given subject will leap into the foreground – and how could a 5th House of SR be in the foreground without a hint of a love affair?

But as I told you, this is absolutely not enough: you also need to create a synergy among several elements of the map of SR.

For this reason my second ace up in my sleeve was to place the Ascendant of the SR in the lady's 7th natal House. This, together with the Sun in the 5th House, corresponds to a newsvendor crying in the street the headlines of events related with the 5th House and the 7th House. Also an Ascendant of SR in the 7th House cannot be considered either positive or negative: it only guarantees that the subject would experience something relevant in that field of her life. We need to play on other elements too.

So let us reflect. Up to this point we have put in strong evidence the 5th and the 7th House while we have two extraordinary transits: Uranus trine to the Moon, and Uranus moving towards its own conjunction with the Descendant. Who told you that its conjunction with the Descendant would necessarily imply the beginning of a steady affair? The answer is: Logic tells that. In fact this subject hasn't got a steady partner and if anything would change radically, it will only change in that direction.

Yet I am considering an aimed birthday with many other supporting points, namely the following ones.

Pluto conjunct to Medium Coeli: it surely helps, within the frame we are moving in, towards the direction of social growth.

Jupiter in Gauquelin zone, i.e. as strong as a Jupiter in the 10th House, supporting and sustaining the action of Pluto in the 10th House.

Venus in the 6th House helps very much protecting health, which is an important point within the frame of the result we wish to be achieved. Unluckily we are forced to insert also Saturn in the 6th House: it is no good for health, but it might also refer to the several troubles that a lady might face, going through pregnancy beyond the age of 45 years.

Last, Uranus on the Ascendant plays a double role: it's a positive element because it heralds turns of events that may be connected with the lady's physical appearance (pregnancy), and it can also play against it because it might expose her physics to sudden downfalls in the widest meaning of this term.

Given the already existing sky, fixed in the ephemerides before we even started considering this project, I believe that this is the best we could do. Let me insist: our aim is always studying the best solution possible – not the perfect solution.

Yet, for this case I have also studied other options.

LUNAR RETURNS AND EARTH RETURNS

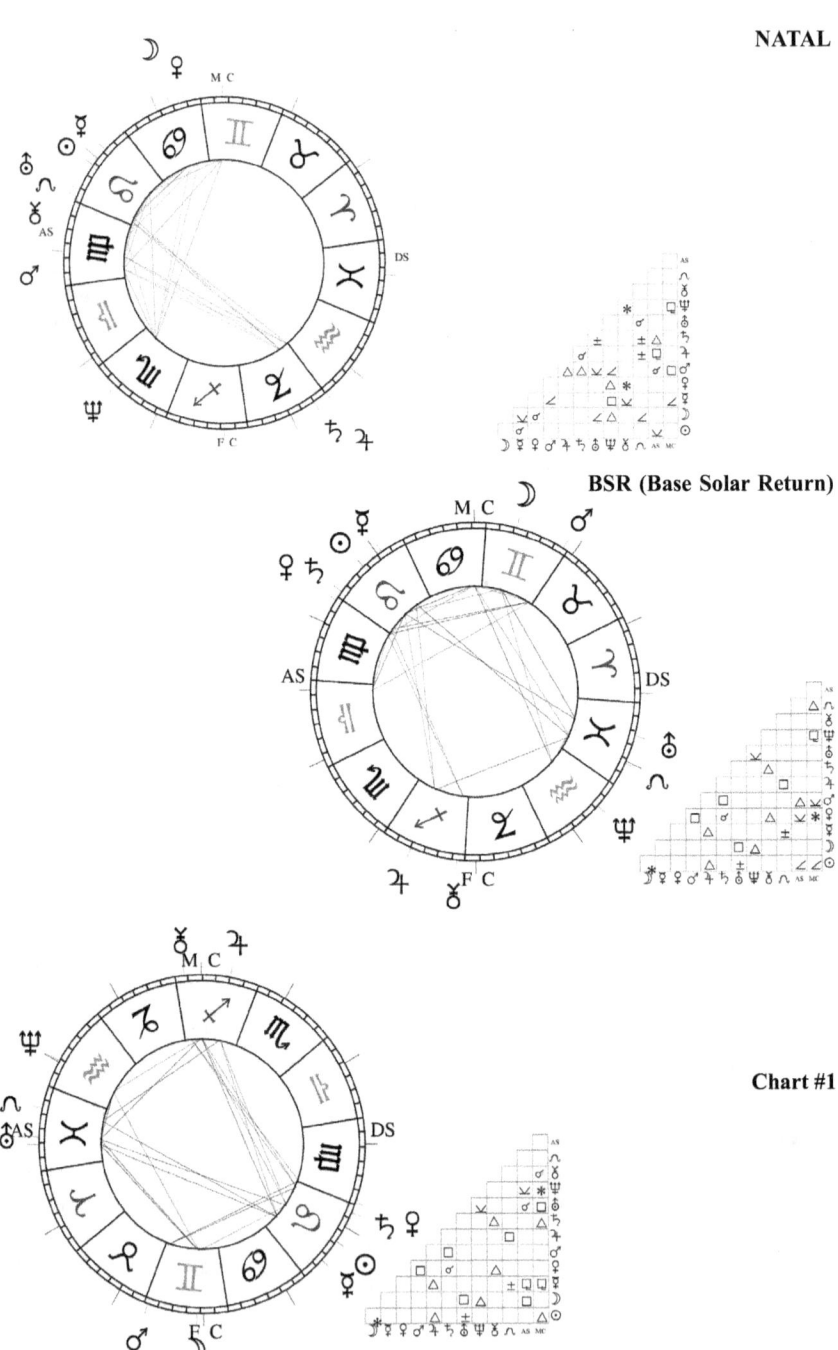

NATAL

BSR (Base Solar Return)

Chart #1

AN ATTEMPT TO GET PREGNANT IN ADVANCED YEARS 231

Also the B option corresponds very well to the different premises on which I had based my previous choice.

Here we have Jupiter very close to the Medium Coeli.

Moreover, we place the Ascendant in the 5th House.

Furthermore, we place a notable cluster of celestials in the 7th House. There's also Saturn there, but this might even be helpful for out project: in fact our lady – for different reasons – might even resolve to marry a man older than she is.

Neptune and Uranus in the 1st House are 'several kilometres' far from the Ascendant, so they should not keep us concerned about her health.

Mars is also quite far from the cusp of the 4th House.

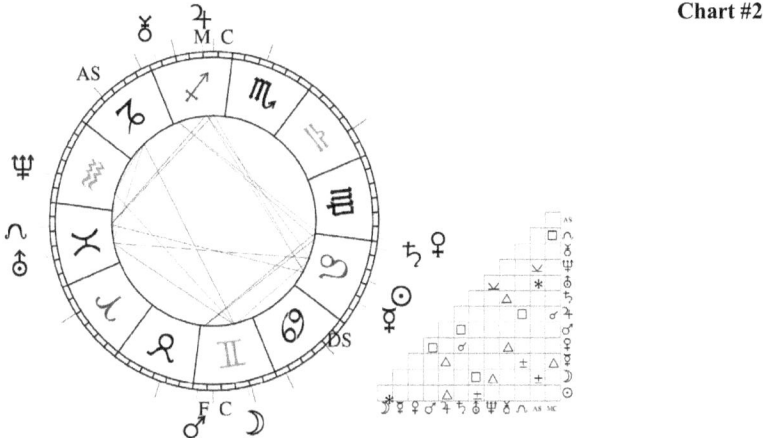

Chart #2

This is the third hypothesis for this ASR, which may take place in two different locations.

The hypothesis of chart #3, such as chart #4, implies the Ascendant of SR in the lady's 10th natal house. I usually do not choose such a position in the presence of dissonant transits of relevance; but in this case it may be good because the possible 'fall connected with to the 10th House' may also refer to the period in which the pregnant subject will be absent from work; and from another point of view, the Ascendant in the 10th House might point to the success of the little miracle of the visit from the stork.

Both chart #3 and chart #4 contain a precious cameo, a rare jewel for such a project: namely Jupiter on the very cusp between the 5th and 6th House of SR – a great protection for love, a great protection for pregnancy, a great protection for health…

The difference between chart #3 and chart #4 is Uranus in the 9th House in the former chart and in the 8th House in the latter chart. In the first case it reduces the danger of sudden death (of the foetus); on the other hand we must accept a minimum of risk because of the presence of Mars in the 11th House. In the chart #4 Uranus is in the 8th House, but we also have another cuspidal position: Pluto on the Descendant, very important for the lady's search of a steady partner.

As I usually do, I only propose everything to the consulting person and as soon as I get her feedback we take our decision together: each of us taking our own responsibility and fully aware of having operated with wisdom, skill, and without infallibility.

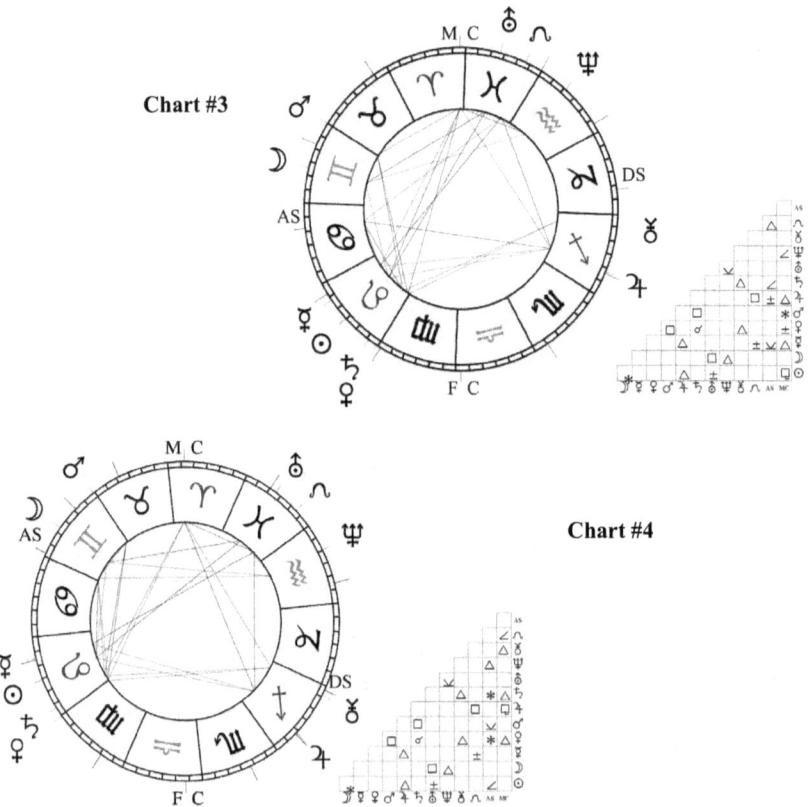

Chart #3

Chart #4

21.
Accuracy of the calculations and lack of passport

In other sections of this volume I have insisted (and I'll always insist) on the great importance of accuracy when casting an ASR.

It is not a display of vanity; I do not intend to show myself to be able to build up – reckoning by hand or with the help of a computer – astral charts of the highest precision. I simply wish to avoid that a poor person runs the risk of having a birthday very far from the one that he, or she, aimed to.

The following example will clarify what I mean.

It's the case of a lady from Emilia-Romagna; she was in legal troubles because of unpaid taxes in connection with her commercial activity.

In spring 2006 she went to the competent Italian authorities to have her passport renewed, but there she was told that due to those legal problems she wouldn't have it renewed. She would have left to aim her following SR in order to enhance her general situation which wasn't doing well and which stood fair chances of getting even worse, in connection with her health, profession, money, love and so on. As you can see, it is not an easy problem to solve, for her BSR contains really dangerous elements for the subject. On the other hand, we all know that here in Europe you cannot travel to any other country without holding your passport, or at least any other document proving your ID.

And if you want to turn a horrible SR into an acceptable, if not excellent, ASR, you need a miracle – and this is where accuracy plays its role.

I then asked for the help of *Aladino*, which I called this way because, just like the Aladdin of the *One Thousand and One Nights*, it's able to perform such wonders that we might well define them 'miracles'.

And there *is* definitely a miracle here, nobody could deny!

You can see it depicted in the following pages.

As you can see, we have avoided very dangerous positions and we have placed gorgeous celestials in the 10th and in the 11th House. Mars in the 10th House may be positive in so far that the native will spend much energy in order to improve her own social and professional condition. Moreover, Jupiter is in the 8th House in a period in which the subject has to do with a sale.

The location of this ASR is Evans in Norway. Its longitude is 16°40' East of Greenwich and its latitude is 68° 29' North of the Equator: much beyond the Arctic Polar Circle. Now, if you tried to get the same astral chart with any other piece of software you would get a very annoying message of error, a sort of 'out of range' or even worse: you would get a chart based on a system of Houses different than Placidus – say Aequalis or Morphyrius – but without getting any specific warning of this change of domification: such a chart would be completely useless for our purposes.

Now the point is – is accuracy an optional, a sort of dandy's vanity? Or is it an absolutely unavoidable requirement for those who practice this branch of astrology?

Do not forget that in the field of ASRs you are dealing with the very life of the subjects, so that you can not claim, later on, «I wasn't aware that...»

Let us put it in another way. Using a much tougher metaphor, consider a carpenter who comes to your place to mount a wardrobe in your bathroom; there he realizes that the wall is made of extremely hard granite, for which he does not have the proper drill bits. What should the carpenter do then? He would buy the proper drill bits, or he would declare that he is simply unable to perform the task.

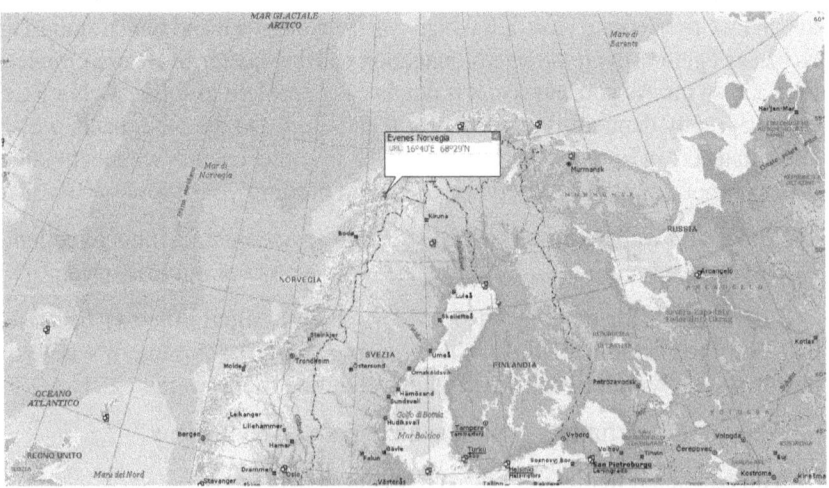

ACCURACY OF THE CALCULATIONS AND LACK OF PASSPORT

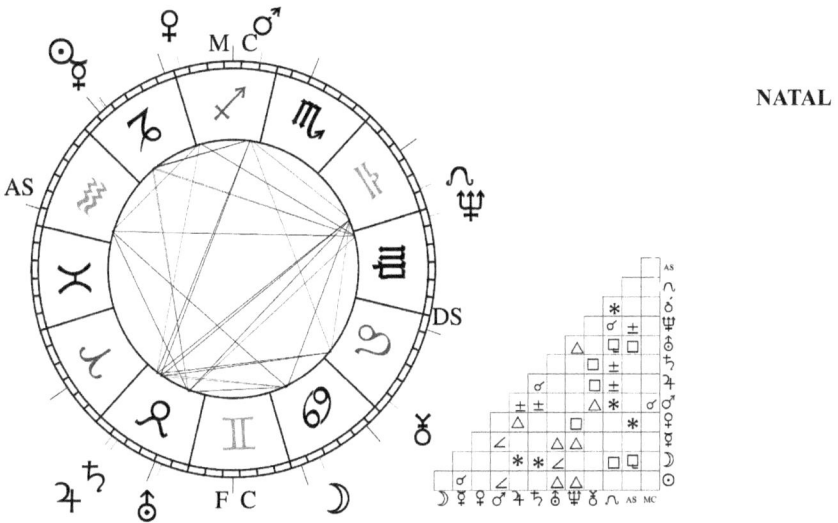

NATAL

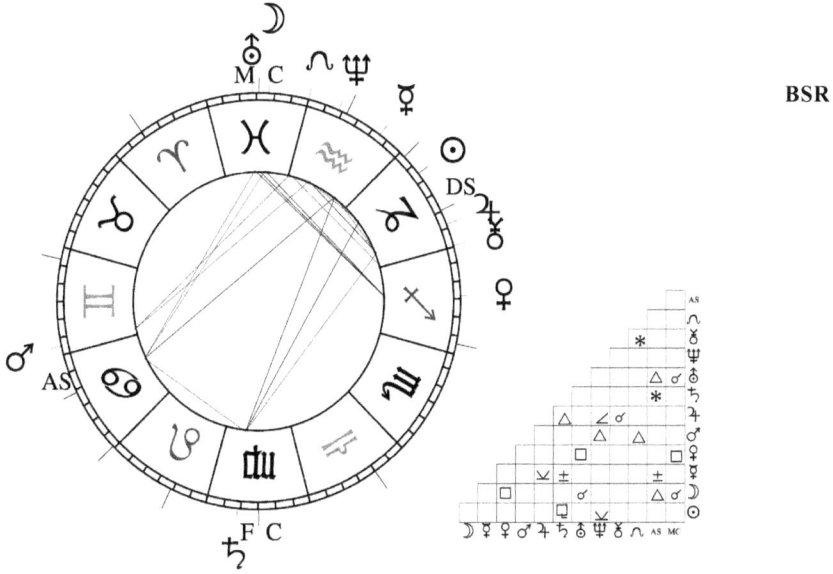

BSR

LUNAR RETURNS AND EARTH RETURNS

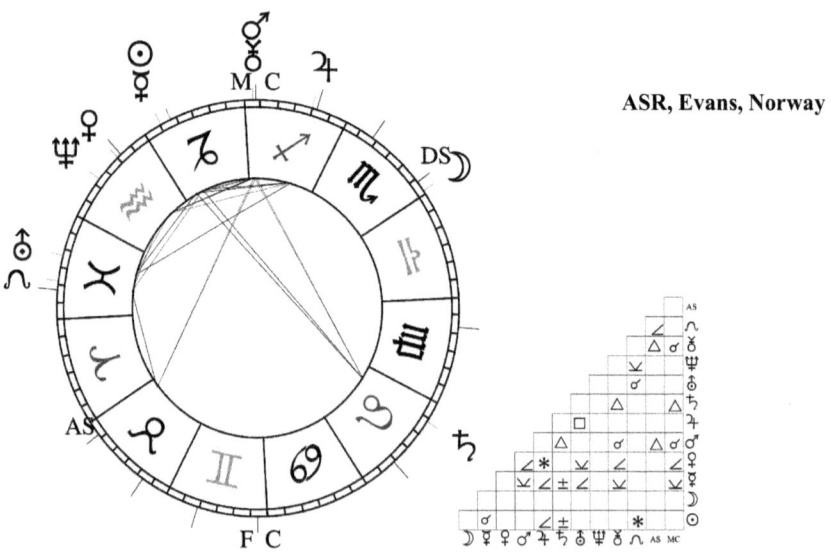

ASR, Evans, Norway

22.
The tragedy of Cogne

Just a few remarks to observe the Cogne homicide especially from the point of view of SRs.

What follows is partly quoted from English Wikipedia and partly retranslated from Italian Wikipedia, according to the text as it appeared there on the 16th June 2007:

The so-called **Cogne case** (known in Italian as *caso Cogne*) involved the death of 3-year-old Samuele Lorenzi in his family home in the mountain village of Montroz near Cogne, a mountain town in Aosta Valley, northern Italy.

The homicide

During the morning of the 30th of January 2008, around 8 am, Annamaria Franzoni found her little son Samuele in agony in his parents' bed, with clear evidence of a serious haemorrhage caused by several blows on Samuele's head.

The mother immediately called the emergency number (118 in Italy) and the family doctor Ada Satragni, who was the first person to reach the scene, where she conjectures that the baby may be a victim of aneurysm.

But as the rescue squad from 118 arrives there (by helicopter) they suspect homicide because of the state of the scene.

They immediately call the national gendarmerie of Italy, the Carabinieri who make the first examinations on the spot. 40 days later the victim's mother Annamaria Franzoni was charged of wilful murder.

The investigations

Neither the innumerable examinations in the family house nor the most sophisticated technologies (such as those based on luminol and the detailed forensic analyses on finger prints, bloodspots etc.) were sufficient to give tangible evidence of any murderer being actually involved. The defence underlined several times that when the fact was discovered there were several individuals on the crime scene, who might have tampered with pieces of evidence in an irreversible way.

At the same time the weapon has never been identified – it's probably a contusive object made of copper, as the forensic examinations on the corpse have shown. Many times suspicion fell upon close neighbours or other people living there, yet the main suspect remained always Annamaria Franzoni, for the other subjects always proved to have an alibi; moreover, according to the prosecution Mrs Franzoni was the only one who might carry out the crime in that span of time. She actually had an alibi of a few minutes: he had taken her elder son Davide to the school bus stop. But the stop is very close to the house and she went back home almost immediately, so – said the prosecution – her alibi might be compatible with the time required to execute the crime.

In July 2004 Mrs Annamaria Franzoni and her husband reported one of their neighbours to the authorities, claiming that he was 'the real murderer'. Please note that the 'real murderer' has been interrogated several times during the years of the investigation and the process, but he has always given the same version of the facts: thus the investigators found his version trustworthy and also his alibi. Due to their reporting him, the Lorenzis have also been reported for false accusation. As we are writing these lines it seems that the defence is avoiding to implicate other persons in the crime: in fact in the recent appeal, that 'real murderer' hasn't been mentioned any longer, although serious allegations have been made against another female neighbour of the Lorenzi's family, with whom Annamaria had had arguments in the past.

Innumerable suppositions have been made about the murderer's identity and the motive for the crime. Somebody argued that the baby became a victim of some sort of satanic cult, or that the crime was somehow inspired by the secret service, or that the baby was killed by some flash-eating raptor such as a large bird of prey. Others suggested – although the evidence contradicts this theory – that it was a natural death caused by cerebral aneurysm or by a seizure of epilepsy that caused the baby to break his head against the headboard, thus actually wounding himself to death…

The trial

In 2004 an Italian court sentenced Samuele's mother Annamaria Franzoni to 30 years in prison for aggravated murder.

The refutation of the truthfulness of certain pieces of evidence given by the defence during their investigation has led to a second, parallel trial called *Cogne bis*. In this latter trial eleven persons have been involved, among them Mrs Franzoni herself, her husband Stefano Lorenzi, and her previous defender attorney Carlo Taormina.

The most recent psychiatric examinations have thrown light on an inner aspect of Mrs Franzoni's personality. Her personality has been defined to be affected by 'hysterical neurosis', that is to say, she tends to theatricality and to simulations, because she's unable to elaborate in a mature way the problems connected with daily life.

On 27 April 2007 the *Corte d'Assise d'appello* in Turin reduced the penalty to Franzoni to 16 years of jail. The reduction has been granted partly because of certain extenuating circumstances, and mainly because of the so called *rito abbreviato* consisting in a sort of summarized, or shortened, trial.

On 21 May 2008 the *Corte di Cassazione* confirmed the decision of the appeal court and Annamaria Franzoni was arrested.

A possible astrological reading of this event

We do not intend to play the role of judges and sentence anybody. We simply wish to point out a few things, especially from the point of view of SRs.

Let me repeat once again that the reading of a SR does not follow the elementary-primitive-simple logic of the Ascendant of SR lying in the 3rd natal House referring to the subject's brother; the Ascendant of SR lying in the 4th natal House referring to the subject's parents; the Ascendant of SR lying in the 5th natal House referring to the subject's sons and daughters; and so on. The map of SR talks to you in a wonderfully complex and mature way, with the thread of its numerous elements.

Let us start with Annamaria Franzoni, sentenced for the death of her little boy Samuele (at the moment in which I am writing these lines her sentence is not yet confirmed).

In her natal chart strong elements of mental disturbance are clear, starting from the almost perfect square between Neptune and the Sun; a fearsome conjunction of the Moon and Pluto in the 12th House; a ruling Uranus, strongly unstable; and so on. Mars is on the cusp of the 5th House and makes it possible to forecast the death of a child. As I have shown with the evidence of thousands of practical examples, the 11th House is much more deadly that the 8th House: and Mrs Franzoni has a stellium in her natal 11th House. Saturn, the ruler of the 5th House, lies in the 8th House: this also refers to the probable death of a son.

Her SR of 2001 (including the day of 30 January 2002) has been cast for Bologna, but it may be almost identical if we cast it for Cogne. It is an impressive map of SR, from our point of view. Mars is in fact glued to the Ascendant! The Sun is in the 8th House of SR: death of a son! Pluto is in the 12th House, opposite to Saturn (aspects are not really important in the maps of SR, still let me mention this aspect for the sake of objectivity): this points certainly to problems of health of an obsessive-destructive kind.

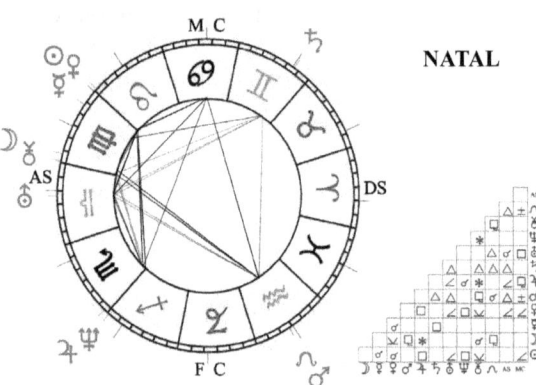

Saturn in the 6th House suggests bad health during the year, either physical or mental health.

Venus and Jupiter in the 7th House may indicate two things; one of them is a blood-curdling detail. In fact they may announce popularity through a trial, or great satisfaction through an act of destruction – as it may be the case of a kamikaze terrorist finding satisfaction in a successful attack.

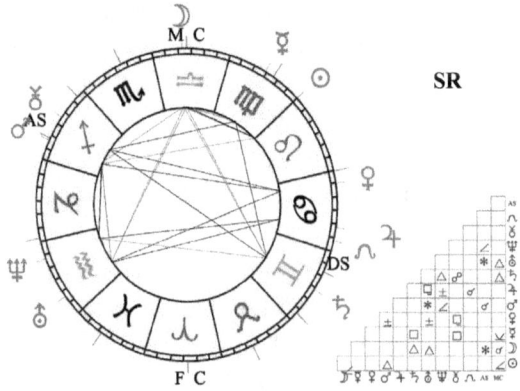

Also the victim's father Stefano Lorenzi's SR has much to do with the tragedy. The Ascendant of his SR lies in his 12th natal House. According to certain, spiritually evolved colleagues this combination should be longed for with pleasure, because it would help people grow.

We don't know how much Stefano Lorenzi grew with his son's slaughter – every reader will be able to form an opinion on this. In his SR Mars is in the 5th House – possible death of a son or violence against a son.

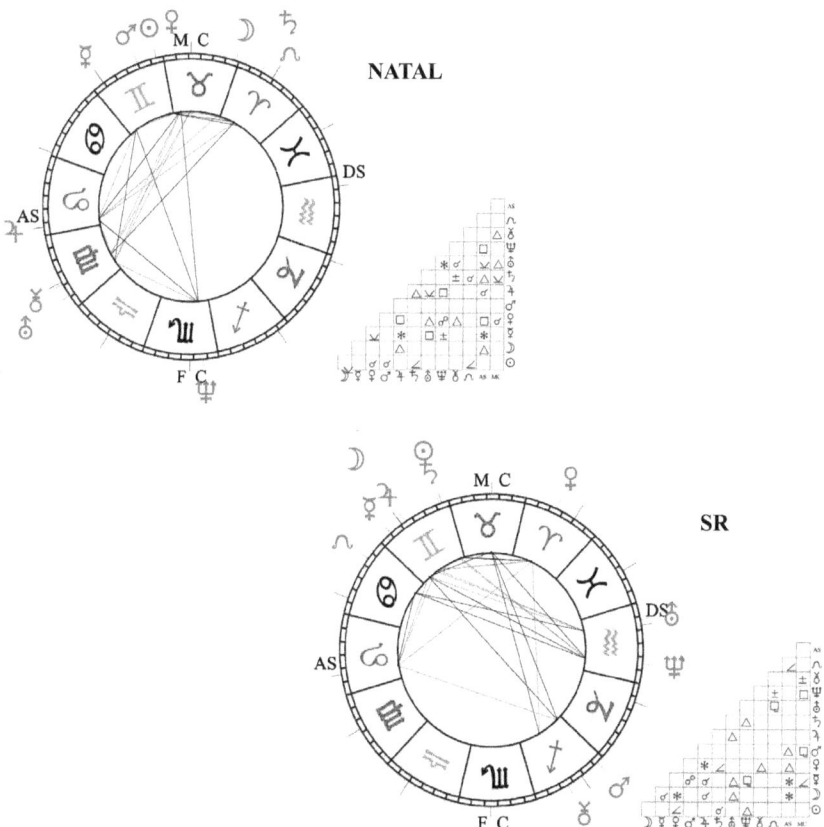

Saturn is conjunct with the Sun in the 10th House of SR: it is my opinion that this represents a terrible fall in society, although the evolutionist astrologers would disagree mentioning some sort of growth instead. To make a long story short, let us underline Uranus glued to the Descendant. This refers to the *coup de théâtre* connected with his wife; her behaviour of breaking all the rules; the sudden change in his wife's life.

Now let us consider the victim. Samuele. When looking for signs of a subject's death, beginners usually expect striking positions such as, in a case like this, finding Mars in the 12th House. Those astrologers who are more experienced with SRs know that it doesn't work this way. A tragedy can surely be recognized in the celestials, but also if you compare the information proceeding from the maps of each member of the family. So in poor Samuele's SR we find Saturn glued to the Medium Coeli – the huge burden for his mother. Of course this may refer to a period previous to his

death or subsequent to his death. It may also mean receiving death from his own mother's hand, but also terrible suffering for his mother's doom. Moreover, Pluto glued to the Imum Coeli may point to strongly destructive impulses for one of the subject's parents (although to my knowledge, his father was never suspected of the murder).

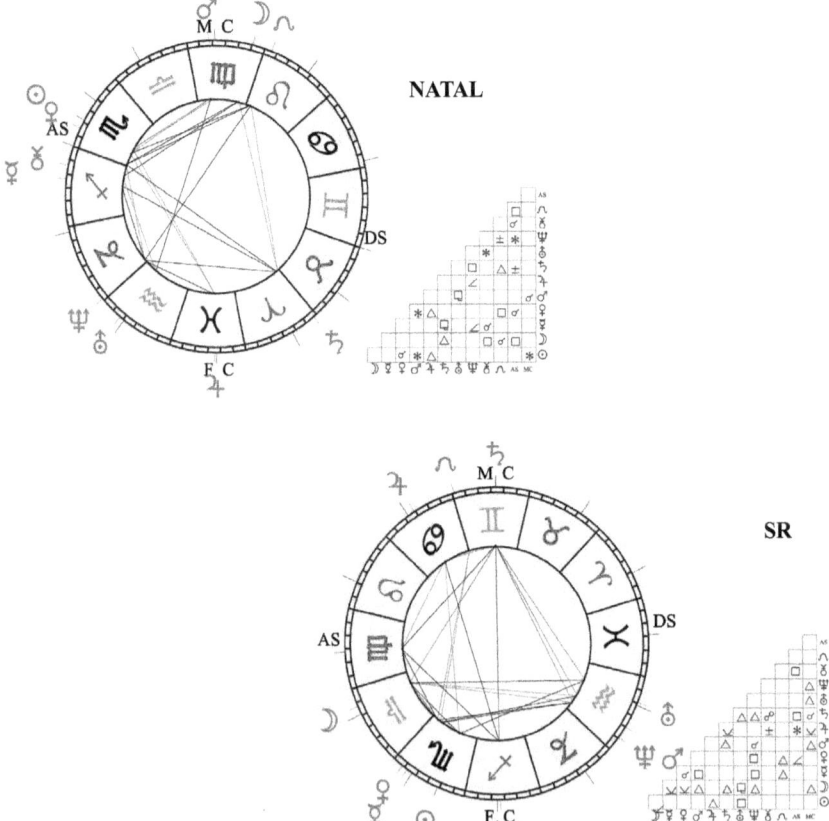

THE TRAGEDY OF COGNE

There are two more little brothers (I don't possess the birth data of all the members of the family), Davide and Gioele – regardless of the fact that they were already born at the time of the crime, or not.

Davide: his Sun of SR is in the 12th House of SR, the Ascendant of SR lies in his 6th natal House. It's two combinations that my school of thought considers deadly, while they would make people grow according to other colleagues.

Mars looks like a captive in a picture: so glued to the Imum Coeli it can only announce destructive, martial events in connection with the parents and the brothers. Jupiter is in the 10th House of SR pointing to his mother's huge popularity. Venus in the 11th House is the possible death of a dear person.

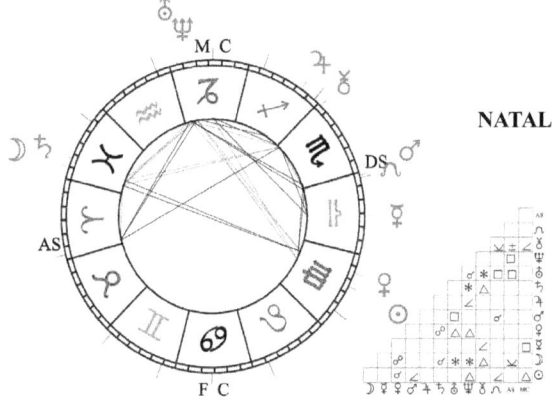

NATAL

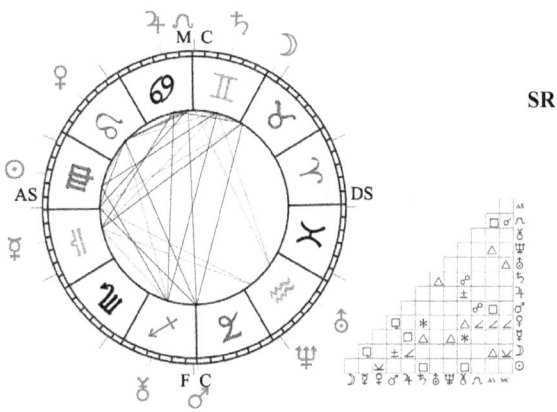

SR

244 LUNAR RETURNS AND EARTH RETURNS

Gioele hadn't been born yet, still his run-over SR talks. The Ascendant of SR lies in his 10th natal House, announcing great popularity. A powerful stellium is on the cusp between the 8th and the 9th House. Mars is on the cusp between the 10th and the 11th House – the mother and death. Don't you think this is enough?

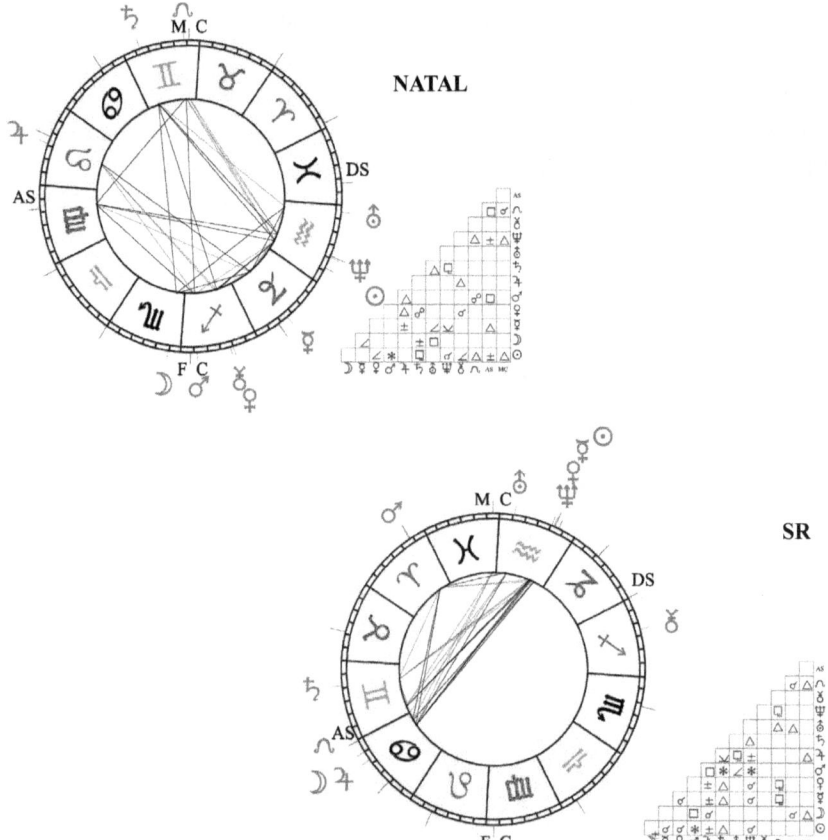

Lastly, consider the graph produced by *AstralDetector* for 2002 for the Lorenzi's family: http://www.cirodiscepolo.it/AstralDetector.htm Astral detector is a piece of software that helps you dating events within one year, by processing the data of the members of a group.

For the 30th of January, to be more precise: for the 30th of January 2002 the graph shows a net peak of depression – remember that a 'peak' means any steep passage from a high value to a low value or vice-versa.

THE TRAGEDY OF COGNE 245

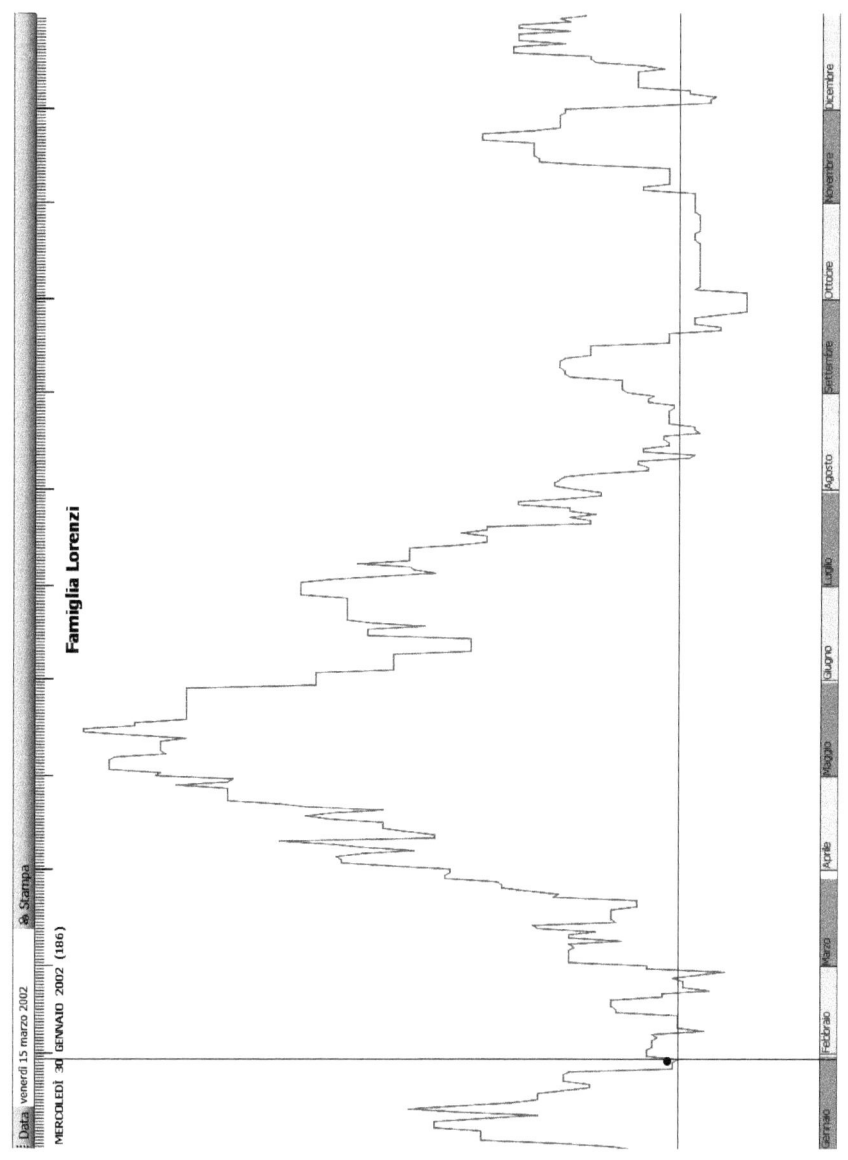

23.
A hard and unsuccessful exercise

The exercise that I'm proposing to you in these pages hasn't been a success, so to say, I did not achieve what I hoped for. I don't mean that I haven't been able to look for it with accuracy – I mean that I was simply looking for the impossible...

Let us proceed step by step.

To begin with, I describe to you how I searched for a good ASR for me for 2008. Making use of my own data of birth makes it possible to reach the following two advantages:

1) I do not involve third persons – although I always do my utmost to protect the privacy of the involved subjects; and

2) I can rely on a very high accuracy because I have been constantly retuning my time of birth for decades.

The following two charts are my natal and my BSR, i.e. the SR that I would have if I spent that day at home in Naples, on July 2008.

At first glance I believe that I could enhance it with a slight relocation. But I immediately realize that a 'slight' change, although apparently it's something quite easy and banal to achieve, in reality it's a mission impossible.

So I look for another valid alternative choice and I find it in Wallis Island, one of the islands of the Territory of Wallis and Futuna Islands, a little eastward from Fiji. There I would have a gorgeous ASR with Jupiter on the cusp between the 7th and the 8th House, also solving what, according to my experience, is a vital need: placing the deadly, very close conjunction of Mars and Saturn only in the 3rd or in the 9th House of a SR. Since I have written much about this detail, I am not elaborating. Many people are very concerned because of placing this conjunction in the Houses traditionally related with accidents. To them I have always told that in my opinion, based on a quite wide practical experience, such a combination is much less dangerous there than anywhere else in the map of SR.

Back to the first option, in Italy. I make a rough correction for estimation and I cross check my idea on the screen of my PC, which confirms that it should be around the city of L'Aquila in central Italy. Yet there I would run a very high risk. In fact, if I had been born only a few minutes later, Jupiter would enter the 1st House of SR, creating a group of three celestials there – and this would correspond to a detrimental combination, virtually equal to the Ascendant of SR lying in the 12th natal House. While if on the contrary, I had been born only few minutes earlier, Mercury would be in the 8th House – creating a group of three in that House of SR, as detrimental as the Ascendant of SR in the 12th natal House.

Yes, I know: I've told you that my time of birth is really accurate so that I'd bet my life on it.

It is true, but in events like this I cannot risk my own life (at the age of sixty it might actually happen) – I'd do it, but only if there weren't any other alternative choice.

Surely Wallis Island is probably the longest and hardest travel on Earth for an Italian, and I am absolutely not amused at the notion of going there – but I cannot run the risk.

And in order not to run any risk, what I need is to place those celestial at a safe distance of at least one degree after and before the cusps. The matter here is not losing that nice Venus close to the cusp of the 8th House, the problem is avoiding the extremely detrimental and dangerous combinations of this SR.

It is common knowledge that at our latitudes and over the span of the year, one degree of the Zodiac corresponds to an average of approximately four minutes of the hour.

In other words, I have to solve the following equation:

Starting from 5:40 am I perform two different searches: one subtracting 4 minutes to this starting time, and the second one adding 4 minutes to this starting time. What I get is two groups of tables. If I find a town in both tables, I've done it.

Such an exceptional tool as *Aladino* would help you perform this search, but you can also perform it manually. In the first case it would take a few minutes, in the second case it might take several months.

So I run the query on Aladino as I've just explained – four minutes more and four minutes less – first scanning Italy, then scanning the whole globe with the option '*Tutto il mondo*'.

I save the results of this search in two different Excel files and together with my smart friend Stefano Briganti I find out the best way to perform a quick search in them. This is what we do:

Open the two Excel files and save them in two separate *DBase V* files, encoding them as *Western Europe* and *International DOS*.

Then start *MS-Access*. Open a new document and save it with any name.

Import the two files (called *A* and *B* in the following screenshots) as *DBase V* files.

Click on *Query*.

Click on *Create Query in structure view*.

Add the previously created files *A* and *B*.

Drag and drop from the letters *TZ* upper left corner to the upper right corner – *TZ* here corresponds to the province of the desired city.

Do the same with *CITTA_*.

You can see two asterisks on the top of the two columns: double click each of them – first the left one, then the right one.

At this point, click on the red exclamation mark among the icons of the upper bar – this actually executes the query.

After the search is performed alas no city is found that exists in both groups.

So I repeat all the procedure, but this time instead of four minutes, with a step of three minutes – i.e. adding and subtracting three minutes to/from the starting time. As you can see from the screenshot, this time hundreds of towns have been found, satisfying the required condition. But the step is three minutes, not four – this is why I considered this result unsuccessful, because I would risk too much, and my own neck, for I consider it a too dangerous hazard.

Thus I must surrender to a little bit of bad luck and choose the (probably) hardest travel of my life.

250 LUNAR RETURNS AND EARTH RETURNS

On the other hand, even if the query gave no positive result, I could show you an *ad hoc* procedure that might help you spare whole days of hard work. In fact, even if you entered the various locations manually one by one, the comparison of the two tables would take whole days searching for the very same town in both tables – not to mention all the different places with the same name: do not forget that, for example, there's a lesser Milano also very close to Perugia…

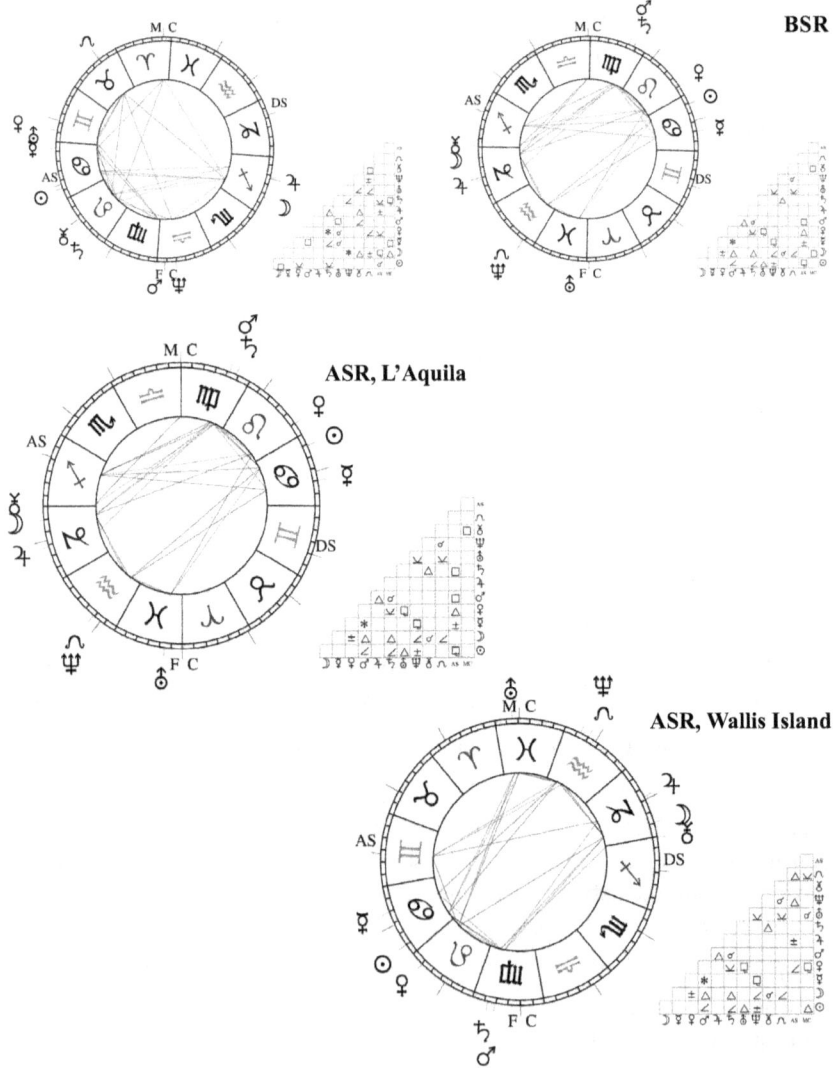

BSR

ASR, L'Aquila

ASR, Wallis Island

Ricerca Località Compleanno

VAL	TZ	-	-	CITTA'	NAZION	LONGITU	LATITUDI	-	-	-
*********/SO8/PLU1/NET2	MC	-	-	Abbadia	IT	-13,24	43,13			
*********/SO8/PLU1/NET2	MC	-	-	Abbadia di Fiastra	IT	-13,24	43,13			
*********/SO8/PLU1/NET2	PE	-	-	Abbateggio	IT	-14,00	42,13			
*********/SO8/PLU1/NET2	MC	-	-	Abbazia di Santa Maria in Selva	IT	-13,24	43,19			
*********/SO8/PLU1/NET2	TE	-	-	Abetemozzo	IT	-13,33	42,38			
*********/SO8/PLU1/NET2	AP	-	-	Abetito	IT	-13,22	42,51			
*********/SO8/PLU1/NET2	PG	-	-	Abeto	IT	-13,03	42,50			
*********/SO8/PLU1/NET2	AQ	-	-	Abruzzi	IT	-13,45	42,15			
*********/SO8/PLU1/NET2	AQ	-	-	Abruzzo	IT	-13,45	42,15			
*********/SO8/PLU1/NET2	AQ	-	-	Abruzzo	IT	-13,45	42,15			
*********/SO8/PLU1/NET2	AQ	-	-	Acciano	IT	-13,43	42,10			
*********/SO8/PLU1/NET2	LT	-	-	Acciarella	IT	-12,45	41,27			
*********/SO8/PLU1/NET2	RI	-	-	Accumoli	IT	-13,15	42,42			
*********/SO8/PLU1/NET2	MC	-	-	Acquacanina	IT	-13,11	43,01			
*********/SO8/PLU1/NET2	TE	-	-	Acquaratola	IT	-13,34	42,42			
*********/SO8/PLU1/NET2	PG	-	-	Acquaro	IT	-13,03	42,52			
*********/SO8/PLU1/NET2	AP	-	-	Acquasanta	IT	-13,24	42,46			
*********/SO8/PLU1/NET2	AP	-	-	Acquasanta Terme	IT	-13,24	42,46			
*********/SO8/PLU1/NET2	AP	-	-	Acquaviva Picena	IT	-13,48	42,56			
*********/SO8/PLU1/NET2	RM	-	-	Acque Albule	IT	-12,43	41,57			
*********/SO8/PLU1/NET2	RM	-	-	Acque Albule Bagni	IT	-12,43	41,57			
*********/SO8/PLU1/NET2	FR	-	-	Acuto	IT	-13,10	41,47			
*********/SO8/PLU1/NET2	RM	-	-	Affile	IT	-13,06	41,53			
*********/SO8/PLU1/NET2	AP	-	-	Agelli	IT	-13,25	42,50			
*********/SO8/PLU1/NET2	TE	-	-	Agnova	IT	-13,30	42,39			
*********/SO8/PLU1/NET2	RM	-	-	Agosta	IT	-13,02	41,59			
*********/SO8/PLU1/NET2	PG	-	-	Agriano	IT	-13,01	42,45			

AVANZAMENTO RICERCA ▓▓▓ interromp

Ricerca Compleanno per : Ciro Discepolo - 3'   GMT compleanno 16 / 7 / 2008   15 2
Condizione Denaro low   Text5   GMT nascita 17 / 07 / 01948   03 3

Ricerca Località Compleanno

VAL	TZ	-	-	CITTA'	NAZION	LONGITUDINE	LATITUDINE	-	-	-
*********/SO8/PLU1/NET2	SI	-	-	Abbadia San Salvadore	IT	-11,41	42,53			
*********/SO8/PLU1/NET2	SI	-	-	Abbadia San Salvatore	IT	-11,41	42,53			
*********/SO8/PLU1/NET2	PG	-	-	Abeto	IT	-13,03	42,50			
*********/SO8/PLU1/NET2	PG	-	-	Acera	IT	-12,50	42,49			
*********/SO8/PLU1/NET2	RM	-	-	Acilia	IT	-12,22	41,47			
*********/SO8/PLU1/NET2	MC	-	-	Acquacanina	IT	-13,11	43,01			
*********/SO8/PLU1/NET2	PG	-	-	Acquaiura	IT	-12,44	42,41			
*********/SO8/PLU1/NET2	PG	-	-	Acqualacastagna	IT	-12,43	42,39			
*********/SO8/PLU1/NET2	PS	-	-	Acqualagna	IT	-12,40	43,37			
*********/SO8/PLU1/NET2	TR	-	-	Acqua Loreto	IT	-12,20	42,44			
*********/SO8/PLU1/NET2	VT	-	-	Acquapendente	IT	-11,52	42,44			
*********/SO8/PLU1/NET2	PG	-	-	Acquaro	IT	-13,03	42,52			
*********/SO8/PLU1/NET2	TR	-	-	Acquasparta	IT	-12,33	42,41			
*********/SO8/PLU1/NET2	AN	-	-	Acquatina	IT	-12,55	43,16			
*********/SO8/PLU1/NET2	SI	-	-	Acquaviva	IT	-11,51	43,07			
*********/SO8/PLU1/NET2	MC	-	-	Acquosi	IT	-13,03	43,15			
*********/SO8/PLU1/NET2	GO	-	-	Adria	IT	-13,31	45,44			
*********/SO8/PLU1/NET2	PG	-	-	Agelio	IT	-12,14	43,04			
*********/SO8/PLU1/NET2	PG	-	-	Agliano	IT	-12,52	42,52			
*********/SO8/PLU1/NET2	PG	-	-	Agriano	IT	-13,01	42,45			
*********/SO8/PLU1/NET2	AN	-	-	Agugliano	IT	-13,23	43,32			
*********/SO8/PLU1/NET2	TR	-	-	Aguzzo	IT	-12,37	42,29			
*********/SO8/PLU1/NET2	UD	-	-	Aiello	IT	-13,22	45,52			
*********/SO8/PLU1/NET2	UD	-	-	Aiello del Friuli	IT	-13,22	45,52			
*********/SO8/PLU1/NET2	AN	-	-	Albacina	IT	-13,01	43,21			
*********/SO8/PLU1/NET2	UD	-	-	Albana	IT	-13,29	46,03			
*********/SO8/PLU1/NET2	GO	-	-	Alberoni	IT	-13,30	45,45			
*********/SO8/PLU1/NET2	SO	-	-	Aldino Secondo	IT	-12,10	44,13			

AVANZAMENTO RICERCA ▓▓▓ interromp

Ricerca Compleanno per : Ciro Discepolo + 3'   GMT compleanno 16 / 7 / 2008   15 3
Condizione Denaro low   Text5   GMT nascita 17 / 07 / 01948   03 4

Excel sheet with the list of towns obtained by subtracting and (following page) adding steps of 3 minutes.

VAL	TZ	-	-	CITTA'	NAZION	LONGITU	LATITUD
*********	MC	-	-	Abbadia	IT	-13,24	43,13
*********	MC	-	-	Abbadia	IT	-13,24	43,13
*********	PE	-	-	Abbategg	IT	-14,00	42,13
*********	MC	-	-	Abbazia	IT	-13,24	43,19
*********	TE	-	-	Abetemo	IT	-13,33	42,38
*********	AP	-	-	Abetito	IT	-13,22	42,51
*********	PG	-	-	Abeto	IT	-13,03	42,50
*********	AQ	-	-	Abruzzi	IT	-13,45	42,15
*********	AQ	-	-	Abruzzo	IT	-13,45	42,15
*********	AQ	-	-	Abruzzo	IT	-13,45	42,15
*********	AQ	-	-	Acciano	IT	-13,43	42,10
*********	LT	-	-	Acciarell	IT	-12,45	41,27
*********	RI	-	-	Accumoli	IT	-13,15	42,42
*********	MC	-	-	Acquaca	IT	-13,11	43,01
*********	TE	-	-	Acquarat	IT	-13,34	42,42
*********	PG	-	-	Acquaro	IT	-13,03	42,52
*********	AP	-	-	Acquasa	IT	-13,24	42,46
*********	AP	-	-	Acquasa	IT	-13,24	42,46
*********	AP	-	-	Acquaviv	IT	-13,48	42,56
*********	RM	-	-	Acque Al	IT	-12,43	41,57
*********	RM	-	-	Acque Al	IT	-12,43	41,57
*********	FR	-	-	Acuto	IT	-13,10	41,47
*********	RM	-	-	Affile	IT	-13,06	41,53
*********	AP	-	-	Agelli	IT	-13,25	42,50
*********	TE	-	-	Agnova	IT	-13,30	42,39
*********	RM	-	-	Agosta	IT	-13,02	41,59
*********	PG	-	-	Agriano	IT	-13,01	42,45
*********	AQ	-	-	Aielli	IT	-13,35	42,04
*********	AQ	-	-	Aielli	IT	-13,18	42,29
*********	TE	-	-	Aiello	IT	-13,30	42,35
*********	PE	-	-	Alanno	IT	-13,58	42,18
*********	FR	-	-	Alatri	IT	-13,21	41,43
*********	RI	-	-	Albaneto	IT	-13,02	42,32
*********	RM	-	-	Albano	IT	-12,39	41,44
*********	RM	-	-	Albano L	IT	-12,39	41,44
*********	AQ	-	-	Albe	IT	-13,24	42,04

VAL	TZ	-	-	CITTA'	NAZION	LONGITU	LATITUD
-	-	-					
*********	SI	-	-	Abbadia	IT	-11,41	42,53
*********	SI	-	-	Abbadia	IT	-11,41	42,53
*********	PG	-	-	Abeto	IT	-13,03	42,50
*********	PG	-	-	Acera	IT	-12,50	42,49
*********	RM	-	-	Acilia	IT	-12,22	41,47
*********	MC	-	-	Acquaca	IT	-13,11	43,01
*********	PG	-	-	Acquaiur	IT	-12,44	42,41
*********	PG	-	-	Acqualac	IT	-12,43	42,39
*********	PS	-	-	Acqualag	IT	-12,40	43,37
*********	TR	-	-	Acqua L	IT	-12,20	42,44
*********	VT	-	-	Acquape	IT	-11,52	42,44
*********	PG	-	-	Acquaro	IT	-13,03	42,52
*********	TR	-	-	Acquasp	IT	-12,33	42,41
*********	AN	-	-	Acquatin	IT	-12,55	43,18
*********	SI	-	-	Acquaviv	IT	-11,51	43,07
*********	MC	-	-	Acquosi	IT	-13,03	43,15
*********	GO	-	-	Adria	IT	-13,31	45,44
*********	PG	-	-	Agello	IT	-12,14	43,04
*********	PG	-	-	Agliano	IT	-12,52	42,52
*********	PG	-	-	Agriano	IT	-13,01	42,45
*********	AN	-	-	Aguglian	IT	-13,23	43,32
*********	TR	-	-	Aguzzo	IT	-12,37	42,29
*********	UD	-	-	Aiello	IT	-13,22	45,52
*********	UD	-	-	Aiello del	IT	-13,22	45,52
*********	AN	-	-	Albacina	IT	-13,01	43,21
*********	UD	-	-	Albana	IT	-13,29	46,03
*********	GO	-	-	Alberoni	IT	-13,30	45,45
*********	FO	-	-	Aldina S	IT	-12,19	44,13
*********	MC	-	-	Ali	IT	-12,56	42,57
*********	PG	-	-	Aliena	IT	-13,02	42,45
*********	TR	-	-	Allerona	IT	-11,58	42,49
*********	RM	-	-	Allumiere	IT	-11,54	42,09
*********	RM	-	-	Alsium	IT	-12,06	41,56
*********	AN	-	-	Alta Mari	IT	-13,20	43,39
*********	UD	-	-	Altana	IT	-13,33	46,06
*********	TR	-	-	Alviano	IT	-12,18	42,35

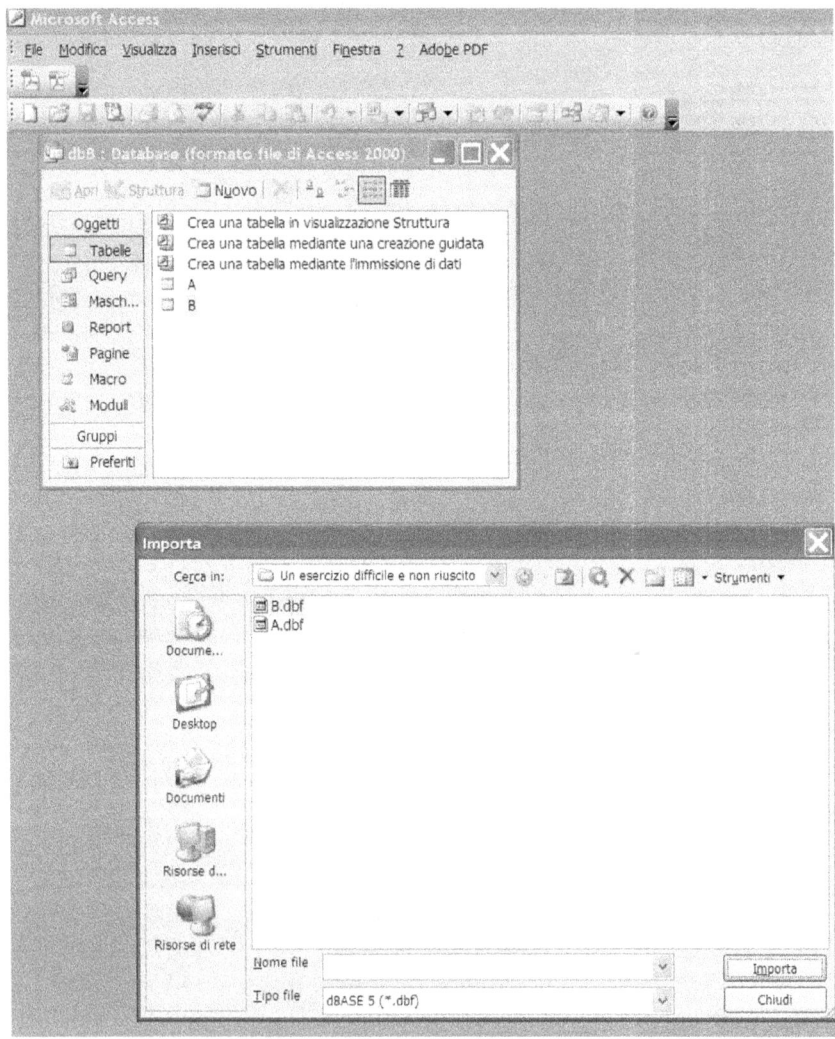

A HARD AND UNSUCCESSFUL EXERCISE 255

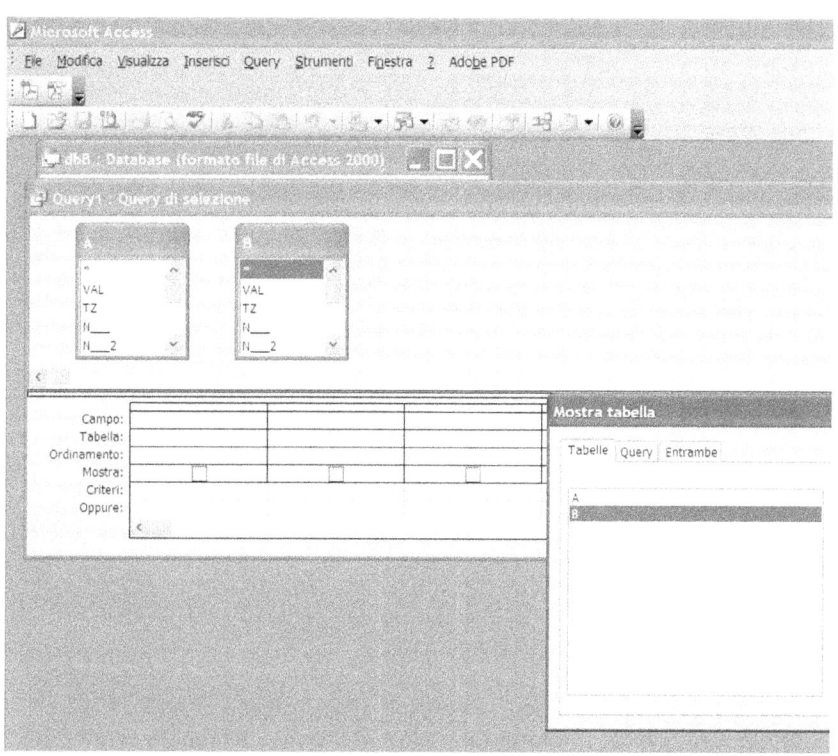

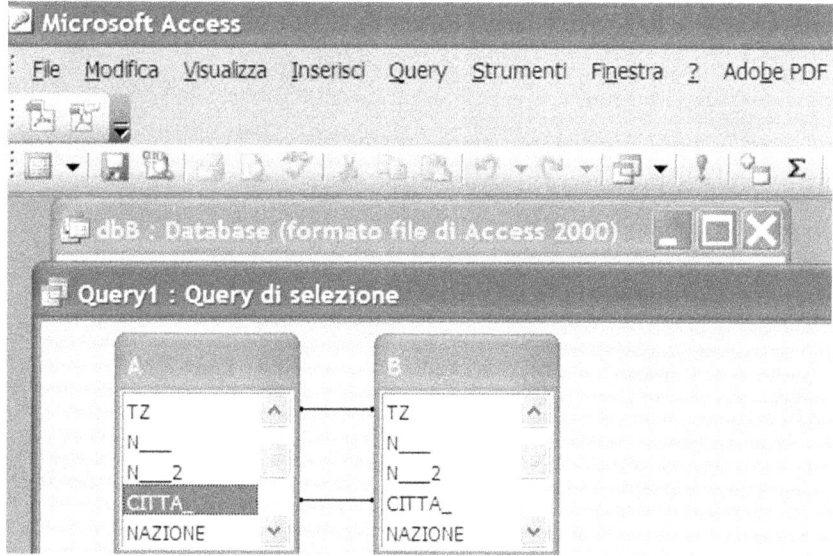

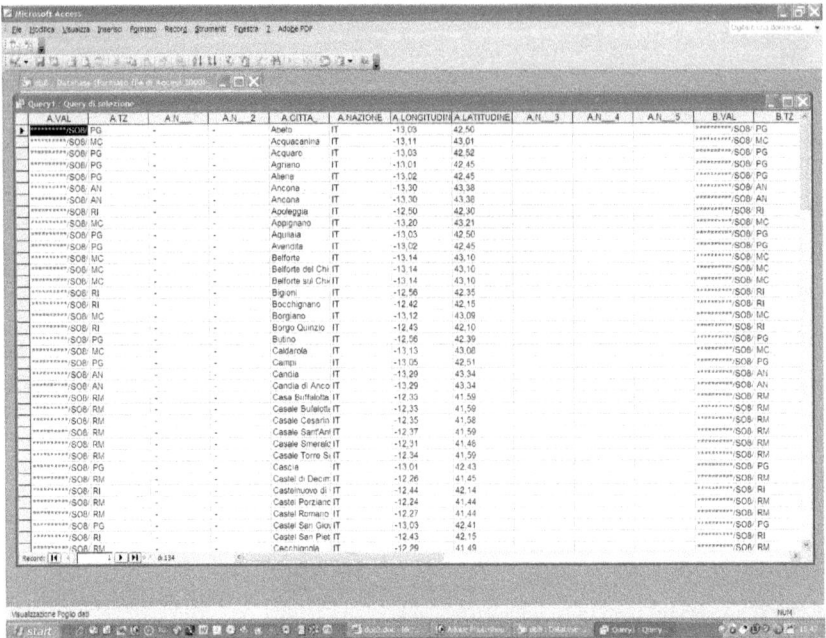

This is the list of the towns existing in the two databases created with steps of –3' and +3'..

There are hundreds of them, yet it is my opinion that they do not solve my problem because the safety margin is too narrow.

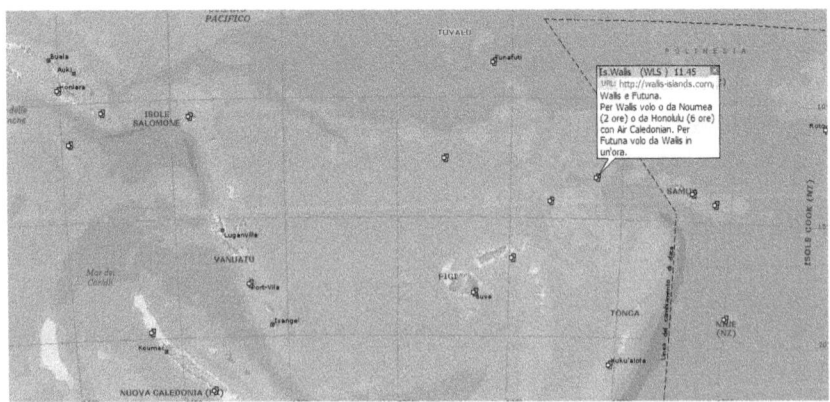

24.
The accuracy of your software when casting a SR

In February 2007 I was abroad for a few days and was told that my friend, actor and showman Marco Columbro had mentioned me in an article published by the Italian magazine *Panorama*. He wrote that from time to time he asks for my advice concerning his aimed birthdays. Besides being a versatile actor and a very brilliant showman, Marco is also a serious student of astrology, he knows and understands SRs and ASRs very well. I would have never made this public, but since he was so nice to write about that, I grasp the occasion and suggest to you the following, little but hard exercise. Marco was born in Lucca on the 28th of June 1950 at 8:30 pm. His birthday of 2006 was a particularly tricky one, whose relocation was very difficult to solve because we aimed at the following results:

- placing Mars and Saturn in the 9th House

- avoiding the Sun in the 8th house but, if only possible, leave Venus there

- placing Jupiter very close to the Ascendant of SR.

With the help of Aladino – besides performing miracles, it's an extremely precise piece of software – I suggested him to spend his SR in Polyarnj, Siberia, 112°03' East and 66°25' North. The relevant chart follows. Nice, isn't it? Now try to carry out the same search on you computer, even if you don't believe in the validity of the aimed birthdays – do it just to test the value and accuracy of your astrological software. Oh but I was joking: so far it's easy, even the good-old module *Molriv* of *Astral* could have solved it – despite having been developed in 1979, it is still much accurate than many other pretentious programmes. So let us make the exercise a little more complex and ask Aladino the same things as before, adding that we want to leave the Sun in the 8th House and Venus in the 7th House of SR. This is a really complex task. The solution offered by our magical piece of software is the following chart: Tiksi in Yakutia, 128°54' East and – mind you – 71°42'

North!!! Test your software and compare the charts – but beware because some astrological programmes play dirty: for example, being unable to process calculations for those latitudes, they draw an astral chart with a different system of House, such as Porfyrius or Aequalis, while we always have to use Placidus.

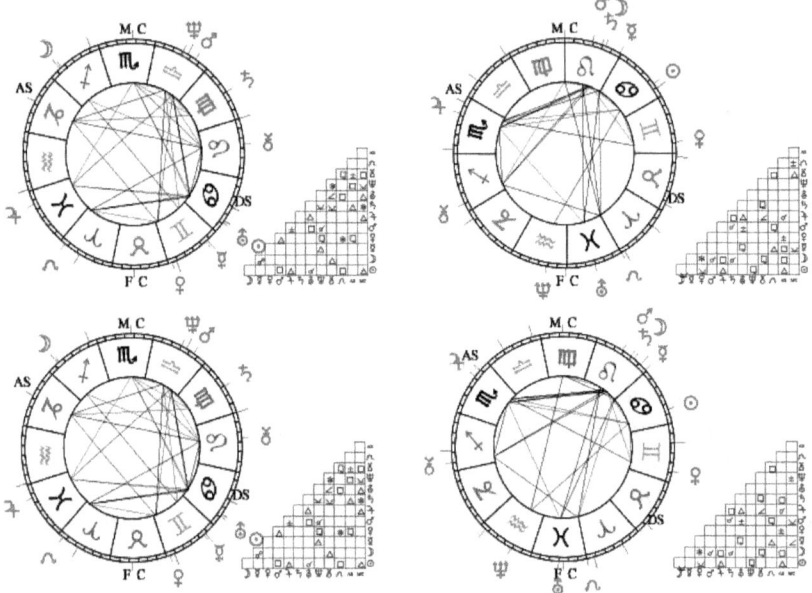

If you find it interesting, with slight amendments this exercise may be useful even if you are among those who believe that the SR must be cast always and only for the subject's place of birth or place of residence. After all, you can always try to cast the SR of an individual born or resident in Tiksi every year for three or four years. It would be interesting to see what you can do with those charts...

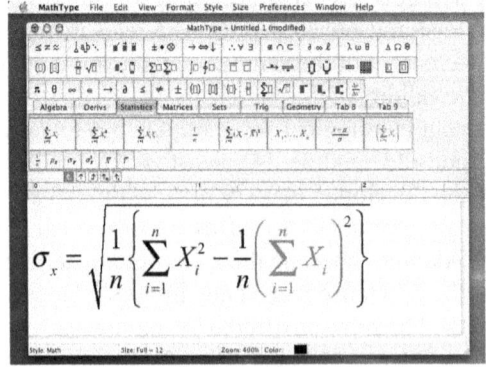

25.
The twenty days before and after the birthday

The twenty days before and after a birthday are usually charged with events, either positive or negative. I have written this in several volumes of mine, as well as in other writings. Those who follow me are perfectly convinced of that, but they (almost everyone) make a huge error of evaluation that I have tried unsuccessfully to correct in the last years, but as the saying goes, «There are none so deaf as those that will not hear.»

The following example will prove what I am repeating for the umpteenth – and hopefully the last – time.

You can see the natal chart of a male subject. He once travelled to a Spanish island for an aimed birthday (see Fig. 3) When he came back he had really extraordinary results and showed his gratefulness to me, yet adding, «Oh well, you have mistaken one point yet. You forecast an accident to me, but the accident took place about twelve hours *before* my birthday, not *after* it. What happened is that I rented a car there and I smashed it against a wall... Nonetheless, as you write in your books, the events of a SR may take place twenty days before or after one's birthday.»

It is so in fact – but always within the frame of the SR 'containing them'!!!

This subject's ASR of the previous year is shown in the chart #2. It has a double position of Sun and mercury in the 9th House, which widely justifies the car accident **that actually had taken place under that SR, not under the following one – for the following SR started after the accident!** Of course also the following SR sought something from the subject: in the following twelve months on several occasions the subject had to give 'offerings' to the stellium in the 3rd House.

So I repeat that the days around the birthday (especially the two or three, and up to twenty days before and twenty days after) 'magnetize' the most relevant events of the year. But each event is connected with the current SR; there is no anticipation of the symbols of the following SR still to come, and there is no 'queue' to the symbols of the previous SR, already over.

If it weren't so this marvellous and very accurate tool of forecasting and analysis of the events would be for nothing.

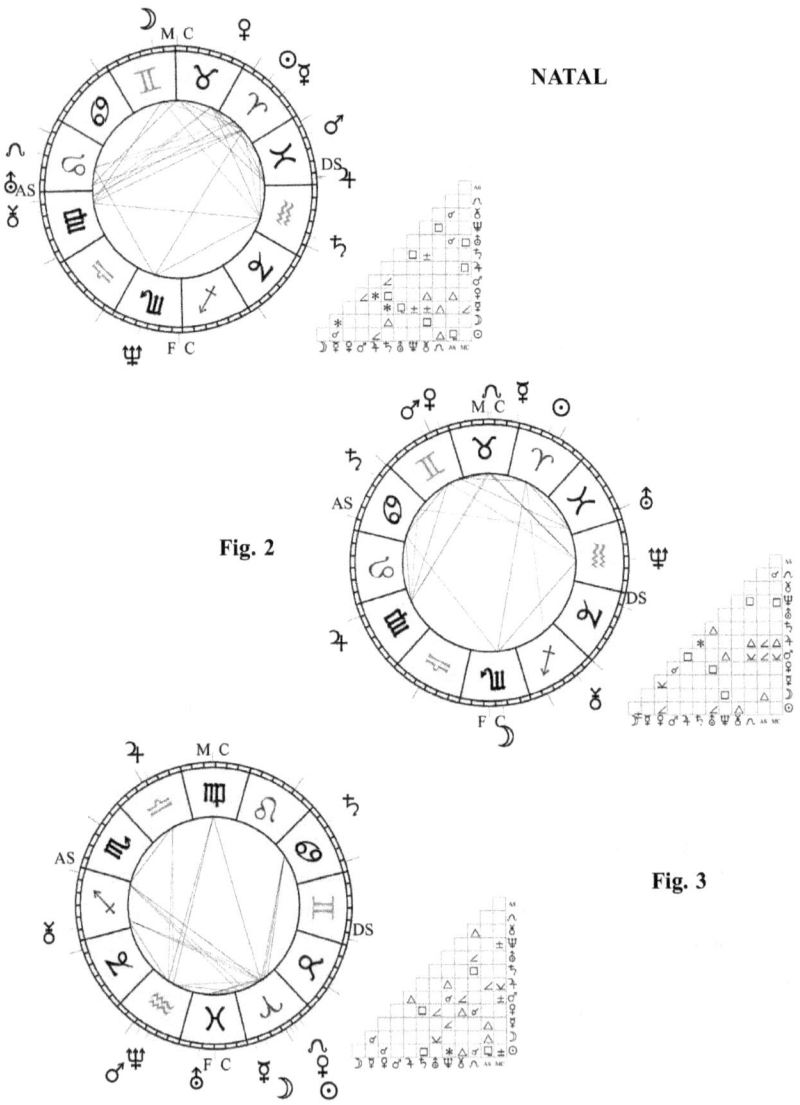

NATAL

Fig. 2

Fig. 3

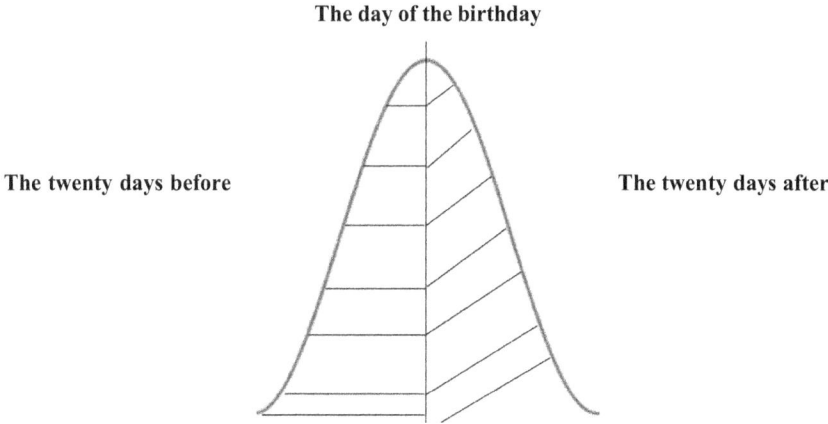

The day of the birthday then, it's even striking in its effects: the chronicles are full of thousands of examples of this. Often media report of a famous person getting married or dying or being elected the day before of his/her birthday. Even so, it is usually the very day of his/her birthday because, astronomically speaking, the Solar Return often takes place the day before the celebration.

PART IV
POSTFACE

26.
Some important subjects for Active Astrology

In this chapter I'll write about certain subjects which are in my opinion, extremely important for the practice of *Active Astrology*.

They are: the Gauquelin sectors; the celestials that are placed in the Gauquelin sectors; the learned usage of the Gauquelin sectors for the exorcism of symbols either in your birth chart or in your charts of Solar Return, Lunar Return, and Earth Return (1); the learned usage of the Gauquelin sectors in order to achieve a correct aiming of a Solar Return, Lunar Return, or Earth Return; the cusps of the Houses and their relevant sectors covering 2.5 degrees before and 2.5 degrees after the cusp; how to consider cusps when a cusp is also a Gauquelin sector; the difference and/or synergies while considering the Gauquelin sectors and the House cusps; the planetary dominants in your birth chart and/or in your charts of Solar Return, Lunar Return, or Earth Return.

Let us start with the Gauquelin sectors

The name of Michel and Françoise Gauquelin will certainly be long remembered in the history of astrology thanks to the massive contribution that the indefatigable work of those French husband and wife has given to Urania's art. As it had already happened in the past with many an innovator of scientific thought, the Gauquelins too must have had confrontations with a widespread and harsh opposition, even more: with many people's mockery. But facts are facts. Despite the blindness of certain masters of the (scientific) steamer, time will surely repay the Gauquelins for their immense work that they have been developing for over 25 years (*Editor's note:* the Author wrote these lines in the '80s).

The credit for the work that I am briefly introducing here now goes mainly to Michel Gauquelin, since only later did his wife Françoise join her husband's researches. First of all, allow me to clear up a misunderstanding. Mr. Gauquelin (the same refers to his wife as well) was *not* an astrologer, as some critic (whose haughtiness is as brilliant as his cleverness) claims. When he was a child he actually took an interest in astrology as a beginner, we might say that he used to play with it. Later on he became a sceptic and he embraced the cause of a critical verification starting from his sceptical position. From then on, we can define him a researcher. All his statistical and critical works were made earlier to his 'crossing the Rubicon'. So it cannot be said that Mr. Gauquelin is favourable to astrology; he is actually one of its most stubborn enemies despite the extremely favourable results obtained by his works. Since he was a secondary-school student he felt the pressing urge of collecting dates of birth to elaborate statistical studies. And this is how his story began: by filling huge books with dates of birth, labelled by professional classes. Hence his first failures: it is not true that one dies more frequently *under* Saturn, or that soldiers were born more substantially in the sign of Aries rather than Libra. At the same time some astrologers were trying to develop their own first attempts of stammering statistical works, and Mr. Gauquelin promptly found out evident errors of methodology in them. In order to avoid making the very same mistakes, he enrolled in the Sorbonne to study the laws of randomness and to learn how to apply them to his own studies in an orthodox way.

In 1955 he published his first work based on the application of scientific criteria, in which he introduced his first exceptional results that would spur him to further develop his research despite the general indifference and hostility. Kepler had foretold that there would be an 'industrious animal' capable of finding a *grain of gold* in the smelly manure of astrology. Michel Gauquelin resolved to find out that grain of gold. And he found it!

To be more precise, he found more than one grain. His own and his wife's task goes on, but up to this date the balance is already a highly positive one. It may be summed up in the following three fundamental discoveries:

1) Great human beings were not born under the same skies as lesser mortals.

2) There are multiple psychological types connected with planets.

3) We all see the light under cosmic conditions resembling those of our parents.

Needless to say that astrologers had known well such 'discoveries' for thousands of years, and that such 'discoveries' were already part of the millenary tradition of astrology; a tradition that also contains several further indications, which one day might be proved scientifically too, if many other little Gauquelins saw the light…

The English translation of the title of Gauquelin's book of 1955 would be 'The influence of the Stars. A critical and experimental study' (2). It collected the dates of birth of about 500 famous French clinicians in which was detected an unjustified overpresence of Mars and Saturn in rising and culminative position, as compared to the values suggested by the law of randomness. It could have been a mistake, so Michel Gauquelin tried to find out that mistake but nobody was able to find it: neither he nor the experts to whom he addressed.

He then repeated the test over another 508 subjects, and the law occurred again with insignificant deviations from the first results. Something important had happened: the young and stubborn researcher had found out a track and he would never abandon it. Before listing the most significant results of Gauquelin's working experiences it is a good thing to make clear the bases of his methods of investigation.

His basic idea was to study the relationship man-star as a function of the hour of the day. To do so, he considered the diurnal movement of planets in correlation to a sort of, say, an astronomical *roulette*. You can see it in Fig. 1). It is a circle subdivided into thirty-six sector (exactly the same number of sectors of the roulette); each sector embraces 360/36 = 10 degrees. Four axes subdivide the circle in four quadrants. They correspond to the most significant passages of a celestial in the sky: namely its rising, its culmination, and the two relevant opposite points.

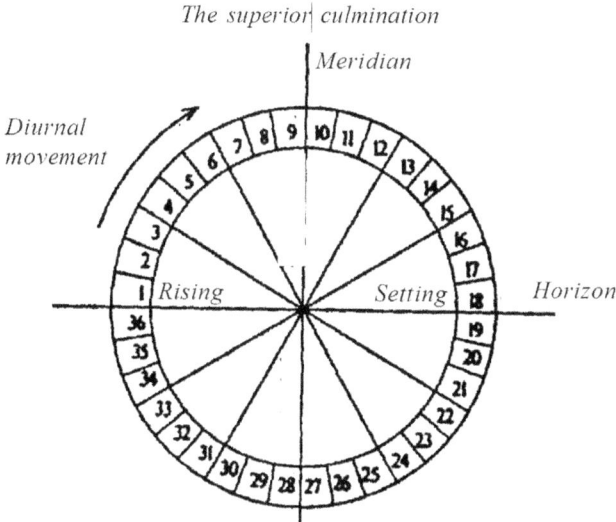

Now, let us consider Mars and a group of one hundred thousand births. Let us consider how many times its presence is detected in each of the 36 sectors. If the births under consideration have been collected randomly, the distribution of Mars follows the laws of randomness. But if we extrapolate from this group the data of a single class (for example: important clinicians) we find that the distribution is no longer averagely uniform, but on the contrary, it shows neat peaks at certain determined points. The points that we are talking about are exactly the four angles of the circle and the areas adjacent to them. This means that in the group of the births of scientists, Mars is definitely more present at rising (Ascendant) and on the meridian, together with Saturn, as indicated also by the astrological tradition. After the first hits, Gauquelin revised his own works and had them revised by experts, because he doubted he could have made some mistake in the method or calculation. Nonetheless, no error was detected. Some experts asked him to proceed with particular double checks, which simply led to identical results. Those experiences were reproduced in several other European countries, the starting group of hundreds was extended to dozens of thousands births; yet the discovered laws reoccurred faithfully. In his later work *Men and Stars*, Mr. Gauquelin formalized his previously discovered general laws. The most significant elements follow.

1) In the group of births of 202 managers of huge companies, 49 times Mars was in the area after the rising point or after the culminating point instead of the average value of 34.6 times (the probability of this event happening by chance is 1 to 200).

2) In a group of 903 journalists, it was found that Jupiter was rising or culminating 185times instead of the average value of 150 (the probability of this event happening by chance is 1 to 100)

3) In 1,352 writers the Moon is very frequently found after rising or after culmination. In fact it is there 292 times instead of the average value of 225 (such a 'crowd' may happen only once every 100,000 possibilities).

4) In 1,409 famous actors, Jupiter is detected in the same sectors of the sky 283 times instead of the average value of 234 (chance of this happening: 1 to 1,000).

5) In 2,088 champions of sports, Mars dominates undisputedly, with striking statistical evidence. In fact you can find it at rising and culmination 452 times instead of 348 times, which leaves to chance only 1 possibility in 5 millions

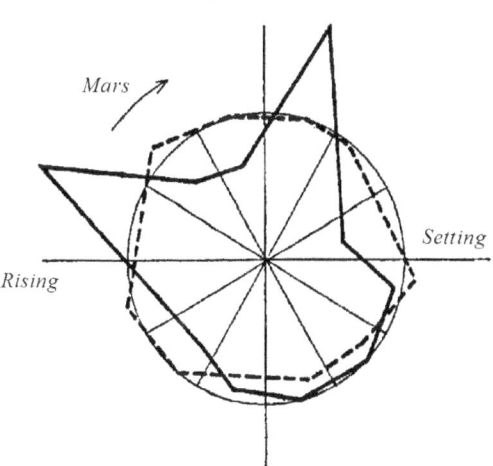

The inferior culmination

This is the distribution of Mars in the hours of day, in a group of 2,088 champions of sports. The circle represents the theoretical values. The solid line shows the presence of Mars at the birth of 2,088 champions of sports (note the very neat peaks corresponding to the rising and the culmination). The broken line represents Mars at the birth of 717 'average' sportsmen: there is no significant peak.

I took these data from M. Gauquelin's *Il dossier delle influenze cosmiche* [The file of cosmic influences], Astrolabio, Rome, 1975, 232 pp. Some people read them and claimed that they were not able to understand how they have been obtained, implying the incompetence of Gauquelin in this field. This should not be surprising; in fact the majority of our censors confine themselves to a quite superficial reading and knowledge of this subject. For example, certain people ignore that in his studies, Mr. Gauquelin subdivided the circle in twelve portions so that in the above mentioned case we have 2088/6 (rising more culmination is $1/12 + 1/12 = 1/6$) = 348. Hence to the random probability of one in 5 millions is a matter of applying formulae. Those who wish to criticize this work should prove to know those formulae. The Gauquelins have carried out very interesting studies also on the so-called astral inheritance; that's to say, the similitude between the birth skies of parents and those of their children. (*Editor's note:* Also Ciro Discepolo and Luigi Miele have attained surprising results in this field by analyzing over 75,000 dates of birth).

According to astrological tradition, in fact, babies do not see the light at any moment; but in the moment closest to a sky which is similar to the birth sky of one or both parents. The French wife and husband wanted to verify this supposed axiom, therefore they analyzed nearly thirty thousand of birth charts of parents & children. The results have been exceptionally favourable to the astrological theses taken as starting point. Not only have they discovered that the baby tends to see the light preferably when a celestial is culminating or rising, such as is it in one of its parents' horoscope. Furthermore, they have even established that this effect doubles itself if both parents have the same natal position. Moreover, from the Gauquelins' studies it is clear that such relationship of analogy ceases to exist if the delivery is piloted: that is to say, if it is artificially postponed or anticipated. At this point it seems useless to stress the importance of these results. Nonetheless, it is useful to underline the following points:

A) The above mentioned statistical studies do not cover a few hundred of cases: they refer to dozens of thousand of them.

B) Specialists in probability theory have performed checks and double checks without detecting any single mistake in method or calculation.

C) All the results and the starting points (including the dates of birth) have been published.

D) To all extents, the described results are incontrovertible pieces of evidence of facts: not mere opinions.

E) The Gauquelins' entire work proves that men were not born under any sky; and that seeing the light at a certain hour or at another hour implies extremely important consequences as far as the native's destiny is concerned. It also proves that, despite what the anti-astrologers have been claiming so far, planets aren't 'rocks', and that they do influence our destiny.

Let us make use of these researches and have them focus on *Active Astrology.*

It is absolutely evident that those who, say, were born with Jupiter 5 to 15 degrees right to the Medium Coeli (i.e. in the minutes following its culmination) or 5 to 15 degrees over the Ascendant (i.e. in the minutes following its rising) those individuals have a dominant Jupiter, and this implies a series of features of destiny and psychological attitudes whose listing and description is not the scope of this chapter.

The same applies to the 5 to 7 degrees after the Descendant (belonging to the 6th House) or after the Imum Coeli (belonging to the 3rd House), although with a definitely lower power.

This first-hand consideration provides us with an insight about the fact that, if every astrologer truly understood its import, there should be no ground whatsoever for misinterpretation.

For example many colleagues believe that a Jupiter placed in the Tenth House is 'the very best' and for their dear ones they would prefer it to be there instead of three degrees beyond the right side of the Medium Coeli, in the Ninth House. This is wrong, because the Gauquelins have proven that a celestial is much stronger **after** it has past over a point of the sky, not **before** its passage. Furthermore, in the mentioned example, Jupiter would be in the 9th House, but due to its strict conjunction to the Medium Coeli, it would have as many '10th-House-like' advantages as '9th-House-like' advantages.

This is fundamental point in the understanding of an astrologer. For if this point is ignored or is rejected deliberately (like certain schools of astrology do, and important ones) then there would be serious mistakes made in any application of astrology.

So, if an astrologer had to choose the most apt sky for the laying the cornerstone of a new industrial plant, he or she would place Jupiter in the 10th House, not in the 9th House, thus losing several points of percentage of its 'fire power'.

Similarly, a less expert astrologer would try at any cost to position Jupiter well inside the 10th House of an Aimed Solar Return, thus giving up the more powerful position of a Jupiter after its own culmination, therefore in the 9th House.

As you can see, we have reached a fundamental point concerning the choice of an Aimed Solar Return, an Aimed Lunar Return, or an Aimed Earth Return. All these rules have already been written; you can find them already published in my volume *Transits and Solar Returns*, *Ricerca '90 Publisher.*

Nevertheless I've been asked several times to elaborate such notions, and this is what I am trying to do.

We have already written about Jupiter. More or less, the same applies to Venus and to the Sun.

Now let us consider Saturn. I think I have always been clear in this regard too. Have you ever read, in any of my volumes, that it's a good or wise or cautious putting Saturn in the 10th House of a SR, LR, or ER? Of course not, you could not have read anything like this!

So how is it that you have doubts if I talk about the hypothesis of placing Saturn, say, 5 to 10 degrees to the right side of the Medium Coeli?

You should not leave Saturn there, even more: you should never leave it closest to 12 degrees from the MC!

Never? *Really* never?

Never, I say. Or better said, virtually never. Say that we refer to a very sick man. Say that it's necessary to have his leg amputated. In this case you might even accept to leave Saturn three or four degrees right to the Medium Coeli provided that at the same time you are able to place Jupiter glued to the to the Ascendant, and why not? Venus in the 6th House!

The situation is different for Mars, but this is also explained in the above mentioned volume in connection with Mars in the 10th House: there you can read that such a combination expresses a noticeable effort of the native to enhance his/her own social-professional condition, his/her own emancipation. If I can avoid it, I do not leave Mars close to the Medium Coeli; on the other hand, I'm not afraid of this position as I would be if Saturn were to be there!

Mars in conjunction with the Ascendant is still another kettle of fish. It is simply ABSOLUTELY FORBIDDEN to leave Mars there, so there's nothing to discuss about it.

What about Uranus, Neptune, and Pluto? The above mentioned volume says it all. If you refer to a native who runs the risk of losing his/her job you had better avoid leaving Uranus close to the Medium Coeli. On the contrary, if you were aiming the chart of a Solar Return in order to achieve a positive and radical change in the native's professional life, well in this case you'd certainly place Uranus very very close to his/her MC in the chart of the Return.

Now let us consider another aspect of the question. If I placed Mars 5 degrees from the Medium Coeli, in the 9th House of a SR, I'd have a SR with a ruling Mars and this would herald twelve months of struggles and battles, but also twelve years of efforts and results achieved 'by frontal attacks'...

Is an ASR with ruling Mars unacceptable? Of course it is acceptable, but if you can, avoid it.

Finding that these further clarifications may be enough for you to understand this subject in full, now let us elaborate on another element that apparently has something to do with the above, while in reality is something completely different.

As you may know, I've always been using Placidus with great satisfaction. The reason is not that I've learnt so from my masters; it has simply proven to work in practice. Now for a long time I've been wondering about the border of the interference between two Houses in Placidus. You can read these considerations in my Italian volume *Nuovo Trattato di Astrologia*, Armenia editore; I believe it's an important work of mine, especially in connection with studying the dating of events within a year as well as my protocol of rectification of the time of birth (3).

So for years I've considered a range of 3.5 degrees. During the following years I've considered a range of 3 degrees. Then 2.5 degrees, then 1.5 degrees. Later, I've resolved to widen my range so that I've considered in subsequent periods 2, then 2.5, then 3 degrees…

As you can see, I can say that I've spent my life on studying it. Now I'm convinced that the right extension of the cusp of a House in Placidus is 2.5 degrees. What does this mean? Among other things, it means that according to my studies, if the native was born with Venus 2.5 degrees above the cusp between the 1st and the 2nd House, during the native's life this Venus proves to 'work' as if it were both in the 1st House *and* in the 2nd House.

Hence numerous, different astrological consequences. First of all, the possibility of aiming a cusp. This means that in an Aimed Solar or Lunar return, you may try and 'kill two birds with one stone' by positioning Venus or Jupiter exactly on the cusp between two adjacent Houses.

On the other hand beware, for if placing Venus or Jupiter exactly over a cusp appears an extremely and useful and fruitful thing to do, placing other celestials (say, Mars or Saturn) over a cusp may represent a real disaster.

As an instance, nobody would find it useful to place Mars over the cusp between the 3rd and the 4th House of an ASR. We know that Mars in the 4th House of a SR often leads to surgery in the following months, so why should you penalize two sectors of the chart at the same time?

Still sticking to the above example, one usually tends to place Mars only in the 3rd House of the return, and not also in the 4th one; unless particular situations require a different decision. But if Mars is placed in the 3rd House, say at four degrees from the Imum Coeli, isn't it in the Gauquelin sector? Of course it is! So what? Being in the Gauquelin sector by the Imum Coeli doesn't mean that the influence of the planet is detectable both in the 3rd and in the 4th House! If it were so, I wouldn't have spent a lifetime to determine the 2.5-degree range that guarantees, virtually 100% results, based on thousands of practical trials repeated several times, that beyond such a range a celestial works only 'before' or 'after' the cusp.

To make a long story short, I'm sure that my readers have understood that (perhaps with the exception of the Medium Coeli, where a few further clarifications were needed) you need not be following anything else than my 'famous' thirty rules.

Yet another thing though.

It is about the Ascendant of Solar or Lunar Return falling in the 10th natal House. I have written so many times and so much about it in my works that there should be no need to add anything else; yet I am asked to do so...

Perhaps this combination is the most difficult to be considered within the choice of an Aimed Solar Return. In my opinion, only the personal experience of a learned astrologer can help establishing whether it is a wise thing to place the Ascendant of an ASR in the 10th House radix. It is usually something very good from virtually any point of view; it's a kind of apotheosis of the 10th House.

Nonetheless, if during the SR having such a celestial combination there are particularly detrimental transits for the native, this combination may lead to a sort of 'reversal' of the traditionally positive values of the 10th House, thus exposing the native to very bad and drastic downfalls, especially in connection with his/her social and professional life.

Let me underline once again that the above only refers to the position of the Ascendant of SR falling in the 10th House of the native's birth chart: it does *not* refer either to the position of the Sun of SR in the 10th House of SR, or Jupiter of SR in the 10th House of SR, or a stellium of SR in the 10th House of SR.

Let us make a practical example. It seems that certain astrologer colleagues of my school have been able to prove, virtually with absolute certainty and beyond any reasonable doubt, that the French *first lady* Ms. Carla Bruni has aimed her own birthday in December 2008, by being there in Rio de Janeiro under apparently extremely favourable celestial combinations.

You should not be surprised about that, since in the last years my works have been translated into several languages so that it is more than probable that Carla's personal astrologer, who may be Italian or French or American, has suggested her to perform such a relocation.

In her ASR of 2008, Ms. Sarkozy would have gained a wonderful 10th House of SR as well as the Ascendant of SR falling into her 10th House radix: but it was a very bad mistake. I'm writing these lines on the 1st of January 2009, and I'm quite sure that facts will prove me right. For it is absolutely wrong to place the Ascendant of SR in your natal 10th House the same year when Pluto passes over your Sun, and Saturn passes over your Moon!

Moreover (and this is really the bottom line) in the last years Madame Sarkozy has been growing so high that one could not possibly grow higher, also considering that her merits are not so valuable after all. Furthermore you should not forget that she has her natal Saturn in her 10th House, which can lead to a complete overthrowing of the native's social life sooner or later. Thus with that Ascendant of SR falling in the 10th House radix, she runs the risk of falling down, and falling down very badly…

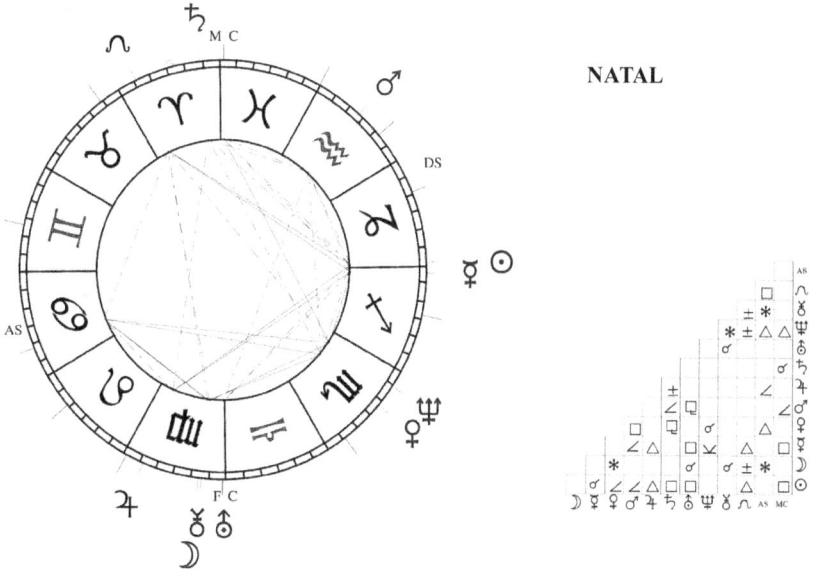

NATAL

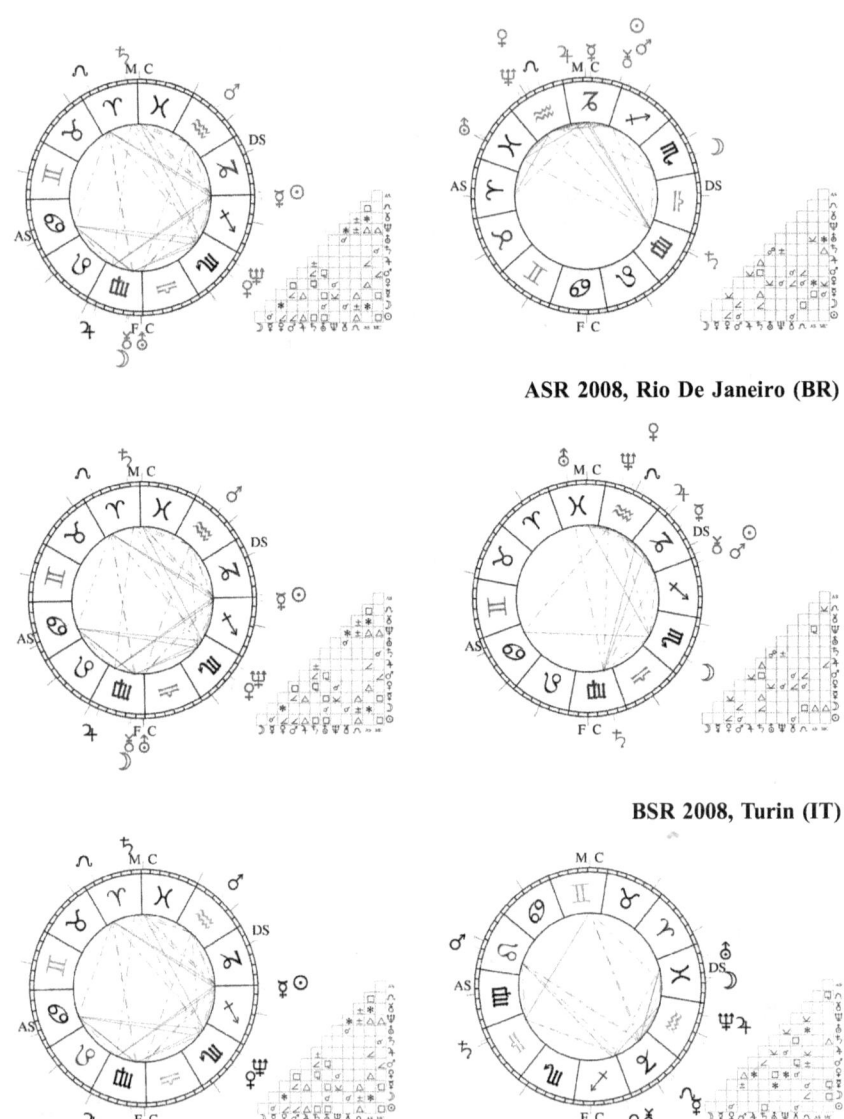

ASR 2008, Rio De Janeiro (BR)

BSR 2008, Turin (IT)

BSR 2008, Paris (FR)

Notes
1) The reader is referred to an explanation of the notion of the exorcism of the symbol in the following article: http://www.cirodiscepolo.it/english_corner/activea.htm.
2) L'Influence des Astres, Etude Critique et Esperimentale, Paris, 1955, published by the Author.
3) Nuovo Trattato di Astrologia, Armenia editore, Milan, 2004, 784 pp.

27.
My school of Astrology

I discovered astrology at the age of 22, during my military service at the airport of Latina in 1970. I dipped into it immediately and with a great passion. I understood that the only way to learn astrology is not by studying dozens of books (which I actually did for many hours a day, yet).

On the contrary, you have to practise it on the field; you have to meet hundreds of people and cast their natal charts; thus making mistakes and learning by mistakes. I don't think that there is any better way to learn astrology. Before meeting somebody I studied his/her chart for hours, dropping notes and wondering how he/she would look like; what would his/her character and cultural interests be, and so on. I eventually met the consulting person, whom in the great majority of cases I didn't know before, and my real study began after he/she had gone away. Then I reconsidered the whole trying to understand what I had mistaken, and why. Such training course was giving me good results and I noticed that, even if the path I was stepping into was boundless, every day I was advancing a little further.

Astrology had become my great passion; it had an even stronger charm on me than informatics – the other nourishment of my soul. But there was one thing that I wasn't able to accept and I couldn't stand at all: often I met people who were to face very hard transits and evidently dramatic situations – and I could do nothing for them! To hide them the truth? This was against my principles: I didn't want to deceive them. To tell them the truth – well I had to, but how? How could I face then their disappointment, their fears? That was the most impelling knotty problem I had to solve if I wanted to keep being an astrologer. During those years I also undertook my first Jungian psychoanalysis and I used to read loads of books on psychology. Very soon I got fascinated by the concept of «constellating a symbol» or, as I named it later on: «exorcization of a symbol».

In psychology to constellate means to activate, i.e. to bring something to life. Once I happened to read with an extraordinary interest the preface that Gianfranco Tedeschi, a Jungian psychoanalyst and a school founder in Italy, wrote to the Italian paperback edition of Jung's study on schizophrenia (Psicologia della schizofrenia, Newton Compton Italiana).

You'll read more about it a little further in this book; then you'll understand how this example can be considered the origin of a good portion of my practice of astrology, which consequently goes under the name of «exorcization of the symbol».

While I was greedily absorbing those readings I also studied the Solar Returns. From the very beginning I discovered that it was possible to change them, even in full, by simply being somewhere else on the day of your birthday. These two coincident discoveries lit a sparkle in me – the desire to follow a way, to try to make light, to check up on some possibilities. I had found a semi-hidden path and I was trying to light it up with a weak torch. That would be my future way. I would never leave it. I'm still trying to improve it every single day since then.

The exorcization of symbols and the Aimed solar returns are the foundation of my Active Astrology.

The exorcization of symbols

I'm sure that the more watchful readers and followers of astrology cannot ignore this current situation. We, the authors, are aligned essentially on three almost incompatible positions that eventually determine one's personal way of understanding and making astrology. The first, yet not the most important school claims that astrology is an instrument of knowledge of the human psyche and it doesn't allow the least prediction. Those who think so argue that Saturn and Uranus have nothing to do with John Smith even if John Smith is being robbed of all his goods the very same moment when these two planets cross the threshold of his natal 2nd House. It's the same as implying that transits, Solar Returns and primary directions are good for nothing.

The second sort or «school» of astrology fully admits the power of transits, to such an extent that it is considered useless to «apply yourself» because everything is already written in your natal chart; and no one can do anything against fate.

Finally, here comes the third school: those who think like me: i.e. that transits, Solar and Lunar Returns, and primary directions work faultlessly, but you have got the chance to antagonize these forces: i.e. to fight against them. Of course, all I wrote in my previous books – and above all in this one – has been borrowed partly from Tradition, partly from my master André Barbault's teachings. It also derives partly from the results of astrological research, partly from my personal experience of almost thirty years of activity; and partly from the personal way I have arranged those pieces of information together, amalgamating them with some aspects of Jungian knowledge, which has been conducting me since the beginning of my studies. I am sure that we can and we must try to weaken the negative transits and to strengthen the positive ones with all the means at our disposal. We can do it mainly with our own knowledge; with the enlightenment, which is the highest form of emancipation at our disposal. Secondarily, we can use the techniques that I have already described elsewhere and that I am about to complete here, in this synthetic work.

The main operation that I am going to describe is what I call the exorcization of the symbol, or if you prefer, the ritualization of the symbol.

«A miracle,» was the cry of a great part of my students after reading the Italian translation of Schicksal als chance [Destiny as Choice] by Thorwald Dethlefsen, published in Italy by Ed. Mediterranee. Still, much of what my German colleague wrote had been published previously in my books over the last two decades, with the exception of the part about reincarnation – something I don't believe in at all.

Let's start from the beginning, by recalling the example that I have already reported in one of my writings, first described by the analytical psychologist Gianfranco Tedeschi in his preface to the Italian edition of Jung's study on schizophrenia (Psicologia della schizofrenia, Ed. Newton Compton Italiana). In his preface, Dr. Tedeschi talks about a Jewish student of medicine in Rome, who had started to manifest symptoms of mental dissociation years before: he had begun to behave like a priest of ancient Jerusalem. Dr. Tedeschi told him that he himself was a Jew too, thus they could celebrate the holy rites together on condition that they strictly followed the rules: fasting first of all; purifying themselves; wearing the right dresses; spreading incense; reading the original scriptures, etc. They did so for many months until the young man abruptly said, «All this is interesting, but – what do the Jews do today?» From then on, having regained interest for actuality, the young man was dismissed from hospital to begin his psychoanalysis with Dr. Tedeschi – who tells the reader that the young man recovered completely and eventually graduated in medicine. The doctor had constellated the symbolism that was pressing from inside the patient: this way the problem had been «exorcized».

Let us consider two further examples whose central characters are two female clients and good friends of mine. The first one is a university professor with a vast general culture and a good knowledge of psycho astrology. During a transit of Saturn over her natal Venus she was left by the man she loved. She felt such a devastating pain that in order to cope with it, in order to detain it somehow, she went into mourning and dressed in black for one whole year. To those who asked her the reason of such a choice she used to say, «I've lost my love.» She went on for one year, exactly the same time required for Saturn to pass beyond her natal Venus; then she went out of mourning – back to normal life.

The second case is another lady professor as cultured and intelligent as the former. As the transit of Saturn on her natal Venus approached, she asked me what she could do to avoid losing her love. Her partner lived in a distant town; they met on a regular basis, say once every fortnight. I advised her to meet as rarely as possible, even further: not to meet at all during the entire coming year. They did so. Thus Saturn «was given» what it required: sentimental mortification, subtraction of loving enthusiasm, temporarily death of sentiment and sex. Then Saturn passed over and everything turned back the way it used to be.

In both cases we can say that the given procedure was to make the «ghost» act; i.e. what in psychoanalysis we could well define the «technique of restraining the field». In the case described by Dr. Tedeschi the principle of identification was employed too – a Jew was the student, and a Jew was the doctor. This procedure has been invented neither by me nor by Dr. Tedeschi or by Jung: it belongs to the rites of any religion; it can be applied very often with excellent results; and it can be compared to the principle of homeopathic medicine similia similibus curantur (the similar cures the similar).

Can we state that all the cases must be treated the same way? No. The above mentioned Thorwald Dethlefsen suggests to wear in black, to visit cemeteries, to meet grave people and so on, in order to cope with a transit of Saturn, say, on your natal Sun. But my personal experience and even the teachings of psychoanalysis don't agree on it. In fact, in many cases one must employ a prosthetic technique: i.e. a technique of compensation. Let me explain. Let's say that the one who copes with the mentioned transit of Saturn is a native Pisces whose Sun or Moon is afflicted by an aspect of Neptune. In this case we are before a psycho labile individual; an extremely fragile person; an emotional sponge who fully absorbs the atmosphere around him/her. It is not wise to advise such a person to read Les Misérables by Victor Hugo and/or to associate with sad people. On the contrary: we'll ask him/her to meet healthy happy people and very equilibrated persons; to watch amusing films such as the American comedies; to read Wodehouse's works all the time. For we must never think that everything has to be read, interpreted and developed in one direction only. Some people react better to allopathic medicine than to homeopathic; similarly we should use the exorcization of the symbol with the strongest individuals and the compensatory technique with the weakest ones. Sometimes the two principles can be melted. In the case of the fragile and vulnerable lady born under the Sign of Pisces, we'd advise her to find help in certain medicines used in psychiatry while spending a few months in a deeper solitude.

The basic principle of the exorcization of the symbol is the notion of sacrifice: exactly the same concept that thousands of years ago made the Greek pastors select and sacrifice the best lamb of their herd in order to contain Zeus' wrath. The bottom line is that you have to pay your due in the same analogical direction of the symbol, and in an expectedly adequate extent in order to discharge the transit. So if you are a female and Uranus transits on your natal Mars in the 5th House, it wouldn't be sufficient to have a dentist fill your cavity – but it would be expectedly enough to undertake an operation and have your some-year-old uterine fibroma removed.

The main piece of advice that I feel like giving to anyone is to «anticipate» the transits; to «offer the sacrifice» when the transit is about to arrive.

Another extraordinary instrument of self-defence in the critical periods – or at least a good way to strengthen the well-promising periods – is to use the Solar Returns in an «aimed» way. That is, to choose the most suitable astral situation to spend your birthday with: i.e. the best annual sky which the horoscope of your following year derives from. For many years I have been advising my clients to use this technique and I have tried it out myself several times – always obtaining excellent results.

I suggest considering the consulting client's general situation about one month before his/her birthday, i.e. when the previous year is coming to an end and the astrologer is adequately updated about the facts that characterized the astral map of his/her prior Return. On the other hand, one month before the birthday one has got time enough to organize even a very exotic journey.

My personal technique is to cast a dozen of Solar Returns maps ranging from Los Angeles to Tokyo scanning all over Europe. If none of them is suitable I explore some «extreme» territories such as Siberia, New Guinea or Easter Island. Farther in this book you'll find suggestions on the right way to proceed, based upon practical cases.

Solar Returns

This is a topic my heart gets inflamed with, because of my significant and satisfactory experience in this field. Since 1970, i.e. my first year of studying astrology, I feel I am on the same spiritual wavelength with this technique. Such a «tuning» would not develop in a fideistic way, but on the base of my practical experience. Nowadays I wouldn't be able to analyse anybody's astral situation without considering at least three maps: the natal chart, the current Solar Return, and the SR map for the next year. Without the three maps the client's situation would appear «blind» to me. In my opinion, understanding the meaning and functioning of a Solar Return allows you to penetrate the secrets of one year of somebody's life; it makes you read the most important and sure events one is about to face during that 12-month period. My first master on Solar Returns was Alexander Volguine, whose fundamental work I asked and obtained to be translated into Italian by my publisher Armenia. Later on I abandoned Volguine's method for the reasons I explained in my Trattato pratico di Rivoluzioni solari, Blue Diamond Publisher. I believe that only few and clearly defined elements of the Solar Return chart need be considered, avoiding to burden its analysis with winding correspondences and analogical mutual links. I do believe that the elements to be considered primarily are the following ones:

1. Where the cusp of the Ascendant of the Return map is within the Houses of the natal chart.

2. Where the Sun of the Return map is within the Houses of the Return map.

3. Where a stellium of the Return map is within the Houses of the Return map.

Then, but only after the above listed elements, one should also consider the planets in the Houses of the Return map, and a little – but very little – of everything else. I believe that not following these rules may lead you to serious oversights. The Solar Return is based on the principle of cycles. In nature we find, as an example, Circadian Rythms of about one day in which cockroaches sleep or are in activity; not to mention the almost monthly

MY SCHOOL OF ASTROLOGY   283

cycles of menstruation in women. Every year the Sun goes back exactly to the same natal position of a person's map and a new year begins for the native, carrying its own special features – the features marked by the native's Solar chart, which the astrologer casts for that moment and that place. According to some colleagues of mine, the Solar Return map should be cast for the native's birthplace, not for the one the native actually is in when the Return takes place. This is nonsense both from the theoretical and from the demonstrative point of view.

You can read about that in my a.m. Trattato. In this chapter I would like to describe one only example that demonstrates the absurdity of my colleagues' view. Let us consider Mata Hari's astral situation. The well known Dutch spy was sentenced to death by the French Government during the WWI. I already exposed this case years ago asking my colleagues to comment on it: having received no remark at all I'm proposing it once again. The stunning spy-dancer-prostitute was born in Leeuwarden on the 7th of August 1876 at 1 p.m. We'll consider one episode of her life for its crystalline cleanness, whatever be the reconstruction that any of you can make of it. The astrologers claiming that Solar Returns are to be cast for the birthplace (instead of the actual place of station of that moment) shall commit themselves and cry aloud to persuade those who disagree. Let's see then. Before becoming a spion and a prostitute, Mata Hari, who was already an amazing dancer, had been married to an official, major MacLeod, who took her with him to Indonesia, precisely to Medan.

There in Medan destiny stroke her tremendously on the 27th of June 1899. A native servant poisoned her two sons. One of them, Norman, died after appalling sufferings. Hence we have got all the ideal conditions to make an accurate comparison. Mata Hari's date of birth is sure – all her horoscope confirms it; we know the precise date of the event we are talking about; and geographically speaking, Leeuwarden and Medan are very distant places.

So what do we observe in Mata Hari's Solar Return map of 1898-1899 drawn for her birthplace, Leeuwarden? Nothing, virtually nothing that may foretell her tragedy – starting from the SR Ascendant in her natal 4th House, which is miles away from the peak events we are examining. Then we see an empty, insignificant 5th House.

Let us consider what her SR map of 1898-99 tells us if we draw it for Medan, i.e. the place where the family actually was at the moment of the murder. In what natal House do you think the Ascendant of SR is? Precisely:

in her natal 8th House. Weren't it enough, we also find Uranus in the 5th House while Mars and Pluto, the two dispositors of the 5th House, are conjunct in the 12th House. If they tell you that they still doubt, they simply lie.

Aimed Solar Return

I shaped this expression myself to indicate the possibility for whoever to go away on the day of his/her own anniversary in order to take advantage of a birthday astral situation better than the one they would experience if they remained on their own place of birth. In the January 1999 issue of the Italian magazine Sirio my colleague Grazia Bordoni published an anthology of declarations about the Aimed solar returns. At the end of the article my friend Grazia was sad to inform me that I had been the only one who expressed the confidence that Solar Return maps are to be cast for the place where you spend your birthday – not for your birthplace.

Actually, this lent me a hand. In fact, when I began claiming it with conviction thirty-one years ago, I had to face the opposite, often fierce opinion of the overwhelming majority of my colleagues. They even derided me for this, harshly and openly criticizing my custom of suggesting Aimed Solar Returns to my clients. Later on, as my works were published in magazines and books, growing legions of readers embraced these studies, swelling the ranks of the persuaded followers of this technique; in order to do that, some of them even disobeyed precise orders of censorship of their own masters – my colleagues. Today an opinion poll would show that the «base», even those belonging to schools other than mine, believes – in the great majority of cases – in Solar Returns and in Aimed Solar Returns.

On the other hand a growing number of Pharisees, who have repeatedly affirmed their own scepticism on this topic until the other day, has suddenly begun to assert that they have always been persuaded of the validity of ASR's; and that this matter is so evident that it is not even worth mentioning. This is the reason why I am particularly glad for the testimonials published on the a.m. issue of Sirio.

Why have I been the first one to embark on this kind of study with such a great fervour – at least compared to my colleagues? There are exactly two reasons. To study an Aimed Solar Return with all the pertinent charts and the calculation required to cast each of them, you must have adequate technical means at your disposal. In the early 1970s I already used tiny Hewlett-Packard pocket computers – the real programmable ancestors of Personal Computer. With the help of professionals on informatics, on such machines I elaborated programs that took full care of the long and laborious calculations necessary to SR's.

Today's program Molriv of ASTRAL is one of those little jewels: it scans the entire terrestrial surface in a few minutes. The other reason that favoured me very much in the study of Aimed Solar Returns is that, differing from the times of Alexander Volguine, nowadays whoever wants to spend a birthday in New York City – now as well as twenty years ago – must not sell his/her own house away any longer, for you can afford it for less than 1,000,000 Italian Liras.

I have been «sending» hundreds of people (more than 14,000 individuals as on January 2001) to spend their birthdays abroad every year for 31 years. The balance I have drawn up is astonishingly positive, as you can read in my book Trattato pratico di Rivoluzioni solari, Blue Diamond Publisher.

28.
Active Astrology

Some astrologers (honestly, few of them and not those belonging to the Hall of Fame of Astrology in the late two centuries) claim that the Solar Returns must be cast for the place where one was born, or for the place of one's residence and not for the place where the native actually is when the Solar return takes place. I disagree, and one can easily find my reasons, supported by hundreds of practical examples, in many of my approximately fifty books. One can change ones destiny by changing ones location of Solar Return.

Let me introduce a case described in my book «Nuovo Trattato delle Rivoluzioni Solari» (Armenia) a really striking case, in my opinion.

My daughter Laura had a peculiar birthday in 2001, compared to that of her astral twin. The latter is one of my friends' daughter who was born in the same town as Laura, only twenty minutes later than Laura. According to my subsequent observations though, I believe that she was born only ten minutes later than my daughter.

Laura was born in Naples on the 27th of May 1975 at 11.25 pm. Both of them would have faced horrible constellations, had they spent their birthday in Naples: perhaps the most awful ones that I could imagine. In fact they would have had the Sun conjunct to Saturn in the 12th House, four celestials in the 12th House, and Mars in the 6th House of SR.

I warned both of them and suggested them to relocate their SR to Australia. In fact my daughter went and visited a very peculiar place called Monkey Mia. Despite its ape like name, it is a magical place with bungalows facing the sea, where you can almost hug dolphins that come to the shore and «befriend» with tourists. Laura spent her birthday there, and two months later married. After that, she found home close to mine; in April she underwent an eye surgery that solved her serious short sightedness; eventually she started looking for a serious job. According to her acquaintances, Laura had the most wonderful year of her life.

Let us see what happened to her astral twin, call her Ilena. She wasn't able to leave and twelve months later she reported that she had had a real *annus horribilis*: the day after her birthday, her brother was urgently hospitalized for a very bad acute illness. He spent one month poised between life and death (she spent much time by his side, in the hospital). Three days after her birthday, while she was eating one of her molar teeth fractures; she had to take antibiotics for one month for a badly cured infection. After years of stable position, she lost her job and spent the whole year in unemployment. After seven years of stable relationship, her boyfriend left her to marry another woman; she fell into depression and spent the rest of the year in bed. According to her acquaintances, Ilena had the most awful year of her life.

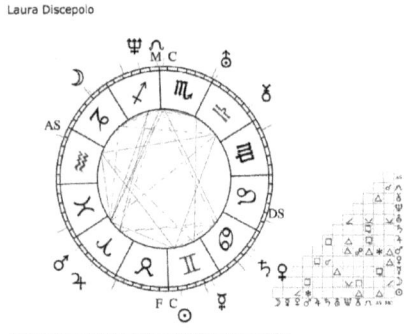

Laura Solar Return For Naples

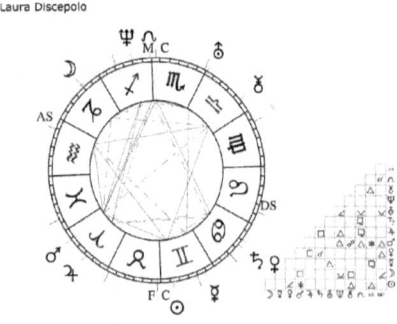

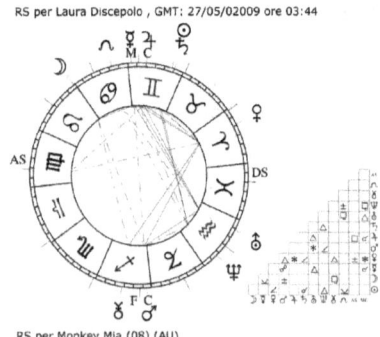

2001 Aimed Birthday Of My Daughter

Now I would like to have this case explained by those who claim that the Solar Return must be domificated for the native's place of birth, or place of steady domicile. Of course, my friend authorized me to release if necessary the real name and astrological data of Ilena, just in case somebody, having no scientific argument to oppose, claimed that this case is a mere fruit of my imagination. Even more, this is what Ilena herself told me: «If anybody doubted of this story I authorize you to publish in future books of yours my birth certificate besides Laura's birth certificate.

Even more: you can add my postal address, my phone number, and even my mobile phone number! And just in case some of your silly colleagues argued that we have invented this story together, I and you, there's no problem: we'll let him verify the date of the hospitalization of my brother at the hospital «Cotugno»; my via *crucis* at the dentist; my dismissal (it has been registered at INPS); the wedding of my former fiancé; and the antidepressant therapy that a real doctor not a virtual one ordered to me.».

If astrology is true and if the «aimed birthdays» do not work, is there any astrologer in the world who's able to explain this case? On the Web, somebody wrote that the ten minute gap between the two horoscopes of the two girls may explain such a huge difference in the Solar Returns of each of them. My comment? If you believe so, you can believe in anything.

Not only: if you follow the non reasoning of such persons, following the same twisted wavelength, could they prove that their life had been different if at the very same Greenwich time they were born in any other part of the world? How could they? Would they live a life with an Italian birth sky and a second life with, say, a Brasilian or Japanese birth sky? If so, we should come to the conclusion that neither classical Astrology is true. If this isn't enough, consider what follows.

Another really difficult case to solve for the opponents of the Aimed Solar Returns is the accident suffered by pop singer Madonna on the day of her birthday in 2005. It is really a puzzling case. Madonna (born in Bay City, MI, USA, 16th of August 1958, at 7:05 am, according to Archivio Bordoni) fell down from a horse on the day of her birthday in 2005, actually a few hours after the Solar Return. She suffered from several fractures. What do you think? Does the Solar Return cast for the States explain the event? Or does the

Solar Return cast for the place where she was actually (near Bristol, in England)? In the latter case she had Uranus over the Ascendant and three celestials in the 6th House, among them the Sun and Saturn. Following: Madonna's birth chart; her SR for the States; and her SR for Bristol, England.

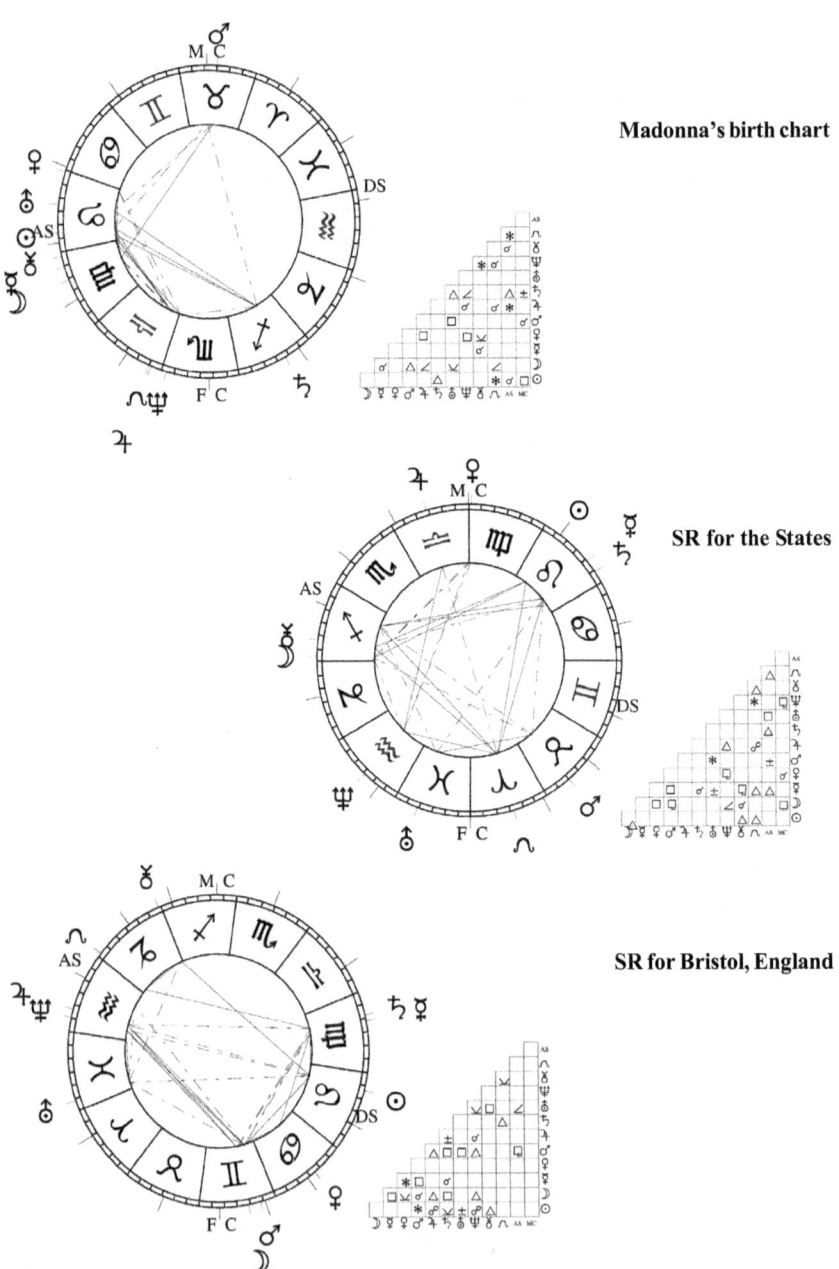

Madonna's birth chart

SR for the States

SR for Bristol, England

Article Published By 'Saptarishis Astrology' – Free Global Astro Magazine – As Read In 96 Countries

29.
Similarities between homeopathic medicine and Lunar Returns

As a conclusion of this work of mine in the English language, I would like to add a few, short considerations about a legitimate (at least in my opinion, it is so) parallelism between homeopathic medicine and Lunar Returns (Lunar, not Solar ones).

In my opinion a Lunar Return can express two important parallelisms with the natural medicine discovered by Christian Friedrich Samuel Hahnemann in 1806 (this is the year in which he published his first important work on this subject).

They are:

1) A mistaken Aimed Lunar Return can not be detrimental to anybody, exactly in the same way as a homeopathic medicine can not be detrimental to the patient if taken by mistake, for the sky of the Lunar Return is always submissive to the sky of the Solar Return. Nothing can happen in the approx. thirty days of a LR if it is also not indicated in the SR.

2) An Aimed Lunar Return can achieve great results if it exploits the synergy, the 'frequency of resonance' with its ruling Solar Return. For example, if you place Jupiter on the Medium Coeli of an ALR within the frame of a current SR having Jupiter also over the Medium

Coeli, the sustaining effect will be the highest that you can attain for the benefit of the native having such skies of Return. Similarly, if a patient is deploying a significant series of medical procedures in order to heal a bone fracture, and in addition to them he or she takes a unique dose of, say, Arnica 1000 CH, the synergic effect in this case also will be highly effective and positive.

30.
An essential astrological bibliography

- Various Authors: *Articles appeared on the quarterly* Ricerca '90 *from 1990 to 2008*, Edizioni Ricerca '90, 128 pp.

- Various Authors: *Special university issue (#45-46) of* l'astrologue, Éditions Traditionnelles, Paris

- John M. Addey: *Ritmi armonici in astrologia [Harmonic rhythms in astrology]*, Elefante ed., Catania, 1979, 352 pp.

- Antonino Anzaldi, Luigi Bazzoli: *Dizionario di Astrologia [Dictionary of astrology]*, BUR, Milan, 1988, 470 pp.

- Francesco Aulizio and Domenico Cafarello: *Considerazioni preliminari su un nuovo modo di studiare l'astrologia [Preliminary considerations about a new way of studying astrology]*, Cattedra di Storia della Medicina dell'Università di Bologna, Edizioni Capone, Turin

- André Barbault, H. Latou, B. Rossi, G. Simon: *Kepler*, Éditions Traditionnelles (l'astrologue *issue #52*), Paris

- André Barbault and Various Authors: *Soleil & Lune en Astrologie [Sun & Moon in Astrology]*, Publications du Centre International d'Astrologie, Paris, 1953, 280 pp.

- André Barbault: *Ariete [Aries]*, La Salamandra, Milan, 1985, 160 pp.

- André Barbault: *Astrologia e orientamento professionale [Astrology and professional orientation]*, Edizioni Ciro Discepolo, Naples, 1984, 93 pp.

- André Barbault: *Astrologia mondiale [World astrology]*, Armenia, Milan, 1980, 272 pp.

- André Barbault: *Dalla psicanalisi all'astrologia [From psychoanalysis to astrology]*, Morin, Siena, 1971, 224 pp.

- André Barbault: *Giove & Saturno [Jupiter & Saturn]*, Edizioni Ciro Discepolo, Naples, 1983, 214 pp.

- André Barbault: *Il pronostico sperimentale in astrologia [The experimental prediction in astrology]*, Mursia, Milan, 1979, 210 pp.

- André Barbault: *La Précession des Équinoxes et l'Astrologie [The precession of the equinoxes and Astrology]*, Centre International d'Astrologie, Paris, 1972, 32 pp.

- André Barbault, *La scienza dell'Astrologia [The science of Astrology]*, Nuovi Orizzonti, Milan, 1989, 186 pp.

- André Barbault: *L'astrologia e la previsione dell'avvenire [Astrology and the forecast of future]*, Armenia, Milan, 1993, 308 pp.

- André Barbault: *L'astrologia e l'avvenire del mondo [Astrology and the future of the world]*, Xenia, Milan, 1996, 212 pp.

- André Barbault: *Toro [Taurus]*, La Salamandra, Milan, 1985, 153 pp.

- André Barbault: *Trattato pratico di astrologia [A practical treatise of astrology]*, Morin, Siena, 1967, 317 pp.

- Armand Barbault: *Technique de l'interprétation [The technique of interpretation]*, Dervy Livres, Croissy-Beaubourg, 1991

- A. Barbault and others: *La luna nei miti e nello zodiaco [The Moon in the myths and in the Zodiac]*, Nuovi Orizzonti, Milan, 1989, 190 pp.

- Enzo Barillà and Ciro Discepolo: *Astrologia: sì e no [Astrology: yes and no]*, Edizioni Ricerca '90, Naples, 1994, 240 pp.

- Angelo Brunini: *L'avvenire non è un mistero [Future is not a mystery]*, published by the Author, Rome, 1964, 528 pp.

- Federico Capone: *Astronomia oroscopica [Horoscopic Astronomy]*, Edizioni Capone, Turin, 1977, 112 pp.

- Federico Capone: *Dizionario Astrologico [Astrological Dictionary]*, Edizioni Capone, Turin, 1978, 224 pp.

- Charles E.O. Carter: *An Introduction to Political Astrology*, Fowler, London, 1951, 104 pp.

- Charles E.O. Carter: *The Astrological Aspects*, Fowler, London, 1930, 160 pp.

- Charles E.O. Carter: *The Astrology of Accidents*, The Theosophical Publishing House Ltd., London, Unknown date of publishing, 124 pp.

- Charles E.O. Carter: *The Principles of Astrology*, The Theosophical Publishing House Ltd., London, 1925, 190 pp.

- Marco Celada: *Articles appeared on the quarterly* Ricerca '90 *from 1990 to 2008*, Edizione Ricerca '90, 128 pp.

- Yves Christiaen: *La Domification [Domification]*, Dervy Livres, Paris, 1978, 40 pp.

- Nicholas De Vore,: *Encyclopedia of Astrology*, Littlefield Adams and Co., New Jersey, U.S.A., 1977

- Arato Di Soli: *I fenomeni ed i pronostici [Phenomena and predictions]*, Arktos, Turin, 1984, 120 pp.

- Ciro Discepolo and Andrea Rossetti: *Astro & Geografia [Astro & Geography]*, Blue Diamond Publisher, Milan, 1996, 102 pp.

- Ciro Discepolo and Various Authors: *Osservazioni politematiche sulle ricerche Discepolo/Miele [Polithematic remarks on the researches of Discepolo & Miele]*, Edizioni Ricerca '90, Naples, 1992, 196 pp.

- Ciro Discepolo and Various Authors: *Per una rifondazione dell'astrologia o per il suo rifiuto [For a refoundation of Astrology or for its refusal]*, Edizioni Ricerca '90, Naples, 1993, 200 pp.

- Ciro Discepolo and Francesco Maggiore: *Elementi di astrology professionale [Elements of professional astrology]*, Blue Diamond Publisher, Milan, 1996, 93 pp.

- Ciro Discepolo and Francesco Maggiore: *Introduzione alla sinastria [An introduction to synastry]*, Blue Diamond Publisher, Milan, 1996, 106 pp.

- Ciro Discepolo and Luigi Galli: *Supporto tecnico alla pratica delle Rivoluzioni solari mirate [Technical support to the practise of Aimed Solar Returns]*, Blue Diamond Publisher, Milan, 2000, 136 pp.*

- Ciro Discepolo: *Astrologia applicata [Applied astrology]*, Armenia, Milan, 1988, 294 pp.

- Ciro Discepolo: *La ricerca dell'ora di nascita [The quest for the time of birth]*, Edizioni Ricerca '90, Naples, 1994, 64 pp.*

- Ciro Discepolo: *Astrologia Attiva [Active Astrology]*, Edizioni Mediterranee, Rome, 1998, 144 pp.*

- Ciro Discepolo: *Come scoprire i segreti di un oroscopo [How to unveil the secrets of a horoscope]*, Albero ed., Milan, 1988, 253 pp.

- Ciro Discepolo: *Esercizi sulle Rivoluzioni solari mirate [Exercises of Aimed Solar Returns]*, Blue Diamond Publisher, Milan, 1996, 96 pp.*

- Ciro Discepolo: *Guida ai transiti* (prima e seconda edizione) *[A guide to transits – 1st and 2nd edition]*, Armenia, Milan, 1984, 510 pp.*

- Ciro Discepolo: *Il sale dell'astrologia [The salt of astrology]*, Edizioni Capone, Turin, 1991, 144 pp.

- Ciro Discepolo: *Nuova guida all'astrologia [A new guide to astrology]*, Armenia, Milan, 2000, 818 pp.*

- Ciro Discepolo: *Nuovo dizionario di astrologia [The new Dictionary of Astrology]*, Armenia, Milan, 1996, 394 pp.*

- Ciro Discepolo: *Nuovo trattato delle Rivoluzioni solari [The new treatise of Solar Returns]*, Armenia, Milan, 2003, 216 pp.*

- Ciro Discepolo: *Piccola guida all'astrologia [A concise guide to astrology]*, Armenia, Milan, 1998, 200 pp.

- Ciro Discepolo: *Suite of software modules ASTRAL*, developed by the Author and Luigi Miele, Naples, 1979-2003

- Ciro Discepolo: *Prontuario calcoli [Ready reckoner]*, Edizioni Capone, Turin, 1979, 72 pp.

- Ciro Discepolo: *Quattro cose sui compleanni mirati [A few facts on Aimed Birthdays]*, Blue Diamond Publisher, Milan, 2001, 104 pp.*

- Ciro Discepolo: *Traité complet d'interprétation des transits et des Révolutions solaires en astrologie*, Éditions Traditionnelles, Paris, 2001, 502 pp.*

- Ciro Discepolo: *Transiti e Rivoluzioni solari [Transits and Solar Returns]*, Armenia, Milan, 1997, 502 pp.*

- Ciro Discepolo: *Trattato pratico di Rivoluzioni solari [A practical treatise of Solar Returns]*, Edizioni Ricerca '90, Naples, 1993, 208 pp.*

- Ciro Discepolo: *Various volumes of ephemerides*, Various publishers

- Ciro Discepolo: *Various volumes of Tables of Houses*, Various publishers

- Ciro Discepolo: *Ci siamo con la datazione informatica degli avvenimenti? [How far have we gone with the computerized dating of events?]*, Edizioni Ricerca '90, 2007, 168 pp.*

- Ciro Discepolo: *365 nap alatt a Föld körül a szolárhoroszkóppal*, DFT-Húngaria, Budapest, May 2006, 190 pp. B5*

- Ciro Discepolo: *Temelji medicinske astrologije: osnove za razumevanje clovekove patologije s pomocjo nebesnih teles*, Zalozba Astroloskega instituta, 2007, pp. 262*

- Ciro Discepolo: *I fondamenti dell'Astrologia Medica [The fundaments of Medical Astrology]*, Armenia, Milan, end of January 2006, 246 pp.*

- Ciro Discepolo: *L'interpretazione del tema natale [Reading the natal chart]*, Armenia, Milan, September 2007, 336 pp.*

- Ciro Discepolo: *Transits and Solar Returns*, Naples, Ricerca '90 Publisher, September 2007, 560 pp.*

- Ciro Discepolo: Russian edition of the 'Nuovo Trattato delle Rivoluzioni solari', end of 2008*

- Ciro Discepolo: *Enquête sur l'hérédité astrale*, issue #67 of *l'astrologue,* Éditions Traditionnelles, Paris, 1984

- Ciro Discepolo: *Statistique sur 834 nominations ministérielles,* issue #67 of *l'astrologue,* Éditions Traditionnelles, Paris, 1986

- Ciro Discepolo: *Nouvelle recherche sur l'hérédité astrale*, issue #106 of *l'astrologue*, Éditions Traditionnelles, Paris, 1994

- Ciro Discepolo: *L'Hérédité astrale sur 50 000 naissances*, and *Astrologie activiste – Réflexions sur l'astrologie*, issue #125 of *l'astrologue*, Éditions Traditionnelles, Paris, 1999

- Reinhold Ebertin: *Cosmobiologia: la nuova astrologia [Cosmobiology: the new Astrology]*, Edizioni C.E.M., Naples, 1982, 208 pp.

- Michael Erlewine: *Manual of Computer Programming for Astrologers*, American Federation of Astrologers, Tempe (Arizona), 1980, 215 pp.

- Hans J. Eysenck, S. Mayo, O. White: *Un metodo empirico sul rapporto tra fattori astrologici e personalità [An empirical method on the relationship between astrological factors and peersonality]*, issue #42 of *Linguaggio astrale*, Turin, 1981

- Serena Foglia: *Prolusione al convegno di studi astrologici tenutosi a Napoli nel 1979 [Opening speech at the congress of astrological studies held in Naples in 1979]*, issue #37 of *Linguaggio Astrale*, Turin

- H. Freiherr Von Klöckler, *Corso di astrologia [Course on Astrology]*, ed. Mediterranee, Rome, 1979

- Luigi Galli and Ciro Discepolo: *Atlante geografico per le Rivoluzioni* *solari [Geographical Atlas for Solar Returns]*, Blue Diamond Publisher, Milan, 2001, 136 pp.*

- Luigi Galli: *Articles appeared on the quarterly* Ricerca '90 *from 1990 to 2008*, Edizioni Ricerca '90, Naples, 128 pp.

- Michel & Françoise Gauquelin: *Actors & politicians*, Laboratoire d'étude des relations entre rythmes cosmiques et psychophysiologiques, Paris, 1970

- Michel Gauquelin: *Il dossier delle influenze cosmiche [The file of cosmic influences]*, Astrolabio, Rome, 1975, 232 pp.

- Michel Gauquelin: *La Cosmopsychologie*, Retz, Paris, 1974, 256 pp.

- Michel Gauquelin: *L'astrologia di fronte alla scienza [Astrology face to science]*, Armenia, Milan, 1981, 312 pp.

- Michel & Françoise Gauquelin: *Méthodes pour étudier la répartition des astres dans le mouvement diurne,* Gauquelin ed., Paris, 1970

- Michel & Françoise Gauquelin: *Painters and musicians*, Laboratoire d'étude des relations entre rythmes cosmiques et psychophysiologiques, Paris, 1970

- Françoise Gauquelin: *Problèmes de l'heure risolus en astrologie*, Guy Trédaniel

- Michel Gauquelin: *Ritmi biologici e ritmi cosmici [Biological rhythms and cosmic rhythms]*, Faenza spa, Faenza, 1976, 226 pp.

- Luigi Gedda and Gianni Brenci: *Cronogenetica [Chronogenetics],* Est-Mondadori, Milan, 1974

- Sergio Ghivarello: *La realtà al di là dell'astrologia [Reality beyond astrology]*, Edizioni Capone, Turin

- Sergio Ghivarello: *L'astrologia e la teoria dei cicli nel quadro dei fenomeni ondulatori [Astrology and the theory of cycles withing the frame of undulatory phenomena]*, C.I.D.A. ed., Turin, 1974

- Sergio Ghivarello: *Lo zodiaco siderale e le costellazioni boreali [Sidereal Zodiac and Boreal constellations]*, #43/44/45, C.I.D.A. ed., Turin, 1981

- Sergio Ghivarello: *Verso una scienza alternativa [Towards an alternative science]*, issue #37 of *Linguaggio Astrale*, Turin, 1979

- Henri J. Gouchon and Jean Reverchon: *Dictionnaire Astrologique – Supplément Technique*, H. Gouchon Éditeur, Paris, 1947, 40 pp.

- Henri J. Gouchon: *Dizionario di astrologia [Dictionary of astrology]*, Siad ed., Milan, 1980

- Henri J. Gouchon: *Les Directions Primaires Simplifiées*, Éditions Traditionnelles, Paris, 1970, ca. 150 pp.

- Henri J. Gouchon: *L'Horoscope Annuel Simplifié*, Dervy Livres, Paris, 1973, 214 pp.

- Hadès: *Guide pratique de l'interprétation en Astrologie*, Éditions Niclaus, Paris, 1969, 228 pp.

- Robert Hand: *I transiti [The transits]*, Armenia, Milan, 1982, 512 pp.

- Eugen Jonas: *Articles appeared on the quarterly* Ricerca '90 *from 1990 to 2008*, Edizioni Ricerca '90, Naples, 128 pp.

- Eugen Jonas: *Il controllo naturale del concepimento [The natural control of conception]*, Blue Diamond Publisher, Milan, 1995, 76 pp.

- Helene Kinauer Saltarini: *Bioritmo [Biorhythm]*, Siad ed., Milan, 1977

- George C. Noonan: *Spherical Astronomy for Astrologers*, American Federation of Astrologers, Washington DC, 1974, 62 pp.

- Tommaso Palamidessi: *Astrologia mondiale [World astrology]*, Archeosofica P., Rome, 1941, 588 pp.

- Johanna Paungger and Thomas Poppe: *La Luna ci insegna a star bene [The Moon teaches us how to be fine]*, Frasnelli - Keitsch, Bolzano/Bozen, 1995, 260 pp.

- Johanna Paungger and Thomas Poppe: *Servirsi della Luna [To use the Moon]*, Frasnelli - Keitsch, Bolzano/Bozen, 1995, 166 pp.

- Mariagrazia Pelaia: *Articles appeared on the quarterly* Ricerca '90 *from 1990 to 2008*, Edizione Ricerca '90, 128 pp.

- Andrea Rossetti: *Articles appeared on the quarterly* Ricerca '90 *from 1990 to 2008*, Edizioni Ricerca '90, Naples, 128 pp.

- Andrea Rossetti: *Breve trattato sui transiti [A concise treatise on transits]*, Blue Diamond Publisher, Milan, 1994, 125 pp.

- Andrea Rossetti: *Transiti, rivoluzioni solari e dasa indù [Transits, Solar Returns, and Hindu Dhasas]*, Blue Diamond Publisher, Milan, 1997, 188 pp.

- Alexander Ruperti: *I cicli del divenire [The cycles of becoming]*, Astrolabio, Rome, 1990, 301 pp.

- Frances Sakoian and Louis Acker: *Transits of Jupiter*, CSA Printing and Bindery Inc., USA, 1974, 72 pp.

- Frances Sakoian and Louis Acker: *Transits of Saturn*, CSA Printing and Bindery Inc., USA, 1973, 76 pp.

- Frances Sakoian and Louis Acker: *Transits of Uranus*, CSA Printing and Bindery Inc., USA, 1973, 78 pp.

- Vanda Sawtell: *Astrology & Biochemistry*, Rustington, Sussex, England, 86 pp.

- Françoise Secret: *Astrologie et alchimie au XVII siecle*, Studi francesi, new serie, vol. 60, issue #3

- Nicola Sementovsky-Kurilo: *Trattato completo di astrologia teorico e pratico [A complete theoretical-practical treatise of astrology]*, Hoepli ed., Milan, 1989

- Heber J. Smith: *Transits*, American Federation of Astrology, Tempe (Arizona), Unknown date of publishing, 42 pp.

- Kichinosuke Tatai: *I bioritmi [The biorhythms]*, ed. Mediterranee, Rome

- George S. Thommen: *Bioritmi [Biorhythms]*, Cesco Ciapanna ed.

- Claudius Ptolemy: *Descrizione della sfera celeste [Description of the Celestial Sphere]*, Arnaldo Forni, Bologna, 1990, 96 pp.

- Claudius Ptolemy: *Tetrabiblos, Le previsioni astrologiche [Tetrabiblos – the astrological predictions]*, Mondadori, Milan, 1985, 490 pp.

- Claudius Ptolemy: *Tetrabiblos*, Arktos, Carmagnola, 1980

- Claudius Ptolemy: *Tetrabiblos*, Arktos, Turin, 1979, 270 pp.

- Alexander Volguine: *Tecnica delle rivoluzioni solari [Technique of Solar Returs]*, Armenia, Milan, 1980, 226 pp.

- Herbert Von Klöckler, *Astrologia, scienza sperimentale [Astrology – an experimental science]*, Mediterranee, Rome, 1993, 183 pp.

- Ritchie R. Ward: *Gli orologi viventi [The living clocks]*, Bompiani, Milan, 1973

- Lyall Watson: *Supernatura [Supernature]*, Rizzoli ed, Milan, 1974

- David Williams: *Simplified Astronomy for Astrologers*, American Federation of Astrologers, Washington DC 1969, 90 pp.

* **These are writings that deal – partly or extensively – with the subject 'Solar Returns' and 'Lunar Returns'.**

Index

Preface to the English Edition .... pag. 7

Preface .... pag. 9

Part I, Lunar Returns

1. The unconscious roots of my passion for the Aimed Solar Returns .. pag. 21
2. Why and how do Solar Returns and Lunar Returns work .... pag. 23
3. Lunar Returns .... pag. 49
4. Twenty trustworthy rules .... pag. 61
5. The concept of modulation .... pag. 65
6. Do Aimed Lunar Returns work? .... pag. 69
7. New fields of research for Lunar Returns .... pag. 73
8. A thrilling Lunar Return .... pag. 83
9. An Aimed Lunar Return for an intervention of rhinoplasty .... pag. 89
10. Lunar Return in San Severo di Foggia .... pag. 93
11. How to choose an ALR for eye surgery .... pag. 99
12. A few practical exercises on the dating of events .... pag. 107
13. SRs and LRs in the attack on Pearl Harbor .... pag. 117
14. Lunar Return on airliners .... pag. 125
15. Lunar Return in Flores .... pag. 131
16. Lunar Return in Peterhead .... pag. 137

Part II, Earth Returns

17. What Earth Returns are and how they work .... pag. 143

18. Table to find out the point *A* in Earth Returns .... pag. 157

Part III, Miscellany and new researches on Solar Returns

19. The significant value of synergy in the aimed birthdays of a whole family .... pag. 213

20. An attempt to get pregnant in advanced years .... pag. 227

21. Accuracy of the calculations and lack of passport .... pag. 233

22. The tragedy of Cogne .... pag. 237

23. A difficult and unsuccessful exercise .... pag. 247

24. The accuracy of your software when casting a SR .... pag. 257

25. The twenty days before and after the birthday .... pag. 259

Part IV, Postface

26. Some important subjects for Active Astrology .... pag. 265

27. Solar Returns Domification .... pag. 277

28. Active Astrology .... pag. 287

29. Similarities between homeopathic medicine and Lunar Returns .... pag. 291

30. An essential astrological bibliography .... pag. 293